DAIMON LIFE

Studies in Continental Thought

John Sallis, general editor

Consulting Editors

DAIMON LIFE

Heidegger and Life-Philosophy

DAVID FARRELL KRELL

Indiana University Press
BLOOMINGTON AND INDIANAPOLIS

The paper used in this publication meets the minimum requirements of American
National Standard for Information Sciences—Permanence of Paper for Printed
Library Materials, ANSI Z39.48-1984.
⊚™

Manufactured in the United States of America

Library of Congress Cataloging-in-Publication Data

Krell, David Farrell.
Daimon life : Heidegger and life-philosophy / David Farrell Krell.
p.   cm. — (Studies in continental thought)
Includes bibliographical references and index.
ISBN 0-253-33147-1 (hard : alk. paper). — ISBN 0-253-20739-8
(pbk. : alk. paper)
1. Heidegger, Martin, 1889–1976.   2. Life—History—20th century.
3. Biology—Philosophy—History—20th century.   I. Title.
II. Series.
B3279.H49K739   1992
193—dc20   91-47493

1 2 3 4 5   96 95 94 93 92

for jd for life

In the ignorance that implies impression that
knits knowledge that finds the nameform
that whets the wits that convey contacts that
sweeten sensation that drives desire that adheres to attachment that dogs death that
bitches birth that entails the ensuance of
existentiality.

—James Joyce, *Finnegans Wake*

CONTENTS

Preface

Daimon life? Does that mean that life is a demon? And that we are going to involve ourselves in something diabolical? Or does the title mean to suggest Heidegger's anathematization of *Lebensphilosophie,* the tradition of "life-philosophy" from Dilthey and Bergson through Nietzsche and Scheler? What precisely does Heidegger's thought, whether elaborating a fundamental ontology of Dasein or meditating on a poetics of being and propriation, have to do with something as vague as "life"? Who or what is this δαίμων?

Diotima of Mantinea opens the classic space of the daimon. To be sure, she invokes the daimon called Ἔρως; yet we may be safe in assuming that Eros has something to do with daimon *life.* Diotima instructs young Socrates in Plato's *Symposium* (202ff.) concerning the nature of love as a "lack" or "deprivation" of the good and beautiful. Love lacks the very qualities that the gods above all possess. Diotima then draws the daimonic consequences:

> "You see, even you don't regard Eros as a god."
> "What can Eros be, then? A mortal?"
> "Far from it."
> "What, then?"
> "As in the other examples, something between a mortal and an immortal."
> "And what is that, Diotima?"
> "A great daimon, Socrates [Δαίμων μέγας, ὦ Σώκρατες]. For the daimonic [τὸ δαιμόνιον] is midway between what is divine and what is mortal."
> "What power does it possess?"
> "It acts as an interpreter and means of communication between gods and mortals. It takes requests and offerings to the gods, and brings back instructions and benefits in return. Occupying this middle position it plays a vital role in holding the world together. It is the medium of all prophecy and religion, whether it concerns sacrifice, forms of worship, incantations, or any kind of divination or sorcery. There is no direct contact between god and mortal. All association and communication between them, waking or sleeping, takes place through Eros. This kind of knowledge is daimonic; any other kind (occupational or artistic, for example) is purely utilitarian. Such δαίμονες are many and varied, and Eros is one of them.[1]

In a lecture course on logic in 1928 Heidegger for the first time (as far as I am aware) mentions τὸ δαιμόνιον, the realm of the daimonic. For a number of years, certainly through the mid-1940s, it serves as a figure that integrates an entire range of themes and subjects that persist in his thought: the finite transcendence of Dasein or human existence, temporality, freedom, anxiety, the overpowering, language, and the holy. My thesis is that these themes and issues all touch on the phenomenon of *life* as it appears in Heidegger's thought from the very outset of his path; further, that however much Heidegger inveighs against life-philosophy his own fundamental ontology and poetics of being thrust him back onto *Lebensphilosophie* again and again; and, finally, that the most powerfully "gathering" figure of his thinking during the years 1928 to 1944, the figure that "plays a role in holding the world together," is that of the daimon—*daimon life.*

Life would therefore be a word that hovers about Heidegger's thought even more hauntingly than the *spirit* with which we have all been so preoccupied of late. That does not mean to gainsay the insights Jacques Derrida's *Of Spirit: Heidegger and the Question* has opened up for us. Nor does it mean to deny that Heidegger's response to the daimon, to life and life-philosophy, invite critical reflection on his politics. The present book, especially in its second part, wants to initiate a new kind of discussion concerning Heidegger's political debacle, a discussion that takes the daimonic as its point of departure. Finally, the great daimon of life should enable us to expand the horizons of our interrogation of Heidegger—back to Plato, then forward to German Idealism, on through Nietzsche and Freud, and onward (beyond Heidegger) to Derrida and Irigaray.

For the most part, this book is a close reading of a number of Heideggerian texts, principally from the late 1920s through the mid-1940s, including *Being and Time* (1927), *Contributions to Philosophy* (*Of Propriation*) (1936–1938), and the lecture courses of 1928 (on Leibniz, logic, and the daimon), 1929–1930 (on theoretical biology), 1942–1943 (on the "daimonic site" in Heidegger's Parmenides lectures), and 1943–1944 (on the Greek sense of life, ζωή as ζά, in the Heraclitus lectures). It allows the larger horizon of daimon life to remain in the background. That horizon, as I have indicated, would encompass Plato's *Timaeus* and all the thinkers and poets of German Romanticism and Idealism, to name but two possible landmarks on the horizon. Only in its introductory and concluding chapters does the present book venture beyond or outside Heidegger's texts, suggesting a number of paths for future research and thought.

Several chapters of the book have appeared earlier in altered form in journals and anthologies, and I would like to thank the editors for permission to use these materials here: John Sallis, editor of *Research in Phenomenology*, XVII and XVIII, for material in the Introduction and in chapter 8; once again, John Sallis, editor of *Reading Heidegger: Commemorations* (Bloomington: Indiana University Press, 1992), for material in chapter 3; and Marcus Brainard, editor of "Heidegger and the Political," a special issue of *The Graduate Faculty Journal*, vols. 14, no. 2 and 15, no. 1, for material in chapter 5.

I am grateful to John Barth for kind permission to quote from his remarkable text, "Lost in the Funhouse," in *Lost in the Funhouse* (Garden City, New York: Doubleday, 1967; reprinted here with the permission of Wylie, Aitken & Stone, Inc.). I owe my retelling of the Gilgamesh epic to a suggestion by Hans Jonas in *The Phenomenon of Life*.[2] I have used the translation by N. K. Sandars, *The Epic of Gilgamesh: An English Version with an Introduction* (1960) with the kind permission of Penguin Books, setting direct quotations in italic type, my paraphrases in Roman. I am grateful to Dover Publications for permission to reproduce a number of stamp images from Jorge Enciso, *Design Motifs of Ancient Mexico* (New York: Dover Publications, 1953): the toad (Tamacolin) from Mexico City, the wizardlizard from Teotihuacan, and the human figure from Tlatilco.

I am also indebted to Jill Lavelle, Joel B. Shapiro, and Anna Vaughn, who helped at every stage, and to John Llewelyn and John Sallis, who read the book in typescript. Finally, my thanks to DePaul University for awarding me a Summer Research Grant in 1991, so that I could complete this work.

D.F.K.

Key to Principal Works Cited

I. Works by Martin Heidegger

AED *Aus der Erfahrung des Denkens.* Pfullingen: G. Neske, 1947.

EM *Einführung in die Metaphysik.* Tübingen: M. Niemeyer, 1953.

EHD *Erläuterungen zu Hölderlins Dichtung.* Fourth, expanded edition. Frankfurt am Main: V. Klostermann, 1971.

G *Gelassenheit.* Pfullingen: G. Neske, 1959.

H *Holzwege.* Frankfurt am Main: V. Klostermann, 1950.

Hk *Heraklit.* With Eugen Fink. Frankfurt am Main: V. Klostermann, 1970.

ID *Identität und Differenz.* Pfullingen: G. Neske, 1957.

NI, NII *Nietzsche.* Two volumes. Pfullingen: G. Neske, 1961.

SA *Schellings Abhandlung über das Wesen der menschlichen Freiheit (1809).* Edited by Hildegard Feick. Tübingen: M. Niemeyer, 1971.

SB *Die Selbstbehauptung der deutschen Universität; Das Rektorat 1933/34: Tatsachen und Gedanken.* Edited by Hermann Heidegger. Frankfurt am Main: V. Klostermann, 1983.

SG *Satz vom Grund.* Pfullingen: G. Neske, 1957.

SZ *Sein und Zeit.* Twelfth edition. Tübingen: M. Niemeyer, 1972, a reprinting of the seventh edition, 1953. I have checked the later editions against the first edition, published in the eighth volume of the *Jahrbuch für Philosophie und phänomenologische Forschung,* edited by Edmund Husserl. Halle a. d. S.: M. Niemeyer, 1927.

UK *Der Ursprung des Kunstwerkes.* Stuttgart: P. Reclam, 1960.

US *Unterwegs zur Sprache.* Pfullingen: G. Neske, 1959.

VA *Vorträge und Aufsätze.* Pfullingen: G. Neske, 1954.

VS *Vier Seminare: Le Thor 1966, 1968, 1969; Zähringen 1973.* Edited by Curd Ochwadt. Frankfurt am Main: V. Klostermann, 1977.

W *Wegmarken.* Frankfurt am Main: V. Klostermann, 1967.

WhD? *Was heißt Denken?* Tübingen: M. Niemeyer, 1954.

ZK *Zollikoner Seminare.* Edited by Medard Boss. Frankfurt am Main: V. Klostermann, 1987.

ZSdD *Zur Sache des Denkens.* Tübingen: M. Niemeyer, 1969.

20 *Prolegomena zur Geschichte des Zeitbegriffs.* Martin Heidegger Gesamtausgabe volume 20. Marburg lecture course, Summer Semester, 1925. Frankfurt am Main: V. Klostermann, 1979.

24 *Die Grundprobleme der Phänomenologie.* Gesamtausgabe volume 24. Marburg lecture course, Summer Semester, 1927. Frankfurt am Main: V. Klostermann, 1975.

26 *Metaphysische Anfangsgründe der Logik im Ausgang von Leibniz.*

Gesamtausgabe volume 26. Marburg lecture course, Summer Semester, 1928. Frankfurt am Main: V. Klostermann, 1978.

29/30 *Die Grundbegriffe der Metaphysik: Welt—Endlichkeit— Einsamkeit.* Gesamtausgabe volume 29/30. Freiburg lecture course, Winter Semester, 1929–1930. Frankfurt am Main: V. Klostermann, 1983.

39 *Hölderlins Hymnen "Germanien" und "Der Rhein."* Gesamtausgabe volume 39. Freiburg lecture course, Winter Semester, 1934–1935. Frankfurt am Main: V. Klostermann, 1980.

52 *Hölderlins Hymne "Andenken."* Gesamtausgabe volume 52. Freiburg lecture course, Winter Semester, 1941–1942. Frankfurt am Main: V. Klostermann, 1982.

53 *Hölderlins Hymne "Der Ister."* Gesamtausgabe volume 53. Freiburg lecture course, Summer Semester, 1942. Frankfurt am Main: V. Klostermann, 1984.

54 *Parmenides.* Gesamtausgabe volume 54. Freiburg lecture course, Winter Semester, 1942–1943. Frankfurt am Main: V. Klostermann, 1982.

55 *Heraklit: (1) Der Anfang des abendländischen Denkens; (2) Logik: Heraklits Lehre vom Logos.* Gesamtausgabe volume 55. Freiburg lecture courses, Summer Semesters, 1943 and 1944. Frankfurt am Main: V. Klostermann, 1979.

56/57 *Zur Bestimmung der Philosophie.* Gesamtausgabe volume 56/57. Early Freiburg lecture courses, War Emergency Semester, 1919, and Summer Semester, 1919. Frankfurt am Main: V. Klostermann, 1987.

61 *Phänomenologische Interpretationen zu Aristotles: Einführung in die phänomenologische Forschung.* Gesamtausgabe volume 61. Early Freiburg lecture course, Winter Semester, 1921–1922. Frankfurt am Main: V. Klostermann, 1985.

63 *Ontologie (Hermeneutik der Faktizität).* Gesamtausgabe volume 63. Early Freiburg lecture course, Summer Semester, 1923. Frankfurt am Main: V. Klostermann, 1988.

65 *Beiträge zur Philosophie (Vom Ereignis).* Gesamtausgabe volume 65. From the years 1936–1938. Frankfurt am Main: V. Klostermann, 1989.

II. English Translations of Heidegger's Works
  BW   *Basic Writings.* New York: Harper and Row, 1977.
  EGT *Early Greek Thinking.* New York: Harper and Row, 1975.
  NI, NII [after the *slash solidus*] *Nietzsche.* Two paperback volumes, reproducing the four-volume hardbound translation. San Francisco: Harper Collins, 1991.

III. Works by Friedrich Nietzsche are cited from the *Kritische Studienausgabe*, 15 volumes, edited by Giorgio Colli and Mazzino Montinari. Berlin and Munich: W. de Gruyter and Deutscher Taschenbuch Verlag, 1980. Cited as KSA, with volume and page. Nietzsche's letters are cited from the *Sämtliche Briefe, Kritische Studienausgabe,* 8 volumes, edited by Giorgio Colli and Mazzino Montinari. Berlin and Munich: W. de Gruyter and Deutscher Taschenbuch Verlag, 1986. Cited as KSAB, with volume and page.

JGB   *Jenseits von Gut und Böse,* 1886.

ZGM   *Zur Genealogie der Moral,* 1887.

WM   *Der Wille zur Macht: Versuch einer Umwertung aller Werte.* Edited
        by Peter Gast, with the assistance of Elisabeth Förster-Nietzsche.
        Stuttgart: A. Kröner, 1964 [the second, expanded edition of
        1906, reprinted in 1930].

IV. Works by Sigmund Freud are cited from the *Studienausgabe,* 11 volumes, edited by Alexander Mitscherlich, Angela Richards, and James Strachey. Frankfurt am Main: Fischer Taschenbuch Verlag, 1982. Cited as StA, with volume and page.

V. Works by Jacques Derrida

Cp   *La Carte postale de Socrate à Freud et au-delà.* Paris: Aubier-
        Flammarion, 1980. *The Post Card: From Socrates to Freud and
        Beyond.* Translated by Alan Bass. Chicago: University of Chi-
        cago Press, 1987.

De   *De l'esprit: Heidegger et la question.* Paris: Galilée, 1987. *Of
        Spirit: Heidegger and the Question.* Translated by Geoff Benning-
        ton and Rachel Bowlby. Chicago: University of Chicago Press,
        1989.

Gs, I–IV   The four "Geschlecht" papers: (1) and (2) are published in *Psyché,*
        with English translations as follows: (1) in *Research in Phenome-
        nology,* XIII, 1983, 65–83; (2) translated by John P. Leavey, Jr.
        in *Deconstruction and Philosophy: The Texts of Jacques Der-
        rida.* Edited by John Sallis. Chicago: University of Chicago Press,
        1987, 161–96. The third "Geschlecht" is not yet published. The
        fourth appears in *Reading Heidegger: Commemorations.* Edited
        by John Sallis. Bloomington: Indiana University Press, 1992.

Ma   *Marges de la philosophie.* Paris: Minuit, 1972. *Margins of Philoso-
        phy.* Translated by Alan Bass. Chicago: University of Chicago
        Press, 1982.

Ps   *Psyché: Inventions de l'autre.* Paris: Galilée, 1987.

An Introduction to Za-ology

Aber Lebendige machen alle den Fehler,
daß sie zu stark unterscheiden. [Yet
living beings all make the same
mistake—they distinguish too sharply.]

　　　　—Rainer Maria Rilke, *Duino Elegy*
　　　　　　　　　　　　　　　　　no. 1

Ist nicht vielleicht der Mensch nur die
Entwicklung des Steines durch das
Medium der Pflanze, Tier? [Might not
human being be the mere development
of stone through the medium of plants—
an animal?]

　　　　—Friedrich Nietzsche, *Fate and*
　　　　　　　　　　　　　　　　History

Heidegger borrows a story from Aristotle. It is the story about Heraclitus warming himself at a stove. And about those frustrated tourists who had come to catch a glimpse of a thinker in action but were chagrined to find him engaged in the undignified activity of warming his . . . well, warming some *part* of himself, Aristotle does not say *which* part, and if Heidegger knows he refuses to tell, although ancient rumor has it that Heraclitus was warming some part of his *body.*

Heidegger recounts this story in his "Letter on Humanism" in response to an observation by Jean Beaufret, whom Heidegger quotes as follows: "What I have been trying to do, for a long time now, is to spell out the relationship between ontology and a possible ethics" (W, 183; BW, 231). In the ensuing discussion Heidegger cites fragment B 119 of Heraclitus, in which the word ἦθος appears. He cites that fragment, he says, because he does not have time to recite the tragedies of Sophocles, which, "in their saying shelter the ἦθος in a more pristine form [*anfänglicher*] than do Aristotle's lectures on 'ethics' " (W, 184; BW, 232–33). Fragment B 119 reads as follows: ἦθος ἀνθρώπῳ δαίμων. "Human beings dwell, insofar as they are human, in the nearness of god." *Der Mensch wohnt, insofern er Mensch ist, in der Nähe Gottes* (W, 185; BW, 233).

Heidegger now narrates the story, which, he says, agrees or is in accord with the saying of Heraclitus, the story that Aristotle "reports," although certainly not in his lectures on ethics. Heidegger cites the source in Aristotle's literary corpus but says not a word about it: *De partibus animalium*, Book I, chapter 5, 645a 17.[1] Heidegger reproduces the story in Greek, along with a translation unmistakably his own, which we might render as follows:

> Concerning Heraclitus the tale is told of what he said to some strangers who wanted to approach him. As they drew near they saw him warming himself at an oven. They stood stock-still, especially when he addressed a word of encouragement to them, those hesitant ones, inviting them to come in with these words: "For here too gods come to presence [εἶναι γὰρ καὶ ἐνταῦθα θεούς: *Auch hier nämlich wesen Götter an*]."

According to Heidegger, this retold tale exhibits all the squalor and austerity of the thinker's life, *die ganze Dürftigkeit seines Lebens,* even though a life in proximity to the δαίμων might well have been thought to be a splendid thing. The present volume will not relate what Heidegger makes of this story, inasmuch as the story "speaks for itself"; nor will it discuss the Heraclitean fragment concerning ἦθος with which the story supposedly is in accord.[2] Instead, the book will recall what Heidegger says earlier in his "Letter" by way of response to Beaufret's *first* question: "How can we once again render some sense to the word *humanism?*" (W, 147; BW, 195). There Heidegger discusses the traditional definition of human being as ζῷον λόγον ἔχον, *animal rationale,* the living being that has speech. Such living being has speech, but not by virtue of its tongue or lips or ears, nor even its hands. Indeed, what could λόγος have to do with these carnal parts, the (modified) parts of animals? In a gesture more than merely reminiscent of Aristotelian entelechy Heidegger will quite often insist that we do not hear because we have acoustical equipment, that is, ears; rather, he says, after the manner of Lamarck, we have ears because we hear. Who has ears to hear, let him ear![3]

Yet how is it with the parts of animals, which, especially in human beings, are (as Heidegger puts it) "in a special situation"? A word about the context of that Heraclitus story. Or, rather, the following extracts from Book I, chapter 5 of Aristotle's *On the Parts of Living Beings,* presented here with very little comment:

> Of beings constituted by nature some are ungenerated and imperishable through all the eons, while others share in generation and decay. The former are excellent beyond compare and are divine, though less accessible to study [θεωρία]. . . . The scanty grasp we have of celestial things gives us, on account of their excellence, more pleasure than all our information about the world in which we live, just as half a glimpse of persons we love is more delightful than a lingering view of other things. . . . And yet . . . the greater nearness and natural affinity to us [of terrestrial things] balances somewhat the loftier interest of philosophy in divine things [τὰ θεῖα]. . . .
>
> We shall now proceed to treat of living creatures [περὶ τῆς ζοικῆς φύσεως] without omitting . . . any of them, however ignoble. For if some of them have no graces to charm the sense, yet even these, by disclosing to our study the craftsmanship of the nature that designed them, give immense pleasure to all who can trace causes and are inclined to philosophy. Indeed, it would be absurd and out of place

if those of us who are capable of discerning causes enjoyed examining the images [εἰκόνας] of these things—because of the painter's or sculptor's craftsmanlike skill [τέχνη]—and yet did not take even more delight in the things themselves constituted by nature. We therefore must not recoil with childish aversion from the examination of the humbler animals. In everything that flourishes, marvels are present [ἐν πᾶσι γὰρ τοῖς φυσικοῖς ἔνεστι τι θαυμαστόν]; and as Heraclitus, when some strangers came to visit him but found him warming himself at the stove in the kitchen and hesitated to go in, is reported to have bidden them not to be afraid to enter, since even in that kitchen divine things were present, so we should venture on the study of every kind of living being without being abashed; for each such being will reveal to us something burgeoning and beautiful [τινὸς φυσικοῦ καὶ καλοῦ]. . . .

If anyone thinks the study of other living creatures an unworthy task, he must go one step further and despise study of himself.

A few brief comments on the context of the Heraclitus story. It begins with the familiar bifurcation of beings into two regions, one encompassing immutable, timeless beings, known to thought rather than sensation, the other embracing beings that come to be and pass away in time, beings concerning which our sensuous knowledge—ἐπιστήμη through αἴσθησις—is vaster, more complete and certain, if less edifying, than knowledge of immutable beings. Yet however much we love to glimpse the ethereal realm, which is like a beloved face to us, the face hidden in a crowd of stars, we are *nearer* to, πλησιαίτερα, and have greater *affinity* with, τῆς φύσεως οἰκειότερα, things here below, on the earth where we dwell; *living* beings; *animals,* as we say.

Question: The "greater nearness" that Aristotle cites—how does it compare with what Heidegger calls nearness to god? Such nearness is the matter of Heraclitus' fragment B 119, ἦθος ἀνθρώπῳ δαίμων. Is the *daimon* of all living beings a god, θεός? Is such a daimon or god alive? Or is it not the crystalline, *ethereal* realm that is eminently godlike, and not at all the earthly region? How then could nearness to animals, the living beings of earth, be the "greater nearness," the proximity that tends to "balance somewhat" our lust for lofty things? Or does the "greater nearness" here point back to our remoteness from and nostalgia for cold crystal? Is "balance" here sheer ballast? Will not Aristotle himself appeal to crystalline transparency? Will he not gaze heavenward and rise on the divine afflatus of theory in order that his researches can take off and leave behind whatever is repulsive in sensation? Are there not throughout Aristotle's text or palimpsest, the palimpsest of metaphysics, ethereal traces of demiurgic causation and formation, traces of the technique that designed living beings as though they were instruments? No doubt, it is as mimetic of τέχνη that living beings themselves should fascinate rather than repel us, us who trace causes. As though the kitchen stove were loftier than what it warms.

A word about that "kitchen" and its "stove" or "oven." The English translations of Aristotle which I have used[4] specify that the stove, furnace, or oven is in the kitchen. Thus the first title of this Introduction was "Someone's in the Kitchen." However, when I saw that Heidegger had neglected to mention the kitchen in his translation—as though anxious to circumvent that room—I took a closer look at the Greek text: θερόμενον πρὸς τῷ ἰπνῷ ("warming himself at the ἰπνός") is all it says, no kitchen mentioned, although if Heraclitus invites the strangers to "drop in" we may well hope that he is talking about the kitchen, talking *in* the kitchen. An ἰπνός, Liddell-Scott informs us, is an oven or stove used especially for heating water for the bath. Which might explain the strangers' embarrassment. Or it may mean "the place of the oven, i.e., the kitchen," presuming that the oven is indoors, inside the house, which was not and is not always the case in Greece. This is a matter of some importance, especially inasmuch as the fourth meaning of the word ἰπνός (=κοπρών) is "dunghill or privy." Which might also explain the strangers' embarrassment.

In a less scatological yet more eschatological vein, the following detail from the 1943 lecture course on Heraclitus is worth recounting. If Heidegger circumvents the kitchen, presuming it *is* a kitchen, he does not avoid the "baking oven," *Backofen*. Indeed, he places Heraclitus not at, near, or even on it, but *inside* it. Πρὸς τῷ ἰπνῷ is here translated as *wie er sich in einem Backofen wärmte* (55, 6–9; 22–23). Heidegger may have been thinking of a *Backstube* (at 55, 10 he writes *Backhaus*), where a baker's apprentice would shake off the early morning chill. Yet it is disconcerting, to say the least (the year is 1943), that Heidegger reiterates the *in* several times, perhaps playing with the ἐν- of ἐνταῦθα. He comes very close to identifying Heraclitus with the loaf of bread that "rises in the heat rays," swelling "into radiance," *in das Erscheinen* (9). Occasionally he uses the preposition *an,* "at," but only in order to emphasize the "undignified everyday appearance" of the philosopher's actions; when Heraclitus is *inside* the oven, as though standing in the firestorm of being, his residence becomes truly *un-geheuer,* uncommon, unheard-of, demonstratively monstrous.

Nor is this the first time Heidegger finds himself drawn to centers of califaction. Two sections of his 1942 lecture course on Hölderlin's hymn *Der Ister* (53, 134–43) are devoted to the stove or hearth, *der Herd*. Heidegger alludes to Hesiod's and Pindar's genealogies of Ἑστία, genealogies that variously name the titaness of the hearth as either "the sister of Zeus the Highest and of Hera who rules with him," in which case something like incest is unavoidable (for how could Hestia be a sister to both Zeus and Hera?), or the eldest daughter of Zeus and Rhea, in which case something like incest is inevitable (for is not Rhea the *mother* of Zeus, Poseidon, Hades, *and* Hera?). Heidegger does not pause to marvel at the monstrous heart(h) of things divinely domestic. Instead, he cites a fragment of Philolaus of Croton, along with Plato's *Phaedrus* (at 246ff., on the feast of gods and daimons) and Sophocles' and Hölderlin's *Antigone*. All these references and quotations celebrate ἑστία as the "stove [or hearth, or foyer] of being":

> The stove, the place in the home that is homey [*die Heimstatt des Heimischen*], is being itself. In its light and sparkle, glow and warmth, all beings have always already gathered themselves. Παρέστιος is the one who, tarrying in the vicinity of

the hearth [or stove], belongs together with those who are familiar with the hearth, so that everyone who belongs around the hearth is like one of the family [*ein Trauter*], whether he is among the "living" or the dead. (53, 143)

When Heidegger rewrites the Heraclitus story for Jean Beaufret three years later, in 1946, he alters the preposition "inside" to at, by, or near (W, 185–86). As though he can hear what Derrida will have said about flame and spirit. However, the alteration only underscores the significance for daimon life of the political, the impact of disconcerting questions concerning spirit and conflagration.5 We shall have to return to the oven—if it *is* an oven—or to the uncanny places and spaces of the Heraclitean daimon. For the moment, let us return to the spirit of the "Letter," and to Beaufret's desire to rehabilitate something like "humanism."

GREATER NEARNESS, ABYSS OF ESSENCE

Early in the "Letter on Humanism" Heidegger writes:

Of all the beings that are, presumably the most difficult to think are living creatures [*das Lebe-Wesen*], because on the one hand they are in a certain way most closely akin to us [*uns . . . am nächsten verwandt*], and on the other hand are at the same time separated from our ek-sistent essence [*Wesen*] by an abyss [*durch einen Abgrund*]. In opposition to them, it might also seem as though the essence of divinity were nearer to us than what is shockingly alien in living creatures [*das Befremdende der Lebe-Wesen*]; nearer, namely, in an essential remoteness [*Wesensferne*] which, while remote, is nonetheless more familiar to our eksistent essence than our scarcely conceivable, abysmal bodily kinship with the beast. (W, 157; BW, 206)

I shall pass over in silence the difficulties involved in translating all these *Wesen* that Heidegger conjures: *Lebe-Wesen*, the shockingly alien "living creature" to which we are akin and in which Aristotle (in contrast to Heidegger) finds "the greater nearness"; *ek-sistentes Wesen*, the "essence" (namely, "ours") that "stands out" ecstatically into the clearing, the nothing, the granting of time and being; *das Wesen des Göttlichen*, the "essence" (or, dare we say, once and for all, the "creature") of the godlike, which, however ethereally remote it may be, seems far more familiar, domestic, *vertraut*, and "kitcheny" to us than what is so foreign, so startlingly alien, both *fremd* and *befremdend*, in the living creatures that dwell so uncannily close to us; and finally, *Wesensferne*, the "essential remoteness," "remoteness of essence," or perhaps "haunting presence" by which what is near seems far, and far near.6 Let me focus instead on the "abyss" that gapes twice in these few lines of Heidegger's "Letter." However akin to us (other) living beings may seem, they are "separated" from us "by an abyss," *durch einen Abgrund*.7 And yet, by a bizarre doubling, this abyss of separation is now invoked to name the very proximity and affinity identified long ago by Aristotle, the nearness and kinship of the human and the bestial: Heidegger refers to our *abysmal* bodily kinship with the beast, *abgründige leibliche Verwandtschaft*.

What about this abyss that separates us from and draws us toward the beasts? Who, us? Are we "Heideggerians" still creatures of the Platonic χωρισμός, the gap that separates being from beings? Are the ontological difference and the proto-ontological difference (between *Sein* and *Seiendes,* and between *Sein* and *Dasein*) a moat dug in order to protect humanity's airy castle from the encroaching beast? How do matters stand (as Heidegger likes to ask) with an abyss of essential separation, a chasm, which at the same time marks an abysmal affinity, a chiasm? Is our abysmal bodily kinship with the beast abysmal precisely because *Verwandtschaft* (from *verwenden*) is one of those oppositional *Urworte,* meaning both to turn away from and to turn toward, both a childish averting and a childlike adverting? And who or what are these "remote" essences or creatures we often take to be "nearer," on our side of the abyss, as it were?

One might at this juncture be tempted into a reading of Goethe's *Wahlver-wandtschaften,* and even more into a reading of Walter Benjamin's remarkable interpretation of that work. I am thinking of Benjamin's commentary on an extended passage from Goethe's *Dichtung und Wahrheit.* On the "plain" of Goethe's "Confessions," according to Benjamin, the concept of the daimonic (*dämonisch*) "stands out like a polished monolith." As though Arthur C. Clarke and Stanley Kubrick found their stunning monolith for *2001: A Space Odyssey* in Benjamin's Goethe! However bizarre a digression it may seem— from our abysmal bodily affinity with the beast to the monolithic daimon—let us digress for an instant. In *Dichtung und Wahrheit* Goethe writes:

> In the course of this biographical narrative the reader has had multiple occasions to see how the child, the boy, the youth tried to approach the supernatural along various paths: first with a view to and an inclination toward a religion of nature; then, through love, his firm attachment to a positive religion; farther on, by means of a retreat into himself, his attempt to get on by dint of his own energies; and finally, his giving himself over [*sich hingeben*] joyfully to a generalized faith. As he wandered back and forth among the interstices of these regions, seeking and casting about in all directions, he confronted many things that may well have belonged to none of those regions; he believed that he could see ever more clearly that it would be better for him to divert his thoughts from these things that were so monstrously vast and ungraspable [*von dem Ungeheueren, Unfaßlichen*].—He believed he discovered something in nature, whether animate or inanimate, besouled or bereft of soul, that manifested itself only in contradictions, and there-fore could be grasped under no concept, much less under a word. That something was not divine, for it seemed to be unreasonable; not human, for it had no understanding; not diabolical, for it was beneficent; not angelical, for it often smiled at others' pain. It was like an accident, for it exhibited no consequent effect; it was similar to Providence, for it gestured toward the way in which things held together [*Zusammenhang*]. Everything that limits us seemed penetrable by it; it seemed to manipulate at will the necessitous elements of our existence; it com-pressed time and expanded space. It seemed to take its pleasure in the impossible alone, and to repel with contempt the possible.—This essence [*Wesen*], which seemed to advance into the midst of all the others, to separate them off, to bind

them together, I called daimonic [*dämonisch*], after the example of the ancients and of those who had experienced something similar. I tried to save myself in the face of this frightful essence. [*Ich suchte mich vor diesem furchtbaren Wesen zu retten.*][8]

Walter Benjamin comments as follows: "Mythic humanity pays the price of anxiety for its involvement with daimonic forces. Such anxiety spoke unmistakably in Goethe on many occasions." Benjamin refers to the "governance of primeval powers [*die Gewalt uralter Mächte*]" in Goethe's life, and to the purest of all anxieties, anxiety in the face of death (*die Angst vorm Tod*), "which encompasses all the others." This is not the only place in which Benjamin begins to sound like Heidegger, for whom he would like to have felt only contempt; this is not the only place where the sake of thinking constrains them both.

The digression, touching Benjamin's Goethe, is no more than a brief indication of the alarming "spread" of the daimonic—of daimonic life, or "daimon life," if you will. If indeed it touches the heart of "mythic humanity," we will find it in the *Gilgamesh* epic, in early Greek thinking through Aristotle, in the Hebraic tradition that culminates in the Cabala and in the Gnostic and Hermetic traditions, on into Goethe and all the romantics and idealists, through Nietzsche, and down to the present. Daimon life will surely touch on plants, animals, humans, and humanists. Yet it could well take us from the *genius* or tutelary figure of antiquity to the mysterious figure of Manes in Hölderlin's third and final draft of his tragedy, *Der Tod des Empedokles*. And the figures of daimon life would not stop proliferating in our own proudly secular yet frazzled age.[9]

The abyss that separates us from all other living beings and yet turns us toward them—returning now to our questions to Heidegger's "Letter"—is it the selfsame abyss that "yawns" in Dasein as "the (nihilative) being-the-ground of a nullity," *das (nichtige) Grund-sein einer Nichtigkeit* (SZ, 285)? Is the abysmal kinship one of those "abysses" in which profound boredom drifts like a muffling fog, removing "all things and human beings and oneself along with it into a remarkable indifference," thus revealing beings as a whole (W, 8; BW, 101)? Is it the selfsame abyss that causes Heidegger's later thinking to somersault beyond all grounds and reasons, the *Ab-Grund* that necessitates a *Satz vom Grund* as the supreme play in which human beings—those who dwell "in nearness to death"—are at stake?[10] The abyss of essence that ostensibly separates Dasein from other forms of life (presupposing that Dasein is alive) will induce us to read Heidegger's *Being and Time* once again, but from a somewhat novel vantage-point, namely, that of life-philosophy. Chapters 1 and 2 will initiate such a reading, though not complete it. For the question of the abyss of essence that separates human beings from just-plain-life is not successfully answered in Heidegger's magnum opus.

In a remarkable lecture course entitled, "The Fundamental Concepts of Metaphysics: World—Finitude—Solitude," delivered during the winter semester of 1929–1930, that is to say, some 120 years after Kleist's *Marionetten-theater*, twelve years after Franz Kafka's "A Report to an Academy," some five years after Thomas Mann's *Magic Mountain*, a tale of time, profound boredom, and consumptive life, two years after Heidegger's own *Being and Time;* and precisely when, on the one hand, Alfred North Whitehead was completing *Process and Reality* and, on the other, Georges Bataille (in *Documents*) was doing impossible things with anthropoid apes, Heidegger undertook a dual challenge: first, he sought to analyze profound boredom, *die tiefe Lange-Weile,* as a founding mood of Dasein; second, he tried to distinguish sharply and in detail among the respective "world-relations" of lifeless stone, living animal, and human Dasein. It was the last time he would try to identify a *Grund-stimmung* that might serve as the fundament for fundamental ontology; it was the first time he tried to say more about animal life than he had said in *Being and Time*, which was that life (as "just-plain-life," *Nur-noch-leben, SZ,* 50) would be what remained after "care" were subtracted from Dasein. Chapter 3 will take up Heidegger's "theoretical biology" in some detail. Suffice it to say by way of introduction that the 1929–1930 course is Heidegger's "most splendid fail-ure."[11] Splendid because Heidegger here tries with remarkable persistence and energy to compare the world-relations of stone, animal, and human being, without collapsing into either crass physicalism or naive vitalism and anthropo-morphism. Yet it is the middle term—animal, ζῷον, living being, just-plain-life—that remains inaccessible, as though an abyss separated the ontologist from it, or as though a ring encircled him or her *within* it, suffocatingly close. "Access" (*Zugang*) is the problem (especially in sections 43, 47, and 49 of the course), just as the kind of access (*Zugangsart*) to the question of the meaning of being and to the everyday existence of Dasein poses the crucial methodological problems for *Being and Time.*[12] After wrestling long and hard with the problem in his lecture course Heidegger eventually concedes that access to the middle term is possible only from *within the circle* of being and the understanding-of-being, that is to say, only from within the abyss that is Dasein (29/30, 371; 394). However, if Dasein is itself an abyss, if its being is the very cleaving of being and the dissolution of all grounds, then what sense can it possibly make to claim that Dasein is separated from the animal by any abyss of essence—one abyss separat-ing another, abysmally, with nothing in between? Life will remain a matter of privation for Heidegger's investigation, "just-plain-life," *Nur-noch-leben.* Her-meneutical encirclement will—like life itself—prove to be full of pitfalls. Let us take a brief look at the lecture course, merely by way of introduction, an intro-duction to something other than zoology.

  At the outset of his theoretical biology (section 51), Heidegger wants very much to resist Wilhelm Roux's reduction of the organic to a *Werk-zeug* or instrumentarium devoid of world-relation. To such mechanism and physi-calism Heidegger opposes a theory of the organ as "capability" rather than "capacity," *Fähigkeit zu* rather than *Fertigkeit für* (sections 52–57). At times the analysis of such capability appears to be leading Heidegger quite close to the world-relation of Dasein, as the creature of the *Wozu, Um-zu,* and *Zu-*

kunft. Indeed, the relation of the organism as a whole to *time* as life-duration seems to remove it altogether from the realm of lifeless beings (29/30, 328). However, Heidegger never expands his theory of organism to the point where it descends into the second great shaft of meanings beneath the words *organ* and *organism*. If ὄργανον is bound up with ἔργον, with the demiurgic world of work and technics, there remains the world (very much closer to Heidegger's own *Grundstimmungen*, one would think) of living beings, the Greek ὀργή, "natural impulse or propensity, temperament, disposition, mood." It is the world in which ὀργάω, "I become ready to bear, grow ripe; of men, to swell with lust, wax wanton, be rampant; of human beings and animals, to be in heat, to desire sexual intercourse"; ὀργάω is presumably related to ὀρέγω, "I reach, stretch out, yearn for," ὄρεξις being Aristotle's word for conation and one of Heidegger's words for care, *Sorge* (SZ, 171), the very "care" that is supposed to be subtracted from Dasein in order to get "just-plain-life." Indeed, a *second*, as yet *untold* history of being lies concealed in the ὀργή; it is a history that commences with the Greek word for life, ζωή, and peters out in the "lived experience" (*Er-lebnis*) of modernity (see chapter 6, below). In spite of its epochal significance for Heidegger's thinking of being—ζωή being one of the principal Greek words for being—Heidegger himself never enters the ὀργάς, never frequents "any well-watered, fertile spot of land, meadow-land, partially wooded, with or without cultivated fields," where daimons are sure to dwell. His *Feldweg* and *Holzwege* seem to circumvent these spots. In his writing—for it is not a question of what "Heidegger" enters into or circumvents, but only of his texts—Heidegger never pursues his bugs and bees back to the nectar-laden ὀργάς. (I mention bugs and bees because they, along with pseudopodia, are Heidegger's favorite animals: not many uncouth mammals here, nor any eagle or serpent, though there is a mole.)

Capability is a reflexive relation of sorts, a *Sich-zu-eigen-sein*, a primitive kind of propriation and particularization (*Eigentum, Eigentümlichkeit*). Yet it is by no means a relation to *self:* Heidegger is careful to reserve selfhood to Dasein. Indeed, the bulk of his analyses set the selfhood of human Dasein in relief against the realm of mere animality. He reserves—for it is clearly a matter of reservations and reserves, retainings and restrainings—the word "comport-ment" (*Verhalten*) to designate the stance or posture of an erect and heroically reticent Dasein in the midst of beings. For the animal realm he selects the words "behavior" and "benumbment" (*Benehmen, Benommenheit*). *Benommen* is the past participle of *Benehmen* and means "disturbed, dazed, dizzy, dazzled, confused, mildly anesthetized, stupefied, stunned"; *benumbed*, as it were, whether by trauma, alcohol, or narcotics. In popular usage the word means dull-witted, stupid. *Benehmen* means to deprive someone of something (see, for example, SZ, 187). Used reflexively, *sich benehmen* means one's behavior, especially in public, as either "socially acceptable" or "boorish" behavior. Heidegger's choice of words—rather odd inasmuch as animals, even well-trained domesticated ones, cannot really be told to "behave themselves" (29/30, 345–46)—seems to rest on the essentially *privative* and *passive* sense and structure of *Benommensein,* not only in the 1929–1930 lectures but also in *Being and Time.* A word about *Benommenheit* and *Benommensein* in *Being and Time,* for these terms will preoccupy us throughout the book.

Heidegger employs the past participle several times in *Being and Time* in order to designate a particularly "fallen" state of the existence of humans—not animals. At SZ, 61, he stresses that being in the world, in taking care or being concerned (*Besorgen*), "is *dazzled* [Heidegger's emphasis] by the things it takes care of," so that a merely theoretical "gaping" at things as though they were merely "at hand" is at first impossible. At SZ, 76, he suggests that in its familiarity with innerworldly beings Dasein can "lose itself" and be "dazed" by those beings. At SZ, 113 (cf. 176 and 271), Heidegger says of the "absorption" (*Aufgehen*) of Dasein in everydayness, "At first and for the most part, Dasein is benumbed by its world." "Dazzled," "dazed," "benumbed" are all trying to translate *benommen:* apparently, for much of the time, Dasein comports itself in the world precisely in the way animals behave in theirs. Nevertheless, in 1929–1930 *Benommensein* will be used to earmark or brand animals as such, animals specifically and exclusively, animals as excluded from all *proper* world-relation, animals as life-and-life-only, just-plain-life, *Nur-noch-leben.*

However, a sixth appearance of the words *benommen, Benommenheit* in *Being and Time* (at 344) radically upsets the sense of the passages we have only now examined. Section 68, "The Temporality of Disclosedness in General," subsection (b), "The Temporality of Disposition [*Befindlichkeit*]," discusses the "mightiness" (*Mächtigkeit*) of anxiety, along with its "peculiar temporality." That temporality is peculiar indeed: it grants the possibility of appropriate Dasein and yet temporalizes not out of the future but out of having-been, *Gewesenheit,* thus subverting the regime of an open resolve that runs ahead, *vorlaufende Entschlossenheit.* In the mood of anxiety, "Dasein is taken back fully to its naked uncanniness and is dazzled by it [*zurückgenommen und von ihr benommen*]. Taken back and taken aback. Yet this bedazzlement [*Benommenheit*] not only *takes* Dasein back from its 'worldly' possibilities but also at the same time *grants* it the possibility of an *appropriate* being-able-to-be [*eines* eigentlichen *Seinkönnens*]." The upshot is that *Benommenheit* is both what bedazzles and distracts Dasein, causing it to be *lost* in the allurements of the world, and what dazzles Dasein with its own uncanniness, thus allowing Dasein to *find* itself as a proper self. In the 1928 lecture course, this positive, "giving" aspect of *Benommenheit* is emphasized quite strongly (26, 13). Throughout *Being and Time* the lost-and-found duplicity of *Benommenheit* is maintained. Dasein as forlorn creature, very like a dazed animal, and Dasein as crystalline, transparent self. In both cases benumbed.

Is this only an accident of misapplied terminology? Has Heidegger quite suddenly and inexplicably grown sloppy in his use of words? Or is something unraveling here, something like the simple oppositions of giving/taking, granting/depriving, finding/losing? Does such unraveling threaten to undo the entire fabric of fundamental ontology? And if the fabric of fundamental ontology frays, can it possibly serve as the stuff of an ontology of life?[13]

The suspicion obtrudes that the deliberate choice of words, the semantic abyss that Heidegger opens in 1929–1930 between human *Verhalten* and brute *Benommenheit,* derives from an ancient prejudice, that Heidegger.'s self-proclaimed *sachliche* interpretation in the biology lectures (29/30, 345) is in fact guided by what Nietzsche would have called a *moral* prejudice—indeed, *the* moral prejudice. Whether Heidegger can be as sanguine about such a prejudice as he appears to be in *Being and Time* (SZ, 310) about the possibility—indeed, the necessity—of a "factical ideal" surreptitiously guiding the ontologist of Dasein is doubtful. The abyss that Heidegger institutes between comportment and behavior is the very abyss that guarantees what a moment ago I called the *proto-ontological difference.* That *Sein* is no kind of *Seiendes* is noted by only one such *Seiendes,* to wit, *daseinsmäßiges Seiendes,* the being that is of-the-measure-of-Dasein. Dasein alone is the being that is not altogether "taken in" by nature, not altogether "benumbed" in the ringdance of beings. The *mäßig* is here superfluous, or perhaps—but this would require a long and difficult exposition—both absolutely necessary, if Dasein is being in a world, and absolutely contingent and accidental, if Dasein is the only such being; the *mäßig* would be, in a word, *supplemental.* In the biology lectures Heidegger also speaks of the *Hingenommenheit* of animals, whose world-relation is only a *quasi*-relation, inasmuch as "relation" is *Verhältnis,* hence reserved for the *Verhalten* of Dasein. Animals "suffer" or "put up with" their world, taking it "in stride." Their *quasi*-world is no more than a "ring of disinhibitions" (*Enthemmungsring*), a closed circle of evasions and eliminations, a theater of deprivation. It is the horrific world in which the female praying mantis suffers the amorous attentions of her mate and then devours him, in both cases bent on evasion and elimination, in both cases *benommen.* Failure of the distinction between comportment and behavior (*Verhalten/ Benehmen*) would mean failure of both the proto-ontological difference (between *Dasein* and every other kind of *Seiendes*) and the ontological difference as such (between *Sein* and *Seiendes*). For the abyss between Dasein and animal is the gap that opens to difference as such: were that abyss to close, the gap that yawns in order to parture the question of the meaning of being would never gape; were the abyss of essence that separates humans from animals not dug, the *question* and *questioning* of being would collapse. However, when the abyss *is* dug, it is always excavated to the specifications of the ontotheological tradition, with gods and angels on one side, demons and beasts on the other, and mortals with a foot in both camps, but leaning toward heaven.

Yet what does gape is the 1929–1930 lecture course itself, its two halves affronting one another stubbornly despite Heidegger's every integrative effort. The benumbed behavior of the organism is contraposed not to *Stimmung,* the fundamentally disclosive attunement of Dasein that is treated in the first half of the course, but to the very Kantian-Husserlian-Schelerian "personality" and "personhood" that Heidegger had criticized in section 10 of *Being and Time.* Indeed, the lecture course has recourse to selfhood, ipseity, the ego, objectivity, representational consciousness, and assertory or apophantic (that is, propositional) discourse—traits and structures that Heidegger tried at least to put in question, if not radically undermine, in his magnum opus. Although he explicitly demands (in section 67 of the course) a return to the earlier analyses of mood and finitude, and thus calls for a closing of the gap in his own lecture course, he still insists that an "abyss" will have to intrude, an abyss to segregate (human) Dasein from (organic) life. Heidegger's abyss would open like Hesiodic χάος in order to let the light of the world shine for Dasein alone, radiating like a flame in a lantern, or like fire in an oven in the kitchen, if it *is* a kitchen:

> We now confront the task of presentifying originarily the moments of the concept of world that we came to know as provisional traits. We shall take up the task by *going back in the direction* opened up to us by our interpretation of *profound boredom* as a founding mood of human Dasein. It will be shown how this founding mood, along with everything encompassed within it, is to be set in relief against what we asserted the essence of animality to be, to wit, benumbed behavior [*Benommenheit*]. Such setting in relief will be all the more decisive for us as the very essence of animality, benumbed behavior, appears to slip into closest proximity [*nächste Nähe*] to what we delineated as a characteristic of profound boredom, what we called the *binding/banning* [Gebanntheit] of Dasein within beings as a whole. It will of course be shown that this closest proximity of the two essential constitutions is merely deceptive, that an abyss lies between them, an abyss that cannot be bridged by any kind of mediation in any way at all. But then the complete bifurcation of the two theses ["The animal is poor in world"; "Human beings shape a world"], and thereby the essence of world, will become luminous to us. (29/30, 409)

However, in what follows (section 68), Heidegger comes very close to seeing how "the entire abyss of Dasein" gapes in such a way as to swallow all "*founding* moods," causing all foundations and grounds, all abysses of essence, to founder. *Abgrund* and *Grund* confront one another in what he clearly recognizes as a "crisis" of fundamental ontology and ontology of life— ontology, if one may say so, *as such*. His own final efforts to define the "as-structure" as the world-shaping peculiarity of human beings, those living beings who have the λόγος—for when Dasein is sunning itself on a rock it knows the sun *as* sun, the rock *as* rock, and this is what makes it different from the benumbed lizard *as* lizard—neatly circumvent the abyss. Postpone the crisis.

I shall not examine the crisis in any detail, not even in chapter 3, below, where all this is elaborated more painstakingly, inasmuch as the question of *Gebanntheit,* the peculiarly *temporal* character of human being, is quite complex. Yet one would be able to show that the 1929–1930 lecture course, with its two parts, parts that very much yearn to become a whole, represents an inversion of the two divisions of *Being and Time*. The materials on profound boredom recover the analyses of appropriateness, time, and the moment of vision, whereas those on animality and organism recover the provisional analysis of worldliness, handiness, and being at hand. Further, one could also show that this inversion solves none of the problems of fundamental ontology. It is not the turnabout or *Umschlag* (26, 196–202) that Heidegger is looking for in 1928; it is not the twisting free or *Herausdrehung* from the tradition that Heidegger requires of Nietzsche and of himself.[14]

Chapters 2 and 3 of the present volume will emphasize only one aspect of the failure, an aspect that Heidegger himself makes certain his students will not overlook. For he openly confesses that he is unable to say anything about the way in which *death* intervenes in both animal and human life. Not only does he find himself resorting to a blatantly metaphysical and even ontotheological appeal to the "as-structure," which here means the apophantic rather than the hermeneutic "as" and the discourse of *Vorhandenheit* more than anything else, but he also catches himself (or *almost* catches himself) reverting to the distinction between human dying and animal perishing, *Sterben* as opposed to *Verenden,* even though it has become clear to all that something very much like the nothing (*das Nichts*) shatters the ring of animal as well as human life. At a crucial juncture in the second half of his course (29/30, 387) Heidegger writes: "The touchstone for determining the suitability and originality of every inquiry into the essence of life and vice-versa [that is, presumably, the life of essence or of the creature] is whether the inquiry has sufficiently grasped the problem of death; and whether it is able to bring that problem in the correct way into the question concerning the essence of life." Heidegger's own verdict (386–87; 395–96) is that his inquiry fails. Fails for precisely the same reason that his earlier search for the unified horizon of ecstatic temporality, the finitude of time, failed—namely, the "difficult problem of death" (24, 387). "Daimon life" is therefore all about the difficult problem of death. Death and dying constitute its very *ethos*—death and dying and all the words that surround these events in the circles of human and animal life.

ZA-, ZER-, ZU: TOO FAR AFIELD

Ἦθος ἀνθρώπῳ δαίμων. Human beings dwell in the nearness of the daimon, of living beings, of death. Who or what is warming itself at the stove, if it *is* a stove? Θεοί, says Heraclitus. Every kind of ζῷον, says Aristotle. Daimonic Dasein, says Heidegger, meaning the mortal. And yet these three answers, whatever the abysses of difference between them, may be the selfsame. Provided we are able to avoid the error of drawing distinctions too sharply, too violently.

In his second Heraclitus essay, entitled "Aletheia," Heidegger invokes gods and daimons, Zeus, mortals, and animals, and tries to think them all together without excessive distinguishings. With remarkable persistence. With scant success.[15] Pursuing through the "grounds and abysses of Greek thinking" his interpretation of φύσις as pure upsurgence (*Aufgehen*) into unconcealment (N.B.: not the *Aufgehen* or absorption in the world that characterizes a bedazzled Dasein), Heidegger recalls "ever-living fire," πῦρ ἀείζωον. It is the fire to which Heraclitus exposes himself every day of his life—as though he were a loaf of leavened bread, himself of the staff of life, as it were, and ready for baking. The thought of ever-living fire thus kindles the question of "life" in general. Life-fire is the *essence* of life, and an inquiry into it would be the new science of za-ology: "How must we understand our word *life* if we accept it as a faithful translation of the Greek word ζῆν? In ζῆν, ζάω, the root ζα- speaks. It is, of course, impossible to conjure up the Greek meaning of 'life' from this sound" (VA, 274; EGT, 116–17). A word about the sound.

Back in 1943 Heidegger had elaborated somewhat upon the impossibility of capturing what is to be said (*das Zu-sagende*) in either spoken or, worse, written or, worst of all, typed words. He said to his students, or read to them what he had written and what his brother Fritz was soon to type, as follows:

> The word of the thinker [in this case, Heraclitus] stands under the protection of the goddess [Artemis]; it is the word as the saying of what is to be said [*die Sage des Zusagenden*]. However, because the word is not grounded in the sounding of the words [*Lauten der Wörter*], because the sounded word resonates as the word that it is solely from out of the primordially soundless word, words and word-configurations can crumble [*zerbrechen*] in writing and in the book [*in der Schrift und im Buch*], whereas the word remains. . . . In the beginning of thinking is the word. (55, 27)

Heidegger repeats this Johannine admonition when the time comes (93) to discuss the root of *za-ology*, the Greek root of life, ζα-, in some detail: "From this phoneme [*Lautgebilde*], itself 'composed' of the consonant ζ and the vowel α, we cannot, of course, spin out the 'essence of life'." Heidegger therefore makes no comment on either the consonant or the vowel, says nothing about either the articulation or the music of Rousseau.[16] Nor does he allude to Plato's *Cratylus* (427a–c), which has thought-provoking things to say about the pneumatic consonant ζ, of all consonants the zephyr, the least occlusive, least demanding and deadly, the most redolent of life and zest, and the mighty aperture of the vowel α, expressive of grandeur. Perhaps he says nothing because he shares Socrates' suspicions about his own wild wisdom, his phonic and manic euphoria, his glossolalia. Yet neither Heidegger nor we can afford to ignore several of Socrates' etymologies and derivations, of Zeus from "life" (396a–b; 410d), of gods from celestial "coursers" (397d), and of daimons and heroes from humans who are superhuman in knowledge and wisdom (398b–c) but also in erotic matters (398c–d). And even in those places where Heidegger would appear to agree with Socrates, the purest thinker of the West, the thinker who never wrote, who never had to take refuge from the storm of being in the shadowy nooks and crannies of literature (WhD? 52, 56), even where Heidegger would agree with Socrates' derivation of *human* from that which looks up and sees (399c), we would be beset by Socrates' worry about all this talk about speech and writing—a worry the Greeks called ὕβρις. However, all this is taking us, as Heidegger will soon say of his own discussion of ζα-, "too far afield." Let us return to "Aletheia":

> Yet we do notice that the Greek language, above all in the speech of Homer and Pindar, uses words like ζάθεος, ζαμενής, ζάπυρος. Linguistics explains that ζα-

signifies an intensification. Ζάθεος accordingly means "most divine," "very holy"; ζαμενής, "very forceful"; ζάπυρος, "most fiery." Yet this "intensification" means neither a mechanical nor a dynamic increase. (VA, 273; EGT, 116)

Before we follow Heidegger in abandoning linguistics and philology for the pure principles of za-ology, let us pause to note the following details. The preposition ζά is the Aeolian (that is, windy!) way to say διά, "through, across, throughout," and the intensifying or emphatic adverb "very, thoroughly"; διά, cognate with δύο and δίς, "two, twice, doubly," expresses both mutual relation and difference, both completing and sundering; it means both that which is in-between or only partly such-and-such and that which is thoroughly, out-and-out, utterly so. Ζά thus implies both intensification and breaching, augmentation and splitting-off, enhancement and dehiscence. We shall have occasion to revert to this ambiguous dilation and dissemination at the end of this Introduction and throughout the book, especially when ζα- takes us to the German zer-, the emphatic prefix. Meanwhile, Heidegger is surely right when he says (55, 93) that there is nothing straightforwardly "mechanical" about ζα-. We may also be certain that there is nothing straightforward about the three "examples" of ζα- words that are here brought to the fore: "most holy," "very forceful and powerful," "doubly fiery." "Aletheia" continues:

> Pindar calls various locales, mountains, meadows, and banks of a river ζάθεος, especially when he wants to say that the gods, the radiant ones who cast a look in [*die scheinend Hereinblickenden*], often permitted themselves to be seen in their proper shapes [*oft und eigentlich*]. They came to presence by appearing here. These locales are especially holy because they arise purely to allow the appearing of the radiant one. So too does ζαμενής mean that which allows the imminently advancing storm to billow up in its full presencing.
>
> Ζα- signifies the pure letting-rise within appearing, gazing into, breaking in upon and advancing, and all their ways. (VA, 274; EGT, 116)

"Aletheia" follows the 1943 course (55, 93–94; 108) quite closely here, although it neglects one further ζα- word, one that is especially striking for a reflection on the essence of life: ζατρεφής, meaning "well-nourished, flourishing, burgeoning." As though what from one point of view looks like an eliminating from another seems to be an enhancing through enjoyment of the fruits of the earth. Moreover, in the same pages of the 1943 lecture course Heidegger risks the assertion that *all* the ζα- words "keep to a unified realm of essence," *halten sich in einem einheitlichen Wesensbereich*, even though further examples and demonstrations would lead him "too far afield," *zu weit*. As an essentially unified realm, ζα- suggests itself as the unified realm of essence as such, the unified realm of φύσις. Za-ology would be nothing else than an inquiry into being as upsurgence in unconcealment.

In neither "Aletheia" nor the 1943 course does Heidegger speculate on the full impact of one of the original ζα- words: ζα-μενής derives from the word μένος, "force, governance, violence" (55, 93: *die Kraft, die Gewalt*), coupled with the emphatic root of life, which some philological speculations, as we

shall see, take to be the most probable origin of the word *daimon*. Δαίμων =
ζα-μένος. Nor does Heidegger pause to wonder whether the German words
zu, zer-, ze-, and z', as intensifying forms and phonemes, the intensifying
structures and sounds of *unserer Sprache,* as it were, are related to the Greek
ζά. In which case one could never go *too* far afield.[17] Nevertheless, he makes
his principal point most forcefully and without hesitation: thought in a Greek
fashion, ζα- means pure upsurgence into radiant appearance, the entry of a
being into unconcealment, the *Herein-* of *Hereinblicken, Hereinschauen,* and
Hereinbrechen. In a word, to repeat, the unified realm of essence in ζα- is
φύσις. Which brings us back to "life" and revives the question of "presencing"
in "Aletheia," as though life and revealing were one:

> The verb ζῆν means rising into the light. Homer says, ζῆν καὶ ὁρᾶν φάος ἠελίοιο,
> "to live, and that means to see the light of the sun." The Greek ζῆν, ζωή, ζῷον
> must not be interpreted in either a zoological sense or a broader biological sense.
> What is named in the Greek ζῷον lies so far from any biologically conceived
> animality that the Greeks could even call their gods ζῷα. How could this be?[18]

"Even their gods," *sogar ihre Götter.* As though nothing could be more
shockingly alien to mortals than the nearness of god and animal to one another. As though the allergic reaction to biology and to "any biologically
conceived animality" in proximity to divinity had nothing to do with the
history of metaphysics and morality. As though the long and tortuous path of
ontotheology did not in the end run up against its ultimate oxymoron—
daimon life. However, as Heidegger is constrained to say, in the dawn of that
tradition the Greeks called their gods daimons, and their daimons they took to
be alive. In his 1951 "Logos" article (VA, 222–24; EGT, 72–74), Heidegger
reminds us that the Heraclitean ῝Εν both accepts and rejects the name *Zeus.*
Perhaps the singular, uniquely gathering One, the unified realm of essence that
is φύσις, would be more amenable to the name *Zeus* if it were written as
Pherecydes of Syros writes it: instead of Ζεύς (Ζήν, Ζάν, Διός, Διί, Δία, etc.)
Pherecydes invokes Ζάς, the titanic, daimonic figure that in its own emphatic
name weds sky and earth, immortals and mortals, perhaps even gods and
dogs.[19]

In the 1943 lecture course (55, 95) Heidegger adds that not only the gods
but also their statues are called ζῷα, for both are "what has surged up, standing there in the open." It is therefore less anomalous that animals too should be
brought into proximity with the gods, although we would do well to recall
Aristotle's words on the relation of art, life, and childish aversion: "Indeed, it
would be absurd and out of place if those of us who are capable of discerning
causes enjoyed examining the images [εἰκόνας] of these things—because of the
painter's or sculptor's craftsmanlike skill [τέχνη]—and yet did not take even
more delight in the things themselves constituted by nature." Heidegger himself protests that the animal "is not being thought in Christian fashion, merely
as something lowly and distinct from something more 'elevated,' to wit, human
beings" (55, 95; cf. 106). Be that as it may, living things such as animals are

surely not pieces of sculpture, statues of stone. No one would confuse the marble horses of a pediment frieze with living creatures. And so Heidegger must in "Aletheia" proceed as follows:

> Those who cast a look in [*Die Hereinblickenden*] are the ones who surge up in gazing [*ins Schauen*]. The gods are not experienced as animals. Yet animality does belong to ζῆν in a special sense. The upsurgence of animals into the free region [*zum Freien*] remains closed and sealed off in a way that is at once shockingly alien [*befremdend*] and captivating [*bestrickend*]. Self-revealing and self-concealing in the animal are one, in such a way that human analysis practically runs out of alternatives when it rejects mechanistic views of animality—which are always feasible—as firmly as it avoids anthropomorphic interpretations. Because the animal does not speak, self-revealing and self-concealing, together with their unity, possess in the case of animals a wholly different life-essence [*ein ganz anderes Lebe-Wesen*]. (VA, 274; EGT, 116)

"Because the animal does not speak." Because it does not have the word, the word that is in the beginning, animal life is an essence that is enigmatically and hermetically sealed within its own undifferentiated self-revealing and self-concealing. As we shall soon see, the animal neither speaks nor sees. Heidegger has of course located the gulf that separates speaking beings from speechless ones decades earlier, in his 1934–1935 Hölderlin course (39, 75). Referring there to the "benumbment" of animal behavior, whereby *numb* and *dumb* constitute something more than a mere rhyme, he writes: "The leap from living animal to speaking human being is as great as, or greater than, that from lifeless stone to living being." As great as, or greater than: ≥, even though the caliper that would measure such abysses in being remains as mysterious as it is handy and peremptory. Problems of za-ology are not so readily solved. For this "wholly different" essence, the "life-essence" of animals, with their "entirely other" mode of self-revealing and self-concealing (the word *self* here translating *sich*, not *Selbst*) does rise in the unique-unifying-One, the solitary sheltering or gathering which Heidegger calls the clearing of being. The issue is whether or not the "life-essence" of animality must rise, insofar as it is living, *as the clearing*, the clearing *as such*. What if the unified realm of essence in ζα-, the unified field of essence as such, the field of φύσις, were *daimon life* rather than what Heidegger prefers to call *Ek-sistenz* or *Da-sein*? What if the clearing and granting of being had to do with neither "man" nor "Dasein" but with all the life that lives and dies on Earth, from dogs through gods, from tadpoles through peoples? What if speech were not the commencement ("In the beginning . . .") and archaic guarantor of presencing (". . . was the surd") but a particularly exotic orchid or muscle, the peculiar property of Spinoza's mosquito with airs? What if the lookers and livers, the gods and dogs, having no particular need of speech, were the proper guardians of the clearing? What if man, the garrulous creature, weak of eye, nose, and wit, were their occasional companion, the plaything of their passing fancy? Daimonically powerful, for the moment, man—who could deny it? The wielder of "smart weapons," who has not felt their firepower? Yet what if the proper guardian of the clearing were a mammal? A mammarian? A body *other* than that of man—that of a woman, for example? What if aligning those human beings called *women* with animals were by no means an insult—no matter how Timaeus meant it, and no matter how widespread the impact of his mysogyny may be—but the highest praise of being? What if all else were man's mere oblivion of air?[20]

How far can Heidegger go with any of these questions? Why does his thinking so often stop short of them? How does Heidegger *know* they are silly?

THE UNIFIED FIELD OF ΦΥΣΙΣ; THE ΔΑΙΜΩΝ

By the late 1930s Heidegger surely cannot entertain any illusions about the failure of fundamental ontology to gain access to just-plain-life. Yet has he succeeded in gaining access to just-plain-φύσις? In the ensuing chapters I shall interrogate these failures once again. But not before returning to the 1943 Heraclitus course, which adduces a number of details to the discussion of animality and unconcealment in "Aletheia."

The upsurgence of animals—in the Greek view that Heidegger is trying to recapture—remains an upsurgence in "peculiar repose" (55, 95). For animals do not speak up. Whatever noises they make, such as those of Kafka's "Josephine," they do not possess the word. And yet. Animals in the ancient Greek view are mysteriously and powerfully expressive, and in manifold ways. (We shall consider one such animal, the horse, in chapter 3, below.) Heidegger's example is the bird, whose hovering and soaring in flight measures the open region of air, and whose song is at once call, announcement, and enchantment. Yet birds, even Aristophanes' rather flighty *Birds,* one might say, are also emblems of mourning and melancholy, harbingers of closure and the dead of night. Heidegger now reveals the sense of the word *bestrickend* (ensnaring, capturing, captivating) in the passage from "Aletheia" cited above, on the alien yet captivating self-revealing and self-concealing of animals: "Flying, singing, the bird is bound to and points to the open [*ins Offene*]. It ensnares [*verstrickt*] in the open. The Greek word σειρά means snare. The Sirens, thought in Greek fashion, are the ones who in multiple senses of the word *ensnare*" (55, 95–96). Heidegger says not a word more about birds and sirens—bronze by gold, face by voice, half woman, half bird, greeting in going—so mysteriously introduced into the clearing. *Into* the clearing, or *as* the clearing? He proceeds to identify ζωή with φύσις, "pure upsurgence" (103), defining the ever-upsurgent (τὸ ἀεὶ φύον) as "the constantly living," the bearer of life-fire, τὸ ἀείζωον (104). Yet the identity of ζωή with φύσις implies the essential proximity (*Wesensnähe*) of life and being as such, "throughout the entire history of Western thought," commencing with Plato and Aristotle and culminating in Leibniz and Nietzsche. In a word, ζωή is a word for being, and the "second" history of being to which I referred earlier is the only history of the only being there ever could be. Aristotle would insist that no question posed in and by such a history is silly, unless they all are.[21]

However, if ζωή is a word for being, perfectly equivalent to φύσις, then the abyss that ostensibly segregates human beings from animals and establishes them in the neighborhood of the gods becomes a troubling sort of gap. The abyss is in fact a *Sprung*, not a leap of pious thought but a crack or fissure in being, what Heidegger in his *Contributions to Philosophy* (discussed in chapter 6, below) calls a cleaving of beyng, *eine Zerklüftung des Seyns*. (*Kluft* is a gap or gully or cleavage, while *Zer-* functions as an intensifier.) If fundamental ontology merely postpones the ontology of just-plain-life, or pretends that life is simply one of the many possible objects of *regional* ontologies, the time will surely come when Heidegger must ask whether there are "stages" or "grada-tions" in being, whether there are stratified gullies or canyons in the putatively "unified field of essence" that is ζά. Such gradations dare not be derived from the forged Leibnizian "chain of being," the great chain that extends from Creator God through angels to humanity, and thence, across a gap of essence that would cleave the field of essence, to the (mere) animal. Surely, Heidegger could not abide the possibility that his "other commencement" and "other thinking" reduplicate beliefs and prejudices that have prevailed throughout the history of metaphysics? Surely, it would be *shattering* to confront the possibil-ity that *Ereignis*, the truth of propriation as granting and unconcealment, might rest on the traditional ordering or hierarchy of beings? For the very distinction between being and beings, and not any grounded order of beings, is now presumably for the first time in all history the spur to thought.

Yet what about this very distinction, what about the "essential unfolding" of the truth of being in the history of being, what about the very order of essence? What does it mean to seek an ordering principle, an articulation or jointure (*Fügung*) for stone, plant, animal, mortal, and god? Can there be a hierarchy of φύσις as self-revealing/concealing? How would such a hierarchy cast off the fetters of the ancient chain that binds all beings to a Creator God, the fetters of ontotheology?

In a lecture course on Parmenides taught during the winter semester of 1942–1943, a semester prior to the course on Heraclitus, Heidegger focuses on two of those ζα- words from the ostensibly unified field of essence that is φύσις. These two words will resonate strongly in the "Letter on Humanism" four years later: θεοί and δαίμονες, gods and daimons. The daimonic, τὸ δαιμόνιον, which first emerges in Heidegger's works in a marginal note to the 1928 Leibniz-logic course, is Heidegger's central concern here. He is quick to cast aside the understanding of the daimon in the sense of the "demonic," that is, in the "Christian" sense (54, 147). The latter he espies, for example, in the timorous condemnation of "state power" (135). (As we shall see in chapter 5, the identification of *Dämonie* and state power dominates Heidegger's thought in the mid-1930s.) The daimonic is not diabolical. It has to do with the *Un-Geheuer*, the vast, colossal, un-common and un-familiar. Heidegger promptly denies that there is anything *Monströses* about this *Un-Geheuer*, which is "radiantly penetrating being" (150: *das hereinscheinende Sein*). The daimonic, passing strange, is actually the nearest of the near, the most intimate and natural thing in the world. It is φύσις itself. "Τὸ δαιμόνιον is the essence and essential ground of the uncommon. It is that which proffers itself to the common and comes to presence in it. Proffering itself [*sich dargeben*], in the sense of indicating and pointing, is the Greek word δαίω (δαίοντες-δαίμονες)" (54, 151).

Liddell-Scott (for we have not tossed philology aside, not just yet) informs us that δαίω is in fact two verbs. The first means to kindle a fire, to burn, presumably with the fire of life, the ever-living ardor of ζάπυρος, "most fiery." The second, in the active voice, means to divide; in the passive voice, to be torn asunder or (when used figuratively) to be distracted (the German word *zerstreut*); in the middle voice, to distribute or allot; in the aorist, to feast on what has been distributed, to consume in celebration. It is clearly the middle voice form of the second verb that both Heidegger and Liddell-Scott emphasize when they suggest that δαίω constitutes the root of δαίμων, preferring this etymology to Plato's in *Cratylus* (398b), which takes δαίμων to be δαήμων, "knowing" or "skilled." Liddell-Scott does not speculate on the connection of δαίω with ζα-, and thus to διά and δίς, nor does Heidegger comment on the possibility, even though the sense of allotment or distribution of destinies— δαίμονες as the divine powers of dispensation—makes the inference plausible. In other words, Heidegger spurns the *difference* implied in the daimonic, the emphatic differing or differentiating that opens the expanse of space-time. He is more intent on showing that the root of δαίω is identical to that of θεάω, "to look," in the middle voice "to offer something to the gaze" or, better, "to offer *itself* to a sighting." The gods, οἱ θεοί, are those who are seen to gaze. Daimons are those who indicate, signal, and show (themselves). The two are in fact selfsame: "Θεοί, the ones we call 'gods,' are those who gaze into the unconcealed and who, thus gazing, signal: θεαόντες, in accord with their essence, are the δαίοντες-δαίμονες, the un-common ones who point into the common."[22] Θέα, the glimpse, the spectacle of theater, is θεά, the goddess Ἀλήθεια. And mortals? Inasmuch as they too gaze uncommonly into the common, are not mortals too θεοί, or, failing that, are they not those who point, δαίμονες? Not quite. Almost. And, after mortals, the animals? Not nearly as nigh, not quite as almost. But why?

In the apparently unified field of essence that is φύσις, in the φύσις that is ζωή and in the ζωή that is the unified realm of essence in ζα-, there is an inexplicable declivity or decline, perhaps a kind of cascade. There is a slippage of generations and of generation that Heidegger does not discuss (just as, before him, Timaeus neglected to account for it), but toward which he gestures when he calls mortals *die Nachkömmlinge*. Mortals are the "afterlings" with respect to daimons, a "posterity" in "posteriority." Mortals have suffered a diminution of essence, perhaps even a de-composition or dis-essencing—what Heidegger later will call *Ver-wesung* (US, 45–47). Yet what about the animals? Do they not also gaze? Or does the slippage of spectation and speech in the divine theater continue unabated? Is there yet another rift in the supposedly unified field of essence, a further plunge?

Here the animal occupies a peculiar position in-between. Animals "look at us," we say. Yet animals do not gaze [*blicken*]. An animal's "espying" or "lowering" or "gaping" and "glaring" is never a self-revelation of being; in its so-called gazing the animal never brings its own upsurgence to accompany that of any being that is revealed to it [*ein Aufgehen seiner selbst in ein ihm entborgenes Seiendes mit*]. (*54,* 158–59)

Presumably, the beasts to which human beings are abysmally akin represent yet another stage in the decline of the divine theater. Gods gaze, daimons gesture, and mortals look up, while the animals graze, gently lowing as cows, dumbly lowering as whales, mouth and eyes humbly lowered.

However, one might pose a range of questions to this "upsurgence of self" in which φύσις, the unified field of essence, is fissured by the theatrical-spectatorial "self" of ontotheology. Let us at least add a word about the odd nature of the animal gaze in Heidegger. For it is still the unseeing glare of the praying/preying mantis—that living parody of priesthood and soothsaying, that sham shamaness who swivels her unseeing head and bites off the head of her mate. It is still a *Spähen, Lauern, Glotzen,* and *Stieren,* nothing like the amicable gaze that embraces peasant and sheep in Chagall's "I and the Village," painted in 1911, while Heidegger was a student of theology. As late as 1968, at Le Thor, in the company of René Char, Heidegger will insist that animals—cows, for example—do not and cannot see (VS, 60). He realizes of course that when an animal stares at us it meets our own gaze in a way no stone ever can. He does not specify what kind of animal he has in mind, but we can be certain that it is now neither bee nor mantis nor pseudopod. It is a mammal, a particular kind of mammal. Not the harmless cow or risible jackass, not the jackass that appears—*adventavit asinus*—in these lecture courses and at the end of "Aletheia" at Heraclitus' (not Nietzsche's) behest. Heidegger concedes—for it is a concession, a deigning to concede and a condescending—that when an animal glares at us we feel "a special concentration of encountering-force [*Begegniskraft*]" (*54,* 159). The "look" of the animal is particularly overpowering and well-nigh demonic in the lowering of a predator, *ein Raubtier,* such as the one portrayed, according to Heidegger, by Oswald Spengler. Let us pause a moment over the theater and theatrics of Spengler's predator; for as we shall see in chapters 4, 5, and 8, the theater is eminently *political.*

Earlier in the 1942–1943 lecture course (*54,* 101), Heidegger cites Spengler's *Der Mensch und die Technik: Beitrag zu einer Philosophie des Lebens* [*Man and Technology: Contribution to a Philosophy of Life*] (1931); he cites it apparently as an illustration of how *not* to go about discussing the ζῷον. I say "apparently," because Heidegger leaves the Spengler quotation without any commentary whatsoever, as though, like the saying of Aristotle concerning Heraclitus, it speaks for itself. Spengler writes: "The character of the predator in the wild [*des freien Raubtieres*] has in its essential traits been transferred from the individual to the organized nation [*das organisierte Volk*], the *animal with one soul and many hands.*" Heidegger does not fail to adduce, again without comment, Spengler's concluding footnote: "And with *one* head, not many." Whatever sarcasm there may be in this citation *sans* commentary, it remains disquieting that Spengler's *Raubtier* returns to Heidegger's lecture course, not as a political or paramilitary metaphor, but as a metonymy for the animal as such. Yet whether as glaring predator in the wild or Leviathan with multiple murderous hands in the city, there is no question but that the animal as such is a (lowly) link in the metonymic and semantic chain of being, and that an abyss of essence will be dug to keep the animal at a distance from the divine onlookers, the daimonic pointers, and the talkers who talk endlessly of primordial soundlessness.[23]

Life is short. It is time to bring these introductory and far too ambitious reflections to a close. Yet it will not do to end without at least mentioning Heidegger's desperate critique of Rainer Maria Rilke's putative "biologism," "anthropomorphism," and naive "Christianity." During the Parmenides lectures (54, 225ff.) Heidegger refers to the eighth *Duino Elegy*. The polemic occurs in the context of a discussion of nothing less than the ontological difference, the abyss of opening and clearing as such. After defining τὸ δαιμόνιον as the gaze, the silent taking-in that characterizes belongingness to being (168–69), and after establishing the etymology of the word *theory* in the daimonic and divine gaze, that is, after constructing the entire theater of theory (219–20; θέα-ὁράω, θεῖον-δαιμόνιον), Heidegger italicizes the following remark: "The *distinction of all distinctions* and the *commencement of all distinguishing* [is] the *distinction between being and the being* [*Der* Unterschied aller Unterschiede *und der* Anfang aller Unterscheidung [*ist*] *der* Unterschied des Seins und des Seienden]" (225). As far as I can see, Heidegger nowhere alludes to the lines from the first *Elegy* that serve as one of the epigrams to this Introduction; that is perplexing, inasmuch as *Unterschied* is here *the* question. Without venturing anything like an account of Heidegger's strained and even hysterical relationship with the poetry of Rilke, I shall simply allow Heidegger's attack to arouse some suspicions.[24]

Is it not uncanny that Heidegger should fault Rilke for having capitulated to a naively "Christian" interpretation of beings as a whole—and then proceed to define the realm of φύσις in such a way that human beings are promised their accustomed nearness to divinity and their traditional eminence vis-à-vis animality? It is as though ἀλήθεια, through the good graces of a theatric and theistic θεωρία, does all the work that Christian ontotheology ever did, so that when Heidegger accuses Rilke (and Nietzsche) of having forgotten ἀλήθεια one must struggle to remember precisely *why* it had to be remembered.

Thus Heidegger, the thinker of bridges (VA, 152–62; BW, 329–39), proceeds to write about those animals beyond the abyss, proceeds as though he had never even posed the question as to the kind of asses' bridge he must now cross. "Man and man alone," he writes, excluding the animals and forgetting those δαίμονες the entire lecture course has been about, "sees into the open." He continues:

In contrast, the animal neither sees nor does it ever catch sight of the open, in the sense of the unconcealment of what is unconcealed. . . . The animal is excluded [*ausgeschlossen*] from the essential domain of the strife between unconcealment and concealment. The sign of this essential exclusion is that no animal and no kind of vegetation "has the word" ["*hat das Wort*," that is to say, "takes the floor" in order to "speak its piece"]. (54, 237)

Never mind the fact that the "sign" of the animal's essential exclusion from the open region can only be a sign of "language," that is to say, a sign that—as another poet says—"is not read." And never mind that Heidegger will not long afterward concede to animals (and plants?) their own peculiar relation to self-revealing/concealing. Here he does admit that forceful exclusion hardly solves the riddle that animals are. "For the animal is related to [*bezogen auf*] the circle within which it nourishes itself, pursues its prey, or mates, in a manner essentially different from that in which the stone is related to the ground on which it lies" (237). Stones lie scattered on the ground; animals hover in the away-from-ground, *Ab-Grund*. Or, at least, they skirt the very verge of the abyss, they prowl the rim. There is in plants and animals a manner of "arousal" or "excitation," and Heidegger now employs a whole series of words based on the root *Regen* in order to delineate it: *Sichregen einer Regsamkeit, Auf-regung, Erregung zu einem Aufgehen* within a circle of *Erregbarkeit*. As we shall see at the end of our investigation, in chapter 9, such arousal and bestirring persist in Heidegger's thinking of language and propriation as the final signs of life in his thought. In the present context, such "bestirring" may seem to represent an advance beyond the "bedazzlement" and "benumbment" of the years 1927 to 1930. However, the principle of exclusion is still operating:

No stirring or excitability of plants and animals ever conducts the living being into the free region in such a way that what is agitated could ever even let what excites it "be" what it is as an excitant, to say nothing about what the living being is prior to or without such excitation. Plants and animals hang suspended in something outside themselves, without ever "seeing" either the outside or the inside; that is, without ever having to stand unconcealed as a gaze [*Anblick*] into the free region of being. (54, 238)

"Without ever seeing the outside or the inside." "Plants and animals hang suspended." Why is the ecstasy of plant and animal inferior to that of human-kind? If it is the essence of Dasein to hang suspended in the nothing of *ek-stasis*, does such suspension of itself guarantee a vision and a voice that delimits "outside" and "inside"? Or is the very appeal to luminous vision and linguistically based interiority itself an indication of the most ancient of metaphysical embroglios? We know that for Heidegger early and late it is the way Dasein or the mortal can initiate itself into mortality, such that it *can* die, such that its death can be a *good* death by dint of these intimations of mortality—it is this that grants the word and the vision to Dasein. Yet the objections raised by Jacques Derrida in *Of Spirit*, in one of those famous footnotes of his (De, 88–

89 n. 2/119–20 n. 3), are telling. They merit repetition, precisely in the context of ζά-ology and φύσι-ology:

> If animals cannot properly question beyond their vital interests, can *Dasein* do so, *properly and in all rigor?* Can it not be demonstrated that the question does no more than *defer*, indeed by the most overdetermined means (through difference *and* the *différance* of difference), the quest and the inquiry, thus only *deflecting* living interest, with alteration and the most discontinuous mutation thus also remaining just a detour? Only being-toward-death *as such* would seem to suspend and liberate the question from its rootedness in life. And this is doubtless what Heidegger would say. Later he was to stress that animals cannot have experience [*erfahren*] of "death as death." Which is why they cannot speak (US, 215). But does *Dasein* have experience of death *as such*, even by anticipation? What could that mean? What is being-toward-death? What is death for a *Dasein* that is never defined *essentially* as a living thing? This is not a matter of opposing death to life, but of wondering what semantic content can be given to death in a discourse for which the relation to death, the experience of death, remains unrelated to the life of the living thing.

We shall soon take up these questions in a reading of *Being and Time*. Yet not before another word about the "circle" in which life *stirs*. The "circle" may also seem to be an advance beyond the "ring of disinhibitions" of 1929–1930, yet not a word appears in the Parmenides course about the *shattering* of that circle, not a word about the difficult problem of death, nothing about the nothing that penetrates animal life. And yet the context of all these lecture courses of the early 1940s certainly involves a confrontation with death, indeed in the very shape of the goddess under whose protection the thinkers in question stand—Heraclitus beneath the sign of Artemis, Parmenides beneath the sign of Aletheia, if not the girdle of Aphrodite.

Heraclitus resides in the nearness of firelight and glowing coals (55, 9). As the thinker of harmony and strife, he stands under the aegis of Artemis, goddess of the lyre and the bow, the bow that is both life and death: recall fragment B 48 on βίος as βιός (cf. 54, 160–61). Of Artemis, Heidegger writes, "Her beauty is that of an elevated, noble appearance," and he adds, alluding to Homer's *Odyssey* (Song 20, l. 71), "The girls she favors grow tall" (16). Artemis is φωσφόρος, the bearer of light; her arrows are " 'sudden,' 'gentle,' and 'lovely' " (17). It is in the nearness of phosphorescent Artemis, the bearer and bestower of life and death, that Heidegger discusses ζωή and ζῷον (17–18): "Life and death run counter to one another [*sind das Gegenwendige*]. To be sure. Yet at the point of extreme opposition, things that run counter turn most intensely toward one another [*das Gegenwendige wendet im äußersten Entgegen eines dem anderen sich innigst zu*]." At some point in our reflections, especially in chapter 7, we will have to confront what both Heidegger and Freud would call *lifedeath*.

Admittedly, life, beauty, and death are not so intertwined in the case of Parmenides' goddess—the single θεά whom Heidegger identifies as Truth, "Aletheia" (VA, 247–48; EGT, 93–94). For Heidegger's solitary θεά is nothing else than θέα, the unfaltering gaze of being. Heidegger will never confuse her, absolutely refuses to confuse her with Aphrodite—as Parmenides, Empedocles, and Nietzsche will always have done. Perhaps as even Hölderlin, the poet of Panthea and Rhea, will have done, though Heidegger would deny this too. Rilke perhaps, but never Hölderlin, would have been guilty of such a confusion of unconcealing and love. In any case, Nietzsche is surely behind all the confusion, for he also abandons Artemis and her brother Apollo in order to revel in a Schopenhauerian distortion of Heraclitus, an interpretation "initiated already by Hegel and then coarsened by Nietzsche and removed to the sphere of the swamp—the 'Dionysian' interpretation of Heraclitean thinking" (55, 18). The swamp? The instant Heidegger nears any well-watered ὀργάς it begins to look like marshland, an abysmal morass, and he circumvents it with disdain. Yet perhaps also in anxiety, if Dionysos is Zagreus, the fragmented *Za*-greus, powerfully mutilated. No doubt an introduction to za-ology, in order to open a path to advanced za-ology, would have to proceed to the "new interpretation of sensuousness" that Heidegger promised at the end of his first lecture course on Nietzsche in 1936–1937, promised but never delivered.[25]

However, it would be churlish of me to let such an introduction end without acknowledging Heidegger's stubborn insistence that the life of the (human) body *must* be thought, even if the body remains the most difficult task for his thinking. Especially in the affair of human embodiment the ghost of Nietzsche will rise to haunt Heidegger with shades of life, daimon life; especially here, with human corporeality, the ghost of Heidegger's 1929–1930 biology course and of the 1942–1943 lectures on ζωή will return to haunt the old man himself. Some extracts from the penultimate session of his and Eugen Fink's 1966–1967 seminar on Heraclitus:

Fink:	. . . The human being differs from all beings. . . . It possesses a double character: on the one hand, it is itself placed in the clearing, and on the other, it is imprisoned in the underground of all clearing,
Heidegger:	That will become comprehensible only through the phenomenon of the body,
Fink:	as in the erotic mode of understanding.
Heidegger:	"Body" is not meant ontically here
Fink:	and not in the Husserlian sense, either,
Heidegger:	but rather in the way Nietzsche thinks the body—even though it remains obscure what the body properly signifies for him.
Fink:	In the section "On the Despisers of the Body," Zarathustra says, "Body am I wholly and entirely, and nothing else besides." Through the body and the senses human beings are close to the earth.
Heidegger:	. . . Can we isolate darkling understanding, which defines our corporeal belonging to the earth, from our being placed in the clearing?

Fink: To be sure, darkling understanding can be addressed only in
               terms of the clearing. But it can no longer be brought to
               language by way of a nicely articulated jointure.

Heidegger: . . . Human beings body forth only if they are alive [*Der
               Mensch leibt nur, wenn er lebt*]. That is the way to under-
               stand "body" in the sense you are using it. At the same time,
               "to live" is meant in an existential sense. Ontic nearness
               does not mean any sort of spatial proximity between two
               things, but a reduced openness [*eine herabgesetzte
               Offenheit*], hence an ontological moment in human beings.
               Nevertheless, you speak of an ontic nearness.

Fink: Back in the days when you first came to Freiburg, you said in
               a lecture course: the animal is poor in world [*das Tier ist
               weltarm*]. At that time you were on the way toward the
               kinship [*Verwandtschaft*] of human beings with nature.

Heidegger: The phenomenon of the body is the most difficult problem.
               (Hk, 232–34)

                                    •

Heidegger uncovers the root of daimon life in ζα-. Eventually he equates it
with "the look" of gods and mortals on the near side of the abyss of essence
that ostensibly separates humans from animals. Yet, if I am right, ζα- is cognate
not with θέα but with δαίω, διά, δίς. And the Latin prefix *dis-, dif-* is at least
in part equivalent to the German intensifying prefix *zer-*, as in *Zer-klüftung,
Zer-streuung,* and so on. Thus something else than the theistic theater of theory
is at stake in daimon life; za-ology will compel us toward a strange and perhaps
shockingly alien logos, a discourse of emphatic life, differentiation, and proliferation. Albeit without excessively sharp distinctions.

῏Ηθος ἀνθρώπῳ δαίμων. Woman and man, the human animals, dwell in
nearness to the daimon. Heidegger first introduces τὸ δαιμόνιον in the 1928
logic course on Leibniz at the place where he is discussing finite transcendence
and the overpowering, *das Übermächtige,* which is his initial way of designating divinity and the holy. *Das Über-mächtige,* the plenipotent, the intensely
powerful, ζα-μενής, δαίμων. Heidegger neglects to mention that earlier in the
logic course (26, 13) he has characterized the fitting mortal gaze upon ethereal
divinity as *benommen,* as a kind of "benumbed behavior." As though a single
look at the blazing sky would be enough to unite—on what Bataille calls the
horizontal axis—god, beast, and humanity.

In the end, Heidegger spurns daimon life, which is the only thing that ever
captivated him. And yet, compensating for this neglect, in a long marginal note
he inserts the following parenthetical remark, as a kind of margin within the
margin, a kind of abyss within abysses: "(It remains for us to consider being
and *the daimonic;* or perhaps understanding-of-being and *the daimonic.* Being
as ground! Being and nothing—anxiety)" (26, 211n.).

How are we to think (within anxiety, and with an occasional burst of laughter, or at least a spray of chuckles) the δαιμόνιον? We can think it, Heidegger replies in this same marginal note, "only in and out of the complete semination [*Streuung,* literally, "bestrewal"] that belongs to the essence of transcendence." He directs our attention to the sixth thesis of section 10 in the logic course. There an "original *semination*" is invoked which would be the "inner possibility" of an intensified "factical dissemination" (*Zer-streuung*) and dispersion (*Zer-streutheit*) of Dasein into "embodiment" and "thereby into sexuality [*Geschlechtlichkeit*]."[26]

That chilly δαίμων there in the kitchen, if it *is* a kitchen; that frigid daimon hovering over the abyss or suspended within it, both disseminating and dispersed: Does it have a body yet? Is it somebody? Some body? Some body who is alive?

PART ONE

Advanced Za-ology

The gods heard the lament of the people of
Uruk: no new bride could satisfy in that first
and last night the lusts of King Gilgamesh,
and no young warrior could satisfy the
King's lust for battle. The goddess therefore
molded from sky and earth a *second self* for
Gilgamesh, and called him *Enkidu.* Enkidu
was a hirsute, wild man, and Gilgamesh
would wrestle with him, would be *drawn to
him as towards a woman.*

When a trapper happened upon the savage
Enkidu at a watering hole, he was struck
dumb, benumbed with terror. The trapper
found in the Temple of Love at Uruk a child of
pleasure. She would civilize Enkidu. Together
they returned to the watering hole and on the
third day of their ambush Enkidu arrived.

*She was not ashamed to take him, she
made herself naked and welcomed his eagerness, she incited the savage to love and
taught him the woman's art. . . . Enkidu
grew weak, for wisdom was in him, and the
thoughts of a man were in his heart. So he
returned and sat down at the woman's feet,
and listened intently to what she said. . . . "O
Enkidu, you who love life, I will show you
Gilgamesh."*

•

Gilgamesh and Enkidu wrestled now in the
bride's doorway. *They snorted like bulls
locked together.* Then one of them threw the
other and they became brothers. One night
Gilgamesh dreamt, and Enkidu interpreted
the dream: "*The meaning of the dream is
this. The father of the gods has given you
kingship, such is your destiny, everlasting life
is not your destiny. Because of this do not be
sad at heart, do not be grieved or oppressed.*"

•

Gilgamesh and Enkidu struck out for the Land of the Living. At its border, a terrible giant guarded the cedar wood. Enkidu grew afraid, but Gilgamesh chided him: *"Where is the man who can clamber to heaven? Only the gods live forever with Shamash the Sun, but as for us men, our days are numbered, our occupations are a breath of wind. How is this, already you are afraid!"*

Yet if Enkidu's limbs were benumbed with terror it was only because he knew that the Land of the Living would not receive his brother Gilgamesh. Enkidu taught his brother the lesson by dying. While Gilgamesh boasted—*"All living creatures born of the flesh shall sit at last in the boat of the West, and when that boat sinks they are gone; but we two shall go forward and fix our eyes on this monster"*—Enkidu fell sick with contagion and withered.

At the very doorpost of death, Enkidu cursed the trapper who had snared him and rebuked the child of pleasure who had given him the wisdom of cities. Shamash the Sun replied by scolding Enkidu, who then revoked his curses. Gilgamesh refused to love Ishtar, the Queen of Heaven, but Enkidu in the end did not refuse: *"Let no man scorn you, striking his thigh in derision. Kings, princes, and nobles shall love you, the old beard will wag his head but the young man will undo his belt. For you gold and carnelian and lapis lazuli lie heaped in the strongroom. On your account the wife, the mother of seven, shall be forsaken. The priests shall make a way for you into the presence of the gods."*

·

Before he died, Enkidu told Gilgamesh his dream. Gilgamesh said, *"The dream was marvelous but the terror was great; we must treasure the dream whatever the terror; for the dream has shown that misery comes at last to the healthy man, that the end of life is sorrow."* And Gilgamesh raised a keen:

Hear me, great ones of Uruk,
I weep for Enkidu, my friend,
Bitterly moaning like a woman in mourning
I weep for my brother.
O Enkidu, the wild ass and the gazelle

That were father and mother,
All four-footed creatures who fed with you
Weep for you,
All the wild things of the plain and the pasture;
The paths that you loved in the forest of cedars
Night and day murmur.
Let the great ones of strong-walled Uruk
Weep for you,
Let the finger of blessing
Be stretched out in mourning. . . .
O my young brother Enkidu, my dearest friend,
What is this sleep which holds you now?
You are lost in the dark and cannot hear me.

"I Call It Death-in-Life . . ."

Reading *Being and Time*

"Life" is not an existential structure of Dasein. Yet Dasein dies. Indeed, it is even born to that end: birth is one of the two ends of an end-like or finite existence—Dasein natal, Dasein fatal. In this regard Heidegger entertains the testimony of a medieval Bohemian peasant, one who has recently become a widower, and who therefore has a complaint against Death. However, Heidegger follows the lead of his anonymous medieval predecessor by allowing Death to have the last word. *Der Ackermann aus Böhmen* begins:

> *Grimmiger tilger aller leute, schedelicher echter aller werlte, freissamer morder aller menschen, ir Tot, euch sei verfluchet!*

> Malevolent subverter of all the people, thoroughly malignant to all the world, murderous devourer of all mankind, thou Death, my curse upon you!

Death, offended by the farmer's vituperation, replies:

> *Weistu des nicht, so wisse es nu: als balde ein mensche geboren wird, als balde hat es den leikauf getrunken, das es sterben sol. Anefanges geswisterde ist das ende. . . . [A]ls schiere ein mensche lebendig wird, als schiere ist es alt genug zu sterben.*

> If you knew it not before, know it now: as soon as a human being is born it has drunk from the proffered chalice, and so it is to die. The end is akin to the beginning. . . . The instant a human being comes to be alive it is old enough to die.[1]

In an early lecture course at Freiburg, Heidegger cites Luther's commentary on *Genesis* to similar effect: *Statim enim ab utero matris mori incipimus.* "For as soon as we abandon our mother's womb we begin to die" (*61, 182*).

We, who? How many of "us" are there? How many mother's sons and mother's daughters? How many peasant men and women? How many living creatures? If the classical and perdurant definition of human being is ζῷον λόγον ἔχον, "the living being that is essentially determined by its capacity to speak," Heidegger nevertheless resists "life" as an earmark of Dasein. The birth and death of Dasein will have to be interpreted in a way that does not depend on the unclarified, unexamined categories of traditional ontologies, especially the category of the "living." For, as Dominique Janicaud writes,

"The definition of man as living [*comme vivant*] is ontic."[2] Almost always, "life" will appear in "scare-quotes" in *Being and Time*. Almost always, "life" will have to be shooed away—for example, in the following moments of the analysis, which we will want to examine quite closely:

(1) Section 10, where the fundamental ontology of Dasein is demarcated or delimited over against anthropology, psychology, and, *a fortiori*, biology;

(2) Section 12, where human being as *embodied* being is affirmed, albeit in a way that leaves the *human* body, the body of Dasein, largely undetermined;

(3) Sections 35–38, on the "falling" of Dasein, which is the very animatedness (*Bewegtheit*) of existence;

(4) Sections 40–42, where *anxiety* and manifold *care* define what it is to be human, even though they spill over into other receptacles of life;

(5) Subsections 43b–c, where the principal ontological problem of "reality" is the being of *nature* and of the sort of thing we call *life;*

(6) Sections 47–49, where the *death* of Dasein is set in relief against the *perishing* of animals and the mere *demise* of a forlorn, inappropriate Dasein;

(7) Subsection 68b, where the ecstatic temporalizing of having-been, mood, and anxiety is made to bedazzle an already bedazzled and benumbed life;

(8) Sections 78–81, in which the path of the life-giving sun rises once again (as it did in section 22), in order to pose the timely question of life to Dasein and eventually to beings as a whole.

(Sections 72–74, where Dasein finally turns to the "end" of its *birth,* as to its destiny, heritage, and history in the world-historical fate of a "generation" and a "nation," I shall hold in reserve for chapter 5, on the politics of daimon life.)

In each of these locations in Heidegger's *Being and Time* "life" proves to be both essential to existential analysis and utterly elusive for it, quite beyond its grasp. Life falls into the gap that yawns between beings that are of the measure of Dasein and beings that are altogether unlike Dasein. Life neither precedes nor succeeds existential analysis but remains outside it, being both necessary to it and inaccessible for it. In short, life supplements Dasein, and like all supplements it is the death of Dasein. Fundamental ontology discovers a kind of being-there that is born and that dies, an existence it "fixes" terminologically as *Dasein;* what it is unable to determine is whether such a being is ever properly alive, or what such "life" might mean.

THE FACTS OF LIFE

Needlessness, heedlessness. Lack of need, lack of heed. Why heed the question of being? Who needs it? *Why* heed it, and *how?* A perverse, remorseless reflexivity and recoil characterize oblivion, as though oblivion were the very air we breathed. If the question of being makes no sense it is because we have never even had to remember to forget it. Oblivion replicates itself and achieves a lethal perfection by which we have always already forgotten being. Oblivion seems to seal the fate of Dasein as unneeding, unheeding. Like Nietzsche's herd of cows at pasture and child at play, like Kafka's ape roaming the rainforest before the circus troupe captures him, oblivious Dasein is *indifferent* to the question of being. A remarkable complacency (*Bedürfnislosigkeit*) surrounds the question with an impenetrable fog; a remarkable lack of need (*Unbedürftigkeit*) characterizes the "they" in their quotidian concerns (SZ, 177, 189). The tradition of philosophy exhibits such complacency in its neglect of the question of being (21, 46); it is as though philosophers too were Cartesian extended substances (92), more like mindless, indifferent stones and animals than vital thinkers.³

However much Dasein declines to heed and neglects to need the question of being, it moves within and is animated by something like an "understanding of being." Not a theoretical observation of entities or a scientific comprehension of their being, to be sure, but an understanding (in) which Dasein *lives*. Being is not only the most universal and undefinable concept, but also the most evident one: "That we in each case already live in an understanding of being and that the meaning of being is at the same time veiled in obscurity demonstrates the fundamental necessity of fetching back again [*wiederholen*] the question concerning 'being' " (4).

What does it mean to "live" (in) an understanding of being? Can we ever understand such "living," if the living itself encompasses (parenthetically) understanding? Can living leap over its own shadow?

Whether or not we can ever understand it, such living within an understanding of being, Heidegger assures us, is a fact (5: *ein Faktum*). Thus the formal structure of the question concerning being yields a particular *facticity* and a certain *movement* or *motion*. We move (*wir bewegen uns*) in a vague and average understanding of being, not insofar as we theorize and construct ontologies, but simply by being alive. Such animation or, better, animatedness (the passive form of *Bewegtheit*, "movedness," is not to be overlooked) is Heidegger's principal preoccupation both before and after *Being and Time*, from the period of his hermeneutics of facticity (roughly 1919 to 1923) to that of his theoretical biology (1929–1930) and well beyond. Moreover, our factical animatedness within an understanding of being, which is an understanding (in) which we *live*, directs us to something very much like *being*. Nietzsche, in a note that will become important for both Heidegger and Derrida, writes as follows: " 'Being'—we have no other notion of it than as 'living.'—For how can something dead 'be'?"⁴

If the earliest form of *Being and Time* is a hermeneutics of facticity, the fact of facticity (to repeat, the facticity by which we understand something like being, which is something like being alive) is a fact of life. Heidegger's project sprouts (in part, but in *good* part) from the soil of Dilthey's philosophy of factical-historical life.⁵ We know that already from the references to Dilthey in sections 10, 43, and 72–77 of *Being and Time*. However, the early Freiburg and Marburg lecture courses demonstrate the point even more forcefully.

For example, during his lecture course on the hermeneutics of facticity in the summer semester of 1923, Heidegger says, "*Facticity* designates the character of the being of 'our' 'own' *Dasein*" (*63*, 7). Why the quotation marks or "scare-quotes" around "our"? Because Dasein lingers or tarries there in each case as *this* particular Dasein: *Jeweiligkeit* is under way to what *Being and Time* will call *Jemeinigkeit,* Dasein whiling away its hour of existence as in each case "my own." Why the scare-quotes around "my" or "our" "own"? Because what may seem to be the property of Dasein is swept away in the larger questions of life, being, and (not quite yet, but lingering on the horizon, *as* the horizon) *time*. For the moment it is *being alive* that captivates Heidegger: "*Sein—transitiv: das faktische Leben sein!*" Being is to be understood transitively: it means that we *are* factical life—not as a soporific solipsism but as active vigilance (*Wachsein*). "If we take 'life' as a way of 'being,' then 'factical life' means our own Dasein [now without scare-quotes] as 'there' in every sort of ontologically explicit manifestation of the character of its being" (*63*, 7).

Yet the larger questions posed to "our" "own" factical Dasein will not disperse, not even in *Being and Time*. If fundamental ontology appears to be constructed on the axis of the proper and the improper, the appropriate and the inappropriate (*Eigentlichkeit/Uneigentlichkeit*), the quotation marks around "own" have in fact already replaced more drastic question marks, or, rather, as we shall see, a single, drastic, ironic exclamation point (!). The scare-quotes and exclamation point cause the axis to tremble and perhaps even to shatter. Any reading of *Being and Time* in terms of "authenticity" would be put to riot by this catastrophe, inasmuch as the only authentic Dasein would be a dead Dasein. And yet such trembling, such shattering of the axis of propriety, would be a sign of *life*.

Hermeneutics is not the chilly science of facticity, not a methodology that allows us coolly to approach life matter-of-factly; rather, hermeneutics *is* factical life surprised in the act, vigilantly caught in the act of interpreting itself. Hermeneutics of facticity is not like the botanics of plants (*63*, 15; cf. SZ, 46), whereby vegetable life is the *object* of botanical science; rather, to say *facticity* is to say *interpretation*—as though Dasein were goldenrod or dill catching itself going to seed. In a sense, the genitive in "hermeneutics *of* facticity" is subjective as well as objective: factical life does the interpreting as well as the living. Yet what does factical life include? What does it exclude? These questions Heidegger does not raise, perhaps because of a certain solidarity of life, solidarity *with* life, or perhaps because of insufficient vigilance. Nevertheless, we gain some insight into the sort of life Heidegger means when we hear him say, toward the end of his lecture course, "Life addresses itself in a worldly way whenever it takes care" (*102*: *Das Leben spricht sich im Sorgen weltlich an*). Life, the sort of life that fascinates Heidegger, is what has a *world*, relates to   *drawn to him as towards a woman*   a world. In his remarks on theoretical biology in 1930, nothing essential will have changed with regard to the world-relation of life. And if among the scattered pages of notes for the 1923 lecture course on the hermeneutics of facticity we find a potpourri of names—Aristotle, the New Testament, Augustine, Luther, Descartes, and

Kierkegaard—two names stand out, to wit, *Dilthey* and *Husserl*. What Heidegger wishes to pursue is a phenomenological hermeneutics of factical historical life, a task that he reduces to two words: *Dilthey destruiert* (*63*, 106–107), "Dilthey deconstructed."

Factical life receives even fuller treatment in the 1921–1922 lecture course, a course whose title ("Phenomenological Interpretations of Aristotle: Introduction to Phenomenological Research") does not do justice to its extraordinary contents. The entire third part of the course is devoted to "factical life" (*61*, 79–155). These pages would amply repay the most meticulous reading. For the moment, I shall recall only a few of the most striking theses on factical life, theses that are well under way to *Being and Time.*

The overarching theme of the course is the imbrication of phenomenological research and factical life. Research cannot extricate itself from its situation; nor should it ever desire to do so. For if it did it would only succeed in being uprooted, after the manner of the neo-Kantian schools of the day, with their doctrines of epistemology, values, and worldviews. Nor can philosophical research simply force its way into life; it must wait upon a maturation or temporal unfolding of its own access to life (*61*, 37: *Zeitigung des Zugangs*). Indeed, phenomenological research is cast adrift on the seas of factical life. Its life is the life of Ishmael:

> Our situation is not that of the rescuing coast; it is a leap into a drifting boat. Everything depends now on our taking the sails' tack into our hands and looking to the wind. It is precisely the difficulties that we must see: illuminating them will first disclose the proper horizon of factical life. Only by appropriating to myself the structure of my having to decide; only by realizing that it is within and upon such having that I shall come to see; only in this way can illumination sustain the fundamental motivation for the temporal unfolding of philosophizing. (*61*, 37)

In this regard, life-philosophy seems to offer phenomenological research some hope, even if its own situation is duplicitous, even hazardous.

On the one hand, Heidegger seems to criticize "modern *Lebensphilosophie*" precisely in the way his mentor, Heinrich Rickert, did in *Die Philosophie des Lebens*.[6] The tendency of Rickert's book is betrayed by its subtitle and its dedication: *A Presentation and Critique of the Fashionable Philosophies of Our Time*, "dedicated to the life of philosophy," rather than to the philosophy of life. Rickert spares none of the enthusiasts of life-philosophy: Schelling, Scheler, Simmel, Dilthey, Bergson, Nietzsche, Spengler, William James, and even Husserl are tainted with it and are accordingly excoriated; all have surrendered rigorously defined concepts and principles for the sake of "the intuitive," "the ingenious" (28). It may well be that some of Heidegger's own polemics against *Lebensphilosophie* (for example, those in the Nietzsche lectures of 1936–1940 and the 1936–1938 *Contributions to Philosophy*) owe something to the tract of his former mentor. Yet for the moment Heidegger champions Scheler, Nietzsche, Bergson, and Dilthey against their stodgy detractor. He cites the penultimate page of Rickert's monograph, where the relationship of research to life touches on the crucial word "repetition," *Wiederholung*. I cite Rickert's text (194) somewhat more fully than Heidegger does (at 61, 80): "One should finally give up trying to see this philosophizing about life as a mere repetition [*ein bloßes Wiederholen*] of life; one should give up trying to measure the value of philosophizing on the basis of its vitality. To philosophize is to create." Heidegger interjects at this point, in good Nietzschean fashion: "Is not creation life?" Rickert's text continues:

> Insight into the distance that separates what is created from the life that is merely lived must leave both life and philosophy content. For even the life-philosophy of our own day has in its own way contributed a great deal to this separation, in spite of its unscientific life-prophecies and the antitheoretical bias of its value accents. Only one who has understood that living life diverges from knowing it can be a philosopher of life—one who both loves life and thinks about it.

Heidegger repudiates such a complacent, not to say smug, separation of living from knowing. In so doing he points to the "repetition" that will characterize his own conception of fundamental ontology. "Repetition" is vigilance, *Wachsein,* somehow fetching itself back from oblivion and complacency. It rescues life from degeneration and decrepitude, "properly" restoring life to itself: " 'Repetition': everything depends on its sense. Philosophy is a fundamental 'how' of life itself [*ein Grundwie des Lebens selbst*], so that in each case it properly retrieves life, snatching it back from decrepitude [*es eigentlich je wieder-holt, aus dem Abfall zurücknimmt*]. Such snatching back, as radical research, is life" (61, 80). In Rickert, cognition and the concept are "sheer ghosts," says Heidegger; and Rickert's philosophy of values and *Weltanschauungen* is as vapid as his anemic life.

On the other hand, Heidegger concedes that the expression "life" is incorrigibly fuzzy—perhaps because life itself, as he will later say, is "hazy" (*diesig*). He sets aside all "biological" conceptions of life, a gesture he will make repeatedly throughout his career, insisting always on the priority of philosophy over the sciences. He attempts to trace the very multiplicity of those familiar uses of the word *life*—he lists a few of them: "political life," "a squandered life," "he's got a hard life," "he lost his life on a sailing voyage," which is, one must hope, not   *All living creatures born of the flesh shall sit at last in the boat of the* *West*   the voyage of the phenomenologist adrift—back to what he takes to be the sense of the *ultimate* meaning of the word. The task of phenomenological research, of philosophy, and even of thinking, will be to show that "life" means something "ultimate"; that "*das Leben*" *ein Letztes bedeutet* (81).

Before he spells out "the fundamental categories of life," Heidegger emphasizes such ultimacy, even if linguistic usage should be ambiguous (82). The verb *leben* may be intransitive: Heidegger's examples are, "he lives intensely," "he lives headlong [*wüst drauflos*]," "he lives a sheltered life [*zurückgezogen*]," "he's only half alive [*er lebt nur halb*],"   *and when that boat sinks they* *are gone*   and "I'm surviving [*man lebt so*]." Yet it may also be used transitively ("to live life," "to live one's mission," "to survive [*überleben*] this or that," "to spend one's years," or "live out one's years," or even "fritter away one's years" [*die Jahre verleben*], and, "above all," Heidegger says, "to undergo a lived experience of something ['*etwas erleben*']"). Yet no matter how we use the word, "a concrete experience [*Erfahrung*] is to be presentified," even if we can account for that experience only as a mere "feeling." Thus Heidegger takes care to defend himself against the charge of grammarification (*Grammatisierung*): even if early on, with the Greeks, grammar was taken over by "a particular theoretical outgrowth and articulation of life," the *grammatical* categories "have their origin in the categories of living speech [*des lebenden Sprechens*], the immanent speech of life itself" (82). If that is so, one may expect that the grammatical categories will be rooted in the fundamental categories of (speaking) life and of what Heidegger later will call "living language." One might also expect two grammatological problems to arise, problems with which the early work of Jacques Derrida has familiarized us: (1) What about those forms of life that do not speak, forms that are not marked by *dem immanenten Sprechen des Lebens selbst,* forms that are deprived of the vaunted interiority in which humanity hears and understands itself (while) speaking? (2) Why and how did the categories of grammar, as soon as they were formulated by the Greeks, become complicit with Stoic logic? We should retain these questions concerning the privilege and the ruination of speaking life and living language as we discuss the fundamental categories of life.

Heidegger begins his analysis with three propositions concerning life: (1) life is a "*sequential unity and process of maturation*" (Einheit der Folge und Zeitigung), the temporalizing of a bounded stretch of time, a process-manifold (*Zeitigung, Erstreckung, Vollzugsmannigfaltigkeit*) that coheres and "hangs together"—even if cohesion occurs by way of an original *distancing* that can become "an original aversion" (*Ursprungsabständlichkeit*) and even "direct hostility";[7] (2) the temporal stretch of life brings with it a sequence of *possibilities,* which are to be taken in a strictly phenomenological sense, not as logical possibilities or as transcendental a priori possibilities; (3) life combines the senses of (1) and (2) by being the collapse—or perhaps the imposition—of possibilities (*möglichkeitsverfallen*), the saddling of life with and by possibilities (*möglichkeitsgeladen und sich selbst ladend*), or ·the very shaping and cultivating of possibilities (*Möglichkeiten bildend;* cf. *weltbildend* in the 1929–1930 biology lectures). The whole (*das Ganze*) of life, as the temporal process of a bounded stretch of possibilities that we shape and that shape and befall us, is called actuality, *Wirklichkeit,* "indeed, reality in its specific imprevisibility as power, destiny [*Schicksal*]." If we try to reduce this complex tripartite description of life into a single assertion, we may say that life proceeds as a bounded stretch of possibilities, some which we choose and cultivate, some with which we are saddled, all such possibilities—but especially those over which we exercise no control—constituting the destined or fateful character of factical life.

One is struck by the dour and even dire mood of Heidegger's analysis of the fundamental categories of life. Life is a bounded stretch, a finite process. It

involves an original distantiation that can readily become aversion and hostility. Itself a sequence of possibilities, life succumbs to possibilities: *verfallen* is
the very first word attached to *Möglichkeit*. If life lives out its days caught on
the horns of the modalities of necessity and possibility, its reality will always be
a bleak one: reality will of necessity hinge upon possibilities that are essentially
susceptible to degeneration. Life is loaded (*geladen*) and is self-burdening. Such
is its reality. Such is the power of its impenetrable destiny. Such are life, existence, and even "being" itself: "Life = Dasein: in and through life '*being*' "
(*61, 85*).

    Heidegger does not speculate on the etiology of the apparently irremediable
degeneration of life. Yet the very parataxis of his style says something about the
source of declivity and decline. That *in* which, *on the basis of* which, *for, with,*
and *toward* which life lives; that *from* which life lives, *on the horizon of* which
it lives, Heidegger calls *world*. "Life in itself is related to the world [*weltbezo-
gen*]" (86). It is the world-relation of life that will continue to haunt Heidegger,
not only in the first division of *Being and Time,* where a modally neutral
description of the everyday life of Dasein continually breaks down and becomes a pejoration of the everyday as somehow "improper," *uneigentlich,* and
not only in the 1929–1930 biology lectures, where the "world-relation" well-
nigh binds the life of Dasein to the squalid life of animals, but also throughout
Heidegger's later career of thought. Here, of course, we are near the outset of
his career. Here the process-meaning of life is its being drawn to the world, as
our everyday speech shows when it identifies *life* and *world*. To stand in the
midst of life is to confront the world; to live in a world of one's own is to lead
one's own special life. Life inevitably interprets itself in the refracted light of
the world. Life, in a word, is reluccent, *reluzent* (61, 117ff.; cf. SZ, 16 and 21).
If much later, in the Nietzsche lectures, Heidegger is suspicious of the ambiguous identity of life, world, and (human) existence, he early on accepts the
concatenation of *Welt, Leben, Dasein,* and *Sein* as evidence of the meaning-
content of life-in-process. Phenomenological research dare not try to forge or
force such concatenations. Nor dare it forget them. It can only respond to the
compelling character of factical life, even if the world-relation of life seems to
contaminate all of life, existence, and being. In the fundamental categories of
life, says Heidegger, suddenly ventriloquized by the spirit of Hegel, "*life comes
to itself*" (88). Yet life tends to misunderstand itself, fall away from itself,
precisely into the relucence of the world. Life is circuitous, full of detours
(*umwegig*); it is, as we have already noted, "hazy" ("*diesig*"). In a word,
relucent life is ruinous. Worse, the very animatedness of life, what Aristotle
calls κίνησις and μεταβολή, is ruinance. From here on it is all downhill, and we
are always already there.

    The entire second chapter of Part III of Heidegger's lectures on factical life
treats of *Ruinanz.* We shall turn to it in a moment in order to confront the
mystery of a life that is both complacently prostrate and passionate to know
itself, both decrepit and upsurgent, both oblivious and perspicuous, both vacuous and vigilant. Meanwhile, Heidegger lends a hostage to fortune. If in only a

few years he drops the expression *life* in favor of *Dasein* and *Existenz,* if he comes to criticize *Leben* in Nietzsche and other life-philosophers as balefully ambiguous, in 1921–1922 he tells his students:

> It merely corresponds to the complacency of factical life itself when interpretation rescues itself from the conceptual tendency it is following by saying that life has manifold meaning and that therefore it cannot be readily grasped in an apt manner. However, we reach the acme of complacency and bankruptcy in philosophy when we enter a plea for the abandonment of this "expression." One shakes off a disturbing premonition—and writes a system.

Is the abandonment or subordination of life to Dasein—the "neutral" term that Heidegger latches onto in *Being and Time* in an abrupt, elliptical, almost brutal fashion[8]—a form of complacency? Is it the very complacency that forgets being? Is fundamental ontology a system, and is it written in order to suppress a disturbing premonition about life?

If *process* is the meaning of life-related-to-world, then the sense of that world-relation is one of care, concern, trouble, renunciation, and deprivation (90: *Sorgen, Bekümmerung, Darbung*). Life as such is restive. Such is its very animation or animatedness, its being prodded from the outside, as it were. A fragmentary marginal note to the 1921–1922 lecture course gives us some insight into the restless movement or movedness of factical life:

> The animatedness of factical life is provisionally interpretable, describable, as *restiveness [die* Unruhe]. The "how" of such restiveness as full phenomenon defines facticity. With regard to life and restiveness, see Pascal, *Pensées,* I–VII; what is valuable here is the description, not the theory and the intention. Above all, [not] soul-body, [not] *le voyage éternel:* to such things existentiell philosophy has no access. Illumination of restiveness, illuminated restiveness; rest-lessness and questionability; the temporalizing powers; restiveness and the wherefore. The restless aspect of restiveness. The unrelieved, undecided "between" of the aspect of factical life: between the surrounding world, sociality, the sphere of the self, ancestry, and posterity [*zwischen Um-, Mit-, Selbst-, Vor-, and Nachwelt*]; something positive. The way in which restiveness trickles through; the configurations and masks of restiveness. Rest—restiveness; phenomenon and movement (cf. the phenomenon of movement in Aristotle).

One cannot but hear in *Unruhe* the fundamental Augustinian tone of restlessness and agitation—*inquietum est cor nostrum, donec requiescat in te*—even if Heidegger would insist that the Augustinian "ontology" of body and soul *everlasting life is not your destiny*   be held at arm's length. For the restiveness of factical life   *do not be grieved or oppressed*   there is no repose.

The animatedness of factical life rises to meet us in the very passivity of the passive voice, *Bewegtheit*. If Aristotle defines life as self-movement, all κίνησις and μεταβολή are nonetheless *moved*. All motion is therefore restive, under way on a voyage eternal, but quite beyond the categories of soul and body. The problem is how to illuminate such restiveness, how to gain access to it, without falling back into complacency and bankruptcy. Interrogation of restiveness must itself be restless. Questioning must be driven by the wherefore, the *Wozu*, the restless aspect of illumination on the expressive face of factical life. It is the face which Hegel once called "absolute dialectical unrest," and which he thought as a skepticism that would somehow accomplish itself and culminate in absolute knowing. By contrast, Heidegger's restiveness marks the first appearance of the daimonic, of the powers of process, the might of maturation, and the potency of timely growth. In a word, *die Zeitigungsmächte*. These are the forces of what I am venturing to call *daimon life*. Somewhere beyond the traditional categories of soul and body, animation and movement, ensoulment and auto-motion, somewhere between ancient lineages and successive generations, between self and other, between life and its spheres, its environs, and its genera—daimon life disseminates. Heidegger says that to inquire into factical life is to leap into a boat adrift. Perhaps in saying so he recalls Nietzsche's great sailing ship, gliding along as silent as a daimonic ghost:

> Oh, what ghostly beauty! With what enchantment its grips me! Could it be? Has all the tranquillity [*Ruhe*] and silence in the world embarked on this ship? Does my happiness itself have its seat there in that quiet place, my "happier" "I," my second, dearly departed [*verewigtes*] self? To be, not dead, yet no longer alive? As a ghostlike, silent, gazing, gliding, hovering daimon [*Mittelwesen*]?

This is of course the passage from *The Gay Science* (KSA, 3, 424–25, no. 60) in which Nietzsche identifies the ship that skims the sea "like a huge butterfly," identifies it in the most unsettling way—*es sind die Frauen*, it's the women. No wonder Rickert wants to keep his distance from life-philosophy! Ironically, distance itself is attributed to women—"Women and Their Action at a Distance"—as though the dimension of the "between" were in some way "of woman." From here it would not be far to Diotima's instruction concerning daimonic ἔρως in *Symposium* (202–203), or to the derivation of the heroic-erotic δαιμόνιον in *Cratylus* (397–98), or the location of the site of the daimonic in *Statesman* (271–72) as between earth and sky, the realm of the overpowering as such. Yet daimon life, for all its overpowering ouranian qualities, is as restive as the sea   *She was not ashamed to take him*   and the eruptive earth, as fecund   *she made herself naked and welcomed his eagerness*   and as given to mourning as the goddesses of the depths. Heidegger makes no explicit reference or even allusion to such a δαιμόνιον, however; the Mother of the Muses, Dame Memory, *die Gedächtnis*, rather than *das Gedächtnis*, and even the ensnaring siren lie much farther down the path (WhD? 6–7). It is high time we reverted to a more sober factical life.

Heidegger's analysis of factical life as relationship to the surrounding world (*Umwelt*), the world of others (*Mitwelt*), and the world of my self (*Selbstwelt*), which is by no means the cogitative "I" or intellectual intuition of reflexive philosophy, deserves the most meticulous study (see 61, 94–100). Yet we will never find our way back to *Being and Time* if this excursion into the early lecture courses goes unchecked. I shall have to content my self with a brief listing of the four fundamental categories of life's "relational meaning," *Bezugssinn,* the sense of its world-relatedness.

(1) *Neigung,* "inclination," "proclivity," or "tendency": life is *drawn* to things, as though by gravity. Such being drawn into the world is the proper meaning or *sens* of life's temporal unfolding. A curious operation of anagram relates inclination to propriation, *Neigung* to *Eignung.* Life "finds itself properly [*eigentlich*] there where it retains its own inclination [*seine eigene Geneigtheit*]" (101). Factical life lets itself be swept away (*mitgenommenwerden*) by the world. This word is cognate with the words Heidegger will use in his 1929–1930 lecture course in order to characterize *animal* life;[9] yet here, in 1921–1922, the power of the world pertains to *factical* life as such. Thus the relations of care both disperse life and preserve life's vigilance. Scattering or dispersion is here counterposed to and yet bound up with vigilant inclination, in what will become the principal mystery of the metaphysics of Dasein, and it is no accident that Heidegger at this juncture (101–102) introduces a series of remarks on metaphysics and on the "devilish" difficulty of gaining access to one's own presuppositions about factical life. Inclination, proclivity, being drawn into and swept away by the world, dispersion in the world, and complacency about it are the "categorial keys" that Heidegger believes will unlock *radical* conceptions of motion—motion as process, stream, flux, life-event, the nexus of process, and temporalization.

(2) *Abstand,* "distance"; or, contrariwise, *Abstandstilgung,* "elimination of distance." With equal originality (*gleichursprünglich*), life covers over and obfuscates its own inclination. It is torn away into dispersion, finds itself (for somehow, inexplicably, it *does* find itself) as dispersed and scattered in its world. Thus life is "in ruinance" (102–103). Life loses its "in the face of," sees itself falsely and in a skewed perspective; as Heidegger will repeat twenty-five years later, in "Poetically Man Dwells . . ." (VA, 195–96), life measures but misses itself (*vermißt sich*). Life chases after rank, success, and position in the world; dreams of overtaking the others and securing advantage; maneuvers itself so as to close the distance yet remains forever distant; devotes itself to calculation, busy-ness, noise, and façade. Here Heidegger uses the very word he will employ in *Being and Time* (SZ, 126), namely, *Abständigkeit,* to designate the consuming passion to put distance between oneself and the others, either by boosting oneself beyond them or by subjugating them. Ironically, in the passion to keep one's distance from the others, one is swept away and becomes *precisely like the others,* who, presumably, are all trying to do the same thing. Thus one winds up without any distance on the others at all. The others? Who are they? Heidegger would have admired Henry David Thoreau's description of the They, had he known it. (If Heidegger in the 1930s bemoans *pragmatic* America, how close to him nevertheless is *puritan* America!)

When I ask for a garment of a particular form, my tailoress tells me gravely, "They do not make them so now," not emphasizing the "They" at all, as if she quoted an authority as impersonal as the Fates, and I find it difficult to get made what I want, simply because she cannot believe that I mean what I say, that I am so rash. When I hear this sentence, I am for a moment absorbed in thought, emphasizing to myself each word separately that I may come at the meaning of it, that I may find out by what degree of consanguinity *They* are related to *me*, and what authority they may have in an affair which affects me so nearly; and, finally, I am inclined to answer her with equal mystery, and without any more emphasis of the "they,"—"It is true, they did not make them so recently, but they do now." Of what use this measuring of me if she does not measure my character, but only the breadth of my shoulders, as it were a peg to hang the coat on? We worship not the Graces, nor the Parcae, but Fashion. She spins and weaves and cuts with full authority. The head monkey at Paris puts on a traveller's cap, and all the monkeys in America do the same. I sometimes despair of getting any thing quite simple and honest done in this world by the help of men.

No doubt the head monkey is headed for a difficult season. Thoreau's prescribed therapy for the "they," a kind of baptism by fire, will be a drastic one, and it will be applied in the name of a "they" without quotation marks, a "they" that follows upon the phrase "by the help of men" so effortlessly that we do not believe that the "they" is being invoked (by one of "them") at all.

> . . . by the help of men. They [*sic*] would have to be passed through a powerful press first, to squeeeze their old notions out of them, so that they [*sic*] would not soon get upon their legs again, and then there would be some one in the company with a maggot in his head, hatched from an egg deposited there nobody knows when, for not even fire kills these things, and you would have lost your labor. Nevertheless, we will not forget that some Egyptian wheat was handed down to us by a mummy.[10]

Yet the effort to isolate maggots from wheat kernels fails. The maggot is hatched of an egg, the living germ in the living ear of wheat. The "they," if they are men, and if men are human beings, and if human beings are for the time being living, are crammed higgledypiggledy with both uncritical "notions" and genuine food for thought. Are matters any different for Heidegger? As much as he would like to purge *das Man* of complacent oblivion, does he not always find the wheat mixed in, so that the "proper" and the "inappropriate" are inextricably intermixed? Is that not part of the sense of the exteriority and passivity that mark *Bewegtheit*, animatedness? Is that not part of the reason why Heidegger will insist over and over again that the analysis of everydayness in the first division of *Being and Time* reveals essentially *neutral* structures, structures that are not to be scorned as "merely" quotidian, "purely" inappropriate?

(3) *Abriegelung*, "bolting" or "locking oneself away," sequestering oneself, and thus producing a situation of enforced isolation. Heidegger assures us that this third characteristic of care and concern is even less perspicuous than the first two, and we believe him. The syntax is odd, as is the thought: *Mit der Neigung in ihrer abstandsverkümmernden Zerstreuung gerät und ist weiter in Verlust was?* "With inclination, in its dispersion, a dispersion that deteriorates distance, something else gets lost and remains lost—what is it?" (105). What gets lost is that which is "before" me, not in a spatial sense, nor even in a

temporal sense. When I live on the basis of something, or explicitly "enjoy" (*ich lebe ausdrücklich von etwas*), my factical self or self-world is co-experienced, if not intellectually apperceived. Yet the "before" of every inclination or velleity is never fully appropriated (106: *unterbleibt die Aneignung des "vor"*), and my relation to things slackens. What gets lost? "In this veiled quality, 'life' speaks." Life speaks behind the muffling mask of its sundry significances. Life is *larvant*. (Is it the mask of grammar and logic, the Stoic and Scholastic mask, that obscures living speech? Are these the larval maggots in the marrow of the wheat?) What gets lost is life itself, as taking trouble and being concerned about itself, *das Leben als sorgendes*. What gets lost is the simple fact that life comes to the fore as such—"the temporalizing of life's proper *Vor-kommen*" (106). Such proper coming to the fore must be appropriated, emphasizes Heidegger once again (*ist . . . anzueignen!*). In hyperbolic pursuit of significance, life avoids itself, evades itself, allows itself to get sidetracked (107: *es geht sich aus dem Wege*). As life closes the distance between itself and other things and people, it *represses* that distance (Heidegger uses the psychoanalytic word, no doubt unwittingly, attaching it to his own variation on Nietzsche's "pathos of distance": *Abstandsverdrängung*). As a result of repression, life gains an illusory self-assurance. In a kind of evasion (107; cf. SZ §40), life preoccupies itself with itself in order to forget itself: "In taking trouble [*Sorgen*], life incarcerates itself from itself [*riegelt sich das Leben gegen sich selbst ab*]. Yet precisely in this incarceration life does not get shut of itself. Averting its glance again and again, life seeks itself, encountering itself precisely where it never guessed it would be, for the most part in masquerade (larvance)." Frenetic in its search for scraps of meaning, for ever-novel significance, life becomes careless of itself. Its most passionate concerns mask a lack of concern (*Unbekümmerung*), which nevertheless is troubled. Restive. Life mistakes itself ceaselessly, makes endless errors, and takes such endlessness to be infinity and the plenitude of eternity. Always more life! Always more than life! Such *infinity* is the mask that factical life holds up to the world. Larvance is the ruse of infinity, as Heidegger will later portray it in the final lines of section 65 of *Being and Time*. He criticizes the unclarified idea of infinity and eternity that vitiates "modern life-philosophy" as a whole. Although he names no names, he is surely thinking of Jaspers's *Psychology of Worldviews* (1919), just as we might think of works in our own time that operate on the basis of uncritical appeals to Eternity and Infinity:

> With this infinity, life blinds itself, enucleates itself. Incarcerating itself, life lets itself go. It falls short. Factical life lets itself go precisely by expressly and positively fending off itself. Incarceration therefore proceeds and temporalizes as *elliptical*. Factical life paves its own way for itself by the way it takes its directives [*Weisungnahme*], inclining, repressing distance, shutting itself off vis-à-vis life. (61, 108)

Which brings us to the final relational category of factical life.

(4) *Das "Leichte,"* the "easy," the "facile." Heidegger cites Aristotle's

Nicomachean Ethics B, 5 (1106b 28ff.) on the limitless ways one can err. The avenues of errancy are many and they are easy to travel, whereas the good is μοναχῶς, unifold, singular, *einfältig*. One can err by either going too far or falling short of the goal: error is either hyperbolic or elliptical. In both cases it is ῥᾴδιον, "easy," like rolling off a log. Life craves security, the security of insouciance. Life is inclined to flee, to make things easy for itself. It swathes its guilt in mists of fog; it tempts itself, falls, and invariably rescues itself for yet another temptation. Life enhances itself, tosses Zarathustra's golden ball fairly far. Yet in so doing it remains elliptical: factical life always falls short of primal decision (109: *Urentscheidung*).

Heidegger now summarizes the categories of relational meaning—that is to say, the categories of life's relation to the world—and (almost parenthetically) indicates the *ruinous* tendency of the whole:

> *Inclination:* proclivity, being swept away, dispersion, self-satisfaction.
> *Distance* (Elimination of): mistaking, miscalculating, remoteness in proclivity (worldly); the hyperbolic.
> *Incarceration:* evading oneself and precisely thereby not being shut of oneself, proliferation of ways to go wrong, blinding oneself; the elliptical.
> (Indication of a unified temporalizing: seeking relief [or: easing up, making things easier, *Erleichterung*]; cf. taking care that one can worry [*Sorge in der Besorgnis*]; appearance, creating masks, so that one "makes life hard" for onself!).
> (61, 109–110)

It is intriguing to wonder whether Heidegger is here engaged not so much in a descriptive phenomenology of factical life as in a *genealogy* of masquerade and ruinous self-deception. We ought to read the 1921–1922 lecture course alongside Nietzsche's "What Do Ascetic Ideals Signify?" (ZGM III). Then the crucial question would be whether Heidegger can allow the kind of *recoil* that characterizes Nietzschean genealogy—for genealogy is always genealogy of the genealogist—to take place in his own analysis of factical life. It is true that Heidegger freely concedes the diabolical difficulty of liberating one's point of departure from inherited ideas and ideals; but when he invokes the masquerade of pretending to "make life hard" for oneself while fleeing constantly to one's own *securitas*—whether it be security in sanctity or security in a priori phenomenological science—is he really thinking of himself and his own project? As Heidegger stalks his own situation, that of a lecturer and researcher in an institution of higher learning, the risk that he will "make discoveries" grows, and so in tandem do the polemic and vituperation grow. In tandem, precisely, it seems, in order to prevent those discoveries from coming home. Such is the unhappy lesson (we shall learn it in chapter 4, below) of Heidegger's "University of Life," of "the spiritual condition" of university life, which is fallen and forever falling farther: "It is not my ambition to make discoveries and to have them patented. Only the belle-lettrists and those corruptors of spiritual life [*Verderber des geistigen Lebens*] who are so sensitive and solicitous about their little treasure chests—only they abuse philosophy today in order thus to expend their vanities" (117–18).

Amen.

How hard Heidegger's life must be, locked into an institution where belle-lettrists and spiritual seducers run free! And yet one might also have to say that Heidegger is here on the verge of a very important discovery, a discovery whose implications embrace the entire project of fundamental ontology. It is a discovery that seems to transcend the very epoch of *Being and Time*, marking that book's limits and soaring beyond them. It is a discovery concerning "appropriateness" or "authenticity," *Eigentlichkeit*, the axis about which the fundamental ontology of *Being and Time* rotates—albeit not always smoothly, not ever "easily." The first chapter of part 3 of the 1921–1922 lecture course, "Factical Life," ends with this discovery of limits—and chapter 2 is called "Ruinance." It is perhaps the ultimate discovery concerning the relational categories of motility, the categories that cluster about life's animatedness (*Bewegtheit*). Heidegger's discovery is that—Aristotle to the contrary notwithstanding—factical life is *not self-moving;* at least, not unambiguously so. "Prestructuring" and "relucence" are inextricably interlaced in factical life. When life takes trouble concerning itself and its world, it becomes embroiled in the very possibilities that such *Sorgen* opens up: life needs the security of possibilities that are already "lived-in," and that it tends to *fixate*. Here is one of the earliest places where Heidegger's understanding of life converges with that of Nietzsche: from 1936 to 1939 Heidegger will focus on Nietzsche's interpretation of life as *Festmachung.*[11] Here, in his own hermeneutics of factical life, Heidegger descries and decries life's tendency "to live by falling into a rut in its world," *sich in seiner Welt festzuleben*. He laments life's self-petrifaction, its congealing or ossifying in its proper possibilities, *Sichfestleben* (13). The result is an anomalous situation with regard to the appropriateness or propriety of life's most proper possibility. Life has its autochthony and its autonomous movement or animatedness, its *Eigenständigkeit* and its *Eigenbewegtheit*, precisely in its living out beyond itself: whatever is life's *own* (*die gerade darin* eigene *ist*) derives from its living *outside* or *out beyond itself* (*daß das Leben* aus sich hinauslebt). In other words, factical life is most properly its own in the very *impropriety* by which it is always already expropriated and exposed to the world. Neither relucence nor ruinance is epiphenomenal. Both pertain to life's essential *Praestruktion*. Thus life's "own" animation is an animatedness that is *not* its own. If anything is contingent here it is the "illumination" that seeks to penetrate the ruinous complacency of propriety and the proper. Thus the ironic exclamation point within parentheses in this final paragraph, after the appearance of the word *eigentlich*, "appropriately," "properly." It marks an irony that would have shaken the entire existentialist account of Heideggerian "authenticity," from Sartre to Macquarrie and Robinson, had the 1921–1922 lecture course been available a generation ago. One might speculate that the irony of a property that is never properly a property(!), a propriety that is always improper(!), would be capable of shattering the most "authentic" readings of Heidegger. Heidegger writes:

> The animatedness is such that, as a motion in itself, it helps itself toward itself [*die als Bewegung in sich selbst sich zu ihr selbst verhilft*]. It is the animatedness of factical life that constitutes life itself; indeed, factical life, living in the world, does not itself properly (!) constitute the movement [*daß das faktische Leben . . . die Bewegung eigentlich (!) nicht selbst macht*]. Rather, factical life lives the world as the in-which, upon-which, and for-which of life [*sondern die Welt als das Worin und Worauf und Wofür des Lebens lebt*]. (61, 130)

Factical life *lives* the world. Or, reading *die Welt* as the *subject* of the sentence, the *world* lives (transitive) factical life. Perhaps this is why Nietzsche and the other life-philosophers find themselves forever confusing life and world. Perhaps this is why when in 1929–1930 Heidegger tries to differentiate the world-relations of various *forms* of life, particularly the forms of life we call *animal* and *human,* his effort is doomed to fail. Factical life lives the world in such a way that the world lives, and not some properly proprietary possibility of authentic ownness. And the world lives and moves factically as *ruina, Ruinanz.*

If we continue to fall with Heidegger's 1921–1922 lecture course we will never be able to escape back (or forward) to *Being and Time.* Therefore, only one word more about ruinance. For ruinance will not help us to read *Being and Time;* it will only hinder us and make things harder. Only one word about ruinance: the word is "nothing," *das Nichts.*

Even though ecstatic temporality has not yet emerged as the enrapturing and rupturing horizon of the meaning of being; and even though no analyses of anxiety and being-unto-death appear in the 1921–1922 course; the crucial word for the analysis of *Ruinanz* is nonetheless "nothing." It is as though a continuous line might be traced from 1921–1922 to the 1928 logic course and the 1929 "What Is Metaphysics?" and "On the Essence of Ground." That line would not circumvent *Being and Time* but pierce it through at one point—the point at which (in section 58, "Understanding the Call, and Guilt") the very being of Dasein is defined as nullity. Guilt is "being the ground of a being that is determined by a not—i.e., *being the ground of a nullity*" (SZ, 283). As thrown projection, Dasein is "the (null) being-the-ground of a nullity" (285). The 1921–1922 "Introduction to Phenomenological Research," after an extraordinary itinerary of ruinance—through plunge and masquerade, through kairological time and the instant of a counterruinance that is always gnawing at life's false securities, always boring away and burrowing, always subverting life's complacency, through the necessity of a phenomenological destruction of all interpretative seductions (particularly those of an ethico-religious sort)—culminates in an account of the "whither" of ruinance (61, 143–48).

Where does factical life land when it falls? Nowhere.

When does ruinance strike home? Never.

What rises to break its free fall? Nothing.

The fall is nothing never nowhere but unobstructed fall, uninterrupted crash (145: *Sturz*). Thus the very animatedness of factical life is nihilation: the nothing of factical life is that which no philosophical dialectic, from Plato's *Sophist* through Hegel's *Phenomenology of Spirit,* has confronted, much less mastered. The nothing cotemporalizes (147: *mitzeitigt*) with the fall, so that life is not only animation but also annihilation—not in any "wild metaphysical" sense, but in the sense of renunciation or doing-without (148: *Darbung*).[12] Life as renunciation, as deprivation, returns to the scene in 1929–1930, when Heidegger tries to think the very essence of *animal* life as deprivation (*Entbehren*). At which point animal and human life will seem very close indeed—in the face of daimon life.

What remains most mysterious in the early Freiburg lecture course is the counterruinance or resistance that enables phenomenological research to struggle against complacency. What *Being and Time* proclaims as its starting-point, namely, the intimacy of *questioning* as an intrinsic mode of being for Dasein, here resists depiction. If life falls but lands nowhere, whence the upsurge and upswing of inquiry? Whence the flourishing of life in the university, whence the university of life?[13] If factical life does without, if *Darbung* is its situation, whence the thrust of phenomenological research? When and how does genuine questioning gnaw its way to the surface—or into the depths? When does life become sufficiently restive? How do we ever know whether or not it is simply an instance of the phenomenologist's thoroughgoing self-deception and rigorous complacency: "Ah, how hard my science is!"?

Let us return to *Being and Time* with the chastening realization that Heidegger's earliest reflections on factical life bring his magnum opus of 1927 to a point of perpetual crisis.

FROM FACTICAL LIFE TO DASEIN

The eight places in *Being and Time* that we indicated earlier as sites where life recurs only to be shooed away by Dasein must now reclaim our attention. First and foremost among them, as is well known by now, is section 10, "Demarcating the Analysis of Dasein over against Anthropology, Psychology, and Biology." Or, as Heidegger says at the end of section 9, over against anthropology, psychology, and "all the more strongly," *a fortiori, und erst recht,* biology. When it comes to avoidance and exclusion, the science of biology seems to possess a certain privilege and distinction. Why?

In section 3 of the introduction, where it is a matter of the "ontological preeminence of the question of being," life appears as merely one area of inquiry (*Sachgebiet*) or region of being (*Bezirk*) among others, such as history, nature, space, Dasein, and language (SZ, 9). Its importance is nevertheless highlighted by the fact that in an earlier "draft" of *Being and Time,* the 1925 *Prolegomena to the History of the Concept of Time* (20, 19), Heidegger formulates his own project in terms of Dilthey's search for a bridge to join the banks of nature and history, a link to forge together the natural and historical sciences—the name of that link or bridge being *life*. Further, as he discusses that crisis in the sciences which can only be resolved by a "perspicuous revision of fundamental concepts," a revision to be undertaken by a fundamental ontology, Heidegger says nothing about anthropology and psychology. He says this about biology: "In *biology* the tendency is awakening to inquire back behind the definitions of organism and life that are provided by mechanism and vitalism, and to determine anew the mode of being of the living as such" (SZ, 10). In 1929–1930 the stalemate of mechanism and vitalism will serve as the point of departure for Heidegger's theoretical biology. Yet why is nothing said or done in *Being and Time* itself to revise the concept of a biology that is already in crisis? Why is nothing about the mode-of-being of living beings as such (*die Seinsart von Lebendem als solchem*) clarified?

The question gains in intensity when Heidegger tells us in section 10 that precisely this failure to clarify concepts is the "fundamental flaw" in all otherwise noteworthy life-philosophy (46). Dilthey, Husserl, and Scheler all share in this failure, to say nothing of thinkers outside the phenomenological and hermeneutical traditions. The question is whether Heidegger's *Being and Time* does not participate in that same failure, and whether the 1929–1930 lecture course is not a belated and even desperate effort to fill in the gap. Yet even in *Being and Time* Heidegger knows that it cannot be a matter of stopgaps. An ontology of life can be neither prior nor posterior to fundamental ontology; it can be neither a presupposition of nor an appendix to fundamental ontology. Throughout *Being and Time* and the 1929–1930 *Fundamental Concepts of Metaphysics*, Heidegger will oscillate between these two impossible positions, this neither/nor, of life vis-à-vis ontology of Dasein. In section 10 of *Being and Time* it is clear to him that the "missing ontological foundation" of psychology and anthropology cannot be supplied by "building these into a general biology" (49). Neither can a general biology be built into fundamental ontology. Nor, finally, can the latter simply be constructed on top of the former. He continues: "In the order of our possible grasping and interpreting, biology, as the 'science of life,' is founded on ontology of Dasein, if not exclusively on it."

Upon what else, "if not exclusively," can the science of life be founded? If the fundamental ontology of Dasein *is* fundamental, what is it that exceeds its grasp and defies its interpreting? Heidegger cannot here be indicating simply that other beings besides Dasein are alive; here it is a matter of foundations, of phenomenological access and hermeneutical precision, of orders of ontological implication, of phenomenological insight, rigorous description, and conceptual grasp. Yet what about this *excess* of life with regard to fundamental ontology? Heidegger continues: "Life is its own mode of being, yet essentially accessible only in Dasein" (50: *Leben ist eine eigene Seinsart, aber wesenhaft nur zugänglich im Dasein*). Life is a proper mode of being, appropriate to itself alone. And yet it encroaches on the appropriateness of a Dasein that can die. To make matters worse, life proper denies us all access to itself—except by way of our (highly problematic) access to Dasein. If access (*Zugang*) to Dasein is exceedingly difficult—and it is, inasmuch as all of *Being and Time* is about the problem of access—then we can expect that access to life by way of human existence will be diabolically difficult. Daimonically difficult.

Heidegger now relates his strategy for going to meet daimon life. It is the familiar strategy of privation, the traditional theological *via negativa.* "The ontology of life proceeds by way of a privative interpretation; it determines what must be, in order that just-plain-life can be" (50: *das, was sein muß, daß so etwas wie Nur-noch-leben sein kann*). Just-plain-life, only-just-life, is ostensibly the remainder of a process of subtraction. It's life-and-life-only, as Bob Dylan used to inform his Ma, that will be reached when something is taken away from Dasein. Heidegger will have to be very careful not to allow that subtractable something to be λόγος. Otherwise he will betray the fact that an ancient prejudice—the very prejudice he wishes to eradicate, that of the ζῷον λόγον ἔχον, the *animal rationale*—guides his own venture from start to finish. And no matter how careful he will be, readers of *Being and Time* will be troubled by this doubt: if life is its own mode of being, *eine eigene Seinsart,* can we get to it *properly* by subtracting anything at all from Dasein? Would that not be to fall into the trap of putatively a posteriori but essentially a priori deduction or derivation? Is not subtraction through privation the very method of deduction, a method that Heidegger himself insists will never restore us to life? Is not all derivation based on deprivation? And is not all de(p)rivation surreptitiously guided by an a priori that here, as in all life-philosophy, lacks foundation?

What sort of being is life? Heidegger writes: "Life is neither pure being at hand [*Vorhandensein*] nor Dasein either" (50). Does that suggest that life is handy, *zuhanden,* like a hammer? Perhaps life is as handy as the handiest of all items—the sun, at which readers of *Being and Time* will soon be required to gaze. We shall gaze at the sun in our next chapter, as though at an a priori of all handy beings, but not before concluding our remarks on this difficult tenth section. Heidegger ends the paragraph, not by defining life as handy but by a syntactically awkward remark about how Dasein for its part is *never* to be interpreted. In other words, Heidegger now doubles up the *via negativa* by declaring what might (never) take us to just-plain-life. "For its part, Dasein is never to be determined ontologically by positing it as life—(ontologically undetermined) and as something else in addition to this." Mere addition will never take us forward from life to Dasein. Yet if this is so, how will subtraction help us to regress to just-plain-life? What if Heidegger's words have to be taken quite literally? That is to say, what if life is its *own* mode of being? Can we be sure that Dasein is alive?

Perhaps there is a way to short-circuit these doubts and methodological difficulties. Would not the human *body* give us access to something like just-plain-life? If Dasein is in each case mine, and if the "mine" is also distributed across the bodies of men and women who exist, would not Dasein always and everywhere be some body who is alive? Let us go back over some of the materials we have only now examined, this time from within the perspective of the human body, if only by way of an *excursus* or digression, if only by way of dispersion and distraction. As though dispersion and dissemination alone might grant us access to the life of Dasein.

SOME BODY IS ALIVE

Thomas Mann published *Der Zauberberg* a scant three years before Heidegger released *Being and Time*. The gnomic hero of Mann's *Magic Mountain* muses on the balcony of a Swiss sanatorium, where inscrutable microbes hollow out the lungs of his cousin and all his companions. Hans Castorp peers into one medical book after another, seeking an explanation, investigating the life that is killing them all.

> He examined deeply, he read while the moon traveled its measured path over the valley formed by high mountains that glistened like crystal; he read of organized matter, the properties of protoplasm, sentient substance preserving itself in a remarkable oscillation of being [*in sonderbarer Seinsschwebe*] between anabolism and catabolism, forming its configurations from primeval yet ever-present fundamental forms; with compelling fervor he read of life and its sacred-impure secret. What was life? They didn't know. . . . [14]

What more can be said of Heidegger's analysis of the body of Dasein after Alphonse de Waelhens's by now familiar and utterly devastating complaint? "Heidegger's reader perceives too late," writes de Waelhens, "that the meticulous acuity in this author's description of the projected world has as its counterpart a total neglect of the world that is 'always-already-there' for us."[15] What more can be said? Only that the "apriori perfect" of the world (SZ, 85)—the world's being always already there for Dasein—was Heidegger's keenest insight and greatest passion from beginning to end. Only, therefore, the gnawing question: Did Heidegger simply fail to see the arm of the everyday body rising in order to hammer shingles onto the roof, did he overlook the quotidian gaze directed toward the ticking watch that overtakes both sun and moon, did he miss the body poised daily in its brazen car, a car equipped with turn signals fabricated by and for the hand and eye of man, did he neglect the human being capable day-in, day-out of moving its body and setting itself in motion? If so, what conclusion must we draw? Surely, the irrefutable conclusion that if indeed "one cannot find thirty lines in *Being and Time* concerning the problem of perception, six lines on the problem of the body" (vi/xix), then Dasein seems destined to share the fate of the cherubim and seraphim, or even worse, the fate of *l'homme*.

In 1972 Medard Boss confronted Heidegger with the objection that "others" had taken over from Jean-Paul Sartre, namely, that in all of *Being and Time* there are only half-a-dozen lines on the body. Heidegger replied: "I can only respond to Sartre's objection by affirming that matters touching the body [*das Leibliche*] are the most difficult, and that at the time I did not know what else to say" (ZK, 292). In a conversation eleven years earlier, Heidegger responded to Sartre's complaint that he (Heidegger) had rendered a "poor treatment" of the body by offering two meager explanations: "First, a treatment of the phenomenon of the body is not at all possible without a sufficient elaboration of the fundamental traits of existential being in the world; second, there does not yet exist an adequately applicable description of the phenomenon of the body, namely, a description that takes being in the world as its point of departure" (ZK, 202). That the *body* as being in the world is the cardinal *ontological* problem is no news to students of Merleau-Ponty, whose work Heidegger knew about, but who plays no role at all in the Zollikon seminars, even though the question of the body is the recurrent theme there. It is also worth noting that when the question of the body is raised, as it is throughout the Zollikon seminars, Heidegger reverts to the vocabulary of existential ontology, of *In-der-Welt-sein*, whereas the aletheiological and topological language of the later Heidegger is left in abeyance: references to φύσις and to the open region are vague and indeterminate, references to propriation and the granting all but absent. Finally, we should insert here the remarks of one of Heidegger's early students, Hans Jonas, who affirms the centrality of the body, and the body's life, as *ontological* issues of the first order:

> The living body that can die, that has world and itself belongs to the world, that feels and itself can be felt, whose outward form is organism and causality, and whose inward form is selfhood and finality: this body is the memento of the still unsolved question of ontology, 'What is being' and must be the canon of coming attempts to solve it. These attempts must move beyond the partial abstractions ("body and soul," "extension and thought," and the like) toward the hidden ground of their unity and thus strive for an integral monism on a plane above the solidified alternatives.

And some pages later, in the same vein:

> In the body, the knot of being is tied which dualism does not unravel but cut. Materialism and idealism, each from its end, try to smooth it out but get caught in it. The central position of the problem of life means not only that it must be accorded a decisive voice in judging any given ontology but also that any treatment of itself must summon the whole of ontology.[16]

However, let us return to *Being and Time* and the complaints of the "others." Let us look for those six lines de Waelhens says are not even there. Let us also observe in passing some of the lines that *are* there, particularly those in sections 12 (on "being-in as such") and 47 (on our ability to experience the death of others). No doubt, the body of Dasein will continue to elude us as a gauzy ghost of the counter-Cartesian: Heidegger will always be able to say what the body is *not*, but will have all too little to say about what it is or might become. Yet if Dasein is (as Heidegger insists throughout his oeuvre) some body, some body who is alive, *wie man leibt und lebt*, stretched between the "ends" of birth and death—Dasein natal, Dasein fatal—then let us scour the text as hard as Hans Castorp scours medical books on his moonlit balcony.

The word for the specifically human body, *der Leib*, with all its concatenated forms (*leiblich, leibhaftig,* etc.) appears twenty-two times in *Being and*

Time; the more neutral term, *der Körper,* corporeal mass in the Galilean-Newtonian sense, appears some twenty-six times.[17] It would certainly be laborious to examine their appearances throughout Heidegger's magnum opus. Let me try to point out a few representative passages, after one or two words by way of introduction.

The only real problem with the body of Dasein is that it is alive. And life, as we heard Heidegger say in the 1921–1922 lecture course, is hazy. Neither Dilthey nor Husserl nor Scheler can penetrate that haze. That is to say, neither Dilthey's conviction that the entirety of life, *das "Ganze des Lebens,"* bridges the gap between the natural and the historical sciences, nor Husserl's tripartite analysis of the constitution of material nature, animal nature, and the spiritual-intellectual world in *Ideen II,* nor Max Scheler's personalistic anthropology can provide access to the global phenomenon of a living being that is bodily being-in-the-world.[18] Heidegger writes in section 10 of *Being and Time:*

> The question remains as to the being of the whole human being, which we are accustomed to grasp as a corporeal-psychic-spiritual unity [*leiblich-seelisch-geistige Einheit*]. Body, soul, and spirit can in turn be designated as phenomenal regions that are isolable from one another thematically with a view to particular investigations; within certain limits their ontological indeterminacy may not tilt the balance. However, when we are asking about the being of human beings [*In der Frage nach dem Sein des Menschen*] we cannot simply add up the component modes of being—body, soul, spirit—each of which has itself yet to be defined. And even an ontological effort that would proceed to define them would have to presuppose an idea of the being of the whole [*eine Idee vom Sein des Ganzen*]. (SZ, 48; cf. 65, no. 193)

Heidegger's fundamental ontology goes in search of that whole, particularly in Division II of *Being and Time,* "Dasein and Temporality." There the whole being of Dasein hides in the enigmatic life of an existence for which death is definitive yet always still outstanding, looming yet always in default. Running ahead into a future that will be the bygones of existence, opened up anxiously by and to the ectases of finite time, Dasein will try to be resolute—but it will succeed only in being bemused and benumbed. Heidegger calls this *readiness.* I call it being on the *verge.*[19]

One of the most bemusing things for an anxious Dasein is the realization that its being toward an end, toward *one* end, is not enough. For Dasein has *two* ends, as Heidegger tells us in section 72 (SZ, 373): first, the end of a death that approaches as Dasein rushes to embrace the proper future toward which it is thrown; and second, the end that every nascent Dasein has always already left "behind," as it were. Our birth, like anxiety itself, comes creeping from behind in order to haunt an otherwise futurebound existence. Stretched and self-stretching between birth and death, the whole being of Dasein is what Dilthey called the nexus of life, *der Zusammenhang des Lebens.* Heidegger does not dwell on the behind of birth, does not gaze on that emergent head glistening with blood, saline water, and cream cheese, the lips and buttocks of the mother   *he returned and sat down at the woman's feet, and listened intently to what she said* one seamless organ of pression pulsion pause retention enhanced pressure and final release, does not regard the purpleveined ochreous tube that invariably connects each slippery new Dasein to its specific Other (Dasein fatal seems to slip into the same, Dasein natal always seems to have slipped into difference, partly because of its own parturition, partly because of its connection with and to its specific [m]other), but he, Heidegger, as we shall see in chapter 5, hurries headlong to join his generation in the shared struggle for a national fate, hastens to accompany those battling progeny who are loyal to their chosen hero (SZ §74, 384–85). So soft at birth, so hard at work on dying. A scant dozen pages of the 437-page *Being and Time* separate Heidegger's somewhat abashed acknowledgment of birth from the bold discovery of a national destiny, and I sometimes think (no doubt too rashly, too impressionistically, after having read too many book reviews in the Sunday supplements) that the nexus of Heidegger's own life stretches out in those dozen pages.

Born, on its feet now, running ahead into its death, Dasein is doubtless alive. Every Bohemian peasant can see that. Yet the ancient designation of human being as ζῷον λόγον ἔχον, *animal rationale*, tells us nothing about its life. Dasein and life *as such,* just-plain-life, as we have heard, cannot be conflated: "Life is its own mode of being [*Leben ist eine eigene Seinsart*], yet essentially accessible only in Dasein [*aber wesenhaft nur zugänglich im Dasein*]" (SZ, 50). Because the entire problem of a fundamental ontology of Dasein is one of access (*Zugang*) to the global phenomenon of being-in-the-world, life is doubly and trebly encrypted and thus hidden from the ontologist. Life is properly its own mode of being. The ring of life and the hermeneutical circle are not coextensive. Moreover, as the lectures on theoretical biology in 1929–1930 will demonstrate, Dasein can never leap out of the *circle* that circumscribes existence into the *ring* of disinhibited drives that constitutes the animal's "world." Nevertheless, Dasein itself, properly speaking, *can* die, presumably because it is alive. Ostensibly because it is in each case my own dying. Putatively because, in other words, Dasein is some specific body, in each case somebody's lived and living body. If access to the global phenomenon of being in the world is difficult, access to life as such is impossible; however, if Dasein is alive, then proper access to living Dasein is denied from the start and fundamental ontology is impossible. Indeed, when the body finally comes to Dasein, or rather, when Dasein "leaps" into its body, a body that is even equipped with something that at least looks like a sex or a sexuality, *Geschlechtlichkeit*, it will be in 1928, when fundamental ontology somersaults into meta-ontology.[10]

Back to the passage that begins by asserting the autochthony of life—*Leben ist eine eigene Seinsart*—and the double-bind of a Dasein that can never leap over its own shadow or outside its hermeneutical encirclement—*aber wesenhaft nur zugänglich im Dasein*. As we heard an instant ago, "The ontology of life proceeds by way of a privative interpretation; it determines what must be, in order that something like just-plain-life [*Nur-noch-leben*] can be." There is, then, or there can be, or perhaps there will someday be an ontology of life. Yet no ontology of life could be fundamental. For the fundament would have to be a *radical* and *original* interpretation of a Dasein which, while dying, for the time being *lives*. No subtraction or addition could get us from one to the other, no algorithm such as $D - x = L$, or $D = x + L$ can be readily applied, no straightforward move from the earlier to the subsequent, or from the posterior back to the prior. Yet if Dasein *is* some body who is alive, we should not need any complex formula or transcendental deduction to move freely between the two.

Concerning life, we heard Heidegger say: "Life is neither pure being at hand nor Dasein either." *Weder pures Vorhandensein noch aber auch Dasein.* This denial will open a chasm that swallows a very important distinction of and for fundamental ontology. At several crucial junctures in *Being and Time* Heidegger rigorously distinguishes what is *daseinsmäßig* (what is of-the-measure-of-Dasein) from what is not so. *Daseinsmäßig* is used some forty times in *Being and Time*, *nichtdaseinsmäßig* some fourteen times. Yet a reference to one is a (negative) reference to the other. Heidegger invokes this binary opposition when it is a matter of crucial distinctions—this sort of death rather than that, this sort of call rather than that, this sort of time rather than that, this appropriate Dasein rather than that inappropriate Dasein. (Never mind what it can mean that an oblivious Dasein can be well-nigh *undaseinsmäßig*, indeed, that at first and for the most part Dasein must be so, almost as though it were a bedazzled animal before it becomes a bedazzled human.) Such a binary measure is of the essence. For the difference between what is of-the-measure-of-Dasein and what is not of that measure constitutes the proto-ontological difference as such: the *difference* between the being that raises the question of the meaning of being and the beings that are *indifferent* to the question implicates the *difference* between beings and being as such. Yet life's neither-nor, its *ne/uter* interrupts and complicates the opposition of *daseinsmäßig* to *nichtdaseinsmäßig*. Life is neither Dasein nor being at hand, neither of-the-measure-of-Dasein nor *not* of that measure. "For its part, Dasein is never to be defined ontologically by positing it as life—(ontologically undetermined) and as something else besides." In the first edition and in all the later editions, the awkward punctuation of the sentence betrays a kind of double distancing of Dasein from life: life (dash, open parenthesis) ontologically undetermined (close parenthesis). No leap from circle to ring and back again will close that fatal distance within which life keeps its secrets. Under the moonlight amid high mountains and stacks of medical books.

Yet where is the human body in all this? It is there in Heidegger's text as the impossible limit between what is of-the-measure-of-Dasein and what is not of that measure. It is there as the negated Galilean, Cartesian, Newtonian bodything (*Körperding*) imbued with a spiritthing (*Geistding*), the outrageous dingaling that our tradition has the temerity to call the *human* body (*der Menschenleib*). No doubt Heidegger scorns that concoction, especially in its Cartesian form—a mental or spiritual *capax mutationum* that guarantees constant perdurance (after the appropriate purgings) for a mind that is inexplicably tied to an execrable body, *ad istam corporis humani . . . coniunctionem* (SZ, 91–92, citing Descartes' *Principia* II, nos. 3–4). After Heidegger carefully excludes the categorial-spatial relation of extended things at hand *in* one another (the dress in the closet, the water in the glass), excludes it as being appropriate only to "beings that are not of the manner of being of Dasein [*Seiendem von nicht daseinsmäßiger Seinsart*]," he elaborates the existential character of "being-in" (54). The ontological constitution of Dasein cannot be thought in terms of "the being at hand of a bodything (the human body)." Rather, "in" must be thought as dwelling, familiarity, cultivation, usufruct, or diligent care. Thus being *in* the world is neither a spiritual and intellectual quality (56: *eine geistige Eigenschaft*) nor a mere epiphenomenon of a bodily being in space, with space as a property of corporeality (*Leiblichkeit*), which for its part "is always at the same time 'founded' on the being of physical mass (*Körperlichkeit*)." The resulting amalgam possesses a "being" that is "*a fortiori* obscure." Heidegger explicitly contrasts human embodiment as spatiality to the existence of minerals in space (*das Vorkommen einer Gesteinsart*). He contrasts it by means of the facticity of that fact which we called a fact of life: "The factuality of the *factum* Dasein . . . we are calling its facticity" (56). Such facticity is the core of the world-relation that is Dasein: the world is that "in which" factical Dasein as such " 'lives'," even if constrained by quotation marks (65). One would no doubt want to contrast the spatial dwelling of Dasein not only with minerals but also with sundry forms of vegetable and animal life. Yet Heidegger does not do so here. He contents himself with the lapidary contrast between stone and Dasein. True, he succumbs for an instant to an anthropological temptation: he refers to " 'the life [*Leben*] of primitive peoples' " (51), a life or living in which the structures of being-in and worldliness might be discerned more clearly, without adornments, free from distractions, stripped of masks, without the veneer of civilization. Primitive life interprets itself naively and forthrightly, in what Ernst Cassirer calls a *Lebensform*.[21] Heidegger squelches the "naive opinion," which is " 'metaphysically' motivated," that the human being (*der Mensch* here being equated with *Dasein*) "is at first a spiritual thing that is then subsequently transposed into a space [*zunächst ein geistiges Ding, das dann nachträglich 'in' einen Raum versetzt wird*]."

Heidegger is able to squelch the naive, metaphysically motivated view—of the spiritthing spirited off into a bodything and then tossed like a stone into space—by virtue of a reference to touching (*Berühren*). A chair can never touch the wall, even if it should be contiguous with it, and not simply because of the infinitesimal spaces that separate molecules of pine from molecules of plaster. A chair can never *encounter* (begegnen) the wall. For the chair has no world, is not there-being (and for the first time in *Being and Time* Heidegger hyphenates the word: *Da-sein*). Two worldless beings in contact with one another can never touch each other. Although the pun is wicked, the following thought is not: no chair is *chair*, the element of "flesh" thought by Merleau-Ponty in terms of the touched-touching paradigm.[22] In *Being and Time* it is as though the entire touched-touching paradigm and the (finite) reversibility of flesh (which can never be immanent, but only imminent, that is, beyond simultaneity) is reduced to the global characterization of worldliness. The stone and the chair cannot touch because they are worldless. One might wonder whether a beast or a god or a daimon could touch. Does Apollo really touch Patroklos when he thwacks him between the angelblades from behind? Can the ape with its prehensile organ—an organ that zoologists, to Heidegger's chagrin, try to pass off as a hand, although it can never apprehend the hand of man—touch the wall of its enclosure? Can it touch the prehensile organ of another ape, say, that of an infant ape it has borne and partured? Kafka's ape says that he became human by shaking hands. If Heidegger (much later, admittedly, in the early 1950s: see WhD? 51) wants to deprive the beast of hands, will it then become a piece of furniture for the human world, can we then shove it against the wall? A wall it will never touch, even if the hairs of its fur sing out something like "wall!" when it backs into a corner? For that matter, if we shoved a Dasein against the wall, would it sing out "worldliness!"?

Frivolous questions. Heidegger certainly does not entertain them here. Here stone and Dasein alone prevail. There are moments when *Being and Time* does invite such frivolity, however: at one point, apropos of touch, Heidegger writes that touching can be performed only by "a being that is of the manner of being of Dasein, or at least of something alive [*zum mindesten eines Lebenden*]" (97). Dasein—or *at least* an animal or plant. As though Dasein touched merely by virtue of its being just plain alive. As though, after all, just-plain-life were *not altogether without* world. In 1929–1930 the animal will intervene between stone and Dasein; it will insinuate itself as a being that is neither of the measure of Dasein nor not of that measure. Yet even then it will not be permitted to touch anything, not the wall, and certainly not Dasein, lest it contaminate human existence. That is to say, in his *Fundamental Concepts of Metaphysics: World—Finitude—Solitude,* the theme of touching is more than merely touched upon, inasmuch as *Berühren* becomes the central phenomenon for Heidegger's nascent attempts to distinguish the world-relations of stone, animal, and Dasein (29/30, 289–90). The stone may be in contact with earth, but it does not touch the ground. The lizard suns itself on the flat rock in the grass near the stream. It is not merely in contact with the earth but, we suppose, senses the warmth expended by the sun and retained by the rock, the warmth now radiating upward through the palpitating belly of the lizard. Yet the lizard never entertains a thought about stone *as* stone, sun *as* sun, or caloric radiation *as* such. Oddly, however, at the moment when Heidegger introduces touching into the 1929–1930 lectures, he does not immediately jump to the *as.* Rather, he introduces Dasein, not as enunciator of the metaphysical or apophantic *as,* of rock *as* rock or being *as* being, but in a rather surprising way: he invokes the hand of one human being touching the head of another. Not a stone on the earth or a lizard on the stone, but a hand on somebody else's head. Perhaps Socrates taking up Phaedo's curls during the one significant philosophical moment in the much-discussed dialogue that bears Phaedo's name. In any case, there is no hand for the lizard, which to Heidegger looks more like a coral snake, more like the death of Dasein, than a lizard *as* lizard.

Meanwhile, something like contamination seems to have occurred already in *Being and Time.* For the facticity of being in the world "has always already dispersed or even splintered [*zerstreut oder gar zersplittert*]" Dasein in certain ways. These are the ways of its everyday concerns and cares, its troubling itself concerning things (*Besorgen*). Heidegger does not fail to mention even the *"deficient* modes" of concern such as ceasing, neglecting, renouncing, or taking a rest: such modes display a Dasein that is "only just . . . ," "*Nur noch.*" He does not cite just-plain-living as one of these deficient modes, even though the identical privative structure applies to both. As for the dispersion of Dasein, *Zerstreuung,* to which Derrida has drawn our attention, we shall focus on it in chapter 5. For the moment we shall have to be satisfied with a remark that will prove to be essential for the 1929–1930 lecture course, a remark concerning what it means to "have" a world. No matter how often we proclaim the fact that human beings "have" an environing world (*Umwelt*), the proclamation is senseless unless and until the meaning of the "having" is determined. Heidegger's analysis of "being-in" aims to determine what it means to possess a world. Heidegger refers to the biologist Karl Ernst von Baer's pioneering use of *Umwelt*—we shall meet von Baer once again in chapter 3. Heidegger is anxious to deny that his own *philosophical* use of the phrase can be construed as "biologism" on his part. The denial establishes a particular rank and order of priority, one that may seem to privilege philosophy but that equally delineates its fate. Heidegger writes:

> For biology too, as a positive science, can never locate and determine this structure [that is, "having an environment"]. Rather, it must always presuppose that structure and must constantly make use of it. Yet the structure itself, as an *a priori* of the thematic object of biology, can become philosophically explicit only if it is comprehended in advance [*zuvor*] as a structure of Dasein. Only by orienting ourselves toward this comprehended ontological structure, and only by way of privation, can the ontological constitution of "life" be demarcated *a priori.* Ontically as well as ontologically, being in the world as concern takes precedence. In the analysis of Dasein this structure undergoes its foundational interpretation. (SZ, 58)

The privilege of priority to which Dasein is condemned, both ontically and ontologically, will not change when two years later Heidegger inquires into the comparative world-relations of stone, animal, and man. In section 13 of *Being and Time* he denies that the structure by which Dasein "has" a world can be called cognition (*Erkennen*). He denies that Dasein merely gapes at the world even when it only-just-tarries alongside beings (61: *Nur-noch-verweilen bei*) in the mode of knowing and scrutinizing them (69: *Nur-noch-hinsehen*), the structure of privation now having been extended to include not only animal life and deficient modes of concern but also cognition—the traditional distinguishing mark of humanity—as such. In contrast to a mere gaping at the world (*ein starres Begaffen*), a cognizant Dasein may be said to be bedazzled by its world, wholly caught up in its refracted light, stunned and stupefied by it, intoxicated with it. Here Heidegger introduces (in italics) the word that in 1929–1930 he will select in order to define the *animal's* having a world, its having-a-world-in-not-having it: "As concern, being-in-the-world is *benumbed* [benommen] by the world of its concerns." Note that such benumbment or bedazzlement is not mere gaping; it is not sheer ignorance, opposed to cognition; it is not what Descartes decries as *hébétude,* Leibniz as *étourdissement.* It is, at least in *Being and Time,* and especially in the first division of *Being and Time,* the eminent mode of having a surrounding world. It is what makes Dasein different from an animal, different from just-plain-life. One might say, without danger of hyperbole, that Dasein is closer to the impoverishment and deprivation of just-plain-life when it goes divinely theoretical, when it only-just-tarries alongside beings in order to just-plain-look-at-them, than when it submits to the fascinations of its world. Whether Heidegger will be able to suffer the proximity of *Nur-noch-leben* to *Nur-noch-hinsehen* and *Nur-noch-verweilen,* or whether he will have to recoil and return to the security of a λόγος that is bound to θεωρία, a private hearing of the λόγος for humankind, is an arresting question. That proximity would perhaps be the death of Dasein, and the death of fundamental ontology as well. Well, then. What about death and the body of Dasein?

If the body of dwelling and the body of touching flesh can be eliminated from ontology of Dasein, postponed as mere aspects of the "spatialization" of Dasein in " 'embodiment' " (SZ, 108: *die Verräumlichung des Daseins in seiner 'Leiblichkeit'*); if the body (like "life" itself, just-plain-life) may be considered as "a problem all its own [*eigene*], not to be treated here," a problem awaiting a *metaphysics of Dasein* and a *meta-ontology of truth;* we must nonetheless be chary of forgetting or even postponing the body that dies. Also wary of forgetting that the puzzle called Dasein is initially posed as an ontologically fuzzy unity of body-soul-spirit. At a particularly dramatic moment in his later biology course, when the chasm Heidegger digs in order to separate Dasein from the animal is all but impassable, he will remember and will remind his students that something like *the nothing* shatters both the circle of Dasein and the ring of life. Life dies. And no handy distinction between dying and perishing, no sleight-of-hand called demise, will prevent such shattering from sending shockwaves across the abyss and through Heidegger's entire project.

Yet one must be fair. Or at least minimally accurate. In *Being and Time* too Heidegger remembers that the body dies. Especially the body of Others. Their fresh cadavers come to grace the dissection table that once belonged to Descartes. These cadavers point back ghostily to the life they once lived. Stranger still, not even death can transform the fresh cadaver utterly into a thing at hand. Eventually, after an unspecified time, the Heideggerian cadaver, no longer so fresh, itself becomes a monumental stone, a tombstone, which in fact is a sign of life. Stone and Dasein become one at last. The stone cries out to the survivors who surround it, "Touch me with solicitude! Touch me   *How is this, already you are afraid!*   with care!" Strange metabolism, curious somersault in being, this death! One final extended passage from *Being and*

Time, on the human body undone, the body no longer alive. For that body still has a few terminal surprises in store for us.

> The being-no-longer-in-the-world of the dead is nonetheless still—understood in the extreme—a being, in the sense of the just-plain-being-at-hand of a bodything we encounter. In the dying of others we can experience the remarkable ontological phenomenon which we may define as the turnabout [*Umschlag*] of a being, from the mode of being of Dasein (or of life) to that of no-longer-Dasein. . . . [23]

Permit me a solicitous intrusion. What was earlier doubly and trebly impossible, namely, access to the autochthonous mode of being called "life," which is a being all its own, is here reduced to sheer apposition, the parenthesis now managing by some sort of punctuational maneuver to elide the circle and the ring: the turnabout of Dasein (open parenthesis) *or* of life (close parenthesis), *des Daseins* (beziehungsweise *des Lebens*). The inconspicuous letters *bzw.*, meaning *beziehungsweise,* the English *resp.,* induce us to read the sentence in the following way: "Dasein or, *to say the same thing in a different way,* life." "Dasein, or, *if you like,* life." Here it is not even a case of Dasein or *at least* life. Here Dasein and life are conflated utterly. Dasein *beziehungsweise* life? That was quick! Death therefore has the dubious advantage of at least seeming to enclose Dasein and all life in the selfsame circle *beziehungsweise* ring. Yet let me continue. For now Heidegger will deny us access to that curious phenomenon whereby Dasein—thought in its extremity by an extreme sort of thinking—apparently turns about into something eminently *nichtdaseinsmäßig.* He will deny us access to the "curious phenomenon" he allowed us to glimpse ever so briefly, the phenomenon that is to found all fundamental ontology. We might wonder what becomes of the crucial distinction between Dasein and no-longer-Dasein, what becomes of *death,* when Heidegger refuses to allow death to catapult existence into mere being-at-hand. We might wonder whether the collapse of the bipolar distinction between *daseinsmäßig* and *nichtdaseinsmäßig* would also entail the collapse of the distinction between Dasein and *Nicht-mehr-Dasein.* But to continue, and to come to a close:

> However, this interpretation of the turnabout from Dasein to just-plain-being-at-hand is mistaken, inasmuch as the phenomenal content, the being that still remains, cannot be represented as a pure bodything. Even the cadaver at hand is, viewed theoretically, still the possible object of anatomical pathology, whose mode of inquiry [*Verstehenstendenz*] remains oriented to the idea of life [*Idee von Leben*]. What is only-at-hand is "more" than a *lifeless* material thing. With it we encounter something *unliving* that has lost its life [*ein des Lebens verlustig gegangenes* Unlebendiges]. (SZ, 238)

In these lines, we may say, paraphrasing Heidegger's judgment of Nietzsche, Descartes celebrates his supreme triumph—viewed theoretically.[24] Yet at this precise moment in his text, Heidegger is disturbed once again by something of-the-measure-of-Dasein. Something impossible, no doubt, inasmuch as the corpse is no-longer-Dasein. Something, no doubt, that *haunts.* As the cadaver points uncannily back to its lost life, indicating how phenomenologically rigor-

ous it has become, the fundamental ontologist, in the mode of phenomenologist, writes as follows:

> The "deceased" ["*Verstorbene*"], who in contrast to the dead one [*Gestorbene*]
> has been torn away from the bereaved, who have been "left behind," is the object
> of "concern," by way of funeral rites and interment, the cult of the grave. And this
> in turn because in its mode of being it is "still more" than a mere handy item that
> concerns us in our environs. Those who remain behind *are with him,* lingering in
> mournful commemoration, in a mode of respectful solicitude. . . . (SZ, 238)

This is the second time, I believe, that the cult of the grave is invoked in
Being and Time. The first time it is conjured, Heidegger is trying to explain
how the sun in its passage from the dawn in the east to the dusk in the west
determines how graves are to be laid out—it is one of the rare moments when
"nature" interrupts the analysis of handy items in our environment, "nature"
and nature's sun intimating the "ownmost possibilities of being for Dasein"
(SZ §22, 104). Here the crypt interrupts the analysis, torques the description of
the "phenomenal basis" once again, in order to push the interpretation beyond
all extremes. Heidegger concludes: "The ontological relation to the dead one
therefore dare not be grasped as being that *concerns itself* with something
handy." Earlier we asked whether life, which is neither a being at hand nor
Dasein, neither of the measure of Dasein nor not of that measure, might be
handy (*zuhanden,* as opposed to the privative and deficient *vorhanden*). The
answer to that question, at least for the life of Dasein, is clear: no, not even
when it is dead, not even when it is *no longer being-there.* There are moments
when life seems to be merely handy, as when Dasein strips hides from animals
and produces leather, thus discovering "nature" in its productive mode (70).
Yet even here, something of nature remains concealed, nature " 'weaving and
striving'," nature overtaking us with the beauty of its landscapes, the flowers of
the grove, "the 'underground stream' " (70). And, perhaps, although Heidegger does not mention them here, the fish in the stream and the horse in the
grove. But let us return to the human realm, the land of the dead.

So many interpreters of *Being and Time* in our own day have expressed
dissatisfaction with Heidegger's notion of proper solicitude for others, as developed in section 26 of that work. They are too impatient. The profound analysis
of proper solicitude, *respectful* solicitude, comes only in Heidegger's reflections
in section 47 on the death of the Other. All proper solicitude comes to him or
her who waits. Of course, there are always those who chomp at the bit, who
insist on haste, who leap ahead solicitously and lay low all life with shibboleths
of ethico-religious discourse. Shibboleths are always on hand, books of prov-
erbs as handy as books of matches, sacred adzes, and flaming swords homing
in on the living. Heidegger does achieve respectful solicitude for the Other,
albeit somewhat late in the day. Most of his time has been spent fending off
publicity, leaping in and leaping ahead for the Other, assuming full responsibility for both the public and the private realms, presuming to be responsible,
presuming to solicit. That is the best one can say. The worst one can say of

Heidegger is that he suffers the same professional deformation as President
Schreber's God, who, "in accord with the order of the cosmos," is doomed to
spend most of his time with cadavers, and who as a result has little or no
understanding of the living.[25]

Not six lines on the animate body. In a book haunted at every juncture, in
each ligature and ligament, by a life that will not be squeezed into any set of
existentials within any hermeneutical circle. Haunted not by spirit but by a
daimon. Daimon life. Forty years after publishing *Being and Time,* Heidegger
turns aside to Eugen Fink during their seminar on Heraclitus; he whispers
something in his usual lapidary fashion, his words barely audible, as though he
were made of stone. He whispers these words, which we heard at the outset of
this chapter, and already   *Enkidu grew weak, for wisdom was in him,
and the thoughts of a man were in his heart*   in the Introduction: "The
phenomenon of the body [*das Leibphänomen*] is the most difficult problem"
(Hk, 243). This, after he has reminded the participants of his favorite oracular
saying, namely, that Dasein *lebt* only insofar as it *leibt,* "lives" only insofar as it
"bodies forth," only as some body who is alive.

Hans Castorp, on the balcony under the waxing moon, still reading by the
pale red lamplight, still researching this maculate yet holy life of ours:

> What was life? Nobody knew. Nobody knew the natural point at which it leapt
> and was enkindled. . . . Between life and inanimate nature an abyss yawned which
> investigators strove in vain to bridge. They struggled to close the abyss with
> theories. The abyss swallowed the theories without surrendering anything of its
> depth and breadth. . . . (291)
>
> Well, then, what was life? . . . It was the being of what was properly not-able-
> to-be [*das Sein des eigentlich Nicht-sein-Könnenden*]. . . . It wasn't material and it
> wasn't spirit. It was something between the two, a phenomenon borne by matter,
> like the rainbow in a waterfall, and like the flame. Although immaterial, it was
> sensuous to the point of lust and nausea: the shamelessness of matter sensible to
> itself, stimulable by itself: the lascivious form of being [*die unzüchtige Form des
> Seins*]. It was a secret sentient arousal in the chaste chill of the universe. . . . (292)
>
> The books lay in a pile on the table by the lamp . . . , and the book Hans
> Castorp had just been researching lay on his belly and oppressed his respiration,
> without however causing his cerebral cortex to issue the order to the responsible
> muscles for its removal. He had read down the page; his chin had reached his
> breast; his lids had drooped over his simple blue eyes. He saw the image of life, saw
> its burgeoning, articulated structure: the beauty borne by flesh [*die fleisch-
> getragene Schönheit*]. (302)

TWO

"... Life-in-Death"

Reading *Being and Time* (II)

Life has appeared thus far in *Being and Time* as the unlikely body of Dasein and the impossible object of ontology. We must now go to encounter life in falling, anxiety, and care. Further, we shall rise to meet it in the ungraspable reality of the resplendent sun, then descend to meet it in bedazzlement, demise, and death. Perhaps even in perishing.

VANUS HEBESCO

The two principal problems of the "everyday being of the 'there' and the falling [*Verfallen*] of Dasein" (SZ, §§35–38) are, first, the difficulty of achieving genuine phenomenological *access* to falling as the movement or animatedness (*Bewegtheit*) of existence and, second, the ease with which the factical ideal of such a fallen yet always still falling existence, an ideal derived from certain strands of the theological and moral-philosophical traditions, surreptitiously guides Heidegger's fundamental ontology. Both problems touch on life. For the falling of Dasein is, as we have seen, the ruinous animation of factical life as such; and the factical ideal of a vigilant, reticent, and resolute Dasein that gets a grip on itself and escapes the snares of the world is an ancient ideal—the ideal of all idealisms and asceticisms since time immemorial, which seek to protect themselves above all from life.

It is intriguing that "life" appears repeatedly in Heidegger's analyses of the craving for novelty (*Neugier*), the ambivalence (*Zweideutigkeit*), and more generally the thrownness and falling (*Geworfenheit, Verfallen*) that character-ize everyday Dasein, and that each time it appears its context is derisory. When Dasein lusts for life by chasing after novelties, it seeks a spurious guarantee that it is indeed genuinely "living life to the full"— *"die Bürgschaft eines vermeint-lich echten 'lebendigen Lebens'"* (173). The very vitality of an altogether lively life is nothing more than frantic curiosity, bustle, dispersion, and distraction, reflecting loss of center and deterioration of roots. When Dasein chatters idly, says Heidegger, it "lives faster" than when it is reticent—if it ever achieves reticence (174). Finally, the very animatedness of an existence that is bedazzled by the world and by its public self (176) "tempts" Dasein—inasmuch as being in the world "is in itself *versucherisch*" (177)—into believing that it is leading "a full and genuine 'life' " (177), a "concrete life" (178). Such temptation and bedazzlement seem to be perfect: Dasein is always already ensnared by the world, so much so that one must wonder by what Odyssean ruse the fundamental ontologist resists its allures and remains vigilant long enough to descry and describe all those pitfalls. Presuming that he has not already fallen. In which case he would not know what he is describing. Presuming then that he has fallen and is still falling, etc.

Heidegger concedes the problem. Falling speaks both for and against the possibility of a phenomenologically accessible "formal idea of existence" (170). "Can Dasein be grasped as a being in whose being there is *involvement* in its being able to be—if this being, precisely in its everydayness, *has lost itself* and, in falling, 'lives' by *turning away from itself* [von sich weg *'lebt'*]?" How does the phenomenologist "live" in such a way as to halt the otherwise perfect aversion of existence to insight? How does one "live" illumination—as Heidegger called it in 1921–1922—if "life" shuns the light? What does the phenomenologist's craving to see betray? Does it manifest a disposition to fundamental ontology? Or is εἰδέναι ὀρέγονται, *die Sorge des Sehens* (the trouble we take to see, even and especially in phenomenological seeing) a *concupiscentia oculorum,* which is to say, a temptation? If the first sentence of metaphysics ordains the desire to see, does not the first sentence of ascetic morality proscribe the lust of the eyes?

When one recalls the tendency of Augustine's suspicion, which is not only of the eyes as such but also of science and the craving *to know,* then the devilishly difficult problems of hermeneutical access to falling and of the factical ideal of (a phenomenological purview of) existence become increasingly poignant. If in his 1920–1921 "Introduction to the Phenomenology of Religion" Heidegger translates Paul's references to ζωή in the first epistle to the Thessalonians (e.g., 1:9, 3:8, 5:10, and especially 4:15–17) as "factical life," is not Heidegger's notion of ruinous life informed by Paul's obsessive vigilance?[1] Is not human life a pernicious trial for Augustine too (X, 28: *temptatio est vita humana*), precisely because his God commands him to "contain himself" from the lust of the flesh, the lust of the eyes, and the ambition of the world (30: *concupiscentia carnis et concupiscentia oculorum et ambitione saeculi*), as though these three were inextricably interwoven in and for life? The incessant refrain of these pages of the *Confessions* is "Give me what you command, and command what you will." How avoid the birdlime of concupiscence when we imbibe it with the mother's milk of faith? How eat our food without tasting it as anything more than bitter physic? How avoid delight in smelling, how purge the infernal ambiguity, as Heidegger says, of "being on the scent" of a thing (SZ, 173: *Auf-der-Spur-sein*)? How suppress the joy of ears that thrill to celestial music played in church? "And so I float between the perils of pleasure and an approved and profitable custom. . ." (X, 33). How see the light while blinding the eye to the beauties of color and shape (34)? Worse, how prevent the lust of the eyes from becoming "a certain vain and curious itch [*vana et curiosa cupiditas*] to experience by way of the flesh [*experiendi per carnem*], an itch that is masked under the palliative titles of knowledge and learning [*nomine cognitionis et scientiae palliata*]" (35)? What happens when phenomenological seeing itself becomes the masked ball of ruinous temptation—beneath the scholar's cap and gown scabrous ambiguity and rasping curiosity?

It is precisely from the thirty-fifth chapter of Book X of *Confessions* that Heidegger extracts that long passage in *Being and Time* on the lust of the eyes (171), surely one of the most extensive quotations in the entire work. The itch to see is the itch to know, the itch of the researcher who is sequestered uncomfortably in the University of Life, the itch of *libido, cupiditas,* and even *morbo cupiditatis,* by which we only-just-tarry-alongside things in order to gaze on them—what Sartre so lubriciously portrays as the Actaeon Complex.[2] The phenomenologist lingers in a vast black forest full of snares and dangers (35: *immensa silva plena insidiarum et periculorum*), tempted by the contemptible, assaulted by the petty throng of beings begging to be unveiled, lusting to know a little bit more each day (*in quam multis minutissimis et contemptibilibus rebus curiositas cotidie*). The copious vanities of the world bedazzle the phenomenologist on all sides. Yet suddenly—who knows when or how?—he or she senses a gnawing in the pit of the stomach and is shaken to vigilance; in an instant he or she overcomes the pervasive tendency to fall. No time to take pride in the recovery, however, "For it is one thing to get up quickly, another thing not to fall at all [*aliud est not cadere*]." Yet to fall is *my* infirmity, *infirmitate mea. Cadere* is the ceaseless cadence of existence. For the phenomenologist there is no concealed uncle, no hidden avuncular father, to heal that infirmity. No guarantor of access or uprightness, no unfailing torch of vigilance. In the midst of the world the fundamental ontologist resists the world. And yet, he confesses, "I dully stand besotted with it." *Vanus hebesco.*

Vanus: pale, wan, empty, hollow, illusory, like a mere shadow or ghost of a man, like Eliot's strawman or Descartes' pumpkinhead. *Hebesco:* I grow dull, livid, faint, insensate; I am dazed, dazzled, bedazzled, benumbed. I become subjected to what Descartes centuries later will deride as animal *hébétude,* a besotting or dulling of the wits; to what hundreds of years later Heidegger still will call *Benommenheit.* Hebetude: worldly beings invading the subject and rutting the very organs by which one would come to know, infecting the project of knowledge or illumination as such. Hebetude as habitude.

When we examine the Pauline and Augustinian background of "everydayness" and "falling," and when we recall those two long notes at the beginning and at the end of chapter 4 of *Civilization and Its Discontents* on "organic repression," notes that depict the legacy of upright posture, suppression of the sense of smell, and upsurgence of visual and facial excitation, then we may wonder whether the pervasive mood of *distrust* of the world and all its vanities, the mood of an essentially *restive* inquiry, does not have to despise and abjure the life that has spawned both existence and ontology. The reward of vigilance is not the virtue of crystalline transparency but a certain jaded quality, the quality that Kafka's urbane ape—reporting to the academy on his accession to humanity—betrays toward the close of his remarks. If his report begins with an account of the handshake, the gesture of "openness" and "the open word," both of which, as we have noted, Heidegger would deny the handless and speechless ape, it concludes with the disturbing account of the apeman's liaison with a half-trained female chimpanzee. Her half-wild, half-domesticated, but altogether confused gaze he cannot endure in broad daylight; at night, in the night behind the night of everydayness, the academician remains the unhappy animal. The *anxious* animal. What Blanchot would call the *writer*. In short, it is as though Heidegger were not making a stupid mistake when in *Being and Time* he constructs the asses' bridge of hebetude between *falling* and *anxiety*— between, that is to say, the epitome of everyday inappropriateness and the apotheosis of the appropriate. It is the asses' bridge that gives and takes everything that a human being can be, and the nameplate on the bridge reads: *Benommenheit.* Vain I may be, utterly forlorn, when lost in the They; yet even when I reappropriate my self to myself—*hebesco.* Here I stand in dull decrepitude; I cannot do otherwise.³

THE ANXIOUS ANIMAL

There are grounds for saying that when in the blink of an eye a human existence achieves the moment of its supreme humanity—it becomes an animal. To be sure, it is *fear* that discloses Dasein by way of privation (SZ, 141: *in privativer Weise*). Fear seems to be *formally* closer to just-plain-life than to Dasein. When Dasein fears some being, some thing in the world, it grows confused and "loses its head" (*Furcht . . . macht 'kopflos'*). Fear is decapitation: the loss of that portion of the body (presuming that the word *head* names only one portion of the body) that houses (according to Timaeus) the heavenly circles of the same, and the wretched instauration of what others have called *Acéphale.*⁴ Fear is thus an instance of hebetude. Yet what happens in anxiety? In anxiety, disclosure and the disclosed coalesce; existence confronts *its own* being in the world. Heidegger emphasizes (186) that in anxiety no intramundane being of any sort comes to the fore. That in the face of which Dasein is anxious remains "wholly indeterminate"; for the situation of anxiety, intramundane beings are quite simply "irrelevant"; the totality of significant relations that constitute the proper world of Dasein as such, the world in which existence *is* as such, the world of things at hand and handy items of equipment is suddenly deprived *as such* of all importance (*als solche überhaupt ohne Belang*). In anxiety, human significance caves in on itself, collapses (*sinkt in sich zusammen*), so that the very world-relation of Dasein loses its polarity, becomes irrelevant, powerless, paralyzed. It is as though the *circle* of forehaving, foresight, and foregrasp, the very circle of hermeneutical understanding and interpretation as such, suddenly becomes an encircling *ring.* It is as though anxiety reduces the very being of Dasein in a radical way. In the 1929 inaugural lecture, "What Is Metaphysics?" Heidegger will say that in anxiety all beings and we ourselves are sucked into an uncanny meaninglessness; in anxiety the world-relation of Dasein vanishes in the fog of . . . nothing at all. In the moment of anxiety Dasein has no hold on this or that being *as such*. Its world suffers a thoroughgoing *deprivation*. In the 1929–1930 lectures on biology, Heidegger will attribute such deprivation—the failure of signification, the evanescence of every relationship to beings *as such*—to the *animal's* world. It is as though anxiety, in the wink of an eye, grants Dasein access to a world that is otherwise blocked to it; as though anxiety were a kind of phenomenological reduction or thinking of releasement. It is as though the animal haunts that deprived and depraved world—the world of thinking—as daimon life.

Because only Dasein comports itself (*verhält sich*) to beings as such, because only Dasein sees the sun *as* the sun, feels the rock beneath its belly *as* rock, hears the gunshot *as* gunshot, only Dasein can suffer animal *fear*. What the animal has no opening upon, namely, beings, it cannot even flee. The animal never loses its head in the face of beings. For neither animals nor things have faces. No mere thing flees another thing. Dasein alone experiences animal fear, whereas anxiety is the animal's. The ring of anxiety has no bounds; it is nowhere; and it is no thing at all. Perhaps, to repeat, it is not merely a stupid mistake when Heidegger says that precisely in anxiety Dasein is *benommen*. And yet the thought that anxiety is the animal's, that the region of openness to being, the region of disclosure as such is roamed by the living, is so *threatening* a thought—whether it breathes in Rilke's elegies or gasps in fits and starts in Heidegger's own meditation on anxiety—that it crowds close and stifles the breath. It is a thought that constricts the flow of air to the lungs; *so nah, daß es beengt und einem den Atem verschlägt—und doch nirgends* (186). Only in *angustia* and *angina*, only in the *Enge* of this narrowness and constriction in the throat and lungs can the coalescence of that *in the face of which* and that *about which* one is anxious transpire; only in that narrow straits between the torso and the head, between the chaos of the heart and the circles of the same in the head, can worldliness (*das Wovor* of anxiety: *In-der-Welt-sein*) and our being able to be in the world (*das Worum* of anxiety: *In-der-Welt-sein-können*) converge (187); only in that shortness of breath does world disclose itself *as* world, that is to say, as no thing at all, and being-in as "*individualized, pure, thrown ability to be*" (188). Heidegger will carry the question of such individuation and simplification (*Vereinzelung, Vereinfachung*) forward into his 1929–1930 course—one of whose three fundamental concepts is solitude or individuation, *Einsamkeit, Vereinzelung*. The particular anxiety of Heidegger's *interpretation* is that individuation (which dare not depend on any unclarified thought of ego, self, or personality), purity (which dare not depend on any asceticism of morality or epistemology) and thrownness (which is a being cast, "dropped," even littered: *Wurf*) may well be *of the animal*. Even if, or precisely because, Hegel denies the animal individuality and selfhood, which are swallowed up in and by the species or universal, Heidegger's own tendency must be toward the animal that philosophy loathes. If for Heidegger anxiety is a being never at home (*das Un-zuhause*), if the uncanny, nomadic sense of *Unheimlichkeit* prevails—and it does prevail, inasmuch as in the 1925 *Prolego-*

mena it is the umbrella concept beneath which even the analysis of anxiety huddles (20, §30, 401–405; 348)—then Dasein is not a domesticated creature, and the metaphorics of dwelling in Heidegger's thought struggles in vain from *Being and Time* through "Building Dwelling Thinking" to tame wild being. For the anxious animal does not think of thinking even as it builds to dwell or dwells to build. The anxious animal is only *there*, like the wind at one's heels, advancing *"hinter" einem her*, creeping up from behind, yet always *schon "da."*

A moment ago we said something about constriction and a narrowing in the throat and lungs—presumably the throat and lungs of a particular mammal that is "there." Toward the end of his discussion of anxiety (190) Heidegger enters two strangely juxtaposed remarks, one (reduced to a footnote) on the importance of anxiety for Christian theology—Augustine's *timor*, Luther's *contritio*, and especially Kierkegaard's *Angst* in the face of "original sin"—and the other on the *physiology* of anxiety and uncanniness. An odd juxtaposition or parataxis of divinity and animality rules in anxiety, similar perhaps to the juxtaposition of the angelic and the bestial in Rilke—and in Trakl. It is particularly odd because Heidegger does not simply dismiss either the theological or physiological with a lordly wave of the hand, a gesture that is otherwise not altogether foreign to him. In the present instance he writes:

> For factically too the mood of uncanniness is usually misunderstood existentielly. Furthermore, "proper" anxiety is a rare item, granted the dominion of falling and publicity. Often anxiety is "physiologically" conditioned. This fact, in its facticity, is an *ontological* problem, and not merely with regard to its ontic etiology and course of development. The physiological occasion [*Auslösung*] of anxiety is possible only because Dasein is anxious [*sich ängstet*] in the ground of its being. (SZ, 190)

It is noteworthy that when endeavoring to solve the ontological problem of the ground of anxiety, the reflexive autoinduction of anxiety in Dasein (*Sichängsten*), Heidegger borrows the medical term *Auslösung*, the "triggering" or "incidental" occasion that causes a dormant disease to awaken. As though some confusion between the fundamental and the contingent, the ground and the figure, were always possible between ontological and physiological explication. Apart from the ontological Lamarckism of the final sentence of the passage, the classical gesture by which ears, eyes, hands, and nervous reactions are subordinated to a reflexive and apparently altogether autonomic self-relation or auto-affection, the passage reverts to the facts and facticity of life, a life whose grounds are abyssal. The *ontological* problem to which Heidegger refers is none other than that of just-plain-life, which is its own mode of being, albeit accessible only in Dasein. A Dasein which, for its part, is "there" only by being some body who is alive. Some body who, for its part, senses a boarding up of the mouth against both inspiration and respiration, a shortness of breath in the lungs, a constriction of the throat, and a rising of the gorge in anxiety. Headless, without knowing what triggers what.

No doubt it is less the *physiology* of anxiety than the *psychoanalytic* and *psychosomatic* readings of such anxiety that Heidegger and Heidegger's readers most need to go to encounter, precisely for the sake of Dasein as some body who is alive. One of the earliest stages of psychoanalysis, its symptomatology of "anxiety neurosis," would be of importance to Heidegger's ontological analysis: *pseudoangina pectoris*, disturbances of breathing, congestion in the lungs—these are among the principal physiological symptoms that impress Freud in 1894 (StA 6, 31). And the mystery of anxiety perdures throughout his late work, *Inhibition, Symptom, and Anxiety* [*Hemmung, Symptom und Angst*] (1926), which is essentially a search for anxiety beyond its physiological constituents (StA 6, 273). The trauma of separation from the mother at birth (*Trennungsangst*) could not be spurned by an ontological analysis that takes birth to be one of the two "ends" of Dasein, especially when the trauma of birth is never left "behind" one, as Freud himself emphasizes (277). Anxiety is *gebürtig* for the duration of existence. Further, it may be that fundamental ontology resists the sexual etiology of anxiety only to the extent that such ontology fails to confront the problem of life, a failure that is marked in its advance to a meta-ontology or metaphysics of Dasein, where something like sexuality awaits. Finally, we ought not be blind to the agreement between Freud and Heidegger that anxiety is distinguished from fear precisely by its *futural* character, its ecstatic projection, its indeterminacy, and its objectlessness (302). Freud had already arrived at the distinction between fear and anxiety in 1920, in *Beyond the Pleasure Principle* (StA 3, 222; cf. 223 n. 1; and see "readiness for anxiety" at 241). No doubt such anxiety, in its uncanny recurrence in neurosis, has to do with that "demonic trait" we identify as destiny or fate in our lives (231; 245–46), perhaps better described as a *daimonic* trait.[5] Freud's fascination with the phylogenetic history of species man and even the cosmic history of the Earth and its relation to the sun, a relationship that has left its mark on humankind and on the development of all organisms (247), and, above all, his fascination with the immanence of death in life—"that every living thing dies and returns to the anorganic because of *inner* grounds" (248)—could not fail to detain the fundamental ontologist. For, however much both the psychoanalyst and the ontologist focus on *human* existence, they are both riddling on the "riddle of life" as such.[6]

COMPULSION

It is odd that when Heidegger comes to define care (*Sorge*) as the being of Dasein and the existential structure in which temporality is already prescribed, that is to say, when he arrives at the structure that should determine all the analyses to follow, he spends less time and care on it than he does fending off "addiction" and "compulsion"—fighting off the animals, as it were (SZ, 193–96). Care, he insists, can never lead us back to, nor can it be constructed out of, "willing and wishing or compulsion and addiction." And yet Heidegger no sooner mentions the fundamental framework of his own analysis than he must ward off the Schelerian anthropological and personalistic categories. These, especially compulsion and addiction (the latter might be rendered more neutrally as "proclivity," reminiscent of the *Neigung* of Heidegger's 1921–1922 analysis of factical life), must be subordinated to care. In the order of ontological implication, care stands above them; in architectonic terms, care undergirds them; but in any case it is ontologically prior to them. A familiar pattern recurs. "That does not preclude the possibility," says Heidegger, "that compulsion and addiction ontologically constitute other beings also, beings that merely 'live' [*Seiendes, . . . das nur 'lebt'*]" (194). Once again Heidegger refers us to the familiar difficulty of fundamental ontology vis-à-vis an ontology of life: "However, the fundamental-ontological constitution of 'living' [*von 'leben'*] is a problem all its own [*ein eignes Problem*]; only by way of a reductive privation can it be developed from the ontology of Dasein" (194; cf. 50). The method must be reduction, privation, subtraction—not cumulation or addition. However, what can be subtracted from care in order to yield addiction and compulsion? *Hang und Drang* would be equal to *Sorge* deprived of something: $H + D = S - x$. Would that "x," that something, be appropriateness, *Eigentlichkeit?* Heidegger's analysis in the latter half of section 42 suggests that this is the case, even though we have been warned not to take inappropriateness as a trait of something unlike Dasein, something inferior to the mode of being of "everyday existence." Dasein hangs on the world, inclines toward it to the point of addiction (195: *Nachhängen, Hang*). Hanging onto the world, Dasein becomes something utterly passive, an object of the transitive verb *leben*. Dasein is "lived" *by* the world. Its danger is *"von der Welt, in der es je ist, 'gelebt' zu werden."* Dasein lets itself be tugged along on the world's leash (*Sichziehenlassen*). Dasein has in its passivity "become blind," is less than a dog, more like a mole on a string.

Compulsion seems to be more active. It is the drive "to live" (*der Drang "zu leben"*), and it seems to carry its own power source (*Antrieb*) with it. Yet compulsion is every bit as "inappropriate" as addiction; it is as little related to the essential future of Dasein as any addiction to present beings is. Compulsion "bowls over" all disposition and understanding. And yet, Heidegger is quick to add, Dasein is never "sheer compulsion." In the following lines of his text (196, ll. 5ff.), he tries desperately to subordinate compulsion to care: compulsion is merely care that is "not yet free," even though care itself must liberate compulsion as an ontological possibility. Care is proclaimed the root structure of Dasein, and yet addiction and compulsion, as possibilities rooted in the thrownness of Dasein, seem to possess a certain genetic autochthony, a certain wild and untamable eminence. "The compulsion 'to live' cannot be annihilated, the inclination to be 'lived' by the world cannot be eradicated." Why are both ineradicables expressed in terms of "life"? Why is *leben* here possessed of a daimonic force that withstands the effects of nihilation, a force that Heidegger is struggling to yoke under the concept of a fully liberated care? Is it only because Heidegger once soiled his hands with life-philosophy, was once compelled by it and well-nigh addicted to it? Or is the problem more deeply interfused?

The compulsion to live and the inclination to be lived cannot be eradicated. (Although why should one want to eradicate compulsion and inclination? What well-rooted factical ideal of existence would be so bent on eradication?) "And yet both, because and only because they are ontologically grounded in care, are to be modified ontico-existentielly by means of care as appropriate [durch diese (die Sorge) als eigentliche ontisch existentiell zu modifizieren]" (196). The parataxis of "appropriate," "ontic," and "existentiell" betrays the utterly mysterious power of care to "modify" the forces of addiction and compulsion that spawn it. "Modification" and "modality" being one (or two) of the names for perdurant mysteries in Heidegger's thought.[7]

Whether these ineradicable forces can be tamed by or yoked under the analysis of care, which would "not yet" be entirely "free" of them, remains the question of "reality as ontological problem" (§43b). Here once again the tradition of life-philosophy (especially Dilthey, Bergson, and Scheler) returns. Dilthey defines the real as impulse and will; more precisely, as resistance or capacity to resist (209). What he is unable to do is to provide an ontological clarification of either will, impulse, or inhibition (Hemmung). Their mode of being (Seinsart) remains in default. "That it remains in default ultimately rests on the fact that Dilthey allows 'life'—which of course we cannot get back 'behind'—to remain in ontological indifference" (209). Whether Heidegger accounts himself among the "we" who cannot "get back 'behind' " life, and (sometimes) he does, does not obscure the fact that the accusation of ontological indifference is Heidegger's challenge to Lebensphilosophie as a whole. However, if life does not allow us to get back behind it, is it not because life, and not Dasein, is the ground of ontological analysis? And would that not imply that the privative approach to it can never grant access to it? At all events, we have by this time seen that Heidegger's fundamental ontology succeeds no better in getting back behind life, which is a mode of being "all its own." "However," Heidegger continues, "ontological interpretation of Dasein does not mean an ontic going back to another being [ein anderes Seiendes]" (209–210). What it does or can mean he declines to say. He turns instead to Max Scheler's interpretation of the reality of the real, his "voluntative theory of existence" as expounded in the sixth part of Erkenntnis und Arbeit (1926).[8] This is the very text that will prove to be important for Heidegger's theoretical biology in 1929–1930. Although Heidegger approves of Scheler's reference to a Seinsverhältnis that cannot be reduced to thought and conceptual grasp, he criticizes the nonfoundational character of Scheler's descriptions. "The fundamental ontological analysis of 'life' cannot be inserted subsequently [nachträglich . . . eingeschoben] as a skeletal structure [Unterbau]" (210).

However, to the extent that the fundamental ontology of Dasein is not the fundamental ontological analysis of life—indeed, to the extent that life can be reached only by way of privation and reduction from a prior ontology of Dasein (50)—to that precise extent Heidegger's complaints concerning Dilthey and Scheler recoil on his own project. Heidegger does try to rectify the situation in 1929–1930 with his comparative "fundamental metaphysical" analysis of world, finitude, and solitude. However, that analysis too seems to be inserted subsequently as a basis or skeletal superstructure for fundamental ontology. Has Heidegger's foundationalism here reached the point of no return, the point of the double-bind, the impossible point between a priori and a posteriori, between the antecedent and the subsequent, between founding and founded, between a transcendentally projected layering and a purely contingent sandwiching-in? Does the ontic-ontological circle, seeking closure, precisely here become vicious? Fundamental ontology of Dasein without an ontology of life is empty; fundamental ontology of life without an ontology of Dasein is blind. Yet such worries arise from an old addiction and compulsion of philosophy.

An indication of the critical impasse is the fact that earlier in *Being and Time* (70–71; 103–104) nature and nature's sun were treated as both "perpetually handy" and absolutely excessive with regard to all handling (recall nature's compulsive "weaving and striving"). Heidegger now (§43c; 211) explicitly denies that nature can be classified as either handy or at hand. Intramundane it is. *Zuhanden, vorhanden,* or *Da-sein* it is not. Yet what mode of being can nature have? Heidegger suggests that only an orientation toward the *positively* interpreted existentiality of Dasein can guarantee "consciousness" and "life" some sort of foundation, some sort of sense of reality—if only an "indifferent sense." Yet how is such *orientation* granted?

It is time to gaze into the sun.

THE SPENDING STAR

Like all the methodologically crucial sections prior to it and after it (e.g., §§9, 28, 45, 61–63, 66, and 83), section 78 begins by conceding the inadequacy of the preceding analysis. Now it is a matter of the origin of the "ordinary concept of time," time as that with which and on which we reckon, and the involvement of both history *and nature* in the project of fundamental ontology as a temporal interpretation of being (404). Heidegger reminds us once again of the source of his own project in Dilthey's quest for a unified inquiry into nature and history, a unified science of life that would have been something perhaps quite different from what the *Geisteswissenschaften* have in fact become. The historical origins of Heidegger's own project are clearly visible in his 1925 lecture course, "Prolegomena to the History of the Concept of Time," and so we shall turn back to that lecture course, by way of an *excursus,* after we have followed the path of the sun in *Being and Time.*

Here we cannot recount the entire story of the "leveling off" of originary time to the ordinary concept of time, the ruinance of time in time by time itself. Nor can we give a full account of ecstatic datability, the ecstatic span or stretch of time, public openness or publicity, and worldliness as the culmination of the Aristotelian analysis of time as "back then, when," "until then, whenever," and "now that" (see §79; cf. 24, §19). Here it will be a matter of gazing, if only for an instant, into the sun. Presumably the sun, too, like the forest, stream, and wind, cannot be reduced to a mere being at hand (70). Presumably it too, like the southwind, is a kind of primeval sign (80). Its being has to do with nearness, regions, and places; or, rather, with their autoproduction. That is to say, it has to do with nearing, regioning, and placing. The sun also has to do with light and warmth, which are both essential to many if not all forms of life. Yet what about this "also" of light and warmth? Why does the granting of regions and places occur as the granting of light and warmth "also"? Why do Heideggerians, who talk so readily of the granting of time and being, generally stay out of the sun and preserve a chilly silence concerning solar dispensation?

In section 22, on the spatiality of handy things in the world, the sun appears to be the handiest of beings:

> Thus the sun, whose light and warmth are in daily use, has its exceptional places, which we discover as we look around us; it has these places on the basis of the changing applicability of that which it donates [*spendet*]: sunrise, midday, sunset, midnight. The places of this handy being, which is handy in changing yet uniformly constant ways, become emphatic "indicators" of the regions that lie in them. These regions of the sky, which do not as yet need to have any geographical sense, provide the antecedent whither for every particular evolution of regions that can be occupied by places. The house has its sunny side and its stormy side; its "rooms" are divided in accord with the orientation to these two sides; the rooms in turn define the "furnishings" that will go into them, each item in accord with its equipmental character. (SZ, 103–104)

So far, Heidegger's analysis of the sun merely inverts that of young Dedalus at his school desk.⁹ Dedalus writes in his book:

> *Stephen Dedalus*
> *Class of Elements*
> *Clongowes Wood College*
> *Sallins*
> *County Kildare*
> *Ireland*
> *Europe*
> *The World*
> *The Universe*

Stephen says that it is very big to think about everywhere, that only God could do that, but Heidegger can do it merely by inserting the sun somewhere between *The Universe* and *The World,* working his way, as it were, by some kind of mirror-play, back to the writing desk. The sun makes places, not simply by moving across the sky and depositing the four temporal regions that will structure both Nietzsche's *Zarathustra* and the farmer's daily round, but also by its donation of light and warmth to all beings on the Earth. The sun is the star that spends itself. Solar extravagance, Georges Bataille calls it. Spending itself, the sun makes both places and signs, "orienting" even at dark of midnight; it also conjures many of the things that occupy places and serve as signs. Heidegger does not pause to address the light of the sun, which he has a good deal to say about elsewhere; nor does he say another word about its warmth, which is the subject of Thoreau's first chapter, "Economy," cited earlier. He does mention the sunny side and the shady or stormy side (*Wetterseite*) of the house. Perhaps he is thinking of that Schwarzwaldhof on the southern slope "toward midday," built for the dwelling and thinking of human animals (VA, 161; BW, 338). Near the Lord God's Corner, into which the windowseats and the dining table are fitted, are the "hallowed places of childbed and the tree of the dead," the places (in the *Stüble*, near the warmth of the *Kunscht*) reserved for childbirth and the laying out of the corpse. Perhaps he is already thinking of those homey yet uncanny places—otherwise we are at a loss to explain why the text of *Being and Time* continues as it does, with the following "example," which we mentioned briefly in the preceding chapter. "Churches and graves, for example, are laid out according to the rising and the setting of the sun, the regions of life and death, in terms of which Dasein is itself determined with a view to its ownmost possibilities of being in the world." *Kirchen und Gräber,* as though these two belonged together even before Nietzsche's *Zarathustra,* churches and tombs belonging together as they always have, *zum Beispiel.* Dawn and dusk are here defined as the regions of life and death, *die Gegenden von Leben und Tod,* long before Dasein "proper" is properly introduced in terms of its most proper possibilities. Nor is there anything about the regions of life and death that one could identify as "biological." Dawn and dusk are regions that orient the building of churches and the digging of graves, which at least in the Black Forest are always laid out from west to east: portal of entry and headstone to the west, high altar and feet to the east. Orientation. Toward the *eigensten Seinsmöglichkeiten* of Dasein, as though the sun had the power to orient us not only in our everyday preoccupations but also in our most original and radically experienced being. To orient and to dazzle us. Such possibilities are given the names "life" and "death." Not the handiest items of equipment, but possibilities that are most our own. Ours, whose? The whale's, for example. *Moby-Dick,* chapter CXVI:

For that strange spectacle observable in all sperm whales dying—the turning sunwards of the head, and so expiring—that strange spectacle, beheld of such a placid evening, somehow to Ahab conveyed a wondrousness unknown before.
"He turns himself to it,—how slowly, but how steadfastly, his homage-rendering and invoking brow, with his last dying motions. He too worships fire; most faithful, broad, baronial vassal of the sun!—Oh that these too-favoring eyes should see these too-favoring sights. Look! here, far waterlocked; beyond all the hum of human weal or woe; in these most candid and impartial seas; where to traditions no rocks furnish tablets; where for long Chinese ages, the billows have still rolled on speechless and unspoken to, as stars that shine upon the Niger's unknown source; here, too, life dies sunwards full of faith; but see! no sooner dead, than death whirls round the corpse and it heads some other way.—
"Oh, thou dark Hindoo half of nature, who of drowned bones has built thy separate throne somewhere in the heart of these unverdured seas; thou art an infidel, thou queen, and too truly speakest to me in the wide-slaughtering Ty-

phoon, and the hushed burial of its after calm. Nor has this thy whale sunwards turned his dying head, and then gone round again, without a lesson to me.

"Oh, trebly hooped and welded hip of power! Oh, high aspiring, rainbowed jet!—that one strivest, this one jettest all in vain! In vain, oh whale, dost thou seek intercedings with yon all-quickening sun, that only calls forth life, but gives it not again. Yet dost thou, darker half, rock me with a prouder, if a darker faith. All thy unnamable imminglings float beneath me here; I am buoyed by breaths of once living things, exhaled as air, but water now.

"Then hail, for ever hail, O sea, in whose eternal tossings the wild fowl finds his only rest. Born of earth, yet suckled by the sea; though hill and valley mothered me, ye billows are my foster-brothers!"

In the later sections of *Being and Time,* with which we are now concerned (see especially SZ, §80, 412), it is not the sun as such that is invoked but the alternation of day and night. That alternation is significant, not only for the time on which we can reckon, but also for the very thrownness (*Geworfenheit*) of Dasein. Existence is exposed or delivered over (*ausgeliefert*) to the reiterated alternation of daylight and dark of night. "The former grants with its brightness possible vision; the latter takes it away" (412). Giving and taking, *geben/ nehmen,* the verbs of bedazzlement, exercise here once again their strange effects: it is surely no accident that the "bright night of the nothing," *die helle Nacht des Nichts* (W, 11; BW, 105) is the oxymoron that dominates the very ambiguity of bedazzlement, which is both the mere distraction and the uncanny focus of a Dasein *distrait.* It is as though Dasein itself were phototropic with regard to both sun and moon; as though Dasein were a higher-order legume.

The datability (*Datierbarkeit:* cf. 24, 370–73) that commences with the dawn of each day, the rising of the sun, has in fact to do with giving or donation: one thinks of Husserlian "dator intuition." Yet it is less the giving of a gift than the expending of a surfeit: one thinks of Zarathustra's honey-bees   *gold and carnelian and lapis lazuli*   and Bataille's potlatch. Its giving is thus a kind of taking. In the same way, Dasein "dates" the time it "takes" to do this or that, and Heidegger now places quotation-marks around the "handiness" of the sun's giving and taking—in a word, its "dating." "Concern makes use of the 'being handy' of the sun, which dispenses light and warmth [*von dem 'Zuhandensein' der Licht und Wärme spendenden Sonne*]." Thus it is not Dasein that "dates" the time it takes, but the sun itself does the dating, the sun spending itself in light and warmth, donating and dating itself: "The sun dates the time that is interpreted in concern" (412–13). It is as though the sun could never be put to use (*Gebrauch*), but only enjoyed, if only for the time being. It is as though the sun were another Dasein.[10]

For its part, the moon does not rise and set with sufficient regularity such that it could "date" the daily grind of men. The only reference to the waxing moon in *Being and Time* is the negative reference to the fourth quarter that has "not yet" emerged from the earth's shadow and is "still outstanding." If the dying of Dasein proves to be unlike a ripening fruit, it will certainly be unlike the waxing and waning moon. Yet there is one phrase in the paragraph that Heidegger devotes to the moon that is quite disarming—even though we readers usually read right on by it. I shall place that phrase in italic here in order to prevent our overlooking it, even though Heidegger himself italicizes part of it, to wit, the word "whole," *ganz:*

> One may for example say that the final quarter of the moon remains outstanding until the full moon. The not-yet diminishes as the concealing shadow vanishes. Yet in this situation the moon is always already at hand as a whole. Setting aside the fact that the moon *even when it is full is never grasped in its* entirety [*nie ganz zu erfassen ist*], the not-yet here . . . has to do solely with the perceptual *grasp.* (SZ, 243)

The moon remains as ungraspable in its being as is Dasein: even when the moon is fully revealed at the full its being remains veiled in a shadow that never diminishes. One might even say that as the moon waxes interpretation wanes, and that the only thing that becomes clearer is its mystery. The moon may be used as a negative analogue of the temporal stretch of Dasein, but that is only because Dasein and the moon are of a piece: the disclosure that encompasses them surpasses the understanding that calculates in terms of everyday possibilities. Which is perhaps why Heidegger will not be entirely deaf to the lunar voice of the sister in Trakl's poetry, never so bedazzled by bronze by gold that he is entirely blind to the silvery figure of Σελήνη, σελάννα.[11]

From the sun's giving and taking, its donation and dating, giving time and guaranteeing obsolescence (which, after all, is a thing's being "dated"), there arises, according to Heidegger, "the 'most natural' time-measure, the day" (413). And if the *Zeitmaß* here still seems to reckon with and on ordinary time, the time on which we can all count, Heidegger adds this: "And because the temporality of Dasein, which has to take its time doing things [*das sich seine Zeit nehmen muß*], is finite, its days are already numbered [*sind seine Tagen auch schon gezählt*]." Here the most earnest of issues in the most earnest of philosophical texts, at the very moment   *as for us men, our days are numbered, our occupations are a breath of wind*   when its thesis concerning a dual temporality and a bipolar appropriate-inappropriate existence is at stake, at the precise point when the thesis concerning the genesis of ordinary time from an originary time is in jeopardy, makes jokes. Good jokes, no doubt. Jokes about giving and taking time, about spending and expending, donating and dating, granting and consuming. The finitude of time and of the existence that *is* its time are announced by way of a casual play on "taking time" and the "numbering" of days that are always already "numbered." Jokes that one might find in poetry, perhaps, indicating that even if my life is measured out in coffee spoons (*kaffeelöffelmäßig*) fundamental possibilities can and do come to the fore. Not in anxiety but in surprise and in the interruption of an otherwise familiar rhythm—reminiscent of the way churches and graves interrupted the analysis of everyday space. Here it is not the everyday in the sense of the daily grind, the quotidian routine, that obtrudes. Rather, a view to the wandering sun opens a perspective on the *day-by-day* occurrence of existence: *tagtägliches Geschehen*. In the tiny gap that separates *alltäglich* and *tagtäglich* we find the incipient cleaving of being, the finitude of time and being as such.

We cannot take the time, as it were, to follow any farther this "star that dispenses light and warmth [*Licht und Wärme spendenden Gestirn*]" (413). We cannot pursue its progress day-by-day across the sky and its donation to the farmer's shadow, the sundial, and the handy digital wristwatch of our own day. No doubt our chasing shadows in Heidegger's text (415–16) could detain us for an eternity—especially "the shadow that constantly accompanies Everyman." Nor can we pursue here an analysis of section 81, "Intratemporality and the Genesis of the Ordinary Concept of Time," especially the curious "circumcision of the now" that is said to take place in Western philosophical interpretations of time from Aristotle onward, the castration of time, its reduction to the ranks of sheer succession.[12]

Nor will we proceed to the yon side of castrated time, to the good that is beyond being, ἐπέκεινα τῆς οὐσίας, which so preoccupies Heidegger after *Being and Time* (see 24, 400–405, for example), even though that is what any glimpse of the sun tempts all knowers since Plato to do (see 26, 143, 237, and 284, for another). The brazen sun bedazzles, benumbs, and even blinds those who would plumb its depths, ascend to its heights, entertain its extravagance. Rather than such heady pursuit, we will be satisfied with a detour and distraction, an *excursus*.

THE LIFE-PHILOSOPHICAL BACKGROUND: DILTHEY, HUSSERL, SCHELER

We have had multiple occasions to mention Heidegger's 1925 lecture course, especially when referring to Dilthey's pervasive influence on Heidegger. Let us take a few moments to examine the early pages of this "first draft" of what is primarily the first division of *Being and Time*—the pages that never made it into the final draft. For these excised pages indicate how deeply Heidegger's fundamental ontology is enmeshed in life-philosophy.

In the first place, the 1925 course begins by declaring nature and history the two regions for investigation, not only for the sciences but also for the *pre-meditation* and *pre-science* of a premeditated and prescient phenomenology, phenomenology as "productive logic." We have just now heard Heidegger say, at the outset of section 78 of *Being and Time*, that the analysis of ecstatic temporality is inadequate because it has left nature and natural processes out of account. Such dissatisfaction with his own analysis is impossible to understand without a sense of the Diltheyan background of the project.[13] A second example. At the end of section 66, as he previews the analyses of temporality that will fill out the remainder of *Being and Time* (temporality and everydayness, chapter 4; temporality and historicity, chapter 5; temporality and intratemporality, chapter 6), analyses that will "relentlessly" expose the "entanglements" in which ontology of Dasein is caught, Heidegger espies something that even his relentless exposition will leave unconsidered. Already at this point he calls for a repetition of the repetition. Why? What sort of thing can have eluded the tentacles and entanglements of temporality?

> As being in the world, Dasein exists factically with and alongside the beings it encounters within the world. The being of Dasein therefore receives its comprehensive ontological transparency only upon the horizon of the clarified being of beings that are not of the measure of Dasein; that is to say, upon the horizon also of that which, being neither handy nor at hand, merely "subsists" [*was, nicht zuhanden und nicht vorhanden, nur "besteht"*]. (SZ, 333)

Would not nature and nature's sun be such a being, as well as all the living and dying things that turn toward the sun, beings presumably unlike Dasein yet sufficiently akin to it to be drawn into the question of being? And, at all events, what could such "subsistence" be—if it is not a sheer regression to the Cartesian ontology that Heidegger has so carefully bracketed out in the first division? How are such "subsistent" beings to be clarified; by whom or by what? The 1925 lectures contain an earlier draft of that now familiar passage in *Being and Time* (10) on the "current crisis" in biology. In 1925 it is described as "the attempt to meditate on the fundamental elements of life," the effort to disabuse ourselves of the prejudices that cause us to define the living organism as physical mass, *ein Körperding*. Even "vitalism" is trapped in mechanistic prejudices, argues Heidegger, and the only hope, a hope he will pursue in his 1929–1930 lectures, is to clarify the meaning of those unhandy beings we call the "living." The only hope lies in a clarification of the *organism*.

Subsection 4c of the 1925 lecture course provides essential background to sections 10 and 43 of *Being and Time*. In the earlier text, Heidegger celebrates Dilthey's response to the positivism of his age in the acclamation of life as actuality, particularly as the reality of history. In *Being and Time* (401) Heidegger will cite Count Yorck to this effect: "The kernal of historicity is the fact that the entire psychophysical given [of human existence] *is* not, but lives." After the italicized word *is*, spurned by Yorck, Heidegger inserts: ". . . being = the being at hand of nature." He concludes the Yorck citation as follows: "Just as I am nature, so also am I history. . . ." However, it is the very emphasis on history over nature, a nature in the possession of the positivists and reductionist psychologists, that comes to haunt Heidegger in and after *Being and Time*. The 1925 lectures, with their account of John Stuart Mill, Wilhelm Dilthey, and Franz Brentano, help us to see why this haunting had to happen, and why the daimon is still not at rest.

Brentano's opposition to positivism and psychologism is vital in this regard. His "classification of psychic phenomena" is motivated by the problem of the psychophysical nexus, the integration of soul and body, the relationship of sense organs and sensuous life to the life of the mind (24). The importance of William James's early work and of Henri Bergson's *Données immédiates* (1889) for Dilthey's 1894 *Ideen zu einer beschreibenden und zergliedernden Psychologie*, and the importance of all these for Husserlian phenomenology, is of course Heidegger's central thesis. His survey of the history is admirable, to say the least, but I will truncate it by noting only one point. Of special interest is the fact that Heidegger's lifelong fascination with Husserl's *Logical Investigations* has Dilthey's own fascination with that book as its prototype: Heidegger's preference for the *Logical Investigations* derives at least in part from the importance of life-philosophical problems for him.

From Heidegger's 150-page account of Husserlian intentionality, categorial intuition, and the a priori, an account that virtually disappears from *Being and Time* (which is unfortunate, inasmuch as it is in many ways the finest introduction to the question of the meaning of being), let me draw out only a few issues. Here the rationale of the division between the sciences of history and the sciences of nature is restored to its rights: Heidegger refers to the regions of those objects that are most often the target of phenomenological description—things from the historically determined environment and the things of nature (20, 53: *das Umweltding, das Naturding*). The bodily givenness or *Leibhaftigkeit* of such things given in intuition particularly interests Heidegger (52–54), and he returns to that theme in the course of his own exposition of the reality of the external world (20, §24; cf. SZ, §43). He criticizes what phenomenology takes to be the apotheosis of self-givenness, namely, the flesh-and-blood presence of an *intentum* in the perceptual *intentio*, as a deficient and in fact bloodless and skeletal privation—what he will later call "merely lingering over" and "only just gaping at" the object. The very division into two intentional regions, the immanent *intentio* and the transcendent object-correlate, becomes the focus of Heidegger's critique. It is not so much an epistemological complaint, however, as a life-philosophical one. In the mode and manner of Husserl's "Philosophy as Rigorous Science," with its invocation of "human or animal consciousnesses" that are "attached" to "human or animal bodies," respectively, Heidegger writes:

> Such consciousness, as a component part of the designated animal unity, is at the same time consciousness of this real nature [*dieser realen Natur*]; it is at one with nature *realiter* in the concretion of every factical creature (human being), but then also at the same time separated from it by an absolute gap. This is what every perception of a thing shows in the distinction between immanence and transcendence. The distinction into two spheres of being is quite odd, because it is precisely the sphere of immanence, the sphere of lived experience, that defines the very possibility within which the transcendent world—from which it is separated by a gap—can assume objective character. (20, 134)

Precisely this odd yet ubiquitous separation is the burning question for Heidegger. Even more oddly, it becomes the burning question for *us* when Heidegger some years later tries to separate man from animal by an abyss of essence. The gap, separation, or cleavage (*Kluft*) between immanence and transcendence is the "neglect" or "oversight" that constitutes the phenomenological object and the phenomenological method. Yet the cloven being of the intentional touches the creature and has an impact on the *Reales* that we are.

We are the animals or the animated ones, *die Animalien,* "the psychic in its factical actuality" (153), possessed of those "empirical units" of personality to which one would have to attribute the barbarism "animal ego," *animalisches Ich* (154). When Husserl, especially in *Ideen II,* divides the intentional objects among the three regions of material nature, animal or living nature, and spirit, he follows the guidelines, strictures, and constraints—the prejudices of the "natural attitude"—that his method can neither overcome nor even descry.

> What is here fixed upon as the given of a natural attitude, namely, the supposition that human beings are given as living beings, as objects of zoology [*der Mensch als Lebewesen, als zoologisches Objekt*] is the product of the very attitude that designates itself as natural. Is it the natural way of observing how we human beings experience one another and ourselves—the way of experiencing ourselves as ζῷον, living being, an object of nature in the widest sense, an object that comes to the fore in the world? To put it bluntly, do human beings experience themselves zoologically when they experience naturally? Is this attitude a *natural attitude,* or is it no such thing? (20, 155)

However great Heidegger's debt to the later Husserlian notion of *Lebenswelt* may be, his response to Husserl's critique of the "natural attitude" is severe: the very dogmatic-theoretical posture of transcendental phenomenology defines the being of acts in terms of the *Realität* of nature (and of the "natural") without itself raising the question of being—the being of acts, of natural nature, and of *Realität* (157). The "primal scission" (*Urscheidung*) of immanence and transcendence precludes the question. "From the point of view of ontology, in Husserlian phenomenology things never change." *Es bleibt ontologisch alles beim Alten* (170). Husserl's *Ideen II* asks about "the relation of soul and body, spiritual and physical nature"; it asks about "the old chestnut, discussed throughout the nineteenth century, namely, psychophysical parallelism"; but what is decisive in the end is "the relativity of nature and the absoluteness of spirit" (171). The upshot is that Heidegger's critique of transcendental phenomenology is a critique "of spirit." His formulation of the neglect of the question of being in phenomenology thus owes a great deal to his preoccupation with something other than a philosophy of spirit, something more akin to life-philosophy. For Heidegger's is nothing other than the question "of the *being of the fully concrete human being."*

> Can its being be *pieced together,* as it were, out of the being of its material underground, the body, of its soul, and of its spirit? Is the being of the person the *product* of the modes of being in these strata of being? Or has it become pellucid that we cannot approach the phenomenon by way of an antecedent parceling out and subsequent collecting, that whatever the tendency toward the personal might imply, the person is precisely here taken as a *multilayered worldthing* [*ein mehrschichtiges Weltding*], the being of which will never be reached, no matter how broadly cast the nets of the reality toward which we are directed? What one retains is always the mere being of a pregiven object, a real object; that is to say, in the end it is always simply a matter of being as objectivity—in the sense of being an object for observation. (20, 173)

Precisely in Husserlian phenomenology the traditional understanding of man as a rational animal and a "person endowed with reason" holds sway. The backdrop for all its questions concerning "the intentional, the psychic, consciousness, lived experience, life, human being, reason, spirit, person, ego, and subject" is the "ancient definition of man—*animal rationale*" (174). Implicit in that ancient definition of human being is a neutralization of the surrounding world (*Entweltlichung der Umwelt*), hence a distortion of history, a reduction and denigration of corporeality (*eine herabgeminderte Leibhaftigkeit*), an illusory model of evidence, and a deposition or degradation of nature as such (*eine herabgesetzte Natur:* 20, 266; cf SZ, 65). Thus when Heidegger takes up the theme of "reality" once again (20, 300–301), it is only to reject the flesh-and-blood givenness of the ghosts of immanence in both history and nature.

Max Scheler's philosophical anthropology, as encapsulated in the 1925 lecture, "The Forms of Knowing, and Culture," follows Dilthey in taking drives, striving, and the correlative resistance as earmarks of reality.[14] Like Dilthey, Scheler wishes to avoid reduction of the "living subject" to a mere theoretician, "an anemic thinkthing [*ein blutleeres Denkding*]," a dessicated thinkingdingaling. Yet Scheler's "voluntative theory of existence" too remains caught in the embroglio of traditional metaphysics. On the positive side, Heidegger vies with Scheler to be the first in his neighborhood to have advanced from a static to a dynamic epistemology, to knowing as a *Seinsverhältnis:* Scheler claims in 1925 to have been teaching his theory of resistance for seven years; Heidegger claims the same for himself and then proclaims both himself and Scheler progeny of the titanic Dilthey. Yet his competition with that older brother is grounded in an enormous respect, a respect Scheler earns precisely because in the problem of the reality of the transcendent world he emphasizes not the bloodless *Leibhaftigkeit* of evidence but "the specific function of embodiment [*Leiblichkeit*]"; that is to say, precisely because Scheler "has worked through these phenomena of biology in an essential direction," his work is irreplaceable. By 1925 Scheler is "perhaps the one who has gone farther than anyone else" in this respect (303). In almost the same breath, however, Heidegger cites Scheler's biological views as the source of his most fatal limitations. It may be that although only the criticisms of Scheler remain in *Being and Time* Heidegger still senses there his indebtedness to him. Perhaps the lectures of 1929–1930, a year after Scheler's death, are a final effort both to acknowledge and to overtake his fraternal rival.

At all events, in the 1925 lectures Heidegger promulgates his own existentials of care and significance (*Sorge und Bedeutsamkeit*) in opposition to Schelerian (and Leibnizian) will and resistance. Although the language of "correlation" is inadequate, slipping as it does into the primal scission of immanence and transcendence, Heidegger speaks of these existentials as the correlation that constitutes "the fundamental structure of life [*die Grundstruktur des Lebens*], which I also designate as *facticity*" (304). Thus the lessons of the 1921–1922 course, the lessons of factical life, are rehearsed once again. Indeed, even in 1927 Heidegger will want to emphasize (SZ, 72 n. 1: "The author may be permitted to observe . . .") that he has been teaching this mainstay of his doctrine since 1919—which is 1925 minus six, if not quite seven, years. Furthermore, the correlation that is not a correlation (care and significance) is not merely one problem among others: it is the key to the thought of *Präsenz*, crucial to Heidegger's analysis of worldliness in 1925 (see 20, §23: *Präsenz, Anwesenheit der Welt, Zuhandenheit, Vorhandenheit, Präsenzwechsel, Besorgtheitspräsenz*), the very heart of his prolegomena to the history of the concept of time. Yet, remarkably, it is the very horizon of time—*Präsenz*—that is expunged from *Being and Time*.[15]

Let this excursus end with Heidegger's own critique of Scheler's alleged biologism:

> Both resistance and bodily presence [*Leibhaftigkeit*] are grounded in an antecedent worldliness. They are particular phenomena of an isolated encountering; that is to say, isolated to a particular mode of access, which is mere striving. Thus the conception of beings in the world as resistance coheres in Scheler's case with his biological orientation, that is, with the question of how the world in general is given for primitive forms of life. In my view, this path, which seeks to explain primitive forms of life by analogy all the way down to one-celled animals, is fundamentally askew. (20, 305)

As we shall see, Heidegger reiterates this critique in his own theoretical biology five years later. At all events, it is important to note here once again the ambivalence of Heidegger's view of Scheler's attention to biology: while his work in biology allows Scheler to advance beyond his peers in the fundamental question of reality, that same work causes him to overestimate the validity of striving as a fundamental concept and to underestimate the labor it will take to liberate that concept from traditional biological or biologistic prejudices. The selfsame ambivalence will characterize Heidegger's response in 1939 to Nietzsche's putative biologism. However, let me return to the account of Scheler, for Heidegger now reiterates the methodological principle that guides his own relation to ontology of life both in *Being and Time* and in the 1929–1930 lectures:

> Only when we have grasped the objectivity of the world that is accessible to us, that is, our relation of being toward the world, can we, perhaps, by means of certain modified modes of observation, also determine the animal's worldliness; but not vice-versa, inasmuch as in the analysis of animals' environment we are always compelled to speak by way of analogy. For this reason, this environment of theirs cannot be the simplest matter for us. (20, 305)

The suggestion here, as in 1929–1930, is that mere privation and subtraction will *not* grant us access to the world-relation of the animal—if privation is the move from a more to a less complex relation. However simple the amoeba's relation to its "culture" may appear to us to be, that relation is (infinitely) complicated by the fact that Dasein can invoke it only analogically. Human culture casts its shadow across the culture of the Petri dish. So much so that Heidegger himself fails to remember this complication from time to time. In his account of the "discoveredness" of beings (20, §28), he makes the following apparently innocuous claim: "A stone never finds itself by way of disposition [*ein Stein befindet sich nie*]; rather, it is merely at hand [*vorhanden*]; as opposed to that, a quite primitive one-celled animal will no doubt find itself [*wird sich schon befinden*], even if its disposition may be as dull and obscure as possible [*wobei diese Befindlichkeit die größtmögliche und dunkelste Dumpfheit sein kann*]; nevertheless, in accord with the structure of its being, it is essentially different from something like the mere being at hand of a thing or state of affairs" (352). Stone, animal, and Dasein are already in place for the 1929–1930 lectures. Yet the animal's dull and obscure world-relation is something that in *Being and Time* and in the 1929–1930 lectures will by no means be classified as *Befindlichkeit*. The exceptional, most broadly cast possibilities of disclosure (SZ, 139) will have nothing to do with primitive life-forms; nothing to do with either theory or dullness of wit, nothing to do with either ῥᾳστώνη and διαγωγή (SZ, 138) or benumbment. (Interestingly, the "dullness" and "obscurity" that Heidegger attributes to the animal's world-relation are precisely the traits that Hegel cites as characterizing the incipient interiority of primitive forms of life, as well as the most primitive level of cognition, namely, feeling or intuition—spirit's *dumpfes Weben*.)[16]

Before we bring this long excursus to a close, we ought to allow the 1925 lectures to remind us of a connection that is quite important also in *Being and Time,* no matter how far-fetched it may seem. In both texts (20, 364–65 and 374; SZ, 166), but more elaborately in the 1925 lectures, Heidegger discusses the λόγος that is "immediately tied to the ζῷον" as itself "vital" and "living"—or, in the case of languages whose world has passed, the λόγος that is "dead." To be sure, "living language" and "dead language" are mere metaphors; yet when Heidegger diagnoses Church Latin as irrecoverably defunct and the Latin of classical Roman times as potentially still alive (for "genuine historical understanding"), and when he sees in poetry "new ontological possibilities of Dasein" (375), we may suspect that the life of living language is essential to living Dasein. What *other* forms of life may be, forms that lack the attachment of λόγος to ζῷον, Heidegger here does not say. It may be that discourse will prove to have more life in it than ζωή itself, whatever the dangers of grammarification. More life than mere living creatures that never speak but always perish. The only remaining doubt, taken up in chapter 9, below, will be whether the stirring of such linguistic life is of spirit or the daimon.

DEATH, DEMISE, AND ANIMAL PERISHING

To Heidegger's chapter on "the possible being a whole of Dasein, and being toward death" (SZ, II, 1) an inquiry into daimon life would have only two questions to pose, and perhaps even these two might boil down to one. First, what are the stakes for all life in the ontological possibility of possibilities for Dasein, namely, death? Second, why must Heidegger's existential-ontological analysis of death exclude "biological death"?

That exclusion becomes palpable in section 46, which takes up the apparent impossibility of grasping and determining the kind of totality or being-a-whole that would be "of the measure of Dasein." In the previous chapter of our own inquiry we anticipated the problem by indicating that Dasein never lies at hand as a finished whole, not even when it is finished forever; not even when there isn't any there there in there-being; not even, in a word, when Dasein is dead. It is almost impossible, Heidegger says, to purge from the vocabulary of existentiality the tendency to think in terms of things at hand: the language of care—of an existence forever "ahead of itself," whose "end" and "wholeness" are always not-yet, always reserved for a future that is still outstanding—remains forever exposed to that danger. However, he now elides all the temptations of *Vorhandenheit* and associates them with the science of biology. Here the temptations are greatest precisely because the object of biology (life) is not and never can be merely at hand. The elision occurs across the trajectory of four questions, presumably a proper sequence of questions (SZ, 237). Heidegger asks: In the question of a possible being-a-whole, have we not "unwittingly posited" Dasein as a being at hand? Has the interpretation of wholeness attained a "genuinely *existential* meaning"? Was the talk of "end" and "wholeness" or "totality" measured upon the measure of Dasein? And, finally, "Did the expression *death* have a biological or an existential-ontological significa-tion, and was its meaning delineated at all adequately and securely?"

What enables Heidegger to counterpose so readily the existential-ontological to the biological? Does the former, particularly in its account of being-toward-death, borrow nothing at all from the latter? What about the discussion of biologically *immanent* death in thinkers like Simmel and researchers like Korschelt, both of whom Heidegger cites in these pages (246 n. 1 and 249 n. 1)? Is it possible that the existential-ontological interpretation derives its most powerful idea, the idea of being toward and unto death, *Sein zum Tode,* precisely from the biology and the life-philosophy that it claims to abjure? Would not such a borrowing or derivation put at risk both the priority of fundamental ontology as the vanguard of science and the priority of Dasein over other forms of life?

It seems I have developed my own sequence of questions. Let me try to respond to them, if only briefly. Admittedly, the talk of "borrowing" is vulgar and naive; no one would scorn it more acerbically than Heidegger. However, in existential-ontological analysis death is the possibility of possibilities for the life of Dasein—the factical life that has eluded fundamental ontology from the outset. How elusive the analysis itself must be, and how intricate its relation to both current science and ancient prejudice, is something Heidegger knows only too well. He also knows the dangers of sleight-of-hand, of an analysis that moves so adroitly that it can suggest that problems have been solved when they have not even been broached. At the end of section 47 Heidegger writes: "Furthermore, when characterizing the transition from Dasein to no-longer-Dasein, it was shown [240: *es zeigte sich*] that the going-out-of-the-world of *Dasein,* in the sense of dying, has to be distinguished from the going-out-of-the-world of what is merely alive [*des Nur-lebenden*]." No doubt, *Aus-der-*

Welt-gehen will be crucial to a being that is defined ontologically as *In-der-Welt-sein*. Presumably, the *exitus* of Dasein from the world of existence will have to be different from the *exitus* of just-plain-life. Accordingly, Heidegger claims that these exi(s)tings have to be distinguished (*unterschieden*) from one another. Yet what is this *exiting* from existence and/or life, this *exi(s)ting*, this *Aus-der-Welt-gehen*, this *exitus* that he is first able to attribute to *both* in order then to call for an important distinction, as though in mimicry of Scholasticism? The reader might very well want to know precisely when and where it "was shown" that such a distinction would have to be made. Heidegger does not say; he passes by quickly.

There are only two possibilities: it was shown either when the cadaver pointed back to the life it once had, thus inviting anatomical scrutiny, or when it solicited the respectful handling of the bereaved, those who remained behind and yet were still with the dead one (238). Presumably, the first possibility will not suffice: every no-longer-living thing points back to the life it has only now lost; every once-living thing invites theory to orient understanding toward the quick as it slices into the still. Not a paramecium bathed in rose or indigo stain that does not say through the looking-glass, "You should have seen me swim! And, oh, how I threw myself into mitosis!" Not a hare wired to the laboratory machines that does not announce, "I leapt like a dancer, and was delicate about my toilette." No, the turnabout (*Umschlag*) in being from beings at hand to Dasein cannot occur merely by way of the anatomical gesture.

The cult of the graves, then. Forgetting Melville's whale, which is a piece of fiction and therefore even less reliable than the science of anatomy. It is the mournful, commemorative lingering of those who are left behind yet still with the dead one, the lingering of those who are still alive, who must have "shown" us the difference in exi(s)ting. It is as though, through the magic of Heidegger's prose, the bereaved had gone over to that undiscovered country from whose bourn no traveler has returned, except for those who travel in *Being and Time*. To be sure, Heidegger takes pains to assure us that the dead themselves will not return, will not go-back-into-the-world: "In such being with the dead [*Mitsein mit dem Toten*] the deceased *himself* is no longer factically 'there' " (238). Factical thereness is not an appurtenance of the corpsebody. The cult of the grave is of and for the factical living. "However," Heidegger now cautions, "being-with always means being with one another [*Miteinandersein*] in the selfsame world." The predicament is thus not so easily escaped. Nor so quickly shown. What is this shared world of the dead and the bereaved? "The deceased has abandoned our 'world,' and left it behind." The issue of a dead Dasein is the issue of an *exitus* from a world that is in each case its own but also *our* own. That is why Heidegger ends the paragraph by conceding that on the basis of *our* world, not *his*, albeit our "world" in quotation-marks, "those who remain behind can still *be with him*." Of course, they could still be with him in *their* world if he (the dead one) were a French poodle or a treasured tropical fish. The fact that Dasein makes funny movies about those who mourn fish called Wanda does not alter the fact that it was never shown in *Being and Time* why the death of Dasein has to be distinguished from the *exitus* of beings that are merely alive. The life that is lost by the one that dies, Heidegger concedes, is a loss of being (*Seinsverlust:* earlier there was talk of *Lebensverlust*—as though being and life were synonymous) that is not accessible (*nicht zugänglich*) to us (239). It is as radically inaccessible, one might say, as the life of animals and plants is to Dasein. Furthermore, whatever one may say about *our* world, our *shared* world, the life that is lost when a living being dies remains inaccessible—whether the living-dying one was Dasein or Diplodocus.

In effect, nothing "was shown." Nothing in the phenomenological descriptions calls for the distinction Heidegger insists we make, the distinction that a tradition of metaphysics, morals, and anthropocentric humanism has already made for him. With an alacrity, not to say brutality, that we recognize as the same alacrity with which he fastened onto the term *Dasein* (7), Heidegger now declares, "The ending of a living being [*das Enden eines Lebendigen*] we shall grasp terminologically as perishing [*Verenden*]" (240). The euphony of the parataxis (*Enden, Lebendigen, Verenden*) should not be allowed to conceal the difficulties. Principal among these is that Heidegger covertly and with no apparent distress drops the word *only* from the phrase "living being." What in the preceding line of text was *Nur-lebenden*, the dubious object of a privative ontology of life that waits upon the ontology of Dasein that ought to found and generate an ontology of life, is now simply a universalized *Lebendiges*. It is as though Dasein in its elevation beyond mere life had lost its life forever in order to make the distinction between it and other forms of life sharper. As for the merely living, its life ends in *Verenden*. In everyday German, that is to say, in the German that is spoken not when one is doing fundamental ontology but when one is lost in everydayness, when one is *benommen* among the Germans, the verb *verenden* means the dying of animals, animal "perishing." The prefix *ver-* suggests a kind of violent deviation, intensification, or truncation. Although *verenden* is intransitive, the action seems to advene from the outside, as though in the case of animals death were always a violent truncation of life advening from the exterior world. Even though *ver-* may derive from πϱό- and πεϱί-, in most cases it comes from the Gothic *fra-*, which suggests causing to disappear, to eliminate or execute.[17] Thus the verb *ver-enden* most likely represents a doubling or intensification of what *enden* already means.[18] *Ver-enden* is a double, haunted and haunting, suggesting a death that is both inside and outside at once; it is a properly za-ological word. Yet the very notion of a death supervening from the exterior, advening from outside, is the one that Heidegger will most resist. Death will prove to be *immanent* in and for both Dasein and all life.

No matter how *verenden* is to be understood "terminologically," the distinction between it and an ending that is of the measure of human existence (241: *des daseinsmäßigen Endens*) can become visible only when the existential-ontological conception of dying (*Sterben*) is demarcated over against "the end of a life" (*das Ende eines Lebens*). Heidegger here refers us back to section 10. Yet the familiar double-bind of privative interpretation returns: how can the ending that measures up to Dasein be counterposed to the emphatic ending or perishing of animals when ontology of life waits upon ontology of Dasein and ontology of Dasein waits upon an existential-ontological interpretation of death? Further, if Dasein cannot experience its own death, much less (in bereavement) the death of its own, when will it ever have anything to say about the death of other forms of life? Unless it should speak too quickly, peremptorily, summarily—by way of execution? Unless it should speak a dead language?

To be sure, the execution here is a matter of rhetoric, a rhetoric that tersely and confidently (or perhaps most anxiously) evades all the problems: "Of course, dying can also be comprehended physiologically and biologically. Yet the medical concept of *exitus* is not coextensive with that of perishing" (241). Presumably, *exitus* is aligned here with the end of Dasein, as though merely living beings never went (medically) out of the world. Simultaneously, the physiology and biology of human dying are reduced to a *zwar* and a merely contingent and inadequate conceptual *auffassen*. Heidegger rightly fears the confusion that threatens his distinction: when we try to conceive of death and dying, beings that are not of the measure, manner, or mode of being of Dasein thrust their way to the fore or insinuate themselves into the analysis; they suggest themselves as structures that can undergird an existential-ontological interpretation of death, as substructures or skeletal frameworks: *Substruktionen*. Heidegger designates two such insinuating structures, assuming that his "or" is distributive here, not collective or appositive: the principal *Substruktionen* are being-at-hand (*Vorhandenheit*) and/or life (*oder Leben*).

Once again, as in section 43b, the dubious, problematical actuality or reality of life comes to the fore. Section 48, "Default, End, and Wholeness," opens with an eminently ontological problem—that of the modes or species of being (*Seinsarten*) and of a regional division or allotment (*Scheidung*) of the "universe of beings" (241). Such an allotment or apportionment of beings requires "a clarified idea of being in general" (241; cf. 333 and 438). Thus the "clarified idea of being" thrusts its way to center-stage in *Being and Time,* demanding to be a superstructure or undergirding substructure of the text well before its time can possibly have come—precisely in the way life thrusts itself to the fore in the analysis of the death of Dasein. It is almost as though *Sein* were *Leben.* Or at least as though the one were as utterly indeterminate and as ubiquitous as the other. It is very much as though the entire topic of the ontological difference were at stake in the question of life. Not only at stake, but also shaken and shattered: to come to an appropriate conclusion concerning "end" and "wholeness" in the life of Dasein, which is one species of being among many in the universe of beings, one would already have to "presuppose as located and recognized" what *Being and Time* is all the while seeking—the meaning of being in general. Such shattering will occupy us later, and it will have to do with the death of Dasein in tandem with the death of the *analysis* of Dasein. For the death of fundamental ontology is implied in the very happenstance that as Heidegger demarcates the death of Dasein from phenomena of completion, plenitude, finish, ripeness, accomplishment, and consummation, and as he counterposes being at an end to being *toward* or *unto* an end, preontological testimony once again confuses Dasein with life. If in the *Cura* fable Dasein is given over to Care "all its life long" (198: *"zeitlebens"*), Heidegger's Bohemian peasant now declares, "As soon as a human being comes to life [*zum Leben kommt*] . . ." (245). Does such unsophisticated, bucolic, post-Classical, whether Hellenistic or Teutonic, preontological testimony simply jumble fundamental-ontological matters? If it does, why does Heidegger call upon it? Is it not rather the case that existential-ontological being *toward* an end has something to do with just plain being alive?

Like section 10, section 49 is all about delineating, demarcating, and drawing spurious borders of inclusion and exclusion. "Demarcating the Existential Analysis of Death over against Other Possible Interpretations of the Phenomenon." It is "interpretation" that is to be demarcated, not death "itself." However, at what point will interpretation and phenomenon touch one another? No doubt, at the point of greatest anxiety. "Death in the widest sense is a phenomenon of life," Heidegger begins (246). Obviously, we may say. Fatefully, we should say, and fatally. Especially for the interpretation. Which is about to die. In Heidegger's own living language, as follows: "Life [*Leben*] has to be understood as a mode of being to which a being in the world belongs [*zu der ein In-der-Welt-sein gehört*]." The reader is, or ought to be, flabbergasted. Earlier, being in the world in general was identified as the fundamental constitution of Dasein (52). Somewhat later, being in the world was called the global phenomenon of Dasein as care, articulated existentially as being ahead of itself in being already in a world alongside present beings (192). However, we now find "a being in the world" attributed to *life*, which, most days of the week, is not of the measure of Dasein. To be sure, by this time we are ready for the demur that is coming: "This mode of being can be fixed ontologically only in a privative orientation toward Dasein." Yet we note something strange about the demur. The orientation toward Dasein is now what is called "privative," whereas earlier it was ontology of life that bore that modifier. The circle of privations may be hermeneutical, but it is assuredly vicious: we have no access to that in privation of which we shall find ourselves oriented toward either life or Dasein. By some sort of miracle Heidegger transforms such vicious circularity, blockage, aporia, or impasse into sheer transparency: "Dasein too permits itself to be observed as pure life."

Perhaps we would be less flabbergasted if we were better prepared; that is, more familiar with the texts that prepare the way toward *Being and Time*. In my long excursus on the 1925 *Prolegomena*, a few pages back, I missed a passage, and must now recuperate it.[19]

The context is transcendental phenomenology, specifically, its appeal to the "sphere of immanence," *Innensphäre*, as the arena of evidence. Heidegger's resistance to the transcendental-phenomenological turn to interiority here appeals to the immanence and interiority of a living creature other than the ζῷον λόγον ἔχον. To wit, the snail. For the snail has something to teach us about intentionality, being-in, dwelling, and world—on which its single foot leaves an unmistakable crystalline or celluloid trace. It is not a matter of equating *Dasein* with *Schnecke,* but of opening the ontological question of the sphere of immanence. "Before we proceed with the analysis," begins Heidegger, "let us explain the phenomenon by way of an analogy that does not lie too far afield [*die selbst nicht allzuweit von der Sache selbst abliegt*], inasmuch as it deals with a being to which we (formally speaking) similarly have to attribute the mode of being of Dasein—'life' " (20, 223).

If no longer flabbergasted, we still need time to draw a breath. Whereas *Being and Time* will attribute to animal life *eine eigene Seinsart,* a mode of being all its own, a mode Heidegger will vainly seek to reach by subtraction and/or addition, he here concedes that one "must attribute" the mode of being that is Dasein to— "life." Heidegger proceeds with his "analogy," which is "not too far afield," hence not really an analogy at all, but something more like the unified field of φύσις. It all begins innocently enough, with a "comparison":

> We shall compare the subject and its sphere of immanence with the snail in its house. I note explicitly that I am not accusing the theories that speak of the immanence of consciousness and of the subject, not accusing them of conceiving such consciousness as a snail in its housing. However, inasmuch as the interior and immanence remain undefined, and because one never discovers what meaning the "in" has, or what ontological relation the subject's "in" has toward the world, our analogy approximates it, negatively speaking, quite well.
>
> One might say that the snail occasionally quits its lodgings while holding onto them. It stretches itself toward something [*Sichausstrecken*], toward nourishment, something it finds on the ground. Does the snail thereby enter into its ontological relation with the world for the first time? No! Its creeping out is but a local modification of its being already in the world. Even when it is in its lodgings, its being is a being outside, if we understand it aright. The snail is not in its house as water is in a glass. Rather, it has the interiority of its house as world, which it bumps against, palpates [*betastet*], in which it stays warm, and so on. Everything that does not hold for the ontological relation of water in the glass—or, if it were fitting, we could say it of water too—everything that would force us to say, "Water has the mode of being of Dasein," would also force us to say, "It has a world." (20, 223–24)

To be sure, Heidegger is not willing to let Dasein dribble through his fingers like water, or to equate hand of man with foot of snail. Yet the horizon of his analogy threatens to expand at every instant to include even what we call the mineral world, the world of water in a glass. It is as though every being showed itself in a unified field of disclosure, as though every being were of a piece. Nevertheless, if the ontological relation is that of "having" a world, Heidegger will soon have to take away with one hand what he has given with the other: the animal, the snail, will prove to *have* a world *in not having it.* Even so, we are tempted to say, Heidegger's recoil in the face of his own analysis will not have a leg to stand on, but only a single foot, with its unmistakable trace. Let us return to section 49 of *Being and Time,* in which a particular form of dying is being prepared for the animal that encroaches on the very being of Dasein.

As we have seen, in *Being and Time* too Dasein "permits itself to be observed as pure life." *Auch das Dasein läßt sich als pures Leben betrachten.* What sort of purity is this? And what sort of "letting," what sort of permission? Surely it is not the purity of just-plain-life, which Dasein presumably never is as long as its proper mode of being prevails. Does the purity pertain to the living or to the observing? Or do the two coalesce in the permission granted by the phenomenon of anxiety? Above all, why has such purity never been discussed prior to this moment in *Being and Time,* the moment that would delineate the dying of Dasein *over against* the perishing of mere life? Or does Heidegger mean that one can *try to* achieve such purity of observation? Does the *läßt sich* really mean "can be coerced and contorted"? The next sentence suggests this when it says, "For the biological, physiological way of posing questions, Dasein then slips into [*rückt in*] the region of being that we know as the animal world and plant world." Data can be gathered on the life-expectancy of plants, animals, and human beings. Such "ontic determinations" enable researchers to make connections among such diverse phenomena as life-span, growth, and reproduction. "The 'species' of death can be investigated, the causes, 'implementations,' and modes of its advent" (SZ, 246). At this point Heidegger cites the data on "life-span, aging, and death" and the interpretations of that data by Eugen Korschelt, a professor of zoology and comparative anatomy at the University of Marburg—thus a former colleague of Heidegger's.[20] In addition to the vast amount and variety of data on animals—from man and other mammals   *All the wild things of the plain and the pasture*   down to sponges and upward from one-celled infusoria to protozoa and metazoa, but with somewhat less reference to the vegetable world—Korschelt inquires into "the problem of death," which   *Night and day murmur*   "touches the foundations of our existence" (1). That problem has many facets, but none more important than the principle of immanence: death is necrobiosis, the final stage of vital development, not advening from outside the organism but indigenous in it, internal and intrinsic to its process, immanent in and for it. Death is the final and (in some sense) the most successful homeostatic adaptation of a living being to its environment (398–99).

Korschelt emphasizes the fact that death is the surrender of individuality. One-celled animals do not "die" as a result of cell-division; yet they do surrender their individuality, and so cannot truly be said to be immortal. The same holds true for germ cells, which remain alive only by abandoning the mother-body, having already abandoned the father-body, at the fitting times—in ejaculation and in birth.[21] In higher organisms, with their colonies and confederations of specialized yet cooperative cells and their radical interdependence of life-functions, death proper may be said to enter on the scene for the first time in the history of life. It advenes when multitudes of highly differentiated cells surrender their capacity for cell-division (that is, their own hope of deathlessness), a surrender that takes place quite early in most cases, as early as birth. The cells of muscle tissue, interstitial tissue, nerve ganglia, and indeed of many kinds of tissue—those of heart and kidney, for example—are bound to degeneration and eventual death. Even the nourishment and replenishment of these cells calls for labor, and hence for the ceaseless metabolic wear-and-tear that inevitably precipitates death. Even when the organism as a whole slips into that mimicry of death we call sleep, these cells expend energy in order to refresh themselves: they court exhaustion during the organism's hours of rest and recuperation. Subjected to the constant threat of self-toxification, that is, inadequate or incomplete excretion, most confederated cells are, like Bohemian peasants, old enough to die the moment they are "born." Their life stretches across a single τόπος, between the two boundaries of "birth" and death, as though confederated cells were homuncular Daseins.

Nevertheless, it is not the death of individual cells that is decisive for most forms of life. If death is the standstill of the organism as a whole, the irrecuperable loss of its life (405: *unwiederbringlicher Verlust*), individual parts and their cells nonetheless continue to live. Korschelt cites instances of the reactivation of the human heart almost twenty-four hours after death, the zombie dream   *The dream was marvelous*   and intensive-care nightmare   *but the terror was great*   of successful resuscitation after brain death. What is missing forever in such reactivation or even continued functioning of isolated organs and cells is the *cohesion* of life (406). The components are still "at hand," *vorhanden,* as Korschelt writes; what is missing is their holding together, their nexus and connection—what Korschelt, like Dilthey before him and Heidegger and Merleau-Ponty after him, calls *Zusammenhang.* Under certain circumstances, a biological researcher can sound exactly like a Bohemian peasant or a phenomenological philosopher. Korschelt cites his confrère Tangl as follows: "In a certain sense, death germinates simultaneously with life" (408). Korschelt himself ruminates on something different from the simultaneity or homogeneity of life and death. The paradox that most intrigues him is this: life arises from and is universally based on cells, and yet death, while essential to the life-process, does not result in *universal* cell death. It is as though Korschelt were reflecting on the possibility   *we must treasure the dream whatever the terror*   of life's being a whole—where the "whole" is by no means a mere aggregation of parts that are "at hand," or a "full" moon, or a "ripe" fruit—and the possibility of death   *that the end of life is sorrow*   as the possible impossibility of such being-a-whole.[22]

If the biologist's formulations at times sound uncannily close to those of the fundamental ontologist's, the formulations of the life-philosopher and social theorist Georg Simmel press even closer. Both Korschelt and Simmel make it seem less likely than ever that the existential-ontological conception of death can be neatly and securely demarcated over against others. For these others are far more complex than one would like to admit, and they contribute directly to the existential conception, which is unthinkable without them—perhaps in the way that it is impossible to think of Dasein without life. Yet if we study these other interpretations of death, the mimetically Scholastic distinction between *Verenden* and *Sterben* (as appropriate to two distinct regions of beings, the "animal" and the "human") may well appear to be wholly specious. However, worse is yet to come. The introduction of "demise" (247: *Ableben*) as the halfway house of a Dasein that can die as both just-plain-life and its proper self marks the demise of existential-ontological demarcation as such. That introduction constitutes one of the many ends of fundamental ontology. For it is also the introduction of a *metaphysics of death*, which Heidegger would like to banish but which will never again quit his thought. From this moment on, a moment already presaged in the 1924 lecture, "The Concept of Time," Heidegger will be haunted by a metaphysics of death. First, however, to Simmel.[23]

Simmel's initial reflections corroborate those of Korschelt. His ultimate reflections lead him to what will become several crucial themes of the fundamental-ontological analysis, anticipating its very vocabulary. First of all, Simmel underscores Korschelt's conclusions concerning the paradox of the death of individuals (which are always conglomerates of cells) without universal cell death: only the "collective life" of cells in a federation admits of death proper, the federation of cells being precisely that which allows for specialization, complexification, division of labor, and enhanced chances for morphological individuation. If death (in existential analysis) is that which individualizes human existence, such individuality (in life-philosophical analysis) itself rests on—or, to put it more neutrally, is at least bound up with—the possibility of the death of the collectivity of cell groups, a collectivity or federation that any "individual" always already *is* (131). The very "individual" that dies as a conglomerate of cells is irrecoverable, writes Simmel, irrecoverable *im Sinne des Unwiederholbaren* (130), as though anticipating the existential-ontological analysis of death in one of its principal traits.

Secondly, Simmel joins Korschelt (along with scores of other researchers and theoreticians cited by the latter, including Bernstein and Weismann, who were so important to Freud) in challenging the very notion of death as *Verenden*, that is to say, as an external or extrinsic truncation of life, a contingent snipping of the thread. Simmel tries instead to define death as a kind of internal boundary or limit to the forms a life can take (99–100). The problem he encounters is that the principle of immanent death defeats the very language of inside and outside. In fact, it is almost as though *Lebensphilosophie* here confronts the central difficulty of deconstruction, grappling with it long before the *domain* of deconstruction—to wit, the metaphysics of presence—has been staked out by Heidegger's philosophy. The very opposition of life and death comes to an end in the idea of immanent death. The putative opposite of life, exclaims Simmel, "stems from nowhere else than life!" (101). Life generates and encompasses death in such a way that the "ends" of birth and death are joined by a single span:

> In every single moment [*Moment*] of life we *are* the ones who will die. That moment would be different if dying were not our endowment, if it were not the determination that is somehow at work in the moment. We are not already there [*da*] at the instant [*Augenblick*] of our birth; rather, something of us is born continuously. In precisely the same way, we do not first come to die in our last instant.[24]

Immanent death, in a word, is *gebürtig*. Dasein natal, Dasein fatal; immanent death, imminent death. Even if *gebürtig* is not Simmel's word, something of the existential-ontological conception is his. For it is the *possibility* of dying, dying *as* necessitous possibility, that first opens what existential analysis will call possibility-being. The distinction between *Verenden* and *Sterben* is the distinction, Simmel would say, between being killed and dying, between *Getötetwerden* and *Sterben* (102), whereby the former is always a merely abbreviated and hence inadequate expression, whether one is speaking of violent or natural death in animals or humans. In contrast to a stone, life has dying as its *possibility*, not as its opposite, contrary, or contradiction. It is a possibility that elides at some unlocatable point with necessity. Thus Simmel alludes to the problem of death and the Kantian problem of the *modalities,* a problem, as we shall see in chapter 6, that occupies Heidegger in his 1936–1938 *Contributions to Philosophy (Of Propriation)*. Simmel finds the elision of death as possibility *and* necessity exhibited in Shakespeare's tragic characters, in Hamlet, Macbeth, and Lear. Their deaths do not advene from an extrinsic fate that threatens from afar. On the contrary, their dying reflects a fatal necessity, the "quality of the entire inner span of their lives" (103). The initially bizarre combination of biology with Shakespearean tragedy in Simmel produces a conception of death that one must recognize as imminently existential-ontological, even if the idea of being is never envisaged there and the question of being never posed: the *that* of our dying is absolutely certain even if, or precisely because, the *when* is absolutely uncertain. Immanent death is inherently imminent. The very position of human being midway between knowledge and ignorance, like daimonic Eros in Plato, is the position first opened by the necessitous possibility of our dying certainly and undeterminably. There we are bound and banned. *Zwischen Wissen und Nichtwissen sind wir gebannt* (105). Such is the very prick of death—as both Simmel (107) and Heidegger agree (20, 438; SZ, 52). O death, where is your sting? It is there in the conjunction of certainty *and* indeterminacy, in the existential *Gewißheit* and temporal *Unbestimmtheit* that constitute the life of existence.

But whose existence? Does not Simmel slip from one region of beings into another, without clearly differentiating them? Is not Heidegger right to chide him for his failure to achieve "a clear apportionment [*Scheidung*]" (SZ, 249 n. 1)? As we heard Heidegger say at the outset of section 48, a clear division, allotment, division, or apportionment of beings needs the already clarified idea of being. In the note on Simmel (and on Paul, Calvin, Dilthey, Jaspers, and Rudolf Unger) he calls for a clear division between "the biological-ontic and the existential-ontological problems." Unfortunately, the clear division of ontic from ontological, and biological from existential, depends upon a scission in being that ostensibly would divide Dasein from just-plain-life without making such life absolutely inaccessible to it. Even more unfortunately, such a scission or gap in being is the dream of metaphysics from Plato through Schelling, the dream that informs the factical ideal of existence that surreptitiously guides Heidegger's analysis from the start.

Simmel touches on the scission that Schelling and Heidegger alike crave in a long footnote to his text (109) over which we might well pause. For it gives us the opportunity to see where daimon life will lead Heidegger after *Being and Time*. Simmel observes that the entanglement or interlacing of death in life, life in death (*die Todesverflochtenheit des Lebens*), should cause us to hesitate to attribute life to the godhead. No matter how enchanting a notion the *living* God may be, it might also be a vulgar stupidity or bedazzlement, *eine Borniertheit*, that lies concealed in all metaphysics as the thought of "spirit" or "life." Nor will it help to think of God as hypervital, superlatively alive, the sur-vivor (*als das Überlebendige*). As we shall see, Heidegger soon after *Being and Time* goes to encounter transcendence in the plenipotent and overpowering, *das Übermächtige*. Whether or not the plenipotent is as doomed as the hypervital will become an arresting question for us. At any rate, Simmel urges his readers to abjure any notions of life, soul, and spirit where the godhead is concerned, and to return to the Schellingian metaphysics of "indifference," or to Spinoza's even more radically ungraspable "infinite attributes," or to the most radical negative theology of the medieval mystics, which is "freer and deeper than all earlier or later dogmatics and philosophies of religion" (109). Whether or not we follow Simmel in that direction (cf. 118–19), as even Heidegger (the reader of Eckhart) would encourage us to do, we might ponder the necessity of another route—the route followed by Schelling, Hölderlin, and Nietzsche, who in the face of evil and nothingness generously grant divinity its last breath of life by letting it die.[25]

I must truncate this discussion of Simmel. Yet not before observing that Heidegger could well have profited by lingering over Simmel's conception of destiny (124: *Schicksal*). Simmel's notion might well have complicated his own, and perhaps even prevented Dasein from marching off in the ranks of its "generation" in order to seek its hero. And not before noting how much Simmel may have contributed to Heidegger's own conception of existence as being in the world—not as potatoes are in a sack, but as sustaining a world-relation, a relation that is both uncanny and incorrigibly tragic (127–29).

Heidegger shortchanges these biological and life-philosophical sources to which his own project refers and out of which it grows. At the same time, he underestimates what they might do to clarify the central problem of *Being and Time*, to wit, the idea of being that will always have to have been clarified before any existential-ontological analysis can proceed. Instead, Heidegger insists on the methodological priority of his project:

> This biological-ontic research into death rests on an ontological problem. It remains for us to ask how the ontological essence of death is determined on the basis of the ontological essence of life. In a certain way, ontic investigation of death has always already decided about it. Preconceptions of life and death are already at work in it, preconceptions that have been more or less clarified. They need the preliminary sketch that the ontology of Dasein provides. Within the ontology of Dasein, which *takes precedence over* an ontology of life, the existential analysis of death in turn is *subsequent to* a characterization of the fundamental constitution of Dasein. (SZ, 246–47)

Ontological analysis depends on this *Vorordnung* and *Nachordnung,* this decision about what comes earlier and later in the order of implications. No doubt, in the lecture courses that follow upon *Being and Time* this very "earlier" and "later" will become part of the problem of the temporality of being. For the moment, Heidegger hopes that an order can be established that will not suffer from the dislocations that arise in *ecstatic* temporality, in the raptures of finite time and the ruptures of "equiprimordiality." We cannot enter here and now into the raptures and ruptures of fundamental ontology. Let us merely note the order on which Heidegger here insists: ontology of Dasein must precede and found ontology of life, must be prior to it, take precedence over it, and undergird it; moreover, in ontology of Dasein a characterization of the fundamental constitution of Dasein as care-ful being in the world must precede, found, undergird, and take precedence over the existential analysis of death—even though ontology of Dasein and the analysis of care are led ineluctably to the analysis of death, *without which they remain essentially incomplete.* The existential conception of death cannot be demarcated over against other interpretations of death until the general characterization of Dasein as care has come to completion; unfortunately, that general characterization heads toward the analysis of death as toward its own life's blood, always too soon, always importunate, always like Agamemnon's shade. Even more unfortunately, an ontology of life cannot commence until these two preliminary investigations are successfully accomplished. Most unfortunately, Heidegger is now asking how the essence of life can define and determine the essence of death. He rushes toward the essence of life as toward the living breath of fundamental ontology. However, before anyone can catch a breath and before any of the work can get done he fixes the meaning of life and death for two regions of being as *Verenden* and *Sterben.* He then, as we have heard, introduces *Ableben,* "demise," as some sort of middle position between the two, an undoing which is even more uncanny than death. Heidegger writes: "We called the ending of what lives *perishing.* Inasmuch as Dasein too 'has' its physiological death, which is of the measure of life [*seinen physiologischen, lebensmäßigen Tod 'hat'*], not ontically isolated, however, but codetermined by its original mode of being [*mitbestimmt durch seine ursprüngliche Seinsart*] . . ." (247).

Let us not allow the sentence to finish just yet. Already it is full of surprises. The new word *lebensmäßig* appears—for the first and last time in *Being and Time*—in order to clarify or befuddle forever the ontological analysis of the death of Dasein. "Has" appears in quotation-marks: if in 1929–1930 the animal "has" a world, Dasein in 1927 "has" a physiological death that is of the order or measure of an as yet utterly unclarified and unclarifiable life. Not in "ontic isolation," not like an isolated ego-subject or tool or mood (Heidegger rejects "isolation" with respect to all these, though never with the word *ontisch* as a modifier), but a physiological death that is always codetermined and codefined by its original. Yet how should an original way to be (*Seinsart*) allow something else to codetermine it? Especially to codefine the very possibility that defines its *ownmost* way to be? Did we not earlier learn that life is its *own* mode of being, albeit accessible only in Dasein? What is Dasein, such that its death is codetermined as physiological *and* existential? Whatever we reply, would not existential death occupy one niche in that dual death which the ontotheological tradition has always made the sole property of composite man, with his *Geistding* trapped inside his *Körperding*? Does Dasein suffer two deaths in order that it may collapse back into the battered body and sullied soul it has always been?

Let us now try to let the sentence finish: "Inasmuch as Dasein too 'has' its physiological death, which is of the measure of life, not ontically isolated, however, but codetermined by its original mode of being; but also inasmuch as Dasein can end without properly dying [*das Dasein aber auch enden kann, ohne daß es eigentlich stirbt*]. : . ." What does Heidegger mean? How can Dasein end without properly dying? To be sure, it can end without being accomplished and consummated, without ending fully (244: *vollendet*). To be sure, Dasein ends for the most part in lack of fulfillment, in oblivion, in frustration, in default. Clearly, Heidegger is here referring to a being toward the end that would be either *appropriate* or *inappropriate*. Dasein can come to an end without dying appropriately or properly. It is therefore *inappropriate* dying that Heidegger is now introducing into the analysis. The sentence therefore ends as follows: "Inasmuch as Dasein too 'has' its physiological death, which is of the measure of life, not ontically isolated, however, but codetermined by its original mode of being; but also inasmuch as Dasein can end without dying properly; and, on the other hand, since as Dasein it does not simply perish, we designate this medial phenomenon as *demise* [*dieses Zwischenphänomen als* Ableben]."

Demise is introduced and inserted in between perishing and dying in order to prevent an inappropriate Dasein from dying like an animal, to preclude its collapsing into just-plain-life when it dies ignobly, but also in order to preserve a certain propriety for Dasein proper when it dies properly. As a "between" phenomenon, however, *Ableben* is closer to the side of *Sterben* than to *Verenden*, as the next several sentences suggest: "Yet *dying* would hold as the rubric for the *manner of being* [Seinsweise] in which Dasein *is*, being *toward* its death [*in der das Dasein* zu *seinem Tode* ist]. Accordingly, we must say that Dasein never perishes. But Dasein can suffer demise only as long as it dies [*nur solange, als es stirbt*]." The phrase *nur solange, als* is troubling. If it means that Dasein can undergo demise only for the time in which it is dying, then the very introduction of demise would be pointless for a Dasein that is dying from the moment it is born, a Dasein that never ceases being born as long as it lives.   *The goddess therefore molded from sky and earth a second self for Gilgamesh, and called him Enkidu.*   Rather, we must assume that *Ableben* is what Dasein does when it is *not* dying *properly.* When it is not *properly* dying. Dasein never perishes. Yet because Dasein does not always sustain a manner of being *toward* its own death it cannot properly be said to be always dying properly. Nevertheless, *Sterben* is proclaimed the ontological foundation of *Ableben,* and such is the ontological force of the phrase *nur solange, als.* Only to the extent that Dasein can properly die does it wither away in demise, though never perish.   *He taught his brother the lesson by dying.*   *Sterben* would be the *ontological* possibility of Dasein, and *Ableben* its ruinous ontic fate. Accordingly, *Ableben* slips unobtrusively into the position formerly occupied by biological-medical *Verenden*. *Ableben* will now have to do, not with inappropriateness, but with biology and medicine! Its position "in-between" now shifts in the direction of perishing. "The medical-biological investigation of demise [*Ableben*, not *Verenden*] can attain results that may also be significant ontologically, provided that the fundamental orientation for an existential interpretation of death is secured." Before we have a chance to ask what in all the world can have secured it   *Enkidu fell sick with contagion and withered*   Heidegger interjects his own question, one that would reduce the ontological status of biology and medicine even farther. "Or must not illness and death in general be grasped—even medically—primarily as existential phenomena?"

In the order of investigation that Heidegger is now trying to enforce—the existential analysis of death *prior to* all biology and ontology of life but *posterior to* the general characterization of the fundamental constitution of Dasein—the distinctions between and among perishing, demise, and dying are somehow fudged. Once introduced, they are taken to be fundamental tools of the analysis. Yet their function in and for that order never becomes clear. What it can mean that Dasein "properly dies" or "dies properly," what "dying itself" can mean, remains entirely mysterious; and yet that mystery (or obfuscation) is to elevate fundamental ontology over all biology, ontology of life, psychology, ethnology, thanatology, and even metaphysics of death. "The existential analysis of death comes first methodologically [*ist methodisch vorgeordnet*], prior to the questions of a biology, psychology, theodicy, and theology of death" (248). Comes *first* in this respect, though *second* with regard to a general characterization of the being of Dasein, which for its part needs several things to have been already clarified, among them *being in general* and *time* as the horizon of *temporal existence, care, life*—and *death.*

At all events, death as the ownmost, nonrelational, impassable, certain and yet indeterminate possibility (further discussed in chapter 7, below) bears certain traces of its biological and theodiceal heritages. A death that is immanent in life confounds every desire to allot and demarcate regions of living beings—or, at least, to distinguish them too sharply.   *Let the finger of blessing/Be stretched out in mourning.*   Death smiles upon such distinctions, smiles ironically, serenely, generously, gravely. Death favors all—dog, god, and Dasein alike.

•

No reading of *Being and Time* ever finishes the book. For that matter, no writing ever finished it. By rights we ought to follow Heidegger's search for ontic attestation of the ontological possibility that constitutes existence, namely, its running ahead into death. Heidegger takes great pains to outline the itinerary of that search, even if the final paragraph of chapter 2 of Division II (SZ, 301) concedes failure. A whole range of things demands our attention here, even if we shall neglect to give it in any systematic way: Heidegger's relentless objections to biology as a foreclosure of the ontological problem and even as the reduction of conscience (269, 275); the important discussion in section 58 of the nothing, *das Nichts,* as the source of all privation (a discussion that goes to the heart of the ostensibly privative relationship that obtains between ontology of life and ontology of Dasein); the mystery of individuation as the formal accusation of guilt in existence, the mystery of a "self"   *a second self*   that miraculously survives both Heidegger's destruction of the history of ontology and the raptures of ecstatic temporality; the dual crisis of the clarified idea of being (which is missing to the very end) and the factical ideal of existence (which is all too present throughout); and the birth of Dasein into its history, heritage, and heroics. All these things come to bear on the project of daimon life; none of them is resolved in Heidegger's magnum opus.

Let us slip away from *Being and Time* and advance to the 1929–1930 lectures on the comparative world-relations of stone, animal, and human being. Nothing we said in chapter 1 reduces the mystery of such "comparative" ontology. Nothing we have said here makes either "comparative" or "privative" ontology more likely to succeed than fundamental ontology. However, let us see how far Heidegger is compelled to take the question of daimon life, or how far the question takes him.   *Together they returned to the watering-hole.*

THREE

Where Deathless Horses Weep

The 1929–1930 Biology Lectures

> ... We often have occasion to observe
> how repugnant it is for a horse to
> trample a living body underfoot; an
> animal never encounters without disquiet
> a dead member of its own species; there
> are even some that extend to their dead
> a kind of interment. ...
>
> —Jean-Jacques Rousseau, *Discours sur*
> *l'origine et les fondements de l'inégalité*
> *parmi les hommes*

Some years ago Charles Scott sent me the draft of a paper on Heidegger and ethics.[1] In it he cited a passage from Homer's *Iliad* on horses and ethics. It became clear that in questions of ethics horses had the edge over Heidegger. For the passage Scott cited is one of the most stunning in all of Homer. It appears twice (not surprisingly, inasmuch as a third of all Homeric verses are repeated verses), first in the sixth song, as Paris gallops through the city on his way to the plain of battle, and then in song fifteen, as his brother Hektor spurs the Trojans to their most successful counterattack. The passage, a literary critic would say, elaborates an "extended metaphor," and it runs as follows:

> As when in its stall a steed that's had its fill of fodder
> Breaks free from its halter and sprints spiritedly across the field
> Toward its accustomed bathing place in the swift-flowing river;
> It is all power. Head held high, mane
> Fluttering to its shoulders, sleek with the fiery spark of youth;
> Its limbs carry it lightly to the herd's familiar grazing ground.
> *Iliad*, 6, 506–11

The words that drew Scott's attention to the passage are εἰωθώς (cf. εἰωθότος, ἔθω) designating the spot where the horse "customarily" bathed, and ἤθεα (cf. τὸ ἦθος), referring to the herd's "familiar" pasture (νομός), its habitat, its "haunts." These words suggest that horses not only *live* but also *dwell*, and that they dwell in nearness to what Heidegger, after Heraclitus, calls the δαίμων. Whether horses have "character," or "ethics," or even worse, "morality," would no doubt be secondary questions for Heidegger; that is to say, not really *questions* at all. What the horses have is *freedom*, now that the halter has been torn; freedom and the pride of power in their sleek flanks.

Yet I abandon this passage and its wild steeds now to the man—or centaur—who uncovered them for me. I shall be concerned here with a different passage and with different horses. They are daimonic horses, albeit under yoke; not prancing free, but standing motionless. They are horses who mourn.

HORSES?

Patroklos is dead. A not so very forthright god stripped him of his armor and left him dazed and naked before the lances of not so very brave men. Apollo, concealed in a cloud of fog, struck him in the back, knocked off his helmet, undid his armor, lopped off his lance, shattered his shield, and let the Trojans clean up the mess.

Human beings are like olive trees. Not the ancient trunks but the tender shoots thrusting from them. These mere slips are transplanted to a lonely place, a vale bubbling with water. Homer depicts the destiny of such an olive shoot as follows:

> Stately tall it grows, rustling softly in the cool of every wafting wind,
> Bristling with shining blossoms,
> Until a wild whirlwind looms, of an instant,
> Uproots the shaft and stretches it out on the earth.
>
> *Iliad, 17, 53–58*

Three words in these last two lines begin with the existential prefix ἐξ-: ἐξετάνυσσε, from τάνυμαι, "to stretch out"; ἐξέστρεψε, from στρέφω, "to twist and tear out"; and ἐξαπίνης (= ἐξαίφνης), "sudden, instantaneous, looming on or out of the instant." The instant is ecstatic rapture, rupture, removal, transport, or "remotion," in and from which Plato seeks ineffable insight (see *Parmenides* 156d and Letter VII, 341d). The instant of time bursts in the rapture that yields all the existential words of Aristotle's treatise on time (*Physics* IV, 10–14). It is the instant of *Entrückung*, rapturous transport, the word by which Heidegger hopes to capture the animatedness of a temporal yet untimely and finite existence.[2]

Patroklos succumbs of an instant—of the rapture that ruptures. The finality of sorceress death veils him (κάλυψε), and his psyche streams from his limbs down to the House of Hades, cut off from manly strength and youthful nobility, lamenting its lot.

An instant earlier, on the field of combat, Patroklos wielded Achilles' weapons, wore his armor, and drove his horses. Rather, it was Achilles' driver, Automedon, who handled the horses for Patroklos.

And what horses they are! Under one yoke, the dappled and the dun, both as fleet as the wind. Indeed, they were sired by Zephyros the Westwind upon the Harpy Podárge as she grazed in a green meadow on the banks of Okeanós, on the outermost rim of earth. Attached to the chariot as a trace-horse is yet a third steed, Pédasos by name. Of Pédasos the poem says, in one of its most puzzling lines, "Even though he was mortal [θνητός], he could keep the pace of immortal horses" (*16, 154*: ἵπποι ἀθανάτοι). Pédasos, the mortal horse who guides the immortals, the horse of the trace, soon demonstrates his mortal lineage: Sarpedon casts his lance at Patroklos but misses and strikes Pédasos instead; the horse whinnies, collapses in the dust, and breathes forth his θυμός (*467–9*). Thus it is not the mortal steed but one of the immortal horses, one of the Harpy's lineage, the dun, who later warns Achilles of his impending demise. Scolded a second time by the driver, Automedon, for reasons we shall soon discover, the deathless dun lowers his head and speaks with the human voice granted him by the shimmering goddess Hera:

> We will rescue you, for the moment, brave Achilles.
> Yet nigh is the day of your demise. We are not to blame,
> But the great god and the mighty fates [θεός τε μέγας καὶ μοῖρα κραταιή]. . . .
> For we race with the panting Westwind,
> Whom they say is swiftest. Yet to you it is allotted
> To be laid low by a man and by a god.
>
> *Iliad, 19, 408–10; 415–17*

Erinyes now silences the steed's resounding, foreboding voice. Achilles is piqued that a horse should play his seer. "I know my part," he snarls, and drives the horses off to battle.

One can understand Automedon's scolding and Achilles' anger. For earlier on, in the thick of the battle over Patroklos' corpse, the immortal horses suddenly lost heart and stood stock-still.

> Yet the horses of Achilles, standing apart from the battle,
> Weep the moment they learn that their master
> Lies in the dust, laid low by the hand of murderous Hektor.
>
> *Iliad, 17, 426–28*

No matter how hard Automedon flails them with the whip, no matter how desperately he curses or coaxes them, they do not move. Homer now sings the passage that stands as the central monument, memorial, or crypt of the present chapter:

> But just as funeral stele stand fixed above the tomb
> As monuments to the dead man or woman,
> They stand motionless and motionless hold the splendid car.
> Their heads are lowered to the ground, tears of mourning
> Run hot from their lids, so painfully do they
> Miss their master. Their luxuriant manes spill
> Over the ring of the yoke and are soiled in the dust.
> It was a painful sight for Zeus, Son of Kronos,
> To see these weeping steeds. Sadly he shook his head and said to his heart:
> "Ah, you wretches! Why did we ever give you to King Peleus,

A mortal, you who are ageless and deathless?
Was it so that you could share in the sufferings of these unhappy humans?
For, truly, there is nothing more wretchedly lamentable than human being,
Amid all the beings that breathe and creep on the earth."

Iliad, 17, 426–47

The profoundly moved yet unmoving horses—like the marbles of a pediment frieze preserved in the Acropolis Museum at Athens—are immortal steeds. Death does not touch them. No spear can dislodge their life, no blast of wind uproot them and lay them low. Yet even immortal horses are susceptible to a mortality they ought not even understand, as though some natural compassion bound them to the fate of lesser creatures whom they might have trampled underfoot. Indeed, the gods themselves are susceptible: immortal Zeus regrets his immortal brother's having given immortal horses to the mortal Peleus, for these immortal horses now weep for Patroklos. The words *mortal* and *immortal* open and close line 444 of song seventeen. They cause that line to seesaw from mortal humanity to deathless divinity, with deathless horses as the fulcrum. These horses are the vicarious sufferers of human death, sharers in the human disaster (445: δυστήνοισι . . . ἀνδράσιν), which the song, now from the mouth of Zeus, goes on to name with unequalled, calamitous clarity: οὐ μὲν γάρ—it must be a Parmenidean pronouncement, we suppose, an anachronistic pronouncement of and by being: οὐ μὲν γάρ τί πού ἐστιν ὀιζυρώτερον ἀνδρός. The pronouncement employs the onomatopoeic word for lamentation, wailing, keening (3, 408: ὀ ἰ ζ ύ ω); "for nothing anywhere is more wretchedly lamentable than man." Here the line breaks, only to have the next line complete the thought with its first word, πάντων, "of all"; and after the strangely inverted prepositional phrase, ὅσσα γαῖαν ἔπι, "of all things the earth upon," comes the cruel close and the collapse of the elevated diction: πνείει τε καὶ ἕρπει, "all that breathes and creeps." A German translation of the entire phrase has this: *Denn kein anderes Wesen wirklich ist mehr zu bejammern / Als der Mensch von allem, was atmet und kriecht auf der Erde.* If toward the end of his life Gustav Mahler had read or heard these lines we would doubtless have had yet another glorious song-symphony *von der Erde.*

Mortals mourned by immortal horses. Do we—with our canned horsemeat and saccharine religions—have any hope of hearing or reading these lines? So much of *The Iliad* is explicitly devoted to the initiation of mortals into their mortality, initiations from the horse's mouth or from a fellow human's. In case Aeneas fails to notice the teeth and skulls cracked by bronze spear-tips, the eyeballs rolling in the dust like forlorn marbles, the brains oozing up the implanted shaft of spear like a runaway fungus, Meriones informs him, "You too are born mortal," θνητὸς δε νυ καὶ σὺ τέτυξαι (16, 622). And poor Hippotheos, whatever his nominal relation to horses and gods, serves as perhaps the first exemplar of what Heidegger will call the *unbezüglichen* or "non-relational" character of death: "For soon enough there rushed upon him the misfortune from which no one could rescue him, however much he may have

desired it" (17, 291–92). Or Hektor's existential-ontological farewell to Andro-
mache: "No mortal, whether noble or common, ever outruns μοῖσα, from the
moment he or she comes to be" (6, 448–49). Or, finally, Odysseus' cheerful
good-bye to his Phaeacian hostess, Queen Arete: "Fare thee well—until the
days of dotage and death which are the human lot" (*Odyssey, 13*, 59–60).

Yet the most humane of these mortal initiations comes once again from
Achilles' deathless steeds. It flows not only from their mouths but also from
their hearts and eyes. Motionless with mourning (ἑσταότες πενθείετον), they
stand troubled of heart, *bekümmert im Herzen,* ἀχνυμένω κῆρ (*Iliad, 23*, 283–
84). That is precisely the phrase used to describe Achilles' grief over Agamemnon's seizure of his prized Briseïs (*19, 57*); or the mourning of the men who lay
Patroklos' corpse on the pyre (*23, 165*); or the terror of the goatherd
Melanthios when the sowherd Eumaios strings him up to the rafters (*Odyssey,
22, 118*). More than "troubled," we must say, in each case; more like "profoundly anxious." *Bekümmerung* is a kind of being stunned, *gebannt,* or
dazed, *benommen,* by the most frightful of κῆρες. Yet if we so much as mention *Bannung* and *Benommenheit,* we are thrust back (or well forward) to the
fundamental concepts of metaphysics as Heidegger conceives of them in his
1929–1930 lecture course.

MOURNING BECOMES LIFE

Life, just-plain-life, Heidegger seems to suggest in *Being and Time,* is Dasein
deprived of care, *Sorge.* He should not have implied that, and he knew it,
inasmuch as the relation of an antecedent fundamental ontology of Dasein to
an ontology of life cannot be expressed in terms of addition, subtraction, or
privation. His enmity toward "philosophy of life" and his promulgation of a
"philosophy of existence" in an effort to escape from the blind alley of the
former must be understood as anxiety in the face of its problem: how to
prevent two millennia of heady philosophy from relegating human beings to a
life lived solely above the eyebrow line. In the face of this problem, intensified
by the neo-Kantian and positivist obsessions with epistemology and rigorous
science, Heidegger too stands there with troubled heart. Whatever the achievements of the fundamental ontology in *Being and Time* may be, they do not ease
this trouble. For if care is the existential-ontological structure of Dasein as
such, then Dasein minus *Sorge* equals, not just-plain-life, but zero. When in
1929–1930 Heidegger once again takes up the question of life by examining
the comparative world-relations or access to beings of stone, animal, and
Dasein, he is, I suspect, oppressed by the sense of his earlier failure to confront
the problems of *Lebensphilosophie.* The quandary will continue to afflict him
throughout his lectures on Nietzsche in the late 1930s. For no recourse to the
categories of body and soul, matter and form, sense and spirit can come to the
aid of existential analysis. If Dasein is some body who is alive, its life will be a
matter of care, time, and death. Yet what of a life-form that is unlike Dasein,

nichtdaseinsmäßiges Leben? The life of a horse, for instance? If deprived of temporally structured care, will horses also be deprived of death?

Of course horses are deathless! Only Dasein dies. Horses merely perish. Well, then, are Achilles' horses deathless because they are immortals or simply because they are animals? Are they gods or dogs? With such questions—as overhasty and as jejune as they may sound—we are perhaps at the very nerve of Western ontotheology. When Heidegger tries to separate Dasein from the animal, or to dig an abyss of essence between them, he causes the whole of his project to collapse back into the congealed categories and oblivious decisions of ontotheology. Yet when he opens up, if only for a brief moment, the "ring of disinhibitions" that links the animal to its limited, impoverished world, opens it up to the possibilities of *time* and *death,* a formidable contingency rises to confront his analysis. It is the chance that may well end all existential analysis and induce a different kind of meditation, a meditation on the trail of the daimonic. A meditation on daimon life would have to follow two sets of traces, to wit, those of overpowering power, *das Übermächtige,* and of the holy, *das Heilige.* These two sets of traces converge in the capacity to mark time and to die. Yet both Homer and Hölderlin would have taught Heidegger that the ability to die also implies the capacity to share a peculiar kind of pain—the capacity to mourn. Readers may think that because I mention mourning I am writing about someone other than Heidegger. I am writing about Heidegger. Pain, mourning, and being able to die: *Schmerz, Trauer und das Sterben-KÖNNEN.* And that means the capacity to be (at times) a horse.

In a moment I shall review those passages in the 1929–1930 lecture course in which the forged ring of animal life, which is the ring of the yoke and halter of ontotheology, cracks and opens. Heidegger himself recognizes the necessity of fissure in the ring, tearing of the halter, and escape of the captive animal. Yet he himself tries to prevent the escape. However, because I will soon lose myself among the trees as I pursue Heidegger's fleeing animal, because I will lose myself among the *Buchstaben* of Heidegger's text; because I will be unable to see the forest, the swift-flowing river, and the pasture; let me state quite baldly, in thesis-form, what I think all this means in the context of Heidegger's long career of thinking.

(1) Even before the mid-1930s Heidegger recognizes the import of Hölderlin's intimation that only as figures of *mourning* can gods become present in a destitute time. However, mourning marks the *mortals,* who sooner attain to the abyss.

(2) Mourning, pain, and joy by the 1950s become something other than fundamental moods or attunements (*Grundstimmungen*) of Da-sein: they become the variable μέλος of language, the singing that sustains the saying of language.

(3) The capacity to mark time and to die are by the 1950s something other than existential structures: they announce the very bestirring (*Regung*) of propriation (*Ereignis*), the agitation or arousal that grants time and being throughout the epochal history of being.

(4) If and when the capacity to mourn abandons thinking; if and when any sort of hope in the rescuing power of history, philosophy, fatherland, emancipatory discourse, or the unending conversation survives; then meditation on τὸ δαιμόνιον will succumb to demonic political power. Not only in 1933 but also in 1993.

(5) Effective against such virulent hopefulness may well be a capacity for mourning that is thoroughly contaminated by a kind of mirth, marred by a peculiar mania, a certain kinky humor. My guess is   *He was a hirsute, wild man*   that such mourning will reflect less sobriety and equanimity than equinimity, horse-sense concerning horseflesh, along with a certain kind of horseplay.

Enough, however, of grand gestures: Monty Python galloping through *The Holy Grail* on coconuts. Let me slow down and examine the principal arguments of the two major parts of Heidegger's 1929–1930 lecture course, published as *The Fundamental Concepts of Metaphysics: World—Finitude—Solitude*. We shall have to follow Heidegger's analysis closely, especially at the point when the ring of disinhibitions (*der Enthemmungsring*), the ring of the animal's access to beings, cracks and opens to time and death.

SLEEP

Heidegger seeks to reawaken metaphysics from its dogmatic slumber and Dasein from its everyday somnolence. The first develops from the deep sleep of the second; the second is the acculturated oblivion of the first. His search *What is this sleep which holds you now?*   takes him into the narrow straits between the Scylla of science (*Wissenschaft*) and the Charybdis of worldview (*Weltanschauung*) on his route toward a mood or attunement that will grant him access to philosophizing as such. "Awakening a fundamental attunement for our philosophizing" becomes the refrain of the 1929–1930 course.

Near the outset Heidegger cites a phrase of Novalis, one that Nietzsche adopted as his own: "Philosophy, properly speaking, is homesickness—*the drive to be at home everywhere.*"[3] Philosophy is homesickness for the homelike, the homey, and the homely; yet it also ventures into the uncanny, its nostalgia interrupted by extramural thinking. *Heimweh, das Heimische, das Unheimliche*—all play a confused and confusing role in *The Fundamental Concepts of Metaphysics: World—Finitude—Solitude,* with the uncanny taking the lead. Finitude and solitude shape the world of Dasein, even if contemporary man seems to have banished all homesickness, seeing to it that he is comfortably lodged everywhere. No surprises. Contemporary man? By that Heidegger means the "man of the city and the ape of civilization" (29/30, 7), or "the animal" who is "the fool of civilization" (9). Ape, fool, animal, and man are jumbled or elided in the polemics that open Heidegger's lecture course, somewhat as in Kafka's "A Report to an Academy." The ape will return to Heidegger's university two decades later as the animal that has prehensile organs but no hands (WhD? 51; Ps, 428). For the moment, it appears as the risible caricature of *homo sapiens sapiens,* as in the early texts of Bataille or the shrill "Trinklied vom Jammer der Erde" in Mahler's *Das Lied von der Erde:*

> *Seht dort hinab! Im Mondschein auf den Gräbern*
> *hockt eine wild-gespenstische Gestalt.*
> *Ein Aff ist's! Hört ihr, wie sein Heulen*
> *hinausgeht in den süßen Duft des Lebens!*

> Look below! In the moonlight on the graves
> squats a savage, ghoulish shape.
> It's an ape! Hear its howl
> contaminate the gentle stir of life!

Mahler's frenzied measures conform to the mood of Heidegger's inquiry. While the question remains the same as that posed in Heidegger's reading of Jaspers ten years earlier—What is the human being? *Was ist der Mensch?*—the mood is now one of suspicion and despair. While the doubt remains the same as that entertained in *Being and Time,* namely, whether one can gain access to the phenomenon to be investigated, the rhetoric is now nothing short of sardonic. Poe has given way to Bierce. Can a fundamental attunement or mood be attained? Do we ever gain access to it? And if our philosophizing depends on our immersion in a fundamental, founding mood, does such immersion promise anything like transparency? How can we know whether we are at home, whether we are truly *there* in there-being? Even regular attendance at Heidegger's lectures will not necessarily help the young men and women of the university who wish to philosophize: whether they attend those lectures or pass right on by them is something that will not even be noticed—it will change nothing.

> What is uncanny is the fact that we do not notice it, that we will never notice the difference; nothing else will happen to us, whether or not we pass it by; we could wander through the halls of the university and make trenchant observations every bit as well as those who do attend philosophy courses and maybe even quote Heidegger. If we don't pass on by, but attend the lectures, is the ambiguity dissolved? Does anything appear to have changed? Don't they all just sit there, equally attentive or equally bored? Are we better than our neighbors because we catch on more quickly, or are we only more clever and more glib; perhaps we've had a few seminars in philosophy and are foxier than the others about the philosophical terminology? And yet, in spite of all that, maybe what is essential is missing in us: perhaps someone else—it might even be some young woman who is now studying at the university [*und sei es auch nur eine Studentin*]—has got it? (29/30, 18)

And her professor? Is he the dispenser of wisdom or the clown? And wouldn't he be the last to know which? All he can be sure of is that he has abandoned his solitude and is now "on the market."

Heidegger repeatedly denies that he is engaged in cultural criticism—*Kulturdiagnostik* (112). Yet the sardonic rhetoric does not abate. It culminates in the language of sortie and attack: one who genuinely philosophizes, that is, one who occupies the site of Da-sein, is engaged in battle with his contemporaries (31: *Angriff auf den Menschen*). The rhetoric, as we shall see in chapter 5, is "hard and heavy," and its polemic is aimed at "awakening an actual, living [*lebendigen*] philosophizing" (87).

What, then, are life and the living? Above all, what is the dogmatic slumber that is everyday life and that needs something more ammoniac than Hume to rouse it? How does one cause a sleepyhead to stir? Or must one *let* the sleeper come round? Moods or attunements cannot be forced, nor ever forcibly altered: only another mood can budge the one we happen to be in, Heidegger says in *Being and Time*. Here (29/30, 89) he emphasizes that one can only let attunement be. Alongside the rhetoric of attack we hear the language of *Gelassenheit* (92; 137). Such language testifies to the fact that in sleep human beings are inevitably bound up with the animal, vegetable, and mineral worlds. Already here, in the question of slumber and somnolence (93–94), those regions of being which by metonymy or synonymy we call *stone, animal,* and *man* come to the fore. Even the essential animatedness (*Bewegtheit*) of existence is mimicked (albeit negatively) in sleep: Aristotle's little treatise on sleep and dreams characterizes sleep as ἀκινησία, immobility.[4] Heidegger will interpret such immobility—the stony sleep that only a bestial Second Coming could vex to nightmare, if not to wakefulness—as a kind of absence or abandonment; both here and in the 1936–1938 *Contributions to Philosophy* he will meditate on "being-there" as "being-gone," *Da-sein* as *Weg-sein*. (See chapter 6, below.)

If Heidegger is not diagnosing his culture, he certainly is not psychologizing about "feelings." These third-class citizens of the philosophic body-politic hold no interest for him (97). Rather, "mood" and "attunement" are taken as modes of *Befindlichkeit*, the primary disclosure that constitutes the *Da-* of Dasein. Heidegger is particularly chary of finding himself in the sleazy company of Oswald Spengler and Ludwig Klages, those paragons of the philosophic feelies. These "philosophers of life" accuse spirit (*Geist*) of having slain both soul and life (105), and their soulful advocacy of life is usually mired in an obfuscating stew and brew of pulsions and drives (*des dunkelnden Brodelns der Triebe*). Heidegger's rhetoric is familiar: it reminds us of his ridicule of Schopenhauer and Wagner, as of Klages and life-philosophy generally, in the Nietzsche lectures of the late 1930s. Indeed, these pages of the first major part of the 1929–1930 lectures (107–11) serve as an excellent introduction to the lectures of 1936–1940; they justify Otto Pöggeler's claim that from 1929 onward Heidegger's thought comes under the spell of Nietzsche.[5] Life-philosophy misinterprets Nietzsche by celebrating Dionysos while neglecting Apollo. Yet such misinterpretation is partly Nietzsche's fault. Even though his brilliance and originality imply that he can withstand the vulgarizations of life-philosophy, that his rigor can "afford" them, as it were, Heidegger does not doubt that Nietzsche's philosophy rests on "a truly vulgar and metaphysically highly dubious 'psychology' " (111).

The accusation of vulgarity and the reference to the bubbly cauldron of life-philosophy might induce us to ask a question, a question we shall have to revive in our later discussions of politics. Whereas Heidegger eschews the facile opposites of "the rational" and "the irrational," his opponents down to the present day invariably accuse him of the latter, never the former: Heidegger is "dangerously irrational." I wonder whether things are in fact quite different from what Jürgen Habermas, for example, supposes. Do the polemics, the attack, and the "hard and heavy" in Heidegger's rhetoric derive from his embrace of irrationalism? Or, on the contrary, is it not his anxiety in the face of the "irrational" life-philosophical readings of Nietzsche, his recoiling from what every enlightened Heidegger-critic supposes Heidegger is tending toward, that is bound up with his militancy and aggression? Is not Heidegger himself an unlikely knight of the pre-Rousseauian, pre-Sadean Enlightenment? Is it not odd that Habermas urges Heideggerians to resist uncritical absorption in worldviews and "unscientific" diagnoses of contemporary culture? Is it not odd—because Heidegger spent the first fifteen years of his career urging his students to resist the very same blandishments by the very same means. Oddest of all is the blithe confidence of critics nowadays that whereas Heidegger failed catastrophically to purge himself of worldviews our enlightened contemporaries will now prevail. If it is not Heidegger's irrationalism but his persistent recoil in the direction of the all-too-rational that spawns his militancy and militarism, his nationalism and decisionism, his sardonic rhetoric of attack and desperate *Gelassenheit*, then matters of enlightenment—awakening from dogmatic slumber—may be more unstoppably dialectical, which is to say, more full of recoil, than we ever imagined.[6]

Heidegger now focuses on the very despair and indifference (*Gleichgültig-keit*) that he senses to be the fundamental mood of his times. No, that is not quite right: indifference pervades all, but it has not yet become a founding mode or mood of our existence. We are anesthetized against our own lack of feeling for being. We are not on Mann's *Magic Mountain* but at Eliot's *Cocktail Party*. The reflexivity that once enlivened cogitation now dulls its wits, ". . . because we ourselves have become *bored* with ourselves [*weil wir selbst, uns selbst*, langweilig *geworden sind*]" (115; cf. 241–42). It is a reflexivity reminiscent of the opening sentence of the preface to Nietzsche's *On the Genealogy of Morals* (1887): "We are unknown to ourselves, we knowers, we ourselves to ourselves [*wir selbst uns selbst*]: there is a good reason for that" (KSA 5, 247). Indeed, it may be that the reminiscence of Nietzsche here is essential: if Heidegger's analysis of boredom is not *Kulturdiagnostik* it is certainly not phenomenology either. Nor is it fundamental ontology. It is closer to genealogy than to anything else. Heidegger scorns both "cultural chit-chat" and "psychological snooping": neither the *weitläufige Kulturgerede* of the George-Circle nor the *Beschnüffelung des Seelischen* of psychoanalysis will serve his kind of genealogical critique (116). Yet what *are* those nineteen tortuous sections of *The Fundamental Concepts of Metaphysics* that treat of profound boredom?[7]

Heidegger begins by associating *Lange-weile* in the Alemannic dialect to what in High German is *Heimweh*, homesickness or nostalgia (120). Profound boredom will thus provide access to the theme of the uncanny in Heidegger's thought, the bizarre conflation of *heimlich* and *un-heimlich* that Freud (taking his cue from Schelling) noted in 1919 (StA 4, 248–50). The unhomelike home of Da-sein is of course what phenomenology calls *world*. Profound boredom is therefore not a mood that "replaces" anxiety in Heidegger's thought; if it occupies the site of anxiety at all it is only in order to conduct Dasein to the identical disclosure. Whether earnestly anxious or bored silly, Dasein is not at home, is ill-at-ease in its world: *es ist einem unheimlich*. Dasein is restive whether being as a whole slips away from it in anxiety or is swathed in the drifting fog of boredom. The quality of the as-a-whole indicates the *horizonal* character of boredom, its way of disclosing the world. Further, the *Weile* of the long while points uncannily to the temporality of the horizonal world (29/30, 130). Even the day-to-day time of diurnal rotation, the clock time of solar nature, is affected by profound boredom: Heidegger notes the uncanny regularity of time, "rolling off like the steady pulsebeat of an impalpable monster" (174), the pulsebeat of Hans Castorp's fantastic Milky Way Monster, the moving image of eternity, which we shall confront in chapter 6. Dasein finds itself captivated by time, held out and suspended in it. *Hingehaltenheit,* itself reminiscent of the *Hinausgehaltenheit in das Nichts* that characterizes anxiety, will soon (149–50) provide a bridge to the second part of the course: if human comportment is *Verhalten,* its "hold" on the world will decisively distinguish it from animal behavior; for *Benehmen* and *Benommenheit* will have as their corollary *Hingenommenheit,* by which animals are "swept away" or "taken in" by their world. *Hingehaltenheit* and *Hingenommenheit,* being held out in the world and being taken in by it, will be the two rims of the abyss that cuts through the ostensibly unified realm of essence and field of φύσις, with humans on one side and animals on the other.

However, the world that holds Dasein in its spell is uncanny. It is a ghost town. Heidegger speaks of a *Hingehaltensein im Leergelassenwerden,* a being held in vacuity, a being abandoned to an emptiness we cannot fill (158). We are held captive, we brave beholders; we are held spellbound in the world of time; we are not so much banished in such captivity as kept under house arrest in the closed spaces of time, inasmuch as there is no other place for us to go but death (170). Once again Heidegger insists that even though he is drumming his fingers on a bone china plate, hoping that the dinner party will not drag on into the night, his descriptions of abandonment and vacuity are not meant as social criticism: rather, boredom *wächst aus der Tiefe* (177), is profound, *de profundis.* In such moments of profound boredom we are abandoned to and held by a determinate emptiness; as we glide away (*weg*) from ourselves we arrive at the "there" of our being, even if, to repeat, when we finally get there there isn't any there there.

It is remarkable that the time of profound boredom is no longer analyzed in terms of *ecstatic temporality.* The only temporal horizon that remains is that of mood or attunement, the finding-oneself-to-be-bored. Thus the sequence of repetitions of the analysis of factical existence and everyday life in the direction of ecstatic temporality—repetitions that began long before *Being and Time* and pervaded that work from its outset—here dwindle to a standstill. It is difficult to know why, but we can be certain that it has to do with "the difficult problem of death." It is as though the existential oxymoron, *wiederholbar-unüberholbar,* the repeatable-impassable, here falls asunder. Yet the irony is that the repeatable-impassable pertains to the ecstasy of having-been, the existential structure of *Befindlichkeit,* to which profound boredom precisely belongs. Should not profound boredom display the horizonal structure, the "ecstematic horizon," of *Gewesenheit* or having-been?[8]

What sorts of beings display themselves on the horizon of profound boredom? At first blush, none at all, inasmuch as everything is muffled and we are left in a vacuum. However, profound boredom is also "telling boredom." It speaks to us of our having been abandoned and left homeless by the very plenipotence of being as a whole, the overpowering character of a life that is subjected to time. Heidegger uses the daimonic words *Übermacht* and *Über-mächtigkeit* to describe such "telling" boredom (205). What does boredom tell us? What does it say? It says that we are bound to be banned. In time, by time, for all time. It says that our being in time is a *Gebanntsein* (218ff.). We are both bound at home in time and banished outside the walls by it; we are both initiated into it and ostracized from it; perfectly accustomed to it and utterly spellbound by it; bonded by, bounded within, banished and banned from it: we are *gebannt,* and the banns of our marriage to time foretell eventual estrangement and divorce. Such is the uncanny release (*Freigeben*) granted by the horizon of all disclosure, the Da- of Dasein, the freedom of existence (223). It transpires in the blink of an eye, as *der Augenblick,* presumably the instant after the blink has yielded to the *Blick,* that is, to an opening onto the world. It transpires as the instant of opened resoluteness toward the world and our being in the world, the instant that reveals the *proper* mode of our existence.

By this time it has become clear that the 1929–1930 lectures invert the order of the two major divisions of *Being and Time.* In the lecture course Heidegger begins with an analysis of the "long while" of boredom, that is to say, with a temporal (albeit not ecstatic) analysis of the appropriate attunement of existence—as in Division II of *Being and Time.* Only then does he pursue the question of the worldliness or worldhood of the being in question—as in the preparatory analysis of Division I of his magnum opus. However, the propriety of appropriate attunement here has effects that differ markedly from those of the second division of *Being and Time.* In 1929–1930 the rhetoric of appropriateness, "authenticity," and resolute openedness is transformed (in spite of Heidegger's own stated intentions) into a diagnosis of contemporary culture—admittedly, against the backdrop of what will soon be called *Seinsgeschichte,* "the history of being." Profound boredom reveals the need and calamity (*die Not*) of our time, which will soon prove to be the need and calamity of being. If our existence, drumming its fingers on dinner plates, is bored out of its mind because it lacks essential thrust (*Bedrängnis*); if every such impetus is in default (*Ausbleiben*); then the words just uttered will soon become words for being in the epoch of nihilism, in which being, effectively banished, comes to nothing.

Not that crises are lacking. "Everywhere we find shattering events [*Erschütter-ungen*], crises, catastrophes, emergencies: the contemporary social plight, politi-cal mayhem, the impotence of science, disemboweled art, the groundlessness of philosophy, the ennervation of religion" (243). While crises abound, compla-cency alone rises to meet them. Needlessness, heedlessness. That is the real spiritual, intellectual, cultural crisis, and news of it pervades Heidegger's dis-course of 1929–1930 as it does that of so many European discourses of the era on "spirit."9

If we attend Eliot's *Cocktail Party*, we do so as the hollow men, whose heads are filled with straw. If we drum our fingers, we also whimper. We lack a sense of mystery (*Geheimnis*). We are not tempered by the inner terror or fright (*innere Schrecken*) that lends Dasein its greatness. We are abysmally content, we run no risks, court no dangers. Our existence is flaccid and neurasthenic; it lacks *Kraft und Macht*. We never dare to occupy the outermost point of the moment of time, *die Spitze*. The hard, the heavy, and the sharp—these virtues of the arena   *They snorted like bulls locked together*   are foreign to us.

Thus ends the first major part of Heidegger's effort to reawaken the mood that will support genuine metaphysical inquiry. Later, in chapter 5, we will have occasion to reflect on its shrill rhetoric, the hard and heavy language of "shattering." For the moment, we must follow Heidegger as he makes the transition to (animal) life and its (impoverished) world.

WORLD POVERTY

As we have seen, the vacuity of contemporary existence, steeped in profound boredom, betrays an emptiness in being as a whole. It exposes a hollowness in what phenomenology has long called *Welt*. What is world? With that question we cross the bridge to the second major division of the course. Heidegger's focus here will be the *world* of Dasein in its *finitude* and *solitude* (251). If in *Being and Time* the path to finitude leads its readers through an analysis of individualizing anxiety and a being toward death that is in each case mine; and if in *Kant and the Problem of Metaphysics* it leads them through an analysis of sensation and intuition in the first *Critique,* in which *Empfindung* and *Anschauung* point to a finitude that is "older" than man; then in 1929–1930 the analysis of profound boredom is meant to lead us to the finitude and individuation of Dasein in its solitary world. To be sure, the course never gets beyond the initial question of *world*. Nevertheless, it is to the "comparative analysis" of the worlds and world-relations of stone, animal, and Dasein, which occupies sections 42 to 63 of the course, to which we must now turn.10

Heidegger seeks a third way to pose the "world question." The first way was the preparatory analysis of the "phenomenon of world" in the first divi-sion of *Being and Time,* an analysis of the referential totality of significance in quotidian existence, the world of our concerns. The second was the history of the word κόσμος and the concept *mundus*, the inquiry carried out in *On the*

Essence of Ground (1929). The third will involve a fundamental duplicity, the dual or double position occupied by human beings in the world: man *has* a world, but is also a *piece* of the world; man is both "master and slave of the world" (262). Heidegger's third way reminds us repeatedly of Merleau-Ponty's attempt to define the reversible flesh of the world—the element with respect to which existence is never wholly free yet never entirely subservient.[11]

The third way is one of "comparative observation" (263). If its point of departure is the question of man as a "piece" of the very world he "has," the route itself is three-pronged, in pursuit of three "theses":

(1) The stone (a metonymy for the material, mineral world) is worldless; that is, it is *without* world; the stone is straightforwardly *weltlos*.

(2) The animal (ostensibly, no metonymy here, inasmuch as "the animal" *means* animality as such) is poor in world; that is, animal life is characterized by a certain world poverty, *Weltarmut*.

(3) Human beings (again, putatively, no metonymy) shape, inform, or constitute their world: *Der Mensch ist weltbildend*.

The third way (not merely the third *thesis*) seems more promising than the two earlier ways, because it appears to offer greater mobility (*Beweglichkeit*) to the analysis. Yet in these matters every advantage entails a cost: if life is animatedness (*Bewegtheit*), then the mobility of the analysis will be mimetic of its object but will also skew the analysis by a kind of sympathetic bias or prejudice. Heidegger is not sanguine about the possibilities of the third way: the likelihood of attaining access is balanced by the equal likelihood of colliding against fundamental aporias. Indeed, he stresses the "special difficulties" that plague the third way. We may be able to name these difficulties, says Heidegger, but we cannot set them aside (264).

Heidegger begins not with metonymic stones but with the presumably essential distinction between human beings and animals in the sphere of what we call, vaguely enough, *life*. His inquiry is not intended to solve any puzzles about evolution or the origin of species: the ape reappears for an instant, but is soon banished (264). Rather, the object of the inquiry is "the essence of the animality of the animal and the essence of the humanity of man," and beyond both, the essence of the vitality of what is alive, *die Lebendigkeit des Lebenden* (265). Heidegger does not yet attempt the sleight-of-hand that will soon accompany his every reference to "essence": he does not here insist that *Wesen* is to be taken verbally, and his insistence that his assertions are not zoological findings but "assertions of essence" (275) only confirms his bold essentialism. The classical metaphysical appeal to essences is reinforced when Heidegger asserts that his *Wesensaussagen* touch on universality; they are not assertions of essence because they are universal; rather, they are universal because they are assertions of essence. Derrida is surely right when throughout the sixth chapter of *De l'esprit* he ties a knot with these two Heideggerian threads, first, the abyss of essence that separates the dumb animal from the questioning human being, and second, the protection of essences (such as *animality* and *humanity*) from contamination by lower echelons of beings. If technology is nothing technical, animality is nothing zoological, and humanity nothing humanistic. The fundamental concepts of metaphysics and fundamental ontology pertain to the order of essences.

Yet however classic the metaphysical gesture here, Heidegger does manage to identify the methodological quandary of his third way: as in the fundamental ontology of Dasein, the problem here too is one of accessibility (*Zugänglichkeit*). Do we have access to the essence of animality? "Or is there no original access here at all?" (266). Clearly, as we head out on our brave third way, we are caught up in circles: the circle of zoology and its always presupposed determination of life; the circle whose center is ἄνθρωπος, a center that is everywhere; the circle of essences and the realms that such essences presumably encompass and define, the oldest of Parmenidean circles. These are the very circles of philosophy. Circling in them makes us ill-at-ease; we feel uncanny in them; and, as Hegel well knew, they make us dizzy. Nevertheless, to dream of stepping outside them is to abdicate; it is to confirm that one is indeed asleep.

The quest for the essence of animality seeks what all zoology presupposes. What in the "Introduction" I called *za-ology*, the quest for the essence of animality and of life in emphatic disclosure, is neither altogether independent of the science of zoology nor simply a part of it. Heidegger does not scorn zoology or any other science. He realizes that without the discourses of the sciences he has nothing to say about beings. He therefore speaks of an *orientation toward* biological science that lacks a grounding *within* that science. The circle doubtless seems increasingly vicious. Heidegger senses that he is moving about its periphery, only occasionally stealing a glance toward the center: "The center, that is, the midpoint and ground, is revealed as the center only in and for a circling about the center" (276). He is unwilling to admit that all talk of "the center" can only be an anthropocentrism or, at best, an *existential* centrism. Nine years later, in his Nietzsche lectures, he will more freely concede that the circle of human existence is not something we can simply doff, in order then to see things more "objectively." Nor does he in 1930 even suspect that moving about the periphery could lead him off on a tangent, so that he would never know in which direction the orienting center lay. Nor, finally, does he recollect Schelling's and Kant's definition of the peripheral as physical and moral evil. He does acknowledge circularity as the unfailing sign of metaphysical *thesis*, and he does spurn the putative linear or zigzag progress of *dialectic* as "the expression of an *embarras*" (276).

After the Christmas break of 1929–1930 Heidegger offers his students a summary of what went before and a transition toward what is to come. Yet the summary—ostensibly on the "founding mood" of profound boredom—introduces a new element into the discussion. Creative philosophizing is now defined as that which takes on a burden or weight, a kind of ballast, providing a center of gravity that not only oppresses but also steadies and stabilizes. The burden weighs heavily on our "heart of hearts"; it is a burden *"an der der Mensch* schwer *trägt im* Gemüt." From the words for heavy and the heart's core (*schwer, Gemüt, zumute*) Heidegger derives the fundamental

metaphysical attunement of "melancholy," *Schwermut*. He cites a fragment of
Aristotle which, referring to Empedocles, Socrates, and Plato (as though Aristotle were as certain of the melancholy of the last two as he is of the first),
wonders aloud why all who achieve merit in philosophy, politics, poetry, or
art appear to have been μελαγχολικοί. However, Heidegger's summary is not
simply a mistake. For "melancholy" is the only possible bridge between the
fundamental attunement of profound boredom and the comparative analysis
of world-relations. On the very last page of his analysis of life, Heidegger will
invoke something very much like melancholy as a universal attribute of living
beings.[12] For the moment, it is clear that *Schwermut* occupies the site of the
fundamental metaphysical attunement. Heidegger resists every temptation to
treat melancholy as an object of depth psychology or as an illness to be
treated. Psychotherapy wishes to eliminate the fundamental attunement of
philosophizing in our time and thus proves to be "the innermost corruptor of
our age" (272).[13]

Heidegger begins (again) *in medias res*. Not with stones or Dasein but, as
we have already indicated, with the world-relation of the animal. Yet he knows
that his inquiry will inevitably be cockeyed, that he will have to keep one eye
on both the inanimate world and the world of Dasein as he studies the world of
the animal. He applauds efforts in the biological science of his time, led by
Jacob Johann von Uexküll and F.J.J. Buytendijk, to resist the total absorption of
life-phenomena by the sciences of physics and chemistry. However, while resisting scientistic mechanism and positivism, Heidegger is careful to abjure vitalism and spiritualism. He makes a point of exposing what he takes to be Max
Scheler's "fundamental error," namely, his all-too-traditional identification of
"man" as the "specifically spiritual" synthesis of all the lower links in the chain
of being—mineral, vegetable, and animal. Heidegger wishes to avoid all such
Leibnizian hierarchies. Yet the means by which he thinks he can do so are
bizarre. He believes he can resist Scheler's divine afflatus by indicating that the
human being can "sink below the level of an animal," that the human being is
eminently corruptible, as though corruptibility and The Fall were not the linch-
pins in the hierarchical structure that places humanity very near the top, immediately below the flawless Father and the only slightly tainted angels. Nevertheless, Heidegger does sense that there are traps   *he was struck dumb,*
benumbed with terror   on all sides: "All this is questionable even as a
question" (287). He rejects all talk of "lower" and "higher" animals, for
example, amoebas and apes. Yet he does not pause to wonder whether his own
highest aspiration, his search for the *essence* of animality and all life in each
amoeba and every ape, is the kind of high-altitude thinking that spawns all the
other hierarchies. Abjuring the "lower," he nevertheless does not hesitate to
introduce "poverty" and "deprivation," *Armut* as *Entbehren*. He defines the
poverty of the animal world in terms of deprivation without for the moment
wondering whether all talk of deprivation does not reinstate all the hierarchies
he would have wanted to dismantle.

Perhaps the most intriguing aspect of his attempt, which is doomed to fail, derives from a simple linguistic homology. Poverty, *Armut,* points to the *Gemüt* that should replace *Geist* as the object of ontological analysis. Recall that Heidegger sketches the project of a deconstruction of the history of ontology on the guidelines of an analysis of "*Gemüt*" (SZ, 25); and recall also Derrida's discussion of this word that *almost* manages to avoid "spirit" (De, 41/21). The analysis of *Gemüt* would have to touch on the *Schwermut* or melancholy that founds philosophizing. Yet the linguistic knot, *Mut,* is not really very encouraging. At the precise moment (288) when it appears to bring together the worlds of animal and man, measuring them on a scale of relative deprivation, an oxymoron rises to shatter the homology. Heidegger asks whether the princely animal "kingdom" can be peopled by "paupers," whether the *Tierreich* can really be *arm.* The juxtaposition of rich and poor can hardly give us courage. Especially when we realize that the original sense of *Mut* is not courage but desire, craving, and striving, which the Greeks called ὀργή and which as often as not has been attributed to the "animal" portion of the human composite.

Weltarm and *weltlos,* world poverty and worldlessness, are alike forms of *not* having a world. Worldlessness is not even a deprivation of world, however, but is a simple absence of it. Thus in his 1936–1938 *Contributions to Philosophy (Of Propriation)*, as we shall see, Heidegger will seek to exclude the stone from all discussion. In 1929–1930, as I have indicated, he emphasizes the meaning of world as "accessibility" to the beings in one's surroundings. The stone has no access to the earth on which it lies: if we toss it into a flooded ditch at the side of the road it will sink into the mire and stay there. The muck will open and part for it but will not be open to it or become a part of it. Yet even here a curious kind of reflexivity marks *Zugang,* a reflexivity of which Hegel would have made much. Access is what opens a being to world, but it is also what the interpreter of world-relations is seeking. We interpreters are searching for access to the world to which other kinds of living beings have access. The world is inaccessible to the stone, and yet the stone seems accessible to interpretation. Heidegger can declare that the stone is marked by *Zugangslosigkeit,* and no hylozoism will rise to complicate his sense of "accessibility." There are moments when for the sake of an endangered species of interpretation he dispenses with his critique of modernity: Galileo and Descartes may initiate the epoch of subjectivity and calculative thinking, but at least they know that matter is extended, the moon pockmarked, and rocks lifeless. Stone has no access to world, and therefore the interpreter-Dasein has easy access to it. Lizards, however, are more recalcitrant.

Heidegger tries to enter into the animal's world. He tries to spell out the difference between the ways lizards and human beings sun themselves. If horses have the edge over Heidegger in questions of ethics, lizards certainly carry the day when it comes to sunbathing. The animal cannot ask about the sun *as* sun, Heidegger repeats over and over again, as though this is what the human sun-worshipper ever does. The animal is incapable of *Nachfragen* (291). Thus the priority of questioning is retained and tied to the issue of world-access. Because the interpreter can ask about the world-relation of the lizard, there must be a way in which the lizard's failure to ask questions can inform and confirm the interpretation: the reflexivity of "access" will guarantee both the deprivation of the lizard interloper and the privilege of the lingering, supine interpreter. Or at least it will *seem to* guarantee these things. The problem is whether and how an interpreter can speak of lizardthings (*Eidechsendinge*) without arrogating to himself or herself an empathy that is ontologically unjustified and psychologically naive and embarrassing. Alternatively, the interpreter of animal worlds must cross out (*durchstreichen*) not only the apophantic and metaphysical *as* but also the words "sun" and "stone" and every other word of language.

Derrida envisages a perverse reading of Heidegger by which one would follow to the letter Heidegger's instructions concerning such crossings out, as though a mechanical rat (I picture it as the turbo-mouse of a word processor, and we will meet it in chapter 8, below) gnawed its way through all the forbidden words the interpreter used (illicitly) to name the animal world: there would of course not be a single word left in the text that treats of the animal world; the turbo-mouse would devour the "ell" that distinguishes *world* from *word,* and the animal wor(l)d would grow as dark as it is silent. Delete ell, delete all. But to return to Heidegger's less perverse, or perhaps less consistent, reading of the animal wor(l)d.

To be sure, *some* sort of "givenness" is there when the lizard suns itself on the rock. Yet nothing is given the lizard *as such.* (No pun on "nothing" intended.) The lizard is not the Lizard King; it cannot do anything. It cannot even enjoy lizardthings. At least, it cannot enjoy metaphysics. At least, that is what those who *can* do metaphysics will always have said of the lizard, which, for its part, is ominously silent.

Heidegger is doubtless unsatisfied with the know-nothing quietism of such an interpretation. Appealing to the range of empirical, ontic information he has at his disposal, thanks to the research of Uexküll and Buytendijk, he asserts that the animal has particular relations—if not with "world" or "environment" as such—with three regions of beings, to wit, "its nourishment and prey, its enemies, and its sex partner" (292). Soon those three regions will be reduced to one, the single relation of "Begone!" (*Weg!*), but for the moment the regions are three. What Heidegger here ignores, however, is the metaphysical commitment that such empirical information already embraces. Is it simply an accident that Heidegger's analyses in what follows mirror to an uncanny degree those of (one of) the last metaphysician(s) of the West? What is the relation of empirical learning and metaphysical lore in Hegel's account of "the animal organism" in the "Philosophy of Nature," the second part of his *Encyclopedia of Philosophical Sciences,* §§350–76? What in the history of being organizes the structures of Hegel's treatment of morphology (§§353–56), assimilation (§§357–66), and the mating-process (§§367–76)? What propels its three-stage dialectic inexorably in the direction of a philosophy of spirit, which is the Phoenix-fire of which nature is but the ashes? Is there anything at all in Heidegger's 1929–1930 course that inaugurates or broaches in any way a deconstruction of the

Hegelian heritage? Has Heidegger thought through those two final sections on the mating process, which treat of "The Illness of the Individual" and "The Death of the Individual from within Itself [or: on the basis of its self, *aus sich selbst*]"? Heidegger's first hint concerning the world-relation of animals bears a fatal resemblance to that of Hegel. The animal, says Heidegger, remains in its "element," as though in a conduit or narrow confine that cannot either shrink or expand. Every animal dwells in a conduit, a pipe or tube·(*Rohr*), a kind of one-way burrow, whether it crawls through the earth or flies as free as a bird in the open sky. Every animal is a metaphysical mole. Which leaves only one question unanswered—that of the literary space of the burrow.[14]

Both animals and humans *have* a world. Yet animals "have a world in *not having* it." The knotty problem (see *29/30*, 293–94: *die Verknotung des Knotens*) is the relation of the second and third propositions, the warp and woof of world poverty and world formation. Heidegger will try to unravel the difficulty by defining the peculiar deprivation (*Entbehren*) of the animal's world, the wretchedness, poverty, or squalor (*Armut*) of that world. Yet the literary space of world poverty rises to haunt him from the start. If he deliberately allows full play to the oxymoron of *Tierreich* and *Armut*, wealth and poverty in the animal kingdom, he nonetheless conceals something about "poverty" in *unserer Sprache*. The adjective *arm*, "poor," is etymologically tied to *Erbe*, "inheritance, legacy, descent," and is itself a descendent of *orbus* and ὀρφανός, "orphaned, abandoned, wretched." As the locutions "poor soul, poor devil, miserable sinner" suggest, the original sense is not squalor and deprivation, not the opposite of *reich*, but *beklagenswert, unglücklich:* unfortunate, miserable, wretchedly lamentable. Indeed, the first word Hermann Paul's *Deutsches Wörterbuch* lists as its "fundamental meaning" (*Grundbedeutung*) is *vereinsamt*, "abandoned or stranded in solitude and loneliness." For Heidegger to ignore the *Grundbedeutung* of poverty (*Vereinsamung*) in the lecture course that elaborates the *Grundbegriffe* of metaphysics, the final fundamental concept being either *Einsamkeit* or *Vereinzelung*, is nothing short of bizarre. If the animal's essential relation to world is one of *Armut*, then the animal partakes in at least two of the fundamental concepts of the metaphysics it never enjoys. The animal has a *world* in not having it, and is abandoned to its absolute *solitude* even as it loses itself for the sake of its species. Which leaves only *finitude* for humanity alone.

Or does the finitude of Dasein leave the animal altogether untouched? Are animals deathless? Does their perishing make them infinite? Or does the nothing invade animal life as well as the life of Dasein? Are world, finitude, and solitude essentially beyond the sharp distinction interpreters make between human beings and other species of life? Are dog and god, viewed metaphysically, or ultrametaphysically, the primordial reversible? With Dasein in the middle, precisely where the human being has always located itself, but now with no chance of escape? And is this being in-between (for example, in-between birth and death) something shared by god, dog, and Da-, something one might call *daimon life*? These are some of the questions that may be haunting Heidegger as he turns to world poverty—to the wretched of the earth—and to the essence of animality in the *living organism*.

THE BEING OF BEEING

The nothing invades animal life even if the animal, like the human, knows nothing of it. That is the insight that will touch Heidegger's analysis to the quick. It will eventually be a matter of touchstones, of testing stones and tombstones—what Heidegger had earlier called "the difficult problem of death" (24, 387). Let us move faster but more systematically now, reporting briefly on each section of Heidegger's analysis of the animal world.

In section 49 he poses the question of a possible "transposition" of Dasein to the respective worlds of stone, animal, and fellow human beings. He rejects the model or method of empathy, so influential in phenomenologies of intersubjectivity, and acknowledges the peculiar difficulty of any transposition to the world of the animal. Can one "go along with" the animal as it "goes about" its living and "goes toward" the beings to which it has something like access? *Mitgang mit dem Zugang und Umgang des Tieres*—is such fellow-traveling possible for any human interpreter? The euphony and homology of *Mitgang, Zugang, Umgang* ought not to conceal the absolute resistance of the animal world to our penetration. Even so, Heidegger refuses to sidestep the problem by turning directly to the world-relation of human beings, a relation from which one might hope to subtract some trait or other in order to arrive (by privation or de-privation) at the animal world (section 50). He refuses   *but we two shall go forward and fix our eyes on this monster*   because of the by now familiar circle: in order to know what to subtract, we would have to know what the primal and proper (*ureigene*) trait of animality *is*.

Theoretical biology informs us that the animal is an organism. Heidegger accepts the identification of animal as organism but rejects the assumption that organs are tools, items of equipment, or machines (section 51). In his zeal to overcome the mechanistic reduction of organisms to sheer automata (in the tradition that extends from Descartes, through LaMettrie, to Wilhelm Roux), Heidegger swings to the opposite extreme: he declares that organs are "capacities for" particular functions, and it is the capacity itself (*die Fähigkeit für . . .*) that equips itself with or cultivates or somehow engenders an organ (section 52).[15]

Heidegger's blatant appeal to entelechy—his Platonico-Leibnizo-Lamarckian strain—becomes somewhat less overt and considerably more convincing in section 53. In a surprising move (given his critique of Scheler in this respect), albeit one that follows the path of Uexküll's *Theoretical Biology*, Heidegger turns to the apparently organless protozoa, the one-celled amoeba and infusoria that have only a relatively undifferentiated protoplasm at their disposal. Here protoplasm temporarily assumes the character of mouth, stomach, bowel, and anus by turns. In other words, the cell generates proto-organs out of its "capacities for" ingestion, digestion, and excretion: the disposition elaborates an organ, rather than the other way round. Organs respond to capabilities. They do not dictate behaviors.[16]

Heidegger notes a dual relation to time in such responses. First, the sequence of organic functions engenders an irreversible series of proto-organs. Second, as the sequence generates a fixed series of articulated organs, which in "higher order" animals become specialized and standardized, the life-duration of the organism (as Korschelt had shown) is more narrowly defined. If capacities enumerate organs, organs number the days of a life. In this way, the organs that serve life also serve to make it finite. Thus the series of organs and sequence of capabilities institute a span between birth and death. Heidegger explicitly relates such institution to the world poverty of the animal, as though the human beings who shape their world were suddenly purged of organs and thus rescued from the constraints of time. Ironically, Heidegger's thesis concerning organs and (finite) temporality militates against his desire to counterpose the poverty of animals to the rich culture (*Bildung, weltbildend*) of human beings. Or, to put it the other way round, if the human beings who shape their world are finite, and if they are living beings with specialized organs, then the essential poverty of the animal world impinges on them. If the nothing comes to invade the animal kingdom in the temporalizing sequence of organ formation, it has certainly always been at home among the human paupers   *the old man will wag his head*   with their livers and their lights.

In section 54 Heidegger emphasizes the *driven* character of animal behavior. The animal's capacity to act opens a dimension of being for the organism, even if that dimension cannot be reduced (or elevated) to "consciousness," "the psychic," or "purposefulness." The "dimensional character of the drive [*Trieb*]" is self-regulating; it brings its rules along with it; it is *regelnd, regelmitbringend*. As Merleau-Ponty will later say in *The Structure of Behavior,* the animal is capability-being, acting always according to norms rather than fixed physical laws. Such norms are "without analogy in the physical order" (*Structure,* 161/148). Heidegger argues that the drive is never merely at hand (*vorhanden*) but is always in some sense peripatetic (*unterwegs zu*), even if we are unable to say anything else about *its* ambience or destination than we can about the *thinking* that is perpetually *unterwegs*. The dimension opened by the drive to see, for example, remains inscrutable: we can photograph what the eye of the lightning bug registers as it clings to a windowpane and "looks" through it to the "garden" and the "church tower" in the distance, but what it "sees" we can never know. We may feel certain that it never sees the churches and graveyards that are oriented toward the rising and setting sun on the beeline of east to west, yet we can never penetrate the dimension of the lightning bug's vision. For us it will always be itself that diminutive sun or meteoric moon that shines, little glow-worm, glimmer, glimmer. Lest too far afield we wander.

However, like a glow-worm, but even more like a moth (365), Heidegger in section 56 draws closer and closer to the flame of reflexivity (*sich in sich . . .*)

and selfhood (. . . *selbst*), the flame that has served as the beacon of modern philosophy since Descartes. Not that Heidegger simply succumbs to the anthropomorphic temptation of cogitative philosophy. Yet he truncates the temptation by peremptorily dividing off the animal's "ownness" (*Sich-zu-eigen-sein*) and "peculiarity" (*Eigentümlichkeit*) from the ostensibly human properties of reflection, self-consciousness, and egoistic ipseity. The animal has no personhood, no personality, but is only the "property" (*Eigentum*) of its world-relation. Every classical philosopheme of anthropocentric metaphysics and morals now intervenes with a vengeance in order to drive the interpreter-moth toward the flame of spirit.

Section 57 develops Heidegger's metaphysical Lamarckism (if we may persist in calling it that) most explicitly: "The organ is not provided with capacities; rather, the capacities create organs for themselves [*die Fähigkeiten schaffen sich Organe*]" (341). Animal organization is a "being capable." Heidegger even attributes to the animal one of the ontological traits heretofore reserved for Dasein: the animal's being is a "can be" (342: *sein Sein ist Können*), which "allows" or "causes" organs to sprout (*sich Organe entwachsen zu lassen*). Once again Heidegger raises the question of the animal's "peculiar" character, its being its "own," a "property" or "propriety" that nevertheless has no relation to consciousness or selfhood. It is nothing less than *the essence of life* that Heidegger designates in such "peculiarity" and "propriety." The analysis of capacity reveals a mode of being (*Seinsart*) that moves toward (*Hin-zu*) beings by moving or being driven away from (*Weg-von*) what anthropocentrism would call a self. It is here, after the reference to the essence of life, that Heidegger almost casually introduces the difficult problem of death:

> Only what is capable, only what is still capable, is alive; what is no longer capable is no longer alive. Whatever does not share this manner of being capable cannot be dead, either. The stone is never dead, because its being is not a being capable in the sense of being bound up with performance and drive [343: *des Dienst- und Triebhaften*]. "Dead matter" is an absurd concept. (29/30, 343)

We shall have to return to this difficult problem and absurd concept in chapter 7.

Section 58 introduces the words *Benehmen* and *Benommenheit,* animal "behavior" and "benumbment" (discussed at length in the Introduction, above), in order to designate the capacity of animal being in contrast to human comportment. Heidegger concedes that the terminology is to a certain extent arbitrary—such fortuitousness is the fortune of all words "in a living language" (345). Once again the metaphor of living language returns in order to haunt the language of life. Yet Heidegger insists that the appropriateness of the terminology can be measured by means of a view to the things themselves, *den Sachen selbst.* Here the thing itself (what Nietzsche called *das Derdiedas,* "the utmost abstract employment of the article in order to designate what in terms of content is purely undeterminable" [KSAB, 4, 47]) is a description of an earthworm fleeing in the face of, or before the snout of, a mole; each animal tunnels through the earth in its own impenetrable and unidirectional conduit, the first in flight, the second in chase. The animals "behavé toward" or "against" one another (sich benehmen gegen) in determinate ways. A stone cannot behave itself with regard to any other being, although a human being can: he or she can "behave well or badly [benimmt sich gut oder schlecht]" (345). Something uncanny happens here as Heidegger's living language struggles to provide a sachliche interpretation of animality in terms of empirically demonstrable animal behavior as bedazzlement and benumbment: the earthworm swings about abruptly and cries out to the mole, "Benimm' dich!", "Behave yourself!" The mole proceeds doggedly. "I am behaving myself!" he mutters. Meanwhile, on the earth's surface overhead, the ass of moral prejudice enters on stage, beautiful and most brave, as Nietzsche says, miming an ancient mystery:

Adventavit asinus, pulcher et fortissimum.

Then the ass came out on stage, beautiful and most brave. (JGB, no. 8; KSA 5, 21)

Heidegger's Derdiedas, his "thing in itself," is to insist on a single sharp divide between animal Benehmen and human Verhalten. That divide follows the fault called moral prejudice: whereas doing and acting, Tun und Handeln, are denied the animal (which has no hands for Handeln), they are reserved for human beings; whereas the life of drives (Triebe, treiben) is reserved for mole and earthworm, human beings are graciously spared the ignominy of Trieben and the   young man will undo his   squalor of Treiben, spared the pulsions and the grubbings of the animal.[17]

As far as life is concerned, matters are for Heidegger precisely as they were for Thomas Aquinas. When Aquinas asks, in the Summa theologiae (I q.91 a.3), whether the human body is fittingly and conveniently disposed, it is man's erect posture, free-swinging arms and hands, and freely flowing speech that he has in mind. Admittedly, animals on all fours sense more accurately and move more adroitly than man does; and many of the animals (if not the earthworm and the mole) have shells or other protective coverings, natural armament to shield them. Yet the erectness of human beings poses a problem. "Further, man is more distant from plants than from brute animals; yet plants have an erect stature, while the brutes have a prone stature. Therefore it seems that human beings should not have erect posture." However, Scripture is adamant: Deus fecit hominem rectum. That last word   striking his thigh in derision   should not be misunderstood. Man's proper and proximate end, namely, "the rational soul and its operations," calls for such erection. As though anticipating modern paleoanthropological and neurophysiological findings, which indicate that those portions of the brain that were formerly occupied by the sense of smell are in homo sapiens sapiens occupied by "higher intelligence," Aquinas replies that although man has the worst sense of smell he has the best brain: pessimum olfactum [sed] maximum cerebrum. As Timaeus long ago observed, the brain's coolness tempers the heat of the heart in man's thermally efficient vertical posture: a cool head is *superior* to, that is, located above, a fiery solar plexis. While he has no horns, talons, feathers, or fur, erect man "has reason and the hand," the latter being for Aquinas, as it was for Aristotle, "the tool of tools." Finally, Aquinas adduces four reasons for the fitting disposition of *homo erectus* as *sapiens sapiens,* doubly wise:

(1) The senses are not for defense alone, but also for knowledge and delectation. Only man experiences the beauty of food and sex, his head being liberated from the prone posture by which animals grub for food and sniff out partners, his face set free to know and enjoy things both terrestrial and celestial. (When Georges Bataille celebrates the pineal eye, he continues to rise and fall on the Thomistic afflatus and the Scholastic axis.)

(2) The brain in man is not lowly and low-down (*depressum*), but is elevated above the rest of the body (*super omnes partes corporis elevatum*).

(3) Were man to scurry about on all fours, very like a mole in its conduit, his hands would be pedestrian utensils, his *utilitas manuum* lost forever.

(4) If his hands were feet, man would have to seize food with his mouth, his head would be oblong, his snout extending far beyond the neck and torso in order to forage, his lips and tongue would be gross and coarse, "lest they be wounded by the world outside." All this, to be sure, would impede the speech of living language, "which is the proper work of reason."

The brief Scholastic interlude indicates the fundamental continuity of Heidegger's thought with that of the tradition. While the mole hounds the earthworm in famished catachresis, the human being pares the nails of its hand and dreams of angels and ontologies. From which the animals, poor devils, will be excluded.

At this point Heidegger once again reminds himself and his students of the fortuitous nature of living languages. The usages of living language are inherently inconsistent, *inkonsequent.* Interestingly, Heidegger's very word for language, *inconséquence,* is the word that the narratrix of Sade's *120 Days of Sodom* (we will meet her, Madame Duclos, once again in chapter 9, below) applies to the libertines' fantasies, tastes, and deeds. Be that as it may, Heidegger notes that language, living language, "pertains to the essence of the finitude of man." It is an interesting remark, for we are accustomed to view "Heidegger-on-language" as an *elevated* discourse: in *Being and Time* language hearkens to silence, and in *On the Way to Language* the word is the very whisper of being and propriation. We are tempted to hear the silence and the whisper as the rustle of angels. Or the discreet intervention of gods. Here too, in the 1929–1930 lectures, the gods are about to speak, albeit in a strange way. Whenever *humans* speak of *animals* they inevitably make an odd negative reference to the very pinnacle of the pyramid, the uppermost link in the great chain of being: "To think of a god speaking to himself is absolute nonsense" (346). Heidegger does not explain why. Perhaps gods are more consistent than Sade's four imperious friends? It would be interesting to speculate on which living or dead language the god might utter to himself or herself, and what the

consequences of such vital, mortal whispers of living language might be. Whatever the case, it is only one step from absolute (divine) nonsense to complete
(animal) benumbment. Heidegger would prefer not to take it.

Animal behavior, unlike human comportment, does not radiate outward
like the rays or beams of the sun. It is contained and constrained (*ein-behalten,
ein-genommen*) within the animal itself, albeit "without reflexivity." "We designate the being-with-itself [*Bei-sich-sein*] that is specific to animals, which possess nothing of that selfhood [*Selbstheit*] that the human being has, inasmuch
as the human being comports himself toward himself as a person [*des sich
verhaltenden Menschen als Person*], and we define the containment of the
animal in itself, in which its every form of behavior is possible, as *benumbment*
[Benommenheit]" (347). We are incredulous. The reader or student at this
juncture surely wishes to swing about and cry out to Heidegger, "*Benimm'
dich!*" For whenever Max Scheler uses the word *person* in the way Heidegger is
now using it he gets his wrist slapped; whenever Hegel appeals to the *Bei-sich-
sein* of spirit in-and-for-itself he gets called a metaphysician. Indeed, Heidegger
here goes to rejoin Descartes and Leibniz, selecting as his name for the essence
of animality the term that could readily be a translation of what Descartes
called bestial *hébétude,* Leibniz *étourdissement* and *confusion,* a being dazed,
bedazzled, or stunned.[18]

For Heidegger, *Benommenheit* is what contains and constrains the animal.
The animal can "behave" in the conduit of its confines, and can even "behave
itself," *aber nie in einer Welt,* "but never in a world" (348). The deprivation is
essential. Even though the word *Benommenheit* is borrowed from psychopathology, here it means not a temporary state of stupor, somewhere between
lucid consciousness and total unconsciousness, but "*the essential moment of
animality*" (29/30, 348; cf. the use of *benommen* at 65, 410).

Section 59 compares the relatedness of animal behavior to human action.
The word *Handeln* (action, "handling") now replaces *Verhalten* (comportment, "holding") and lends humanity a hand in order to suppress animality
and drive it away. Animal behavior is itself a being driven away (349:
Hingetriebensein, Weggetriebensein). Heidegger's exemplary animal is now the
honeybee. The worker bee flies from clover blossom to clover blossom, ignoring the blandishments of the Forget-Me-Nots. It is faithful to clover, driven by
odor and color to go to that blossom alone and away from all the others. After
it has sucked up the available nectar it flies off. What drives it away? Does it
"observe" that no more nectar is "at hand"? Heidegger reports the results of
an experiment: if an entire bowl of honey is placed at the worker's disposal it
remains at work until it realizes that it cannot take on board any more food. It
then abandons the bowl in order to call other bees to its aid. However, if one
"carefully severs" the bee's abdomen   *Because of this do not be sad at
heart*   while it is sucking up the honey, so that the sweet amber liquid
flows freely through the aperture at the end of the thorax, exiting before its
time, as it were, the bee will remain "calmly" at work. The worker notes
neither the being at hand of always-more-honey nor the no longer being at

hand of its own abdomen. Heidegger does not extrapolate in the direction of the human difference, does not engage in a meditation in the direction of Ernst Jünger's *Der Arbeiter,* even though one might wonder about the possibilities of severed abdomens and/or catheters at the assembly line in Chaplin's *Modern Times.* The feeding machine would either function flawlessly or not be needed at all. As for the worker-bee, it is "simply taken in [*hingenommen*] by its food" (352), rather than the other way round. It is in some sense consumed by its food, driven toward it, totally absorbed by it. Further, the worker-bee is "taken in" by the researcher's scalpel, which merely exacerbates the bee's being driven to eat. The bee never determines the *Vorhandensein* of anything, never counterposes itself (*sich gegenüberstellen*) to its source of nourishment (353). Its drive to consume the liquid can be suppressed only if its satiety is somehow inhibited—for example, by removing its abdomen. Pulsion and inhibition or disinhibition here reign supreme: nothing is at hand for the bee, no thing *as a* thing. When the drive to return to the hive is disinhibited, the nondisemboweled honeybee heads for its hive. Bearing all the scars of spirit, having become the negation of a negation, the long-suffering dialectical bug goes home.

Heidegger neglects to mention a traditional equivalent to abdominal amputation, which (ever since Plato) is neglect of philosophy. For the truncated honeybee could as easily be said to have failed to practice philosophy. Study of philosophy and pursuit of culture indicates that the free flow of nectar through the body has ceased and solidified, as Plato's *Timaeus* relates, in a strange yet very powerful passage. The passage contains the *second* appearance in the dialogue of the "receptacle" (ὑποδοχή), which earlier on (at 49–52) is acknowledged to be the matrix of the universe, where being meets becoming. If the receptacle is earlier identified as the womb and nurse of becoming, a matrix that stanches in some inexplicable way the flow of life's blood, it is now identified as the lower abdomen, the place where diarrhea (literally, "flow-through," German *Durchfall*) ends and philosophy begins. The worker bee *is a* worker bee, and not a pig, precisely because its abdomen stops the flow. Likewise the toilsome philosopher, who raises his head from the feeding trough, πρὸς τῷ ἱπνῷ, long enough to gaze on the starry skies and engage in dialogue:

The authors of our race were aware that we should be intemperate in eating and drinking, and take in a good deal more than was necessary or proper, by reason of gluttony. In order then that disease might not quickly destroy us, and lest our mortal race should perish without fulfilling its ends—intending to provide against this, the gods made what is called the lower belly [73a 2–3: κάτω κοιλίαν] to be a receptacle [3: ὑποδοχήν] for superfluous meat and drink, and formed the convolution of the bowels, so that food might be prevented from passing quickly through and compelling the body to require more food, thus producing insatiable gluttony and making the whole race an enemy to philosophy and culture [6: ἀφιλόσοφον καὶ ἄμουσαν], and rebellious against the divinest element within us. (*Timaeus,* 72e–73a)

Excise the philosopher's belly and bowel and he or she becomes the benumbed worker bee; sever the bee's belly and bowel and it becomes a pig. Κοῖ
is the squealing of piglets; κοιλιοδαίμων is "he who makes a god of his belly."
However, let us set pigs and philosophers aside and return to the nondisemboweled disinhibited honeybee, who, now sated, is on its way home.

Yet *how* does it find its way home? Not by following the scent of the
blossoms it has visited while outwardbound on its journey; nor, or at least not
usually, by following the colors and shapes of landmarks on its way. Rather, it
orients itself by means of the sun (356). If only several minutes pass between
the bee's setting forth from the hive and its return, the diurnal rotation of the
Earth will not have altered excessively the bee's reading of the sun's position. If
a researcher puts down the scalpel and takes up a black box, capturing the
bee   *Gilgamesh and Enkidu set out for the Land of the Living, where a
terrible giant guarded the cedar wood*   and holding it captive for several
hours, the bee   *You are lost in the dark and cannot hear me*   may
never find its way home after its release. It follows the beeline to where its hive
would have been at the moment of its capture: when the proper distance is
traversed, the bee abandons the beeline and searches in vain for its truant hive.

For a brief moment Heidegger allows himself to slip back into the living
language of (human) comportment: the bee "comports itself" toward the sun
(*verhält sich zur Sonne*). Later he will be guilty of the same *lapsus calami*, when
the female praying mantis devours her mate. Yet he quickly recovers and
asserts that the bee is "*simply delivered over to* the sun   *Only the gods
live for ever with Shamash*   and to the duration of its flight [359: einfach
überlassen]." No matter how clever its operation, no matter how precise its
reading of the sun's position, the bee is compelled and benumbed. Heidegger
never takes up the possibility of the bee's attunement, its *Gestimmtsein*, concerning which the first half of his course has had so much to say. For the bee
fails the test of ἀπόφανσις, it does not take the floor in order to speak up and
defend itself, and nothing more can be said of its essence, not even in an
inconsistent living language. The bee is not open to beeing. And no poor pun
will salvage it.

THE TOUCHSTONE

In section 60 Heidegger introduces the figure of the *ring* that circumscribes and
encompasses (*umringt*) the animal. No doubt he means the dimension of its
driven behavior, rather than the circumscribing but disorienting black box. As
the verb *ringen* ("to struggle or wrestle") suggests, within the ring of animal
behavior the principal mode is elimination or eradication (*Beseitigen*). One
sample of the kind of elimination or setting aside that Heidegger has in mind is
the following:

> . . . All animal behavior [*Benehmen*] is animated within this fundamental trait of
> eliminating [*Beseitigen*] or, as we also say, not-getting-into something [*sich nicht*

Einlassen auf . . .]. One of the most striking examples of this peculiar eliminative trait in all behavior is the comportment [*Verhalten:* surely a slip of the pen on Heidegger's part, a slip into the abyss of livid language that wants to keep the bee or mantis at bay] of insects within their own surroundings which we call the sex drive [*Geschlechtstrieb*]. It is well known that many females gobble up the male after copulation. For after copulation the sexual trait vanishes; the male takes on the characteristics of prey and is eliminated. The other animal is never there for the first-mentioned animal [i.e., specifically, the female?] as merely alive: it is either a sex partner [*Geschlechtsgenosse*] or prey; in either case it is in one way or another already 'gone' [*in irgendeiner Form des 'weg'*]. Behavior as such in each case is in itself an eliminating.[19]

Heidegger's example of eradication reminds us of the final pages of Freud's *Beyond the Pleasure Principle* (discussed in chapter 7, below), in which the "exquisite dualism" of Eros and the death-drive becomes very difficult to sustain; or of the pages in *The Ego and the Id* (StA, 3, 314) in which the noise of Eros is finally hushed and quelled by death. If the separation of germ plasm from the body of the male in ejaculation is a mimetic enactment of the individual's demise, a "little death," as the courtly tradition has it, the female praying mantis, now a *preying* mantis, merely mimes the mime and renders explicit the moral of life and death: *weg!*

Is the death of the eliminated animal therefore evidence of a relation to the nothing (*das Nichts*)? Heidegger denies it vigorously: *Nein!* he cries (368). However, the animal's mimicry of death will soon return to haunt the ring of animal life and the circle of Heidegger's comparative observation of world-relations. Heidegger does not define the life of drives with any originality or penetration: he accepts the common notion of the drive as a tension resulting from a surfeit of energy, a damming up of force (370). The animal wrestles (*ringt*) in the ring of its world-relation, its having in not-having; wrestles in order to eradicate beings that were never there at hand for it in the first place. It is driven to wrestle in the ring whenever its drives are uncapped and released, unimpeded, "disinhibited" (*enthemmt*). Even if the nothing does not penetrate the ring of animal behavior (*Nein!* he cries, but why the need to shout?), animal behavior is marked by negation and negation of negation. As we shall see when we examine the 1928 logic course in chapters 5 and 6, the ring of "disinhibitions" has its immediate provenance in the work of Dilthey and Scheler; yet the notion points us back beyond Scheler's "felicitous expression" to Leibniz's notion of *vis primitiva et activa* as *per se ipsam in operationem fertur*, requiring no external aid, *sed sola sublatione impedimenti.*[20]

Near the end of his account of the "openness of [animal] behavior," an openness that is hemmed in by the ring of a having-in-not-having, Heidegger reasserts in a surprisingly forceful way the *richness* of the animal's world poverty (371). He reiterates his thesis that only a deconstructive study (*eine abbauende Betrachtung*) can gain access to the essence of life. Once again he denies any intention to denigrate life or to relegate it to "a lower stage" than that occupied by human Dasein. The question of possible stages, steps, or levels in being will return to haunt him: the ostensibly unified field of φύσις will crack and deracinate in order to expose strata in being. For the moment, however, Heidegger is cautious about denigrating life in the usual ways, and his caution goes fairly far: "It is rather the case that life is a realm [*Bereich*] that possesses a wealth of openness [*ein Reichtum des Offenseins*], perhaps in ways the human world can never know" (371–72). If the animal has a world in not having it, the human world may never know either the having or the lacking. Nevertheless, Heidegger immediately slips back into the most familiar sorts of prejudgments and prejudices: animal disinhibition is eminently transitory, he says, and lacks a stable object, being utterly dependent on a stimulus. No matter how royally rich the animal's world may appear to be, the world-relation of the animal is one of struggle within the closed ring of its essentially impoverished and slavish possibilities. The animal is there to eradicate, in a realm where all is elimination and nothing is truly at hand. Perhaps we need to take a closer look at the nothing and the pervasive negatives of animal life?[21]

The three sections of Heidegger's 1929–1930 lecture course that must now concern us are section 61, which tries to bring to a conclusion the analysis of the organism; section 62, which reiterates the openness to the world that characterizes animal behavior even as benumbed behavior; and especially section 63, which raises an objection to the thesis concerning the animal's impoverished world. The objection, as far as I can see, is not met. It is circumvented in a way that both challenges the analysis beyond its capacity to respond and draws it back into the realm of ontotheology—the tradition that extends, let us say, from Saint Paul to Schelling. The objection, unmet as it is, indicates that the course's entire undertaking is a colossal failure, a *daimonic* failure. To repeat what Heidegger indicates at the outset of the course, and not merely by way of *politesse*: to designate a problem is not to overcome it (264).

Section 61c concedes that the effort to delineate the essence of the animal organism is "incomplete." The description of benumbed behavior (*Benommenheit*) fails to render in a positive way the peculiar animation and animatedness (*Bewegtheit*) of life. A whole series of questions remains to be taken up; for example, the Hegelian question of the individual organism's relationship with its species and its specific *history*. (To repeat: it is remarkable that both here and in the *Contributions to Philosophy* Heidegger remains almost entirely within the confines of Hegel's meditation on the mating-process and species-identity, without ever citing Hegel's extraordinary analyses.) Yet there is one question on which the entire analysis of organism and world-relation hangs, one "moment," Heidegger says, "which belongs to the innermost essence of life, and which we designate as *death*" (387). He continues—in a passage we have already cited in the Introduction, but which bears repeating here: "The touchstone [*Prüfstein*] for determining the suitability and originality of every inquiry into the essence of life and vice-versa [that is, presumably, the life of essence or of the creature] is whether the inquiry has sufficiently grasped the problem of death; and whether it is able to bring that problem in the correct way into the question concerning the essence of life."[22]

Two remarks. First, recall the parallel passage in Heidegger's Nietzsche lectures (NI, 460/2, 195) in which the problem of "the nothing" (*das Nichts*) is declared the testing-stone (*Probierstein*) that determines whether we gain entry into the realm of philosophy or remain barred from it. What might seem to be a merely regional issue, the question of death in "theoretical biology," in fact embraces both the existential-ontological project and Heidegger's incipient "other" thinking. Second, recall that Heidegger's attempt three years earlier to identify the unified horizon of ecstatic temporality failed to confront what Heidegger called, in that classic understatement, the "difficult problem of death" (24, 387). Once again it is *death* that should reveal the innermost animatedness and vitality of life's essence, its *élan*, its *Schwung* and *Schwingung*, precisely as it should have revealed the existential truth of *time*. Yet rather than confront the challenge of a unified field of ἔκστασις, Heidegger once again falls back to the distinction between *Sterben* and *Verenden*, "dying" as opposed to "perishing." Benumbed behavior "prescribes *altogether determined possibilities* [ganz bestimmte Möglichkeiten] of *death*, of *coming-to-death*" (388). Although Heidegger employs the plural here, perishing remains the sole possibility of animal life. He immediately relates this problem (as he does in *Being and Time*) to the theoretical-biological thesis of immanent death, that is, a death that is intrinsic to life. Like Freud, Heidegger is much exercised by the death that is *in* life, *in sich selbst*; unlike Freud, Heidegger is careful not to go too far, *zu weit*, with the thesis of immanent death. (Clearly, a long story waits to be told here, the story of *Heidegger* and what Derrida has called "the menace of the psyche"; see the final sections of chapter 7, below.)

If section 62 insists on the openness (*Offensein*) of benumbed behavior and the access to beings that an organism indubitably exhibits, it is also forced to fall back to a position that *Being and Time* itself showed to be inadequate. The animal does not experience being *as* being, does not have access to beings *as such* (390–91). Here and throughout the final hours of the lecture course Heidegger appeals to the animal's lack of ἀπόφανσις, its lack of λόγος, as the secret of its benumbed behavior in an impoverished world. Not the foundational hermeneutical-as but the derivative apophantic-as comes to dominate— and undo—fundamental ontology; furthermore, as Heidegger himself here suspects, his earlier labors to establish a "fundamental attunement" for metaphysics will have been in vain. Human beings are no longer those who are benumbed with anxiety in the face of their uncanny existence (see the references to *Benommenheit* in *Being and Time*, recorded in the Introduction); nor are they the beings who are bedazzled by the overpowering power of the δαιμόνιον (see 26, 13, discussed in chapter 5, below); rather, human beings are once again those logical, logistical living beings who have the word and who take the floor to declare that animals inhabit an impoverished world, that their conduct plays itself out in a circle of drives and a ring of disinhibitions within which they dispatch their prey and propagate their species, bedazzled, unbothered, and bewildered. Yet perhaps also bewitched. Which is what bothers Heidegger.

Section 63 is entitled (not by Heidegger, *nota bene*) "Self-objection against the thesis of the animal's not having a world as a deprivation, and of its being poor; the nullification [*Entkräftung*] of this objection." Brave words. Words of a solicitor. Yet something other than confident refutation is happening in Heidegger's text and to his entire effort. There will be no "nullification" of the objection but only an infinite postponement of the difficult problem of death. A postponement, but also a change of venue for Heidegger's meditation, a surprising shift in the direction of Schelling.

What is wrong with the thesis of world poverty? Clearly, it is blatantly anthropocentric: the animal's behavior appears to be benumbed only against the backdrop of a putatively more vigorous and vital stance toward beings as such; the animal's world reflects a deprivation only on the set of a richer, more varied and abundant openness to being. However, as Heidegger will insist throughout his Nietzsche lectures, especially the third course, "The Will to Power as Knowledge," the charge of anthropomorphism and anthropocentrism is essentially duplicitous, for it always presupposes that a thinking could, if only it were rigorous enough, erase the human backdrop and expunge the set of (human) existence. Heidegger's self-imposed task is to think the "positive side" of this duplicitous state of affairs (394). It is not that the thesis concerning the animal's world poverty goes too far and has to be "wound down" or even "renounced"; it is that a certain possibility touching the touchstone has to be "left open" (395). Heidegger hints at that possibility in two passages, the first early on in the "self-objection" (393), the second at its culmination (396). The first passage:

> If deprivation [*das Entbehren*], in certain of its transformations, is a suffering [*ein Leiden*]; and if a being deprived of world, as well as poverty, belong to the animal's being; then a suffering and a sorrow [*ein Leiden und ein Leid*] would have to permeate the entire animal kingdom and the realm of life in general. Biology knows absolutely nothing about this. To fabulate on such things is perhaps the poets' privilege. [*Von dergleichen zu fabeln, ist vielleicht ein Vorrecht der Dichter.*] (29/30, 393)

Which fabulists is Heidegger thinking of? He does not say. Yet who can read this passage and not be reminded of the fabulous Schelling and his *Schleier der Schwermut*, the weighty veil of melancholy draped over all life, the veil woven in vain at the origin of all weaving, as both Freud and Schelling know, in order to occlude the bifurcated essence of God?

If *I* seem to be spinning veils—and tales—here, if *I* appear to be a Schleiermacher, let this second passage unsettle my readers as much as it unnerves me:

> The fact that biology knows nothing of this is no counterproof against metaphysics. That perhaps only poets occasionally speak of it is an argument that dare not be allowed to cast metaphysics to the winds. In the end, one does not really need Christian faith in order to understand something of those words that Paul (in Romans 19) writes concerning the ἀποκαραδοκία τῆς κτίσεως, the creatures' and

all creation's longing gaze [*von dem sehnsüchtigen Ausspähen der Geschöpfe und der Schöpfung*]; for the ways of creation, as the Book of Esra (IV, 7, 12) also says, have in this eon become narrow, mournful, and arduous (*schmal, traurig und mühselig*]. (29/30, 396)

The word *sehnsüchtig*, "characterized by longing and languishing," cannot but lead us (as it presumably led Heidegger) to Schelling. Something else, an Other, *ein Anderes*, will also soon lead us there. Note for the moment the fabulous use of Paul, whose faith one need not share in order to grasp the suffering and the longing that pervade life, Paul being here corroborated by the apocryphal, fabulous Book of Esra: Old and New Testaments, as well as authentic and apocryphal Scriptures, conjoined in something that could never be called "tepid paganism," not even by the most sectarian of religionists,[23] to testify to—or to fabulate upon—the ways of life and all creation. Which are *traurig*. "Sad, sorrowful," we would normally say. Here I would render it more literally as "full of mourning." Continuing the passage to its unnerving conclusion:

Nor do we need any sort of pessimism in order to be able to develop the *world poverty of the animal as an intrinsic problem of animality itself*. For with the animal's openness to that which disinhibits [*Offensein . . . für das Enthemmende*], the animal in its benumbed behavior is essentially exposed to an Other [*wesenhaft hinausgestellt in ein Anderes*], something that can never be revealed to it as either a being or a nonbeing, yet which, disinhibiting, and with all the transformations of disinhibition that it encompasses, introduces an *essential shattering* into the essence of the animal [*eine* wesenhafte Erschütterung *in das Wesen des Tieres*]. (29/30, 396)

Two remarks. *Hinausgestellt in ein Anderes.* Is that not at least reminiscent of *Hinausgehaltenheit in das Nichts*, as though the animal were suspended within anxiety? *Eine wesenhafte Erschütterung.* What is this essential "shattering" of animal life? We will not understand the openness and the world-relation of benumbed behavior, will not understand the organism in all its transformations, "as long as we fail to bring into play the fundamental phenomenon of the life-process, and thereby of death [*und damit des Todes*]" (396). After several years have passed, Heidegger will identify this fundamental phenomenon of life as a "bestirring" and "excitability" (*Regung, Erregbarkeit*, which we will take up in chapter 9), and he will continue to associate these words with "shattering" (*Erschütterung*). To feel the force of this essential shattering, one would have to trace the use of the words *Scheitern* and *Erschütterung* in *Being and Time* as the touchstones of existential analysis as such, but also in the 1935 *Introduction to Metaphysics*, where Dasein is defined as shattering in the face of the overpowering, the uncanny, the daimonic. And, of course, also in the 1933 rectoral address, where "the most intense stirring" meets with "the most extensive shattering." A massive undertaking, and a dispiriting one, perhaps even a shattering one. We shall begin to undertake it in chapter 5.

WHICH HORSES?

Where deathless horses weep. Horses? Which horses?

Perhaps the blinded horses of Peter Shaffer's *Equus*, horses nonetheless relentless in their demands, *Give me none of your archetypal waffle, nothing of your primal drives your equestrian erotism your lifedeath, explain me as I am in all my particulars, account for my hide my froth my reek my square teeth my velvet muzzle my look even my blinded eyes*, horses with tears, tears mixed with gore, where eyes should be.

Perhaps Jewel's horse in *As I Lay Dying*, both Jewel and Jewel's horse—Faulkner's "two figures carved for a tableau savage in the sun":

> When Jewel can almost touch him, the horse stands on his hind legs and slashes down at Jewel. Then Jewel is enclosed by a glittering maze of hooves as by an illusion of wings; among them, beneath the upreared chest, he moves with the flashing limberness of the snake.[24]

Yes, perhaps Jewel's horse, for who can forget the horse that kicks and bites like an immortal mortal? And perhaps furious Jewel too, who, Darl says, is the only mortal Bundren who mourns his mother as she lies.

Not, however, Raskolnikov's nag. Not the piteous horse, the dray horse that Nietzsche conjures in a letter dated 13 May 1888 to Reinhart von Seydlitz:

> Yesterday I dreamed up an image of *moralité larmoyante* [a weepy moralism], as Diderot puts its. Winter landscape. An ancient drayman, with an expression of the most brutal cynicism, harsher still than the winter that surrounds him, relieves himself upon his own horse. The horse—the poor, berated creature—looks about, grateful, *very* grateful—. (KSAB *8*, 314)

No, not the gratefully submissive whipping-horse of a lacrimonious morality, but a horse that weeps bitter tears. A horse that mourns a man who collapses one January morning in the streets of Torino.

Perhaps also the spirited sorrel ridden by a woman who only the most pinched and embittered souls would deny was outrageously beautiful, a woman who even riding bareback could reach from her mount the first cherries of summer and who said that when she bit into the first cherry the first drops of blood began to flow and she wasn't really surprised because time had made her as ripe as the cherry but startled nonetheless by the drops as always never really expecting them and who in this instant—stretched out in it so suddenly—thought or rather felt four things in her life to be perfectly consonant: the cherry, the blood, the friend she loved, and the horse. Which four things in their unity she invited him to contemplate, knowing full well that he would be as baffled and bewitched in that fourfold as she was.

Horses? Which horses?

Why should any horse, whether animal or god, care about Patroklos? Why should any horse or man or horseman pause to disobey the command to cast a cold eye on life, on death, on death-in-life and life-in-death, the command to pass by? What immortal mortal animal or mortal immortal god could share in the plight of Patroklos, which is twofold: first, that he is older than Achilles yet loves him as a younger man ought, the most trying situation for a Greek male, as Alcibiades (and Socrates?) knew well; second, that a god has knocked him silly from behind, followed by men from the front, back, and flanks, wherever like vultures they can get in on the kill. Yet it is not out of shame over their luminous, treacherous Olympian kin that these horses weep, nor in rage at the blackguards who strike that defenseless body. Not shame and rage, but persistent, unsuccessful mourning moves them. Paralyzes them. The obsessive desire for a being they can neither introject nor incorporate. Mourning as longing, languor, and languishment.

At the culminating moment of his 1936 lectures on Schelling, Heidegger considers Schelling's daring thesis that the essence of ground in God is longing, *die Sehnsucht*. He can no doubt sense the resistance in his hearers, their twitching flanks, their flaring nostrils and spooked eyes. He employs every rhetorical trick he knows in order to overcome their skittishness:

> The essence of ground in God is longing? We can scarcely restrain the objection that this statement projects a human condition onto God—. Ah, yes! *But* it could also be otherwise. For who has ever verified the supposition that longing is something merely human? And who has ever refuted thoroughly and with sufficient reason the possibility that what we call *longing*, which is where we are, in the end is something other than we ourselves? Does not longing conceal something that denies us *any* grounds for limiting it to humankind, something that would sooner give us cause to grasp it as that in which we human beings are unfettered *out beyond ourselves* [über uns weg *entschränkt*]? Is it not precisely longing that proves the human being to be Other, other than a mere human being? (SA, 150)

To the resurgent, derisive cries of *Schleier-macher! Schleier-macher!* Heidegger could retort—although he never would, but then why not?—that the "beyond" of "out beyond ourselves," the *weg* of *über uns weg*, might lead us, not to the outermost crystalline spheres of divinity, but precisely to the *animal's* disinhibited openness to beings—*weg!* (29/30, 364). Likewise, he could indicate that the word that Luther used to translate the ἀποκαραδοκία of creatures is not "longing gaze" but *das engstliche harren*, a persistent yet *anxious* looking-out-for . . . , as though animals were capable not only of the longing gaze but also of the *anxiety* that opens Dasein or mortality to its essence.[25] Finally, the *Regung* or "bestirring" of longing in the ground of God's essence has as we shall see everything to do with the untrammeled, unfettered essence of just-plain-life: *Regung* is destined to be a word in Heidegger's theoretical biology (see especially 54, 237–38), in his Schellingian meditation on ontotheology (SA, 151, 159, and 161), and in the language of φύσις and *Ereignis* (US, 257–58 and 264, all these passages discussed in chapter 9, below). And if the movement of bestirring or longing should lead us to the outermost spheres, it would not be a question of merely anyone's God, but of Aristotle's and Schelling's and Hölderlin's God, on the verge of discovering its flanks, its sexes and sexualities, its fatal commitment to mortality, and its ineluctable subjection to the granting, to the bestirring of time and being, to downgoing. And thus to a mortality whose "fundamental mood" would be a *Schmerz* beyond *Schwermut*, a pain, rather than suffering and sorrow, an impossible mourning that is always and everywhere a *Sehnsucht*, a languor and a longing. Less a "fundamental mood" than a mode, motif, motet, or melody, *eine Weise*; perhaps what Whitman calls a *threnody*, Irigaray an *air*.

Pain, mourning, and the ability to die. If death invades animal life too and shatters it, what blindness and what wisdom long ago sang ageless, deathless horses? confused mortals with immortal steeds? granted the immortal horse a mortal voice, borrowed from immortal Hera, and where did *she* get it from?

Never mind, for the moment, that voice. Mind equine tears, the water shed—the water shed over the impossible, impassable, abyssal watershed that Heidegger, like most philosophers before him, hopes will segregate human beings from the animals. Homer's horses tread the watershed. Always they go to the brink. Occasionally they stand very still.

What world-relation do these mournful horses have? Freud says that in mourning the *human* world suddenly becomes impoverished, the *human* being poor in world. What would Heidegger say to that? What world-relation do these weeping horses sustain? Answer: they sustain *every possible* relation.

First, that of stone:

> But just as funeral stele stand fixed above the tomb
> As monuments to the dead man or woman,
> They stand motionless and motionless hold the splendid car. . . .

Second, that of the god:

> It was a painful sight for Zeus, Son of Kronos,
> To see these weeping steeds. . . .
> "Ah, you wretches!"

Third and finally, inevitably, that of humans and other living beings:

> "Was it so that you could share in the sufferings of these unhappy humans?
> For, truly, there is nothing more wretchedly lamentable than human being,
> Amid all the beings that breathe and creep on the earth."

PART TWO

Toward a Politics of Life

The death of Enkidu left Gilgamesh bereft. The end of all bravado. Emaciated, haggard, he set out alone to find Utnapishtim the Faraway, the only mortal whose family had survived the flood. Gilgamesh said, *"I have a desire to question him concerning the living and the dead."* After passing through leagues of thick darkness, Gilgamesh arrived at the Garden of the Gods.

As he walked in the Garden by the edge of the sea, Shamash the Sun saw him. He saw that Gilgamesh was dressed in the skins of animals and that he ate their flesh. He was distressed, and he spoke to himself and said, "No mortal man has gone this way before, nor will, as long as the winds drive over the sea." And to Gilgamesh he said, "You will never find the life for which you are searching." Gilgamesh said to glorious Shamash, "Now that I have toiled and strayed so far over the wilderness, am I to sleep and let the earth cover my head for ever? Let my eyes see the sun until they are dazzled with looking. Although I am no better than a dead man, still let me see the light of the sun."

•

When the ferryman remarked on the king's weary appearance, Gilgamesh replied, *"Why should not my cheeks be starved and my face drawn? Despair is in my heart, and my face is the face of one who has made a long journey. I was burned with heat and cold. Why should I not wander over the pastures? . . . Enkidu my brother whom I love, the end of mortality has overtaken him. I wept for him seven days and nights until the worm fastened on him. Because of my brother I am afraid of death, because of my brother I stray through the wilderness. His fate lies heavy upon me. How can I be silent, how can I rest? He is dust and I too shall die and be laid in the earth for ever."*

·

At long last Gilgamesh found Utnapishtim the Faraway. He addressed him as father and posed his question concerning the living and the dead. He confided in the survivor and told him of the life he sought. Utnapishtim replied elliptically and hyperbolically at once, saying: *"There is no permanence. Do we build a house to stand for ever, do we seal a contract to hold for all time? Do brothers divide an inheritance to keep for ever, does the flood-tide of rivers endure? It is only the nymph of the dragon-fly who sheds her larva and sees the sun in glory. From days of old there is no permanence. The sleeping and the dead, how alike they are, they are like a painted death. What is there between the master and the servant when both have fulfilled their doom? When the Annunaki, the judges, come together, and Mammetun, the mother of destinies, jointly they decree the fates of men. Life and death they allot but the day of death they do not disclose."*

And Gilgamesh replied: *"What shall I do, O Utnapishtim, where shall I go? Already the thief in the night has hold of my limbs, death inhabits my room; wherever my foot rests, there I find death."*

·

The destiny was fulfilled which the father of the gods, Enlil of the Mountain, had decreed for Gilgamesh: "In nether-earth the darkness will show him a light. . . . The heroes, the wise men, like the new moon have their waxing and waning. . . . As in the dark month, the month of shadows, so without him there is no light. O Gilgamesh, this was the meaning of your dream. You were given the kingship, such was your destiny, everlasting life was not your destiny. Because of this do not be sad at heart, do not be grieved or oppressed; he has given you power to bind and to loose, to be the darkness and the light of mankind. . . . But do not abuse this power, deal justly with your servants in the palace, deal justly before the face of the Sun."

FOUR

"You in front of Me, I in front of You"

Heidegger in the University of Life

Heidegger and politics. The theme is dreariness itself, dreariness relieved only by disgust. My aim in this chapter, which is on the way toward a politics of *life,* is threefold. First, I want to write something—very little, very briefly, very carefully—about Heidegger's silence after 1945 concerning the Extermination. It is of course foolish to write summarily about something that cries for time, thought, and recognition; but it is death itself to perpetuate that silence and to forget the enormous consequences of a topic I have just called "dreary." Second, I want to report on several of Heidegger's activities as rector in 1933–1934 that have only recently, that is, in the past five or six years, come to light. I mean his efforts to precipitate the end of the "liberal" constitution of the German university, as envisaged in Kant's *Conflict of the Faculties (Der Streit der Fakultäten,* first published in 1798), by eliminating the frontier between power and knowledge, state and university, heteronymy and autonomy. His efforts can be summed up in a single very ugly word, *Gleichschaltung,* the "streamlining" of the university, the "meshing of gears" between Party-State and university, the "synchronizing," better, the total submission to Party and to state power by the German university between 1933 and 1935. Or, if irony might help us to confront and bear ugliness, the *rectification* (from *Recht,* right, far right, erectile, rectal, rectoral) of the German university. Third, I want to discuss one of Heidegger's earliest statements concerning the university in a lecture course taught at Freiburg in 1921–1922, "Introduction to Phenomenological Research." Whereas the 1929 inaugural address, "What Is Metaphysics?" (W, 1–19; BW, 91–112), the 1933 rectoral address, Heidegger's 1945 plea in his own defense, and the *Spiegel* interview of 1966 have long been available, this early text, only recently published, is Heidegger's most detailed and most astonishing avowal concerning the university—as the university of *life.*[1]

Note that my three topics regress in time, from 1945 and after to the summer of 1933, and then back to the winter of 1921–1922. "If like a crab we could go backward. . . ." It is, I hope, neither to flee history nor to dream of pinpointing origins in history that I go backward. Nevertheless, there is an irrepressible *desire* to go back, in order to seek alternatives and conjure up all sorts of what-might-have-beens for the dismal theme of Heidegger and politics. There is much that is entirely contingent in and about this chapter, and I am all but certain that the three topics will not really cohere; even more certain that no "thesis" will jell, no grand explanation in terms of either life-philosophy or just plain life, no final adjudication and ultimate settling of "The Strange Case of Dr. Heidegger." Let it therefore be simply three more specimens of journalism, at a time when philosophers the world over seem bent on producing poor journalism, and—if things should go very well—a preparation of some disturbing questions.

THE SILENCE

I cannot begin to write of Heidegger's silence, not even   *How can I be silent, how can I rest?*   in the ways undertaken recently by Philippe Lacoue-Labarthe and Jacques Derrida.[2] I shall hold to what must seem a shocking understatement and evasion. Nevertheless, I shall say what I believe would hurt Heidegger most—that his silence concerning the fate of European Jewry between 1933 and 1945 is a failure of thinking, *ein Versagen des Denkens.* More than that, worse than that, yes, but at least that. I want to locate for discussion three places in the Heideggerian text where failure to break the silence concerning the Holocaust or Extermination implies a failure of the thinking itself. I will not subject these passages to an analysis of the rhetoric of the text, although they certainly merit that; for I still believe that in Heidegger's texts *there is thinking,* and that when the *thinking* fails an abyss opens right there on the page. The three places I want to indicate—though surely there are more—are:

(1) "The Question Concerning Technology," at the point where Heidegger expands his analysis of *Bestand,* "stockpile" or "standing reserve," to include the phenomenon of human "resources," human "materials" (VA, 25–27; BW, 299–301). My question is this: If it is the essence or historic unfolding of technology (*Wesen* in its verbal sense) to reduce mortals to stockpiled raw materials, what is the historic unfolding that negates this ostensibly essential reduction by enforcing the sheer *wastage* of human beings? In the historic unfolding of technology, whence that *particular form* of devastation?

Let me try to sharpen the question. Heidegger does not actually say that in the age of technology humanity is totally reduced to a stockpiled resource, a "standing reserve"; quite to the contrary, he believes that the primal phenomenon of revealing (*Entbergen*) will survive the reduction. He writes:

> Only to the extent that man for his part is already challenged to exploit the energies of nature can this revealing that orders happen. If man is challenged, ordered, to do this, then does not man himself belong even more originally than nature within the standing-reserve? The current talk about human resources,

about the supply of patients for a clinic, gives evidence of this. . . . Yet precisely because man is challenged more originally than are the energies of nature, i.e., into the process of ordering, he never is transformed into mere standing-reserve. Since man drives technology forward, he takes part in ordering as a way of revealing. Yet the unconcealment itself within which ordering unfolds is never a human handiwork, any more than is the realm man traverses every time he as a subject relates to an object.

Where and how does this revealing happen if it is no mere handiwork of man? We need not look far. We need only apprehend in an unbiased way what has already claimed man so decisively that he can only be man at any given time as the one so claimed. Wherever man opens his eyes and ears, unlocks his heart, and gives himself over to meditating and striving, shaping and working, entreating and thanking, he finds himself everywhere already brought into the unconcealed.

If we think of the supply of human materials for a hospital, we may have some hope in the opening of eyes and ears and even hearts: doctors too are sometimes patients, and they may yet learn patience. However, if we think of the supply of human materials for a death-camp, can the rhetoric of the unlocked heart survive? Or are we left with a hollow hyperhumanism incapable of confronting a reduction—in the chemical sense of that word—more devastating than the reduction of human beings to stockpiled *resources?* Is Heidegger's thought heterologous enough to broach the question of such a reduction, a wastage and a purge beyond wickedness and imagination? What do we confront in the technology of the camp, the chamber; what, precisely there, among brick ovens, barbed wire, and the chain of command, unfolds essentially? The Heideggerian discourse of destiny, freedom, danger and rescue, of revealing, concealing, and questioning melts away into silence. What could break *that* silence? Apparently, not even "Heidegger" "himself" could break it.

In a remark made after the war, in the course of his Bremen lectures on "Insight into What Is," remarks that are often cited and universally condemned nowadays for their callousness and "scandalous, piteous insufficiency," Heidegger invokes the wastage of human beings in the context of planetary technology. He is quoted (by Wolfgang Schirmacher, cited here by Philippe Lacoue-Labarthe) as saying: "Agriculture is now a motorized alimentary industry, in terms of essence the same thing as the fabrication of cadavers in the gas chambers and extermination camps, the same thing as a military blockade and the reduction of a nation to famine, the same thing as the fabrication of hydrogen bombs."[3]

While Lacoue-Labarthe indulges in the rhetoric of indignation, he fails to reflect on the phrase of Hannah Arendt's that he has cited on the previous page: ". . . I am speaking of the systematic fabrication of cadavers, etc.; I needn't elaborate any further on this subject." Rather than inveigh against the callousness or insufficiency of Heidegger's remarks, in the way we might also condemn John Steinbeck for bemoaning "the rape of the land" in *The Grapes of Wrath,* I would prefer that we try to think about them. If we can even begin to do so, we will notice a strange discrepancy between this identification of the "fabrication of cadavers" and other forms of technological reduction, a discrepancy between the reduction of raw materials to a standing-reserve or stockpile and the reduction of human beings (even when reduced to human resources) to mass graves. Failure to think through this massive discrepancy I take to be a serious failure, a failure of thinking so devastating that it seems a failure of *life*, a *daimonic* failure. Neither the rhetoric of the open heart nor the rhetoric of indignation would compensate for or do justice to the failure.⁴

(2) "The Letter on Humanism," at the conclusion (W, 189; BW, 237), where Heidegger writes about the appearance of evil (*das Böse*) in the clearing of being: "The essence of evil does not consist in the mere baseness of human action but rather in the malice of rage [*im Bösartigen des Grimmes*]." And later: "To healing, being first grants ascent into grace; to raging, its compulsion to malignancy [*und Andrang zum Unheil dem Grimm*]." Are malice, the rage of evil, and malignancy anything more than noxious flowers of rhetoric in Heidegger's text? All that rage on the page—who or what is it about? We can be sure that it involves the *Katastrophe* that devastated Germany and the Germans—*die Katastrophe* [*die*] *über sie* [*die Deutschen*] *hereingebrochen ist* (SB, 43). Yet does not the very word "catastrophe," flowing from the pen of Heidegger—the avid reader of Greek tragedy and the thinker who pursues Schelling's question concerning the essence of *evil*—compel us to ask with some persistence how the knots were tied, how, where, and by whom? Not in the expectation that the question of guilt, *die Schuldfrage*, will be resolved, or even broached in ways to which we are accustomed—even though *Schuld* fascinated Heidegger throughout his life and writing—but simply in the anxiety that words like *Unheil, das Böse*, and *Grimm* can be clichés, must be clichés, if unaccompanied by the command to think. And so:

(3) *Was heißt Denken?* "What Calls for Thinking?" What commands and commends thought, gives us to think, calls for our thinking? Such commending to thought Heidegger calls *Mnemosyne*, the gathering of commemorative thought, remembrance, thought thinking back, *Nachdenken, Andenken, Versammlung des Denkens*. While elaborating the gathering of commemorative thought during the transition from the sixth to the seventh lecture hours (WhD? 63–70), Heidegger confirms Nietzsche's suspicion that humanity is ill-prepared to assume dominion over the earth. He speaks of "imminent decisions" that are about to challenge humanity, then asks: "What did the Second World War really decide—if we remain silent about its terrible consequences for our fatherland [*furchtbaren Folgen für unser Vaterland*], especially the way it has been rent down the middle?" The rift (*Riß*) through the middle (*durch seine Mitte*) reminds us of the European "middle," to wit, interwar Germany, which Heidegger in 1935 invokes as the only hope for a Europe torn between American pragmatico-technocracy and Russian Bolshevism. Even after the Second World War he appears to cling to this hope concerning the fatherland: the father nation, which (alone?) has suffered the frightful consequences of the War, has been defeated by outsiders, and the son will remain loyal. In Heidegger's fatherland, the *Riß* is an open wound: Germany's rending is per-

haps a metaphysical event (see *Riß, Zerrissenheit,* at WhD? 34). And, to make the most obvious point, by announcing that he will be silent (*um . . . zu schweigen*) about these terrible consequences of the war, Heidegger of course *breaks* his silence. By breaking his silence on the frightful consequences for his fatherland, he reinforces in an absolutely frightful way that other silence.

To his own (rhetorical) question Heidegger replies that World War II "has decided nothing" about the "essential destiny" of humankind in the face of technological danger. Our "sociopolitical" and "moral" categories are too constraining (*engbrüstig:* "narrow-chested," hence short-winded, without stamina) for meditation on that danger. Heidegger specifically criticizes the "European intellectual world," or the "way of conceiving things in Europe," *die europäische Vorstellungswelt,* "between 1920 and 1930," for being inadequate to the crises it had to confront. "Between 1920 and 1930." Why stop at 1930? Why not (also? especially?) 1933 or 1935? Why not 1938 or 1945? Which crises does Heidegger have in mind? Does he wish to suggest that he himself remained immured from the woefully insufficient European *Vorstellungswelt* of the Weimar Republic, even though the rhetoric of his rectoral address and of his 1935 *Introduction to Metaphysics* betrays a fatal affinity with its "period"? Or is he here, on the contrary, confessing the bankruptcy of his own hopes for "resurgence" in the early 1930s? Why no clear word on his own relation to those "European" notions—presuming that Germany, France, England, and all the other nations of Europe shared the identical set of representations? Whatever the reason, Heidegger is more disposed to admonish his listeners in 1951 that those representations will even now make Europe a plaything (*ein Spaß*) for the "powers" and the "vast populations" of "the East." Presumably, "the East" is China after 1949, or Russia after 1917—the Bolshevik "red threat" of the European mental set between 1920 and 1930. Heidegger does not pause to allow such recoil to take effect, does not allow it to call for thinking, but instead cites a long passage from Nietzsche's *Twilight of the Idols* (KSA 6, 140–141). It is a passage that, in Nietzsche's own words, is "antiliberal to the point of wickedness." Heidegger does not flinch as Nietzsche makes an ironic reference to the "Deutsches Reich" (the Second, however, not the Third). All Heidegger wants to do, with Nietzsche's help, is to expose the decrepit politics of the European nation states, *die Nationalstaaterei.* He does not pause to ask whether his own fears for his fatherland remain altogether untainted by *Nationalstaaterei.*

A whole series of troubling questions might arise to detain us here, but let me press on to the point that Heidegger himself wants to make: his sole concern is "an as yet unspoken gathering [*Versammlung*] of Western destiny in its entirety," a gathering that will enable the Occident or "evening land" to confront "coming decisions" (WhD? 67). He finds that unspoken gathering presaged in Hölderlin's late hymns, with their confraternity of the gods. The brotherhood of Christ, Heracles, and Dionysos is an intimation of what Heidegger in the late 1930s was calling "the last god," *der letzte Gott.* That god's coming, an epiphany of ultimate withdrawal, would be the passing-by of all divinity. As intriguing as the thought of divine *Vorbeigang* is, I feel constrained to ask: Is such "high-altitude" gathering, the gathering of Western destiny, the gathering that fraternizes with the passing gods of Greece and Hölderlinian Germany—for the last god has his *Volk*, a chosen people who will be the "futural ones" on this earth—is this the thinking that gathers us? Gathers *us* here and now? But who, us?—as Heidegger repeatedly asks. What if that which calls on us to think, pointing as it does into its own withdrawal, cannot be gathered, does not give itself to be gathered? What if the call is like ashes, like the odor of wetted ashes, *liliata rutilantium*, an ashen breath? I will not say anything here about mourning, memory, and impossible thought, impossible perhaps not only for Heidegger; but as that thought begins to appear in other texts, texts not by Heidegger, I confess that I am riveted by them, see the only possible future for Heideggerian commemorative thought or *gathering* in the very *dispersal* they suffer. I am talking of course about *Schibboleth: For Paul Celan, Memoires: For Paul de Man, Feu la cendre,* and other recent texts by Jacques Derrida.⁵

I shall now pass on to my second theme, if only so that I can escape the first, and finally get to the third. For it is high time that I say this: I am writing (too quickly, rashly) of a radical failure of thought within the Heideggerian text, and I shall in a moment comment on a radical failure of action within the Heideggerian academic regime, only because Heidegger's thought remains for me the most radical example in our century of what thinking can and should be. I am hardly alone in that belief, so that a disclaimer like this seems superfluous and even absurd. Yet so many have by now lit the match and tossed it into the faggots they have hastily and even gleefully gathered about Heidegger's feet that such a declaration seems to be necessary. I therefore remind myself and my readers of Heidegger's *thinking* as we pass disconsolately from one failure to another, from the silence to cacaphony.

THE NOISE

I had always *believed* Heidegger's protestations that he accepted the nomination as rector of the University of Freiburg only reluctantly and that his sole aim was to preserve its integrity against the Party's crudest interventions and manipulations. After reading the recent accounts by Hugo Ott and Bernd Martin, based in part on their research at the Freiburg University archive, I am, to say the least, no longer convinced.⁶

If Ott and Martin are correct, Heidegger was offered the post precisely because of his outspoken support of the National-Socialist regime. His predecessor, Wilhelm von Möllendorff, felt unable to carry out the order of the Baden *Reichskommissar,* dated April 5, 1933, to retire all non-Aryan civil servants (in Germany that includes university professors) and to reconstitute the university senate, the principal decision-making body in the German university. "Synchronization" was the order of the day, and Heidegger the man to carry it out. Ex-Rectors Möllendorff and Josef Sauer, along with Walter

Eucken and others, hoped to resist total capitulation to the Party by active resistance in the senate. Heidegger's willful demolition of that body was perhaps his most dubious "achievement" as rector. It is that undoing I wish to stress in the context of these pages, even though Heidegger's equally active engagement in the *Gleichschaltung* of the student union and the student body generally—symptomatic here is his leadership in the paramilitary "Science Camps" project—is perhaps even more profoundly disturbing. Heidegger accepted the nomination, according to Ott and Martin, not reluctantly and on the defensive, as it were, but because he wanted to be *Führer.* Führer of the university.   *You were given the kingship, such was your destiny, everlasting life was not your destiny.*   Spiritual-intellectual *(geistiger)* Führer.   *But do not abuse this power.*   These historians do not hesitate to identify Heidegger, apparently without irony or acrimony, as the *Führer-Rektor,* as though that were a legitimate academic or administrative title.

Significant in this regard is the telegram Heidegger sent to Hitler on May 20, soon after his election to the rectorate, a telegram from *Führer-Rektor* to *Führer-Führer.* He urged Hitler to postpone an imminent national meeting of the Confederation of German Institutes of Higher Education "until the leadership of the Confederation has undergone the *Gleichschaltung* which particularly here is so necessary" (HO, 350). In telegraphing Hitler, Heidegger showed that he did not hesitate to go to the top, presumably because he believed that in the German university he himself *was* the spiritual-intellectual top. His ambitions doubtless extended far beyond Freiburg-im-Breisgau, and the reorganization plan he proposed and carried out in his *alma mater* served as the most radical—the most rectified—model in all Germany. Even the Bavarian proposal for university "reform" was more modest than Heidegger's for that "model state," *Musterländle,* Baden. When it was all over, at summer's end, Josef Sauer—theologian, sometime rector of the University of Freiburg, and a mentor and staunch supporter of the young Heidegger since 1911—jotted into his journal, *"Finis universitatum!"*

I cannot in the present context spin out a lengthy narrative about the summer of 1933 in Freiburg. Some details. By October Heidegger had rejected two calls to be professor of philosophy in Berlin; his colleague Alfred Baeumler was not so choosy, but he, Heidegger, would remain in the provinces and "try to shape the new possibilities" at home, *an unserer Universität* (HO, 353). His consistent aim nevertheless was "to prepare the unified structure [*den einheitlichen Aufbau*] of future higher education throughout Germany" (HO, 353). Such a shaping of "new possibilities" is what Heidegger's notorious rectoral address is all about. Allow me therefore to refer briefly to two aspects of that address.[7]

I found on rereading *The Self-Assertion of the German University* that the words that disturbed me most were the cognates of "unity" or "one," as just now in *einheitlicher Aufbau,* echoed in the Bavarian reform plan entitled "The Simplification [*Vereinfachung*] of the University Administration in Bavaria." Even more than the words *Geist* and *geistig,* the following words were most

disconcerting to me: *einzig,* singly or uniquely; *Vereinfachung,* simplification
or a making onefold, as in the phrase, "Questioning then compels the extreme
Vereinfachung of one's view toward that which cannot be circumvented" (SB,
13); *Einfachheit,* simplicity, as in the phrase ". . . the essentiality and simplicity
of questioning in the midst of the historical-spiritual world of the people" (SB,
17); and even the article *ein,* especially when it is italicized, as it is more than
once in the rectoral address, thus becoming a "one": "But of *one* thing we can
be sure, [namely] . . . that the German university [must respond to] *one* formative force" (SB, 18); and "The faculty will be a faculty . . . when it shapes the
powers of Dasein that surround *it* into the *one* spiritual world of the people
[*die* eine *geistige Welt des Volkes*]" (SB, 17). A motley crowd of ghosts or
Geister may be a lovely, spirited thing; but one *Geist,* a univocal and sin-
glemindedly purposeful *Geist der Einigkeit und der Einfachheit,* bodes ill.

In the second paragraph of this same rectoral address (SB, 9), seeking the
essence of the German university, Heidegger comments that one commonly
perceives that essence to be the university's self-administration, *Selbstver-
waltung,* what Kant would have called its "autonomy." Concerning that autonomy Heidegger pledges perfunctorily, as though only a brief reminder suffices
to reconfirm a long-standing   *Do we build a house to stand for ever, do
we seal a contract to hold for all time?*   promise, *die soll erhalten
bleiben*—the university's autonomy "is to be preserved." Perhaps no one in
Germany could have seen to the preservation of administrative autonomy in
the university or in the Confederation of Institutes of Higher Learning; yet it
now seems clear that no one could have done more to destroy it than Martin
Heidegger did.

Heidegger first began to undermine the authority of the *Freiburger Senat*
simply by neglecting to convene it. It met once during his year in office. Yet the
constitutional changes he himself engineered on behalf of the ministry of culture in Karlsruhe go well beyond neglect. I will detail some of those changes in
a moment. However, allow me to set the tone for them by reproducing here
Heidegger's letter of July 3, 1933 (FrU, 56) to the collective institutes of higher
education in Germany, a letter addressed to the institutions themselves, not to
any of their elected officers or duly appointed representatives, nor even to any
chancellors, hence a letter to everyone and no one, as a sign of things to come:

An sämtliche deutsche Hochschulen
Der Herr Minister des Kultus, des Unterrichts und der Justiz hat mich mit Erlaß
vom 22 Juni 1933 ermächtigt, für die Dauer meines Rektorates aus der Dozenten-
schaft der Universität zu meiner Unterstützung einen Kanzler zu ernennen. Die
Bestimmung des Aufgabenbereiches des Kanzlers ist mir überlassen worden. Der
Kanzler hat innerhalb seiner Aufgaben "im Auftrage" des Rektors zu zeichnen,
meine Verantwortlichkeit für die Führung der Rektoratsgeschäfte bleibt hierdurch
unberührt. Zum Kanzler habe ich den a. o. Professor der Geologie Dr. Julius
Wilser ernannt.

Heidegger

To All German Institutes of Higher Education:
The Minister of Culture, Instruction, and Justice in his decree of 22nd June 1933 has empowered me to designate a chancellor [that is to say, the chief officer of the university administration and the *representative of the state* in the German university, normally not an academic but a civil servant proper] from among the university staff in order to assist me. Determination of the scope of the chancellor's duties has been left to me. In the fulfillment of his duties the chancellor is to sign his name with the phrase "acting on behalf of the Rector"; my responsibility for leadership in conducting the affairs of the rectorate thereby remains untouched. I have designated as chancellor an associate professor of geology, Dr. Julius Wilser.

Heidegger

Self-assertion of the German university: the chief representative of the state apparatus—to which, incidentally, Kant referred all power—is here made subordinate to the chief academic officer of the university, the rector—who, after all, is merely the elected representative of the faculties. To be sure, this rector is a *Führer-Rektor*, even if he does come, not from the superior faculties of theology, law, and medicine, but from the inferior faculty of philosophy. *Rectification* of the German university: even though Heidegger insists at the end of his rectoral address, "Every obeying contains in itself resistance [*den Widerstand*]," this particular philosopher is not of the left, not of the loyal opposition, not a member of the resistance, which, assembled in the university senate, Heidegger will now neutralize.

No common plan for university reform was ready for implementation at the *Reichsministerium* in Berlin during the summer of 1933. Karlsruhe, in *Musterländle* Baden, and Heidegger, stepped into the breach. On August 24, 1933 Heidegger circulated to university staff (and apparently to colleagues throughout Germany) a ministerial decree dated August 21 (FrU, 62–64). According to some sources, Heidegger himself composed the preamble to the government decree; it appears certain that he is the principal architect of the plan. The relationship between rector, deans, and senate is its main object, and while I will not drag readers through the entire document, there are certain points in it that merit scrutiny. In his introductory letter Heidegger celebrates the decree as the "initial foundation" for the "inner construction" of the university "in accord with the entire range of tasks we face in our education in the learned disciplines." The document itself begins by proclaiming the necessity of a re-formation (*Umgestaltung*) of the constitutions of universities throughout Germany, *im ganzen Reiche,* a renewal that will have to be "unified and thoroughgoing" (*einheitlich und umfassend*). Ironically, the question of reform in and among the faculties themselves—which is where Heidegger's genuine interest had always lain—is in effect postponed, even though the question of deanships touches on the matter of the division of the university into various faculties and academic sections: whereas Kant had called the deans the "regents" of their respective faculties, Heidegger would appoint these minor royalty himself, and they would be mere "heads of sections,"

Abteilungsleiter, "conductors" of a sort. Some excerpts and details now from the decree's four articles:

I. The Rector
1. The Rector is the leader [*Führer*] of the institution: all the rights and privileges of the Senate as it has been constituted heretofore in both its smaller and larger convocations revert to him. He will be designated and appointed by the Minister of Culture, Instruction, and Justice from among the range of full professors. . . . [The rector's right to appoint the chancellor and deans and to conduct all the affairs of the university is then briefly outlined.]

II. The Senate
1. As an advisory body, the Senate stands at the rector's disposal. [*Als beratende Körperschaft steht dem Rektor der Senat zur Verfügung.*]
2. The Senate shall consist of the Rector, the Chancellor, the Deans (section heads) . . . [and now comes a slip of the Minister's *Schreibmaschine,* a *Tippfehler,* a wonderful slip of the Party-State apparatus, for the next words of the document, hastily corrected by the ministry in its next decree, are these: listing the members of Senate, all of them so far appointed by the *Führer-Rektor,* the document now grants senate membership to *den Fakultäten (Abteilungen),* in other words, to all the faculties and hence to every member of the faculties! In order to avoid another "conflict of faculties" the ministry wisely altered the phrase to "heads," *Leiter,* the centrally appointed "leaders" or "conductors" of the faculty sections] . . . and five other Senators to be designated by the Rector.

In the rectoral address (SB, 18) Heidegger quotes Clausewitz to this effect: "I reject the frivolous hope that the hand of contingency will aid us." Heidegger and the Minister, one must say, left nothing to chance.

Also of interest in the August 21 Karlsruhe decree is the fact that the reformed—that is, "synchronized"—student body is generously represented in the newly selected (rather than elected) senate: use of student pressure against recalcitrant professors was an essential part of Heidegger's—and not only Heidegger's—university "reform." It is this organization of the radical *Studentenschaft* that in our own (past? gone forever?) days of student activism gives cause for considerable discomfiture and concern. (I am thinking of some soul-searching questions that one can find, for example, in Gérard Granel, *De l'université.*[8]) However, let us leap to paragraph five of article II, which is succinct and decisive: "5. The Senate will pass no resolutions. Votes therefore will not take place [*Der Senat fasst keine Beschlüsse. Abstimmungen erfolgen daher nicht*]." Many further details deserve our attention, but what I have presented thus far surely communicates a sense of the document, allows us to taste the flavor of it. It concludes as follows (article IV, paragraph 5): "All prior determinations to the contrary are hereby declared null and void; in particular, the smaller and larger convocations of Senate, along with the staff's General Assembly, will no longer convene. (Signed:) Dr. Wacker."

Along with the somewhat less radical *Vereinfachung der bayrischen Hochschulverwaltung,* the *Karlsruher Erlass* of August 21, 1933 served, as I have mentioned, as the paradigm for the rectification of the German university throughout the Reich. By the end of 1933, with the establishment of the *Reichsverband der Deutschen Hochschulen,* "synchronization" had by and large been achieved, although only on August 3, 1935 did the *Reichsministerium* "simplify" the entire system. When it needed a Minister of Science *Deal justly before the face of the Sun* to take up residence in Berlin, Karlsruhe's Minister of Culture, Dr. Wacker, got the nod, and he did not elect to stay in that model province of Baden. (*Wacker* in German, incidentally, means something like "stout-hearted," as in, "Give me some men who are. . . .")

The story of the quarrels and disagreements that compelled Heidegger to resign after only one year in office cannot be told here, but it is certainly a less heroic tale of *The heroes, the wise men, like the new moon, have their waxing and waning* demission or defenestration than Heidegger himself has made it seem in his various retrospects. The lapidary remark of historian Bernd Martin (FrU, 69) seems apt: *ungeeignet zum Führen,* "unfit to lead." Martin's judgment accords with what Hannah Arendt told me in Freiburg years ago: "He was a lousy administrator. The only thing he was able to get done was that ski lodge for the Student Union up on Schauinsland." (In my journal, where I recorded our conversation, I expressed doubts about this eyewitness account, thinking that it might have been distorted: it seemed almost banal. . . . I confess I even used the word "myopic." *Let my eyes see the sun until they are dazzled with looking.* All these years later, fifteen of them, I find her glauconic [with an "n," not an "m"] judgment confirmed.) Let me pass, then, to my third and final topic, the one that brings me closest to the book's proper theme, namely, daimon life. *Although I am no better than a dead man, still let me see the light of the sun.*

THE UNIVERSITY OF LIFE

The first detailed account of Heidegger's 1921–1922 Freiburg lecture course that reached me was Hans-Georg Gadamer's lecture to the Collegium Phaenomenologicum in Perugia, Italy, in 1986. In the middle of that lecture Gadamer paused and said something like this: "I have read this text, but it is very difficult and I do not understand it well yet. And so I shall have to live a few years longer!" I wish Gadamer those years! Even though we have examined the text at the outset of chapter 1, above, I still feel shy about condensing into a few pages—and dismal pages at that, pages on the dreariness of Heidegger and politics—this most extraordinary text, published as volume 61 in the Martin Heidegger Gesamtausgabe.⁹

Heidegger's "Introduction to Phenomenological Research" wants to do a lot, and in a hurry; it is laced with the most sardonic polemics; ultimately, in the perspective of the ontology of Dasein that is to come, it is perhaps more promise than fulfillment. Its proper theme? Phenomenological research. Into what? Into methodology, Aristotle, the university, and life. Above all, life, "factical life," *das faktische Leben.* Yet what has life to do with the university, or the university with life? Let me begin at the beginning of the course, in order to follow some of its major moves.

The course will ostensibly be about Aristotle's philosophy, but not before a few preliminary questions are resolved. For example, what is *history* of philosophy? What it should be is confrontation with what is truly historic in and about philosophy; but that can be grasped only when we ourselves are philosophizing. The history of philosophy "is graspable only as existence, accessible only in terms of purely factical life . . ." (61, 1). Accessible, *zugänglich:* "access" or *Zugang* is one of the course's leitmotivs. Recall that at the outset of *Being and Time* (SZ, 6, 7, 16, 21, 36) it is an interpreter's *Zugang* to the question of the meaning of being that Heidegger most carefully analyzes; recall too that access to the world-relation of the animal is precisely what resists comparative analysis; recall finally that beings in the world are inaccessible *as such* to the animal. In the 1921–1922 lecture course "access" will tie this presumably stratospheric philosophical question—concerning history and existence—to the familiar and yet uncanny and sometimes monstrous institution we call *the university.*

Phenomenological research into the historic import of philosophy leads naturally enough to the even broader question, What is philosophy? (61, 11–12). The task of defining philosophy is quite commonly both overestimated and underestimated: overestimated by formalists and methodology fanatics, underestimated by philosophy professors who encourage their pupils to get out there and have an *Erlebnis,* never mind what sort, never mind how. Heidegger's scorn ranges and rages over both, but especially over the latter, not because he despises fundamental existentiell experience (*existentielle Grunderfahrung*) but precisely because that is what he most needs. His polemic against *Lebensphilosophie* can be understood only against the backdrop of his own conviction that rigorous research into, say, philosophical categories or the history of philosophy can bear fruit only if it is rooted in, and constantly refers back to, *dem faktischen Leben, der Situation des Lebens.* The very bitterness of his polemics—against Rickert, Spengler (although Spengler is treated more generously here than anywhere else in Heidegger's oeuvre), Jaspers, Bergson, Nietzsche (although Nietzsche is already an exceptional puzzlement to Heidegger), and Scheler—testifies to his conviction that philosophy is "illumination of factical life" (26), and nothing else.

However, what should such "illumination" (*Erhellung*) be, and why should it be necessary? It should be something that grows out of, grows together with, factical life itself: it should be *concrete.* But then why is it necessary? Because life is hazy (*diesig*). Already we discern the paradox: factical life—our lives as we live them—is the only resource for philosophical problematics and phenomenological research; yet that resource is for essential reasons obscured by a mist and is most often inaccessible to us. Philosophical questioning should ripen or temporalize naturally: *Zeitigung,* maturation or temporalization, is already a fundamental category for Heidegger. (More than a category, we must say, inasmuch as it binds research to life; later on, Heidegger will call it an *existential.*) It almost seems as though the meaning of being as *time* will emerge simply as a result of the persistence of the word *Zeitigung* in Heidegger's text, *Zeit-igung* being literally the timing of time. Research is fundamentally a life-process, *ein Vollzug des Lebens,* and not some mad dash after "theory" for its own sake. Yet why is this natural process so rare? Why does it need the toilsome supplement that is philosophizing? Why does it need the embarrassment of *university* philosophy? All that professorial waffle? There can be no doubt that maturation, temporalization, and process also bring with them philosophical senescence (that incessant talk about inanities in the philosophy classroom), decrepitude (that perpetuation of vapid traditional problematics— "Hey, kids, how do we know whether that chair is *really* there?"), and ultimately *rigor mortis* (the worship of "eternal" truths and "eternal" values to which the philosopher pays lip and knee service). Heidegger is already by 1921 absorbed in the practice of a *Destruktion* of inherited categories, methods, and norms; by now he knows full well that philosophical questioning always falls prey to a *Fehltendenz,* a tendency to lose itself in things that seem "evident" to "everybody." How resist that tendency? How cultivate the maturation of life's genuine questionability (*Fraglichkeit*)? How assist or accelerate the ripening of insight; how supplement the temporalization of access (*die Zeitigung des Zugangs*)?

Heidegger prescribes a certain kind of appropriation (*Aneignung*) of the tradition to our own life-situation. "Our" own? As we shall see, or hear, his lectures invariably communicate the sense that professor and students must join in the shared task of appropriation. That word *appropriation* will remain essential to the fundamental ontology of Dasein. Appropriation is the making-our-own of the situation in which we understand (41ff.: *die Aneignung der Verstehenssituation*). Such appropriation is doubtless highly complex. In addition to the destructuring of the entire tradition from Plato and Aristotle onward, it instigates a whole range of detailed phenomenological descriptions, many of which will perdure through *Being and Time*. It is in this complex discussion of the appropriation of the situation in which we understand, a situation that is in part natural process and in part existentiell engagement, that Heidegger first mentions the university (50). He speaks as one who until very recently was himself a student. To study philosophy as it is taught in the universities is to confront a corpus—most often a corpse—of doctrines. It is to suffer the schizophrenia of "systematic philosophy" versus "history of philosophy." Yet Plato's φιλοσοφία μουσική means, according to Heidegger, something else: it means a certain way to behave, a certain manner of comportment; it means how we adopt a stance toward beings, beings of any kind whatsoever. Philosophy is, or should be, *ein Wie des Sichverhaltens,* and "how we comport ourselves" is simply *to philosophize*. Even in 1921–1922 one notices a certain preference on Heidegger's part for *Sichverhalten*, comportment, over mere behavior. *Philosophieren* is an intransitive verb, like *musizieren,* "to make music." After the manner of Socrates. The phenomenon of philosophy, however grotesque its appearance in the university, has an *archontic* sense—the sense of its being, ὄντως ὄν, from the origin, ἀρχή. Yet archontic sense, which is anything but anarchic, will not be found fixed and mounted in the pages of Plato and Aristotle, at least not there alone; factical life will have to come to bear on philology and history, the genuine questionability of life will have to gnaw its way to the surface, if there is to be philosophizing. Indeed, the image of something "gnawing," an image Heidegger no doubt finds in Protestant devotional and spiritual-ascetic texts, is extremely important in his lectures (see, for example, 61, 137–40). It constitutes a kind of negative-dispositive of the "kairological character" of time (which he describes as "sitting still, being able to wait" for the arrival of the "fitting time"), as an enhancement of what he will soon call "ruination"; thus "gnawing" is related in some myterious way (mysterious in the way that all matters of the genealogy of morals are mysterious) to what he will then call "counterruination," the counterthrust that philosophizing is, inasmuch as it "eats away" at life's false sense of security. And *where* is such rodent-like factical life, infesting the walls and gnawing its way to the surface? In the university.

Before we enter Heidegger's university, or our own, let us dwell a moment on this strange notion, *das faktische Leben,* which we met in the first two chapters of the present book. "Factical" is a term apparently derived from Dilthey.[10] The bulk of Heidegger's 1921–1922 course is devoted to it. Whose factical life? Once again, "our own." In a biological sense? No, not until 1929–1930, as we have seen, does Heidegger teach a course in the philosophy of biology—one of his most brilliantly conceived and maddeningly disappointing endeavors. What, then, is our own factical life? It is a life of passion (*Leidenschaft*) for all the things one can come to know (*Wissenschaft*). Passion and science constitute the odd couple that will dominate Heidegger's inaugural address, "What Is Metaphysics?", delivered eight years later, after his sojourn at Marburg and return to Freiburg. However, factical life is more than—but also perhaps less than—the consuming passion to know, and Heidegger now elaborates a whole series of fundamental categories concerning life, *Grundkategorien des Lebens* (84ff.). They are so far from being pellucid, even in the retrospect granted by *Being and Time,* that we might suspect that Heidegger has succeeded primarily in capturing life's haze. Nevertheless, in the history of philosophy, nothing ever quite like this, as far as I can see, has ever been thought. Here especially I will do Heidegger grave injustice, since I am anxious to get to the university. A quick sketch, then, no more than that, simply to remind ourselves of material we have already considered.

Factical life is a sequential unity, a maturation process, a temporalizing of a certain stretch (*Erstreckung*) of time, a certain coherence of time. That coherent sequence consists of possibilities, some of which we can shape, some to which we are simply delivered over. In the latter we confront a certain actuality or reality of life (*Wirklichkeit*), a certain power (*Macht*) that we call fate or destiny (*Schicksal*). Such power our vision never penetrates. Destiny is *undurchsichtig*. Later Heidegger will identify the power of destiny in life as a certain "mightiness"; later still he will identify the mightiness of being as a whole as "plenipotence," *Übermacht,* the hyperpower of the holy. I note in passing that the famous analyses of anxiety, uncanniness, and being-unto-death in Heidegger's *Being and Time* do not appear in this course, even though factical life is clearly identified as *Existenz, Da-sein*, and even *"Sein"* as such (*61, 85*). Many of the fundamental structures of *Being and Time* do appear here in their nascent form: world, care and taking-care, repetition or recovery, environment, being with others in a common world (*Mitwelt*), and so on. Yet here, as in the 1929–1930 course on biology, the dominant thought of the analysis is the animation or animatedness, *die Bewegtheit*, the χίνησις of factical life as temporalization. Such animatedness cannot be described in linear fashion. Rather, life is tendency—and it is tendentious. There is something about it that always entails dispersion and a squandering of forces. Life is restless, loves detours: it is *unruhig* and *umwegig* (93, 88). Among the fundamental categories that pertain to life in motion are, we recall, the following: *Neigung,* inclination or proclivity; *Abstandstilgung,* elimination of distance; *Abriegelung,* enforced isolationism, a bolting or locking oneself away; *das "Leichte,"* the facile or easy.

Let us dwell a moment longer on this last fundamental category of factical life. Aristotle says that bad things, faults and errors, are easy, there are so many to choose from, and no matter where you land, you are liable to meet one; whereas what is fitting is usually just one, μοναχῶς, and when pursuing it we usually either go too far or fall too short of it. Factical life for the most part is either   *Utnapishtim replied*   hyperbolic or elliptical. Thus Heidegger complains to Jaspers in the mid-1920s that his life in the "foggy nest" of Marburg (meaning the *University* of Marburg) is too easy: "The flimsy facile stuff down here ruins one in the long run [*dieses weiche leichte Zeug hier unten ruiniert einen auf die Dauer*]."[11] Facility means ruination, *das Leichte = Ruinanz.* The fitting, the good, is apparently never light and easy but always heavy and hard.

Because of our obsession with security—recall that fifteen years later, in his lectures on Nietzsche (NII, 141–47/4, 96–101), Heidegger writes of the fundamental early-modern transition from security-in-sanctity to security-in-certitude—we fall short of, or pass on by, the primal decision (*Urentscheidung*) that would enable us to stop running, stop evading. Life is "prestructured" in such a way that it sees itself only as mirrored in the world. Factical life is *reluzent* (61, 100, 106, 123; cf. SZ, 16, 21). It is more moon than sun. Further, life plunges (131: *stürzt*) into the world, struggles for "success, status, advantage, position, attainment" (121), all the while plummeting in ignomiry. Factical life is *Ab-fall*, downfall and throwaway. Lapsing, plunging, squandering its resources, factical life masks its own drive to security, clutches its eternal values, eternal truths, eternal gods; and, as we have heard, when it plunges it prevaricates, procrastinates, evades, and sighs, "How hard my life is!" Factical life is *Larvanz*, a play of masks, *Maskenspiel*, mummery and mime. Meanwhile, nothing can conceal the fact that life chases after something that eludes it. Life must in fact do without. It is *Darbung*, something between sheer deficiency (almost an *Entbehren*, deprivation, one might say) and willful abnegation, *privatio, carentia.* Plunging, lapsing, falling, fleeing, masking, renouncing, factical life is *Ruinanz* (from *ruina, Sturz:* a fall or plunge). As we recall from our earlier discussion, life collides against nothing, nothing at all (143–48). Existence bottoms out, life plummets without cease, until death.

Whence, then, in all the world the counterthrust of questioning—whence phenomenological research? And where will we find this mysterious supplement at work, gnawing its way forward like a rat or a highly charged mouse? In the university. Not simply in authenticity or appropriateness, *Eigentlichkeit,* as we might expect in the perspective of *Being and Time.* Indeed, as we saw in chapter 1, the binary structure *Eigentlichkeit/Uneigentlichkeit* is forcefully and even fatefully challenged here, six years before Heidegger makes it the supporting pillar or central axis of fundamental ontology, by the operation of one of those rare exclamation marks. The animatedness of factical life, however autonomous and autochthonous it may appear to be, "does not itself properly (!) make the movement." What is proper to the proper animatedness of factical life proper is that its movement is *properly not its own.* If life itself, and human life in particular, have since Aristotle been defined as *self*-movement and autonomous agency, then the passive voice of "animatedness," *Bewegtheit,* will send reverberations through everything we call philosophical anthropology and even through metaphysics as such. Self-movement proper properly depends on a force that is simultaneously extrinsic and intrinsic to it, a force something like death. A diabolical dependency, indeed, not so much on the *world* as on *time*—which, however, does not yet stand at the center of Heidegger's inquiry. Even so, it is high time we entered the university. Of *life.*

If life is as Pauline, Augustinian, Lutheran, and Kierkegaardian as Heidegger suggests, whence in all the world the passion for science, the lust for illumination? Whence the passion that will enable us to test in some way the fundamental categories of factical life? This question conducts us to the question of the university as the site of testing, probing, and questioning. Derrida's hypothesis in "*Mochlos,*" to the effect that the trajectory of Heidegger's relation to the university and the sciences describes an arc away from both of these toward an encounter with intimations of beyng (*Seyn*) itself, is surely sound. However, in 1921–1922 we are near the outset of that trajectory, and here the university is still quite vital.[12]

Let me now take a step even farther back toward the outset of that trajectory, interrupting my account of the 1921–1922 course by referring to the opening remarks of the oldest recorded lecture course by Heidegger that we have. In the "War-Emergency Semester" of 1919, which lasted from January 25 till April 16, Heidegger lectured on "The Idea of Philosophy and the Problem of the Worldview [*das Weltanschauungsproblem*]" (56/57, 1–117). He opened his course with a "Preliminary Observation" on "Science and University Reform." As we read this text, it soon becomes clear that what Heidegger has in mind bears no relation to *reform* of the university faculties, the senate, or the administration. His concern is what it means to be a scholar and teacher in a time of cultural crisis and collapse—a time when neo-Kantian value theory threatens to reduce philosophy to the mere classification of "worldviews."

Heidegger strives against the epistemologies and value theories of Windelband, Cohen, and Rickert (all of them discussed here in detail), hoping to replace them with a program of phenomenological research that will constitute a "pretheoretical primal science" of philosophy, *eine vortheoretische Urwissenschaft*. I cannot do justice here to Heidegger's vision, but can only emphasize what this "reform" of university philosophy is *not*.

While theory and the philosophical life generally can be described as the *habitus* of a personal existence (which Heidegger is already calling *Dasein*), such personal existence finds itself caught up in a prevailing environment consisting of sundry things and fellow human beings, the environment of a predominant society, *Gesellschaft*. The scholar is not isolated, but is also a member of the other half of the Tönniesian distinction, that is, a member of a community or *Gemeinschaft* of researchers who also are striving toward the ideals of science and learning. The scholar is organized by and into scientific academies and universities (56/57, 4). To be sure, these are threatened by the crises precipitated by the war and the turmoil of postwar Germany. I cite Heidegger's "Preliminary Observation," in which the influence of Dilthey ("generation," "nexus of life," etc.) is palpable, at length:

> University reform, much discussed of late, is altogether misguided. It totally misconceives what constitutes every genuine revolutionizing of the spirit [*Revolutionierung des Geistes*] when it spreads abroad its manifestos, protest meetings, programs, societies, and confederations. For these are counterspiritual means [*geistwidrige Mittel*], serving ephemeral goals.
>
> We are not mature enough today to achieve *genuine* reforms in the university sphere. Such maturation is a matter for an *entire generation*. Renewal of the university means rebirth of genuine scientific consciousness and of a nexus of life [*Lebenszusammenhang*]. Yet life-relations renew themselves by going back to the genuine origins of spirit; as historical phenomena, they need the calm and the security [*Ruhe und Sicherheit*] of a genetic crystallization [*genetischen Sichverfestigens*]. In other words, they need the inner veracity of a highly valued, self-constructing life. Life alone—and not the hullabaloo surrounding overhasty culture-programs—is "epoch-making." Such life is inhibited by the "active spirit" of young men who are a bit too free with the pen [*schreibgewandte Jünglinge*]; it is counterfeited by the attempt—visible in all the learned disciplines, from biology to the history of literature and art—to help themselves to a "worldview" by borrowing phrases and constructions from a philosophy that is itself in disrepair.
>
> However, just as tremendous awe causes the religious man to be silent about his ultimate mystery; and just as the genuine artist lives only as long as he is giving shape to something and refraining from talk, despising all effete chatter; just so, the scholar [*der wissenschaftliche Mensch*] achieves an impact only through the vitality of genuine research [*die Lebendigkeit echter Forschung*]. (56/57, 4–5)

No doubt the ideal of genuine research—phenomenology, not as a methodology that has been refined to a point where it can no longer be applied to history and culture, but as a philosophical *questioning* arising out of and returning to the nexus of life—remains Heidegger's ideal during the 1920s, the years that culminate in *Being and Time*. However, let me return now to the

1921–1922 course, "Introduction to Phenomenological Research," and its essential context, "factical life."

Precisely when it grows together with factical life, coming to fruition in "kairological time," the unpredictable, fitting time, philosophical questioning within the university burgeons *against* the downward pull of false security, mirror, mask, and plunge. Philosophizing is—or at least can be—*gegenruinant*, counterruinous (176). Life embraces a capacity for resistance (177: *Widerständigkeit*). (Recall the notion of *Widerstand* in the rectoral address, and in Kant's *Conflict of the Faculties*). The university is the home of that resistance, and nowhere more so than in its philosophy faculty. To be sure, even in that faculty possible progress toward proper understanding finds itself swamped in dailiness (*Täglichkeit*); yet there is at least a chance that in the university we can bring matters to the light of day. We do not yet properly possess understanding, but we are already on the scene, incipiently questioning, "in the nexus and process in which we now are currently moving" (62). We? We, who?

> Our endeavors are not brought to completion sometime, somewhere, and by somebody. Rather, here and now we are living in these endeavors—in this very place, in this lecture hall. You in front of me, I in front of you, we together. We designate this initially determinable (self-worldly), with-worldly, and environmental situation, or the nexus of life that prevails and properly lives in this situation, with the term *university*. (61, 63)

Whether the life-situation in the university and the lecture hall will provide *access* to genuine questions, whether it will open itself to its own being and its own origin, its archontic sense, is not yet decided—*es ist damit noch nichts entschieden* (64). (Compare the peroration of the rectoral address [SB, 19], where the young people, the students, *die junge und jüngste Kraft des Volkes*, have "already decided.") Of course, there are "difficulties" and "doubts" about life in the university. The philosophy taught there—is it really philosophy? Heidegger's polemics against the Marburg philosophers and his own mentor Heinrich Rickert appear to have answered that question already. (And I remember my own first philosophy course at university, taught by a man of the cloth who had returned from the missions in order to be put out to academic pasture, a course that caused me to write in my journal, "The philosopher—what an incredible mixture of arrogance and naïveté," and I knew then that I would never have anything to do with that discipline, but something happened, I plunged, life has detours and is hazy.) Philosophy in the university has ossified, even if some famous contemporary philosophers think it is a cultural value, proclaim it edifying, insist that the endless babble continue. Nevertheless, it will not do to flee the university into the hothouse of the belle-lettrists, to seek refuge among the literary types. In a fallen world, where ease prevails, "it is easy to run away from the university." *Von der Universität weglaufen ist leicht* (66). However, it could be that new possibilities of access will arise within the university, that our situation will become "radically relevant and free," not merely allowing but demanding and enabling the most radical development of philosophy. Not that struggle and polemic will ever become dispensable: there will always have to be *Destruktion*, inasmuch as *Da-sein* itself is a kind of polemic. *Polemik . . . als solche durch da-sein* (67). We shall return to the matter of polemic in later chapters.

However, a second wave of "difficulty" and "doubt" rises (68, 114): Is not the university's situation an accident of history, and has it not so deteriorated that the institution as such and as a whole appears to be in demise? Precisely this demise is our situation, we live it, and anything we come to understand will have its (crumbling) "ground" here. No doubt the situation will differ from university to university; luckily, Freiburg differs from the others, there is genuine questioning occurring there, Husserl and phenomenology are at work, it would be worthwhile writing a book about philosophy in the university for one's Freiburg colleagues (187, 190–93). However, as in the Postwar trimester of 1919, the factical life-situation in the university or in the classroom today, in 1921, has nothing to do with the brouhaha surrounding a general *university reform* (69ff.): all these discussions about reform are "uncritical," they avoid the question as to who is competent to judge these matters and they forget the question as to the fitting time for change. And Heidegger, the future Führer-Rector of the University of Freiburg, now makes a remarkable statement— remember that this is 1921: "For us, here, it is a matter of seeing philosophically the situation proper, without anyone playing prophet, without the coquettish charms of a 'leader' [*ohne Prophetentum und Führerallüren*]. (People today are writing about the Führer problem! [*Man schreibt heute über das Führer-problem!*])" (70).[13]

Yet if prophets and Führers cannot shore up the sinking level of the students' spiritual-mental preparation (*geistig-seelische Vorbereitung*) for life, neither can insipid agreements negotiated in faculty meetings and confirmed by majority votes (Heidegger plays with the words *Stimmungen* and *Abstimmungen* here) prevent the university from foundering. What is needed is the full engagement of a life, *der Einsatz eines Lebens*—what in later lectures at Marburg University Heidegger will call *existenzieller Einsatz*, "existential engagement or commitment" (26, 176)—genuine passion, and a certain resoluteness in understanding. True, factical life proper is always in flight from investigation into matters of principle. It will therefore always be a matter of preliminary, preparatory labors   *does the flood-tide of rivers endure?*   against the floodtide, as it were. Yet Heidegger has some confidence that his own generation—and "generation" is a crucial category here, as it was in 1919 and will be in section 74 of *Being and Time*—with its highly developed historical sense will be better prepared than any prior generation to perform this work. In a marginal note he sketches a route from the university of "today" back to that of the epoch of German Idealism, to the ages of Humanism, Reformation, and High Scholasticism, and on back to Alexandria, the Lykeion, and the Akademia; he even invokes the possibility of an "objective comparison" of what "objectively has been" (61, 73) with regard to the university. Elsewhere, however, he notes that the dream of "theoretical objectivity" is that corner of the world's masked ball that is reserved for philosophers (90, 155). And even in these pages (72) he notes that "education" or "formation" at the university is ambiguous: *Bildung* and *Ausbildung* have to do with *Bilder,* images that are always prefigured (or disfigured) in the world, and thus *reluzent* (128). There is no prophesying how those images will now temporalize, no telling how they will construe. One can hope that "tradition" will not be mere mummery, reflected glory, self-deception, and plunge for us who are in the university, not mere *Larvanz, Reluzenz,* and *Ruinanz;* one can hope that the tradition will make a genuine claim on us. Yet Heidegger closes these remarks on the university (76) with a series of troubling questions. What part or aspect of the university is here in question, which is supposed to measure itself against a glorious past? What *is* the university itself? Who are you in front of me, who am I in front of you? He replies:

> We said that the university is a *nexus of life* [*ein* Lebenszusammenhang], something lived in. How do matters stand with this 'living' at and in the university? Shall we take up the university and experience it? However, this question is always and everywhere to be posed concretely, as we take it here and now, as we live it. We live it in the way we ourselves are, on the basis of, and within, our *factical Dasein.* (61, 76)

What does Heidegger want? Does he want us all to *live in* the university? To be boarders? Or does he want us all to *live the university?* Can we   *You will never find the life for which you are searching*   any longer say that our passion is science? Do we dare yet say that what we most desire to know is all-consuming passion? What Augustine clearly would have regarded as concupiscence? What, after all, has the university to do with life? Will anything in the *tradition* of the university help us to answer such questions?

The question of tradition, university tradition, will have to be held in abeyance, observes Heidegger, until we have some sense of the *being* of the university, today, for us. Otherwise we will never know what is fitting or what is fatal about it as a situation for the fundamental experience of questioning. Whether we might learn anything from history and tradition, whether like a crab we can go   *There is no permanence*   backwards, will depend on such questioning within facticity, without anything   *From days of old there is no permanence*   that even vaguely resembles security.

One must return to one's own university, then, you in front of me, I trailing along behind, hoping that it is one of the very few universities where thinking flourishes, where there are colleagues worth writing books for, and where it is worthwhile plunging into university work. So many students to teach and papers to sign! And, oh, those insipid meetings of Senate. . . . How hard our life is! Perhaps we shall find a moment or two in the midst of it all to ask what our passion is. We know that then we shall be close to life. . . .

All the same, we might try to remember that as dubious a character as Heidegger may be, it is often best to allow him the last word, precisely because his analyses never culminate in definitive results. For his categorial analysis of factical life has not in fact arrived at a categorical result. Factical life has not been squeezed into a ball and rolled toward some overwhelming conception of university education. Nothing has been decided about the way in which we shall *live* the university. Nothing has been decided, nothing rectified, once and for all. It is still a matter of you in front of me, I in front of you. Or, as Heidegger also says, of *us together*. That much we know. The rest is masked.   *It is only the nymph of the dragon-fly who sheds her larva and sees the sun in glory.*   The formulae are scattered, the clay tablets shattered. Here are the foreboding concluding words of the 1921–1922 lecture course (61, 155), with which I shall close this chapter:

> Or is not the objective and ontological meaning of factical life, if the genuine mode of access to it lives in the process of questionability, in categorial terms precisely *not* univocal? Does not factical life fend off as a matter of principle any thorough-going or pure functionalism as regards the relations to be defined? Is it not, as far as meaning is concerned, shattered [*zerbrochen*]?

ADDENDUM TO CHAPTER FOUR

ON THE HARD *GESCHLECHT*

Remarks on Hugo Ott, *Martin Heidegger: Unterwegs zu seiner Biographie*
(1988),
Jürgen Habermas, "Foreword" to Victor Farías, *Heidegger und der Nationalsozialismus* (1989),
Philippe Lacoue-Labarthe, *La fiction du politique: Heidegger, l'art et la politique* (1987),
and Dominique Janicaud, *L'ombre de cette pensée: Heidegger et la question politique* (1990).[14]

Pflichtlektüre. "Required reading." Hugo Ott's *Martin Heidegger: On the Way to His Biography* is required reading for every serious student of Heidegger's philosophy, precisely because his is not a philosophical book and does not pretend to be one. There are no doubt moments when one must object to Ott's embarrassing attempts to say more than the results of his research sanction. Yet on balance the book gathers together and interprets meticulously documents that are otherwise impossible to come by, documents that remove the "Heidegger Scandal" from the realms of yellow journalism and hagiographic whitewash alike. Ott's book will please no one, neither the Heidegger Haters and Baiters nor the Holy Heideggerians, neither the Heidegger Bashers nor the Heideggerians of the Strict Persuasion, and that is a good thing. After the dishonest book by Victor Farías—recently granted an *Imprimatur* by the leading advocate of emancipatory discourse and communicative praxis, and recently released with high entrepreneurial hopes onto the American "market"—and the equally dishonest efforts by Heidegger-Gesellschaft members to suppress evidence and avoid consequences, one can only welcome Ott's book. In this brief Addendum (in the context of *daimon life*) there can be no question of an adequate review of this book or any of the others. Allow me to single out six strengths and six weaknesses, as I see them. First, the weaknesses:

(1) Ott develops in depth only two stations of his way toward a Heidegger biography, namely, Heidegger's early religious education and his activities as rector of Freiburg University. One senses the gap that opens up between these two stations (for example, between pages 128 and 129) and swallows so many things that would have to come under scrutiny—among them, to be sure, Heidegger's *thinking*.

(2) So little appears about Heidegger's family life, either his parental home or the household he established with Elfride, about his friends, colleagues, intimates, and so on. Ott also seems to want to reduce Elfride's role in Heidegger's political engagement to an ironic reference or two, which, as even the French Occupation Forces knew, is hardly sufficient. And if Ott dreams of demonstrating what he calls "an ambivalence in the structure of Heidegger's personality" (162–63), he supplies far too little evidence and himself possesses far too little of the requisite psychological acumen to establish the point. In short, Ott's book is not really on the way to being an adequate biography. For that larger task—which is itself highly problematic, inasmuch as biography and autobiography are among the genres that have by now lost whatever theoretical innocence they may once have had, and which is for all practical purposes impossible as long as Heidegger's correspondence remains shut away in the Archive—a writer and researcher with more generous gifts will be necessary.

(3) Although Ott prides himself in the skills of his historian's craft, he is often insufficiently critical of his sources. The worst instance is his taking always and everywhere at face value Jaspers's criticisms of Heidegger (see 177 and 244ff.), whereas Jaspers himself always takes pains to admit how dubious and precarious he finds his own judgments of Heidegger to be, precisely because they arise from the source of his greatest suffering and self-doubt.[15]

(4) Ott often crosses wires, confusing events that occur at quite distinct levels, taking such crossings and confusions as telling evidence: (a) he overestimates Theodor Haecker's *Was ist der Mensch?* as a catalyst for Heidegger's 1935 *Einführung in die Metaphysik* (255ff.); (b) he traces Heidegger's anticlericalism back to his failure to receive an appointment to the Freiburg professorship in Medieval (Catholic) Philosophy, as though there were no other larger issues involved; (c) he conflates Heidegger's politics with his "seductive language," here too following Jaspers's lead (and a cliché of our time) quite uncritically; (d) he wonders aloud whether the fact that Heidegger gives Hans Jantzen a biography of Hermann Göring in 1933 and that the 1951 "Logos" essay is Heidegger's contribution to Jantzen's Festschrift means that Göring and Heraclitus somehow form a pair and are joined (*sich fügen*) in Heidegger's thought; (e) he associates Heidegger's relatively lenient treatment by the French *épuration* process with Jean-Paul Sartre's "importation" of Heidegger into

France, so that the duped French from Sartre to Derrida (*die Wacht am Rhein,* revisited) are seen as responsible for Heidegger's otherwise inexplicable "comeback" in Germany. Etc., etc.

(5) If Ott's book has a philosophical thesis, it is that Heidegger serves as the Secretary of Beyng, By Appointment to Its Majesty, in such a way that Heidegger is himself the one who arranges the advent of *Seyn;* thus, according to Ott, Heidegger believes himself to be at a safe remove from the possibility of errancy, and, with truth as correctness having been supplanted by truth as disclosure (= anything goes = Tugendhat for the People), Heidegger then wanders the ways of political wickedness. It is actually *fortunate* that Ott has very little to say about Heidegger's thought.

(6) Ott says he wants to ask about the relation of *Werk* to *Mensch* (131). Yet he is ill-placed to do so, because he is barred by dearth of familiarity from the former and has at the end of the day precious little insight into the latter. While he would like to demonstrate *eine Ambivalenz in der Persönlichkeitsstruktur Heideggers,* to repeat, he has little sense of what either ambivalence or personality might mean. We are not dealing here with an author of great psychological penetration.

No, the book's strengths lie elsewhere.

(1) The account of Heidegger's early schooling, especially his religious education, is detailed and carefully drawn; the matter is of enormous importance for many if not all aspects of Heidegger's thinking. (Heidegger's interest in arithmetic, mathematics, physics, and chemistry—and his competence in these areas—also receives its due.)[16]

(2) Heidegger's relations with Husserl, even though they are treated in absolute ignorance of the issues of phenomenology and hermeneutical ontology, receive an informed consideration here. Likewise Heidegger's academic career in Freiburg and Marburg, although, again, without insight into scholarly and philosophical matters. In general, Ott is at his very best when discussing academic politics and intra-university disputes, intrigues, and campaigns. These abound, and anyone who thinks that Heidegger must have been above that sort of thing is in for a rude surprise.

(3) Ott's treatment of the rectorate, of Heidegger's relations to the Party during and after 1933–1934, is superb. The accounts of the denunciations of Eduard Baumgarten and Hermann Staudinger ("Aktion Sternheim"), even though the former is incomplete, are simply devastating—here Jaspers's judgment of Heidegger seems to have been entirely accurate, and it modifies my own earlier judgments (cited in note 15) on the Heidegger-Jaspers relationship.

(4) Ott's account of Heidegger's admiration of military or soldierly qualities, his adulation of World War I heroes (one of whom he was not), coupled with his chronically endangered health, is revealing. That account would no doubt have been better balanced had it heeded the *identical revelations* by Jaspers's *Philosophical Autobiography* in this regard. In the end, it is not Heidegger's "private" (that is, problematic and eccentric) nazism that strikes the most terrifying chords: it is his ideological militancy and militarism, his

unbridled and uncritical nationalism and chauvinism, and his unrestrained personal ambition and expediency. If one insists on pushing the question, "Was Heidegger a Nazi, or was he not?" Ott's book suggests the inevitable answer: Heidegger was too much a nazi to have been a Nazi, too rigorous and radical in his view of the "Movement," too bemused about the possibility of his own role of leadership in it, and too selective about what he took the "inner truth and greatness" of National Socialism to be.

(5) One of the merits of Ott's book is that it discusses in an honest and balanced way (after Farías' "emancipated" version) the question of Heidegger's (possible) antisemitism. If Ott is unable, as he says, to provide "a unified picture," it is because the picture is not unified (180ff.). One of the book's achievements is to put to rest rumors and calumnies that have been around so long that eveyone assumes they *must* be true (the moralizing rumormonger's mainstay), and he does this without the least hint of "protectionism" or "beautification." Ott's response in this regard is neither devastating nor reassuring, and it is probably the best response we will ever get. Was Heidegger an antisemite? Sometimes it seems so—especially when (as we will see in chapter 5) he wants to "trim" the intelligentsia; at other times it seems utterly out of the question. Was he a vicious racist of the Hitler-Goebbels ilk? Never. Yet this question above all, alas, needs further examination.

(6) By presenting many documents and texts heretofore unavailable, Ott offers much food for thought to readers who are not historians but philosophers or literary critics. Nasty food. Necessary food. I shall close this portion of the Addendum with two nasty samples: (a) When the minister of culture in Karlsruhe congratulates Heidegger on his official entry into the Party, Heidegger replies:

> My most hearty thanks for your greetings upon my entry into the Party. We must now devote all our energies to the conquest of the world of the academicians and scholars for the sake of the new national-political spirit [*den neuen national-politischen Geist*]. That will not be an easy skirmish [*Waffengang*]. Sieg Heil. Martin Heidegger.

Why does the discourse of spirit mesh so readily, so easily (recall Heidegger's discussion of *das Leichte*) with that of weaponry, battle, and conquest? Why does spirit enjoin devotion to the hard and the heavy in Heidegger's discourse, *Härte und Schwere*, heavy metal, stalwart mettle, and stolid gravity? Will it ever be enough to murmur *Gelassenheit* in the presence of such a spirit? (b) When Heidegger addresses the student body in Tübingen on November 30, 1933, he criticizes Nazism for being insufficiently rigorous and vigorous, in a word, insufficiently nazi. His peroration:

> We today are in battle for the new reality. We are but a transition, a sacrifice. As fighters in this fight we must have a hard *Geschlecht* [generation? race? tribe? sex?], one that no longer clings to its own [*nichts Eigenem*], one that attaches itself firmly to the basis of the *Volk*. . . . We are fighting heart by heart, man by man.

Wir kämpfen Herz bei Herz, Mann bei Mann. Why the hearty, manly struggle, side-by-side? You beside me. I beside you.   *Then one threw the other.*   We together. Why the struggle against what Heidegger elsewhere treasures, to wit, *das Eigene,* what is one's own? What does it mean when the thinker of ruinance, mummery, and deprivation craves *ein hartes Geschlecht?* Why the kerygmatic call for sacrifice, sacrifice of whom or what, and for which reality? Why, from the thinker of radical individuation and letting-be, *das harte Geschlecht?* At the risk of excessive and unpleasant repetition, I shall open the next chapter of the present book with this same dismal passage and the same dreary questions.

For no one who reads Hugo Ott's book will be able to escape from the terrors of such questions. Questions which, the more one thinks about them, become uncannily contemporary, especially for those of us who are under academic contract. However, let me now turn to Jürgen Habermas' "Foreword" to the Farías book.

•

Why did Habermas attach his name to this book of bad journalism? He knew of Hugo Ott's serious research, much of it available in published articles at the time Habermas was writing. Did he not know of the impending book? Did he have to hurry in order to lend the force of the Habermas Machine to a dishonest and disreputable publication? That he knew of Farías' "questionable methods" and errors of fact is clear from two of his remarks (37; 400 n. 80). That he hopes such dubious methods and culpable errors can have a "wholesome enlightening effect" is unwholesome benighted expediency. That said, and it must be said, Habermas' "Foreword" is a more serious piece of analysis than anything one can find in *The Philosophical Discourse of Modernity* (1985). Indeed, Habermas has read Ott, Pöggeler, and Franzen—if not Heidegger— with care and insight. Thus his "Foreword" to the Farías book is doubly out of place. I cannot summarize it here, but will have to settle for a few brief questions and remarks.

(1) Habermas insists that there should be "no categorial denigration" (12) of Heidegger (such as that undertaken in the book he is introducing to the German public); indeed, that the "new beginning" ushered in by Heidegger's *Being and Time* in 1927 "makes the most profound penetration into German philosophy since Hegel" (13). Furthermore, Heidegger's thought contains *"perdurant* insights" (34). Does Habermas' work anywhere demonstrate that he has studied this most profound penetration since Hegel with the same diligence he has shown with regard to other thinkers—Hegel, for example? That he has absorbed in any way those "perdurant insights"?

(2) Habermas' thesis is that from about 1929 onward the innovative insights of *Being and Time* suffer a kind of *Verweltanschaulichung,* a contamination by a particular (i.e., the *jungkonservative)* worldview (18–19). A critical reading of Heidegger would therefore endeavor to extract the scientifically

tested arguments from that worldview (34), which, for its part, contains a series of "scientifically untested diagnoses" of his times (20) and an "uninhibited fetishizing of spirit [*Geist*]" (22). Three remarks:

(a) Habermas apparently has not noticed that Heidegger's own conception of his task as a university lecturer in phenomenological philosophy was from the very start to purge from his scientifically tested propositions all uncritically accepted *Weltanschauungen*.[17] Habermas' counsel therefore unwittingly borrows from Heidegger the very strategy it would wittingly turn against him. If that strategy failed to protect the innovative insights of Heidegger's "new beginning" from seductive worldviews, will anything be able to protect social-critical discourse? For all its scientifically tested hypotheses?

(b) If Habermas wants to learn about the disastrous consequences of fetishizing *spirit,* he will have to *read* Derrida. Now that he has finished *writing* about him.

(c) Habermas' belief that 1929 is the crucial year of a contaminating "turn," which is based on a reading of Pöggeler's more considered remarks, has to be refined: as we have seen, Heidegger's pedagogical politics are under way by 1919 and do not have to wait upon a reading of Nietzsche (which, at all events, commenced in Heidegger's student days) or upon the 1929 "What Is Metaphysics?" Here too Derrida's insights concerning Heidegger's relations with the university are crucial, and Habermas needs to read them. Firsthand.

(3) There is a curious inconsistency in Habermas' critique of Heidegger's view of "morality": at first he says that for Heidegger morality is merely a derivative, reified value-system that has to be rejected (18); then he suggests that (especially after 1929) Heidegger combines truth *and morality* in one authoritarian gesture (35). Does this inconsistency betray Heidegger's confusion and amorality? Or does it betray a vacillation at the heart of an enlightened, rational, and terribly moral social-critical discourse? Which, however, claims to be altogether free of "scientifically untested diagnoses" of its times?

(4) Even though he depends excessively on Pöggeler's and Franzen's "periodizations" of Heidegger's thought, rather than on an independent reading of Heidegger's texts, Habermas does have his own very powerful interpretation of Heidegger's career of thought: the *messianic* tone of the early writings (through *Being and Time*), which also exhibits a certain *decisionism*, becomes at some point an *apocalyptic* tone, which also betrays a certain *passivism*. Habermas is uncertain as to when this "turn" occurs,[18] yet is convinced that it culminates in the incapacity (common among intellectuals of the Adenauer era) to confront the past thoughtfully, or, as others have said, to mourn it. The pivot of such a turn in Heidegger's thought would be the question as to whether the "inner truth and greatness" of National Socialism, to wit, a thoughtful confrontation with global technicity, remains possible for "the Movement." My request to Habermas would be that he read the *Contributions to Philosophy* (1936–1938) very carefully: his reading Heidegger rather than the secondary sources would actually be an event of some importance. As matters stand, Habermas' failure to read means that his call to his own generation, the call to read

Heidegger *critically,* remains what Marx would have called the *farcical repetition* of a *tragedy*—Heidegger's call to his own generation.

Meanwhile, Habermas spurs me to ask whether Heidegger's political failure(s) would not come more clearly to light if we considered them in terms of what Heidegger in *Being and Time* calls *Wiederholung,* an appropriate relation to what-has-been. Is Heidegger's failure a failure to repeat? Or do repetition, readiness for anxiety, and resolute openedness never temporalize, never happen, so that the very dream   *The dream was marvelous but the terror was great*   of reprise is the failure from which none of us has yet awakened?

(5) When Habermas takes up Franzen's thesis concerning the history of being (*Seinsgeschichte*), he turns to the question of "collective destiny." What happens, on the one hand, when the rhetoric of "collective destiny" contaminates the radical individuation of an appropriate Dasein? And what happens, on the other hand, to social-critical discourse when it takes "collective destiny" not as the flower of an atomized bourgeois worldview but the cornerstone of its own critical thought about discourse? Is it enough for Habermas to utter a pious word or two about the perdurant insights of *Being and Time* and then to evade every possible recoil of Heidegger's thought on his own? Is it not indeed time to read?

(6) In 1953 Habermas, the student, asked in the *Frankfurter Allgemeine Zeitung* for July 25 whether "the planned murder of millions of human beings" could be made "comprehensible in terms of the history of being." The question is so little answered today that Habermas is right to repeat it. I myself (dreaming of reprise?) have fetched the question back again, or fetched it forward, in the very first moments of this chapter. The Extermination or Holocaust challenges Heidegger's thought on technicity (but perhaps also on propriety and appropriateness [*Eigentlichkeit*]) by exposing its own humanistic confidence that "man" will not be reduced to standing-reserves. For there are other kinds of reduction. When Philippe Lacoue-Labarthe wonders whether this *humanism* of Heidegger's is not a highly dubious and dangerous *nihilism,* the nihilism of *metaphysics,* Habermas lashes out in a note (397 n. 30) against "Heidegger's French apologists" (Oh, those French, those dupes, from Sartre to Derrida, who made the return of the monster possible! To the Rhine! To the Rhine!) who "turn things on their heads." Once again, reading would be better than slamming, even if one must read with one's head, on one's head, like a patient Hegelian.—Allow me, then, to turn for a brief moment to Philippe Lacoue-Labarthe's *La fiction du politique.*

•

If my response to Lacoue-Labarthe's *La poésie comme expérience* and *La fiction du politique* were that in these books he has moved through too many questions far too quickly, how absurd these few remarks of my own would be! Whatever doubts I entertain about Lacoue-Labarthe's effort, there is no doubt that he is one of the very few (one thinks of Derrida, to be discussed below in chapter 8, Janicaud, discussed below, and Pöggeler, who *ought* to have been discussed here)[19] who have inquired into the *philosophical* presuppositions and consequences of Heidegger's political engagement. Let these few remarks of mine on *La fiction du politique*—for the moment—suffice.

(1) I acknowledge Lacoue-Labarthe's insights as far as the two extremes of the question are concerned: he too proclaims the dishonesty of the Farías book (moreover, he demonstrates it convincingly: see 175–88, esp. 175 and 178) on the one hand, and identifies Heidegger's engagement as *une faute à l'égard de la pensée*, on the other (180).

(2) Lacoue-Labarthe's *question* encompasses nothing less than the (problematic) end of philosophy as such and as a whole—both as *university* philosophy and as the production of philosophico-literary *texts* (13–31). His hypothesis is that a residue of metaphysical humanism and nostalgia for pure presence linger in "the allure [again that word *Allüren!*] and the style of the engagement of 1933" as eminently *philosophical,* that is to say, as "authorizing itself by means of the idea of an hegemony of the spiritual and the philosophical over political hegemony itself (it is the motif of a *Führung* of *Führung,* or of the Führers), which goes back at least as far as the Platonic *basileia* if not to Empedocles" (28–29; cf. 47). Such philosophico-spiritualist hegemony is bound up with the traditional philosophical hegemony over rhetoric and literature, a hegemony that expresses itself as the pervasive "mimetology" of our tradition, which is Lacoue-Labarthe's long-standing concern. Thus when one calls for a "philosophical" response to Heidegger's engagement, Lacoue-Labarthe would be quick to point out the double edge, the violent edge, of philosophical tyranny, which never ceases to cut.

(3) A large part of Lacoue-Labarthe's book is devoted to the question of the adherence of Heidegger's thought to, and even absolute coherence with, National Socialism, including its antisemitic core, if not its crude racism and biologism (38, 55, 77). While Heidegger tries to distance himself from the most blatant forms of biologism and racism, Lacoue-Labarthe wonders whether such an effort can ever wholly succeed. Yet unlike Adorno, who remains content with a biologistic metaphor whose double edge not only cuts deep but also boomerangs (Heidegger, ". . . *dessen Philosophie bis in ihre innersten Zellen faschistisch ist*" [151n.]), Lacoue-Labarthe tries to be both vigilant and faithful.

(4) Lacoue-Labarthe recognizes that the question "How to judge?" is in full crisis in our time, when all ethical discourse teeters on the brink. Yet his own rhetoric of the horror of the Extermination and of Heidegger's silence is itself a rhetoric of indignation—*scandaleusement, piteusement insuffisante; intolérable*—and it often fails to pose questions of contamination and recoil precisely when they most need to be posed. (I am aware that my own remarks here occasionally avail themselves of such a rhetoric, even in their interrogative mode, and I know, from the sick man's pallet, as it were, how inevitable such contamination is.) As we have seen, he cites both Hannah Arendt and Heidegger as employing the phrase *fabrication des cadavres,* yet condemns the latter alone for its usage (57–58). Naturally enough. Yet what here is "natural"? He defines the extermination of European Jewry as the culmination of "the spiritual logic of

the West" (59), then tries (woefully unsuccessfully) to isolate the Hebraic tradition from the Graeco-Christian tradition, to rescue it from all *captation héllenistique*, in order to preserve the status of the Jewish people as pure outsiders, pure witnesses, and pure victims. He does this with the purest of intentions, without recognizing in such a will-to-purity the murderous logic that arouses his indignation and grief in the first place (62–63; 76–77).

(5) Perhaps the (admittedly diffuse) discussion of "National Aestheticism," based on ideas of Walter Benjamin and Berthold Brecht, yet venturing into the troubled waters of Hans Jürgen Syberberg's *Hitler, ein Film von Deutschland,* is the most remarkable of the book. I would only ask an old question (it is perhaps the question posed decades ago by Ashley Montagu, Erich Fromm, Georges Bataille, Herbert Marcuse, Wilhelm Reich, and, more recently, by Klaus Theweleit): Does not the inquiry into national *aestheticism* at crucial junctures (e.g., 110, 111–113 n. 25) necessitate speculation on what one might have to call "National *Erotism*"—an inquiry into the twisted erotic dynamism of nationalism, antisemitism, fascism, and nazism?[20]

(6) Two final observations:

(a) Have Lacoue-Labarthe and Jean-Luc Nancy simply turned things on their heads, as Habermas complains, by identifying national aestheticism as an area for future thought? Or is this not the very "turn" and contamination-by-worldview that Habermas wants to think about but is rather helpless to define? However, by stylizing certain aspects of Heidegger's encounter with art (for example, by stylizing Paul Celan as a pure victim confronting the impenetrable silence of an impenitent Heidegger, by turning Heidegger's meetings with Celan into an emblem, a tableau, for his own efforts to cope with the Extermination—and Lacoue-Labarthe has done this, I believe, in *La poésie comme expérience*), the inquiry often enough merely reproduces a certain rhetoric of scandalized indignation and a deadly logic of purity and *épuration.* Indignation is *indigne,* for purity is *pyrification.*

(b) Nevertheless, Lacoue-Labarthe does achieve some formulations of such simplicity and directness that he enables us to return to Heidegger's texts with new and significant questions. Hugo Ott, Jürgen Habermas, and Lacoue-Labarthe all want us to make that return. For example, to *Being and Time,* §74 (SZ, 384), with the following very powerful question in mind: "Why does historical Dasein determine itself as a *people*?" (*Fiction,* 164). Is not that determination the eminent fiction of the political? At a time when the United States is celebrating the purge of its "Vietnam depression" and convalescing euphorically in the "Desert Storm"; at a time when all "the West" is as jubilant over the "collapse of Communism" in "the East" as, say, Heidegger would have been; would not the question of the fiction of the political be the sort of question *we* ought to take back with us, back to *our* universities?

•

One word more. Perhaps the most sustained and thoughtful of all the books mentioned here—although I am by no means claiming to "cover the literature," which is vast, and vastly uneven—is that of Dominique Janicaud. Fortunately, plans are currently afoot to have his volume translated into English, although as far as I know the publisher has not yet been decided. Janicaud's is an eminently *philosophical* book: especially in its opening and closing pages, his meditation expands in scope beyond the debacle and disaster of Heidegger's politics; again and again it brings its questions *home*, as it were, to the author and to the reader. It is also very carefully researched and written and contains a wealth of historical and political information. It certainly does not replace Ott, which is not its intention, but complements his work. It also responds at length and in detail to Habermas and (especially) to Lacoue-Labarthe. Here once again I shall limit myself to a handful of kudos and a more meager handful of complaints. First, the bravos.

(1) A good part of the book's excellence probably derives from the fact that Janicaud had no desire to write it. He notes that the book was written à *contrecoeur* (11). He describes his intention as "the will to confront calmly a task that exceeds the personal case of Heidegger, a task in which our capacity to assume the terrible legacy of our century is at stake, a task that should prepare us to think—on renewed bases—of the role of philosophical rationality in the City" (11). Thus Janicaud's book is a further application of thoughts developed in his *La puissance du rationnel.*[21]

(2) Janicaud traces the background of the ascent of philosophy and the philosopher since the Enlightenment to the position of moral arbiter. After all, "Why believe in a philosopher?" (14). Why the expectation of and demand for political and moral wisdom in the case of those who study philosophy? In a sense, of course, those expectations and demands go back to Empedocles and Socrates. Nevertheless, in a secular society such as ours, where the churches no longer serve as powerful centers of "dogmatic authority and moral propagation" (or is this wishful thinking on Janicaud's part?), the philosopher (or, in the United States, perhaps the professor of literature) is expected to serve as an exemplar. Hence the universal fascination with biography (32), although that too goes back beyond Diogenes Laertius. And hence the shock over Heidegger's often banal and occasionally quite malign example. Janicaud quotes Paul Veyne's "salutary insolence" as follows: "We confront the embarrassment of having to concede that one of the greatest metaphysicians who ever lived was also capable of being a contemptible imbecile" (17). Janicaud's effort in the face of "this schizoid situation" is to ask, calmly, as he says, and by way of "patient work with the texts" (23), to what extent the imbecility infects Heidegger's thought.

(3) One of Janicaud's most noteworthy traits is his refusal to indulge in the rhetoric of indignation and purification. With an eye educated in part by Nietzsche, Janicaud spurns the joys of rebuke. "We would be lost without recourse in an operation of rejection, whose radically purificative character certain people find tempting; they forget that purges are liquidations of thought, Goebbels' posthumous victories in the topsy-turvy hell of our culture" (19). Janicaud's purpose throughout, and his achievement, is to avoid "the

intellectual terrorism that would be a very sad replica of the flaws it claims to castigate" (156). If Janicaud is a Heideggerian apostle, however, his role is that of Thomas—". . . calmly taking measure of the problem, drawing our finger along the length of the wound" (25).

(4) As Janicaud reads the texts of the 1930s, especially the rectoral address and all the jaded blooms of the Schneeberger *Nachlese*, he notes that what is truly disconcerting about Heidegger's engagement is not the initial enthusiasm but the "caricatural" nature of his argumentation in favor of the Party, his exploitation and spoliation of his own earlier work. "What is terrible is to discover beneath the philosopher's pen this rhetoric (and the manner of his denials), a rhetoric become *pathos*, a *pathos* of the most violently sophistical type" (48).

(5) At this juncture, Janicaud begins his rereading of *Being and Time* (in chapter 3, "The Unfindable Politics?"). He then proceeds to a reading of *Introduction to Metaphysics*, focusing on the notorious and spurious "parenthetical remark" on the "truth and greatness" of National Socialism, that is, its response to technicity (in chapter 4, "The Purloined Letter"). In chapter 5 ("The Last Circle") he turns to Heidegger's lecture courses on Schelling and Hölderlin in order to examine there something like an implicit theologico-political treatise. He concludes by engaging in a serious debate with Philippe Lacoue-Labarthe (in chapter 6, "Caesuras") and by trying to gain some distance on the entire question of Heidegger and politics (in chapter 7, "At a Distance"). Of all the materials he discusses, the Hölderlin lectures, it seems to me, grant Janicaud the occasion for his most thought-provoking and original insights. These remarks are particularly difficult to summarize. Suffice it to say that they have to do with Heidegger's quasi-political appeal to the poet Hölderlin as the avatar of the very future of Germany and Europe (134–41). For Hölderlin is in some extraordinary way the basis of Heidegger's "theologico-political boondoggle [*méprise*]" (141–52).

(6) What Janicaud finds "fundamentally objectionable" in Heidegger's theologico-political history of being as nihilism and the essential unfolding of technology and oblivion of being is "not the accent it places on historicity, but *its exclusive and unconditioned character,* which leads it in turn to too global a conception of planetary nihilism" (119). Heidegger's history of being is *necessitarian,* after the manner of Hegel, and its "destinal historialism" operates by *coup de force* (120). Janicaud therefore poses the following questions: "What authorizes thought to pass from the transcendental realm to the mundane, historical domain? What price does it have to pay for this veritable transgression of finitude? What type of pretensions does it raise, in spite of the apparent modesty of its 'rejection' of metaphysics?" (121). It is here that *the shadow of this thought* reverts to adumbrations of Heidegger's own doubts. Janicaud quotes Heidegger's *Introduction to Metaphysics* (EM, 152): "Nobody leaps over his own shadow." Janicaud comments: "Metaphysics does not so readily release its own, if indeed it is true that Heidegger is never content merely to deconstruct it, and never succeeds in wholly surmounting it. Decidedly, 'no one can leap over their own shadow' " (121).

(7) Janicaud's critical discussion of Lacoue-Labarthe's *La fiction du politique* is one of the highlights of the book. Janicaud is able to show how Lacoue-Labarthe's moral indignation vis-à-vis Heidegger appeals to a number of suppressed convictions of a moral or ethical character—however vigorously Lacoue-Labarthe seeks to deny it. "It is difficult to find a text more rigorist in its morality, and more rigorously ethical, than *The Fiction of the Political*" (127). Yet whether Janicaud goes far enough in his uncovering of Lacoue-Labarthe's ethical double-bind is a question that might lead us toward some more critical responses to his work.

Among the difficulties Janicaud's task confronts, I find the following ones most noteworthy.

(1) Janicaud's thesis is that what leads Heidegger to his political error (and it *is* an "errancy," says Janicaud, whatever its "internal 'logic' ") is bound up with "the radically historial-destinal character of his thought" (96). Yet Janicaud also contrasts Heidegger's history of being, in all its amplitude and profundity, with the wretched pettiness of his face-saving attempts in 1953 (the notorious tampering with the text of *Introduction to Metaphysics*) and 1966 (the *Spiegel* interview). Obviously, it is the profound conception of a history of being that one values in Heidegger. Yet how could Heidegger's redoubtable *Seinsgeschichte* be purged of its historial-destinal character? What of its amplitude and profundity would remain? And, to push matters in a direction Janicaud would hesitate to follow, is there something petty and banal precisely in Heidegger's history of being—something in which the pettiness and banality of his political failure would be rooted? Could a second history of being, one that heeded the destiny of ζωή, help to alleviate the dilemma, help to release some of the tension that runs through Janicaud's account? Only, it seems clear, if such a second history declines to insist on the *destinal* necessity of its analyses; only, it seems transparent, if it settles for a more abashed hermeneutic of history and a more multifaceted view upon being as φύσις. (We shall return to this in chapters 6 through 9.)

(2) As far as I can see, Janicaud nowhere takes up the thesis of Reiner Schürmann's *Heidegger on Being and Acting*. Yet Schürmann's reading of the Heideggerian history of being is too strongly opposed to his own for Janicaud to ignore it. If Schürmann can argue that the historial-destinal character of Heidegger's later thought culminates in the end of all epochal principles and the instauration of truly an-archic thought, then Janicaud must confront him with his own fears concerning the essentially *tyrannical* character of destinal historialism, the *reaction* of Heideggerian "sending." Even though he does not refer to Schürmann, Janicaud has already addressed "the heart of the debate," to wit: ". . . a destinal thought (integral historialism) makes an incision (from the ontological point of view, displaced in the direction of the [propriative] 'event') between the things that do not depend on us (the course of the world) and those that do (thinking). A quite Stoic division, not at all to be spurned, but whose elevated point of view itself soars beyond (or avoids) considerable difficulties" (101).

(3) Nevertheless, the debate concerning the greatness and the hazards of "destinal historialism" rages within Janicaud's own text. For he *affirms* the power of Heidegger's historial-destinal thinking of being as much as he *fears* it. Toward the close of his sixth chapter, Janicaud again takes up "the profoundly ambiguous character of destinal historialism" (149). If for a brief instant he is tempted merely to subtract Heidegger's "political writings" from the "considerable oeuvre" that would remain, the bulk of which would simply "exceed or defy politics" (156), at which point Janicaud would have to confront Schürmann's insistence that Heidegger's oeuvre is as much about (political) acting as it is about (ontological) thinking, Janicaud's considered view is more nuanced: "The fragility of Heideggerian thought in its political aspect is thus the index of risks run by a thought that confronts its destiny" (157). In other words, Heidegger's *destinal* historialism itself *confronts a destiny,* one to which at least in part Heidegger can only *respond* in thought, so that the distinction between "the course of the world" and "thinking" breaks down where one most needed it. To be sure, the "fragility" of Heidegger's thinking "is inseparable from its grandeur . . ." (157).

(4) Historial-destinal matters are often even more confounding than Janicaud will allow. Whereas he tries to develop a clear chronological sequence, the texts of 1933–1935 manifesting Heidegger's "enthusiasm" for National Socialism, the texts of 1936–1938 [i.e., the *Contributions to Philosophy (Of Propriation)*] exhibiting Heidegger's "disillusionment," one cannot always sustain such a sequence. The darkness of Heidegger's polemic in 1936–1938 is part of the shadow cast in 1933–1935 as well; and the apocalyptic tone of the final sections of the *Contributions,* "The Futural Ones" and "The Last God," are assuredly not purged of enthusiasm. Nevertheless, it is true that the later texts are increasingly somber, increasingly drastic. In chapter 6, below, I shall refer to them as "paranoetic."

(5) Janicaud challenges Lacoue-Labarthe's moral indignation quite ably (130: "In the face of the Extermination itself, do moral condemnations suffice?"); he demonstrates that the destinal historialism of Lacoue-Labarthe outdoes that of Heidegger himself (131: "At no moment does Lacoue-Labarthe doubt this interpretation of the destiny of the Occident," to wit, that ever since Plato's *Republic* it was bound for Auschwitz); finally, he challenges Lacoue-Labarthe's interpretation of *tragedy* in the context of National Socialism (132: "Why the recourse to a concept which this event [or counterevent] entirely escapes?"). Yet I find Janicaud's criticisms sometimes too harsh, sometimes too mild. "Too mild" I find his criticism that Lacoue-Labarthe transforms "Auschwitz" into a "pure in-itself": it is rather the case that Lacoue-Labarthe's *emblematic* use of Auschwitz (as also—terrible irony—of Paul Celan's poetry) is a peculiar form of the *ontotypological representation* that Lacoue-Labarthe himself is always at pains to unmask in others. It is also the case, I believe, that his moral indignation not only "does not suffice" but also borrows its energetic rhetoric of condemnation from the very sources that he himself most wants to condemn. "Too strong" I find Janicaud's view that "national aestheticism" is a

mere "alibi of National Socialism." It is potentially much more than that, and very much worth pursuing, as, moreover, Janicaud himself later in his book seems to concede (159, 176).

Janicaud concludes his book with a fair, balanced, and yet relentless judgment concerning Heidegger's apolitical or antipolitical stance, his silences, his futile and self-serving apologies, his nationalism, his militancy, and, above all, his refusal to learn the lessons of his own involvement in National Socialism, the lessons of "this terrible experience" (159). While his theme is "this other Heidegger, the shadow of the first" (164), and while he never allows himself to be distracted from the dismal case at hand, Janicaud also never allows his reader to bask in the cheering sunlight of moral(izing) superiority. Instead, he assigns his readers a task. The task is to develop a sense of a *rational* politics beyond all rationalisms, and a sense of political destiny "precisely as an absence of destiny" (171). He leaves his readers with an "incessant reminder of the constitutive limits of the possible" (175). Doubtless, readers will insist on knowing whether such constitutive limits are ontological givens, or elements of a destinal history of being, or something else altogether. Janicaud does not reply to such impatient either/or questions. He poses his own more supple ones:

> Can metaphysics be deciphered by a unified discourse? What is the connection between the metaphysical character of Occidental languages and our ethnocentrism? Can thought as such find a unity in its solitary interrogation? How would it articulate itself alongside the critical project? What shall we retain as the more decisive characteristic concerning time, its irreversibility or its granting? And if rationality is our part, has it any right (or every obligation) to transcend entirely the conditions of its provenance? (174)

The mood, or "air," of such questions has nothing about it of self-righteous reprimand; it is not about meting out good or bad points.   *His fate lies heavy upon me.*   Janicaud's book is genuinely philosophical in that it responds to pain (*douleur*) and suffering (*souffrance*), the pain and suffering of life in the face of questions that defeat reason but—as Janicaud hopes—do not put it to rout (179).

Shattering

Heidegger's Rhetoric in the 1930s

No doubt Heidegger's texts of the 1920s and 1930s betray a penchant for the hard and heavy, for metal, mettle, and melancholy—*Härte und Schwere*. No doubt such a penchant is troubling, especially when one discerns the debility and morbid sentimentality of all hard nationalisms and heavy fanaticisms. When Heidegger pleads for *das harte Geschlecht,* mustered "heart by heart, man by man," one can only suffer pangs of embarrassment and then turn away in shame or disgust or pity or self-recognition. Once again, Rector Heidegger addressing the student body at the University of Tübingen on November 30, 1933: "We today are in pitched battle for the new reality. We are but a transition, a sacrifice. As fighters in this fight we must have a hard *Geschlecht,* one that no longer clings to anything of its own, one that attaches itself firmly to the basis of the *Volk.* . . . We are fighting heart by heart, man by man."[1]

Winfried Franzen analyzes the motif of a "yearning for the hard and heavy" in Heidegger's 1929–1930 lecture course, *The Fundamental Concepts of Metaphysics: World—Finitude—Solitude,* which occupied us in chapter 3 and which remains crucial for our inquiry into daimon life.[2] Here the mood of melancholy (*Schwermut*) predominates—melancholy in, of all things, biology. Franzen tries very hard to provide a fair and balanced account, threading his way warily between the Assassins and the Acolytes. Yet at almost every turn in his essay, with almost every "verdict" and "judgment," one senses that he has either gone too far or fallen short—something that, as both Aristotle and Heidegger agree, is "easy" (61, 108–10).

One may well share Franzen's suspicion concerning Heidegger's "existentiell heroism." One may well entertain doubts about that rigorous "ideal of existence" which at the end of section 62 in *Being and Time* Heidegger confesses he has, the ideal that causes him to scorn what Franzen calls (apparently without embarrassment) "practical-bourgeois life" and "normalcy" (85). It is surely true that Heidegger despises complacency, and that he adjudges most of us complacent. It is perhaps also true that he wishes to spur Dasein to "a permanent condition of existentiell hypertension" (85). It is certainly true that authoritarian leaders of political and religious mass movements in our own century have known how to channel such contempt and fervor. It is also undeniably true that Heidegger's "unrestrained nationalism and cult of *Deutschtum*" (87) are profoundly worrying. Worse, they are an inconceivable stupidity, as inane, for example, as the unrestrained and blissfully ignorant American chauvinism of our own day, the undying cult of the American Adam. Finally, Franzen is doubtless right to worry about Heidegger's ambition to overshadow all his contemporaries and to outbid all past thought (88): that passion smacks of the will-to-will, of the "gigantism" and "machination" that Heidegger so acerbically criticizes in this age of worldviews, calculative representations, and technological challengings and orderings.

Yet it is intriguing that Franzen misses altogether the culminating moment of section 38 of that lecture course, the section he finds so dubious politically; he misses the moment in which Heidegger confesses himself to be uncertain of the prodding effect of his own questioning. For the capacity to inquire is what section 38 is all about, and its polemics reach a point of radical recoil to which one must attend: "Yet we cannot, we can never, objectively determine and assert that this vacuity [i.e., the emptiness that arises in profound boredom and melancholy] empties us out and thereby compels us to the very point of the moment of vision. . . . We cannot register the profound boredom of our existence as a factual state of affairs" (29/30, 247). "We can only ask whether in the end this profound boredom pervades our existence. . . . We can only ask

> whether human beings today have always already broken off, bent, and dulled the *point of the most penetrating moment* by reacting precipitately, by hastily concocting their agendas, confusing their own haste and hubbub for the resoluteness of the moment. We cannot locate profound boredom in the existence of contemporary humanity; we can only ask whether or not people today—precisely in and through all the instances of our contemporary humaneness—are in fact suppressing that profound boredom; and that means, concealing their own existence as such from themselves. . . . (29/30, 248)

One really does wish that Heidegger were less stern, less severe, less glinty and steely, although one would hate to see him become one of the squooshy thinkers—who outnumber him mightily. The difficulty is that as we rush to judgment, hastening to say how dangerous it is for a thinker to condemn his time as incapable of summoning the courage to be bored with itself; as we scamper to find the book of matches that will settle in one grand conflagration all the old scores with Heidegger; that flinty disagreeable irascible hypertense thinker makes us worry about our own haste, makes us rue the unbearable vacuity that is scarcely concealed behind our bustle and our righteousness. "We have invented the happiness of the Heidegger Scandal," say the Last Men, and they blink. With steely retribution in their squooshy hearts.[3]

What characterizes the hardness and heaviness, the brittle severity, austerity, and gravity, of this unpleasant and highly disturbing Heidegger? Answer: failure. Failure or foundering. *Scheitern*. Failure as a trembling or agitation to the point of disintegration. *Erschütterung*. In a word, shattering.

Ironically, and perversely, shattering constitutes the very hardness and heaviness for which Heidegger yearns and which we debile thinkers find so suspect. Why not a touch of *légèreté*, a hint of legerdemain, a breezy levitation with Being, instead? Why not make one's peace, why not return to traditional ontotheological and ethical systems? Why not embrace the normalcy of moral pretense and social-critical p(r)ose? Why not the old I'm OK You're Not So OK philosophy? Why insist on perpetual exposure to one's own failure, as Heidegger always does? Why insist on shattering, especially when success has never enjoyed better repute?

SCHEITERN

Scheitern and *Erschütterung* appear to be related linguistically, although the actions of *Scheiden* and *Schütten* upon which they are based seem to be opposed, the first meaning to split open, the second to cover up. However, *Scheitern* is related to *Schaudern,* to shiver and quiver; *Erschütterung* is related to *Schütteln,* to shake or agitate. Heidegger employs *Scheitern* nine times in *Being and Time,* always in telling places, in contexts we will want to examine quite closely.⁴ *Erschütterung* appears only once (SZ, 254, line 39), in that famous footnote on Tolstoy's "The Death of Ivan Ilyich," a note that is notoriously difficult to interpret.⁵ *Scheitern*—foundering, failing, shattering—appears regularly in *Being and Time* when it is a question of the methodological conduct of Heidegger's own existential hermeneutic of Dasein. As we shall now see.

(1) At the end of section 31, "Dasein as Understanding," Heidegger indicates that projection upon being is always itself cast or thrown, always already attuned. Does not the *geworfener Entwurf* of Dasein contain a conundrum, is it not even more enigmatic than the analysis thus far has taken it to be? "It is indeed. We must first allow the enigmatic character of its being to come fully to the fore, if only in order to be able to founder in a genuine way [*in echter Weise scheitern zu können*] in our efforts to 'solve' it and to pose afresh the question of the being of thrown-projective being in the world." Such thrownness of all projections upon being is a *Faktum*—a fact of life for Dasein. Especially for the Dasein that philosophizes.

(2) In section 35, "Chatter," Heidegger suggests that chit-chat is what allows us to succeed in the public world. "Chatter is the possibility of understanding everything without first having to pay it any mind." Chatter rescues us from the hazard that when we try to pay heed to something, when in dedication we turn devotedly to a thing, precisely then we may well fail or suffer shipwreck (*bei einer solchen Zueignung zu scheitern*). Things elude us even when we most want to heed them. The empty talk helps us not to notice. Notice what? The fact that shattering has taken place.

(3) In the most diabolical of the three sections on the "falling," "lapsing," or even "decomposing" (*Verfallen*) of everyday Dasein, most diabolical because most recoiling, section 37, "Ambiguity," Heidegger indicates how devilishly difficult it is to know "what is disclosed in genuine understanding and what is not." Everything *seems* to be genuinely understood, especially at those

philosophy conferences we all attend so assiduously. In his 1925 lecture course Heidegger describes the philosophy conference thus:

> Today we decide about metaphysics and about even more elevated things at philosophy conferences. For everything that is to be done these days we first have a meeting, and here is how it works: people come together, constantly come together, and they all wait for one another to turn up so that the others will tell them how it is, and if it doesn't get said, never mind, everyone has had their say. It may very well be that all the talkers who are having their say have understood little of the matter in question, but still we believe that if we accumulate all that misunderstanding something like understanding will leap forth at the end of the day. Thus there are people today who travel from one meeting to the next and who are sustained by the confidence that something is really happening, that they've actually done something; whereas, at bottom, they've merely ducked out of work, seeking in chatter a place to build a nest for their helplessness—a helplessness, it is true, that they will never understand. (20, 376)

Härte und Schwere on the line for the philosophy professors. Heidegger. Maybe we regular conference-attenders *should* burn the bastard?

But we were speaking of *Scheitern*. To shatter and to chatter. Chatter "lives faster" than genuine understanding. Understanding, deliberate and taciturn, bends to the task at hand and risks "genuine failure." *In der Verschwiegenheit der Durchführung und des echten Scheiterns. . . .*

(4) In the next section, §38, "Falling and Thrownness," Heidegger depicts those modes of being that tempt, tranquilize, and alienate quotidian Dasein. These modes seduce Dasein into thinking that it is living life to the full, living real life, concrete life (SZ, 177–78), when in fact it is plummeting through groundlessness and nullity—what Heidegger earlier in his career called *Absturz* and *Ruinanz*, the principal animation (thanks to gravity) of everyday existence. The uttermost alienation of Dasein, in which existence is benumbed by the They (SZ, 176, l. 6), does not however arise from involvements with beings unlike Dasein; it does not arise from reification; rather, it occurs when Dasein analyzes itself to death (*"Selbstzergliederung"*), trying out on itself every conceivable sort of interpretation—such as, one might interpolate, the interpretation of dreams—and losing itself in "characterologies" and "typologies." Clearly, Heidegger is talking about either psychoanalysis (which he elsewhere condemns in similar terms, "elsewhere" meaning precisely §38 of *The Fundamental Concepts of Metaphysics: World—Finitude—Solitude* [(29/30, 248, at the very point where we broke off the quotation]) or traditional Protestant Christianity. Heidegger does not pause to compare the self-dissection of psychotherapy with that of the Catholic pietism and puritanism of his own background, even though his passion for Augustine, Luther, Pascal, and Kierkegaard would suggest the potential richness of such a comparison. It is evidently psychoanalysis alone—the "possibility of interpretation" that (along with Nietzschean and Foucaultian genealogy) competes most intensely with his own hermeneutics of facticity—that Heidegger here condemns. His reason for denouncing it is that such psychologistic vivisection closes off the possibility that

is proper to Dasein, the possibility of "genuine shattering." Freud dreams of transmuting hysterical misery into normal unhappiness. *Why should not my cheeks be starved and my face drawn?* Heidegger dreams of something more closely akin to total breakdown, although he would doubtless scorn even that frantic masquerade of a proper existential-ontological crisis. Facial tic, numbness in the extremities, and nausea would be but sentimental effusions compared to a steeled, taciturn, reticent, and impassively resolute Dasein. Whose very genuineness, the genuineness of its understanding, is guaranteed precisely insofar as it genuinely shatters. Whose endurance and center of gravity, *Härte und Schwere,* consist in the possibility of genuine questioning, *Fragen.* That is no doubt the proper privilege of questioning: malleability and responsiveness alloyed mysteriously with impermeable metal, always on the verge of genuine shattering. Questioning finds its sole felicity in proximity to failure, in the neighborhood of precipitate ruinance.

(5) Whose failure? At a crucial juncture in *Being and Time,* at the point where Heidegger is taking stock of "the results of the preparatory fundamental analysis of Dasein" and portraying the "task of an original existential interpretation of that being" (§45), the question of failure becomes the failure of the question. If a *radical* and *original* inquiry must grasp the *whole being* of Dasein, and if Dasein is the elusive "in between" of birth and death, then is not an "original ontological interpretation of Dasein doomed to shatter—on the very mode of being of the thematic being [i.e., Dasein] itself"? The possibility of genuine shipwreck is no longer the possibility that pertains to the proper *object* of the inquiry, namely, appropriate Dasein, but the proper possibility of the inquiry itself. An odd situation results: every time we say that Heidegger's *Being and Time* fails to attain its self-proclaimed goal, we corroborate in some perverse way its approximation to the unmitigated failure that Heidegger prizes above all things. Does a factical ideal of existence slip unbeknownst into his analysis, surreptitiously guiding the inquiry through all its twists and turns? *Echtes Scheitern.* Does the analysis of ecstatic temporality founder when it tries to assert the priorities of the future over having-been and of original time over derivative, inappropriate, "vulgar" time? *Echtes Scheitern.* Is there a confusion of modalities (for example, of carelessness and neutral indifference) and of grounds and groundings (for example, of appropriateness in inappropriateness and vice versa)? *Echtes Scheitern.* Is the circuitry of a resolute readiness for anxiety and an anxiously resolute openedness in fact a vicious circle, so that the flash of an eye is always only on the verge of vigilance? *Echtes Scheitern.* Does the profusion of repetitions of the question of being's meaning dissipate into the vaporous cloud of an "idea of being" that will always have to have been clarified ahead of time? *Echtes Scheitern.*

If nothing fails like success, nothing succeeds like genuine shattering.

(6) In section 47, "Experiencing the Other's Death, and the Possibility of Grasping a Whole Dasein," Heidegger takes special care to observe that in a world where They take one another to be infinitely substitutable—this bus driver replacing that one in the daily run, this philosopher filling in for that one

on the conference circuit—no Dasein can "represent" another in its dying. The possibility of death-by-proxy, of an *arrêt de mort* that would arrest death rather than execute the sentence of mortality, shatters. *Indes scheitert diese Vertretungsmöglichkeit völlig. . . .*

(7) Questions of methodology return uncannily often to the analysis of being-unto-death. Yet such a return yields anything but a totality, anything but a graspable whole. Any such totality or whole shatters from the outset. Section 48, "Default [*Ausstand*], End, and Totality," begins by noting that the metaphysical passion to divide and segregate distinct regions of beings is a futile passion. The desire to divide and rule *shatters*, not only because of the plethora of beings but also because "a clarified idea of being in general" must always be presupposed for such a dividing—even if it always eludes our understanding. Eludes it in the way that death eludes the understanding of a Bohemian peasant widower, inasmuch as death is not being *at* an end but a being *toward* it and *unto* it—not *Zu-Ende-sein* but *ein Sein zum Ende* (245).

(8) Shattering conducts questions of methodology and existential-ontological hermeneutics to the uncanny being-toward-death of Dasein. The care structure itself disallows every representational grasp of the whole being of Dasein. The effort to get a grip on the phenomenal whole of Dasein shatters at the very moment when what is disclosed and disclosure as such converge, that is to say, in the moment of anxiety. Thus in Heidegger's courses after *Being and Time*, as we have seen, the invariable "touchstone" (*Prüfstein* or *Probier-stein*) for the genuineness of a questioning is its anxious proximity to *the nothing* and to *death*.

(9) As long as we think the nexus of a Dasein that lives "between" birth and death as a being at hand in temporal succession, the *Zusammenhang des Lebens* eludes us. All ontology fails, lets us down (*läßt scheitern*). It is here, "between" birth and death, that we must resolve Dilthey's problem; it is here that we must think *life* not as a being at hand but as a radically finite historizing. Life—and shattering?

After this final invocation of *Scheitern* in *Being and Time* Heidegger writes:

> Dasein does not first of all fill up a path or stretch of life that is somehow at hand with phases of momentary actuality. Rather, it *stretches itself* in such a way that its own being is constituted from the outset as spanning. The "between" that is tied up with birth and death is already harbored *in the being* of Dasein. . . . Understood existentially, birth is not and can never be something bygone, in the sense of something no longer at hand; just as little does death submit itself to the mode of being of what is not yet at hand but is approaching, though still outstanding. Factical Dasein exists natally, and natally it is already dying, in the sense of being toward death.

Das faktische Dasein existiert gebürtig, und gebürtig stirbt es auch schon im Sinne des Seins zum Tode. Dasein natal, Dasein fatal. That is life. That is hard. That is shattering.

Dasein stretches itself, but is always already stretched, spans its temporally animated life between a birth and a death it will never have chosen for itself. An anomalous amalgam of perdurance and animatedness, *Beharrlichkeit* and *Bewegtheit,* hardness and lightness, Dasein perdures—perdures as the self that is always moved in and as ecstatic temporality. Dasein perdures in the raptures and ruptures of time. Perdures precisely by shattering. That is the way Dasein happens (*geschieht*), and its happening is history (*Geschichte*).

From the birth of history in the perdurance and animatedness of Dasein it is but a dozen pages to those troubling passages in *Being and Time* that treat of Dasein as inheritance (*Erbe*), destiny (*Schicksal*), communal fate (*Geschick*), and nation or people (*Volk*). Dasein assumes its inheritance, takes over its legacy, freights itself, weights itself, ceases to take itself "lightly" (SZ, 385: *Leichtnehmen;* cf. *"das Leichte,"* 61, 108–110). When Dasein commits itself to its destiny, it regains a relation to its heritage and tradition (*Überlieferung*). It can now bear the slings and arrows of a radically individualized destiny, steeled by this new and resolute relation to tradition (*die sich überliefernde Entschlossenheit*). Almost imperceptibly, and so soon after its birth, Dasein goes to meet its *Deutschtum* in the heavy armor of an unwieldy syntax: "When Dasein, running ahead, allows death to become mighty in it [*in sich mächtig werden läßt*], it understands itself, free for death, in the plenipotence [*Übermacht*] of its own finite freedom, in order to take over the *impotence* [Ohnmacht] of its being left to itself, in the freedom that in each case only 'is' in the having-chosen of a given choice [*die je nur 'ist' im Gewählthaben der Wahl*], and in order to become perspicuous about the contingencies of the situation that is disclosed to it" (SZ, 384). *Mächtig, Übermacht,* and *Ohnmacht* engage in a curious ringdance of power and debility, usurpation and obeisance, durability and shattering. In such a ringdance, anything but fleet of foot, election has always already occurred, and it has occurred for the elect:

> Yet if the Dasein that is bound up with its destiny [*das schicksalhafte Dasein*] exists as being in the world essentially in being-with with others [*im Mitsein mit Anderen*], then its happening is a co-happening and is determined as *fate.* That is how we designate the happening of community, of the people [*das Geschehen der Gemeinschaft, des Volkes*]. Fate is not pieced together out of many individual destinies; just as little can our being-with-one-another be grasped as the collective occurrence of a plurality of subjects. (SZ, 384)

At this point Heidegger refers to section 26, "The Dasein-with of Others, and Everyday Being-with." The shortcomings of that section are discussed so often nowadays that we need not rehearse them here.[6] Suffice it to say that "proper solicitude" is now (in section 74) undercut by a legacy that is always already determinative of being-with: "In being with one another in the same world and in resolute openedness for particular possibilities, destinies are from the outset already guided [*im vorhinein schon geleitet*]." Dasein natal is constituted from the start as spanning; yet the radically individualized spanning of a Dasein that is in each case my own is constituted from the outset as a *shared* legacy. An *empowered* legacy. "In communication and in struggle the power of fate first becomes free. [*In der Mitteilung und im Kampf wird die Macht des Geschickes erst frei.*] The destined fate of Dasein in and with its 'generation' constitutes the full, appropriate happening of Dasein."[7]

Things are happening very quickly, and very oddly. Things are solidifying, gaining weight. Shattering suddenly seems remote. For the past 150 pages of *Being and Time* we have been trying to isolate Dasein in its own proper, radically individualized, and thrown existence as anxious, resolutely open, and irreplaceable. The shattering that is death has seemed to be coextensive with the shattering of fundamental ontology itself, as though the *fundamentum* of the existential hermeneutics of Dasein were eminently concussible. Now the word *Scheitern* has done its work and has gone into abeyance. No doubt a very similar word emerges in reminiscence of it, a word with a similar ring, similar though somewhat more crystalline. Heidegger writes, in italics and in spaced type: "*Only a being that is essentially f u t u r a l in its being, such that, free for its death, it can let itself be thrown back onto its factical 'there,' splintering on its death* [zerschellend an ihm] . . . " (385). *Zerschellend.* Splintering like a ship against the craggy shore or a crystal goblet on the floor, breaking into myriad pieces with an exploding, ringing sound. "*That is to say, only a futural being that is with equal originality h a v i n g - b e e n [g e w e s e n d] can hand it-self over to its inherited possibility, take over its own throwness and a c h i e v e t h e   m o m e n t   o f   v i s i o n for 'its time' [a u g e n b l i c k l i c h sein für 'seine Zeit'].*" If the perfect and perfection of having-been as thrownness once upon a time disturbed the analysis of a futurebound, projective understanding hard on the brink of shattering, it now returns to reassure. By a heavy-handed sleight-of-hand, Dasein now inherits a possibility that allows it to pick itself up by its own bootstraps and leap over its own shadow. By legerdemain Dasein becomes *augenblicklich* in such a way that "its moment" stretches immeasurably beyond the finitude of "its time" in order to embrace "its times," the times of an entire generation,[8] the inherited times of its forebearers, and well-nigh "the times" of news and newspapers. What good is it if Heidegger reminds himself and us of the *finitude* of proper temporality once that sleight-of-hand has done for Dasein precisely what the relation to the Infinite has always done for human beings in the past, namely, granted them the license to perpetrate infinite violence?

Thus the tradition becomes explicit, is repeated, and an armorplated Dasein marches off rhinocerously to choose its hero. The hero with delicate hands. Spengler's predator, with myriad hands but only one head. Open resolve, running ahead, makes its choice, the choice that liberates it for those successors who engage in struggle (*die kämpfende Nachfolge*) and who are loyal to the tradition that is to be repeated (*Treue zum Wiederholbaren*). What such repeatability can mean in the face of a mortality that is insurmountable remains unclear. That the Dasein that shatters and splinters can so readily congeal into a people—a people who never really succeed in becoming the rhinocerous, a people who therefore need tanks and armored cars—this can only disturb and haunt us. Even though section 74, like most other sections of *Being and Time*,

closes with pentrating questions about the nexus of life, questions that admittedly have not been satisfactorily answered, one fears that the analysis has not
shattered sufficiently, that it has succeeded too well.

Dasein natal is Dasein fatal. Its nativity implies nationality, and its nationality, at least in Heidegger's case, although certainly not in his alone, entails a
nationalism. Heidegger's nationalism, the inherited hellenized *Deutschtum* of
the George-Kreis, the hard and heavy legacy of what Philippe Lacoue-Labarthe
and Jean-Luc Nancy have called a "national aestheticism," will escape un-
scathed the rigors to which Heidegger almost everywhere else subjects his
heritage.[9]

ERSCHÜTTERUNG

The spirit of Heidegger's "spiritual leadership" of the German university in
1933 has been analyzed closely and thoughtfully in Derrida's *Of Spirit:
Heidegger and the Question.* In the previous chapter I tried to point out the
intimate relation of such a spirit to Heidegger's early conception of "factical
life" as a life in and of the university, and of the role of phenomenological
research in such a living institution. Here it will be something more than an
insistent gnawing, goading life at the university, serving as a counterthrust
against ruinance. Here it will be a matter of life's shattering. Whether in or out
of the university.

In one perspective, the rectoral address is all about shattering and failure,
precisely in its self-assertive leadership claims, its claims upon the spirit.
Heidegger cites Aeschylus' *Prometheus,* in which that archetypal daimon proclaims knowing (τέχνη) far less powerful than necessity (ἀνάγκη). Heidegger
comments: "That is to say, every knowing of things remains exposed from the
outset to the plenipotence [*Übermacht*] of destiny and fails in the face of it [*und
versagt vor ihr*]" (SB, 11). He adds: "Precisely for that reason, knowing must
unfold its supreme despite [*seinen höchsten Trotz*], for which alone the entire
might of concealment in beings arises, in order then actually to fail [*um
wirklich zu versagen*]."

Whenever after 1945 accusations were made against Heidegger's trium-
phant "Self-Assertion," Heidegger himself liked to point to this and similar
passages in order to indicate that his was no inflated triumphalism but an
essentially tragic attitude toward life, knowledge, and the institutions of knowledge. The concealed, the dubious, the question-worthy were his passion, the
uncertainty of beings as a whole, which called forth nothing if not supreme
despite (SB, 14). And which, as we shall see, elicited nothing so much as
shattering.

Among the world-shaping powers of historical human existence Heidegger
counts not only spirit, history, and language; nation, ethical community, and
state; poetizing, thinking, and believing; law, economy, and technology; but also
illness, delusion, and death: *Krankheit, Wahnsinn, Tod* (13–14). How bizarre to
find these three listed among the "blessings" and "fecundities" of cornucopious

being! Yet precisely this bizarrerie calls forth Heidegger's thinking—as spite thrusting against ruinance. A truly spiritual world is one that thrives on danger, on "the innermost and uttermost danger." A danger that will now take us to our second word for shattering, *Erschütterung*.

> For "spirit" is neither empty perspicacity nor the uncommitted play of wit, nor the boundless pursuit of analytical intelligence, nor even cosmic reason. Rather, spirit is originally attuned, cognizant, resolute openedness to the essence of being. And the *spiritual world* of a people is not the superstructure of a culture; just as little is it the arsenal of applicable insights and values. Rather, it is the power that most profoundly preserves a people's forces of earth and blood, the power that most intensely heightens and most extensively shatters its Dasein [*Macht der innersten Erregung und weitesten Erschütterung*]. Only a spiritual world guarantees a people greatness. For it compels the ongoing decision between the will to greatness and complacent acceptance of decline [*Gewährenlassen des Verfalls*] to count cadence for the march that our people has begun, the march into its coming history. (SB, 14)

Spirit is power, albeit the power of resolute openedness. A resolutely spiritual world preserves forces—forces that are bound up with the earth and with blood (*erd- und bluthaften Kräfte*)—as the power of both heightened arousal or excitation (*Erregung*) and the most widespread shattering (*Erschütterung*), the power that is both *innerste* and *weiteste*. Earth, blood, and excitation: is there a suppressed biologism in Heidegger? *Erregung* is a word that we find in reference to the animal, to God, and to propriation (*Ereignis*), and we shall hear its various resonances in chapter 9, below. However, these lines of the rectoral address that take us closest to National-Socialist *Blut und Boden* are strangely bloodless and ethereal. Heidegger is in search of, not a race or bloodline or breed, but historical greatness, even grandeur. Greatness is the prize awarded those who march in perpetual decision, not an either/or decision for this rather than that, but de-cision as the rhythmic law of a will to grandeur in the face of the haltless advance of corruption. Heidegger finds such grandeur in the "boldness" or even "recklessness" of which Dasein is (occasionally) capable.[10] Thus even shattering does not happen, does not take place, once and for all. It is the relentless exposure to *Entscheidung*, the shattering trek across the abyssal watershed of decision, that counts. (Recall the etymological connection between *Scheitern, Scheiden, Erschütterung, Schütten,* and *Schütteln*.) Relentless exposure to the shattering plenipotence of beings.

The overpowering thrust of beings, what one might call and what indeed was long called their *transcendent* power, preoccupies Heidegger from the time of his 1928 lecture course on logic. The theme of plenipotence extends beyond his 1935 *Introduction to Metaphysics* in order to obsess his 1936–1938 *Contributions to Philosophy (Of Propriation)*. I certainly cannot survey here in any adequate way these complex texts. I shall refer to the 1928 logic course, to a roughly contemporary review of Ernst Cassirer's *Mythic Thought*, and only indirectly to the 1936–1938 *Contributions to Philosophy*, which will occupy us in the following chapter, before returning to the 1935 lecture course. What I wish to broach is the possible connection (a connection that may prove to be tenuous and that in any case is not clear to me) between what I am calling "shattering" and the following matters:

• the "overpowering" of existence by plenipotent beings as a whole;

• the "semination" or "bestrewal" of transcendence, the primal dispersion of Dasein as *Streuung;*

• the overcoming of thought on the "ontological difference" in a thinking of "the sundering [or cleaving] of beyng," *die Zerklüftung des Seyns;*

• the way in which "plenipotence," "semination," and "cleaving of beyng" exhibit not so much the divine or holy, the "transcendent" in any of its traditional senses, but the *daimonic,* what Heidegger calls τὸ δαιμόνιον;

• and, by way of anticipation of matters to be discussed in chapters 6 and 9, the principal trait of daimon *life,* which is life lived in the element of *air.*

PLENIPOTENCE: THE OVERPOWERING

In 1928 Heidegger identifies Aristotle's "double determination of philosophy" as (1) *ontology,* not yet defined terminologically as such, of course, but at all events a "science of being," a λόγος of τὸ ὄν; and (2) *theology,* which he takes to mean the science of ouranian or celestial beings.[11] The heavens, as the sovereign realm of perdurant being, encompass and overwhelm the philosopher. It is from the sky that (most) gods sweep down in order to look in on mortal affairs. The sky is thus *das Umgreifende und Überwältigende.*

Oddly, the impact of the heavens on the philosopher is described by the very word that in *Being and Time* portrays a Dasein that is both bedazzled by the world and stunned by anxiety, the very word that one year later (in 1929–1930) will be used to designate the essence of *animal* behavior. As though all life, from gods, through humans, to horses and dogs, radiated bedazzlement. When a glimpse of heaven seizes the philosopher he or she is *benommen,* both taken from and given to himself or herself, "benumbed," "bedazzled," or simply "dazed." In 1928 Heidegger *my face is the face of one who has made a long journey* identifies such benumbment as an encounter not with dogs but with gods. Further, he explicitly relates the overpowering—celestial plenipotence—to what in *Being and Time* is called "thrownness," *Geworfenheit,* the factical cast of the very *life* of Dasein. Such overpowering thrownness brings the projects of Dasein—including, as we have seen, its projects of ontology—to the brink of shattering. Much later in the logic course he relates thrownness not to Dasein but to the *ground* of being as such, as though being itself were on the brink (278).

The overpowering comes to the fore once again in a long note, a footnote or marginal insertion in section 11 of the 1928 logic course, "The Transcendence of Dasein" (26, 211 n. 3). Heidegger notes:

The problem of transcendence is to be taken back to the question concerning temporality and freedom. Only on that basis can we show in what way transcendence itself, as essentially ontologically differentiating [*zur Transzendenz selbst, als wesentlich ontologisch differenter:* the syntax of *differenter* is difficult, but suggests the feminine, dative, present-participial form of differencing, so that there would be every reason, especially because of the relation to temporality, to translate it as *différance*], implies the understanding of being as *plenipotence,* as holiness [*von Sein qua* Übermächtigem, *qua Heiligkeit*].

Transcendence devolves upon the questions of ecstatic temporality and freedom (as both the freedom toward death of *Being and Time* and the freedom of revealing and concealing in "On the Essence of Truth" at its earliest stage, circa 1930). What pertains to transcendence as such is an understanding of being as the sacred in the sense of the plenipotent or overpowering—the ouranian canopy that dazzles us. But to continue:

> It is not a matter of demonstrating the divine ontically in its "existence" ['*Dasein*']. Rather, it is a matter of illuminating the origin of this understanding of being in terms of the transcendence of Dasein; that is to say, of illuminating the cohesion of this idea of being with the general understanding of being. (Cf. now Scheler's idea of such a genesis.)[12] Only on the basis of the essence of "being" and transcendence, only within and on the basis of the full bestrewal [*Streuung*] (cf. §10, guiding statement no. 6) that pertains to the essence of transcendence, can this idea of being as plenipotence [*Übermacht*] be understood; yet not by interpreting it in the direction of an absolute Thou, nor as the good, nor as value, nor as the eternal.

In these marginal lines (and more starkly in the final lines of the note, which for reasons of space I will not cite) Heidegger distances himself from every "confessional" or "ontic" belief in God, in order to identify a realm of the holy as superlative power; yet it is not in the blazing sky that he seeks such a realm, nor in the starry heavens above his heart and head, not in either of the diurnal realms of the celestial flame, but in the bestrewal, strewing, scattering, sowing, or seminating that occurs in and as transcendence. He refers his students to those remarkable passages on semination and dissemination that appear earlier in the logic course, passages to which Derrida's first "Geschlecht" article has drawn attention and to which we gestured at the end of our "Introduction to Za-ology." *Streuung* has to do with the scattering not only of a bemused and distracted quotidian existence but also of the essence of an anxiously attuned and resolute Dasein into embodiment and sexuality. Or at least into something like carnality and sexuality. *Streuung* involves nothing less than a scattering of the very *ground* of existence and being. It is doubtless bound up with "transcendence," which Heidegger in his 1929 inaugural lecture, "What Is Metaphysics?", identifies as the *finitude* of being (W, 17: . . . *weil das Sein selbst im Wesen endlich ist* . . .], and which the *Contributions* will identify as the cleaving or fissuring of beyng.

Yet the parenthetical remark which Heidegger now introduces, to which I have referred elsewhere,[13] binds these apparently disparate themes (transcendence, temporality, freedom, plenipotence, the holy, abyssal ground, sexuality, embodiment, and bestrewal) into a kind of daimonic knot. A knot of the Ariadnic thread. I continue quoting:

(Zu bedenken bleiben: Sein und δαιμόνιον bzw. Seinsverständnis und δαιμόνιον. Sein qua Grund! Sein und Nichts—Angst.)

(It remains for us to consider being and the daimonic, or understanding-of-being and the daimonic. Being as ground! Being and Nothing—anxiety.)

The second-order margin of the daimon, the daimonic note to a note on transcendence, suddenly puts us in touch with the theme of daimon life. Life as the site of confrontation with the overpowering, life as the plenipotent scattering of the ground of being in multifaceted embodiment and sexuality, life (as we shall see in the next chapter) as the network of space-time and the tearing of that network, life as the (finite) source of both revealing/concealing and shattering.

A second sighting of that daimon occurs in Heidegger's 1928 review of the second volume of Cassirer's *Philosophy of Symbolic Forms*.[14] Particularly striking in Heidegger's review is his attention to the ways in which primitive or mythical Dasein is benumbed or bedazzled (*benommen*) by what comes to presence in its world—what anthropologists (and Cassirer too, following them) call the mana-effect of magical potency and the overpowering. The primitive is stupefied by his or her world in the way that, in ours, only the poet and thinker are struck. Perhaps that is why in *Being and Time* Heidegger wanted to examine the "self-interpretation" of the world of primitive Dasein. For here the poetic experience is foundational. Out of an "original *Benommenheit*" the "primitive" unfolds his or her conception of time, space, and number; on the basis of such stupefaction, the sacred and taboo regions of being come into relief; the very alternation of day and night (see chapter 2, above) occurs within such bedazzlement. *Benommensein* and *Mächtigkeit* are the chief categories—rather, the principal *existentials*—of the primitive world, in which the daimon is as close as the nearest rock, tree, or outrigger canoe paddle. More specifically, the daimon hovers in the reflected or refracted light of the plenipotent world (*Rückstrahlung;* cf. SZ, 16 and *Reluzenz* in the 1921–1922 lectures).

Cassirer recognizes stages of daimonic sophistication in primitive thought: Heidegger paraphrases his assertion that "only at the higher stages does the magical daimon become δαιμόνιον and *genius,* so that, in the end, Dasein is determined not by an alien power but by what it is freely capable of, as an ethical subject free for itself" (1006). One senses that Heidegger himself is suspicious of the philosophical underpinnings—or, rather, the lack of such—in Cassirer's speculations, which allow such an interfusion of anthropological and ethical motifs. In his critical response to Cassirer (1007ff.), Heidegger repeats a familiar question: "How does it stand with regard to the ontological elaboration—an elaboration not to be found anywhere here—of the constitution and the mode of being of what are indiscriminately enough called 'consciousness,' 'life,' and 'reason'?" In short, the experience of mana should not be conceived of as a form of representation, whether of intuition or of the under-standing. As a *Lebensform*, mana is in fact *an understanding of being* (1009: Seinsverständnis). Thus one must push the question of primitive or mythical "life" as such, of this life and its particular "thrownness." Heidegger writes:

> The thrownness of Dasein implies a being delivered over to the world in such a way that being in the world is overwhelmed by that to which it is transposed. Plenipotence can announce itself as such and in general only to a being that is delivered over to. . . . In its dependence on the overpowering, Dasein is benumbed by it; only as akin to such a reality, only by belonging to it, can Dasein experience itself. Accordingly, in thrownness every being that is in any way unveiled possesses the ontological trait of plenipotence (mana). (1009–10)

A whole interpretation of temporality lies concealed in such thrownness and unveiling, an interpretation that would help us to understand the spontaneity and instantaneous character ("*Augenblicklichkeit*") of so-called primitive life. And further, beyond temporality, the very *transcendence* that is operative in primitive life needs to be illuminated. For the being bedazzled or benumbed (*Benommensein*) of primitive life cannot be understood in terms of the Kantian or neo-Kantian subject-object relation, nor by any other ontic approach. Be-numbment or bedazzlement expresses an ontological attunement, a mode of being (*eine Seinsart*) in which the epistemological, valuative, and cultural catego-ries of subjectivity dissolve. Indeed, benumbment may hold the key that will unlock the door that leads beyond both Kant and Hegel: as Cassirer expresses a hope in the *Hegelian* confidence that spirit must first externalize and objectify itself in order to establish its interiority, Heidegger repeats his early, persistent question about what in 1921–1922 he called "prestructuring" and "relucence": "What is the ontological constitution of human Dasein in general, such that it comes to its proper self, as it were, only by way of the detour through the world?" (1011). After considering the 1928 logic course and the Cassirer review, we may add: Why is the world-relation of Dasein essentially overpowering, essentially daimonic? How is that world-relation bound up with transcendence, the holy, and, of all things—the body and sexuality? How could the word that means the universal (and not simply "primitive") impact of unveiling, the revela-tory thrownness that defines humanity as such, come to be attributed
Why should I not wander over the pastures?   to the *animal's* world?

BESTREWAL

Heidegger's projected "metaphysics of the Dasein" (26, 171ff.) takes not "man" but the "neutral term" *das Dasein* as its theme, the Dasein that is somehow "prior to all factical concretion." Somehow. For does not such prior-ity mean, one must ask, prior to life? Prior to the between of birth and death? The very first determination to be neutralized, the first "example" of factical concretion, the first aspect of life that must be preceded or anteceded or gotten back behind, is something like a dual sexuality: ". . . that the Dasein is neither of the two sexes [*keines von beiden Geschlechtern ist*] (172)." Such sexlessness (*Geschlechtslosigkeit*, assuming here that Heidegger's reference to "the two" is sufficient to identify *Geschlecht* as sex rather than, say, *das harte Geschlecht* of a mustered generation, tribe, clan, or race) is nothing indifferent or negative. It is "the original positivity and might of essence," *die ursprüngliche Positivität und Mächtigkeit des Wesens*. Derrida therefore appears to be justified in identifying the *duality* of the sexes as the seed of negativity—especially inasmuch as his reading of these lines in the 1928 logic course is already "magnetized" by Heidegger's 1953 Trakl essay and its "gentleness of a simple [or unifold] duality," *die Sanftmut* [N.B.: something less than hard and heavy] *einer einfältigen Zwiefalt*.[15] Indeed, even if such a reading were magnetized back in the direction of Hegel's philosophy of nature, duality would nonetheless remain the seed of death in natural life. Certainly the reference Heidegger is about to make to "proliferation," *Mannigfaltigung*, suggests that duality is degeneration and decrepitude. Or is duality—duality and multiplication of the manifold—the very mark of daimon life? And duplicitous, multifaceted life the very mark of a riven being, a strewn and bestrewing ground, the oxymoron of the fertile abyss?

The sixth guiding principle of Heidegger's metaphysics of the Dasein begins as follows: "6. The Dasein in general harbors the inner possibility of factical dispersion [*Zerstreuung*] into embodiment and thereby into sexuality," *in die Leiblichkeit und damit in die Geschlechtlichkeit*, again presuming that the last word can be said and thought as "sexuality." A host of problems arises, among them the very meaning of "inner possibility" and the relation of "factical concretion" to "factical dispersion." How are the concrete and the dispersed related? Or are they one and the same? If they are two, can both be factical? What is the relation of dispersion or emphatic bestrewal (*Zer-streuung*) to the bestrewal of transcendence itself as the plenipotence of ground? And why should all these things be linked preeminently (if only by way of eminent *negation*) with such ostensibly ontic matters as embodiment and sex, generation, tribe, and race? Which sex? Which race? The human? How would the "human race," *das Menschengeschlecht*, be related to factical life, just-plain-life, daimonic life? Are all these forms of "life" the same? Are they "forms" at all? Are there "stages" of finite being? Does φύσις exhibit "levels" or "grades" of revelation and concealment?

Perhaps the ambiguity of *Streuung/Zer-streuung* can be clarified by some of Heidegger's earliest remarks on the subject. In his 1921–1922 lecture course, "Phenomenological Interpretations of Aristotle: An Introduction to Phenomenological Research" (discussed earlier, in chapters 1 and 4), Heidegger elaborates on dispersion as a category of movement in the sense of inclination (*Neigung*). Such dispersion is twofold: (1) life disperses itself in the world, thus "prestructuring" its possibilities; (2) life returns to itself only in the reflected and refracted light of these dispersed possibilities, returns to itself as "relucence." "Self-dispersing life encounters its world as 'dispersion,' as dispersing, manifold, replete, preoccupying, vacuous, monotonous." Indeed, the nascent structures of ecstatic temporality can be seen through the fog of duplicitous dispersion: when life inclines to this or that possibility, it moves (toward) itself, *auf sich zu*, the prepositions that in *Being and Time* mark the future ecstasis. When life takes care or trouble concerning the things closest to it at present, it radiates back upon itself, *auf sich selbst zurück*, the prepositions that mark the ecstasis of having-been. Thus the animatedness of inclination is both the quagmire of distraction or diversion and the seedbed of human temporality proper. In the margin of his lecture notes Heidegger writes: "The specific larvance [i.e., mask and masquerade] in the ambiguity of linguistic expressions of the categories of facticity is not accidental. *Zerstreuung:* (1) dispersing itself (prestructuring); (2) the dispersal (relucent)." The implication is that relucent dispersal is the unavoidable effect exerted by things in the world on factical life, whereas the reflexive *sich zerstreuen* functions as an inevitable, necessary, and a priori structure, a prestructuring, *Praestruktion*. A tension remains between the prior, potent, "prestructuring" dispersion or (if we may say so) bestrewal of factical life in its concerns and the subsequent, reactive, structurally posterior dispersal or (if we may say so) distraction of that same life. Factical life sows the seeds of its own dissipation and ruin. The "fundamental peculiarity of life's animatedness" is "ruinance, petrifaction" (61, 120). And yet, as life locks itself away from itself, incarcerates itself in the prison of an endlessly distracting world, it experiences an inchoate form of transcendence: factical life, precisely in duplicitous dispersion, is "*away from itself,*" "*outside itself*" (123: "Von-sich-weg," "Aus-sich-hinaus"). Such nascent transcendence is mighty. "The mightiness of relucence in the very movement of incarceration . . . wins from this flight from itself the modes in which it occupies itself with the world and with itself." Thus the seeds of ruin are invariably the seeds strewn by the primal, abyssal ground of existence, by (if we may say so) daimon life herself.—But to return to the 1928 logic course and "the problem of transcendence."

Heidegger attempts to locate the "properly concrete" source of the Dasein, the origin and font of existence, which is "not yet" factical concretion, "not yet" factical dispersion. No doubt that "not yet" threatens to remove his *temporal* interpretation of transcendence to the horizon of the Aristotelian "no longer/not yet," which derives from an unexamined acceptance of the present "now" as the standard for being, an acceptance that in Heidegger's own view founds both metaphysics and *vulgar* time. As factical, the Dasein is, among other things (none of these other things are specified, however), "splintered into a body and, at one with that, among other things [once again unspecified], split in twain [*zwiespältig*] in each case into one particular sexuality" (26, 173). Heidegger hastily denies that any of these *Zer-* words (*zersplittert, zerspalten,* etc.) are negative concepts, a denial that is one of his most characteristic gestures.[16] The emphatic prefix *Zer-* means no more than the "inner possibility" of a "proliferation" or "multiplication," a *Mannigfaltigung* or *Vermannig-faltigung,* not a Kantian manifold but a profusion of facets, a multifaceting. Heidegger's "guiding principles" will culminate in a discussion of *space* as an eminent site of such proliferation. We will have to affirm what Derrida hesitates to proclaim: both *Streuung* and emphatic *Zer-streuung* in the 1928 logic course (if not in *Being and Time*) must be thought as eminently (if not entirely) *positive* modalities, forces, or potencies.[17]

Such proliferation in and of embodiment, sexuality, and space does not occur because some "primal creature [or primal essence: *Urwesen*] is sundered in twain," as in Aristophanes' myth in Plato's *Symposium*. (Heidegger does not make the allusion a specific reference—perhaps because it is too obvious, or perhaps because it would embroil his discourse in an unsavory Platonic-Freudian context.) Rather, the possibility of proliferation lies in each Dasein as such. Embodiment may be viewed as an "organizational factor" of such multifaceting, rather than as one-result-among-others of factical dispersion. Furthermore, the multiplication in question is not merely a characteristic of the Dasein; rather, the manifold (the forbidden Kantian word returns) "pertains to being itself," *gehört zum Sein selbst*. Being itself is not one but many. Which would suggest that being itself is not the font and origin. That hint will soon induce Heidegger to designate being itself (*das Sein selbst*) as finite (*endlich*). "In other words," writes Heidegger, concluding the thought, "to the essence of the Dasein. . . ." Being itself "in other words" is Dasein. *Sein selbst: das Dasein?!* How will we ever again be able to distinguish between *Sein* and *Dasein?* Are they not here conflated, and does not such conflation spell the end, not the beginning, of a thought of ontological difference? At least, is not the proto-ontological difference (*Sein/Dasein*) left behind by a thinking of the cleaving of beyng (*Zerklüftung des Seyns*)? Yet what can a thinking of ontological difference (*Sein/Seiendes*) be when the proto-ontological difference has been left behind by the leap to meta-ontology—which, as we shall see, is the leap to bestrewal, semination, and dissemination? Heidegger writes: "In other words, to the essential unfolding of the Dasein . . . in general there belongs, in accord with its metaphysically neutral concept, an original *bestrewal,* which in one altogether determined respect is *dispersion* [*eine ursprüngliche* Streuung, *die in einer ganz bestimmten Hinsicht* Zerstreuung *ist*]" (173). Whether or not emphatic bestrewal or dispersion is the one altogether determined respect we call *sexuality,* the mystery of proliferation surely pertains to being itself. As though being itself were gaping in dehiscence. As open as the living air.

The final use of *Streuung* (I have found only three references in Heidegger's oeuvre, in contrast to the dozens of references to the emphatic *Zerstreuung*) occurs at the end of the 1928 lecture course, in section 13, "Transcendence and the Essence of the Ground" (278). Here Heidegger identifies "two domains of problems" that eventuate from his discussion of transcendence and ecstatic-ecstematic temporality as the *nihil originarium*.[18]

First, "clarification of the origin of the multiplicity [*Mannigfaltigkeit*] of grounds, of the forms of ground; that is to say, of the bestrewal of ground [*Streuung von Grund*]." The manifold that was earlier associated with the embodiment, sexuality, and spatiality of the Dasein in and through a seminal leap, a leap of origins itself susceptible to emphatic dissemination or dispersion (*Zerstreuung*), is here attributed to ground as such. *Grund* here means *der*

Grund des Grundes (277), the point of convergence of freedom, temporality, the nothing—and anxiety. The point of τὸ δαιμόνιον. The ground of ground will of course prove   *After passing through leagues of thick darkness* to be a fecund abyss, *Grund/Ab-grund.* Heidegger refers to such an abyssal ground as the "primal phenomenon" and "primal *factum*" of a "primal history" and a "primal time" (270, 274); the mysterious, daimonic point of convergence, which is not a point at all, unless perhaps in Hegel's sense, will prove to be "primal propriation," *das Urereignis* (274). Thus the first domain of problems embraces virtually all the questions that will culminate ten years later in the *Contributions to Philosophy* (*Of Propriation*). A glance ahead to that text reveals the single most evocative figure of bestrewal, a figure that will return to dominate the closing pages of the "Letter on Humanism" in yet again ten more years. That figure serves as the disseminative partner of the peasant woman who in 1935 treads the field at dusk in Van Gogh's shoes, she and he both being figures of the *thinker* as such. In the *Contributions* we read:

> Yet how does the thinker safeguard the truth of beyng, if not in the patient, heavy footfall of his questioning steps and their concatenated sequence [*in die schwere Langsamkeit des Ganges seiner fragenden Schritte und ihrer gebundenen Folge*]? Inconspicuous as the sower [*der Sämann*] who on a lonely field beneath the vault of the sky paces the length of the furrows with a heavy and hesitant step, reticent in each moment, measuring and shaping with each arching toss of his arm the concealed space of all growth and ripening. Who among us can still perform this function in his thinking—as the most primordial exertion of his force and his supreme future? (65, 19)

For Heidegger, the thinking that thinks *shattering* is *seminal* thinking. Such thinking elevates the thinker. He or she, the peasant woman or man who scatters seed, is needed and used by the gods. Or by the daimon. Elevated, needed, and used, the thinker   *Emaciated, haggard, he set out alone to find Utnapishtim the Faraway*   is also crushed—*durch diese Erhöhung zerschmettert werden* (65, 87). If the thinker salvages the truth of being, rescues it from utter oblivion, such salvaging "is never practicable without a shattering [*nie . . . ohne eine Erschütterung*]" (65, 389).

Second, "interpretation of the essential retrogression of the ground into one ground (thrownness in itself)." The factical thrownness of Dasein (in each case my own), of factical life, and even of just-plain-life, the *Wurf* of *Geworfenheit,* the litter of life cast or dropped on the earth, now applies to the essential retrogression of ecstematic horizons in the Dasein, to there-being as such. A (finite) *Da-sein* that is no longer readily distinguishable from (finite) *Sein.* Suspended in the vibrancy of the ecstasies or raptures of time, transcendent Dasein, metaphysically isolated, is impotent (*ohnmächtig*). "The impotence is metaphysical . . ." (279). It is nonetheless shattering. For the "world entry" (*Welteingang*) or "worlding of the world" (*Welten*), the worlding that springs from the originary nothing, is itself tied to both daimonic plenipotence and anxiety. World *entry* is simultaneously what the Stoics called ἐκπύρωσις, the conflagration that consumes one universe in order to release another from its ashes. In the raptures of such world aperture and closure, the ground of Dasein is the site of both plenipotence and impotence, of everything and nothing. Its privileged yet parlous position is captured in the very ambivalence of dissemination, seminal *Streuung* and emphatic, daimonic *Zer-streuung*. How to conceive of the Dasein universal-ontologically as both the central-vigilant and the peripheral-dormant monad, as both being-in-totality and utterly individualized, metaphysically isolated, and benumbed being-there, as both overpowering and shattering   *I was burned with heat and cold*   in the face of the overpowering? Heidegger will turn to that question in his 1935 *Introduction to Metaphysics* and in his 1936–1938 *Contributions to Philosophy*. In 1928 the question is "still altogether obscure" to him (26, 271).

THE CLEAVING OF (FINITE) BEYNG

The daimonic weft of transcendence (temporality, freedom, plenipotence, the holy, embodiment and sexuality, being, and the nothing—anxiety) is anything but readily raveled. Yet Heidegger's "self-critique" of his own 1935 lecture course, published as an "Appendix" to the *Gesamtausgabe* edition of *Einführung in die Metaphysik*, is helpful in making a first approach to the daunting *Beiträge zur Philosophie (Vom Ereignis)*, which we shall take up in the next chapter.[19]

What Heidegger appears to regret concerning his 1935 course is that its Leibnizian beginning ("Why are there beings at all, and why not far rather nothing?") is insufficiently cast in terms of the history of being, insufficiently *seinsgeschichtlich*. It fails to pose the crucial questions of the disenfranchisement (*Entmachtung*) of φύσις—rather than, one must say, the disempowering of ψυχή or *spirit*—and the essential unfolding of the truth of being (*die Wesung des Seins*). Not only do the upsurgence of beings into unconcealment and the disappearance of beings into concealment have to be heeded, but so also does the utter disregard for such revealing and concealing in the history of being as such. Thus Heidegger wishes to overcome his earlier points of departure, to wit, understanding-of-being (*Seinsverständnis*), which dominates the period of *Being and Time*, and ontological difference (*die Unterscheidung*), which dominates the lecture courses that follow immediately after *Being and Time*, in favor of a thinking of the *happening of being* (Seinsgeschehnis), a happening or occurring that constitutes the essential unfolding of the history of being as such. His self-critique twice deploys the word *Erschütterung* to express the desired overcoming:

> Thus this question ["How does it stand with being?"], viewed as a whole, is the attempt to shatter the "difference," and *not* simply to *pursue its other side!* For the tendency of the whole shifts away from understanding-of-being to *happening-of-being*—to that extent, therefore, the *overcoming of understanding-of-being* is decisive!

On the other hand, we must for all that do some serious work on the forgotten and unquestioned Platonic-Aristotelian-Kantian (P-A-K) fundamental position—understanding-of-being *located* as *historical* fact and yet at the same time shattered.[20]

Does the attempt to shatter ontological difference and understanding-of-being relate to the shatterings discussed in the 1935 lecture course itself? I shall cite only two instances of such shattering, one involving *Scheitern,* the other *Erschütterung,* both in the remarkable third part of the fourth chapter of *An Introduction to Metaphysics,* "The Limitation of Being—Being and Thinking."

Shattering occurs at the culmination of Heidegger's *second* approach to the first choral song of Sophocles' *Antigone,* with its celebration of the most monstrous, violent, and uncanny of living creatures among gods and animals. Life has been present from the outset of the lecture course, as the vibrant élan (*Schwungkraft*) that streams through plants and animals (EM, 4), as the tree which we conceptualize as "alive," and as the nerve (the dendrites, as it were) of "life" itself (61), as the λόγος that is once again to be thought in accord with φύσις, according to which "the being of life is at the same time death" (100), and as the familiar, fatal definition of man as *animal rationale,* ζῷον λόγον ἔχον—

> At bottom the designated definition of man is zoological. The ζῷον of this zoology remains in many respects worthy of question. In the sole framework of *this* definition of man, the Western doctrine of man—all psychology, ethics, epistemology, and anthropology—has been constructed. For a long time now we have been adrift in a confused wash of notions and conceptions drawn from these disciplines. (EM, 108)

The life of that same living creature called *Mensch* will perdure throughout the 1935 lecture course as the *transformed* zoology of a rethought "man." If the *end* of the definition of man as rational animal (". . . a definition not shattered even today . . . " [134]) yields to an incipient thought of φύσις, then the *beginning* of that definition (in Parmenides, Heraclitus, Sophocles—and Heidegger) is φύσις = λόγος ἄνθρωπον ἔχον, a coinage Heidegger translates as follows: "Being, the overwhelming to-appear [i.e., φύσις], necessitates [i.e., ἔχον] the gathering that indwells and grounds [i.e., λόγος as λέγειν] the being of human beings [i.e., ἄνθρωπον, in the accusative]" (134). Such logistical gathering initially appears as the hard, even violent subjugation of other living beings, as portrayed in the antistrophe of Sophocles' song. Heidegger comments:

> (. . .) It names the birds swarming in the breeze, living creatures in the water, the bull and the stallion in the hills. The living being, suspended dreamily in itself and in its environs [*leichtträumend in sich und in seinem Umkreis schwingt*], constantly streaming beyond itself in ever novel configurations, renewing itself yet persisting in its *one* orbit, knows the place where it grazes through the night and wanders by day. As living, it is enmeshed in the sovereign sway of sea and earth. Into such living, which rotates about its own axis, not truly dwelling [*ungewöhnlich*] in its own circle and articulation and ground, man tosses his snares and nets;

he tears life out of its ordered place and shuts it away in pens and corrals, placing it under yoke. . . . (EM, 118)

Note how problematic the reading of that sentence concerning the "unfamiliar," "strange," or "not truly dwelling," *ungewöhnlich,* is. Is it the living creature in the seas and the mountains that is "unfamiliar," "not dwelling"? Or is it not *man* who is the least familiar, most uncanny, most monstrous, most violent, most nomadic and least homey of creatures? The position of the phrase *im eigenen Kreis* (the name *Mensch* appearing only after the entire phrase) certainly suggests that it is the animal that does not dwell in its own rotating circle, articulation, and ground, the animal that hovers lightly in dreams, somnambulating effortlessly in its one (not even two) orbit(s). However, the dative case follows the violent accusative (*In dieses . . . Leben, dahinein wirft der Mensch . . .*) and thus may nevertheless imply that it is *man* who does not dwell (*In dieses in sich rollende Leben, im eigenen Kreis und Gefüge und Grund ungewöhnlich, dahinein wirft der Mensch . . .*). What decides the dwelling or not dwelling, the familiarity or foreignness, of animals ("life") and human beings? Shattering. *Scheitern.* Which nevertheless concerns them both, as the culminating lines of Heidegger's 1929–1930 analysis of the animal's "ring" attest. At the end of this second approach to Sophocles' choral song Heidegger writes:

> All violent governance immediately shatters [*scheitert*] against but *one* thing. That is death. Death accomplishes beyond all accomplishment, sets bounds beyond all boundaries. . . . Yet this uncanny thing [*dieses Un-heimliche*], which displaces us once and for all from everything familiar, without recourse, is not some special propriation [*Sonderereignis*] that has to be listed among others merely because, at the end, it too advenes. Man is without exit in the face of death not merely when he comes to die but always and essentially. As long as man *is,* he stands in the exitlessness of death. Thus the Da-sein is the very occurrence of uncanniness. (EM, 121)

The shattering of (proto)ontological difference and understanding-of-being as starting-points and ruling perspectives for inquiry into the history and truth of being is at one with the shattering of human existence in the uncanniness of death, which is both   *Life and death they allot but the day of death they do not disclose*   certain and indeterminate as to its when. Yet even more uncanny than the death of Dasein is the fact that in the face of the plenipotence of being Dasein is not alone. For whatever sees the light of day or follows the path of the sun confronts in some way or at least is vulnerable   *Already the thief in the night has hold of my limbs, death inhabits my room; wherever my foot rests, there I find death*   to the shattering interruption of its circle or the penetration of its ring. Not the *exitus* as such, but *exitlessness,* is shattering. Life natal is life fatal. Whatever cleaves to being cleaves to the cleaving of being, both in a single lifetime and in the entire history and unfolding of being.

Heidegger's *third* approach to the choral song preserves the thought of shattering in the "breaking" (*Zerbrechen*) and "breach" (*die Bresche*) that imply not only the collapse of man but the rending of being as such (EM, 124), a cleaving or sundering of being that the *Contributions to Philosophy* will continue to accentuate. The essential unfolding of being thus itself entails a shattering and breaching, and any attempt to secure human dying from animal perishing   *how alike they are, they are like a painted death*   would be sheer subterfuge. All such attempts would operate under the aegis of what Nietzsche analyzes as "the ascetic ideal."[21]

However, let me truncate the extensive first account of shattering in *An Introduction to Metaphysics*. As that course turns from φύσις to λόγος, abandoning the difficult problem of death for questions of interpretation, students of the course may sense a certain dissatisfaction, a certain suspicion—Irigaray will cultivate it in chapter 9, below—that in spite of the focus on shattering the sundering of λόγος from φύσις is also being played out in Heidegger's own thought, in 1935 as well as back in 1929–1930, in the biology course. Which would corroborate the thesis that Heidegger's is at least in part a thought *of spirit*. Let me refer briefly to a second instance of shattering in *An Introduction to Metaphysics*.

The second instance has to do with the demotion of daimon life into sheer demonism, the demonism that surfaces when spirit is summoned back from its disenfranchisement. Suddenly "the metaphysical people" finds itself sandwiched in between the mediocre routines and subversive measures that bear the names *America* and *Russia*. Heidegger calls the malignant destruction of rank and the flattening of spirit *das Dämonische* and *die Dämonie* (EM, 35). Have these anything to do with the δαιμόνιον that Heidegger identifies in 1928 as the overpowering and the holy, the very site of being and abyssal ground? Perhaps they are a mere mummery of being's unfolding, a topsy-turvy carnival of life? In the early 1920s, we remember, Heidegger calls such mummery *Larvanz* (61, 93, 106–107, 110). In the destitute time of Bolshevism and Pragmatism, the demonry of spirit—spirit reduced to mere "intelligence"—bedevils not only the λόγος but also the ζῷον that is man. Heidegger describes the way in which for Marxism and Positivism spirit becomes a vacuous superstructure of the animal. Yes, in what follows he is speaking of Marxism, though also, albeit by way of indirection, of Nazism. And, yes, we are circling back from meta-ontological bestrewal and the cleaving of finite being to our own "hard and heavy" beginning in politics. He is speaking of Russia and America, though also, albeit once more by way of indirection, of the Germany of 1935, a Germany looking forward to the Summer Olympics of 1936:

> If one understands spirit as intelligence, as Marxism in its most extreme form has done, then, by way of defense against this, it is entirely correct to say that spirit, i.e., intelligence, must in the hierarchy of effective forces in human Dasein always be subordinated to sound physical fitness [*gesunden leiblichen Tüchtigkeit*] and also to character. Yet this hierarchy becomes untrue as soon as one grasps the essence of spirit in its truth. For all true force and beauty of body, all sureness and boldness of sword, and also all genuineness and perspicacity of understanding are grounded in spirit, finding their elevation and degeneration only in the respective power or impotence of spirit. . . . (EM, 36)

"Force and beauty of body," *Kraft und Schönheit des Leibes.* The phrase is continuous, contiguous, and in absolute symmetry with "sureness and bold-ness of sword," *Sicherheit und Kühnheit des Schwertes*—as the truth and essence of comprehending spirit. Body beautiful bespeaks force, deftness, or agility, along with rakish boldness. Of the sword. It is interesting to recall that Heidegger at about this time in his career accuses *Nietzsche* of "brachial brutal-ity" (NII, 200; 294–95/4, 147–48; 3, 218–19). Where now in Heidegger's hard and heavy rhetoric of the brave new *Geschlecht* do we find shattering?

We find it in the third part of the fourth chapter once again (EM, 93). Here Heidegger refers to a certain "reaction of spirit" that may well become a "seedbed" for "political reaction." It seems unlikely that by "political reac-tion" Heidegger is referring to the reactionary *right:* by 1935 all "reaction" is coming from the other side. The danger of reaction and reactionary thinking arises in the very battle against "intellectualism," a pitched battle in which Heidegger is fully engaged. Intellectualism is merely an "offshoot" or "scion" of Western metaphysics. However, just as the anthropological definition of man has not yet been shattered (134), so here too shattering is still in default: "Trimming the excrescences of contemporary intellectualism is important." *Die Beschneidung der Auswüchse....* "Trimming" could be replaced here by words translating the more usual senses of *Beschneidung,* especially when one thinks of that *Geschlecht* of men and women against whom the charge of "intellectualism" is most often levied in the Germany of the 1920s and 1930s. *Beschneidung* means circumcision or castration. The malignant growth of de-monic intellectualism must be circumcised, or perhaps even more radically trimmed. With a keen sword. That is important. Even so, warns Heidegger, the position of intellectualism in culture "will not thereby in the least be shattered [*erschüttert*]; it will not even be struck a blow" (93).

Thus the dangers of political reaction, reaction against the most reaction-ary. Heidegger fears that his resistance to reaction will be both plenipotent and impotent at once, ever elliptical, always falling short. Some of the dangers of some kinds of political reaction Heidegger dimly descries; others quite close by he apparently never sees. Readers of Heidegger will have to become accus-tomed to unbearable juxtapositions.

A DIFFICULT BIRTH

One of the most disconcerting juxtapositions in the history of the Third Reich is the contrast between the two state-sponsored art exhibitions of 1937, the Nazi-endorsed "Grand German Art Exhibition" (*Grosse Deutsche Kunstaus-stellung*) and the execrated "Degenerate Art" exhibition (*"Entartete Kunst"*). It is difficult to locate Heidegger in such a contrast. His rhetoric of the 1930s, including not only his "heart by heart, man by man" and his "sureness and boldness of sword" but also his "setting-into-the-work of truth" and his "deed that founds the state" (UK, 62–69), is reminiscent of what George L. Mosse calls "beauty without sensuality."[22] And yet Heidegger's lifelong heroes of art are doubtless all of them among the censured artists—for example, Paul Klee. When one juxtaposes Josef Thorak's sculpture, "Comradeship," displayed prominently in the gallery of the Party-sponsored exhibition, alongside Karl Hofer's magnificent canvases, "Men Friends" and "Women Friends," canvases first confiscated and then exposed to ridicule in the "Degenerate Art" exhibition, the shocking ambiguity of Heidegger's own position in Germany in the 1930s becomes palpable. The streamlined and antiseptic phantasm of the iron-pumping *Männerbund* confronts and affronts what Freud calls the two streams of eroticism, tenderness and sensuality; the aggressive fantasy of the militant male group damns and dams both streams, which are themselves (according to Freud) most often in conflict. Earlier on, in chapter 3, we speculated on Heidegger's excessive "rationalism," in the sense of his "enlightened" flight from all things "irrational" and sensual, as a possible subtext of his polemic against life-philosophy *and* his political militarism and militancy. It is not a question of homoeroticism, but of a *national erotism*, a purged and pyrified bonding, tempered yet intemperate when it comes to violence, if not sensuality, a bonding in which the sole energizing force is an aggressive sense of mission. A militant mission *for* the nation and *under* a leader but *against* the disruptive sensuality of the body, against polymorphous life, against the enemies who have always already stolen the *jouissance* we never possessed, against the free play of shapes in art, against effusions of color (for color can thrill and threaten), against the unexpected and the disarming, against ecstasy, delicacy, and humor. There is no absolutely convincing way to demonstrate the dire political significance of pristine moral "respectability" and militant "ethicality," of the moralizing fight to suppress life and body on behalf of spirit and homeland. Yet the connections—even if they amount to a hollow, a certain core of nothingness called *desire*—are there. And as Mosse suggests, these connections, vacuums, and vacuities are as disconcerting and as shattering in the United States and the England of the 1990s as they were in the Germany of the Nazi era.[23]

Shattering hangs suspended in the terrible twilight of historical overpowering. In its most derisory modes it appears as the rhetoric and politics of demonism and antidemonism in Heidegger's text, the inflexible sentimentalities of a *Geschlecht* that confuses itself with the sword. It is a rhetoric worthy of an exchange between a cynical diabolizing rockstar and an exercised exorcising archbishop. In its most exacting mode, however, it appears as a metaphysics of the daimonic, calling for a nascent politics of life as the fundamental form of disclosure, a nascent politics of the unified field of φύσις.

A nascent politics of life? Life as disclosure? A politics of the unified field of φύσις? I have to acknowledge that even though this second part (now two-thirds complete) of the book pledges to sketch such a politics, it does not do so. It does not because it cannot. Yet from the moment (I believe it was at the outset of chapter 2) there was talk of Dasein natal, Dasein fatal; or even from the moment when (in chapter 1) there was mention of saline solution and the neophyte, the slippery Dasein smeared with cream cheese;—from that moment on the spirit of Hannah Arendt's *Vita activa* (in America called *The Human Condition*) at least ought to have been present.²⁴ For Arendt emphasizes the *birth* rather than the death of the human being as the proper inspiration for the political task. The birth of a new human being provides more hands for labor, another world for work, and another destiny for public life and political action. It also introduces an inexpungeable pledge or a gage to remembrance and history. A history, it is true, not of heavy metal, stolid mettle, and irremediable melancholy, nor of tremendous feats and public glory, *tantae molis erat,* but of a lumpier, crazier mix, from diapers to bookbags to adventures to possible public impact to inevitable private catastrophe. Maudlin histories, the collectivist will say, ineffectual late-capitalist suburban yuppie histories. Nevertheless, birth initiates the only kind of history we will ever have, and public life begins by noticing it. "Labor and work, as well as action, are also rooted in natality in so far as they have the task to provide and preserve the world for, to foresee and reckon with, the constant influx of newcomers who are born into the world as strangers" (10). Political action plays a special role with regard to natality, inasmuch as "the new beginning inherent in birth can make itself felt in the world only because the newcomer possesses the capacity of beginning something anew, that is, of acting" (10–11). Arendt therefore proposes that "natality, and not mortality, may be the central category of political, as distinguished from metaphysical, thought" (11).

However, if Dasein fatal is Dasein natal, should metaphysical thought be that far removed from political thought? *Can* it be? Perhaps all the fuss concerning the dying/perishing opposition should be left in abeyance, and more attention paid to the *Wurf* of *Geworfenheit,* the dropping of the litter by which so many sorts of mammals are thrown into the world. Perhaps one should wonder how the *human* condition might open its doors and its horizons to all sorts of allanthropic births, parturings, hatchings, and dehiscences. Arendt's august and austere political realm seems far removed from the urgency of life in process of giving birth, difficult birth, far removed even from *human* birth (29), and one must imagine it even more remote from the exigency of unicellular, meiotic life, as Freud, for example, wrote of it. Yet if all three of Arendt's categories (labor, work, action) revert again and again to natality, then the distance between metaphysics, politics, and life must from time to time be closed, or at least diminished. It cannot be closed if we scorn birth as the instauration of a life "which man shares with other living things and which forever retains the cyclical movement of nature" (85); if we close a Leibnizian eye to the natality that introduces us to fatality, "the over-all gigantic circle of nature herself, where no beginning and no end exist and where all natural things swing in changeless, deathless repetition" (84); if we insist upon Aristotle's distinction between βίος (a life *in between* birth and death that is chock full of stories about feats and achievements in the public sphere) "as distinguished from mere ζωή" (85). Mere Zoe. Mère Zoé. Mere mother life. Poor Zoe, the whore of Nighttown, befriender of Bloom, no feats to show for it, banished from the New Bloomusalem of public action. And yet *daimonic.*

Metaphysics impinges negatively on politics and the *vita activa* whenever such traditional hierarchies make their mark even on a thinker of natality: linear action toward hard and fast results over passive, repetitive nature, straight-line politics over cyclical life, political biography over za-ology. It is difficult to know where to turn. It is certainly not a matter of jettisoning Heidegger and opting for another philosophical hero—choosing heroes is Heidegger's scenario anyway. There are no short-cuts. In the next chapter, which turns to Heidegger's *Contributions to Philosophy (Of Propriation)*, in the vague hope that they will also contribute something to *life,* shattering will doubtless continue to prevail over natality. Shattering will characterize the essential unfolding of the history of the truth of being as such. *Erschütterung* will raise the din of what otherwise seems to be the pious euphony of intimation and resonance (65, 108: *der Anklang*). Shattering will prove to be the sundering, cleaving, or gaping of being as such, *die Zerklüftung des Seyns.* Being, written now as *beyng,* will gape precisely as though its historic unfolding were a birthing, or a shattering. As the abyss of beyng yawns, the animal that is beside or outside itself, literally littered outside itself—Luce Irigaray calls it the *animal extatique à lui-même*—will lose the ground beneath its feet and head, and all beyng, suddenly riven and rending, will be in free-fall through the air, abandoned to the very element of daimon life:

> The air remains—it is what resuscitates life, yet at first under the form of an absence: nothing is there but what it is, and it does not appear. This provenance of life, this mediation and milieu of life—these give themselves without appearing as such. The first time they give themselves, they are felt as pain. The open air represents the possibility of life, yet it is also the sign of the loss of that which—or of her who—gave everything without distance, without hesitation, and without chagrin. The air, the open, is, in the beginning, the limitless immensity of mourning. There all is lost.[25]

SIX

Paranoetic Thinking

"Life" in the 1936–1938 *Contributions to Philosophy (Of Propriation)*

In the foregoing chapter we cast our nets wide—excessively wide, no doubt—in search of the daimon. We found the daimonic site, τὸ δαιμόνιον, in the 1928 logic course, in the thicket of transcendence, freedom, temporality, the over-powering, the nothing, and the holy. The common element of these apparently disparate items proved to be "strewing" or "bestrewal," *Streuung,* the root of emphatic *Zer-streuung,* dissemination, dispersion, and distraction. If the fore-going chapter spread itself too thin across too many texts, the present one will concentrate its forces and focus sharply on but two or three pages of a vast text, on some fifty lines in a book over five hundred pages long. We shall examine only two of the 281 sections or aphorisms of Heidegger's 1936–1938 *Contributions to Philosophy (Of Propriation).* Both appear in Part IV, "The Leap" (if *Sprung* means "leap"), the two aphorisms that treat of "life." And we shall permit nothing to disturb our focus.

Herewith, then, a preliminary reading of sections 153–154 of the *Beiträge zur Philosophie (Vom Ereignis).* These sections or aphorisms appear well after the mid-point of "The Leap," perhaps three-quarters of the way through it, at the moment when a leaping animal—say, a deer or a horse—extends its folded forelegs in anticipation of the shock of landing. The animal hopes that it will land on the farther rim of the gap that is to be leapt, trusts that it will not plummet into the abyss. Of the four key words of the *Contributions,* "the intimation" or "resonance," "the assist" or "interplay," "the leap" or "the fissure," and "the grounding" or "founding" (*der Anklang, das Zuspiel, der Sprung, die Gründung*), the leap or fissure is itself the third of four, on the descending arc, on the *chute.*[1]

THE FISSURE OF LIFE

At that point in the trajectory of "The Leap," three-quarters of the way through it, something unanticipated rises to meet us. "The Leap" consists of fifty-two aphorisms, most of them, while not familiar (for every leap is full of surprises), at least suggesting a trajectory. The leap of thinking, sustained by its

fundamental mood of awe and reticence and propelled by the fundamental
mood of a time in transition, which is a mood compounded of terror and
jubilation, aims to surmount the guiding question of metaphysics (τί τὸ ὄν,
What is the being?) in the direction of the fundamental question—the question
of the history, truth, or essential unfolding of being (or, as Heidegger now
writes it, almost as an affectation, of "beyng"). "The Essential Unfolding of
Seyn" is the farther rim of the abyss that the leap of thinking hopes to attain.[1]

Thinking thus leaps across a fissure in beyng, a yawning cleavage in the
earth, *die Zerklüftung* (§§127 and 156–59). This title appears at two different
moments of "The Leap," in the first quarter, in order to introduce a discussion
of "the nothing," then immediately before the shock of landing on the farther
side, the side on which "the grounding" is to commence. There it introduces a
discussion of "beyng unto death." Near the conclusion of its leap, which
stretches from "the nothing" to "beyng unto death," something uncanny
springs from the abyss to interrupt Heidegger's thinking.   *Daniel Paul
Schreber's* Denkwürdigkeiten eines Nervenkranken[3] *propels us in two direc-
tions at once: back to Johann Georg Hamann's 1759* Sokratische Denkwürdigkeiten *and forward to Heidegger's reflections on what is worthy of thought,*
denkwürdig. *The full title of Hamann's text would propel us forward in any
case to Heidegger's 1929–1930 lecture course, the first half of which, as we
have seen, depicts the fundamental mood of philosophizing as melancholy and
profound boredom. Hamann's title is:* Sokratische Denkwürdigkeiten für die
lange Weile des Publicums, zusammengetragen von einem Liebhaber der
langen Weile. *For the moment, in this context, the context of the leap and the
abyssal cleavage or fissure of beyng, it will be Schreber over Hamann, not by
any means in order to declare Heidegger's* Contributions to Philosophy *de-
mented, but in order to probe the limits of a thinking that undergoes what
Heidegger himself calls* Zwang *and* Verrückung, *"compulsion" and "rapturous
rupture." These violent swings in (fundamental) mood or attunement occur
not because of some personal tic in either Hamann or Heidegger, perhaps not
even in Schreber, but because of "the inception of an essential unfolding of
beyng," an unfolding that "compels us, provided we have become mature
enough for it, into a thinking* [was uns . . . in ein Denken zwingt]*" (65, 243; cf.
416, on* das Zwingende, *"the compelling").*

What is uncanny is the irruption of the two aphorisms on "life." Section
153 is called "Living," *Leben.* Section 154 is entitled " 'Life'," "*Das Leben.*"
No other aphorisms among the 281 of the whole share these titles—in a
meditation that consists almost entirely of repetitions.   *At each moment
of every hour Schreber can feel the miracle that is taking place in his body.*

Of course, "life" and living are mentioned elsewhere in the *Contributions,* although almost exclusively as something to be avoided and kept at a
distance. "Closeness to life" is the contemptible claim of a besotted and sentimental *Lebensphilosophie,* the wretched legacy of a bankrupt neo-Kantianism,
an inane *Weltanschauungsphilosophie,* and a flaccid *Existenzphilosophie,* the
last palsied offshoot of a moribund Platonism and Idealism, a mere shadow of

the regnant technophiliac positivism that is bedazzled by its own machinations and *Er-lebnissen,* both positivism and life-philosophy benumbed by their contrived "lived experiences."⁴

The sheer mass of Heidegger's spontaneous, compelling, repetitive polemics against *Erlebnis* and *Lebensphilosophie,* always passionate, often heavy-handed, at times even sardonic, suggests a kind of compulsion, *Zwang,* which is but the shadow side of the sensitive and even docile Heideggerian thinking of response, letting-be, releasement, and pious acceptance. Sarcasm and contumely are the obverse of an otherwise unresisting acquiescence that feels itself seized, transported, and delivered over to what is to be thought. We shall have to ponder this odd alternating current of piety and polemic in what I will call Heidegger's *paranoetic* thinking. Not *paranoid* thinking, inasmuch as here there is no being, no *Seiendes,* to be feared and hated. For Heidegger's "other" thinking, there can be no being—no thing or person—that is available for the mechanisms or strategems of fixation, repression by reversal, return of the repressed, and reconstruction ("I love him," "He loves me but I hate him," "He hates me and persecutes me," "Such is my wretched universe"). Not paranoid thinking, inasmuch as in Heidegger's case there is no being that can be sought out and blamed for the unspeakable catastrophe that is about to advene.   *Schreber senses that the end of the world is at hand, a Stoic* ἐκπύρωσις, *a* Weltuntergang: *the final 212 years of the 14,000-year cosmic cycle have run out. He is the only human being left.*   Not paranoid, to repeat, but *paranoetic,* a thinking that must surrender every noematic correlate, every noetic structure, every conceivable being, and all guiding questions concerning beings and their grounding. It is a thinking, no longer even of ontological difference, but of beyng, which has never shown its face, which has no face.

However, there are one or two moments in the earlier parts of the *Contributions* where living and "life" command thought in potentially more positive ways. First, in a discussion of truth in the "Preliminary View" (71), Heidegger refers to the "sheltering" or "salvaging" (*Bergung*) of "stone, plant, animal, and human being," of both the "inanimate and the animate," which are to be "taken back into the self-occluding earth." The earth, first introduced in the 1935–1936 lectures on the "Origin of the Work of Art," is introduced into "The Leap" immediately before and after discussion of "life" and the living. Earth is therefore introduced—soon we shall hear its voice—in proximity to "the nothing," "the cleavage of beyng," and "beyng unto death." Second, in the context of a detailed discussion of the history of being (or beyng) from Platonism through German Idealism (see aphorism no. 110), Heidegger relates Plato's "one," the ἕν, through κοινωνία, to the unifying thought of γένη, the "genus" and "species" of all classification of "*Gattungen*"; the unifying being beyond beings is thus the source of human felicity, εὐδαιμονία (two of the rare appearances of this word in Heidegger's thinking occur here, in aphorism no. 110; 65, 210–11); thus the Platonic ἀγαθόν, "the good," "the fitting," *das Taugliche,* is a "condition of 'life,' of the soul, and thereby of the essence of life and the soul as such"; the soul, in Platonism, yearns for the good and the beautiful, and such yearning is daimonic ἔρως. "Because the essence of beings is gathered in ψυχή, the ψυχή itself is the ἀρχή ζωῆς [that is, the dominant principle of life], and life is the fundamental figure [*Grundgestalt*] of beings" (210; cf. 214 and 221–22). In these pages of the *Contributions* Heidegger sketches a trajectory for the history of beyng that has more to do with reproduction than production; life than technicity; organism than the organon. His sketch identifies τὸ ὄν with ζωή, beings as a whole with life. Not until his lectures in the early 1940s on the early Greek thinkers, especially Heraclitus, will he return to this lightly limned yet never fleshed out sketch.

These two sets of remarks invite us to ask whether the principal plot of the history of beyng—the captation of truth in the ἰδέα and its subjugation under the yoke (ζυγόν) of correctness, the ancient model of production eventually leading to the hegemony of technology in the epoch of representation—does not neglect the equally fundamental figure of being(ness) as life and generation. For is not the Demiurge both craftsman and father? Does not the Demiurge go to meet, if only in fear and trembling, the mighty Ἀνάγκη? Is not τέχνη always and everywhere haunted and hounded by τίκτειν, production by reproduction?

The essential step toward the mission of redemption, according to Schreber, is that the savior undergo metamorphosis into a woman, die Verwandlung zum Weibe. *Freud suspects that the savior's passion, the entire mission of redemption, derives from his desire for such a metamorphosis. Schreber retorts that personally he would far rather retain the honorific status that his life as a male guarantees him than risk transfiguration. Yet he realizes that no thinker thinks by personal preference, but only in response to what is sent.*   It is important to remember that Heidegger has not simply forgotten τίκτειν. In "Building Dwelling Thinking" (VA, 160; BW, 337), he notes in the final pages, immediately before his introduction of the Schwarzwaldhof, that production or bringing-forth, *Hervorbringen,* is the Greek word τίκτειν. *Hervorbringen heißt griechisch* τίκτω, he says, peremptorily. He makes no further reference to the word, however, but going straight for its root, *tec,* he relates it to τέχνη, which now becomes *the* word for *Hervorbringen.* Technics, techtonics, architecture, and technology now slip into place, usurping the at least equally original throne of τίκτειν as though by divine right. In Heidegger's history of beyng there appears to be but one scion of *tec,* and it is not τίκτω, "I engender." Yet does not τίκτειν discreetly accompany the technical organon all the while? Are not the organon and all the ergics and energics of organism accompanied by the court jester of orgiastics, with craving (ὄρεξις) as its fundamental mood (ὀργή)?   *Schreber knows that every soothsayer must surrender the prophetic vision of* Κάλχας *for the blind insight of* Τειρεσίας.   Does German Idealism simply peter out into positivism and "philosophy of life"? Or does not Schelling, for example, think beyng as willing, willing as the will of love, love as languor and longing, and languishment as the divine body of woman?[5]   *Schreber stands before the mirror. Costume jewelry and ribbons bedeck his naked torso. Beneath the soft skin of the hollow between his breasts he can feel a woman's voluptuosity-nerves. He knows that these used to be the nerves of God.* Whatever the excesses a Ludwig Klages (Robert Musil's "Meingast") may have perpetrated in and against life-philosophy, is there not a *history of beyng as life* that has to be traced as meticulously as Heidegger has traced the history of beyng as the oblivion of revealing? Just as Heidegger concedes that *Being and Time* is less a refutation than a culmination of modern metaphysical subjectivity, must he not concede that life, " 'life' as the totality of the living and at the same time human 'life' " (65, 221), is the culminating point in the history of metaphysics? (It is number 27 in his 27-point analysis.) The fact that this culminating point is decried as degenerate *Er-lebnis* and *Lebensphilosophie* is an indication, not that life is without importance for the history of beyng, but that it remains to be positively entertained by a thinking at the "other commencement." Is not *Seynsverlassenheit,* that is, the abandonment of beings   *Like Newton, Schreber believes that after performing the work of creation God withdrew from the world, abandoning it, growing utterly remote*   by beyng, as much a "family novel" as a tale of technics and forgetfulness? Is not *Seynsvergessenheit,* that is, oblivion of beyng, at work in and as Heidegger's own history of being as production, representation, ontotypology, enframing, and nihilism? Has not Heidegger's own history of being, between the moments of commencement and end, between ζωή and *Erlebnis,* left virtually everything undiscussed? Is not the Heideggerian history of being trapped in the very frame it aims and claims to shatter? Would not such a shattering of the technicist frame have to eventuate through a history of and meditation on beyng as *contributions to life?* One is tempted to say of Heidegger what he says of Nietzsche in *Being and Time* (§76, 396), namely, that he knew more than he let on—except that what Heidegger knows can be thought only within unrelieved anxiety, only paranoetically.

The sudden upsurgence of living and of "life" three-quarters of the way through "The Leap" remains unnerving. Especially if we recall that in the meta-ontology of 1928 something like a "primal leap" (*Ursprung*) first initiates Dasein to embodiment and sexuality.[6] These brief and enigmatic invocations of life in the *Contributions* serve to mediate the discussion of the essential unfolding of beyng (which discussion they interrupt) and to introduce for a second time the fissure or cleavage (*die Zerklüftung*) of beyng.

The cleft of beyng releases beings but occludes itself. That the essential unfolding of beyng occurs as radical cleavage and sundering is perhaps the very essence of the leap—"*der Sprung* erspringt *die Zerklüftung des Seyns.*" Indeed, the more one thinks *Zerklüftung* the less certain one becomes of "the leap." For *der Sprung* is (also) the crack, rent, or fissure in beyng. One does not get over it, even and especially through a leap of thinking.   *At one time, according to Schreber, Flechsig's soul showed forty to sixty cleavages* (Abspalt-ungen), *as though all beyng were cloven.*   Just as Heidegger radicalizes *Kluft, Klüftung,* and *erklüftende* by means of the emphatic prefix *Zer-* (see 65, 103, 1. 6 f.b.; 231, 1. 10 f.b.), so we must think every *Erspringen* as a

Zerspringen, not as some brave leap of faith or thought but as the shattering, cracking, or cleaving of a *Riß* or rift. Is it an accident that throughout the *Contributions* we read again and again of ecstatic *Entrückung, Berückung,* and *Verrückung?*

One might well wish that the leap—if it is a leap—pursued clearly defined *steps* or *stages.* Yet the overdetermined gaping of the truth of beyng shows none. During the time of transition to the other beginning we have had to think that cleft or cleavage of beyng as the ontological difference. Such difference itself now dissolves into sundry differences and relationships *sans rapport,* among them: (1) the difference between *Sein* (as "beingness," *Seiendheit*) and *Seienden;* (2) the difference between *Sein* (as radiant appearance) and *Seyn* as the essential unfolding of the truth of, and history of words for, beyng, *die Wesung;* (3) the difference between *Sein* and *Da-sein* as the "instantaneous place" of the leap or fissure; (4) the difference within the clearing, as *die verbergende Lichtung,* between the self-obfuscation of beyng and the *showing* of such obfuscation, as well as between concealment (*Sichverbergen, Verborgenheit*) and sheltering, shepherding, or salvaging (*Bergung*); and finally, (5) difference as the striving of earth and world, the agon wherein the gods come to be, struggle, pass by, and pass away. And a sixth difference would possibly arise, with the traditional (Kantian) modalities of possibility, actuality, and necessity—thought in a non-traditional manner as accesses of death, excesses of mortality.

Indeed, if we were to fall into the abyss of the cleavage, we would confront, as we hurtled by, all the strata of the modalities, where the possible and the necessary affront one another (65, 75). We would descry while falling through the air something very much like death (283: *Der Zusammenstoß von Notwendigkeit und Möglichkeit;* see §§160–63 on being-toward-death). In the abyssal *Zerklüftung* modalities proliferate even beyond necessity and possibility, engendering what Heidegger calls singularity, rarity, instantaneity, contingency and seizure, reticence and freedom, preservation and necessity (118: *Einzigkeit, Seltenheit, Augenblicklichkeit, Zufall und Anfall, Verhaltenheit und Freiheit, Verwahrung und Notwendigkeit*); or, as another list has it, refusal and default, seizure and contingency, reticence and transfiguration, freedom and compulsion (280: *Verweigerung und Ausbleib, Anfall und Zufall, Verhalten-heit und Verklärung   Flechsig's rays have destroyed Schreber's stomach and intestines, lanced his lungs, split his esophagus, burst his bladder, fractured his ribs   Freiheit und Verzwingung   and yet Schreber submits utterly to the compulsion to think, accepts ceaseless Denkzwang, because every time he pauses, God (Flechsig) believes that he (Schreber) has lost his (Schreber's) mind. Somewhat after the manner of Descartes   ).* Further-more, the play of space and time in all decision occurs within the fissure or cleavage of beyng itself (103: *Das* Zeit-raum-hafte *der Entscheidung als aufbrechende Klüftung des Seyns selbst*). Indeed, *Zerklüftung* gapes in the turning of propriation as such (231: Im anderen Anfang *gilt es den Sprung in die erklüftende Mitte der Kehre des Ereignisses*). What looks like a leap *over* the gorge is instead a plunge *into* its abyssal fissure—*Zerklüftung* is the fission of propriation (235–39). Thus, finally and most mysteriously, *Zerklüftung* is the trembling of the godhead in conception and nativity (239: *die Erzitterung des Götterns*), the very unfolding, flexing, and parturing of the godhead. More than nativity: natality. Daimon natal, daimon fatal.   *Schreber senses that there are gaps or cleavages in the cosmic order, such that God's flexibility is threatened, his perfection flawed, his species endangered.*   The shudder of the godhead in agonistic struggle and decision (244: *das Entscheidungsreich für den Kampf der Götter . . . , in welchem Kampf die Götter erst göttern und ihren Gott zur Entscheidung stellen*) marks both the coming-to-be and the passing-by (as passing-away) of "the last god." In the verb *Göttern* we may hear the "gathering" of godhead in ἀγαθόν, in *gattern, Gattung*, and *begatten,* the untold tale of the history of beyng as ἔρως. Trembling at conception and birth, but also in refusal and flight, *"quivering in excessive refusal"* (244–45: *Götterung [Verweigerung] . . . als Übermaß der reinen Verweigerung*), the godhead eventually goes to meet a violent demise in the net-work of space and time:

> Das Er-eignis und seine Erfügung in der Abgründigkeit des Zeit-Raumes ist das Netz, in das der letzte Gott sich selbst hängt, um es zu zerreißen und in seiner Einzigkeit enden zu lassen, göttlich und seltsam und das Fremdeste in allem Seienden.
> Das plötzliche Verlöschen des großen Feuers . . . (65, 263)

> Propriation and the enjoining of propriation in the abyssal character of time-space is the net in which the last god hangs himself, rending the net, letting himself [itself?] come to an end in his [its?] singularity, godlike and rare and the strangest thing among all beings.
> Sudden smoldering of the conflagration . . .

The death of the shivering godhead marks the end of an era.   *I emerge as victor from the apparently unequal struggle of a single weak human being against God Himself, albeit after much bitter suffering and deprivation, because the order of the cosmos is on my side.*   Perhaps it is the end of the history of beyng as we (fail to) know it. The death of the last god, portrayed in the two brief concluding sections of the *Contributions,* is both the most terrifying and the most jubilant event of propriation, inasmuch as death is the supreme witness of beyng (230; 284). Thus, "the most frightful jubilation must be the dying of a god," and, reading the sentence as a speculative proposition, a speculative leap (*Satz*), "the dying of a god must be the most frightful jubilation" (230: *Der furchtbarste Jubel muß das Sterben eines Gottes sein*).

No, we shall not fall into such an abyss here and now unless we are compelled to do so; unless the daimonic fissure opens beneath our feet and head or below our leaping bodies. For if we did fall, then Heidegger's tepid paganism (Levinas, Jonas) would become the whiteheat of solar extravagance, and his theodicy a journey quite beyond compulsive polemics into a specular realm where the masters are few and most of them shut away. If we did fall, we would have to develop a full discussion of a possible *daimonic politics* of life (although not a theologico-political treatise), even if that discussion would have to be largely negative, largely apotropaic. We would have to ask why when "the futural ones" find their god they become a *Volk*, and whether if they should find their god shivering in natality and fatality they might become a gentler *Volk*. Further, we would have to ask why this particular people's last god gets caught up in questions of *Geschlecht*, a word and an issue of troubling complexity, as Derrida has taught us in his recent texts. One of the many passages in Heidegger's oeuvre that Derrida would have to add to his repertory is the following one on "the essence of the people [*Volk*] and Da-sein":

> The essence of the people is grounded in the historicity of those who belong to *themselves* on the *basis* of their belonging to the god. From the propriation in which such belonging is historically grounded there originates first of all the grounds as to why "life" and the body, sexual reproduction and *Geschlecht*, lineage and—to say it by way of a fundamental word—the earth, belong to history. . . . (65, 399)

There can be no doubt that the daimonic nexus of god and *Geschlecht*, life and the body, sex and reproduction is for Heidegger a *volkisch*, though not *völkisch*, node. That daimonic knot is as inextricable as it is hopelessly tangled in Heidegger's thought. No, let us not fall into such a fissure, not even for the sake of our gentler *Geschlecht*.

(DE)GRADATIONS OF BEYNG

Let us instead allow the daimon that is called variously "life" and "living" to interrupt the leap or fissure of thinking and beyng. It all begins innocently enough with a recollection and subtle mutation of the gradations, stages, or hierarchies that traditional metaphysical systems (from Plato's *Republic*, through Philo and Plotinus, to Christian theology and ontology) express in and as the great chain of being—*die Stufen des Seyns*. Heidegger refers to the relation in Leibniz's *Monadology* of the "central monad" (God) to the "sleeping monads" on the periphery.

In his 1928 logic course Heidegger had invoked the central monad and the preestablished harmony that pervades every monad, "each according the stage [*Stufe*] of its wakefulness" (26, 119). Such vigilance or alertness (*Wachsein*), which had fascinated Heidegger early on in his career, even during the early Freiburg period, and the impulse (*Drang*) of *vis primitiva*, imply that the monad, "as a force, is something living" (112: *etwas Lebendiges*). As a living pulsion, the atomic monad is ecstatic: it seems to explode, expending its energies to the point where inside and outside become indistinguishable, as though the monad were limitlessly vast and imperceptibly small at the same time, the incalculable *aleph* of all space. Leibniz's monadological, cosmotheological metaphysics returns in the 1928 lectures when Heidegger ponders transcendence, temporality, and the source of the world—in what he calls the *nihil originarium* (26, 271ff.). If one thinks of the dark side of those stages of wakefulness, one may recall what Leibniz calls "a prolonged state of unconsciousness [*étourdissement*]," or "the profound and dreamless sleep" into which a soul may "swoon," the soul being "stunned" or "dazed" by myriad *petites perceptions,* which cause it to suffer both vertigo and—at least in the case of animals—something approximating death.[7]

In the 1936–1938 *Contributions,* Heidegger's own question, set in spaced type or italics, is as follows: "*Are there, from the vantage-point of the question concerning the truth of being as propriation, gradations of this kind at all; are there even gradations of beyng?*" To be sure, such a hierarchy would no longer be a great chain of being(s), descending from the Supreme Being by analogy or emanation from angels through mortals to monstrous fish at the bottom of the muddy sea. It would be a hierarchy in the force of truth (*Wahrheitskraft*), a graded originality in the salvaging of beyng (*Bergungsursprünglichkeit*), or an order of rank in the essential unfolding of propriation itself (*Erwesung des Ereignisses*).[8] However, Heidegger will soon deny that, properly speaking, there can be such a hierarchy. In later essays, as we have seen, he will insist on the "unified field" of φύσις.[9] Yet the question remains as to how "the living, how 'nature' and nature's inanimate components, such as equipment, contrivance, work, deed, and sacrifice . . . are to be ordered [*zu ordnen sind*]" (65, 274). The very frontier between animate and inanimate nature, between astral and maternal Earth, seems to be as uncertain in this new universe of thought as it was in the old. Heidegger feels compelled to risk such an ordering of disclosive power, even though he rightly fears the family tree of all such (de)gradations and hierarchies:

> Nevertheless, does there not still remain a way, at least provisionally, of creating a spectrum within the projection of being [*einen Gesichtskreis des seinsmäßigen Entwurfs zu schaffen*], after the manner of "ontologies" of the various "realms" (nature, history), so that we can experience these realms afresh? Such a thing can become necessary as a *transition.* Yet it remains an embroglio, because it is easy to slip from such a spectrum into the systematics of an earlier style.

Heidegger will soon give us occasion to remember the dangers of the slippage to which philosophies of life—whether in Leibniz, Schelling, or Scheler—are prone. For the moment, he tries to think order as enjoining (*Fügung*) and as the striving of world and earth (*die Bestreitung des Streites von Welt und Erde*), in recollection of (what will become) "The Anaximander Fragment" and (what has by 1936–1938 become) "The Origin of the Work of Art."[10]

I shall forego all comment on the notion of *Fug* and *sich fügen* in "The Anaximander Fragment" in order to recall briefly the striving and the strife of world and earth in "The Origin of the Work of Art" (UK, 41–45). Perhaps that striving can best be recollected by means of a certain rift in the image of earth that Heidegger himself invokes; it is an architectural image of a work that does a great deal of work in Heidegger's text—the Greek temple. The Greek temple is supported by the earth, more specifically, by a cliff, and more specifically still, by a cloven earth, by cliff and cleft. The temple "simply stands there in the midst of the cloven vale of rock," *inmitten des zerklüfteten Felsentales.* If the temple stands there in relief as something inconcussible, something that resists all shattering (*Das Unerschütterte des Werkes steht ab*), the earth itself is the memory of all rendings and strivings, the monument, we might say, to what Heidegger in 1936–1938 calls *die Zerklüftung des Seyns.* In "The Origin of the Work of Art," Heidegger does not invoke such a terrestrial memory; he emphasizes the solidity and support of the earth. Yet the hewn stone of the temple columns itself recalls the cleavage of earth and the fissure of beyng. Out of that cleavage and fissure arise life and the living. Among the beings that the temple gathers into presencing are the god, the holy, birth and death, disaster and blessing, victory and disgrace, perdurance and decrepitude; also, Heidegger adduces, the raging storm, the grace of the sun, the light of day (a second invocation of birth, at least in the language of Homer), the expanse of the sky, the gloom of night, and the swelling sea. Then Heidegger says this: "Tree and grass, eagle and bull, snake and cricket first enter into their configured relief [*gehen erst in ihre abgehobene Gestalt ein*] and thus come to the fore as they are" (UK, 42). Such advent and upsurgence into the zoographics of bas-relief in a temple frieze, he concludes, are what the Greeks long ago called φύσις.

I shall interrupt Heidegger's meditation on the work of art here by posing a question. With the upsurgence of *the living* into the clearing, can it be merely a matter of yet another configuration and low relief? Do the living beings that come to the fore in beyng constitute a *tableau mort?* Or must not φύσις, onto which the cloven earth too opens, embrace the coming-to-presence of (but "of" now as *genitivus subiectivus,* that is to say, now as the multiple and varied presencings of *and to*) what are called cricket and snake, bull and eagle, stallion of the mountain, and, yes, even the rooted tree and the leaves of grass? Could these living things be disclosed and assume their proper shapes if they themselves were deprived of all disclosure, if they themselves assumed the figure of cadavers? Or is not the question of an order and rank in disclosive power, of gradations in beyng, however dangerous it may be, absolutely essential to a meditation on φύσις? Is there not something like a variegated *flesh* of disclosure?[11]—But let me truncate the interruption and return now to the *Contributions.*

For the moment, Heidegger does not seem to be worried about a distinction that slips into his own thinking directly from the pages of the *Monadology* (§49), to wit, that of activity and passivity: earth is proclaimed "in one respect *more original* than nature," because it is "related to history." The passive voice of *geschichtsbezogen* conceals the essential *activity* of human history, which raises earth above the sheer impassivity of what Leibniz and Hegel hold to be "swooning" nature.   *Schreber believes that the hyperactive Flechsig will never withdraw from him, will never abandon him again, so that like Kierkegaard he is condemned forever to adopt a feminine position before Him. Freud believes that if he does not analyze Schreber's* Denkwürdigkeiten *he will be in the ridiculous position of the man Kant portrays in his* Critique of Pure Reason, *who bends to hold the sieve while his mate milks the billygoat.*

Further, *world* is proclaimed "higher" than both nature and earth, inasmuch as world is *"formative of history* [geschichtsbildend] and thus closest to propriation" (65, 275). Recall that in the remarks on theoretical biology in 1929– 1930 Heidegger had distinguished between the passivity of brute *Benommenheit* and the activity of a *weltbildenden* humankind. He neglected at that time to indicate that in *Being and Time* he had used the word *benommen* to designate both a passive Dasein enamored of the world and a vigilant Dasein stunned by its radical individuation in anxiety. A dazed Dasein, while not yet resolutely open, not yet fully present to its own mortality, poises on the verge of anxiety proper.[12] By 1929–1930, Dasein has found its feet. It adopts a braver stance toward beings. It holds and keeps itself (*verhält sich*) in the openness of being, while the animal ostensibly remains ensnared in the closed ring of what both Leibniz and Scheler, according to Heidegger, call "disinhibitions" (26, 103, ll. 10–14: *Enthemmungen*). At least until something like death shatters that ring. In 1936–1938 Heidegger is worried about the technologized animal called man, who can neither shape a world nor find his big toe nor be stunned by his own mortality: "Is technology the historical path toward *the end, to the regression of the last man to the technologized animal, the animal that loses even the original animality of the integral animal* [die ursprüngliche Tierheit des eingefügten Tieres]; *or can it, if taken ahead of time as salvaging* [Bergung], *be integrated* [eingefügt werden] *into the grounding of Da-sein?"* (65, 275; cf. 98). If the animal called *man* cannot be so enjoined, it is destined to be, not the "as yet undetermined animal" of Nietzsche's reflections, not *das noch nicht festgestellte Tier*, but the already distorted animality of the rational animal. Early in the *Contributions* (28) Heidegger asks whether "the beginning of the last man drives humanity into distorted animality [*verstellte Tierheit*] and denies historical humanity its last god." Heidegger's hope is that the essence of technology can be enjoined to the world of man as the animal is enjoined in its world—the world that it has in not having it (in 1929–1930), and which, as we shall see, it may not have at all (in 1936–1938 and throughout the 1950s).

THE OTHER REVERBERATION OF DA-SEIN

Aphorism 153, *Leben*, without quotation marks, rejects the reduction of life to organism, of organism to the realm of the corporeal (*das Leibliche*), of the corporeal to mass (*der Körper*), and of mass to Galilean-Newtonian mechanics. That rejection appears to be a constant in Heidegger's thought, whether in 1927, 1929–1930, 1936–1938, or the 1940s and 50s. What now occupies him is the question of a fundamental relation to the living (*Grundverhältnis zum Lebendigen*). What are plants and animals, once we cease using them to decorate and entertain the lives of the regressive, technologized animals? Heidegger's first reply to the question is as unforeseen as everything must be on a leap that is a fissuring of the very gap to be leapt. He wonders whether once we have stepped back from machination, in which everything is laborious (*das Mühsame*), we will finally be able to descry the effortlessness (*das Mühelose*) of the living. That reply is surprising because in 1930 he quoted both Paul and the apocryphal Book of Esra in order to suggest that the ways of life, reflected in the longing gaze of all creation's creatures, are laborious (29/30, 396: *mühselig*). That is one of the rare moments in Heidegger's theoretical biology when the fundamental mood of philosophizing (discussed throughout the first half of the 1929–1930 course) spreads its veil of melancholy over the whole; it is one of the rare moments when it seems at least possible to integrate the difficult problem and invaluable touchstone of *death* into the discussion of life (29/30, 270–71, 387, 396). Now, in 1936–1938, as all the world, even beyond Europe, dims, life appears to be "effortless."   *As long as he remains a male, Schreber is not subject to the travail of mortality. Only after he has mothered a new breed of humanity, a new* Geschlecht, *will he die a natural death and be assumed, bodies and soul, into heaven.*   However, the fundamental relation of Dasein to the living is anything but effortless: echoes of a problem unresolved in *Being and Time*, to wit, the way in which the living is to become "the other reverberation of Da-sein" (*65, 276: zum anderen Widerklang des Da-seins*). "Life" runs and hides from ontology as well as from biology, precisely in the way that beyng withdraws from the thinker (293). Onward, then, to reticent, reverberant "life," in quotation-marks:

154. "Das Leben"

a "mode" of the beingness (beyng) of beings. The incipient opening of beings to it [*beginnliche Eröffnung des Seienden auf es zu*] in the safe-keeping of the self. The first darkening [*Erdunkelung*] in the safe-keeping of the self is grounded in the benumbment of the living, in which all stimulation and excitation run their course, along with the sundry stages of the dark and its unfolding.

"Life" is the strife of opening and closing, of a brightening and darkening, as Schelling long ago affirmed. "Life" is some sort of opening to beings: the words *auf es zu* suggest the ecstatic futurity of Dasein, which runs ahead by letting what-is-to-come approach it and confront its ecstatic "self." "Life," at some stage (for the gradients or stages of being will *have to be* preserved for beyng in order to fend off the dark, no matter how grave the danger that we may slip into the miasmas of past systems), safeguards and keeps the self.

Schreber is willing and able to wait centuries. At some point, finally unmanned, he will bear divine fruit. Freud says his wish-fulfillment is asymptotic.   "Life" at some stage (but at which stage? can there be stages of openness in the unified realm of essence?) safeguards and secures the ecstatic self that is outside itself, the "self" that perdures in section 64 of *Being and Time*, having withstood as though by magic the "destruction" of all personhood, subjectivity, humanism, psychic interiority, and spiritualism, as well as the dismantling of the meaning of being as perdurant presence (*beständige Anwesenheit*). The "self" survives (in) the *Contributions* as well, survives more efficaciously than "life."

After the very first sentence on "life" in the *Contributions*, "life" as incipient opening, the perspective is suddenly reversed: as quickly as one might slip into a gap or gully, Heidegger writes of a first darkening (*Erdunkelung*). Barely opened, not yet wholly safeguarded, the neophyte self now regresses to the benumbment of the (merely) living. Barely in the ascendant, "life" regresses. It succumbs to stimulation and excitation, which, as Freud showed in the 1895 "Project" and throughout his metapsychological writings, are always incitements to death.   *Schreber's overexcited nerves jangle so wildly that even divinity is distracted; Flechsig deviates, descends, invades Apollo-like from behind; Schreber sometimes wishes that the cosmic order had left excitability to the animal stage of being.*   The sundry steps or stages of the living proceed *downward,* as steps of a ladder descending into the great dark. Yet from what Archimedian point, from what point or aperture, do they proceed downward? From the *summum ens?* From the *animal rationale?* From *homo techno-habilis?* Can these beings be distinguished by a technologized animal that is no longer enjoined even to its own brutishness? And which slippage constitutes the graver danger to life—slipping into the abyss of essence that ostensibly separates Dasein from the animal, or slipping into the as yet unthought of metaphysics, slipping into systems that made distinction after distinction—inside from outside, activity from passivity,   *Freud finds Schreber's* Denkwürdigkeiten *to be full of hair-splitting distinctions, as in all theodicies*   speech from writing, presence from absence—in order to rescue human beings from life? Would not the desire to separate animality from Dasein be the metaphysical desire to preserve intact the full presence of an "inside" from the death that invades from the "outside"? No matter how minute such an "inside" may become, or how monstrously vast an "outside"? As Thomas Mann's Hans Castorp reflects, on the *Magic Mountain:*

> The "minuteness" of the innercosmic stellar bodies would be an altogether invalid objection, for the standard that measured large and small had slipped through our fingers by the time the cosmic nature of the "smallest" particles of matter revealed itself. Likewise, the concepts of outside and inside had suffered a blow to their stability. The world of the atom was an outside, just as the planet Earth on which we dwelled was in all probability, from an organic point of view, a profound inside. (*Der Zauberberg*, 301)

Let us continue our descent into *154. "Das Leben":*

> *Darkening* and the essence of *instinct.* The *safe-keeping* of the self and the *preeminence of the "species,"* which does not recognize any "individual" as selflike.

Here we have an unmistakable reminiscence of "life" in the Hegelian system, in which the respective *Gattung* (genus or species) is preeminent over each *Einzelnes,* the latter containing within its "self" both the seed of death and the universal impotence of all merely "natural" species. From the ashes of such life, Phoenix-like, spirit as such must rise.[13] The safeguarding and securing of the self as individuality cannot occur in animal life, Hegel teaches, and Heidegger presumably concurs.

However, does Heidegger simply accept the Hegelian preeminence of

Gattung, or is there here a faint intimation, perhaps the faintest living *Widerklang,* of the untold history of beyng as ζωή, ἀγαθόν, and ἔρως, the erotic gathering of life? Does Heidegger simply repeat the identification of instinct and occlusion, the life of drives as fundamental passivity, as *weg! sein,* that is to say, a form of being that is always already bygone? Or does he affirm precisely in Da-sein a *being away,* an ecstatic *Weg-sein,* as the very opening of a disclosure that is invariably in the vicinity of death, *Seyn zum Tode?*[14] Is what seems effortlessly alive, precisely in its vulnerability and transiency, precisely in its being-away-toward-death, the site of disclosure? Is such eminently exposed disclosure a shared εὐδαιμονία, the very blessedness of "life"?   *Schreber believes that he is called upon to redeem the world, to restore its vanished happiness, felicity, or blessedness, Seligkeit. He would affirm what another has written of such daimonic felicity: "Blessed are they who dare to belong to the unblessedness of [the] cleavage" (65, 416), that is to say, to the cleaving of beyng.*

Let us therefore fall farther:

> Darkening [*Erdunkelung*] and *worldlessness.* (Earlier as *world poverty!* Misleading. The stone not even worldless, because it is altogether without darkening.)

Here Heidegger revises—tentatively, telegraphically—his earlier theses (from the 1929–1930 biology lectures) that the stone is worldless and the animal poor in world. Both realms of being, both animate and inanimate nature, are dropped down a peg, as it were, in the order of disclosure. Dropped down a peg, reduced in rank—in spite of the fact that the darkening of the earth in death (what *is* this *Erdunkelung?*) is what grants all "life" its aperture on beings. It now appears to be the case that the stone is less than worldless (although what could be less than least, lower than last?), and that the animal is no longer merely destitute, no longer having-in-not-having, but absolutely stonily deprived of world. Perhaps in this absolute deprivation the animal finds its lapidary ease? Perhaps Heidegger has here signed a temporary truce with Rilke—before the final outbreak of hostilities in 1943?[15] At all events, we are now approaching the end of the aphorism, the very bottom of the *Zerklüftung* of "life":

> Petrifaction and regression of life from the incipient opening. Accordingly, no occlusion either [*Demgemäß auch keine Verschließung*], as long as the living is not in accompaniment—"earth" (stone, plant, animal). Stone and stream not without plant, animal. How does the decision to "life" stand and fall? Meditation on "the biological."

Does a second reversal stir here, perhaps in favor of "life"? "Life" on the upswing? In recognition of the happenstance that closure and disclosure are (of) life? That the *darkening* of life in death is the lighting of both revelatory world and occluding earth? That upsurgent φύσις is plenipotence (190: "... φύσις is so overpowering")? It is difficult to say. The aphorism ends, clipped and cryptic, yet also gaping. Identifying "earth" (*die Erde*) as the site of the "darkening" (*die Erdunkelung*) of stone, plant, and animal. Calling for a meditation on "the biological," which the *Contributions* has rejected all along in the most sardonic terms.[16]

THE CROAKING OF THE EARTH

"Life," scarcely begun, falls back, turns to stone, is paralyzed, ossified, petrified. Yet in that very regression and occlusion a kind of reversal seems to occur. Heidegger concedes that there can be no closure, *keine Verschließung,* unless "life" accompanies, *mitzugenommen wird.* "Life" is essential to the *earth* that the thinking of beyng and propriation tries to think. Earth, as the self-occlusion that juts forth and shows itself, is the supportive site of stone, but also of *plant* and *animal,* that is to say, of particular kinds of *showing.* Hölderlin's stone, not without stream, and stream not without lizard, lichen, and fish. As though every being and all beyng were precisely as an earlier system of metaphysics and an earlier regional ontology of nature portrayed them. Leibniz, *Monadology,* §§66–69:

66. Whence we see that there is a world of creatures, of living beings, of animals, of entelechies, of souls, in the smallest particle of matter.
67. Each portion of matter may be conceived of as a garden full of plants, and like a pond full of fishes. Yet each branch of the plant, each member of the animal, each drop of its humors is also such a garden or pond.
68. And although the earth and air which lie between the plants of the garden, or the water between the fish of the pond, is neither plant nor fish, they yet contain more of them, but for the most part so subtilized as to be imperceptible to us.
69. Therefore there is nothing fallow, nothing sterile, nothing dead in the universe, no Chaos, no confusions, except in appearance; somewhat as a pond would appear from a distance, in which we might see the confused movement and swarming, so to speak, of the fishes in the pond, without discerning the fish themselves.[17]

All of which leads Leibniz to say that "all bodies are, like rivers, in perpetual flux, and parts are entering into them and departing from them continually" (§71), so that "there is strictly speaking neither absolute birth nor complete death . . ." (§72). "What we call *birth,*" concludes the thinker of the regressive stages or the infinitesimal links in the great chain of being, "is development or growth, as what we call *death* is envelopment and diminution" (§73). Life fatal, life natal, in a universe where large and small, dark and bright, wave and particle, organic and anorganic, self and other are most often difficult to distinguish. Hans Castorp, for his final moonlight appearance:

Had not one bold and visionary researcher spoken of "Milky Way Animals," cosmic monsters whose flesh, bone, and brain were constructed of solar systems? Yet if that were so, concluded Hans Castorp, then the moment you thought you'd come to the edge, the whole thing would start all over again! Perhaps young Hans Castorp was hiding once again in the innermost recesses of his own self, a hundred times over, huddled warmly on his balcony with a view of mountain crags in the moonlight of a frosty night, where, frozen of finger and flushed of face, enthralled with the humanistic science of medicine, he studied the life of bodies? (301)

Heidegger's *Contributions to Philosophy* does not take up the "end" of Dasein as birth, alluded to so cryptically in section 72 of *Being and Time*. However, precisely now, precisely when Heidegger returns to the cleavage or fissure of beyng, he does take up the end of death, presumably not as envelopment and diminution, but as "the supreme and uttermost testimony of beyng" (65, 230 and 284). Such testimony the gods too must render. Their dying is joined to beyng-toward-death as such by "the shortest route" (282, 414: *die kürzeste Bahn*). Daimonic testimony therefore only confirms the experience of mortals, rendering evidence not of nihilism but of affirmation (284: *Bejahbarkeit*) and creative yes-saying (246 and 266–67: *das wesentliche, "schaffende" Jasagen*). If the human being's bodily kinship with the beast is, as the "Letter on Humanism" says, abyssal and abysmal, *ab-gründig*, it is because Da-sein is the *ab-gründige Grund* (65, 286), the abyss that envelops (?!) both of the stages of beyng that we call *the human* and *the animal*, though not to forget *the vegetable*, stages that are not stages at all but infinite differencings of infinitesimal (?!) life. Or of "life." "Life" being the kind of disclosure that Max Scheler once saw and felt as he watched a speed-up film about plants. On March 3, 1926, during the period of his final cosmological and anth(rop)ological musings, he wrote the following to Märit Furtwängler:

> I saw a film on plant life, a film in which twenty-four hours of life were compressed to a few seconds. It was wonderful! You could see the plants breathing, burgeoning, and dying. The natural impression we all have—that plants possess no soul—vanished altogether. You could see the entire drama of life, all its unheard-of exertions. The most beautiful thing was to see the creepers that were planted near little four-runged trellises. Their turbulent "search" for a hold, the "satisfaction" when they found the rungs of the trellis, their frustrated attempts (often one tendril tried to find a hold in the tendrils of another plant, which was in as precarious a position as the first, so that they both collapsed), and, above all, the following phenomenon: when they reached the fourth rung they would cast about in "desperation," searching and searching, until (incredibly!) after repeated failures they would return to the fourth rung. It shattered me so [*erschütterte mich so*], that it was all I could do to hold back tears. Oh, life is everywhere of the same sweetness, everywhere enchanting, everywhere painful. . . . And all of it, all of life, is one.[18]

In the end, of course, life does have as much to do with birth as with death, with flourishing as with decay. In his discussion of "the cleavage and the 'modalities' " (65, 281), Heidegger discusses possibility and necessity as the two "horns" of actuality or ἐνέργεια. He pauses in order to sketch in a few lines "the kernal of Aristotle's 'ontology.' " If actuality is thought on the basis of a dynamic yet undeveloped φύσις, then it is conceived in the light of change, turnabout, or overturning, μεταβολή. In other words, it is thought ecstatically. Such ecstatic metabolism seems to be the counterpart or the foil to what we take to be the prototypical Aristotelian conception of being, namely, constancy and presence, especially when μεταβολή takes the form of φορά. Φορά means gestation, carrying, and bearing; it means a being borne or swept along in rapid motion, as a planet is swept along in its orbit; it means a rush, pulse, pulsion, or impulse. Aristotelian being as οὐσία, permanence of presence, would thus be in tension with metabolic life, and a frenetic and restive life could only cleave (to) such being.

Must not such a tension—between permanence of presence and the ephemeral modalities of metabolism—be thought paranoetically? Heidegger's thought, I repeat, is not paranoid. Its situation is more dire than that. For as we have seen, there is no being that has conspired to engineer beyng's abandonment of beings, no being to be excoriated in projections of insane hatred. Not even an oblivious humanity can be blamed, so that the vituperative polemic is all in vain and must succumb to the piety that it energizes. Paranoetic thinking finds no paranoematic correlate on which to pin its hopes or project its phobias. If the last god seems available for sacrifice, it is only in passing by, *Vorbeigang,* a passing by that is a passing away, a passing away into the absolute past of everything that is *Vorbei!* The last god signals in withdrawal, forever out of reach, and tantalizes thought.   *During the lengthy process of his purification, Schreber learns a new language: his speech no longer projects Jehovah-rays and Zoroaster-beams, but sparkles with the idiom spoken by God Himself. Schreber speaks* die Grundsprache, *which, according to Freud, is* "a somewhat archaic yet quite forceful German, particularly remarkable for the wealth of euphemisms it contains."   The fundamental attunement of the language of paranoetic thinking, responding to the god's ultimate withdrawal, is the cacaphony of scurrilous sarcasm interspersed with piety; such an attunement inevitably produces a grating sound, the *Mißton,* as Heidegger calls it in one of his essays on Nietzsche, of quietism interrupted by a compulsive polemical screech, or a snarl suddenly relaxing into pious prattle. Occasionally the *Contributions* succeeds in integrating the two linguistic modes, the result being a hilarious parody of Zarathustra's parody of the Biblical idiom: "For the last god despiseth these above all [. . . *denn all dieses hasset der letzte Gott zuerst*]" (406).

What Heidegger *wishes* to think, and what he *must* think, is an οὐσία that would no longer be counterposed to μεταβολή and φορά. The forgotten beyng, the beyng that has abandoned beings such as ourselves like a gigolo abandoning his bastards along with their mother, is the object of his dreams and the demon of his nightmares in the apocalypse of "the other commencement." Such metabolic beyng, as disclosure, would not be without life; the very story of revealing and concealing, the story of the truth of beyng, would be a life-story. The story of propriation, *Ereignis,* would be a tale of the granting of time and being to those beings—whether gods or mortals or the mortal godhead or daimon—who can be cultivated and used, if only for a finite time.

God suffered from the fact that in accord with the very order of things He enjoyed social intercourse only with cadavers. It was never granted Him to know a living human being. No wonder He was so awkward with Schreber.

"Daimon life" would name that region of beings for which revealing and concealing, growth and decline, lightening and darkening, animatedness and shattering would come to the fore and into question. And, beyond questioning, into anxious heed and patient response.

Amid the overwrought, distraught polemics, amid the outcries against the publicists, pundits, and Babbits of modern life-philosophy, against the nihilists and know-it-alls of positivism, Bolshevism, biologism, and racism, of pragmatism, value-philosophy, and Weltanschauungen; not altogether muffled by the prattle of piety, by the sentimentalities of nationalism, quietism, and pietism; Heidegger hears the raucous sound of the jubilant dying god, the expiring god suddenly passing, the last god croaking like a real toad in imaginary Leibnizian gardens. For if the word *Erdunkelung* is cloven otherwise, cloven as *Erd-unkelung*, then it is not (only) darkening but (also) the throaty song of the Earth. *Erdunkelung* is (also) *Erd-unkelung,* which is to say, *das Unken der Erde*. Because *die Unke* is a toad; figuratively, a croaker, a Jeremiah. Though not, as the dictionaries say, a grouse.

PART THREE

Vital Signs

Beside the sea she lives, the woman of the vine, the maker of wine; Siduri sits in the Garden at the edge of the sea. . . . She is covered with a veil; and where she sits she sees Gilgamesh coming towards her, wearing skins, the flesh of gods in his body but despair in his heart, and his face like the face of one who has made a long journey. . . . "Gilgamesh, where are you hurrying to? You will never find that life for which you are looking. When the gods created man they allotted him death, but life they retained in their own keeping. As for you, Gilgamesh, fill your belly with good things; day and night, night and day, dance and be merry, feast and rejoice. Let your clothes be fresh, bathe yourself in water, cherish the little child that holds your hand, and make your wife happy in your embrace; for this too is the lot of man."

But Gilgamesh said to Siduri, the young woman, "How can I be silent, how can I rest, when Enkidu whom I love is dust, and I too shall die and be laid in the earth for ever."

.

From the bottom of the sea Gilgamesh recovered a plant which when eaten restored youth. He did not eat of it, however, but set out on his homeward journey. *Gilgamesh saw a well of cool water and he went down and bathed; but deep in the pool there lay a serpent, and the serpent sensed the sweetness of the flower. It rose out of the water and snatched it away, and immediately it sloughed its skin and returned to the well. Then Gilgamesh sat down and wept. . . . "Was it for this that I toiled with my hands, is it for this I have wrung out my heart's*

*blood? For myself I have gained nothing; not
I, but the beast of the earth has joy of it
now. Already the stream has carried it twenty
leagues back to the channels where I found
it. I found a sign and now I have lost it. . . .*

•

*He was wise, he saw mysteries and knew se-
cret things, he brought us a tale of the days
before the flood. He went on a long journey,
was weary, worn out with labor, and returning he engraved on a stone the whole story.*

•

*The king has laid himself down and will not rise again,
The Lord of Kullab will not rise again;
He overcame evil, he will not come again;
Though he was strong of arm he will not rise again;
He had wisdom and a comely face, he will not come again;
He is gone into the mountain, he will not come again;
On the bed of fate he lies, he will not rise again,
From the couch of many colors he will not come again.*

•

*The people of the city, great and small, are
not silent; they lift up the lament, all men of
flesh and blood lift up the lament. Fate has
spoken; like a hooked fish he lies stretched
on the bed, like a gazelle that is caught in the
noose.*

•

*Gilgamesh, the son of Ninsun, lies in the
tomb.*

SEVEN

Lifedeath

Heidegger, Nietzsche, Freud

Earlier we noted how disconcerting it was for life-philosophers such as Georg Simmel who became convinced that death could no longer be regarded as standing apart from life as its opposite. Studies by biologists on the life-duration of individual members of the various genuses and species suggested that the causes of dissolution and death were immanent in life; if not the τέλος of life's unfolding, death was certainly not a merely contingent truncation of a vital development that was in principle endless. Neurophysiological research on nerve tissue and germ plasm and psychoanalytic speculations on the types of drives and pulsions at work in living creatures expanded on these medical and biological studies, which, as we have seen, had already (especially through Eugen Korschelt) had their impact on Heidegger's existential ontology. If Dasein was reborn at each instant of its ecstatic existence, and if it was dying in each such instant as well, then the immanence and imminence of its death had to alter whatever sense its factical "life" might possess.

Nevertheless, Heidegger's fundamental ontology leaves the question of immanent and imminent death untouched insofar as it suppresses or at least subordinates "ontology of life." If existential ontology always needs the question of being (*die Frage nach dem Sein*) to have been "clarified beforehand" (SZ, 13, 333, 436), it also always needs "life" to have been clarified in precisely the same way. As though *being* and *life* were inseparably joined—perhaps one and the same. For Nietzsche, as we heard, they were: " 'Being'—we have no other way of representing this than as *'living.'*—How can anything dead 'be'?" (WM, 582). Heidegger, however, who explicitly acknowledges the circularity of ontology of Dasein and the question of *being*, holds the circles of the *living* at a distance, no matter how persistently and incorrigibly Dasein dies.

For both Nietzsche and Freud, as we know, death is immanent in life. Life "itself" and death "itself" can be written only as *lifedeath*. In the present chapter we shall turn to Heidegger's lectures on Nietzsche from 1936 to 1940, in which the issues of life and death arise, albeit without a full acknowledgement of lifedeath on Heidegger's part. As we shall see, Heidegger is more concerned to keep "biologism" and "animality" remote from what he calls *thinking* than to push the question of lifedeath. Biological science he would have nearby, to be sure, but safely in tow. Finally, it goes without saying that thinking will abjure psychoanalysis, the final outpouring of rampant subjectivism, sentimental "lived-experience," and a wrongheaded insistence on therapy. Heidegger never goes to encounter Freud's thinking of lifedeath, not even at Zollikon.[1]

Nietzsche's thought of lifedeath—of becoming and of life bodying forth from chaos and ash—arises from a thinking that according to Heidegger is not biological but eminently metaphysical. One first sees Nietzsche's thought taking recognizable shape in the notebook in which Nietzsche jotted down his thoughts from the spring to the fall of 1881, the gestation period of *The Gay Science*. The notebook bears the Mette-catalogue number M III 1. It is one of the most valued pieces of the *Nachlaß*, because it contains some of the earliest formulations of Nietzsche's "thought of thoughts," namely, the eternal recurrence of the same. Heidegger knows of the notebook and often turns to it in his account of eternal return and Nietzschean chaos. He would certainly not object if we occasionally allowed fragments from notebook M III 1 to intrude upon our account of his Nietzsche lectures. In the final portions of the chapter, when we turn to Freud's *Beyond the Pleasure Principle*, the intrusions will come from elsewhere.

THE NEW INTERPRETATION OF SENSUOUSNESS

It would not be difficult to show that in virtually all of Heidegger's lectures and essays on Nietzsche the issues of life and life-philosophy are very much at the center. Nietzsche's account of nihilism as the devaluation of the highest values hitherto leaves no doubt that the initial instauration of those values arises from a *degeneration* of life. If art is the essential countermovement to nihilism, that is because artistic creativity is an effulgence of *regenerative* life. Each of the "five main rubrics" of Heidegger's 1940 course on "European Nihilism" (nihilism, revaluation of all values hitherto, will to power, eternal recurrence of the same, and overman) devolves upon Nietzsche's understanding of being as *becoming*, becoming as *chaos*, and chaos as sensuous, sensate *life* (NII, 38–40/4, 8–9).

At the end of the very first course on Nietzsche, "The Will to Power as Art," Heidegger writes a kind of promissory note: he pledges to develop Nietzsche's "new interpretation of sensuousness." For Heidegger does not simply accuse Nietzsche of merely inverting the Platonic hierarchy that elevated the supersensuous above the realm of the sensuous. As Heidegger brings his course to a close he stresses that the sensuous realm cannot be regarded as a merely "rehabilitated" realm, a kingdom to which at long last sovereignty has been restored. If indeed the "true world" has finally become a "fable," the sensuous world does not suddenly become the fabulous substitute for a defunct Platonism. In particular, the customary way we divide the sensuous world into inanimate and animate sectors no longer serves. In the final moments of the course (NI 244–45/1, 212–13) Heidegger acknowledges that for Nietzsche's "perspectivism" the very distinction between organic and inorganic falls away: the inorganic too has its own perspective, and all becoming   *Let us be on guard!*   must be acknowledged as perspectival. Heidegger explains as follows: "The mechanistic representation of 'inanimate' nature is only a hypothesis for purposes of calculation; it overlooks the fact that here too relations of forces and concatenations of perspectives hold sway." Thus for Nietzsche there is no inorganic world; whatever is in any way "real" is alive, that is, "perspectival."

Not surprisingly, Heidegger relates Nietzsche's new interpretation of comprehensive sensuousness to Leibnizian monadology, except of course that now truth and semblance fall on the same side of an impossible distinction, so that the very difference between truth and error collapses along with the distinction between the living and nonliving. If a residual distinction between the inanimate and animate realms persists, it is only in order to stress the equation of truth with error: "*Truth is the kind of error* without which a certain kind of living being could not live. The value for *life* ultimately decides" (WM, 493). The new interpretation of sensuousness would take as its starting-point *Simplification is the chief need of the organic . . .* "*Error" is the means to the* happy accident!   a "more profound meditation," one which would acknowledge that all semblance, error, and (mere) appearance are possible "only if something comes to the fore and shows itself at all" (NI, 247/1, 215). Heidegger's thought of the unified realm of φύσις, as upsurgence into radiant shining and withdrawal into concealment and mystery, promises to be the new interpretation of sensuousness. It will have to respond to what Nietzsche calls the raging discordance between truth and art. That is to say, Heidegger will have to resolve the discordance between truth and art without collapsing into a supine Platonism, without that "hidden maneuver" by which Platonism paints the discordance as a felicitous one (230–31/1, 198–99; cf. 65, 182; 218–19). Further, Heidegger will have to resolve the discordance between truth and art while still affirming the privilege of art in the question of truth as revealing and concealing.

His formulation of the Nietzschean discordance is powerful, and is by no means to be rejected out of hand: "*Art, as transfiguration, is more enhancing to life than truth, as fixation of an apparition*" (250/217). Yet that formulation will have to submit to all sorts of doubts and questions. Is art something other than fixation? Whose art? Is art the province of humankind alone, is it a mere technique of man the technician? Do other forms of life merely fixate on apparitions; or, if the essence of life demands enhancement and transfiguration as well as preservation, do other forms of life participate in what "we" call "art"? Is the very meaning of art to undergo radical transformation?   *As opposed to the art of artworks, I want to teach a superior art: that of the invention of feasts.*   Finally, if life-enhancing art undergoes essential redefinition, will not the sense of revealing and concealing, world and earth, rift and clearing have to shed their anthropomorphic and theomorphic skins?   *Deus nudus* est.   Will not the traditional appeal to language, the λόγος possessed by only one type of ζῷον (= ἄνθρωπος) or perhaps, at most, by one additional type as well (= θεός), have to subside. Would not a new interpretation of sensuousness place demands on Heidegger's thinking of art, poetry, and language to which his thought is unequal?   *Let us be on guard!*   Which is not to say that any other thinking is equal to those demands. . . . Heidegger will doubtless continue to privilege art as the setting-to-work of truth, but only insofar as he can think truth as radiant shining rather than as fixating *adaequatio*. However, because the discordance between enhancement and fixation occurs in Nietzsche's view on and as the scene of *life*, Heidegger cannot suppress forever the questions of (1) ontology of life, (2) the unified field of φύσις as upsurgence of *life* into revealing, and withdrawal of *life* into concealing, and (3) the particular form of *excess* that is at the root of ζωή, to wit, ζα-. Which would call for za-ology, that is, for a *living in excess* of language and a *living in*   Paracelsi mirabilia. *Recounted by F.N.*   *the excesses* of living language.

In the final hour of the 1936 course Heidegger adopts a phrase from Nietzsche's preface to the 1886 edition of *The Birth of Tragedy*, the preface entitled "Attempt at a Self-Criticism." Whatever the criticism, Nietzsche proclaims that he is able to affirm the task of his "audacious book," which he now defines as follows: "*. . . to see science under the optics of the artist, but art under the optics of life*" (KSA 1, 14). Heidegger comments:

> Half a century has elapsed for Europe since these words were penned. During the decades in question the passage has been misread again and again, precisely by those people who exerted themselves to resist the increasing uprooting and devastation of science. From Nietzsche's words they gathered the following: the sciences may no longer be conducted in an arid, humdrum manner, they may no longer "gather dust," far removed from "life"; they have to be shaped "artistically," so that they are attractive, pleasing, and in good taste—all that, because the artistically shaped sciences must be related to "life," remain in proximity to "life," and be readily useful for "life."
>
> Above all, the generation that studied at the German universities between 1909 and 1914 heard the passage interpreted in this way. Even in the form of the misinterpretation it was a help to us. But there was no one about who could have provided the correct reading of it. That would have required re-asking the grounding question of Occidental philosophy, questioning in the direction of being by way of actual inquiry. (NI, 252–53/1, 218–19)

Heidegger depicts a pedagogical scene for his students in 1936, on the eve of World War II, the scene of a generation—his own—that came of age between 1909 and 1914. Heidegger himself would have been twenty to twenty-five years of age during those years on the eve of what was thereafter called "the Great War." He would have been a contemporary of Clarisse and Walter, two characters in Robert Musil's *Der Mann ohne Eigenschaften* who have a highly charged relation to will to power as art. In the year 1913 Clarisse and

Walter fall under the spell of Professor Meingast, Musil's name *à clef* for the life-philosopher Ludwig Klages. For Clarisse, entranced by Meingast, Nietzsche is the new prophet of burgeoning life, whose spirit of music will induce her to spurn her Wagnerian husband and embrace the cause of Moosbrugger, a genial psychopath. It is impossible to recapture the mesmerizing effect on Clarisse of Musil's Meingast-Klages, but it is easy to see why such enthusiasm and flamboyant life-philosophy should have repelled Heidegger. Indeed, the lecture courses of 1936 to 1940 may be viewed as endeavors to liberate Nietzsche not only from the uses and abuses of National Socialism but also from necromancers such as Ludwig Klages and Ernst Bertram. The first course ends by sketching quite briefly and cryptically the new interpretation of sensuousness that will acknowledge and enhance Nietzsche's twisting free of Platonism yet resist the perfervid contortions of the life-philosophers.

Science under the optics of the artist, but art under the optics of life. "Science" means knowing as such, hence all relation to truth. "Optics" means the perspectival character of being as becoming. "Art" means creation in the grand style, as effulgence and transfiguration of "life." The final words of the lecture course relate the grand style of art to the rigors of thinking. Yet what about "life," which needs both perspectival fixing and transfiguring of being, both fixation of and on an apparition (for the sake of survival and maintenance) and artistic creation (for the sake of enhancement and surpassing)? What does "life" mean?

It means "neither mere animal and vegetable being," Heidegger avers, without justifying the "mere"; neither animal and vegetable life "nor that readily comprehensible and compulsive busyness of everyday existence" that he had earlier called *das faktische Leben* and later on the quotidian life of an "improper Dasein," a Dasein that deludes itself into thinking that it is living life to the hilt. Neither this nor that, but "life" as becoming, *das Werden*. " 'Life' is neither 'biologically' nor 'practically' intended; it is meant metaphysically. The equation of being and life is not some sort of unjustified expansion of the biological, although it often seems that way, but a transformed interpretation of the biological on the basis of being, grasped in a superior way—this, of course, not fully mastered, in the timeworn schema of 'being and becoming' " (NI, 253/1, 219). The new interpretation of sensuousness does not mean that truth and knowledge are to be subjected "to aesthetic rehabilitation." It means that nihilism is to be overcome in a creative thinking of being as φύσις, a creative thinking that for Nietzsche could only be a thinking of   *Humanity! Your entire life will be inverted again and again like an hourglass and again and again it will run out—one vast minute of time in between, until all the conditions from which you came to be will converge once again in the world's circulation. And then you will find again every pain and every pleasure and every friend and foe and every hope and every error and every leaf of grass and every glance of the sun, the entire nexus of all things*   the eternal recurrence of the same.

CHAOS AND ASH

The genesis, communication, configuration, and domain of the doctrine of
eternal return constitute the four foci of Heidegger's *second* Nietzsche course,
"The Eternal Recurrence of the Same" (1937). Halfway through his treatment
of Nietzsche's principal thought, Heidegger offers a "summary presentation"
of the thought of recurrence on the basis of notes from the *Nachlaß* concerning
"being as a whole [*das Seiende im Ganzen*] as life and force; the world as
chaos" (NI, 339; 2, 82). Heidegger observes that the editors of the *Großoktav-
ausgabe* of Nietzsche's literary remains *Let us be on guard!* present the manuscript of M III 1 in a "misleading" manner, then comments: "We
shall try to avoid being misled. Nevertheless, Nietzsche's manuscript offers no
secure guidelines" (341; 2, 83). The very first point of Heidegger's ten-point
summary presentation is crucial for the theme of lifedeath. Heidegger begins:

> *What stands in view?* We reply: *The world in its collective character.* What all
> pertains to that? The whole of inanimate and animate existence, whereby "ani-
> mate" encompasses not only plants and animals but human beings as well. Inani-
> mate and animate things are not juxtaposed as two separate regions. Nor are they
> laminated one on top of the other. Rather, they are represented as interwoven in
> one vast nexus of becoming. Is the unity of that nexus "living" or "lifeless"?
> Nietzsche writes (XII, number 112): "Our whole world is the *ash* of countless
> *living* creatures: and even if the animate seems so miniscule in comparison to the
> whole, it is nonetheless the case that *everything* has already been transposed into
> life—and so it goes." *If we assume an eternal duration and consequently an
> eternal transformation of matter—* Apparently opposed to this is a thought
> expressed in *The Gay Science* (number 109: "Let us guard against saying that
> death is the opposite of life; the living creature is simply a kind of dead creature,
> and a very rare kind." In these passsages lies the suggestion that in terms of
> quantity the living creature is something slight, in terms of its occurrence some-
> thing rare, when we cast a glance toward the whole. Yet this rare and slight
> something remains forever the firebrand that yields an enormous quantity of ash.
> Accordingly, one would have to say that what is dead constitutes a kind of living
> existence, and not at all the reverse. At the same time, however, the reverse also
> holds, inasmuch as what is dead comes from the animate and in its preponderance
> continues to condition the animate. Thus the animate is only a kind of metamor-
> phosis and creative force of life, and death is an intermediate state. To be sure, such
> an interpretation does not capture perfectly Nietzsche's thought during this period.
> Furthermore, a contradiction obtains between these two thoughts, which we can
> formulate as follows: What is dead is the ashes of countless living creatures; *and*
> life is merely a kind of of death. In the first case, the living determines the prove-
> nance of the dead; in the second, the dead determines the manner of life of the
> living. The dead takes preeminence in the second, whereas in the first it becomes
> subordinate to the living. (NI, 341–42/2, 84–85)

It is important to note that "the dead," *das Tote,* is the neuter singular, not
the plural: it is therefore to be read not in the sense of Gogol's *Dead Souls,* as
those who were once alive but are now deceased, but in either of the following

two senses. Either *das Tote* refers to the collectivity of once living but now defunct creatures; or it embraces also those beings that as far as we know were never alive, the whole of inanimate nature, the "billiard ball universe" from Galileo through David Hartley. Yet it is this "as far as we know"   *We cannot think becoming otherwise than as passage from one perdurant state of "death" to another perdurant state of "death." Oh, we call the "dead" something motionless! As though there were anything that is motionless! The living is not the opposite of the dead, but a special case*   that is in question, our very (lack of) knowledge concerning the ostensibly inanimate universe.[2]

We have already caught a glimpse of Hans Castorp's Milky Way Monster, a product of some general, mysterious, post-Leibnizian corpuscular animism, indeterminably astronomical and microscopic, occupying the place Twain described as "the Greak Dark." For Heidegger it is not a matter of reverting to such animisms. Above all, it is a matter of discerning the limits of our knowledge. For from antiquity through modernity the will to know has had a secret predilection for "the dead," which at least appears to stay in place. *Fundamentally false estimate of the* value *of the* dead *by the* sensate *world. Because the latter is* us! *We belong to it! And yet with sensation comes* superficiality, *swindle: what have pain and pleasure to do with the actual event! They are a mere supplement, they do not penetrate into the depths! Yet we call them the* inner, *and the dead world we see as* exterior—*quite falsely! The "dead" world! Eternally and unerringly it moves, force pitted against force! And in the sensate world all is false, all is conceit! It is a* feast *to pass from this world into the "dead world"—and the greatest cravings of our knowledge seek to counterpose to this false and puffed-up world the eternal laws wherein no pleasure no pain no swindle reside. Is this the root of self-denial of sensation in the intellect? The meaning of truth is to understand sensation as the exterior side of existence, as an oversight of being, an adventure. Admittedly, it doesn't last long! Let us see through this comedy, and so enjoy it! Let us not think of our return to the insensate as a regression! We shall become altogether* true, *we shall consummate ourselves.* Death *is to be* interpreted otherwise! *That way we shall* reconcile *ourselves with the actual, which is to say, with the dead world.*   Heidegger's first point in the summary presentation of Nietzsche's thought of chaos and ash as the site of eternal return continues as follows:

Perhaps two different views of the dead are in play here. If that is the case, then the very possibility of contradiction becomes superfluous. If the dead is taken with a view to its knowability, and if knowing is conceived as a firm grasp on what is permanent, identifiable, and unequivocal, then the dead assumes preeminence as an object of knowledge, whereas the animate, being equivocal and ambiguous, is only a kind—and a subordinate kind—of the dead. If, on the contrary, the dead itself is thought in terms of its provenance, then it is but the ashes of what is alive. The fact that the living remains subordinate to the dead in quantitative terms and in terms of preponderance does not refute the fact that it is the origin of the dead, especially since it is proper to the essence of what is higher that it remain rare, less common. From all this we discern one decisive point: by setting the lifeless in relief against the living, along the guidelines of any single aspect, we do not do justice to the state of affairs—the world is more enigmatic than our calculating intellect would like to admit. (NI, 342–43/2, 85)

It is important to note that at least under one of his many "signatures" Heidegger does not disdain life, does not suppress it and flee from it, simply in order to make his own life less complicated.[3]   *To be redeemed from life and to become dead nature once again: this can be felt to be a* feast—*by one who wills to die. To love nature! To honor once again what is dead! It is not the contrary but the womb, the rule that has more meaning than the exception: for unreason and pain come to the fore only in the so-called "purposeful" world, only in the living.*   It is not Nietzsche's inconsistency concerning the origins of life and death that intrigues Heidegger, but the many faces and protean shapes of lifedeath.   *To attain the advantages of a dead man*—*no one bothering about us, neither for us nor against us. To imagine oneself vanished from humanity, to learn to forget cravings of every kind: and to apply the entire superfluity of one's energy to* spectation! *To be the* invisible specta-tor!!   Lifedeath designates the world in its riddlesome collective char-acter; our calculating intellect is never equal to its collective complexity.

In the remaining points of his summary presentation, Heidegger encapsu-lates Nietzsche's conception of the totality of beings as finite force in a bounded magnitude forever in a state of becoming, never attaining equilib-rium, producing unlimited and hence unsurveyable effects over an unlimited expanse of time. The effects are unlimited, yet not, strictly speaking, infinite. The "space" of such effects we take to be boundless, if only because we conceive of space as empty. Space remains "an imaginary, imaginative bit of imagery" (347/2, 89). Heidegger suggests that here Nietzsche is groping to-ward a conception of the *void,* a space-time that is both engendered by and in remotion from *world.* He cryptically refers to an *Ent-stehen* of space-time in the worlding of world, related in some way to his own existential conception of *Ent-fernung* in *Being and Time,* which is both distance and undistancing, both a moving away and an approaching, both a cleaving and an annealing of the fissure. At all events, *time* for Nietzsche is actual, as opposed to imaginary, even if it is essentialy boundless and infinite, even if it can be called by the name *eternity.*[4]

As Heidegger approaches the tenth and final point of his summary presenta-tion he expresses the hope that he will "attain solid footing for our concluding interpretation of the world" as Nietzsche sees it (349/2, 91). He now intro-duces a second phrase from aphorism 109 of *The Gay Science,* one that prom-ises solid footing: "The collective character of the world is, on the contrary, to all eternity—chaos."

Now that "solid footing" has been introduced, it seems an opportune moment to point out one of the most puzzling aspects   *In short,* **wait and see** *to what extent* knowledge *and* truth *can be* **incorporated**—*and to what extent a transformation of human being advenes, whereby such being ulti-*

mately lives only in order to know   of M III 1, from which Heidegger is deriving much of the material for his ten-point summary. As I mentioned, this notebook contains many passages on the nascent thought of the eternal return of the same. At the same time, in contrapuntal fashion, within a maddeningly intricate fugue, Nietzsche sketches other passages on the fundamental error of metaphysics—its supposition that any two things or events can be identical or the same (*gleich*). Thus the pages that give birth to the affirmative thought of eternal recurrence of the same (*des Gleichen*) contain, often in boldface type (indicating multiple underlinings), the most devastatingly convincing demonstrations that   *There would be no suffering if there were nothing organic; that is to say, without belief in the same, that is to say, without* this error there would be no pain in the world!   nothing is ever the same. Not even in the eternal recurrence of the. In other words, the Procrustean bed of eternal return is strewn with ashes. It is difficult   *Error is the father of the living! This* primal error *is to be understood as an* accident! *Guess what it is!*   to attain solid footing in chaos.

Whatever others might assert concerning chaos—that it is quasi-Heraclitean flux or the Hesiodic gap that yawns between sky and earth—Nietzsche uses the word *chaos*   *Let us be on guard!*   in order to ward off the most common "humanizations" of beings as a whole. Both moralizing and technical explanations (the beneficent Demiurge) fall away, and aesthetic habits are denied their free exercise (presumably, and Heidegger insists on this, Nietzschean transfiguration and artistic effulgence are not mere aesthetic habits); moral-juridical "laws" and intellectual anarchy, purposefulness and aimlessness, rationalism and irrationalism—all are equally barred from chaos. At the end of the list of pervasive bad intellectual and aesthetic habits Heidegger reverts to the very first of his ten points, the familiar yet unfounded opposition of organic to anorganic existence.

> Finally, the notion of the collective character of the world as an "organism" is out of the question, not only because it is a special case that dare not be taken to represent the whole, and not only because human notions about what an organism is are modeled on human beings themselves, but above all because an organism always necessarily requires something other than itself, something outside itself, for sustenance and nourishment. Yet what could subsist outside the world as a whole, understood as "organism"? "The supposition that the universe is an organism is belied by the *essence of the organic*". . . . (NI, 351/2, 93)

In a word, or in a refrain, all one can say of chaos is, "Let us be on guard. . . ." Let us be on guard against interpreting the collective character of the world as anything at all. "Let us shield ourselves," adduces Heidegger, "from the tendency to project any fortuitous notion about ourselves, any human capacity, onto beings" (351/2, 93).

We pause to observe that this Nietzschean refrain is quite close to that of Heidegger in his 1929–1930 biology lectures. Let us shield ourselves from every tendency to project the world-relation of Dasein onto that of the animal;

but let us also guard against the supposition and presumption that we can ever shield ourselves so successfully that we gain unmediated access to animality. World poverty is the squalor of Dasein. We have met the wretched of the earth, and they are us.[5]

To be sure, Heidegger shares with Nietzsche the task of a dedivinization and dehumanization of beings as a whole. If anything, Heidegger becomes increasingly dubious about Nietzsche's dedication to the task, suspecting that the latter's desire (in the project of overman) to master the world stops short of radical dedeification. Nor does Heidegger accept that dedivinization is atheism. "The most fundamental point to be made about Nietzsche's notion of chaos is the following: only a thinking that is utterly lacking in stamina will deduce a will to godlessness from the will to a dedeification of beings. On the contrary, truly metaphysical thinking, at the outermost point of dedeification, allowing itself no subterfuge and eschewing all mystification, will uncover that path on which alone gods will be encountered—if they are to be encountered ever again in the history of mankind" (NI, 352–53/2, 94). Heidegger goes so far as to attribute to Nietzsche a kind of "negative theology," albeit one purged of the Christian God. The world as a whole is an ἄρρητος, an ineffable τόπος and topic beyond the reaches of all rhetoric and logic (352/2, 95). Surely, the the reference to ἄρρητον foreshadows the *sigetics* with which the lecture course will close—reference to "telling silence" (*Erschweigen*) as the proper medium of a thinking that dwells in the vicinity of poetry. For the moment, Heidegger is satisfied to restrict his remarks concerning Nietzsche's "defensive" posture in the thinking of eternal return and choas to the following cryptic sentences: "Such a defensive procedure represents the very opposite of despair concerning the possibility of knowledge, the very opposite of an unmitigated predilection for denial and destruction. The procedure therefore becomes a salient feature in every instance of great thought, appearing again and again under different guises; nor can it be directly refuted, as long as it perseveres in its style and refrains from leaping over the barriers it has established for itself" (NII, 352/2, 95). However recondite the invocation of negative theology may appear to be, Heidegger insists that the thought of chaos is as inscrutable as it is essential. It is somehow tied up with finite force, bounded space, endless time, and becoming—yet it resists even these notions to the extent that they are "humanizations." It seems that all we can say of chaos and ash is *nothing*. "Or is 'the nothing' perhaps the most human of all humanizations?" asks Heidegger, twisting *das Nichts* as he is wont to do, but this time in a way that endangers his own protracted meditation on the *nihil*—which not only pervades human comportment toward beings but also *seems* to shatter the ring of animal behavior.

Of course, Nietzsche does attribute a kind of *necessity* to chaos, not in the sense of purposive world order, but in the sense of μοῖρα and *fatum*, perhaps in the sense of what the ancients call 'Ανάγκη. Heidegger's tenth and final point is: "*Cosmic chaos is in itself necessity.*" He concedes that none of the points explicitly mentions the thought of eternal return, yet intimates that a "field" has been opened for Nietzsche's fundamental thought:

> For one thing, we have circumscribed the field in which the thought of return belongs and which the thought as such concerns: we have surveyed this field of being as a whole and determined it as the interlacing unity of the animate and the lifeless. For another, we have shown how in its foundations being as a whole—as the unity of animate and inanimate—is structured and articulated: it is constituted by the character of force and the finitude of the whole (at one with infinity) that is implied in the character of force—which is to say, the immeasurability of the "phenomenal effects." Now—and we can proceed with the following only on the basis of what we have already worked out—we must show how being as a whole, which is deployed in its field and in its constitution in the manner we have indicated, is *susceptible* of the eternal return of the same; we must show how eternal return may be ascribed to being as a whole, *demonstrated* of it. At all events, this is the only possible arrangement by which we can proceed in an orderly fashion through the entire labyrinth of Nietzsche's thoughts, mastering that labyrinth as we proceed—presupposing, of course, that we wish to proceed in the way that is prescribed by the inner lawfulness of the guiding question of philosophy, the question of the being as such. (NI, 355–56/2, 96–97)

Mastering the labyrinth? Prescribed by the inner lawfulness of the *guiding* question? The guiding question (*die Leitfrage:* "What is the being?") is by no means Heidegger's own question. And one wonders whether he would ever speak of mastering the *Grundfrage* or the *Vorfrage* of metaphysics. However ironic Heidegger's remarks here may be, we may take it that the field of eternal recurrence of the same—where precisely "the same" is anything but assured—is marked by a curious interpenetration   *How foreign and superior we take ourselves to be vis-à-vis the dead, the anorganic. Meanwhile, we are seventy-five percent pillars of water and have anorganic salts in us that may have more power over our being well or ill than the society of all living things!*   of living and lifeless, animate and inanimate. The unified field of eternal return—which can only be the unified field of φύσις—is chaos and ash unto all eternity: lifedeath.

"NIETZSCHE'S ALLEGED BIOLOGISM"

It would certainly be worthwhile following Heidegger's trajectory throughout this second lecture course. For "The Eternal Recurrence of the Same" is remarkable in at least four respects: first, it shows us a Heidegger who reads *Thus Spoke Zarathustra* and other Nietzschean texts in a way that some recent commentators have insisted Heidegger *never* reads, is never *able* to read;[6] second, it brings Heidegger's own thinking of mortality and downgoing (*Übergang* as *Untergang*) as close to Nietzsche's thinking as Heidegger ever comes (if such judgments can ever be made); the Nietzsche who truly matters to Heidegger is the one who thinks the *tragic thought* of recurrence; third, it enables us to assess the strengths and weaknesses of Heidegger's extensive but not uncritical use of the Nietzschean *Nachlaß;* fourth and finally, it not only gives us the clearest account of what Heidegger calls Nietzsche's "fundamental metaphysical position" but also provides us with the means for pushing beyond that position to *another* Nietzsche—for example, Nietzsche the philosopher of Dionysos. Heidegger's students, in their sole recorded intervention in the Nietzsche lectures, insist that Heidegger recount more about this god (NI, 467–68/2, 203–204). However, let us advance to that section of the *third* lecture course, "The Will to Power as Knowledge," in which Heidegger asks about Nietzsche's putative biologism.

The question arises throughout the third lecture course, and occasionally in all the others. Yet it is put most insistently in the sixth and sixteenth sections, "Nietzsche's Alleged Biologism" and "Nietzsche's 'Biological' Interpretation of Knowledge" (NI, 517–27; 590–602/3, 39–47; 101–10). At first blush, nothing can rescue Nietzsche from the accusation of biologism. The optics of life obtrude as plainly as the spectacles on Nietzsche's nose *Noses are thinkable* when he equates *world* with *life*. He uses both words as names for being as a whole. His genealogical thinking is sheer bio-graphy, his dallyings with the popular sciences of his day (with Roux, Boscovitch, Spencer, et al.) are transparent bio-logism. So it seems. Moreover, his invocation of the "splendid blond beast" in the eleventh section of the first treatise of *On the Genealogy of Morals* (KSA, 5, 275–76) indicates that Nietzsche's biologism is not a "harmless opinion" but "the innermost will of his thought" (NI, 518/3, 40). So it seems.

Heidegger now introduces Nietzsche's equation of being and becoming, being *as* becoming, with the living. Once again he concedes, as though under duress, that the ambiguous and even specious term *biologism* "obviously gets to the core of Nietzsche's thinking." It would be a "very forced and even vain endeavor" to conceal or downplay Nietzsche's persistent use of biological language. Yet what seems obvious about Nietzsche's thinking proves, as it always does in Heidegger's interpretations of great figures in the history of philosophy, to be "the *main obstacle* to our penetrating to his fundamental thought" (519/3, 41).

Among the rubrics of the day that are to be avoided, because utterly misleading, are "biologism," "life-philosophy" (*Lebensphilosophie*), and "metaphysics of life." As for the science of biology, Heidegger notes once again what he argues consistently from *Being and Time* through the later work about every science: "The essential realm in which biology moves can itself never be posited and grounded by biology as a science, but can only be presupposed, adopted, and confirmed. This is true of every science." The question of a science's realm, and that realm's boundaries, is a question of and for *metaphysics,* which "thinks beings as a whole." Only a science that submits to such questioning can be "pregnant with decision," so that it can advance beyond hack work and "help to create history." Only a science that poses questions concerning its own foundations and limits, formulating what Heidegger calls "field propositions"

(*Gebietssätze*), can forge ahead. The self-critical scientist will know that no complacent precision can rescue science from these apparently inchoate and often very vague questions (521/3, 42). Metaphysical questioning requires a *leap*, says Heidegger, as though he were expecting scientists to dance. For what plodders cannot perform they must pooh-pooh.

Heidegger's leap may seem closer to Kierkegaard's leap of faith than to Freud's limp; yet we should not forget that *der Sprung* also means a crack or fissure. These are the very years in which Heidegger is thinking the cleaving (not merely the *clearing*) of being, being as abyss—*die Zerklüftung des Seins,* discussed in the previous chapter. It is not that when philosophers become kings scientists will become metaphysicians. It is that the scientist must acknowledge "the higher knowledge concealed in every science, on which the worth of that science rests" (523/3, 43–44). It is not that science and philosophy stand side-by-side as neighboring stately edifices. Rather, "*Science and reflection on the specific field are both historically grounded on the actual dominance of a particular interpretation of being, and they always move in the dominant circle of a particular conception of the essence of truth.* In every fundamental self-reflection of the sciences it is always a matter of passage through metaphysical decisions that were either made long ago or are being prepared now" (523/3, 44).

What has this long disquisition on scientism and positivism—"The idea of a 'scientifically founded worldview' is a characteristic offshoot of the intellectual confusion in the public mind that emerged more and more strikingly in the last third of the previous century and attained remarkable success in those half-educated circles who indulged in popular science"—to do with Nietzsche? No doubt, Nietzsche indulged.   *The melancholic lacks kalium sulfate or kalium phosphate.*   Yet his circles were hardly half-educated. Indeed, what would it mean to be wholly educated—in either mansion, in any science or in several selected areas of philosophy? Would an academic elitism or even snobbism, you in front of me, I in front of you, resolve the problem of the nebulous boundary between science and philosophy? Heidegger elsewhere explicitly repudiates such academic elitism, although there is ostensibly nothing outside the walls that can illuminate the life inside. Only one thing will help, and in an essential way it implicates Nietzsche: "If we think Nietzsche's fundamental thought decisively enough we will catch sight of the ground of this confused relationship," namely, that of science and philosophy, a relationship that is deeply concealed "in the essence of modernity." For Nietzsche does not simply misapply concepts of biology beyond their proper limits. He is not unaware of the metaphysical decisions that lie impacted in all concepts of life and the life-sciences.

Heidegger even wonders whether Nietzsche is on the lookout for a ground of life "that has nothing more to do with the phenomena of life in plants and animals" (526/3, 46). *Nietzsche thinks not biologically   The inorganic* conditions *us from top to toe: water air soil terrain electricity etc. Under such conditions we are plants   but metaphysically.* Nietzsche brings to a point of culmination the Western thought of being as φύσις. For the moment, Heidegger is satisfied to issue a warning:

> Whether one votes yes or no on Nietzsche's "biologism," one always gets stuck in the foreground of his thinking. The predilection for this state of affairs is supported by the form of Nietzsche's own publications. His words and sentences provoke, fascinate, penetrate, and stimulate. One thinks that if only one pursues one's impressions one has understood Nietzsche. We must first unlearn this abuse that is supported by current catchwords like *biologism*. We must learn to "read." (527/3, 47)

READING CHAOS

Nietzsche's putative biologism conceals his fundamental thought concerning life, a thought that places him in closest proximity to the unified field of φύσις. If Western metaphysical thought is logic in the broadest sense, that is, thought's turning toward λόγος, Nietzsche's thinking reverts to the precincts of life: the categories of logic must be thought as schemata devised by and for the preservation of a certain species of life. However, Heidegger argues that if the residual claim is made that such schemata distort becoming by petrifying its flux, then some sort of notion of truth as correctness is retained and the primal question of truth as disclosure suppressed.[7]

What "is" becoming? No matter how vigilantly we remain on guard in posing or replying to such a question, and we must remain   *Let us be on guard!*   on guard, Nietzsche's considered reply is that becoming, the recurrence of life from ash and ash from life, can be thought only as chaos. Yet Heidegger now pushes beyond the question of the organic and the inorganic in the chaos of becoming. He now insists on the thought of "bodying life," *das leibende Leben,* in chaos. Human being is the being of some body who is alive. Yet the bodying forth of life cannot be reduced to sheer humanization, anthropomorphism, organicism,   *The modern scientific sideshow to belief in God is belief in the* universe as organism: *that nauseates me*   or biologism. Indeed, as we shall soon see, the bodying forth of life conducts Heidegger back to the fundamental challenge of "will to power as art," to wit, the still-outstanding "new interpretation of sensuousness." For in his very first lecture course on Nietzsche, which concludes with a reading of Plato's *Phaedrus,* Heidegger agrees with Socrates that human beings "cannot body forth" as "living being" (ζῷον) unless they have already caught sight of being, as though being itself were somehow bound up with life (NI, 223–25/ 1, 192–94).

It will not be possible here and now to follow Heidegger's third lecture course in the direction of Nietzsche's (possible) "twisting free" from Platonic structures, in the direction of his creative-artistic interpretation of truth as harmony or concord (*Einstimmigkeit*) with becoming, and this as the extreme transformation of *adaequatio* and ὁμοίωσις in the history of metaphysics. Nor will we be able to take up the question of "justice" (*Gerechtigkeit*) as

Heidegger's final word for the commanding-poetizing perspective that in Nietzsche's view would settle the discord that rages between truth and art.[8]

To be sure, the specter of biologism continues to haunt Heidegger's account of "Nietzsche's 'Biological' Interpretation of Knowledge." There can be no doubt that for Nietzsche the logical category is an expression of life's preservation, if not its enhancement; the psychological faculty of reason is the purveyor of "laws" in a world always already reduced to bite-size, that is, "justified" chunks. "Just as certain sea animals, for example, jellyfish, develop and extend their tentacles for grasping and catching, the animal 'man' uses reason and its grasping instrument, the law of contradiction, in order to find his way around in his environment, in that way securing his own permanence" (NI, 593/3, 103). Yet for Nietzsche such ostensibly biological asseverations concerning the law of the excluded middle are in effect metaphysical speculations on the being of beings—on what beings can and cannot be. Underlying the "law" of (non)contradiction is the *command* issued by one species of being that all being *be* by way of (non)contradiction, the command itself expressing an inability or incapacity of that particular species   *Guess what it is!*   to deal with beings except as fixed and permanentized as the "same." Is that one species all "life"? Or merely "human" life? Or merely the human "philosopher's" life? Heidegger once again suggests that the term *biological* may well mean "something other than what is alive, representing the latter as plant and animal" (615/3, 122). Life is a poetizing and commanding "perspectivism," which cannot be reduced to any familiar biological notion, much less any cliché-ridden "biologism."

> *Nietzsche thinks the "biological," the essence of what is alive, in the direction of commanding and poetizing, of the perspectival and horizonal: in the direction of freedom.* He does *not* think the biological, that is, the essence of what is alive, biologically at all. So little is Nietzsche's thinking in danger of biologism that on the contrary he rather tends to interpret what is biological in the true and strict sense—the plant and animal—*nonbiologically,* that is, *humanly,* preeminently in terms of the determinations of perspective, horizon, commanding, and poetizing— in general, in terms of the representing of beings. Yet this verdict concerning Nietzsche's biologism would need a more comprehensive clarification and foundation. (NI, 615/3, 122)

Whether Heidegger's account of truth as "justice" can supply such a foundation is dubious, to say the least. Whether his equation of the "human" with the "nonbiological" and his restriction of biology "in the strict sense" to plants and (other) animals can help to secure such a foundation is perhaps worse than dubious. Yet when Heidegger notes the "humanization" that is implied in Nietzschean poetizing and commanding perspectivism, this should not be taken as a mere slap against Nietzsche. It reminds us of something very strange about an earlier moment in Heidegger's own "Will to Power as Knowledge," a moment that tarries with life's bodying forth in and as the *human body.* To which we now return. As to a moonlit balcony.

   In the course of renewed discussion of chaos in section 12 of his lectures, Heidegger says something uncanny about the human body, about the life that bodies forth in human being. Human life and the human body cannot, after all, be so readily counterposed to the properly biological, the plant and animal. Nietzsche's concern with "life as knowing" and with knowing as "schematizing a chaos in accordance with practical need" (551/3, 67–68) indicates that it is invariably and inevitably the life of *human* being that is in question here. Once again Heidegger refers to Hesiod's *Theogony* and to χάος as "the gaping," that is, as "a measureless, supportless, and groundless yawning-open," words that are indeed reminiscent of the cleaving of beyng (563/3, 77). In the Kantian and neo-Kantian world, where knowledge begins with a "mass of sensations," chaos takes on its distinctly modern sense, by which the body and its senses *appear* to assume special importance, albeit only to be regimented by pure forms, sensible concepts, intelligible categories, and transcendental schematisms. However, Heidegger now suddenly leaps from the Kantian to the Nietzschean body. "Perhaps this body as it lives and bodies forth [*dieser Leib, wie er leibt und lebt*] is what is 'most certain' (WM, 659) in us, more certain than the 'soul' and 'spirit,' and perhaps it is this body and not the soul about which we say that it is 'inspired' ['*begeistert*']" (565/3, 79).

   Heidegger here seems to be speaking in Nietzsche's voice. It seems therefore that Nietzsche is "ventriloquizing" Heidegger. Yet the ventriloquy is so successful that it puts at risk any interpretation of Heidegger's thought as a thought "of flame" and "of spirit" (see chapter 8,   *In the learned circles of the north the epidemic of* winter *rages. Maybe the stoves have been poisoning us all the while! When compared to the French, the German looks like a degenerate potbelly lover*   below). The Heidegger-Nietzsche ventriloquy is not so readily sorted out: let her or him who will search for the master voice speaking through the dummy; let him or her who will expose themselves as wood or worse. That ventriloquy now produces some of the strangest effects of heidegger's nietzsche and nietzsche's heidegger, effects of the human body, of some body who is alive.

   Life lives in that it bodies forth. We know by now perhaps a great deal—almost more than we can encompass—about what we call the body, without having seriously thought about what *bodying* is. It is something more and different from merely "carrying a body around with one"; it is that in which everything that we ascertain in the processes and appearances in the body of a living thing first receives its own process-character. It may be that *bodying* is initially an obscure term, but it names something that is *immediately* and *constantly* experienced in the knowledge of living things, and it must be kept in mind.
   As simple and as obscure as what we know as gravitation is, gravity and the falling of bodies, the bodying of a living being is just as simple and just as obscure, though quite different and correspondingly more essential. The bodying of life is nothing separate by itself, encapsulated in the "physical mass" [*Körper*] in which the body can appear to us; the body [*der Leib*] is seepage and passage at the same time. Through this body flows a stream of life of which we feel but a small and

fleeting portion, in accordance with the receptivity of the momentary state of the body. Our body itself is admitted into this stream of life, floating in it, and is carried off and snatched away by this stream or else pushed to the banks. That chaos of our region of sensibility which we know as the region of the body is only *one section* of the great chaos that the "world" itself is. (NI, 565–66/3, 79–80)

Seepage and passage, *Durchlaß und Durchgang,* letting through and passing through. Floating in the stream of life, beyond or beneath any distinction between activity and passivity, chaos spiraling on into larger circles of chaos. One is reminded of some lines of poetry in the American language—the permanently impermanent floodtide and the stream of lifedeath that is Walt Whitman's "Crossing Brooklyn Ferry," the fifth strophe of which reads as follows:

What is it then between us?
What is the count of the scores or hundreds of years between us?

Whatever it is, it avails not—distance avails not, and place avails not,
I too lived, Brooklyn of ample hills was mine,
I too walk'd the streets of Manhattan island, and bathed in the waters around it,
I too felt the curious abrupt questionings stir within me,
In the day among crowds of people sometimes they came upon me,
In my walks home late at night or as I lay in my bed they came upon me,
I too had been struck from the float forever held in solution,
I too had receiv'd identity by my body,
That I was I knew was of my body, and what I should be I knew I should be of my body.[9]

Nietzschean chaos is not a mass of sensations. It is not Galilean turbulence. It is not the Hobbesian state of siege. It is neither a jumble nor a jungle of impingements. "Chaos is the name for bodying life, life as bodying writ large" (566/3, 80). Poetizing as commanding perspectivism is the semiotics of life as bodying, semiotics writ small on the vast palimpsest of chaos. Heidegger's reading of will to power as knowledge reads what is writ large as chaos, and even if that reading should dwindle to talk of "justice," it reads chaos as "what urges, flows, and is animated, whose order is *concealed,* whose law we do not descry straightaway." Darwinism is not its law, as it was not the law for Nietzsche. Once again Darwin's (or Thomas Huxley's or Nast's or Mahler's or Kafka's) ape is shooed away: "Above all, Nietzsche's idea of viewing man and world as such primarily from the perspective of the body and animality in no way means that man originates from the animal and more precisely from the 'ape'—as if such a 'doctrine of origin' could say anything about man at all!" (567/3, 80). (Exclamation points are rare in Heidegger; the ape wrings this one from him.) Heidegger introduces a note from the *Nachlaß* in support of his own horror of Darwinism: "The apes are too good-natured for man to have originated from them." The ensuing laughter   tranquilizing effect *(as with blue)*   drowns out the difference in tone that distinguishes Nietzsche from Heidegger in this respect: whereas Nietzsche, like Nast, moves to champion the ape against the Darwinian calumny, Heidegger moves always and everywhere to keep the animal's prehensile organs off human lapels: "The animality of man has a deeper metaphysical ground than could be inferred biologically and scientifically by referring man to an existent animal species that appears to be similar to him in certain external respects."[10]

Heidegger's point on the "deeper metaphysical ground" of man's animality is well taken, if he is responding to the conception of a mere homology or isomorphism of man and anthropoid apes. Yet what "externality" frames the "similarity" of animal and man? What "deeper metaphysical ground" prevents the human hand from clasping the grasping organ of the ape—or prevents the latter from getting a grip on the former? Presumably, a "new interpretation of sensuousness" would have to take up such queries, overcoming all its allergies to plants and (other) animals alike. *Noses are thinkable the olfactory nerves of which would be tickled only by the effluvia of a volcano.* It is no doubt significant that Heidegger now for the first time reverts to the theme of will to power as *art*, and art as the bodying forth of life. It is Heidegger's way of interpreting science (hence, knowledge and truth) under the optics of the artist, and art under the optics of life. He writes:

> "Chaos," the world as chaos, means beings as a whole projected relative to the body and its bodying. In laying this foundation for world projection, everything decisive is included. Thus the thinking that as revaluation of all values strives for a new valuation also includes the positing of the highest value. If truth cannot be the highest value, that highest value must be yet above truth, that is, in the sense of the traditional concept of truth: it must be nearer and more in accordance with true beings, that is, with what becomes. The highest value is *art*, in contradistinction to knowledge and truth. It does not copy what is at hand, does not explain matters in terms of beings at hand. But art transfigures life, moves it into higher, as yet unlived, possibilities. These do not hover "above" life; rather, they awaken life anew out of itself and make it vigilant. . . . (NI, 567–68/3, 81)

The afflatus of such vigilant, creative, artistic life is poetic enchantment. Heidegger cites a line from Stefan George's "The Human Being and the Wood Sprite," which warns against the fatal Faustian optimism bound up with technological mastery over nature: "For 'only through magic does life remain awake.' " Life's magic is art, which according to Nietzsche is "an excess and overflow of blossoming bodily being into the world of images and desires" (WM, 802; NI, 568/3, 81). Such an overflow is of course reminiscent of Dionysian excess and Apollinian "form-engendering force."

It is therefore regrettable that two years earlier, in 1937, Heidegger frustrated his students' request to hear more about Dionysos—more about the tragic daimon and the cloven realm of τὸ δαιμόνιον. No doubt, Heidegger feared that Professor Meingast had made himself an uncanny guest in Freiburg as well, that his own students were in danger of becoming Clarisses, Walters, or even Moosbruggers. However, it could be that those students of 1937, in the course entitled "The Eternal Recurrence of the Same," had also been present at the initial course of 1936, "The Will to Power as Art," and that they now knew what an interpretation of sensuousness entailed. It is regrettable that these students failed to intervene in the third course, that of 1939, "The Will to Power as Knowledge," precisely at this point, in order to remind Heidegger that in 1936 he himself, and not Klages, had insisted that artistic rapture *bodies forth* as *embodied attunement* to beings as a whole (NI, 125–26; 143/1, 105; 121). It is unfortunate that Heidegger's students failed to indicate that the magic of George's dramatic poem is Dionysian magic, and that its excess need not degenerate into a Wagnerian *Klage(s)lied*. Excess might once again become truth, as Nietzsche wrote in *The Birth of Tragedy*, the truth of tragic art in the "mating" or "crossing" of Apollo and Dionysos.[11]

In retrospect, it appears that Heidegger comes closest to the bodying forth of artistic rapture in his discussion of Plato's *Phaedrus* (in section 23 of the *first* lecture course on Nietzsche: NI, 223–31/1, 192–99), which defines the work of art (or rather, the work of its beauty) as τὸ ἐκφανέστατον καὶ ἐρασμιώτατον, "what is most radiant and most enchanting." Beautiful appearance is "the most rapturous," *das Entrückendste*, the most erotic. Heidegger translates the Platonic "superlatively erotic" with the word he himself chooses in *Being and Time* to designate the animatedness of human temporality. *Entrückung* usually means erotic or mystical transport, enchantment, or rapture. He adds to the nominalized present-participial form of the word (*das Entrückende*) the pendant or counterweight, *das Berückende*. What is most erotic is oxymoronically *berückend-entrückend*, both "captivating" and "liberating." In Plato's account, the beauty of the sensuous world both captivates us, fascinating and fettering us to beings here below, and liberates us for the view upon nonsensuous being. If there is any discordance between art and truth, beauty blesses the discordance, which is therefore "felicitous." Nietzsche's twisting free of Platonism occurs in his exposure of the "hidden maneuver" by which Plato guarantees the happy end of the story of the gap between being and becoming. Precisely *how* Nietzsche exposes the hidden maneuver, or how that maneuver comes to *show itself* at the end of metaphysics, is Heidegger's question. Yet precisely here he makes little headway. Precisely here his students must have wanted to press him, press him on the most erotic, press him on the superlatively rapturous, which rages in the discordance between what others will call "art" and "truth," press him on the discordance of chaotic *life*.

Art under the optics of life, art viewed metaphysically, is more true to life, as it were, than truth as fixation and immobilization. "Art ventures and wins chaos," not merely as the confused throng of sense-data not yet ordered by intellect, but as "the concealed, self-overflowing, unmastered superabundance of life," as the chaos encountered in bodily states (NI, 569/3, 82), and not merely as something set over against us as an ob-ject (*Gegen-stand*). "We do not first simply encounter chaos in bodily states; but, living, our body bodies forth as a wave in the stream of chaos." Such a wave suggests *periodicity* rather than perfect presence, and lifedeath rather than the *nunc stans* of a paralytic eternity. It alters forever the very sense of "knowing." Heidegger concludes this section of his course with a recollection of Leibniz:

These living beings are, when thought in a Leibnizian way, "living mirrors," "metaphysical points" in which the whole of the world gathers and shows itself in the circumscribed luminosity of each perspective. In trying to clarify how chaos came to be posited as what is knowable and to be known, we happened to stumble across what knows—the living being that grasps the world and takes it over. That is not a matter of chance, for what is knowable and what knows are each determined in their essence in a unified way from the same essential ground. We may not separate either one, nor wish to encounter them separately. Knowing is not like a bridge that somehow subsequently connects two existent banks of a stream, but is itself a stream that in its flow first creates the banks and turns them *toward* each other in a more original way than a bridge ever could. (NI, 569–70/3, 82–83)

In the following sections, Heidegger investigates the tension between the urge to *stabilize* becoming in the rushing stream of chaos and the urge to *overcome* and *surpass* every moment of stabilization. Life is as much the one as the other, as much "propulsion toward the permanent" as "this pure streaming of drives and pulsions, proclivities and inclinations, needs and demands, impressions and views, wishes and commands," the vitality of life that "pulls and sucks the living itself into its own stream, there to exhaust its surge and flow" (570–71/3, 84–85). Life at its most vital is lifedeath, the surge and oblivion of whorls and eddies in the pool of chaos. Robert Musil describes the mind and memory of Moosbrugger, the madman who unites the banks of the stream as no mossy bridge ever could, as himself a stream: "One can easily picture a human being's life as a flowing stream. However, the movement Moosbrugger perceived in his own life was the flow of a stream through a vast body of standing water: driving forward, the stream was also drawn back in eddies, and there the proper course of his life all but vanished."[12] If life requires the security of stability, the formation of horizons or of islands in the stream, then schemata are necessary "with a view to stabilizing the onrushing and oppressing torrent" (573/3, 86). Once again Heidegger notes the ambiguity of "life" in Nietzsche's texts—often indistinguishably plant, animal, and human life—as furious flux and cold clinker, flame and chill, fire and ash, struck from the phosphorous float forever held in solution. Always the tension of a dual tendency.   *Principal tendencies: (1) To cultivate love of life, of one's own life, in every way! And* whatever *each individual concocts to that end must be tolerated by the other—we must appropriate to ourselves a new and magnificent toleration. No matter how much it offends our own taste when we as individuals truly augment the joy we take in our life!/(2) To be united in enmity against everything and everyone who tries to make the value of life suspect: against the Gloomy Gusses and malcontents and Grumbling Gerties. To prevent them from reproducing! Yet our enmity must itself be a means to our joy! And so, laugh, mock, annihilate without bitterness! This is our* mortal struggle./This life—your eternal life!

Once again Heidegger indicates that Nietzsche, like all metaphysicians before him, fails to pass beyond "life" to "a *more original essential configuration of human being* (in Da-sein)" (574/3, 87). Yet neither here nor in what follows does Heidegger take up the essential configuration of Dasein as bodying forth *in* and *as* the stream of life, life as chaos, life as the lifedeath of eternal return. Nowhere does he pursue the problem to which Nietzsche's prodding, persistent thought has led him. That is why we have read the third lecture course in such an odd way, eddying forward and back from the sixth and sixteenth sections (on Nietzsche's putative biologism, in fact his *metaphysics* of being as becoming and becoming as life) to the sections on the world as chaos and human existence as bodying forth. What gets lost in the Heideggerian meditation is the very first point that Heidegger raised in his earlier treatment of chaos in the 1937 lecture course, chaos as the stream of ashes from once living things, and ash as the barest trace of a life that can only be universal lifedeath.

Daimon life is life in which death is both immanent and imminent—both always already there (hence, immanent) and always only on the verge of advent (hence, imminent). To follow the stream of Heidegger's thinking of Nietzsche in ways that do body forth in the lectures yet are never pursued with any persistence there would bring us to locales where Heidegger himself never ventured. For instance, the locale of lifedeath in the final speculations of Freudian psychoanalysis.

IMMANENT DEATH, IMMINENT DEATH: BEYOND THE PP

"What now follows is speculation," Freud begins in chapter 4 of *Beyond the Pleasure Principle* (StA 3, 234). As though his long detour through medicine and natural science—the detour he calls *psychoanalysis*—were coming to an end. Coming to an end in the speculative domain that in our own day has come to *its* end, the somewhat seedy domain of philosophy.

In the *Selbstdarstellung* of 1924–1925, Freud said of even his most speculative writings, "I have assiduously avoided all approaches to philosophy proper [*die eigentliche Philosophie*]," adding that such avoidance was made easier for him by his "constitutional incapacity" for philosophy.[13] Three decades earlier, in his letter to Fließ of January 1, 1896, the claim was quite different: Freud congratulated his friend for having advanced through medicine to physiology by taking medicine as a kind of "detour," conceding that his own use of the medicinal detour would ultimately conduct him back to *his* "initial goal," which, he confessed, was *Philosophie*.

Constitutional incapacity or skillful navigation of the detour? Final destination or initial goal? Progress or regress? Innovation or restoration to an earlier state?

Later on in the *Selbstdarstellung* Freud makes another confession, perhaps a more ironic one: his speculations on society and religion, which served him as "yet another platform" (*eine weitere Bühne*) on which psychoanalysis could produce its kind of theater, represent a "regressive development" in him (98). At all events, whether backward or forward, something *is* coming to an end in the *Beyond*. Here the coming to an end of a detour would be not a return to the highroad of life but the specular arrival of something I have been calling *lifedeath*. An arrival that could only be *imminent*, that is, always merely on the verge of coming to presence, and *immanent*, ensconced in the innermost interior of a fortress-like crypt. There *is* something cryptic about the detour, something catachretic. In the published version of the Freud-Fließ correspondence a bizarre typo alters the word "detour," *Umweg*, to "impassable path," *Unweg*.[14] Fließ's deft way-around becomes a daft no-way. The printer might just as well have botched the whole thing and set the word *Holzweg*, meaning a timber track that leads nowhere, a *chemin qui ne mène nulle part*, or quite simply the word *weg!* Unless, of course, Freud really made no slip at all: perhaps he was trying to lead his friend, who like Heidegger was inclined to solar speculation, by the nose   *Noses are thinkable*   back to proper biological science and medicine. We would have to see the original letter in order to scrutinize the *m* of *Umweg* or the *n* of *Unweg*, on which the entire odyssey of psychoanalysis through medicine would depend. And even when we saw the extra stroke that makes of *n* an *m*, we still would not know whether it was a detour or a parapraxis.—But enough of this cryptic philological limping along: it is time for the speculative somersault, time once again for what Hegel called *der spekulative Satz*.   *For whom is the funhouse fun? Perhaps for lovers. For Ambrose it is* a place of fear and confusion.

In these final portions of a chapter on "lifedeath," I shall ask whether the principle of immanent death in chapters 5 and 6 of Freud's *Beyond the Pleasure Principle* is mirrored in Heidegger's existential-ontological interpretation of death in *Being and Time*. As obvious as the question is, there is some risk in it, as there is in any frontal collision. For just as Freud abjures philosophy, so Heidegger—as we recall from our discussion in chapters 1 and 2—demarcates existential analysis over against any psychological or biological speculation on death. To bring Freud and Heidegger together is to make a scene. Or two scenes. On the one hand, a Lacanian scene: the unconscious, structured as a λόγος, is both gathered and gathering to the overwhelming *truth* of being, to wit, unfulfillable *desire*.   *To say that Ambrose's and Peter's mother was* pretty *is to accomplish nothing; the reader may acknowledge the proposition, but his imagination is not engaged. Besides, Magda was also pretty, yet in an altogether different way.*   On the other hand, a Derridian scene: two cantankerous old grandfathers, *deux pépés*, two cranky schoolmasters and unpleasurable principals, PP x 2, cannot decide whether they want to be radical revolutionaries or postal authorities of the Pleasure Principle.   *You think you're yourself, but there are other persons in you. Ambrose gets hard when Ambrose doesn't want to,* and obversely. *Ambrose watches them disagree; Ambrose watches him watch. In the funhouse mirror-room you can't see yourself go on forever, because no matter how long you stand, your head gets in the way.*   "To make a scene" is in German *Theater machen*. It promises something of the theater, something of a Dionysian scene. Lacan would welcome it, would relish its cruelties. Derrida, for his part, would discourage our making a scene, even though he himself is a kind of maenad. He would discourage our making a scene, not because Freud and Heidegger have nothing to do with one another, in the way that Freud insisted on having nothing (or precious little) to do with Nietzsche, but precisely because, as they turn their backs on one another in a bootless *a tergo,* they have to do with one another more than with anything or anyone else. In "Spéculer—sur 'Freud,' " Derrida writes:

> Correspondence, here, between two who, according to the usual criteria, never read each other, much less met one another. Freud and Heidegger, Heidegger and Freud. We have embarked into a region where we navigate by this historic correspondence—and at bottom I am certain that these two "texts," indicated by these proper names but also, I am sure, overflowing them for reasons I am busying myself with here, are preoccupied with one another, spending all their time deciphering one another, coming to resemble one another, as one ends up resembling what one excludes or the deceased in absolute mourning. They could not read each other—therefore they have spent all their time and exhausted all their energies in doing so. Let that go. There are a thousand ways to settle accounts with Freud and Heidegger, between Freud and Heidegger. Not to worry, it happens by itself, without our taking the slightest initiative. (Cp, 379–80/357)

Derrida is right. Hence the rather obvious, flat, and frontal nature of these final remarks on immanent, imminent death, however tenuous and laborious they may be. And yet. Derrida's own "Spéculer" picks up with the words, "Everything remains to be done. . . ," so that my own question may be given the go-ahead, encouraged to make a little scene about death.   *We should be much farther along than we are; something has gone wrong; not much of this preliminary rambling seems relevant. Yet everyone begins in the same place; how is it that most go along without difficulty but a few lose their way?*

Let me begin with some Heideggerian theatrics, inasmuch as Freud's bobbin-on-a-string in the *fort/da* game at the beginning of *Beyond the Pleasure Principle* and his urbane invocation of Aristophanes at the end are so well known by now. Let me begin with a scene that Heidegger makes in his *Contributions to Philosophy,* which we examined in the preceding chapter for its paranoetic thinking of life in the cleavage or fissure of being. The years 1936–1938 themselves constitute part of a larger scene—Freud leaving Austria two months after the *Anschluß,* eight years after he is awarded the Goethe-Preis, and five after the first burning of his books in Berlin—but I shall restrict myself to the scene of Todtnauberg, "Dead Meadow Mountain," where Heidegger during the years 1936–1938 is spending more and more of his time.

Nobody likes a pedant.   This scene, the scene of the *Contributions,* has at first blush nothing to do with Freud and the question of the immanence of death in life. Yet it does have to do with war. A war of words. Polemic. As I argued in the foregoing chapter, one of the most interesting aspects of the *Contributions* is its juxtaposition of some of Heidegger's most inspired speculation—the "intimations" of beyng, the "futural ones," and "the last god"—alongside some of his most sardonic polemics. When we recall the strictures of *What Calls for Thinking?* (1951–1952) against polemic ("Every form of polemic fails from the outset to attain to the stature of thinking" [WhD? 49]), then the violence of the repetitious, compulsive polemics is anomalous, even astonishing. For two reasons. First, the most strident polemics are directed against *Lebensphilosophie,* even though (or precisely because), as we have seen, Heidegger's ontology of Dasein springs in some significant measure from the soil prepared by Dilthey, Bergson, Simmel, Scheler, and Nietzsche. Second, the energy exerted in such polemics (Freud would have spoken of their *Aufwand*) is so great that it seems somehow to propel and energize the most daring and delicate thoughts of the *Contributions*—the history of beyng as abandonment of beings, the cleaving of beyng, and beyng's finitude. Heidegger's *thinking* in this work of 1936–1938 I have called *paranoetic* thinking. Not paranoid thinking, to repeat, not Schreber's *Denkwürdigkeiten,* but something far more desperate than paranoid thinking: Heidegger's situation is more harrowing than Schreber's worst nightmares, inasmuch as Schreber at least knows where his God is, speculatively speaking. Not paranoid, but *paranoetic* thinking: no being can serve as its objective correlative, its tribunal of reason, or its ground. No *Seiendes,* and not even *Seyn,* which is a name for default, omission, nothing at all—the history of our epoch, for which even the name *nihilism* is nonessential. In paranoetic thinking, all names are lacking, every signature forged, no one is in charge, and every communication has to be signed by an other, p.p.'d.   *There's no point in going farther; this isn't getting anybody anywhere; they haven't even come to the funhouse yet. Ambrose is off the track, in some new or old part of the place that's not supposed to be used; he strayed into it by some one-in-a-million chance, like the time the roller-coaster car left the tracks in the nineteen-teens against all the laws of physics and sailed over the boardwalk in the dark. And they can't locate him because they don't know where to look.*

Late in the *Contributions,* Heidegger's polemic outdoes itself, producing a kind of theater (65, 347). Ironically, the polemic is directed against "theatrics" and "staging" (*Bühne*), and it has eminent (if overdetermined) political implications. For the gigantism (*das Riesenhafte*) of National Socialism is the national-aesthetic expression of that movement's machination (*Machenschaft*) and unbridled will-to-will. Such gigantism, which is all theatrics and staging, is all that is left of what Heidegger had recently been celebrating with such hard and heavy rhetoric as the grounding and founding of a state. A politics of gigantism and colossal theater—even though what is being discussed is the most speculative of Heidegger's themes, to wit, the way in which nonessence, dis-essencing, and decomposition (*Un-wesen, Ver-wesung*) plague the essential unfolding of truth (*die Wesung der Wahrheit*): "If truth unfolds essentially as the clearing of that which conceals itself, and if *nonessence* pertains to essence as a measure of the nullity of being, then would not the perversion of essence prate and prance [*sich breit machen*] in essential unfolding? Would it not do so precisely by distorting the clearing, dissimulating essence, driving distortion to the extreme by placing it at center-stage and in the limelight—all surface, all show? *Theatrics*—configuration of the actual as the task of the stage-manager!" (65, 347).

For Heidegger such theatrics—which wring yet another exclamation from him—are immanent in the theater of (un)truth. In the section of the *Contributions* called "The Grounding," truth and untruth are brought back to the being-unto-death of Dasein. We would be able to see this quite clearly if we worked through sections 201–202 of the *Contributions* (65, 323–25), on *Dasein* as *Wegsein*, being-there as being-gone. While Freud's grandson and Heidegger agree *mutatis mutandis* about the character of the *da*, what playful Ernst calls *fort* the more earnest Heidegger calls the emphatic and even imperative *weg!* Being-there is always already being-begone, being-bygone. Without regard, one might almost say, but say very softly, *pianissimo, pp,* to the presence or absence of the mother. Study of these sections of the *Contributions* and chapter 2 of the *Beyond* would link these remarks of mine on *Bühne* and paranoetic polemic to the proper theme of this chapter, if one can say so, the theme of the immanence and imminence of death as lifedeath. Let the suggestion serve as the deed. *So far there's been no real dialogue, very little sensory detail, and nothing in the way of a theme. And a long time has gone by already without anything happening; it makes a person wonder. We haven't even reached Ocean City yet: we will never get out of the funhouse.*

For Freud's speculation, no insight is more compelling than the immanence of death in life. For Heidegger, no insight is more compelling than the imminence of one's own death. Let me begin with Freud, rehearsing matters that are by now quite familiar.

The immanence of death in life: Freud is here profoundly influenced by the research and speculation of August Weismann, himself one of the most important sources for Eugen Korschelt, Professor of Anatomy and Zoology at the University of Marburg—that colleague of Heidegger's whom we met in chapter 2. A genealogy embracing Weismann and Korschelt would enable us to link Freud and Heidegger in a way heretofore unsuspected: the two grandfathers might indeed be brothers, at least as regards the idea of biologically immanent death. For all theoretical biology and life-philosophy of the late nineteenth century, as we have reiterated, no speculation is more unsettling than that involving the immanence of death in life. As Georg Simmel puts it, death is not the *Parzenschnitt*, not the thread of Atropos cut from above and outside the organism; death is not the extrinsic and contingent truncation of life introduced from the environment; death is not murder or being killed, *Getötetwerden;* rather, it is the culminating stage of organic development as such, life's essential unfolding, varying in its precise operation within each species yet always inherent in that species' life. The idea is so common today that it is difficult for us to experience its power in the way Simmel did when he exclaimed, "But this opposite of life derives from nowhere else than life itself! Life itself has produced it and includes it."[15] And let us not abandon Simmel before recalling once again how influential the idea of immanent death as imminent death must have been for the existential-ontological analysis of birth and death, of human being and *finite* time, in Heidegger. How much of the existential analysis is immanent in life-philosophy? Enough perhaps to explain Heidegger's polemic against it.

No sooner is the idea of immanent death born, however, than monstrous problems arise. If death is in some sense the τέλος of life, the essential unfolding of life as such, immanent in it and proper to it, then the very opposition of life and death becomes untenable, meaningless. One of the nagging doubts that Freud's 1895 "Project" had refused to confront   *He envisions a truly astonishing funhouse, incredibly complex yet utterly controlled from a great central switchboard like the console of a pipe organ*   was suggested by the very rubric of *die Not des Lebens,* the exigency of life considered as "primary process." Life emergent (but from what?) is in a perpetual state of emergency, "from the outset," inasmuch as the very means by which it secures its ascendancy constitute the gravest menace to it. Even in the "Project" that menace seems to come less from the outside, less from the penetration of the *Reizschutz* by unfiltered energy quanta than from the internal dynamics of system ψ, the dynamics of trauma, hallucination, and starvation. The system of life seems to be geared to autodestruct.

By 1920 and *Beyond the Pleasure Principle,* Freud is invoking "inner drives," *Triebe aus dem Innern,* as the most formidable challenge to Fechnerian constancy. Yet even here his speculation does not really push the question of absolute constancy as stasis and stasis as death—the question of lifedeath. When in chapter 5 of *Beyond* Freud defines the drive as an indigenous compulsion in the animate organism to restore a former state (3, 346: *ein dem belebten Organischen innewohnender Drang zur Wiederherstellung eines früheren Zustandes*), it is the intrinsic residence of the compulsion, *das Innewohnen,* the dwelling-within, *im-manēre,* that is most mysterious. It is what is cryptic as such. For it compels Freud's speculation, not *beyond* the PP, and not inside or outside it, but somewhere behind and beneath it. Exigent life is indigent, and death is indigenous to it. From the outset to the end.

No, Heidegger would interject at this point, not to the bitter end, inasmuch as death is interpretable only as a possibility of Dasein, and as a possibility it can only be *imminent.* Freud would rejoin by agreeing that the abstract notion of time, the punctilious time of the time-line in the tradition that stretches from Aristotle through Husserl, is derivative of consciousness and secondary process, that it therefore does not suffice for speculation on lifedeath from the "outset" to the "end." Freud, like Heidegger, dreams of a more profound temporality, born of periodicity and a kind of rhythm. However, Freud is uncertain as to whether Heidegger's notion of kairotic, appropriate temporality does not remain punctilious. Heidegger would reply that the kairotic is only a stepping-stone to the far side of *ecstatic* temporality, time as the ἐκστατικόν, but this sounds too oceanic to Freud's ear, and the two of them go back and forth on it interminably, full of mutual mistrust, as brothers often are. And well they should be, if they are speculators. In a temporal scheme such as Freud is dreaming of, which is itself rather oceanic if the truth be told, neither the PP nor the so-called death-drive (a pleonasm, inasmuch as Eros too, insofar at it *is* a drive, contains its imminent, immanent death), neither a PP nor a beyond-the-PP are punctuated and available as evidence. Immanence itself is displaced, and imminence postponed, derailed onto the verge of each dimension of time. What would speculation on the verge of lifedeath be like?

To be sure, the entire speculation—on the pleasure and reality principles, the priority of the lifeless (for Freud does not advance to the stream of Nietzschean ash), the detour to death as the proper (*eigenen*) path of a specific organism, on the subordination of the partial drives of self-preservation, power, and self-assertion to the immanent and ownmost possibility of return to the anorganic, and finally, the particularly unnerving speculation on the identity of the ambiguous "partial drives," which serve as both lifeguard and psychopath, bodyguard and hit-man, angel and executioner (*3, 249: "auch diese Lebenswächter sind ursprünglich Trabanten des Todes gewesen"*)—the entire speculation, I repeat, hangs on the supposition of immanence: *Wenn wir es als ausnahmslose Erfahrung annehmen dürfen, daß alles Lebende aus* inneren *Gründen stirbt.* . . . "If we may take it as an experience that admits of no exception that every living thing dies because of *inner* reasons. . . " (248). Never mind that this "inner," at least in the case of vertebrates, means no more than an invaginated exteriority, the spinal gray and the cortex of the brain being those *exterior* surfaces that house the deepest *interiority* of metaphysical man. Never mind, because it is precisely those inner reasons, the putative immanence of death, that Freud himself purports to doubt in chapter 6 of *Beyond:*

> We have constructed a range of conclusions on the basis of a presupposition that all living things must die due to inner causes. We accepted the supposition without concern because it did not seem to us to be a supposition. We are accustomed to thinking this way—our poets confirm this tendency of ours. Perhaps we are determined to believe this supposition because it harbors some consolation.

Allow me to interrupt in order to highlight two odd aspects of Freud's doubt. First, what biological science regards as a major advance in its conception of death, the immanence of decline and demise, Freud now identifies as a customary, familiar idea, an old saw that "the poets" have seduced us into believing. The final truth of Eros and the death-drives is indeed taken from the mouth of one of our oldest poets, and a comic poet at that, a comic poet figured by a very tricky philosopher writing a very tricky text. Second, we recall that when Heidegger develops the idea of the essential inherence in life of death, which he does in his lectures on theoretical biology in 1929–1930, he professes the idea *precisely because* it is an idea of poets rather than biologists. The immanence of death in life is an idea of poets—and worse than poets: we recall that Heidegger cites an epistle of Paul and the apocryphal Book of Esra from the Old Testament to corroborate his biological meditation.—But to continue the passage from the *Beyond:*

If one is oneself to die and to surrender to death those one loves most, then one would rather succumb to a merciless law of nature, to awesome 'Aνάγκη, than to a contingency one might have been able to avoid. However, this belief in the inner conformity to law [*die innere Gesetzmäßigkeit*] of dying is perhaps no more than one of the illusions we have created "in order to bear the burden of existence." (254)

To be sure, in order to lend credence to his own suspicion of notions implanted in us by *poets* "in order to bear the burden of existence," Freud here cites *Schiller*. When it comes to tricky writers, Freud does not stand behind Plato—except insofar as plato [*sic*] stands behind Socrates. Yet no one who has studied Heidegger's existential-ontological analysis should evade the devilish point Freud is making. The very necessity that drives Heidegger to insist on appropriateness, resolve, openness to one's own finitude, readiness to assume the burden of an existence that is suspended over an abyss of nullity—this very necessity Freud reduces to a comfort and a consolation, as though the very backbone of fundamental ontology were invaginated superficiality; as though it were no more than what Heidegger in section 62 of *Being and Time* calls "a factical ideal of existence," that is to say, an inherited idea about what existence *should* be, a received idea and ideal that covertly guides and thus distorts the entire analysis. Readiness for anxiety? Reticence and resolution? Guilt and conscience? *Echtes Scheitern?* Mere conjurings of a necessitous possibility fabricated in order to make the burden of contingency easier to bear. Hard and heavy armorplate in order to shield the soft underbelly of life.

I will not follow any farther Freud's diabolical and daimonic text, so overdetermined, so merciless in its exposure of other's illusions, so scrupulous *and* blasé about its own contradictions and castles in the air.   *I'll never be an author. It's been forever already, everybody's gone home, Ocean City's deserted, the ghost-crabs are tickling across the beach and down the littered cold streets. And the empty halls of clapboard hotels and abandoned funhouses.*   Allow me to return now to Heidegger's *Being and Time,* specifically to those pages that separate what Heidegger calls the preliminary sketch (*Vorzeichnung*) and the full concept (*voller Begriff*) of being-toward-death, discussed briefly in chapter 1. At the outset, as it were.

ΖΑΘΗΝΤΟΣ

I wish to make the transition by acknowledging my debt once again to Derrida's "Spéculer—sur 'Freud.' " Derrida's text derives from a seminar entitled "life death," *la vie la mort,* in which it becomes clear that there is no getting beyond the pleasure principle (PP) to something one might properly identify as a death-drive proper. In a text that functions "athetically," with no thesis but with countless "hypotheses," a text that proceeds by a singular drifting and diabolical limping, *er-hinken,*   *"What are you limping for?" Magda inquired of Ambrose. He supposed in a husky tone that his foot had gone to sleep in the car. . . . How long is this going to take?*   the very notion of propriety, along with the logics of opposition, contradiction, and dialectic disperse.

Derrida does not so much challenge the notion of the immanence of death in life—we have seen that Freud himself does that—as challenge the interiority to which immanence inevitably appeals. If the mirrorplay of speculation toys with the demonic in Freud's text, with the uncanny eternal return of the daimon, with the drivenness of drives and compulsive repetition as essentially demonic, with the hopping devil of Freud's *Beyond the Pleasure Principle* as a whole, it is because the demonic enjoins an uncanny doubling of all its doubles and institutes an illimitable specular haunting. "Life Death," "Eros Todestriebe," "Protector and Pallbearer," "quasi-immortality," "death-process"—these rubrics are less demonic than daimonic: they hover hermetically and hermeneutically in between all the identity poles, as Hermes, Dionysos, and Hades hover between heaven and earth, but also between earth and underworld.

When Derrida interprets the *fort* of the *fort/da* game as the emphatic *weg!* (be gone! be bygone! go bye-bye! bye!) he unwittingly underscores Heidegger's insistence in the *Contributions* (published nine years later than "Spéculer") that *Da-sein* is *Weg-sein*, and not simply by way of opposition, contradiction, dialectic, or paradox. However, the very propriety and identity that Freud's *Beyond the Pleasure Principle* undermines serves as the axis of Heidegger's fundamental ontology in *Being and Time*. If *Freud*'s text is daimonic, so too the δαιμόνιον to which Heidegger himself refers in his 1928 logic lectures will not leave intact the axis of appropriateness. For that axis is fixed in the slippery sockets of lifedeath. Discussing the detour that is self-preserving life, life maintaining itself by means of partial or component drives, Derrida worries about the "immanence" of the death that would be "proper" to a particular organism:

> The component drives [*Partialtriebe*] are *destined* to *ensure* that the organism dies *its own death*, that it follows its proper path toward death. That it arrives at death according to its proper pace (*eigenen Todesweg*). That all the possibilities of a return to the inorganic that would not be "immanent" in it are kept at a distance from it (*weg!* we might say, *fernzuhalten* he says). The nihilative pace [*pas*] must come to pass within it, from it to it, between it and itself. Thus the nonproper must be held at a distance, one must reappropriate oneself, one must cause to return (*da!*) unto one's death. One must send oneself the message of one's own death. . . . Not in order to keep oneself from death, or to maintain oneself against death, but only in order to avoid a death that would not revert to oneself, to cut off a death that would not be one's own or of one's own kind. In the detour of the pace, in the pace of the detour, the organism keeps itself from that other which might still steal its death from it. It keeps itself from the other that might give it the death that, by itself, it would not have given to itself (for this is a theory of suicide deferred, or suicide by correspondence). . . . The drive of the proper would be stronger than life *and* death. (Cp, 378–79/355–56)

Yet precisely this propriety—the drive of the proper—is undone in the Freudian text:

> . . . the most driven drive is the drive of the proper, in other words, the drive that tends to reappropriate itself. . . . The proper is the tendency to appropriate itself.

Whatever the combinatory of these tautologies or analytic statements, they can never be reduced to the form S *is* P. Each time, in the case of drive, force, movement, tendency, or τέλος, a division must be maintained. . . . Heterology is involved, and this is why there is force, and this is why there is legacy and scene of writing, distancing from the self and delegation, sending. The proper is not the proper, and if it appropriates itself it is because it disappropriates itself—properly, improperly. Life death are no longer opposed in it. (Cp, 379/356–57)

The very immanence of lifedeath undergoes interminable suspense, the indeterminacy of a death that can only be the event of an uncertain future, an imminent death. The death-drives *and* the PP operate by way of exappropriation; they belong to a domain that exceeds all oppositions and identities, "so that we no longer know precisely what we are saying when we say proper, law of the proper, economy, etc." (Cp, 419/393).

What must such exappropriation mean for a fundamental ontology that revolves about the appropriation of one's own (proper) being-toward-death? Even if one does not properly (!) move oneself proper. We recall that section 50, "Preliminary Sketch of the Existential-Ontological Structure of Death," elaborates three decisive traits of death as the possibility of the sheer impossibility of being-there. Death is the *ownmost* (eigenste) possibility of Dasein. In the very first trait we hear the root of *Eigentlichkeit*, appropriateness. If existence is in each case my own, the possibility of death must be more proper to me than anything else. My own death, as the ownmost possibility of my being in the world, bears no relation (*Bezug*) to any other existence; death is (second trait) *nonrelational* (unbezüglich). Ownmost, without relation, the death of Dasein is uttermost, outermost, *die äußerste Möglichkeit*. It cannot be surmounted or surpassed, cannot be overtaken or passed by; death is (third trait) *impassable* (unüberholbar). Uncanny—this impassable possibility that is driven by necessity. No wonder lucid analytical philosophers write articles and even books about Heidegger's obvious confusion of the Kantian modalities.

So much for the "preliminary sketch." Yet two more fundamental traits have to be added if we are to grasp the full existential concept of death. We remember that section 52 counterposes the "full existential concept" to the "everyday being toward the end." The discussion has to do with the very certainty (*Gewißheit*) of death. Precisely this certitude, as Freud indicated, comforts quotidian Dasein. "Death" becomes the pendant to "taxes." Heidegger's discussion of such equivocal certitude, conviction, taking-to-be-true, and even apodicticity of evidence serves as a repetition of section 44, on "truth," the truth of an existence that is always simultaneously in untruth. Nowhere does Heidegger's project veer so close to its Cartesian legacy; nowhere does it repudiate that legacy so decisively. For the *certitude* of death (fourth trait) has something peculiar (*eigentümlich*) about it (SZ, 258). No cogitation, no experience, no mental manipulation, no confrontation is equal to it. For the certainty of death is accompanied always by (fifth trait) "*indeterminacy* as to its when" (258). No, not merely accompanied. The fifth and final trait is not simply hooked onto the fourth, as the fourth is not merely appended to the first three.

Impassable indeterminacy is the crucial determination of all the traits, the order of which now changes. Heidegger writes in italics the following definition of "the full existential-ontological concept of *death*": "*Death, as the end of Dasein, is the ownmost, nonrelational, certain and as such indeterminate, impassable possibility of Dasein*" (258–59). The third trait, *Unüberholbarkeit*, shifts now to fifth and final position. Or perhaps to *fourth* and final position: are the traits of certitude and indeterminacy two or one? *Gewisse und als solche unbestimmte:* certain and, precisely as certain, indeterminate. One might object that indeterminacy as to the *when* of death does not render death as such indeterminate; however, the imminence of death, which as existential possibility is always still outstanding, renders problematic every form of immanence, including the immanence of death. The "peculiar" nature of death's certitude, the *Eigentümlichkeit* of indeterminacy as to its "when," displaces the propriety of precisely this most proper possibility.   *This can't go on much longer; it can go on forever.*   Heidegger will doubtless continue to insist on the reciprocal grounding of appropriate and inappropriate forms of existence. Yet the peculiar haunts the proper and undermines all the fundaments of fundamental ontology; the indeterminate imminent, which is a name for finite transcendence, τὸ δαιμόνιον, haunts all immanence. Existential certitude can never proceed as the firm footfall of confident interpretation. It can only limp along with its nihilative pace in the face of the overpowering, in the face of daimon lifedeath, Ζωήθάνατος; it can only be what Heidegger himself calls an excessive demand and an utter phantasm, *eine phantastische Zumutung.* The imp of the perverse is always at home in such certitude. Which is perhaps why even nowadays *Being and Time* is a difficult book to obliterate.

When immanence is displaced in ecstasis to an "outside itself" in-and-foritself (SZ, 329), what transpires? Let us speculate. Certitude seems to be held in suspension; it finds itself on the verge, where, in the end, naught nowhere was never reached. It is a little like wandering through the mirrormaze at an amusement park, very much like being "lost in the funhouse." That is the title of a short story or brief text by John Barth, and I have been reading it obsessively all the while I ought to have been pursuing pure speculation with Freud and Heidegger.   *He wonders: will he become a regular person? Something has gone wrong; his vaccination didn't take; at the Boy-Scout initiation campfire he only pretended to be deeply moved, as he pretends to this hour that it is not so bad after all in the funhouse, and that he has a little limp. How long will it last?*

Two paces more, if readers will allow. It is no surprise that Heidegger should lend himself to a speculation on the death-drives. Yet can the full existential conception of death in any way be immanent in or imminent to Eros? How can it be, when Heidegger maintains the most stubborn silence concerning that area which Socrates, "the purest thinker of the West" (WhD? 52), claimed to be his sole area of expertise—τὰ ἐρωτικά?

Heidegger seldom invokes the daimon Eros by name. We have already had occasion to recall very briefly his remarks on ἔρως and τὸ ἐρασμιώτατον, "the

superlatively rapturous," in the final hours of his first Nietzsche course, "The
Will to Power as Art," remarks made when the need for a new interpretation of
sensuousness becomes palpable. The scant references to ἔρως in the *Contributions to Philosophy* only serve to remind us that one must elaborate *another
history of being*, a history of being as φύσις and ζωή, running beneath the overt
history of λόγος and ἀλήθεια. According to that overt history, truth as
unconcealment is subjected to the yoke of ὁμοίωσις, *adaequatio*, and "correctness of representation." The untold, covert history would presumably involve
the yoking of ἔρως, φύσις, and ζωή under a regime of repression, asceticism,
and technism, in an economy of production, exchange, scarcity, and oppression.
With this other, more covert history of being as φύσις and ζωή, an excess that is
never isolated from ἔρως, Heidegger offers little help. As we shall see in chapter
8, the Trakl essay of 1953 never conjures daimonic Eros, whatever it may say
concerning the "discord of the sexes" and an envisaged return to a "gentler
childhood" and a "more confluent twofold." Where is there a spark of Eros in
Heidegger to which a death-drive could attach itself like a virus? Where in
Heidegger is there any hope of viral contamination by   *Noses are thinkable*   an Aristophanic sneeze?   *Naturally he didn't have enough
nerve to ask Magda to go through the funhouse with him. With incredible nerve
and to everyone's surprise he invited Magda, quietly and politely, to go through
the funhouse with him. "I warn you, I've never been through it before," he
added, laughing easily; "but I reckon we can manage somehow. The important
thing to remember, after all, is that it's meant to be a funhouse; that is, a place of
amusement. If people really got lost or injured or too badly frightened in it, the
owner'd go out of business. There'd even be lawsuits. No character in a work of
fiction can make a speech this long without interruption or acknowledgement
from the other characters."*

There is of course one place where Heidegger early on does discuss something like Eros. I mean the 1928 logic lectures, discussed in chapter 5, on τὸ
δαιμόνιον. In these lectures, we recall, Heidegger provides some guidelines for
his "preparatory analysis" of Dasein. It is an analysis, he says, not of human
beings but of *das Dasein*, a neutral and neuter-gendered phenomenon whose
name guards the peculiar neutrality and indifference of what otherwise would
be called *man*. As Derrida has emphasized, the very first thing toward which
Dasein is proclaimed indifferent and with respect to which Dasein is declared
essentially neutral is *Geschlecht*. Because Heidegger mentions "both *Geschlechter*," and because we assume that the sexes are two, and because this is a logic
class, we infer that Dasein is neutral and indifferent vis-à-vis sexuality. Such
neutrality is nothing negative, insists Heidegger, but, as we have also heard, is
"the original positivity and might of essence," *die ursprüngliche Positivität und
Mächtigkeit des Wesens*.   *No reader would put up with such prolix-
ity*.   If the daimonic drivenness of drives in Freud has to do with power,
mastery, or at least coping with a world that both spawns and menaces life,
then we may surmise that Heidegger's nascent "metaphysics of Dasein" has
indeed slipped into the speculative realm of Eros. That realm lies behind or

beneath the ego of any egoism or of any isolationist individualism. Its isolation is metaphysical. (In the logic lectures, incidentally, it seems as though an idea were being daimonically driven to its speculative uttermost, simply out of curiosity, in some uncanny isolation.) At the heart of this penisolate realm is the primal font, *der Urquell,* from which all factical concretion flows. Factical concretion? Existences like yours and mine, bodies concrescent, organisms assimilatory and erotized. (I am going too fast, I know, but it is a fast idea.) What are the dynamics of factical concretion? Factical concretion is—to speak an ancient language, a language Aristophanes knew and parodied—both condensation and rarefaction, both convergence and dispersion. Yet even if Heidegger is avowed the thinker of gathering (*Versammlung*), the two words he chooses in order to designate the dynamics of factical concretion are, as we recall, semination and dissemination, *Streuung* and *Zer-streuung,* literally, strewing and emphatic bestrewal or scattering. Strewing of what into what? That is hard to say. Emphatic bestrewal disseminates embodiment and thereby sexuality, which also enjoins a scattering or dispersal into space and into language, the language not of propositions but of prepositions. Emphatic bestrewal sounds like something negative, even if *dis-* (from δύο, δυσ-), one of the progeny of ζα-, means doubly or utterly, and is essentially positive. *Zerstreuung* is an unfolding of facets, hence an aggregation of sorts. Scattering, dispersion, and distraction devolve upon an original semination, *Zer-streuung* upon *Streuung* as such. Without even *whispering* the name *Aristophanes,*   *Italics should be used* sparingly   for that would cause *gastric upset,*   *Italics mine*   Heidegger writes: ". . . it is not a question of imagining some vast primal creature [*ein großes Urwesen*] that would have its simplicity split [*zerspaltet*] into many particulars . . ." (26, 173). Rather, strewing is original multiplication; it is that which allows multifaceted, manifold being; *Zer-streuung* is therefore the ultimate modality, the necessitous possibility of all actual possibles.

However, the dynamism that projects Dasein into a dual sexuality inaugurates the never-ending scene of the drive or drives that constitute the mating process (26, 175: *die gattungshafte Einigung*), which for Heidegger as for Hegel drags on into and as wretched infinity. The dynamism of a driven or strewn Dasein produces a scene—a polemical scene—in which the narrowing, compelling, obscuring, and obfuscating of *other* possibilities (the possibilities of the *other,* of the *other sex,* for example) is the rule. Heidegger wonders aloud why our being-with-one-another has to be "crowded close [*gedrängt*] into this particular factical direction in which other possibilities are left in the shadows or remain altogether closed [*abgeblendet werden oder verschlossen bleiben*]" (26, 175). Multiplication, even of one by two, yields dispersion. Assimilation or gathering yields disaggregation. Concentration yields distraction. *Streuung* yields *Zerstreuung.* The emphatic *Zer-* is daimonic, it is the ζα- of ζωή, the redoubled force of ζαθνητός, and it is unstoppable. It blasts every contact barrier and obliterates the stores of all cathexis; it restores the delirious reign of chaos and extravagant expenditure.

Streuung ought to have been predicated of life alone, and *Zerstreuung* uniquely of death. Yet Heidegger's putative dualism is as futile as Freud's. "From the outset," boasts Freud in chapter 6 of the *Beyond*, "our conception was a *dualistic* one, and today it is so more keenly [*schärfer*] than ever before." Freud's *Beyond* is full of "sharp distinctions," if only in order that Freud may take a swipe at Jung's libidinal "monism." Yet how bizarre Freud's sharp distinctions are, forever trying to balance an equation consisting of two unknowns, "life" and "death," presuming that they are two (3, 266). How full of bravura and *miserere* is his limping text: "We are coming under suspicion of having tried all the while at any price to escape from an embarrassment" (3, 263).   *A long time ago we should have passed the apex of Freitag's Triangle and made brief work of the* dénouement; *the plot doesn't rise by meaningful steps but winds upon itself, digresses, retreats, hesitates, sighs, collapses, expires.*   Earlier in chapter 6 he calls his conception of the life of drives (*Triebleben*) an "exquisitely dualistic conception" (258). *Exquisit dualistisch. Exquisit* means either "exceptional" and "profoundly thought-through" or "contrived," "belabored." It also means a painful examination, and refers to the excruciating pain of torture, as with the exquisite pain of the dentist's drill. Freud's speculation is *exquisitely* dualistic, barely able to withstand the pain of difference yet incapable of collapsing into supine monistic immanence. For the lifedeath of drives is as far beyond beings as beyng ever was, and the thinking that broaches it can only be exquisitely paranoetic.

Recall, finally, that for the Heidegger of the early Freiburg period, especially between the years 1919 and 1923, factical life is essentially ruinous, or as he says, *ruinant*. To resist such *Ruinanz* he posits a *Gegenruinanz*, a homologue to Freud's *Gegenbesetzung*, the effort by intensified investment to stem psychic trauma. Neither Freud nor Heidegger dreams of an effortless existence, not even for animals—regardless of what Heidegger says in the *Contributions* about their "ease." *Die Not des Lebens* is for both thinkers *die Notwendigkeit*, the exigency of life is the turning and turning of need, and the mysteries of primal repression and primary process are mysteries of being, whether one thinks being as ruinance, care, destitution, or calamity.

To be sure, the journalist in us is ready by way of *dénouement* to reduce both Heidegger and Freud to some determinate *Zeitgeist*, some nice niche in the pan-German Ideology. Some very nice ni(etzs)che? I wonder whether, once we have finished speculating on the two of them (Freud and Heidegger), or all three of them (Freud, Nietzsche, and Heidegger), as though *we* were the stage-managers of the world-historical *Bühne*, their crypts will gape once again and they will rise to haunt us with things we thought we knew and had under control by now, things still secret even after they have been utterly disclosed, things both homey and monstrous at once, things both within and without our ken, both canny and uncanny—in a word, a word beloved of Nietzsche, Freud, and Heidegger, things *unheimlich*. If death is immanent in life precisely because it is ever imminent, we will never feel at home with these three grandpapas who scarcely ever speak to one another, these three irascible heroes and daimons, these guardian angels and godfathers of lifedeath, these several grand pépés.   *He wishes he had never entered the funhouse. But he has. Then he wishes he were dead. But he's not. Therefore he will construct funhouses for others and be their secret operator—though he would rather be among the lovers for whom funhouses are designed.*

EIGHT

Something like Sexes, Something like Spirit

Heidegger and Derrida

> Goethe says: "It is not always necessary
> for the true to be embodied: enough if it
> hovers like a spirit [*geistig*] and produces
> accord; enough if it wafts through the
> air, earnest and amicable, like the sound
> of a bell."
>
> —Martin Heidegger, "Art and Space"

At various points in this meditation on daimon life we have been drawn to Derrida's discussions of *Geschlecht*—sex, race, tribe, and generation are some of its meanings—and *spirit*. How could the daimon not have to do with spirit? How could sexuality and generation not touch on life? Or something *like* the sexes and sexuality, something *like* spirit? Heidegger says in 1929 that he is searching for something like *being*. Yet on his quest for being he encounters   *the flesh of the gods in his body but despair in his heart* something like sexes, something like spirit.

Thus far we have seen four generations of Derrida's "Geschlecht," the third as yet unpublished; we also have the volume that interrupts the genetic transmission from the (unpublished) third to the (recently published) fourth generation. There is neither time nor space for a full-scale review or detailed reading of the five texts in question, four generations of *Geschlecht* and one generation *Of Spirit*, but it may advance our reflections on daimon life if we remind ourselves of Derrida's as yet uncompleted and as always inimitable itinerary.

FOUR GENERATIONS OF "GESCHLECHT"

The first generation of "Geschlecht," written in 1983, indicates something that is true of all five texts. All are "magnetized" (*aimanté*) by Heidegger's 1953 Trakl essay, "Language in the Poem: A Placement of Georg Trakl's Poem [*Die Sprache im Gedicht: Eine Erörterung von Georg Trakls Gedicht*]" (US, 35–

82). The other, "nearer" pole of the first-generation "Geschlecht" is Heidegger's 1928 logic course, especially those pages that rehearse a number of "guidelines" for the fundamental-ontological interpretation of Dasein, the pages we examined in chapters 5 and 7. Thus the entire *Geschlecht* series and *Of Spirit* traverse a kind a magnetic field between these two poles: *aimant* means both "magnet" or "lodestone" and "loving, affectionate." The distance traversed in Heidegger's career from "logic" to a "placement of poetry" is measured by the distance between a metaphysics of Dasein from which sexuality (though not potency and positive might of essence) is apparently extruded and a discourse on the poem of a *poète maudit*. It is also the immeasurable, unmeasurable distance traversed between ontological and sexual difference. Thus Heidegger's notorious "silence" in the face of the sexuality of Dasein—the accusation brought against *Being and Time* long ago by Jean-Paul Sartre and since then by scores of others—is actually a highly charged silence. It matters little whether an interpreter stands closer to the earlier or the later pole, whether he or she is an "existentialist" Heideggerian or a fellow poet and mystagogue of being and *Ereignis*. Derrida is of course neither, or at least no more one than the other, and any attempt to identify 1928 or 1953 as the pole to which the "Geschlecht" series is more powerfully drawn is bound to fail: the most remarkable aspect of the first-generation *Geschlecht* in particular is that it moves with apparent (which is to say, deceptive) effortlessness between metaphysics of Dasein and placement of poetry.

That ease of movement produces an extraordinarily generous reading of Heidegger's *Being and Time* and 1928 logic course. Derrida attributes to Heidegger, or wishes him, the thought of a "pre-differential, or, rather, pre-dual sexuality" (Ps, 402/72). That is to say, Derrida is willing to grant that Heidegger's banishing of sexuality and embodiment from ontology of Dasein may in fact be a purging of the uncritically accepted dualisms of male/female sexuality and spirit/body incarnation. Thus Derrida would see the "original positivity of essence" in sexuality being drawn toward what the later pole of the magnetic field calls the "unifold" or "simple twofold" (*die einfältige Zwiefalt*) of brother and sister in Trakl's poetry (US, 50). However, the generosity of Derrida's double reading entails an act of supreme self-cruelty: the very first generation of *Geschlecht* (the word and the thing, as Derrida likes to say) lends hostages to fortune, surrenders a *gage* that will engage his own future without limit; the very first generation demands of all the succeeding generations of *Geschlecht* that they approach brother and sister as major figures in Trakl's poetry as well as in Heidegger's placement of Trakl's "poem." Neither the complete line of Derridian *Geschlechter* thus far (I through IV) nor the book *Of Spirit* succeeds in sustaining such an approach. Brother and sister— whom Trakl also calls the lovers—in fact recede as the *Geschlecht* series progresses, and *Of Spirit* dallies, as is perhaps meet and just, with theologians rather than lovers or siblings. In other words, the generosity of the initial *Geschlecht*, which finds the "binary sexual mark" falling on *one* side of the difference (the nearer side, the safe side, the side of absolute duality), and which urges a meditation on sexual as well as ontological difference, almost inevitably sows the seeds of a waxing neglect in the generations to come. As Mrs. Jason Compson laments, "What have I done to have been given children like these. . . ."

On the less generous side of the double reading of *Being and Time* and the 1928 logic course we have Derrida's devastating demonstration in "Geschlecht I" of the futility of Heidegger's effort to protect ontological dissemination or bestrewal (*Streuung*) from ontic dispersion and distraction. As we noted in the "Introduction to Za-ology," the prefix *Zer-* does precisely what the root of ζωή (ζά) does: it intensifies rather than negates, so that dissemination embraces both fecundating and scattering, and bestrewal encompasses both sowing and squandering. In a more innocent age we would have said that these all have a common origin; now we would say that *Zer-streuung* lies back behind or is anterior to any origin, as a "nonorigin of origins." *Zer-streuung* is emphatic *Streuung*, redoubled bestrewal, the fecundity of essence, the *con-* of *concrescere* (*Konkretion* and *das Konkrete* are Heidegger's desiderata in the 1928 "guidelines"). However, bestrewal is also the dissipation and petering out of essence, the *con* of *con-taminatio, con-tangere*. How to think this *con*, or even pronounce it? Heidegger would always hear it as the *cum*, the together-with (*zu-sammen*) derived from the Gothic *sama* and the Greek ἅμα, which makes even solitary oneness (*ein-sam*) a gathering (*gemein-sam, Ver-samm-lung*) of community (US, 265). For Heidegger the *con* would always be evidence of the gathering of thinking and what-is-to-be-thought, even in its most irrecusable withdrawal. For his part, Derrida would stress the mutual touching and inter-penetration of concrescence and contamination. The *dis-* and *zer-* appear to escape Heidegger even as he employs them; or, rather, *he* appears to escape from *their* devastating consequences. Even Derrida himself hesitates and is reluctant to perform the operations of double reading on *Zer-streuung*. In "Geschlecht I" he announces that he "would hesitate" to attribute a "positive or affirmative sense" to the *dis-* and *zer-*. The present book is creating its own hostages   *You will never find that life for which you are looking*   to fortune and the future by refusing to hesitate.

Dis- and *zer-* are not comfortably housed in either fundamental ontology or poetics of being, nor even in deconstruction. They compel a thinking and a reading of the daimon. Daimon life is the *con* of both Heideggerian concres-cence and Derridian contamination. Beyond both, daimon life is the positive semination and scattering of origins in *dis-* and *zer-*, a scattering intimated by Hegel when he says that the stars are scattered across the night sky not in order to edify moralists but as an effect of cosmic leprosy. No absolute line of differentiation, no straightforward opposition, no confident affirmation or negation can undergird such reading and thinking. It takes more than two to *con-tango*, more than two to contaminate essences thoroughly, more than two to fecundate, more than two to leave the blissful or pious fecundities behind. Inasmuch as the mark of duality always falls on the one side, the safe and near side, it takes something beyond the positive/disparaging and affirmative/

negative oppositions, something beyond either hesitation or precipitate speed, something beyond the poles of every magnetism, something beyond childish aversion and adversion to read and think the daimon.

When toward the end of "Geschlecht I" Derrida returns to *Being and Time*, in order to expand the horizon of his problem from sexuality to *life* as such (Ps, 410–12/80–81), another kind of generosity in his reading strikes us. Indeed, the project in which I am engaged in this text, at this moment, is initiated precisely here (411/80), with Derrida's description of "this enormous problem" of the relation of Dasein to just-plain-life: it is important to jettison all talk of leaving behind and moving beyond, except insofar as one generation of "Geschlecht" succeeds upon another. Derrida's own sense of the "religious" and "ethical" dimension of the problem, which is closely allied with the *political* dimension, points him in the direction of the second-generation of *Geschlecht*.

"Heidegger's Hand (Geschlecht II)" adroitly demonstrates the heavyhand-edness of Heidegger's own need to reinforce the traditional humanistic and ontotheological distinction between animality and humanity. At the same time, it demonstrates the political clout of such an enforced distinction. The philo-sophical nationality and nationalism of the entire *Geschlecht* of German think-ers from Fichte through Heidegger, who define their Germanity so liberally as to embrace the entire right-thinking and right-speaking *Menschengeschlecht*, the race of mankind and all *humanitas*, become compellingly clear in the opening pages of "Heidegger's Hand" (Ps, 415–20/161–65). The rigorous opposition of such humanity to animality is of course not merely a Germanic obsession, although the German contempt for all things Latin and Mediterra-nean (such as *humanitas?*) inevitably complicates the story of the hand of man. Indeed, the hand of man becomes several kinds of monster (*montre, monstre*).

To be sure, the complicity of eye and hand in reading and writing has long fascinated the author of the *Grammatology* (see especially Part II, chapter 4, of that work). How the hand of man touches the matter of sexual desire or sexual difference, the theme of the first-generation *Geschlecht*, is not so readily dis-cernible, even though Derrida alludes to these themes here (Ps, 423/168). His masterful reading of the hand of man as opposed to the prehensile organ of the ape need not detain us: suffice it to say that the appendage we call the *hand* raises the question of the relation of human embodiment to the *handicraft* of thinking. One might be forgiven the awful pun if it could be shown how important it is for Heidegger that the fundamental sign (*signe*) of human-ity   *I found a sign and now I have lost it*   be kept at a distance from the ape (*singe*): for a *signe singe* would wreck the elevation of Heidegger's thought. Yet the very *hauteur* of his hyperhumanistic thinking is freighted with what Derrida calls an "empirico-dogmatic ἅπαξ λεγόμενον [i.e., a pronounce-ment made once and only once]" (428/173): the single, peremptory, and abso-lute oppositional limit between humanity and animality marked by the hand of Heidegger obviates the necessity of his marking multiple differences among living beings, as though that absolute oppositional limit did not appeal either to zoological findings or to the "common sense" that Heidegger would never own up to but by virtue of which he writes.

The hand, singular, is the unique sign of thinking-speaking man. Even when there are two hands in Heidegger they fold into one (*falten sich*) in a gesture that points to the great onefold (*Einfalt*). The allusion to the farther pole of the magnetic field is clear: instead of the *einfältige Zwiefalt* of sister and brother we have the folding of one pair of hands into simple oneness—as in the famous Dürer drawing. If I have a residual worry about the way *Of Spirit* ends, and I shall return to this, it is that the discussion among the theologians (who are so utterly fraternal, the Christian with the Messianic Jew, a single *Geschlecht*, it seems, so much so that one must wonder why it has not always worked this way) reinforces the very piety that always signs away the life of the animal—or of the other human being.[1]

There is no need to rehearse here Derrida's convincing reminders that Heidegger's singular hand, his writing hand, relies on the confidence of the proximity of hand, eye, ear, and throat, a proximity that bolsters all Western logocentrism and phonocentrism (437/181). The second hand of Derrida's text, that is to say, its second part,[2] returns to the questions of dispersion, duality, and sexuality raised by the first-generation *Geschlecht*. It is here (439/183) that Derrida also says something about "Geschlecht III," a typescript distributed to the participants at the conference during which "Geschlecht II" was presented. It is in the brief references to the third-generation *Geschlecht* and in that typescript itself that one feels the pull of Heidegger's 1953 Trakl text most strongly.

I will focus on only one trait of the second pole of that force-field called *Geschlecht*, the pole and pull of Heidegger's "Language in the Poem." It is the redoubled trait of *Zwiefalt, das Zwiefache, Zwietracht,* and *Zwist*: twofold, duality, discord, and altercation. Indeed, it is the crescendo of violence in these *Zwie-* words of Heidegger's Trakl text, commencing with a tender twosome and terminating in bitter logomachy, that captivates Derrida. Heidegger introduces the duality and duplicity in the following paragraph of his "placement":

> By what is this *Geschlecht* struck, that is, cursed? The Greek word for curse is πλήγη, the German word *Schlag*. The curse of the decomposing *Geschlecht* consists in the fact that this ancient *Geschlecht* has been dispersed in the discord of the *Geschlechter*. Within such discord each of the *Geschlechter* seeks the unchecked tumult of individualized and utter savagery. Not the twofold as such, but discord, is the curse. From the tumult of blind savagery, discord casts the *Geschlecht* into abscission and imprisons it in unchecked individuation. So ravaged, so severed in twain, the "fallen *Geschlecht*" can on its own no longer find its way into the right *Schlag*. It can find its way only as that *Geschlecht* whose twofold nature wanders forth out of discord into the gentleness of a confluent twofold. That *Geschlecht* is "foreign," and it follows the stranger. (US, 50)

Derrida comments as follows in his fifth and final note on the *Schlag* (stroke, blow, coup, coinage) that constitutes *Geschlecht*, the word and the thing, as though they were two:

What comes to *Geschlecht* as its decomposition (*Verwesung*), its corruption, is a *second blow* that comes to strike the sexual difference and to transform it into dissension, war, savage opposition. The primordial sexual difference is tender, gentle, peaceful; when that difference is struck down by a "curse" (*Fluch*, a word of Trakl taken up and interpreted by Heidegger), the duality or the duplicity of the two becomes unleashed and even bestial opposition. This schema, which I reduce here to its most summary expression, Heidegger claims, despite all the appearances and signs of which he is well aware, is neither Platonic nor Christian. This schema would come under neither metaphysical theology nor ecclesial theology. But the primordiality (pre-Platonic, pre-metaphysical, or pre-Christian) to which Heidegger recalls us and in which he situates the proper site of Trakl *has no other content and no other language* than that of Platonism and Christianity. This primordiality is simply that starting from which things like metaphysics and Christianity are possible and thinkable. But what constitutes their archi-matutinal origin and their ultra-Occidental horizon is nothing other than this hollow of a repetition, in the strongest and most unusual sense of this term. (Ps, 451/193)

Derrida's concluding objections to Heidegger's effort to rescue Trakl's poem from its Christian-Platonic matrix are the seedbed of both the *third*-generation *Geschlecht* and the book *Of Spirit*, the book that interrupts the line of transmission from the third to the fourth. It would be indiscreet to say much about the third, inasmuch as it is not only unpublished but also only partially transcribed. Indeed, Derrida emphasizes in the typescript that his third *Geschlecht* covers only a fragment of the itinerary that it has projected for itself. Nevertheless, "Geschlecht III" comes closest to attaining that *rhythm* of which Heidegger's Trakl essay itself speaks. Derrida follows Heidegger's lead in pursuit of the wave of the concealed locale that rises and falls, flows backward, and frustrates all forward, assertive saying. Before we follow Derrida following Heidegger in "Geschlecht III," we ought to take a moment to examine the most recent arrival of the *Geschlechter*, "Heidegger's Ear: Philopolemology (Geschlecht IV)."

"Geschlecht IV" meditates on friendship and discord in Heidegger's thought. It begins with an odd phrase from section 34 of *Being and Time*, ". . . as in hearing the voice of the friend that every Dasein carries with itself." Derrida is intrigued by the voice, the "carry" of the voice, and the undisclosed and uncontextualized "friend" behind the voice in Heidegger's text. Derrida's fourth *Geschlecht* moves in the direction of Heidegger's lectures on the early Greek thinkers, especially Heraclitus, and on the matters of thought identified by Heidegger as φιλεῖο and πόλεμος. Thus the subtitle of "Geschlecht IV," "Philopolemology." The main title (inasmuch as "Geschlecht IV" is but a parenthetical subsubtitle) reflects both Derrida's fascination with the voice of the friend in *Being and Time* and the lineage of "Geschlecht" itself: if "Geschlecht II" tries to grasp "Heidegger's Hand" *for this too is the lot of man* the fourth-generation *Geschlecht* listens in on "Heidegger's Ear."

Derrida notes the facelessness and sexlessness of Heidegger's aural friend, the otobiographical friend Dasein always carries with itself. He also relates (very briefly, very tenuously, in a passage we shall consider in a moment) the question of "friend" and "voice" with "the brother" and "the stranger" in Trakl's poetry. If Derrida neglects Trakl's "sister," it is probably because he is listening *with* Heidegger's ear, that is to say, with an ear perhaps too finely attuned to the Heideggerian discourse. Doubtless, the sister   *She is covered with a veil*   is neglected—in spite of the fact that the "carrying" of the friend, as *Austrag* and *Austragen,* involves a gesture of gestation, carrying-to-term, and giving birth, *Gebär(d)en.* Ultimately, it seems, Heidegger agrees with Aristotle: friendship is an affair of equals, an affair to which women and animals are not equal:

> ... there is friendship par excellence (*prote philia* or *teleia philia*) only between men: not between gods and men, not between animal and man, not between gods, not between animals. On this point, Heidegger would remain Aristotelian: *Dasein* alone has a friend, *Dasein* alone can carry it [the voice] *bei sich,* man alone as *Dasein* pricks up, opens, or lends an ear to the voice of the friend, since this voice is what permits *Dasein* to open itself to its own potentiality-for-being. The animal has no friend, man has no friendship properly so called for the animal. The animal that is "world poor," that has neither language nor experience of death, etc., the animal that has no hand, the animal that has no friend has no ear either, the ear capable of hearing and of carrying the friend, the ear that also opens *Dasein* to its own potentiality-for-being and that, as we'll hear in a moment, is the ear of being, the ear for being. (ms. 22)

Because the animal is poor in world and lacks an experience of the "as such," it is dismantled limb from limb like the unfortunate Lemuel Pitkin: no hand, no ear, no voice, no friend. Does the human animal   *like a hooked fish he lies stretched on the bed, like a gazelle that is caught in the noose*   whom Timaeus and all metaphysicians since define as *woman* undergo the same dismantling? (See "An Introduction to Za-ology," page 18, above.)

Derrida's most sustained comment on the apparent sexlessness of the friend and of friendship "as such" occurs in the second part of "Geschlecht IV." Here he discusses Heidegger's Heraclitus lectures of the 1940s and the 1955 lecture at Cerisy-la-Salle, *Qu'est-ce que la philosophie, Was ist das—die Philosophie?* At issue is Heidegger's treatment of φιλεῖο as putatively *prior to* both φιλία and ἔρως, φιλεῖο being taken as the bestowing or favoring (*die Gunst*) of being. Derrida rejoins the itinerary of the *Geschlecht* series when he remarks on the apparent sexlessness of Heideggerian fraternity and fraternizing:

> But in supposing a sort of pre-erotic moment of *philein,* does not Heidegger point to a kind of *Lieben* or loving [*aimance;* recall the *aimant* and *aimanté* of the entire *Geschlecht* series, as a "magnetized" itinerary] that would still fall not only short of *philia* and of the different types of friendship distinguished by Aristotle (according to virtue, political interest, or pleasure), but short of the distinguishing mark [*insigne*] and the enigmatic distinction between love and friendship, this last resembling perhaps in its canonic model, as I have tried to show elsewhere, the homo- or monosexual de-erotization or sublimation of fraternity, that is, of the virile duo.

Where then, in this respect, is the voice of the friend placed, the friend that each *Dasein bei sich trägt?* Is this voice pre-erotic or not? What can that mean? What about its *Geschlecht* and its relation to fraternity? (ms. 66)

The implications of such sublimated fraternity   *when Enkidu whom I love is dust*   for Heidegger's work as a whole radiate outward in every direction. Derrida points back to Heidegger's *Being and Time* in the following telling remark: "If *Sein und Zeit* were the book of the friend, it would also be the most and the least erotic book given us to read in this century" (ms. 68). The same might be said of the 1953 Trakl essay, to which Derrida has already turned "in another place," as he loves to write, the site of the *third* "Geschlecht."

Perhaps we can regress now to "Geschlecht III" if only because, being unpublished, it may turn out to be more laden with future than its published posterity. In "Geschlecht III," Derrida tries to follow Heidegger's odd rhythm, follow it in the way that Heidegger claims to be following the stranger, the brother, and the sister in Trakl's poem. At the same time, Derrida multiplies the precautions any listener, interpreter, or interloper must take: adrift between poetizing and thinking, commentary and placement, one scarcely knows which way to move, hardly knows what to say or to write about the farther pole of the magnetic field. Perhaps it is fair to say that the third-generation *Geschlecht* gets caught up if not wholly entangled in what others would call the "hermeneutics" of *Dichten und Denken.* For even though a reciprocity appears to govern the two pairs, poetizing/thinking and commentary/placement, the fundamental or foundational character of *Erörterung* or placement (as opposed to *Erläuterung,* commentary, *explication de texte*) betrays the privileging of what Heidegger the thinker—in all modesty, with all the rhetoric of the "merely provisional" and "preparatory"—is himself writing. In his "Conversation with a Japanese" (US, 121), the personage called the "Questioner," the most humble and diffident of the three personae, the one who rules the text with an iron hand in the velvet glove of *Gelassenheit,* speaks of a process in which "commentary can pass over into placement." The Questioner thus indicates the order of implication that elevates placement over commentary: anyone and everyone comments—such is the democracy of literary criticism—whereas thinking *places.*

The third-generation *Geschlecht* scarcely proceeds beyond the first three pages of Heidegger's placement, its preamble, as it were. Not that the preamble is unimportant. Here, for example, Heidegger defines the place of placement (*Ort/Erörterung*) in terms of its "original sense." The "original meaning" of *Ort* is "tip of the spear" (US, 37). Heidegger does not pause long enough to allow any other discourse to intervene, and certainly not the discourse of psychoanalysis, which he resists with a resistance that would have pleased and intrigued Freud. If Heidegger himself walks blithely over the abyss of the unconscious when he cites the "original meaning" of *Ort* as "speartip," over both the spear and the abyss of psychoanalytic thinking; that is to say, if

Heidegger unconcernedly strides beyond the edge of the cliff like a cartoon character who will plunge only when he looks down; then Derrida himself fails to take the plunge. He gets lost in the issue of the *Zwie-gespräch* or dialogue of thinking and poetry, without falling into the abyssal *Zwie-falt* of the hymen and the *Zwie-tracht* of the sexes that he, Derrida, more than anyone else has taught us to heed. No doubt the *rhythm* of Heidegger's placement is terribly important: our reflection on the daimon could well take rhythm as one of the final signs of life in Heidegger's thought.[3] Yet the itinerary of "Geschlecht III" does not take Derrida to Heidegger's unaccountable encounter with the stranger, the brother, and the sister, at least not yet, and this is unfortunate. The first three pages of Heidegger's text do not decide everything.

There remain questions of downgoing (*Untergang*) and apartness (*Abgeschiedenheit*), questions of the solitary *Geschlecht* that Heidegger sees on the horizon of the decomposing race. There remain questions concerning the mortality and animality of the new *Geschlecht,* which is said to be no longer a stranger on earth, questions about Heidegger's evident desire to domesticate the new race of *ek-sistent* humanity, to make retroactive the curse, blow, plague, and wound (*plaie*) that he designates with the Greek word πλήγη. Whatever it is, and whatever strewing or bestrewal caused it, the πλήγη transforms the twofold of sexuality into tumultuous struggle and discord. Derrida begins to engage these questions about two-thirds of the way through his "Geschlecht III" with a discussion of the foreign, of strangeness and the stranger. However, the engagement both here and in *Of Spirit* is, as we shall see, truncated by Derrida's effort to challenge Heidegger's "dechristianizing" of Trakl. One cannot deny the importance of Derrida's objections; yet one must be troubled by what his strategic decision bypasses. It passes on by something or someone that is most important to Trakl, something or someone whose burning significance even Heidegger perceives—which is why his 1953 Trakl essay magnetizes in the first place. That the Heideggerian discourse of finitude and downgoing is pitted with traps and snares is doubtless true; yet it is every bit as true that Trakl's figures of the stranger, the brother, and the sister draw Heidegger in their wake—*in Ruh und Schweigen unter,* "downward to stillness and silence." Derrida, himself the thinker of thanatography, resists the downgoing of Trakl's poetry in the direction of sister, lover, defunct brother, and moribund father. One might say that he resists the *teeth* of Trakl's poem, that he circumvents the wooded site toward which Trakl's wolves are loping and the secluded corner to which Trakl's rats are scurrying; in such avoidance and circumvention Derrida's reading is either still too close to or always too remote from Heidegger's own reading of Trakl.[4]

That said, the final pages of "Geschlecht III" demonstrate that Heidegger's reading of "azure game," the blue deer that haunts the forest rim, suppresses any possible residual bestiality, brutishness, or animality in Trakl's figure. *Heidegger's* animal is gathered in cerulean holiness (US, 44–45), a holiness which for its part seems to have less to do with the overpowering or daimonic than with the providential sending of being. Its blue grows lovelier line by line in Heidegger's text, ever more gentle, powdery, serene; in a word, ever more *denkerisch.* As its blue lightens in hue, becoming more faintly pastel tranquilizing effect *(as with blue)* than any creature in Gauguin or *les fauves,* the relation of its animality to decomposition and dis-essencing (*Verwesung*) is left to hover in obscurity. Indeed, Heidegger seems to take decomposition to be a property of the *bygone* coinage of humanity, as though the new *Geschlecht,* in its fidelity to the earth, could slough off its essential dis-essencing, its *Ver-wesung,* and as though Heidegger's *Contributions* had not insisted that the new *Geschlecht* of Da-sein is Weg-sein. As the new Heideggerian race rises from the ashes of Platonism, its banner bears the ouranian color of the ancient *Geschlecht* it is said to have replaced.

Yet no sooner does Derrida announce the theme of brother and sister, the theme of the "more tender" sexual difference, than he also announces his own remorse over the need to hasten to a conclusion. Remorse is doubtless necessary, inasmuch as Heidegger's text (especially after its "preamble") becomes problematic in a way that no discussion of "placement *vs.* commentary" could ever have anticipated. Derrida's "Geschlecht III," at its *chute* or *envoi,* focuses all too briefly on the following lines from Trakl's *Herbstseele,* "Autumnal Soul":

> *Bald entgleitet Fisch und Wild.*
> *Blaue Seele, dunkles Wandern*
> *Schied uns bald von Lieben, Andern.*
> *Abend wechselt Sinn und Bild.*
>
> Soon slip away fish and game.
> Azure soul, dark wandering
> Soon parted us from dear ones, others.
> Evening alters sense and image.

Heidegger comments: "The wanderers, who follow the stranger, quickly find themselves separated from 'dear ones,' who are 'others' for them. The others—that is the coinage of the decomposed figure of man [*der Schlag der verwesten Gestalt des Menschen*]" (US, 49). Derrida marks Heidegger's hasty identification of the loved ones, the others, with the decomposed, notes it but hesitates to elaborate on it. Yet why does Heidegger refrain from asking why Trakl calls the "others," from whom wandering separated "us," *Lieben,* loved ones, or those who are "dear to us"? Why does Heidegger neglect to say a word about the loved ones whom he has so hastily identified with the corrupt? Is he so certain that "the others" are now *unloved,* that a brave new *Geschlecht* is about to abandon them to indifference? Further, is the possible gender difference of the "others" preserved in any way in Heidegger's reading of Trakl? Or does that reading prefer to abandon the horizontality of lovers, of the "incestuous" brother and sister, for a vertical-historial reading? Does it prefer that a uniform *Geschlecht* supplant the decomposed form of a sexually riven humanity?

Derrida's "Geschlecht III" breaks off at the point where the second major division of Heidegger's placement begins. That is to say, it treats only the preamble and first part of Heidegger's fourfold text. I would like to gesture toward three passages in the *second* part of Heidegger's placement that deserve a place in Derrida's itinerary, which has never been fixed and booked in advance. Neither the final chapters of *De l'esprit* nor "Geschlecht IV" touch on these passages. I present them here along with a few questions, looking forward to a *fifth*-generation *Geschlecht* that might rejoin the closing questions of the *third*.

First, Heidegger refers to the more tranquil childhood of Elis, the departed youth. Such a childhood ostensibly "shelters and safeguards in itself the gentle twofold of the sexes, of the youth as well as 'the golden figure of the girl [*Jünglingin*]' " (US, 55). The more tranquil childhood that promises something like simplicity, something like brother and sister without a seam or pleat or fold to divide them—is it not the dream of a uniformity (*Einfalt*), of unending latency, that cannot bear the inevitable, impending disruption? Is it not the dream of Caddy's brother Quentin, who can only gnash his teeth when confronted with her first lover: "Not that blackguard, Caddy." Does not the dream of infinite latency, of a *Nachträglichkeit* instituted absolutely and thereby postponed forever, desperately try to suppress the mark or re-mark of sexual difference? Does it not try to replace the horizontality of the difference and of differences with a narrative of vertical creatures who rise to fulfill the heroic and historic destiny   *He went on a long journey, was weary, worn out with labor, and returning he engraved on a stone the whole story*   of generations that assemble heart by heart and man by man in order to rescue "man" and the "human essence," though not the sister, and never woman, who always moves on, who always shifts her ground?

Second, Heidegger refers to the "flame of spirit" that "gathers in apartness" (US, 66–67). It is the selfsame flame that obsesses Derrida in *Of Spirit*. Yet here Heidegger himself brings the thought of spirit as flame to bear on the thought or dream of a more tranquil childhood for brother and sister. The flame of spirit, as gathering,

> conducts the essence of the mortals back into their more tranquil childhood, sheltering it there as the coinage that has not yet been struck, the coinage that will stamp the coming generation. The gathering of apartness safeguards the unborn child from what has already withered away, conducting the child toward a resurrection of the human coinage, a resurrection advening from the dawn. The gathering, as the spirit of the gentle, at the same time soothes [*stillt*] the spirit of evil. The tumult of evil surges to utmost malignancy whenever it escapes from the domain of discord between the sexes [*Geschlechter*] and penetrates the realm of fraternity and sorority [*das Geschwisterliche*]. (US, 66–67)

To be sure, each *Schlag* ("coinage") and each *Geschlecht* (the word and the thing) in the above passage needs to be translated multifariously, not merely as "generation" or "sex" as the proximate sense dictates. There is still something to be said for a reading of discord between the *Geschlechter* that hears in that word not "the sexes" but the European nations of 1914–1918, attending the

discordant feast of their own immolation.⁵ That said, the questions too multi-
ply themselves. The tranquillity of a pristine Greek childhood for mankind, the
dawn behind the long day that declines into the land of evening (Occident,
Poniente, Abendland), promises a future "resurrection," as in William Butler
Yeats's play of that name, yet without the play's ironies and confusions of
identity. Yet why does the flame of spirit soothe or suckle (for *stillen* is "to
nurse") the spirit of evil? And to what end? Why is the epitome of evil said to
be the penetration of a discord hitherto restricted to the *Geschlechter* into the
otherwise peaceable *Geschwisterliche,* the irruption of sexual discord into the
children's corner, into the realm of the siblings, the "sisterly," the domain of
sister and brother alike? Is the *geschwisterliche Zwiefalt* to which Heidegger
refers in the following lines of his placement the twofold of the *first blow* of the
double set?—recall, "Not the twofold as such, but discord, is the curse." Does
the *second blow* (the curse, the plague, the wound of discord), that is to say,
duplicity proper, occur not only when latency ends and the struggle between
the sexes in general begins but also and especially when discord erupts between
brother and sister? Is *incest* the utmost evil, evil redoubled, evil most furious
(ζάπυρος), the malignancy to end all malevolence? Is the horizon and horizontality of brother and sister, the dear ones, for that reason to be abandoned, and
the avatars of the accursed race left to decompose   *and will not rise
again*   and disappear forever? However, if exogamy and prohibition of
incest characterize the very figure of humanity as it has heretofore constituted
itself, the very coinage of humanity that is said to have decomposed by now,
why the *revenant* or specter of incest? Or, contrariwise, if one were to transport
precisely the definition of consummate evil (as incest) from the former race to
the future one, would not the seed of contamination, "from the dawn," wreck
the millennial dreams of the ostensibly new human coinage? Would not any
future coinage of humankind have to confront the ineluctable necessity (*Weg!*)
of its decomposition and dis-essencing? Or, to put the question in a somewhat
more decisive form: Is it incest or incest-prohibition that is a forgetting of
being? How can Heidegger be so certain that it is the first? Or, as metaphysics
would ask the question, What is πλήγη? And how many are its strokes?

Third, Heidegger writes of the "friend" who becomes a brother to the
stranger who sings the "Song of the Departed" (US, 69–70). The stranger's
new brother   *because of my brother I stray through the wilderness*
thus becomes a brother to the stranger's *sister,* precisely through his nascent
fraternity with the brother. *Der Bruder des Fremdlings [wird] durch diesen erst
zum Bruder seiner Schwester.* . . . The fraternity of brothers is assured by the
stranger's invitation to join a conversation, and by the friend's seeing and
overhearing the stranger (*Einladung zum Gespräch, Anschauen, Nachlau-
schen*). Yet the new affiliation with the *sister,* the new fraternity with her
sorority, Heidegger leaves altogether without description or explanation. Except to say that the wanderer will become a brother to his future brother's
sister, or to *his own* sister (for the word *seiner* is ambiguous), only through the
medium of fraternity, that is, only (*erst*) through some sort of compact between

friend and stranger. It is as though the wanderer gains a sister by marrying a brother-in-law. Except that here the sister's womanly qualities and possibilities, whatever they may be and however they may "crowd close," are precisely what seem to be excluded from sorority.

How would such exclusion compare with Creon's execution of Antigone on the brink of her adolescence? Or with the symposiasts' banishment of the young women who play the flute? Or with Hegel's ostracism of *Venus vaga*, the undomesticated woman he sees lurking in the figure of Schlegel's *Lucinde*, the vagabond woman, the gypsy, who threatens all civil society? Clearly, Heidegger's sister has little in common with Lucinde, and is much closer to Hegel's Antigone, albeit much younger and far less strident. Yet how far removed all these figures are from Trakl's lunar sister! Precisely how does Heidegger's wanderer, the one who follows the stranger, become a belated brother to the sister, a brother to the one who speaks with the voice of the moon? Is there any hint at all in Heidegger's text about whether one can eavesdrop on such a voice or solicit its invitation to a conversation—whatever such a conversation might be about? Is there any hint concerning what it means when brother-and-sister-to-be look at and intuit (*anschauen*) one another in their vertical postures? Or does such overhearing and talking and looking always occur *durch diesen erst,* only through the medium of the brother?

To be sure, Heidegger himself broaches none of these questions—to which his "placement" nonetheless brings us. No questions could be more relevant to the itinerary of Derrida's *Geschlecht,* at least insofar as that genealogical line commences with "Geschlecht I." And yet neither Heidegger nor Derrida pose them with any persistence. "Response: later," writes Derrida, laconically. (With an "o.") Later than the third and fourth generations of "Geschlecht," later also than *Of Spirit.* To which we shall soon turn. Not forgetting remorse. For it is insufficient to distinguish between the two strokes, the "friendly" or "neutral" stroke that is as neutral as the primal *Streuung* that disseminates Dasein into embodiment and sexuality, the neutral blow that coins the gentle twofold of brother and sister, and the "accursed" stroke that is as plaguey as the dispersion and distraction (*Zerstreuung*) that follow hard on the heels of every dissemination, the "accursed" blow that instigates the discord of the *Geschlechter.* Perhaps there are not two strokes at all, but only one, precisely as there is but one temporality. Schelling, for example, whom we shall discuss in chapter 9, interprets human corporeality as the outcome of a single stroke, a single "eternal deed"; man and woman are created *in Einem magischen Schlag,* "in one magical stroke [or coinage]." That one stroke is more original than any oppositional thinking can ponder, including the oppositional thought of good and evil. Schelling recognizes that the *indifference* of that single blow puts him in touch with the daimonic, with the body of his God, and like Goethe he is afraid.[6]

Derrida is no doubt right to perceive Heidegger's own repressed or suppressed Christianity and Platonism in the πλήγη of the *second* stroke, the accursed stroke of evil that ostensibly sets brother and sister on the rocky road of sexual struggle and discord. Far from removing Trakl's poem from the Platonic-Christian context and tradition, Heidegger's need for and insistence on *two* strokes locks the poem in that tradition. Yet Derrida's own "Geschlecht" series does not do nearly enough to expose the limitations and the double binds of the redoubled strokes and blows of Heideggerian sexuality. Does the interruption called *Of Spirit* improve the chances of such exposure and questioning? Does *Of Spirit* put the questions that need to be put—or at least "placed"?

ONE GENERATION OF "SPIRIT"

Of *spirit?* Spirit and *Heidegger?* What is this apparent confusion of Heidegger with Hegel? Derrida's *Of Spirit* shows ten sections. It spans Heidegger's *Being and Time* and the same Trakl essay of 1953, "Language in the Poem." Its major way-stations include the rectoral address of 1933 and the *Introduction to Metaphysics* of 1935. Yet Derrida also manages to draw Heidegger's Nietzsche, Hölderlin, and Schelling interpretations into his account and to touch on scores of other themes and figures in the Heideggerian text. I shall begin with a brief account of the book's gestation, then report on its ten sections, posing a number of questions along the way, especially concerning the final turns the book takes in the direction of Georg Trakl.

Of Spirit is *not* a member of the *Geschlecht* series, even though the word and thing called *Geschlecht* in Trakl's poetry is the pole to which the book as a whole is drawn. It is the text of a lecture delivered in March of 1987 at a colloquium organized by the Collège International de Philosophie under the title "Heidegger: Open Questions." A private seminar at Yale and a talk at the University of Essex colloquium, "Reading Heidegger,"[7] in the Spring of 1986 were significant stages in the preparation of the book. These in turn arose from work done in seminars during the past several years at the École des Hautes Études en Sciences Sociales on "Philosophical Nationality and Nationalism." No doubt the four principal "threads" of *De l'esprit* (A. The question of the *question* in Heidegger's texts; B. The contamination of all essences, such as the "essence" of technology; C. Animality and the philosophy of life; D. The problem of the "epochality" of being) are visible in earlier works of Derrida's, such as the various *Geschlecht* papers, "Envoi,"[8] "The *Retrait* of Metaphor,"[9] and *Spurs: Nietzsche's Styles.*[10] These texts, culminating at least in part in *Of Spirit*, complicate and deepen Derrida's earlier work on Heidegger, best known through the articles, "The Ends of Man" and "Ousia and Gramme" (Ma, 129–64/109–36; 31–78/29–67). Yet in none of these earlier texts, nor even in the talks immediately preceding *Of Spirit*, is there evidence of the spirit that is haunting Derrida. For that one would have to turn to *Glas, The Post Card,* and the recently published works, *Mémoires: For Paul de Man, Schibboleth: For Paul Celan, Ulysse gramophone, Parages,* and *Feu la Cendre.*[11] Yet I shall here restrict myself to a brief introduction to *Of Spirit*, with its four threads and ten sections. Although the third thread, on animality and life-philosophy, is most

germane to the present undertaking, all four threads remain relevant to it—
they are indeed knotted together in a daimonic knot.

(1) "Spirit" is a word Heidegger advises the fundamental ontologist to
avoid. It is one of those words like *subject, person, rational animal, consciousness,* and *ego* that most needs deconstruction. In *Being and Time* he often
places the word "spirit" in quotation marks, as though mentioning it without
using it; these "scare-quotes" and other means of avoiding a word (crossing
through, erasing, employing the subjunctive mood, and so on) preoccupy Derrida throughout his text. In choosing the title *De l'esprit,* he is emphasizing
another kind of avoidance—or at all events another sort of lack or dis-
symmetry. The title is unmistakably French, and not merely because the word
esprit belongs to the French language. The treatise form *De...* (cf. *Traité
de...,*) conjures the French scholarly and essayist traditions of the Classical
Age; *De l'esprit* is the title of a book by Helvétius burned (the book, not the
author, not quite) on the steps of the Palais de Justice in 1759. The formula is
ultimately Ciceronian, hence utterly *Latinate,* so that the gap between *spiritus*
and *Geist*—the entire problem of translation—opens at the center of the book.
To be sure, the apparently academic and scholarly problem of translation is
saturated with prejudices involving nationalities and national languages and
cultures, principally the Latin-Romance-Mediterranean as opposed to or opposed by the Hyperborean-Nordic-Deutsch. *Of Spirit* is a *political* book
through and through, even though readers hoping for easy answers to hasty
questions are inevitably disappointed by it.

(2) Derrida makes his contribution to the colloquium on "open questions"
concerning Heidegger his own *hesitations* or points of indecision in reading
Heidegger—"moments of gravest perplexity" (De, 21/7). He asks how the four
threads of hesitation (to repeat: the question, essence, animality, and epochality) can be tied in a knot; he hypothesizes that the word *Geist,* a word
largely *avoided* in the Heideggerian text, may serve as that node. For *Geist* is
there wherever many are gathered (*versammelt*) by and into the unifying One.
Not only for Hegel, but also for Heidegger—so that it is not a case of Derrida's
merely confusing these two thinkers. Herewith an initial presentation of the
four threads:
(A) Questioning is the piety of thinking, says Heidegger at the end of "The
Question Concerning Technology" (VA, 44; BW, 317). In *Being and Time* he
had identified Dasein as the exemplary interrogating-interrogated being, so
that the questioning of being—and not some property of spirit—served as the
appropriate starting-point for an analysis of human being. It was not until very
late in the day (see "The Essence of Language," 1958 [US, 157–216]) that
Heidegger challenged the supreme dignity of the question by asserting the
preeminence of the address and assent of and to language (*Zuspruch, Zusage*),
language prior to all explicit questioning. (The long note dedicated to Françoise Dastur, in section 9 of the book, is essential in this respect, and we shall

have to pay special attention to it below). Here is the site on which Derrida joins Heidegger's efforts in thinking with greatest sympathy and engagement, reflecting on the *promise* that the call of thinking and language enjoins. For Derrida, that promise is a double affirmation, perhaps more in Blanchot's than in Deleuze's sense, a "yes, yes" that somehow *engages* questioning. As the subtitle of *De l'esprit* betrays, this first guiding thread is also the most persistent in Derrida's text. "Thus I shall try to show," writes Derrida (De, 25–26/ 10), "that *Geist* is perhaps the name that Heidegger gives, beyond every other name, to this unquestioned possibility of the question."

(B) The *essence* of technology is nothing technical, says Heidegger in that same essay. A recurrent strategem of his, one that would preserve the realm of essences (in the science of ontology as well as in poetizing thinking) from the merely contingent, the ontic, the prosaic. Similarly, at a certain point in his trajectory, in the early-to-mid-1930s, Heidegger is keen to rescue *Geist* from a certain destitution, disenfranchisement, and decrepitude, *Entmachtung*. He will try to rescue it by force of an "essential will" or "will to essence," *Wesen-wille*. Derrida even sees that same desire to preserve spirit from "disessence" or decomposition, *Verwesung*, at work in the 1953 Trakl essay.

(C) The discourse on animality in which Heidegger participates but which he by no means masters is perhaps the second most visible thread in *Of Spirit*. How could it be otherwise, if "spirit" is traditionally defined in opposition to nature, materiality, and bestiality; and if, as "On the Essence and Concept of φύσις" indicates, *Geist* is aligned with "grace," the "supernatural," "art," and "history"?[12] However much the animality of "mere life" appears to be excluded from the purview of fundamental ontology; however much life too appears to be a matter that necessitates avoidance (precisely because life is neither Dasein nor what is handy nor the at-hand); animality remains a problem that returns again and again to haunt Heidegger's thought, haunt it to the point where the ontological difference itself is made to tremble. Even in later texts such as *What Calls for Thinking?* Heidegger's discourse on man and animality surrenders to a rhetoric so "peremptory and authoritarian" that it appears to be "dissimulation in the face of an impasse" (De, 28/11). That impasse—reminiscent of Freud's "embarrassment" in the *Beyond*—becomes most visible in the 1929–1930 lectures on "The Fundamental Concepts of Metaphysics," which occupied us in chapter 3, above, in which Heidegger tries to compare the world-relations of stone, animal, and Dasein. If the stone is worldless, and humanity world-shaping, animality is both *with* and *without* world—animality is "poor in world." Such "world poverty" is no doubt related to the animal's lack of essential "technique," which is a lack of "know-how," bound up with its inability to pose questions: thus the first three threads begin to twist and knot themselves, as it were; inasmuch as they have always done so in our history, viewed as the history of being, they point to the fourth and final thread.

(D) The epochality of Heidegger's history of being preserves traces of a certain teleological thinking, especially in what it "forecloses" for thinking.

Derrida sees such foreclosure at work in Heidegger's interpretation of the
Platonic χῶρα as a preparation of the Cartesian interpretation of beings in
space as *extensio,* and also in Heidegger's tendency to exclude recalcitrant
figures from the history of being, figures such as Spinoza, who cannot be
readily subordinated to the epoch of subjectivity. The *telos* of Derrida's own
book—if it is fair and accurate to apply the same word to his endeavors here,
as I believe it is—is to put in question or to suspend Heidegger's rejection of the
entire Platonic-Christian tradition in his effort to hear the word *geistlich* (but
not *geistig*) in Trakl's poetry.

That *Geist, geistig, geistlich* knot these four threads Derrida claims to know
"ahead of time," *comme par avance* (24/19). The word "hypothesis" is there
merely out of courtesy. Yet if he knows *Geist* to be the truth of being, the
gathering of both Heidegger's and his own thought, the result of such knowledge is as fatal as it is paradoxical. Derrida's only surety is a "negative certitude," and *Geist* remains his hypothesis: the certitude is "not understanding
very well what ultimately regulates the *spiritual* idiom in Heidegger," and the
hypothesis that an excessive clarity, "the ambiguous clarity of the flame,"
ζάπυρος, we would say, will take us to the knot formed by these four threads
(29–30/12–13). The catachresis of knot and flame, woven as a daimonic wick
or fuse, will haunt us to the end.

(3) Heidegger does not often try to define *Geist.* He employs the word
axiomatically. Yet whenever he does try to define it the results are dramatic. In
Being and Time it is, as we have said, a matter of avoiding *Geist.* The word
belongs to the ontotheological tradition and must undergo *Destruktion;* it
pertains particularly to the Cartesian *res cogitans,* whose being—the being of
the *sum*—has suffered neglect. Derrida works carefully through section 10,
"Delimiting Dasein from Anthropology, Psychology, and Biology," in which
Heidegger emphasizes the complacency or ostensible needlessness (*Bedürfnislosigkeit*) that has characterized the question of "the *being* of the subject, of the
soul, of consciousness, of spirit, of the person" (SZ, 46). Even when Heidegger
uses the word *Geist* without quotation marks, he is mentioning it only in order
to enforce avoidance of it. Dasein, and not spirit, raises the question of being—
Dasein, and not some dogma of spirit, is to be the concrete starting-point for
fundamental ontology.

Here Derrida reverts to a suspicion he has entertained at least since the
1968 "Ends of Man" essay: "This exemplarity [i.e., of *Dasein* as the privileged
questioner of *Sein*] can become, or can remain, problematic" (Ma, 36/17.) The
suspicion itself cannot readily become a question, as Heidegger would wish,
inasmuch as a kind of "reflection" of questioning is in play here. How *question*
the structure of *Fragen* without on the one hand confirming its power and on
the other begging the question? Precisely what one has always found most
compelling about *Being and Time*—the fact that the fundamental ontologist
begins by thinking about what he or she is doing and so engages phenomenology to factical life—can also become terribly disquieting. How could one

possibly test the "legitimacy or axiomatic necessity" (De, 37/18) of this point of departure? A questioning of being-able-to-question: would not such a reflexivity undermine the very order of existential analysis and all its demonstrations, derivations, ordering, hierarchies, groundings, and descriptions? Derrida is right to remind us that this issue of the proper starting-point, which Heidegger calls *den rechten Ansatz,* and of the appropriate access, *angemessenen Zugang,* obsesses Heidegger before, during, and after the Marburg years in which *Being and Time* has its genesis. It dominates the 1921–1922 analysis of factical life and the 1929–1930 lectures on the animal world as much as it does *Being and Time.*

The principal issue elaborated by Derrida in this section is the problem of indifference (*Gleichgültigkeit,* but also *Indifferenz*): the indifference of every being at-hand toward its own being, the indifference (*Indifferenz*) that belongs to Dasein structurally and is essential to the *modal* structure of existential analysis, and indifference (*Bedürfnislosigkeit*) to the question of the meaning of being. It is indifference in these three senses that causes *Geist* (along with consciousness, subjectivity, person, and so on) to be interpreted as some thing at hand. Existential-ontological analysis as a whole can be viewed as an effort to deconstruct *Geist* by removing it from handy assertions and relocating it in the direction of *Gemüt* (one's "heart of hearts" or innermost core), and *Gemüt* in turn in the direction of *Existenz:* "The apparently new beginning of philosophizing [in Descartes] reveals itself to be the sowing of a fatal prejudice, as a result of which succeeding ages neglected a thematic ontological analysis of 'Gemüt' along the guidelines of the question of being and also as a critical confrontation with the ontology inherited from antiquity" (SZ, 25); ". . . the 'substance' of human being is not spirit, as the synthesis of soul and body, but *existence*" (SZ, 117). Here one can readily see how the issues of *essence* and of the *question* implicate the third thread, animality and the philosophy of life, as well as the fourth, epochality. And it is also clear that the shift from *Geist* to *Gemüt,* the latter being even less translatable than the former, more fraught with melancholy (*Schwermut*), leads us to suspect that the matter of "spirit" in *Being and Time* is, as it were, a closed book. Spirit? And *Heidegger?*

(4) Yet spirit does return. Returns to haunt. *L'esprit revient.* Glorious, veiled in the sheerest raiment, transfigured, having shed its corporeal integument of quotation marks. Although Heidegger begins by avoiding the word, it becomes clear that "something of spirit can be subtracted from the Cartesian-Hegelian metaphysics of subjectivity, something that points in the direction of [*faire signe vers*] the *Gemüt*" (44/23). Spirit's return occurs not only after *Being and Time* but also within it; for example, when Heidegger refers to the "spiritual" nature of Dasein's spatiality after having insisted that Dasein is not a *Geistding* encapsulated in a *Körperding* (SZ, 56). In section 70 he writes: "Rather, because it is 'spiritual' ['geistig,' still in quotation marks, to be sure], *and only for that reason,* Dasein can be spatial in a way that remains essentially impossible for an extended corporeal thing" (SZ, 368).

Spirit also returns as the epitome of the vulgar understanding of time—falling as one thing at hand into time as another such thing (SZ, section 82). Quotation marks continue to constrain *Geist* here, yet the privileged horizon of *time* requires that the position of "spirit" and "time" not be symmetrical with that of "spirituality" and "spatiality." Heidegger writes, near the conclusion of section 82 (SZ, 436): " 'Spirit' does not first of all [*nicht erst*] fall into time, but *exists as* the original *temporalizing* of temporality." "*Geist*" appears in quotation marks, as Hegel's word. Yet something can be translated from the latter's superlatively metaphysical text into Heidegger's own analysis of the *Zeitigung* of Dasein; something can be subtracted from the vulgar conception of a plummeting spirit and so saved for an existential analysis of falling, *Verfallen*. Whether and how such "subtraction" might be tied up with the "privation" we saw repeatedly failing in chapters 1 and 2 is difficult to say. " 'Spirit' does not fall *into* time; rather, factical existence 'falls' as lapsing [*verfallende*] *from* original, appropriate temporality." The fall is, as Derrida notes, "displaced," becoming a lapsus from one mode of temporalizing to another, although whether Heidegger can sustain *two* modes of temporalizing is doubtful, to say the least.[13] All reverts to *time*—just as, much later, in 1953, both good and evil will revert to the *flame* of spirit (now fully divested of its "scare-quotes").

It is precisely here that a close reading of Heidegger's 1921–1922 lecture course ("Phenomenological Interpretations of Aristotle: An Introduction to Phenomenological Research," discussed in the first and fourth chapters of the present book) supports Derrida's *Of Spirit*. Factical life is *animated* as falling; its very *Bewegtheit* or κίνησις is *Ruinanz*. Mirrored in the world by a kind of reflected light or *Reluzenz*, seduced by the carnival or masked ball of what in *Being and Time* he will call inappropriate everyday existence but here *Larvanz*, life plunges into the nothing, "*the nothing of factical life*." The mystery and miracle in such a fallen and falling world is that a counterthrust, *Gegenruinanz*, can occur. It transpires in philosophy's tendency to seek illumination, *Erhellung*. As a result of some inexplicable "gnawing" at its restive innards, life becomes aware of its factical failings and lacks, its *Darbung*, and struggles against the plunge. If *Geist* remains virtually unnamed in such a scenario, the *Erhellungstendenz* of knowing and philosophizing remains the only force by which total distraction, dispersion, and diffusion (*Zerstreuung*) can be countered. Significantly, spirit does appear in this early lecture course when it is a question of "leadership" (*das Führerproblem*—which, however, as we recall, is laughed to scorn) of the university, of the "spiritual-intellectual preparation" of students (which is no laughing matter), as opposed to the fatuous wit of mere "*Geistigkeit*," in quotation marks; or of the "spiritual condition we find ourselves in"; or of "the corruptors of spiritual life," who abuse philosophy (61, 70, 117–18).

(5) *Of Spirit* now takes one of its most dramatic turns. The problem of quotation marks—one that has long preoccupied deconstruction, which embraces "paleonymy" and inaugurates the "epochal regime of scare-quotes"—

reaches a kind of crisis. For in the 1933 rectoral address, *The Self-Assertion of the German University*, of which this section is a close reading, Heidegger drops the scare-quotes. Derrida pictures them as pins holding a curtain that is lowered before a stage: as the pins fall away, the curtain, which was always raised a crack, opens onto the political play of spirit itself. On the *Bühne* of the gigantesque, though by no means as Agit-prop. The raising of the curtain introduces a scene of academic-political solemnity: Spirit itself, in procession, appears in mortarboard and ermine in order to confirm the self-affirmation (which, as we saw in chapter 4 is more a *rectification*) of the German university. The prudence and methodological rigor of *Being and Time* bow low to the fervent rhetoric of the newly ordained *spiritus rector*.

The spiritual mission of the German university under its new leadership (*Führung*) sanctions the end of those constraints (" ") that bind *Geist* and *geistig* in *Being and Time*. Two decades after the *Rektoratsrede*, in the Trakl essay of 1953, Heidegger will counterpose Trakl's word *geistlich* to the term *geistig*, because the latter remains embroiled, according to Heidegger, in the Platonic-Christian ontotheological tradition. However, in 1933 Heidegger sets *geistig*, not *geistlich*, in italics, underlines and stresses it rather than setting it off in constraining scare-quotes; he ignores *geistlich* (which of course would be odd outside the strictly clerical or ecclesiastical context), and does not suggest that *geistig* has anything to do with a tradition that has to be deconstructed. *Geistige Führung* will not be concerned preeminently with such a *Destruktion*. At the core of the rectoral address Heidegger defines *Geist*, not in a Cartesian or Hegelian sense, but in terms of the mission (*Auftrag*) of the German university as such. Derrida singles out four predicates contained in the definition of spirit which, in spite of the apparent distance of the rectoral address from *Being and Time*, stand in discomfiting proximity to it: (1) spirit is a *questioning*, understood as a will to knowledge and a will to essence (*Fragen, Wissenschaft, Wesenswille*); (2) spirit expresses the *spiritual world* of the people (*geistige Welt*, the latter word being a crucial "existential" of *Being and Time*); (3) spirit is nourished by the forces of earth and blood—even in the august, elevated German university (*erd- und bluthaften Kräfte als Macht*); (4) spirit is resolve or resolute openedness (*Entschlossenheit*, one of the most important structures of *Being and Time*, retained also, although Derrida does not mention it, in *Gelassenheit* [G, 19]).

Derrida cites a long passage from the rectoral address (SB, 14), describing it as a celebration, exaltation, and kerygmatic proclamation of spirit. As we saw in chapters 4 and 5, it is a text of superlatives, of singulars, of the essence, and of the utmost gravity: *Geist ist ursprünglich gestimmte, wissende Entschlossenheit zum Wesen des Seins*. "Spirit is originally attuned, cognizant resolute openedness to the essence of being." Also of utmost violence and danger: *Und die* geistige Welt *eines Volkes . . . ist Macht der tiefsten Bewahrung seiner erd- und bluthaften Kräfte als Macht der innersten Erregung und weitesten Erschütterung seines Daseins.* "And the *spiritual world* of a people . . . is the power that most profoundly preserves a people's forces of earth and blood, the power that most intensely heightens and most extensively shatters its Dasein." Here Heidegger erects and exalts "the highest," *le plus haut*. With these words, *le plus haut*, one cannot help but think of *le Très-Haut* in the ethico-religious discourse of Levinas, and one will have to think of it again in the closing pages of *De l'esprit*, where Derrida imagines a colloquy between Heidegger and a group of theologians. For the moment he indicates the highs and lows that often dominate Heidegger's discourse: one might think of that extended passage in his Nietzsche lectures in which he comments on Zarathustra's *high* mountains and *deep* seas, the former having emerged from the latter and pointing back to the depths (NI, 291–92/2, 39–40). In the *Rektoratsrede* of 1933 it is a matter of the elevated historic destiny and the *hauteur* of a people gathered in *dieser hohen Schule* over the depths of earth-and-blood forces. Spirit here has nothing to do with metaphysical subjectivity—at least in Heidegger's own judgment. "No contradiction with *Being and Time* in this respect," remarks Derrida (De, 61/37). There remains of course the possibility that the new rector's "massive voluntarism" remains embroiled precisely in the decisionism and will to election of *Subiectität*, and that the union of *Geist* and *Geschichte* (*geistig-geschichtliches Dasein, geschichtlich-geistige Welt*) cannot so easily be disentangled from the Hegelian context. Yet how disastrous such a context would be for both fundamental ontology and Heidegger's "other" thinking! For if *Dasein* and *Welt* are unified in *Geist;* if the global phenomenon of being-in-the-world is willful spirit; if openedness to the essential unfolding of the truth of beyng is *Geist;* if the history of being is the existence of spirit (*Dasein des Geistes*); then Heidegger's thinking is the mere epiphenomenal flurry of a certain right-wing Hegelianism, and, once again, the confusion will not have been Derrida's.

Derrida does not dream of suggesting such a reduction. Not for nothing has he been a kind of "envoy," insisting that his French and American colleagues read and study Heidegger with the greatest care. For the growing number of philosophers in the English-speaking world who disdain reading except when it comes to books and articles of bad journalism, Derrida as an envoy is no doubt tainted. There is absolutely nothing in *Of Spirit* that the boulevard press in Paris and certain academic presses in America and England will be able to tout as evidence of "Heidegger the Nazi." And yet the entire text is haunted by the ghostly return of a *Geist* that always means more than either Heidegger or Derrida himself can control. As though spirit were a kind of fungus, a mushroom thrusting its head through pine needles on a forest floor.

Spirit and history unite for Heidegger in *essential questioning*. The first and second threads of Derrida's hesitation and perplexity therefore return again in the weft of *The Self-Assertion of the German University*. Science is *das fragende Standhalten* in the midst of beings as a whole (12). Such science obligates the one who assumes leadership (*geistige Führung*) "to the essentiality and simplicity of questioning," *zur Wesentlichkeit und Einfachheit des Fragens* (17). Such questioning understands itself as response—response to the call to responsibility. Once again, echoes of an ethico-religious discourse, echoes that will return in section 9 when Derrida himself invokes the responsibility of engagement. Thus Heidegger's discourse of spirit would legitimize National Socialism. One could turn against Heidegger the charge he brings against Nietzsche in "Who Is Nietzsche's Zarathustra?" when he writes of Nietzsche's "supremely spiritualized spirit of revenge," *höchst vergeistigter Geist der Rache* (VA, 117; N,2,228). And yet one must also acknowledge that in this very same gesture Heidegger takes his distance from National Socialism, interrupts his commitment to what will prove to be anything but a *spiritualized* politics of "earth and blood." Ultimately, however, one cannot separate off spiritualism from biologism and naturalism, and it is this *contamination* of the discourse of "freedom of the spirit" and the "rights of man," this *complicity* in which all such discourses are inevitably caught, that haunts Derrida's *Of Spirit*. No doubt one must choose the least hazardous of such complicities and contaminations as best one can, even though choice itself is the greatest hazard; to dream of escape from the necessity and the hazard of choice would be to give up the ghost. And so the other ghost, the ghost of spirit, always returns, doubles itself, passes into its opposite, ventriloquizes. "Metaphysics returns," writes Derrida, "and I understand this as a returning-to-haunt; *Geist* is the most fatal figure of this haunting return" (De, 66/40). Even Heidegger, with all his scare-quotes, all his *Anführungszeichen* and *Gänsefüßchen*, cannot escape it: such equivocity is of spirit, *de l'esprit*. It returns almost immediately, in the 1935 lectures on metaphysics, and decades later, in the 1953 "Language in the Poem."

Spiritual *Führung* is intro-duction into metaphysics, understood as *Hineinführen in das Fragen der Grundfrage*. Heidegger's geopolitical analysis of spirit in 1935, an analysis conducted from the apparently sole possible vantage point of "the metaphysical nation" (EM, 29), oscillates between the despair-beyond-pessimism of "the darkening world" and the hope-beyond-optimism of "new historical *spiritual* forces from the middle." Derrida continues his analysis of this text, *An Introduction to Metaphysics*, in section 7 of *De l'esprit*. Having cited Heidegger's "*Weltpolitik* of spirit" and *Weltverdüsterung* of "spiritual decline," Derrida now picks up another thread, the third, which asks how the spiritual world is related to the world of beings that are ostensibly unlike Dasein. Animals, for instance. *Other* animals.

(6) Derrida treats at some length the analyses of animality and the world-relation of animals as Heidegger develops them in his 1929–1930 lecture course, which we examined in chapter 3, *The Fundamental Concepts of Metaphysics: World—Finitude—Solitude*. He emphasizes Heidegger's hostility to *Lebensphilosophie*, emphasizes it perhaps excessively, inasmuch as Heidegger's discomfiture with transcendental phenomenology and his advance through *Existenzphilosophie* to fundamental ontology has much to do with his early conviction that philosophy must flourish on the basis of factical life and be at one with it. This is not to say that Heidegger is a *Lebensphilosoph*, a life-philosopher of the Bergsonian, Nietzschean, or Schelerian sort, much less a Spenglerian or Lamentarian (= Klages). However, it does mean that the po-

lemic arises from a need and a frustration at the heart of Heidegger's own thinking. Derrida's analysis fails to do justice to the Diltheyan, Schelerian, and even Leibnizian background to the question of life and animality; it thus misses something of the centrality of this particular thread—the thread of daimon life.

A second difficulty with Derrida's analysis here is that it begins by anticipating the "raising of the curtain" on *Geist* in 1933–1935. He projects the 1935 proclamation, "*Welt ist* geistige *Welt. Das Tier hat keine Welt, auch keine Umwelt*" (EM, 34), back onto the 1929–1930 lectures. That the animal has no world, or has-it-in-not-having-it, or is poor in world, would according to Derrida amount to saying that the animal is poor in spirit. World-poverty would be spiritual poverty. While I believe that Heidegger's thought does betray this tendency, and am therefore wholly in accord with the essential thrust of the analysis, I believe it is essential not to confuse 1935 with 1929. The very poignancy of Heidegger's lectures on animal life derives from the fact that there he does *not* appeal to spirit. There, as in *Being and Time*, it is a matter of avoiding *Geist*, even when it seems most appropriate to introduce it. As far as I can see, Heidegger does not even introduce the word negatively, in scare-quotes: he opposes the use of the words *Seele* and *Bewußtsein* in his discussion of animality, but leaves *Geist* altogether out of account. Now, it is precisely Derrida who teaches us the importance of observing scrupulously the use or nonuse of the *geistigen* vocabulary, and such scrupulous care is called for here, especially here: when at the end of his 1929–1930 course Heidegger tries to define the *human* relation to world as *Weltbildung*, he engages in a long analysis of speech as apophantic discourse, of the "as" that introduces human beings to the realm of essences (the rock *as* rock, sunlight *as* sunlight, lizard
deep in the pool there lay a serpent   *as* lizard); yet he never appeals to the *Geist* that used to guarantee the traditional route of access to that realm. It is precisely in the *avoidance* of the word that one senses the hovering Hegelian spirit, not so much in the wings as suspended in the machinery above center-stage, the machinery labeled "*Gattung.*" What Heidegger does introduce in the final part of his course are the following notions, each designed to specify the *human* relation to the world and to exclude the animal from it: freedom, openness to the world (*Weltoffenheit*) and the ruling sway of the world (*Walten der Welt*), the difference (*Unterschied*) between being and beings, the confrontation or encountering "hold" that is established between human beings and all other beings (*Entgegengehaltenheit*), and the project and projection (*Entwurf*) of being into beings that constitutes a human life. None of this appeals overtly to *Geist*, to *geistigen* or *geistlichen* matters. If *Weltoffenheit* characterizes humanity, *Weltoffensein* characterizes animality. Yet how does -*sein* differ from -*heit*, indeed in such a way that Heidegger can be assured that an "abyss" separates human beings from animals, as though the world were constructed like one of those modern, cageless, animal-friendly zoos? Precisely   *the serpent sensed the sweetness of the flower*   in this *non-naming* of *Geist* the spirit of metaphysics (objective and subjective genitive) returns. As we have seen, Heidegger tries to reduce the *Offensein* of animality to its enclosure

within a ring of disinhibitions, of passive subjections and preprogrammed responses (*Hingenommensein, Eingenommensein*), a closed circle of benumbed behavior (*Benommensein*). Yet the circle is, as we have also seen, continually undone, the ring repeatedly shattered. By something like *time,* and something very much like *death.*

Derrida's case is made all the stronger if we insist on prolonging—as Heidegger does—the avoidance of spirit. Heidegger's effort to distinguish the world-relations of humanity and animality is fundamentally aporetic; it is, as Derrida says, "nonplussed," *embarrassé.* By reintroducing the notions of *lack* or *privation,* the very notions that he employed in order to subordinate the problem of "just-plain-life" (*Nur-noch-leben*) in *Being and Time* (SZ, 50 and passim), Heidegger reverts willy nilly to the measure of Dasein. Although Derrida does not state the matter as baldly as I shall here, I believe he would agree that the very effort to define the *singular difference* between humanity and animality inevitably obfuscates the *proto-ontological* and ontological *differences.* I would stress far more than he does the fact that Heidegger uses the very same word to describe the world-relation of animals and the appropriate comportment toward being that characterizes Dasein: if the lizard sunning itself on a rock is benumbed (*benommen*), so is Dasein, not only when it succumbs to the world's distractions and goes sunbathing but also precisely when it confronts the uncanniness of its existence in anxiety. Appropriate Dasein, rapt to the ownmost possibility of its existence, is an animal.

Here perhaps is where the ghost of metaphysics descends, not merely as a return of Hegelian spirit but as an epiphany of the δαίμων that captivated Heidegger throughout his life of thought. The nothing invades animal life and disrupts the ring. Death shatters that ring and signals the way in which time— the marking of time—always bears a fundamental relation to the animal's life. The animal is thrown by way of its litter (*Wurf*), cast into its life and projected toward its death as no stone is ever thrown; the effects of that invasion, disruption, and shattering of the ring by (something like) the nothing are felt also at the center of the vital and hermeneutic circles of Dasein. Those circles and the ring of animality suddenly become coextensive, if only for a fleeting instant, not for *knowledge* but in *daimonic passion.* If Heidegger returns to his bugs and his bees, apparently confident that the world of humankind will prove to be essentially different, just as Hegel (and Jörgensen) were confident that spirit would assume essentially higher forms; if in other words the "troubling affinities" of Heidegger, Hegel, and the ontotheological tradition on the question of animality continue to plague us (as we noted, there are passages from the *Contributions to Philosophy* that seem to be lifted directly from the spirit and letter of Hegel's *Encyclopedia*); it remains the case that the daimonic, τὸ δαιμόνιον, combines for Heidegger in mysterious ways the matters of godhead, animality, factical life, embodiment, sexuality, and the abyss of anxiety.

Derrida more than anyone else would want us to recall the note from the 1928 logic course (26, 211n.) that weaves a complex web of knots with the themes of semination and dissemination (*Streuung, Zerstreuung*), the overpowering (das Übermächtige), the holy and divine (Heiligkeit, das Göttliche), τὸ δαιμόνιον, the nothing, and anxiety. Whereas Derrida stresses throughout Of Spirit that spirit is a gathering into a unifying one (Versammlung), we must also acknowledge Heidegger's insight during the period 1928–1930 that transcendence is dissemination or bestrewal into factical concretion, embodiment, spatiality, and (something like) sexuality (26, 173). Semination and dissemination, bestrewal, distraction, and dispersion, Streuung/Zer-streuung, are also "of spirit." Insofar as Geist is daimonic, it is no less disseminative than it is gathering. It flickers like a flame. This qualification does not cause Of Spirit to tremble, much less to shatter, but it does perhaps suggest that Derrida's Geschlecht project remains the more radical one. At the end of these remarks I will try to show why the latter project must continue. And it ought to continue, not with an imagined dialogue between Heidegger and the theologians—those diffident demonists—but with the already initiated negotiations between sisters and brothers. For example, in Trakl's magnetizing poetry.

Toward the end of section 6 Derrida's threads twist together to form several very tight knots. The animal (thread 3) lacks both the experience and the language of the as such, the language of essence (thread 2); lacking language, the lizard poses no questions about the rock across which it stretches (thread 1); it is as though one must cross through (durchstreichen) the word rock for the lizard, just as the word Sein will have to be crossed through as one confronts the epochality of the granting in propriation (thread 4). These knots, tied even before 1933–1935, will have profound political consequences. Profound yet utterly equivocal consequences. To distinguish Dasein from animality might of course be taken as the very best means of refuting the prevalent biologistic and racist ideologies; yet that distinguishing, in Heidegger's case, is aimed at least as much against Rilke, who poetizes animality as an opening onto being. Such distinguishing rests in fact on the most traditional sorts of teleological humanisms, on hierarchizations and evaluations, however ostensibly humane these may be. Derrida is therefore troubled by the complicity and contamination that prevail between humanistic and racist discourses, "the terrifying mechanisms of this program, all the double constraints that structure it" (De, 87). The epochal question as to whether that "program" can be transformed once and for all (thread 4) belongs to the web of questions thus far woven, including the question of the question: "There is no animal Dasein, inasmuch as Dasein is characterized by access to the 'as such' of beings and to the correlative possibility of questioning. It is clear that the animal can be in search of prey, can calculate, hesitate, track or follow a scent; but it would not properly know how to question. In the same way, it can use things, instrumentalize them, but it would not know how to gain access to a τέχνη" (88/56–57). However, that epochal question, to repeat, is an eminently political one. Precisely because the animal is neither Dasein nor Zuhandensein nor Vorhandensein, because one can think animality in terms of neither existentials nor categories, the existential ontology of Being and Time fails in the face of life. (One can schematize the matter in the following way, even though Derrida does not:

precisely because the animal is neither *daseinsmäßig* nor *nichtdaseinsmäßig,* at which point the word *mäßig* becomes a mere *supplement,* both necessary to and futile for ontological analysis, animal life puts the very notion of the [*proto-*]*ontological difference* at risk.) Derrida asks: "Could not one therefore say that all deconstruction of ontology, the kind of ontology that is developed in *Being and Time,* the kind that in some way dislocates the Cartesian-Hegelian *spiritus* in existential analysis, here finds itself threatened in its order, its very instauration, its conceptual framework, threatened by that which is still called, obscurely enough, the animal?" (89/57). Precisely that obscurity finds its darkest concentration in what Heidegger soon calls *spirit,* without quotation marks, *Geist* and *geistig,* though not yet *geistlich.*

(7) After having looped back in time to the 1929–1930 lectures on animality, Derrida returns to the political scene of 1933–1935, the scene not of world-poverty but of world-darkening, *Weltverdüsterung.* He cites a long passage from *Introduction to Metaphysics* (EM, 34–35) on the misinterpretation and debilitation, deposition, or disenfranchisement (*Entmachtung*) of *Geist.* In one of the most controversial developments of his text Derrida compares these famous pages with less well-known passages from other authors. He cites Husserl's attempt to define "European humanity" in terms of its "spiritual meaning": spiritual Europe includes the English Dominions and the United States, but excludes the Eskimos and the Indians "who are on display at the fairs [*Indianer der Jahrmarktsmenagerien:* a *Jahrmarkt* is a fair or traveling show, *Menagerie* is an animal display]"; Husserl also excludes "the gypsies who are constantly roving about Europe [*die dauernd in Europa herumvagabundieren*]." This "sinister passage," comments Derrida, appears in a public lecture delivered in Vienna in 1935. Derrida also cites at length Paul Valéry's *Variété* as an exemplary text for the era 1919–1939, in which discourses on "Europe" and "Spirit" abound. Derrida's purpose is not to reduce the differences in the situations of Husserl, Heidegger, Valéry, and the others (one thinks of all the discourses on *Geist* in the Weimar years, commencing with those of the Mann brothers and the Stefan George Circle, culminating in those of the *Jungkonservativen*), yet he does not shy from posing the question, "Which is worse?" "Where do we find the worst?"[14]

It is difficult to do justice to these analyses, as rich and nuanced as they are provocative, inasmuch as the breadth of material on which they draw (materials gathered in the seminar on "Philosophical Nationality and Nationalism") stretches far beyond my competence. However, I do wish to add one complication to Derrida's discussion of "the demonic" in *Introduction to Metaphysics* (EM, 35). It is not enough to contrast Heidegger's *das Dämonische* and *diese Dämonie* to the *malin génie* of Descartes, even though Derrida shows brilliantly that the Cartesian *cogito* (Oh, those French!) and the hegemony of the *subiectum* are precisely the evil spirit of Heidegger's history of being. It would also be necessary to relate the demonic to the daimonic (of 1928), of which, I suspect, it is a monstrous mutant. In other words, when Heidegger in the early

1940s refers to the demonic in terms of Spengler's predator (*Raubtier*) or to the violence of intra-European conflict in the epoch of spirit's debility, this has direct implications for the questions of both animality and theology: *Dämonie/daimonion* may well be the royal road to *esprit* as *Geist* and *revenant*, spirit and ghoul rising out of the epochal conjunction between god and dog, the epochal convergence of dog, god, and the da-. Derrida is right to recognize here traces of the problem of evil in Schelling's philosophy of the Indifferent. I shall proceed to that theme at the cost of ignoring Derrida's trenchant analysis of the "four misinterpretations of spirit" in *An Introduction to Metaphysics* (EM, 35–37; De, 103–5/64–65), but not before highlighting the apotheosis of Heidegger's lament concerning the darkening of the world. For that very darkening announces the onset of the drama of spirit, the raising of the curtain, the flash of blinding floodlights: Our nation, says Heidegger, will assume its historic mission as the midpoint of the West (*Übernehmen der geschichtlichen Sendung unseres Volkes der abendländischen Mitte* [EM, 38]). Derrida's analysis of that mission of "our people" and "our language" is one of the most powerful and subtle of *De l'esprit*.

Heidegger's constant references to *unserer Sprache*, "our language," and the reference here to *unserem Volk*, "our nation," prompt Derrida to pose with particular urgency the question of *translation*, especially the question of the illusion that translation can be a reduction to *the same*.[15] *Of Spirit* is obsessed, one might say, *vom Geiste*. Derrida follows closely the development of the concluding pages of chapter 1 of *An Introduction to Metaphysics* (EM, 38–39): "Our question" is the question of being, as the question of "our Dasein," "our whole constitution," "our history"; no doubt all three are jeopardized by "our totally false relation to language." *Unsere Frage, unser Dasein, unsere ganze Verfassung, unsere Geschichte, unser gesamtes Mißverhältnis zur Sprache.* Heidegger does not here explicitly refer to *unserer Sprache*, as he no doubt often will do, especially in the Trakl essay of 1953; toward which *Of Spirit* is on its way; yet the mutual implication of nation, language, and philosophical task is in Heidegger's view undeniable: "Because the destiny of language is grounded in the given *relation* [Bezug] of a nation to *being*, the question of *being* will for us be inextricably bound up with the question of *language* [*wird sich uns . . . verschlingen*]" (EM, 39). Derrida is no doubt acutely conscious of the fact that as a thoughtful speaker of *French* he should in Heidegger's view (the view addressed to the mirrorplay of the *Spiegel*) slip into *German* every time he tries to *think*. He is also acutely aware, especially when speaking and writing English or American, that he would actually rather slip into *French*. Heidegger's privileging of *unserer Sprache* is therefore in its mild-mannered presumptuousness simultaneously frightening and funny: *terriblement dangereux et follement drôle, tranquillement arrogante*, a bit naive and ultimately without much *esprit*, observes Derrida wryly. He reports the admonition of a Prussian professor in Matthew Arnold's *Friendship's Garland*, who urges that we should all *"Get Geist."* Ironically, Derrida's English (or American) is better than the Prussian's, so that the word *get* proves to be as overdetermined as the *Geist* that is to be got.

At stake of course is Heidegger's dual claim (EM, 43) that the grammar of Occidental languages arose from "Greek meditation on the *Greek* language," and that the Greek language, viewed in terms of "the possibilities for thinking," is, "alongside German, the most powerful and the most spiritual at once." Derrida emphasizes two asymmetries in Heidegger's claim. First, Greek and German are set in opposition to all the other languages on the face of the earth, and identified as languages "called by" being; Heidegger, however, signs his name and seals his claim in only *one* of them; of course, if Heidegger is merely insisting that *Geist, Denken,* and *Sein* are not reducible to *esprit, penser,* and *être,* or to *spirit, thinking,* and *being,* Derrida would be the first to concur. Yet are they really any more reducible to πνεῦμα, νοεῖο, and οὐσία? Second, the Graeco-German axis is broken in any case in 1953, when Heidegger claims that the Greek has no word for *geistlich. Geist* will prove to be not the Greek πνεῦμα but an intense, Germanic *Flamme,* "flame."

I interrupt Derrida's exposition precisely at this point in order to indicate something that *Of Spirit* unveils but then wraps in silence: *Geist,* the untranslatable word, *is Flamme, flamme,* flame. *Flamme* is of course a word that cannot be translated from German into French . . . because *it is the same word in both languages,* both morphologically and semantically. *Geist ist (die/la) F(f)lamme. L'esprit est (la/die) f(F)lamme.* If Nietzsche concludes his poem *Ecce homo* with the line *Flamme bin ich sicherlich,* he does so precisely as a good European, one who would have preferred to write *Also sprach Zarathustra* in French. In a note jotted down during the year 1939 Heidegger complains that Nietzsche is insufficiently *deutsch.* Perhaps that is because Nietzsche, who knew something about stoves, also knows that *Flamme* is *flamme.* Derrida's book is therefore about two sides, at least two sides, of untranslatability.

To claim in 1935 that what the Greek and German languages share is *Macht* and *Geist* is in fact to accentuate the asymmetry. Derrida doubts whether the Greek ever dreamed of waiting an epoch or two in order to acclaim, empower, and enfranchise German as its pneumatico-noetic equal. Not even as its parapneumaticonoetic equal. The Greek had more wit than that; as πολύτροπος, the Greek was more agile.

(8) Derrida inserts a brief interlude after the second major "act" of the drama *Of Spirit.* If Act I is "Avoidance: 1927;" and Act II is "Geist: 1933–1935," Act III will be "Flame: 1953." The interlude turns (all too briefly) to Nietzsche, Schelling, and Hölderlin, as Heidegger reads them in the late 1930s and throughout the 1940s. While Heidegger sometimes accuses Nietzsche of (merely) overturning the Platonic schema of the intelligible and sensible, of rejecting rationality (and thus *Geist*) in order to affirm the *brutalitas* of *bestialitas,* he nonetheless tries to affirm Nietzsche's "metaphysical" interpretation of the "thought of race," *Rassengedanke.*[16] Derrida wonders whether this avoidance of biologism and naturalism on Heidegger's part is any less grave in its consequences than the things it avoids. However, he holds the question "in suspense."

The relation of *Geist* to *Seele* in Heidegger's *Nietzsche,* especially in his opposition to Ludwig Klages, leads Derrida to Heidegger's lectures on Hölderlin's *Der Ister* in 1942. In the context of Hölderlin's *Stromdichtungen,* Heidegger (53, 157) cites a line that defines *Geist* as "spirit" that "is at home / not in the beginning, not at the source." Nevertheless, this very spirit is a *gathering,* the gathering of a community, a history, and a thinking. The reading of *Geist* in Hölderlin is thus continuous with Heidegger's 1936 lectures on Schelling's 1809 treatise *On Human Freedom,* in which Heidegger defines *Geist* as "originally unifying unity," a unity that encompasses the poles of existence and ground in the essence of God. "As such unity, spirit is πνεῦμα" (SA, 154). It is of course precisely this pneumatic interpretation of *Geist* that will be undone in Act III.

There can be no doubt that this brief entr'acte leaves much unsaid. One could, for example, conduct Heidegger's designation of Schellingian *Geist* as *bildender Wille* back to thread 3, on humanity as *weltbildend.* At that point the overtly humanistic prejudice that Heidegger shares with German Idealism would become clear, however much his "Letter on Humanism" insists on rethinking the ontological privilege of human being as *ek-sistence.* Indeed, there would be some grounds for arguing that German Idealism and Romanticism (one thinks of Hölderlin, Novalis, the Schlegel brothers, and Johann Georg Hamann—to mention only a few) offer opportunities for thinking the comparative world-relations of humanity and of other forms of life that Heidegger simply cannot match. Derrida himself is clear about the merely suggestive character of the interlude, which has but two aims: first, to exhibit the profound continuity of Heidegger's own discourse with that of German Idealism, which is as much an invocation of fire and flame as a thought of spirit; and second, to put into question the borderline that Heidegger will soon wish to draw between an ontotheological, Platonic-Christian tradition of πνεῦμα and *spiritus,* on the one hand, and a more originary thought of *Geist* as *Flamme,* on the other.

(9) "What is spirit?" The being of spirit, according to Derrida, does not cease to occupy Heidegger after 1933, once the quotation marks have been removed. Heidegger's final answer, after twenty years, years not untouched by fire, is: *Geist* is fire, flame, immolation, conflagration. That final answer has more to do with commencement than with end, however, when years themselves are spiriting, *geistliche Jahre.*

It will not be possible here to recount in detail Derrida's response in *Of Spirit* to the Trakl essay, the farther pole of the magnetic-erotic field, and one of Heidegger's most difficult texts. Derrida focuses on Heidegger's definition of spirit and spiriting (*Geist/geistliche*) as flame, a "definition," to be sure, that arises out of a conversation with poetry. Almost in desperation, one suspects, Derrida insists that the definition of spirit as flame is a pronouncement (*énoncé*) by Heidegger, an endorsement or signing by Heidegger, even though Trakl's verses appear to induce the pronouncement. Twice in his discussion

(De, 137/86–87; 178/108), Derrida explicitly promises to continue his study of the Trakl essay, and to return to it in later writings of his own. Because we will want to hold him to that promise, I present the earlier, more detailed pledge here:

> This *Erörterung* of Trakl's *Gedicht* is, it seems to me, one of Heidegger's richest texts: subtle, overdetermined, more untranslatable than ever. And of course one of the most problematic. With a violence I can neither dissimulate nor assume, I shall set about extracting from it the specter that responds to the names and attributes of spirit (*Geist, geistig, geistlich*). Because I shall continue to study this text elsewhere, with a patience that is more decent, I hope to be able one day to render justice to it (beyond the scope that this conference today allows me), by analyzing its gesture, its mode, or its status (if indeed it has one), its relation to philosophical discourse, hermeneutics, or poetics; but also by analyzing what it says about *Geschlecht*, about the word *Geschlecht*, and also about place (*Ort*), as well as animality. For the moment, I shall pursue only the passage of spirit [*le passage de l'esprit*].

Not spirit but *soul* dominates Heidegger's Trakl essay, which responds to Trakl's line, *Es ist die Seele ein Fremdes auf Erden,* "Something strange is the soul on earth." Heidegger's effort is to resist the "Platonic-Christian" understanding of the line as a reinforcement of the "Vale of Tears" tradition: the "soul" of Trakl's poem *seeks* the earth, is under way *toward* it. *Geist* is introduced in that same poem (*Frühling der Seele*) in the phrase, *Geistlich dämmert,* dawn rises, or dusk descends, "spiritually," "spiritingly." Heidegger refers to the "*essential* essential unfolding" (*wesentlichen Wesens*) of this twilight, and we are reminded of Derrida's second thread: Heidegger will everywhere insist that his conversation with Trakl touches on the *essentials. Geistlich* is also said of two other moments, "night" and "year." The latter is especially important for Heidegger's reading of Trakl: he traces the word "year" in *das geistliche Jahr* to *ier,* ἰέναι, *gehen:* to go or pass. Such passage (*gehen, Gang*) might well have reminded Derrida of the passage of "the wandering sun" in *Being and Time,* a passage (we examined it in chapter 2, above) that is so important for the *spacing of time,* precisely in a "nature" that is neither *daseinsmäßig* nor simply *vorhanden* but in an altogether exceptional way *zuhanden,* a way more than merely reminiscent of *animality* (SZ, 70, 80, 103, 211, and 413).

Derrida hastily summarizes his interpretation of the two "blows" or "strokes" of *Geschlecht,* into (1) the *duality* and (2) the *discord* of what seem to be the two sexes, *die Geschlechter.* He proceeds to the question of the dawn, *die Frühe,* the morning before all mornings, the *archi-origin* and essence of primal, primaveral time. Such time is in Heidegger's estimation *geistlich,* not in any ecclesiastical sense, but in the sense of a promise. Here Derrida takes up a theme that appears in all his recent work, namely, that of the double-yes or promise that in some sense precedes all questioning: precisely at the point where Heidegger attempts "a more originary thinking of time" than that broached in *Being and Time,* Derrida himself focuses on the "more promising" (*versprechender*) precedence that guides his own thinking. Here we find ourselves very close to the provocation, the regnant spirit or tutelary genius, of *De l'esprit*, "the promise that, opening all speech, renders possible even the question. . . : the asymmetry of an affirmation, of a *yes* prior to all opposition of *yes* and *no* . . ., prior to every question," the promise that would be "*une promesse de l'esprit*" (De, 147/94).

Here Derrida inserts a remarkable footnote (dedicated to a remarkable scholar, Françoise Dastur, whose discussions with Derrida sparked the note); it is the note I mentioned earlier in this chapter, and it is undeniably one of those footnotes that would merit close scrutiny, perhaps even a "note on a note." The note states the book's thesis and then goes on to identify a passage in *On the Way to Language* that supports that thesis. Finally, it poses a number of challenges to Heidegger's thinking of language and of propriation, the recurrent themes of his later thought. The note begins:

> Well, then: prior to every question. It is precisely in this place that the "question of the question" vacillates, the question that has hounded us from the outset. It vacillates the instant it is no longer a question. Not that it is subtracted from the unlimited legitimacy of questioning; rather, it slips into the memory of a language, of an experience of language that is "older" than the question, always anterior and presupposed, so ancient that it never was present in an "experience" or an "act of language"—in the current sense of these words. This moment—which is not a moment—is *marked* in Heidegger's text. (De, 147 n.1/129 n.5)

An experience that is not an "experience," a moment that is no moment, a priority that is merely what Rodolphe Gasché[17] would call *quasi-transcendental*: Derrida sees it in Heidegger's thought of the granting, the *Es gibt,* and in those pages of *On the Way to Language* (US, 174–76; 180–81) where the interrogation mark is suppressed, or at least subordinated, and the piety of thinking (as questioning) recedes before what Heidegger calls the *Zusage* or *Zuspruch* of language. The questioning attitude depends on a prior address by language and a readiness on the part of the addressee to hear and affirm what is to be thought. Heidegger writes: "What do we experience when we consider the matter sufficiently? That questioning [*das Fragen*] is not the appropriate gesture of thinking [*nicht die eigentliche Gebärde des Denkens ist*]; rather, [the appropriate gesture is] hearing the affirmation of what is to come into question [*sondern—das Hören der Zusage dessen, was in die Frage kommen soll*]" (US, 175). Interrogation is not the last word of language, even if in 1927 it was the character of Dasein as *questioner* that seemed to guarantee a proper starting-point for fundamental ontology. The *Zusage* is in Derrida's view the "yes" that engages us in questioning, without necessarily being spoken aloud or written explicitly, yet always in a particular language; he calls it *le gage,* a forfeit, surety, guarantee, assurance, pledge, or promise. The forfeit paid to language is not a prelinguistic silence. Quite the reverse: it is en-gage-ment in language and responsibility to it. A singular event, more than simply reminiscent of the *singulare tantum* of *propriation,* more like the earliest stirrings (*Regungen*) of propriation (*Ereignis*) in the telling silences of language—"an event the memory of which precedes all remembering [*dont la mémoire devance tout souvenir*] and to which we are bound by a faith that defies all telling [*une foi qui défie tout récit*]" (De, 149/130). Here erasure becomes impossible. Here the guiding pulsion of deconstruction itself appears to be stilled—at least for a spiriting moment. Nothing can erase the always antecedent pledge of and to language. There is no getting back behind the forfeit to language. "*Aucune rature n'est pas possible pour un tel gage. Aucun retour en arrière*" (149/130).

I will not continue to comment on this remarkable note (it has only just begun), which goes on to discuss the "turning" (only in order to reject it as a strategy for interpreting Heidegger's path of thought) and a new topology for rereading Heidegger, a new series of tasks for thinking, centering on issues of responsibility, *Schuldigsein*, resolve, reliability, affirmation, promise, and propriation. Needless to say, there is a great deal of future in this note, an enormous amount of promise, a hostage to Derrida's own future and to ours.

Ours? I mean that of anyone who has ever read any of Heidegger's texts   *He was wise, he saw mysteries and knew secret things*   with some care.

As Derrida enters the final phase of *De l'esprit*, the fourth of his threads of hesitation—epochality—comes to predominate. Heidegger insists that Trakl's poetry stands outside the Platonic-Christian epoch, outside the χωρισμός that separates the intelligible from the sensible, beyond the decomposed *Geschlecht* of ontotheology. Derrida accuses Heidegger of a "massive and gross" reduction of that tradition and tries to restore the Heidegger-Trakl dialogue to the broader context of a conversation with representatives of the Hebraeo-Christian theological tradition(s). One can sense the necessity of such an attempt, and one marvels at Derrida's dexterity in fashioning such an imagined conversation.

Yet is Heidegger's compelling need to extract Trakl from ontotheology as gross and as caricatural as Derrida suggests? Does not Heidegger demand such extraction within a specific context of *Trakl-Rezeption*, which Derrida, for his part, totally ignores? Is not Heidegger responding to the religiously committed *Brenner*-circle and to critics and commentators such as Friedrich Georg Jünger, all of whom are keen to gather Trakl into the fold? How will we judge whether Heidegger, in an essay Derrida acknowledges to be one of his subtlest and most challenging, proves to be a crude reductionist? Is Heidegger a crass dechristianizer of Trakl, precisely this same Heidegger who since his youth is so fatefully and fatally drawn to the flame of *Geist*? Or does he manage to gesture toward a figure beyond *Geist*, beyond *spiritus*, perhaps even beyond the Hebraic *ruah* these words may be trying to "translate," as Derrida says, a figure and a "haunting shadow" to which Derrida himself has been drawn in the past and to which he must let himself be drawn again? Heidegger writes:

Whether, to what extent, and in what sense Trakl's poetry speaks in a Christian way; in what manner the poet was a "Christian"; what "Christian," "Christianity," "Christendom," the "Christian character" mean here, or anywhere—all this

encompasses essential questions. However, a situating of them hangs suspended in
empty space as long as the site of the poem has not been located thoughtfully.
Furthermore, situating them demands a meditation for which neither the concepts
of metaphysics nor those of Church theology are adequate.

A judgment concerning the Christian character of Trakl's poem would above
all have to consider his two final creations, "Lament" and "Grodek." It would
have to ask, Why does the poet, here, in the uttermost need of his final saying, not
call on God and Christ if he is such a decided Christian? Why instead does he
designate "the haunting shadow of the sister," the sister as "the one who greets"?
Why does the song end, not with the confident prospect of Christian redemption,
but with an allusion to the "unborn grandchildren"? Why does the sister also
appear in the other final poem, "Lament"? Why is "eternity" here called "the icy
wave"? Is that thought in a Christian way? It is not even Christian despair. (US,
75–76)

Is Heidegger here crude, brutal, gross, massive, caricatural? One perhaps
ought to postpone the reply until Derrida responds to the sister, to the lunar
voice, and to ice in Heidegger's subtlest and most challenging text. Until, that is
to say, the typescript of "Geschlecht III" is expanded and prepared for publication. For the moment he is preoccupied with fire and *Geist*. He cites a long
passage (US, 59–60) on spirit as flame, ecstatically outside itself, glowing and
consuming at once, a bright light and the white of ashes. Here Heidegger
moves boldly back behind the pneumatic tradition to that of fire, apparently
not by turning to Empedocles or even Heraclitus but by having recourse to the
resources of the German language alone: *Geist* in its "original sense" is *gheis*,
stirred up, en-raged, being-outside-oneself. (Hermann Paul's *Deutsches Wörterbuch* does not cite the form *gheis* but mentions the Gothic *usgaisjan*, "to drive
one outside oneself," and the Old Nordic *geisa*, "to rage." Yet I cannot find
any direct attribution of fire or flame to *Geist*. Wherever *gheis* may ultimately
hail from, I wonder whether it or these "Gothic" and "Old Nordic" words
truly belong to *unserer Sprache*. The *Oxford English Dictionary* cites *gheis* as a
"root" of *Geist* and *ghost*, apparently pre-Teutonic in origin and related to the
Sanskrit *hedas*, "anger," "fury," which might of course get us eventually to
"fire.") Thus *Geist* is both the highest good, the sunlight beyond being, and the
worst evil, the sunspot of explosion and ash. The Greeks didn't have a word for
it, however, even if almost all the other words for being are Greek words. For
example, all the words that haunt the unified realm of essence that is ζα-. One
of Derrida's insights is that such equivocal, duplicitous fire and flame may be
found elsewhere, in a tradition both inside and outside Germany and *unserer
Sprache*.

(10) Spirit? And *Heidegger*? Do the words *Geist, geistig, geistlich* in fact
dominate Heidegger's thought after 1933? In the *Contributions to Philosophy*
of 1936–1938, which we examined in chapter 6, is "spirit" the missing link
joining *Anklang* and *Zuspiel, Sprung* and *Gründung*? Do *Da-sein* and *die
Wesung (bzw. Zerklüftung) des Seyns* prove to be "spiritual"? Do the "futural

ones" who attend to the "passing" of "the last god" show themselves as *geistlich?* Only if "passing," *Vorbeigang,* be interpreted in the retrospect of 1953 as the *spiriting of a shivering godhead.* Otherwise, no, the drama of spirit-resurrected-from-quotation-marks will not be the exclusive drama to which we will give the title "Heidegger."

One can write what I have only now written, however, and still be totally convinced of the importance of Derrida's effort, as an effort of *thinking.* For there may be an even more significant drama than any to which we would give the title "Of Spirit," with "Heidegger" as the playwrite. There is a drama one may eventually be able to call "Daimon Life," with Heidegger, Derrida, Nietzsche, Freud, Irigaray, and others as the playwrites. I turn now to the final pages of *De l'esprit.*

Derrida is rapt to Heidegger's fires, as he is elsewhere to Hegel's. The German nation as guardian of the sacred fire of philosophy, of the ancestral hearth of thought, of the domesticity of spirit, of *Geist* in one sole language: a certain continuity of the pyric tradition in Europe's middle. As though Europa had reincarnated as Panthea, the woman whom the physician and thaumaturge, Empedocles, cures by preserving and nurturing the warmth that resides in the belly of her otherwise chill corpsebody. (Incidentally, Derrida neglects to cite the most heartwarming fire and the most scorching flame in Heidegger's text: the theme of *der Herd* in the 1942 lectures on Hölderlin's hymn, "Der Ister" [53, 134–43; 151], where the rhetoric of Romantic domesticity flickers and crackles in Heidegger's text, and the unnerving and even horrific juxtaposition of bread and Heraclitus in the baker's oven.[18]) Yet Derrida complicates the picture of this continuity: even in Aristotle, πνεῦμα is not merely breath, but is related to vapor or gas and an ardent, life-sustaining exhalation. Heidegger would have to concede, perhaps upon the urging of Eugen Fink, that πῦρ ἀείζωον, "ever-living fire," and the Homeric-Pindaric ζάπυρος do not need to wait upon the German *Geist.* The larger point is that Heidegger is locked into a "linguistico-historical triangle" represented by the words πνεῦμα, *spiritus,* and *Geist,* a triangle that he himself would wish to be rigorously closed. Yet what if these three words—at least, during and after the time of the evangelists—are attempting to translate the Hebrew word *ruah?* In any case, *can* the triangle be closed? What would one make of the ironic fact that the theme of *fire* is ubiquitous in Jewish prophetic texts? Can Heidegger, *from within* the triangle, decide anything about a thought of *Geist* that would transgress the boundaries of Europe and transform the meaning of both Orient and Occident? (Recall that this last claim is made also in the 1936 "Anaximander Fragment," where the thought of the eschatology of being, the gathering into the "land of evening," *das Abendland,* is said to "overwhelm Occident and Orient alike" (H, 300; EGT, 17). Such questions form nodes along that fourth thread of hesitation and suspense called "epochality."

Derrida also poses questions to Heidegger's indebtedness to *Schelling* in Heidegger's account (in the 1953 Trakl essay) of good and evil in the solitary flame of spirit. Here the same gesture occurs: Heidegger tries to remove

Schelling's metaphysics from the site of Christian ontotheology, just as he will later seek to rescue Trakl's poetry from it. While Derrida is surely right about the continuity of this "metaphysics of evil" in Heidegger's thought with the thought of Schelling, and while such continuities obviously jeopardize every notion of epochality, I am uncertain about what to make of his point. Is there not some sense in which Schelling's thought of evil in the 1809 treatise *On Human Freedom* (see chapter 9, below) is a *radical* one? Is it not very difficult indeed to *place* Schelling's most radical thinking in any Christian context—no matter how differentiated or nuanced that context may be for us? Does not Schelling dislocate and displace that context—perhaps as Trakl's poetry displaces and dislocates the word "Christian"? When Schelling comes to give an account of the blow or stroke of evil as an "eternal deed" performed once and for all in a time before time, in a life before life, a deed—like creation itself—performed "in one magic stroke," *in Einem magischen Schlag* (*Werke*, 7, 386–87), would we not find it as difficult as Heidegger does to discuss Schelling in the context of "Christianity"? (It is that single *Schlag* in Schelling, incidentally, that ought to fascinate the thinker of *Geschlecht*—not two strokes, here, but one; recall that the one magic stroke defines "the manner and quality of his [i.e. *des Menschen*] corporization.") Neither here nor in the case of Trakl should we be too quick to adjudge Heidegger's efforts to "dechristianize" the site "crude" or "conventional." [19]

Yet one must admit that Derrida is never quick to judge. He acknowledges that *one* of Heidegger's paths leads him to a thought of another beginning, another *Geschlecht*, one that is heterogeneous with regard to origins. That path promises to lead us to the thought of "something altogether other," something "provocative, disruptive, irruptive" (De, 177/107). The second path, by which Heidegger would rescue Trakl from the swamp of Christendom, Derrida does find forced, "laborious," "caricatural," and "conventional." He concludes *Of Spirit* with an imagined dialogue between Heidegger and a group of aggrieved theologians, who find everywhere in Heidegger's presumably dechristianized Trakl-interpretation a vast array of religious symbols and theological themes: the promise, an origin   *he brought us a tale of the days before the flood*   earlier than all origins, an apocalyptic end of former history and the commencement of a new history; a falling and a curse, but then a *Zuspruch* that Trakl places in the mouth of God, an affirmation that Heidegger himself cites:

> *Gott sprach eine sanfte Flamme zu seinem Herzen: O Mensch!*

> God spoke a gentle flame to his heart: O Humanity!

A falling and a curse, a resurrection, a rescuing stroke, and—to put an end to the list—a writing of fire. Which elicits "a similar echo from my friend and coreligionist, the Messianic Jew" (De, 181/111). The response that Derrida imagines for Heidegger, his response to these patient/ impatient theologians, is by no means caricatural. Yet no student of Heidegger will take Derrida's imagined dialogue as the "last word" on the subject, which of course would be the last thing its conjuror had in mind. Because Derrida concludes his astonishing effort by invoking once again "the path of the altogether other," I myself want to conclude with two gestures toward this "other."

The first gesture is in reply to a particularly disarming passage in *Of Spirit* that evokes alterity in the form of terrifying violence; the second responds to one of Derrida's *future* works, as it were, perhaps to the missing *third* generation of *Geschlecht* which he has promised and which we will not allow him to forget. The first passage, on the alterity of an unimaginable violence:

> It involves "events" past, present, and to come, a composition of forces and of discourses that seem to wage a war without mercy (for example from 1933 to our own day). It involves a program and a combinatory whose power remains abyssal. Such power allows none of these discourses to be innocent in any strict sense; discourses can only exchange their power. Such power leaves no site untouched, no site which might support a seat of judgment. Nazism was not born in the desert. We know it well, but it is always necessary to recall it. And even if, far from every desert, it had sprouted like a mushroom in the silence of a European forest, it would have done so in the shadow of great trees, in the shadow of their silence or their indifference, but in the same soil. I will not draw up the account of these trees which in Europe people an immense black forest. I will not count the varieties. For essential reasons, their presentation defies the space of a tableau. In their burgeoning taxonomy they would bear the names of religions, philosophies, political regimes, economic structures, religious or academic institutions. In short, what we also call, confusedly enough, culture or the world of spirit. (De, 179/109–10)

To be sure, not in the desert. Yet the desert too has often enough run red at the sound of "sibboleth," a sound uttered without hope in many tongues, sounds made by soldiers on their knees, trying to surrender, so many of them that they "get in the way" of advancing armies. The prophetic discourses of the ageless desert, propagated now in other lands, farther west, have often enough served as clarion calls to close the triangle and open fire.

That immense black forest has by now been devastated   *he will not rise again*   by ghosts of the past, ghosts that never will, or certainly never should, be laid to rest. Immediately after the line, "Something strange is the soul on earth," Trakl writes:

> *Geistlich dämmert*
> *Bläue über dem verhauenen Wald und es läutet*
> *Lange eine dunkle Glocke im Dorf; friedlich Geleit.*
> *Stille blüht die Myrthe über den weißen Lidern des Toten.*

> Spiriting twilight
> Turns to blue above the devastated wood and long tolls
> A deep-throated bell in the village; boon companion.
> Myrtle blooms in silence over the white lids of the dead one.

OF SISTERS

In the strophe that immediately precedes the line *Es ist die Seele ein Fremdes auf Erden,* Trakl invokes the sister, the greeting figure that haunts Heidegger's "Language in the Poem" and to whom—this is my second, my concluding gesture—Derrida will have to return. *Of Spirit* is in fact published simultaneously with a book entitled *Psyché.* There is no *Geist* without *Seele,* says Heidegger, and Derrida's *Of Spirit* (172–73/104–105) notes the all-too-traditional account in Heidegger of the soul's "femininity," of the soul as the "protectress" and "nurse" of the spirit. The soul apparently *gathers* in the same way that spirit does; the soul too is ostensibly the unifying one.

And yet. Heidegger does try to heed what Trakl's *Frühling der Seele* says:

> *Schwester, da ich dich fand an einsamer Lichtung*
> *Des Waldes und Mittag war und groß das Schweigen des Tiers;*
> *Weiße unter wilder Eiche, und es blühte silbern der Dorn.*
> *Gewaltiges Sterben und die singende Flamme im Herzen.*

> Sister, when I found you in a lonely clearing
> Of the forest and it was noon and vast the animal's silence;
> White under wild oak, and silver blossomed the thorn.
> Horrific dying and the flame singing in the heart.

It is not clear that the sister—for example, the one called upon in Trakl's final, icy poems, among the many sisters in his works—is an avatar of spirit. Or of "spirit." And yet Heidegger's "Language in the Poem" points to her again and again, precisely when it appears to be a matter of *Geist,* in a way that Derrida's *Of Spirit* scarcely betrays and certainly does not elaborate. After reprinting the poem *Geistliche Dämmerung* in its entirety, a poem that ends with the lines, "Always the sister's lunar voice resounds / Through the spiriting night [*Immer tönt der Schwester mondene Stimme / Durch die geistliche Nacht*]," Heidegger comments as follows:

> The starry heavens are depicted in the poetic image of the nocturnal weir. That is the way our ordinary mode of representation puts it. However, the night sky, in the truth of its essence, is this weir. Whatever else we may call the night remains a mere image, that is to say, a pale and anemic afterimage of its essence. In the poem of this poet the weir and its mirroring surface recur again and again. The water, sometimes blue, sometimes black, shows man his own face, his returning gaze. But in the nocturnal weir of the starry sky the glistening blue of the spiriting night scintillates. Its shimmer is cool.
>
> The chill light derives from the shining of her who is the moon [*dem Scheinen der Möndin*] (σελάννα). As ancient Greek verses tell us, in the precincts of her luminosity even the stars grow pale and frigid. All becomes "lunar." The stranger who treads through the night is called "the lunar one [*der Mondene*]." The brother hears the "lunar voice" of the sister when, on his bark, which itself is "black" and scarcely lit by the stranger's golden sheen, he tries to follow the stranger on the stranger's nocturnal voyage on the weir. (US, 48–49)

This is one of the rare moments in Heidegger's text when the curious interplay emerges between brother, sister, stranger, and the one who tries to follow. It is surely the case that the silver thread of the sister is cut too abruptly in Heidegger's text. However, my question to Derrida is whether one should not follow precisely this silver thread that Heidegger (none other than he) has espied in Trakl's poetry, in the direction not of the solar theologians but the sister. If Heidegger does not follow the lunar voice with sufficient concentration and distraction, neither *Of Spirit* nor the *Geschlecht* series will greatly improve our hearing. Other texts of Derrida's do help us in this regard, and so we may be asked to perform some sort of strange grafting operation on "spirit." Even if one suspects that Heidegger struggles constantly to transform the horizontal position of brother, sister, and lovers in Trakl's poems into the vertical posture of his own history of being, it remains true that he has tried to respond to the pallid argentine of the sister, her shining as σελάννα. He has struggled to hear the "lunar voice" of the sister through the spiriting night, no matter how many will condemn such an effort out of hand as decadent romanticism.

Among those who do *not* condemn, among those who instead spur the question, is Luce Irigaray. In her *L'oubli de l'air: Chez Martin Heidegger,* Irigaray has the following to say about Heidegger's Trakl essay:

> That man is heading into his decline, into the decomposition of whatever up to now has gathered man—this he has said. At least, by way of the poet Trakl. . . . That the dusk would offer the chance of a new dawn, that this November would offer the hope of a new Spring to come, which would be granted by a gaze that is lost in the night—this he has said. Again, that the destiny of this other sunrise has been confided to something foreign [à l'étrange], where all will be gathered, sheltered, and safeguarded otherwise. Where will the sojourn find another site? Where will habitation take place, no longer on the site of hate, but in the lodgings of the only tenderness there is?
>
> Yet it is in the young boy, dead in order to safeguard a profound childhood, that this setting and rising would find their possible future. A young boy, demented: sensitized otherwise than man, the old man of the West. A dream that is dead at morningtide, a dream for the insurrection of spirit [de l'esprit]. Abandoned to the passageways of an underground memory.
>
> The apparition and evanescence of a profound childhood, ungenerated by the difference between boy and girl, would find their place in the figure of an adolescent. It would be on the side of man's having yet to be engendered that a chance would be reserved for what is to come. Would it still be of man [Encore de l'homme]? (OA, 108–109)

In the light of Heidegger's effort, if not his unequivocal success, would not an imagined dialogue between Heidegger and the Trakl children (who spoke *French* with one another and with their Alsatian governess, "Mademoiselle," French, and not German, not *unsere Sprache*), a dialogue led by the *sister,* serve as an effective conclusion to some future work? Would not the lunar voice of the sister challenge thought in a way no solar theologian   *he will not come again*   or desert prophet ever has? Would Heidegger ever be able to *retreat* before that voice, when at least *one* of the paths he takes in the Trakl essay leads him—perhaps reluctantly, perhaps in turbulent anxiety, perhaps benumbed and bedazzled (*benommen*)—to the sister? Might not this dialogue proceed in such a way that the "regular, typical, and recurrent signs" (De, 182/ 112) of Heidegger's usual way of responding would never again   *he will not rise again*   come to the fore? Might not the sister, whom Trakl calls *ein flammender Dämon*, demand of Heidegger:

> You are reading me as a cipher in your *vertical, historical* account, as a character in your tale of being, oblivion of being, and reappropriation. Yet what if you should find me—*me,* and not my brother—on the *horizontal,* as your nearest and most distant horizon? What if you should find me not *geschichtlich* but *geschlechtlich?*
>
> The gentleness you yearn for, that stiller childhood of your nostalgia; your homecoming, your homeland and its forces of earth and blood; am I simply that for you, and no more? Your Valkyrie in calico? Have you forgotten those pillows yellowed by incense, love's old sweet song? The brotherly-sisterly twofold to which I, the sister, give my name, *die geschwisterliche Zwiefalt:* why do you seek it in the more gentle onefold of us children? One fold? Isn't that puerile, isn't that *einfältig?*
>
> What curse do you fear from my lips? Come. Don't be afraid. Tell me. The discord that makes you tremble, the restoration you crave, the reduction of a twofold humanity to a concordant One, the return to the dawn of a demented, departed youth, a dead boy in whom you find me unmanned, unwomaned—is it not the dream of a *latency* unmarked by difference?
>
> You lust after the antique past.
>
> You lust after the distant future.
>
> You lust after everything but lust.
>
> In your clearing, where you sought the secret of being and solicited the mysterious event, I and the silent animal at my side waited. The daimons white under wild oak were still. You approached, turned aside, circumvented us. You bore the torch of spirit, the singing and singeing flame of the sun. You hoped we would follow in train; you feared we would follow in your wake. You wagered you would win me, hoped you might become me, through mastery, through my brother. You believed that by heeding the

stranger's song you would become *his*
brother and thus a brother to *his*
sister[, making her *your own* sister . . .] *durch
diesen erst zum Bruder seiner Schwester
werden.*

You are looking for my brother? For the
remnants of a life? You expect me to say that
he lies unburied on the plain outside the city;
you are certain that I go to greet him with
dust. Come. Take up this thread of mine,
don't tie yourself in knots.

The lunar song you hear is mine, not
his. . . . Both his and mine, how can we tell,
why should we ever want to tell?
Consonance of the spiriting years, the years
that will take us both. Come. By my
contractions, by my waves, by my rhythms of
joy and pain; by the burning in my belly, by
my aloofness and chill; by my apartness; by
my hand in your mouth you will know me, if
ever you do know me, O my . . . brother?

NINE

Final Signs of Life

Heidegger and Irigaray

In chapters 6 and 7 some nonsense was uttered about a second history of being, a "more covert" history of φύσις and ζωή. Evidently, such a second history of being, appealing as it does to a distinction between overt and covert, surreptitiously reverts to the first, which is based on the opposition of revealing and concealing, openness and closure. One would have to be both more careful and more reckless about such talk. More careful: a history of za-ology cannot simply be rattled off without the most painstaking research and reflection. If Heidegger took three or four decades (or five, or six) to elaborate the first, no one should expect less of the chronicler of the second. Guarantees against old age, decrepitude, and lifedeath would have to be written into the contract. More reckless: an *other* history of being, of being as φύσις, but of φύσις as ζωή, and of ζωή as ζά, might well have to cast off every pious appurtenance of Heideggerian *Geschichte* and *Geschick*, abjure every appeal to "essence" and "fateful sending," renounce the comforts of epochality, propriety, and propriation, and overcome both the temptations of fundamental ontology and the blandishments of an ostensibly *other* thinking of beyng—or of its history. In short, such a second history of being would have to lose both history and being to anarchy. For as long as a history of being recounts the story of being as *destinal*, as a *sending*, the "suspension of epochal principles," as Reiner Schürmann calls it, and calls *for* it, is a sometime thing. A truly an-archic thinking will occur only at the moments of interruption in any recounting of any history of being. A second history of being would therefore have to be *ludic*, and perhaps even *ludicrous*; it would have to persevere without face-saving strategies of any kind. Disarmed by life, as it were, in the way an adolescent is disarmed by love; without recourse, destined only to continue in the face of inevitable interruption.

Having lost both history and being, such a second history of being would perhaps have to lose Heidegger as well; or, if not, it would have to accept some strange bedfellows for him: Nietzsche's *On the Genealogy of Morals*, Foucault's *History of Sexuality*, Derrida's *Post Card* and *Glas*, Bataille's 1929–1930 texts on mythological anthropology, Irigaray's fluid mechanics of woman and God in *Speculum* and *Ce sexe*, along with Sade's Duclos, the narratrix of *120 Days of Sodom*.

On the twenty-fourth day of her narrations, Madame Duclos tells the tale of the only mortal man who ever achieved an authentic confrontation with his own death. Anxious, resolved, resolutely open, ready and willing to encounter the ultimate, this man is ready to be made even more anxious than he already is, which is more anxious than most mortals are ever likely to be. Duclos gives him no name, but I call him *l'homme au Sein-zum-Tode,* and this is his passion:

> The scene took place at his little house in Roule. I was admitted to his bedroom, a room dark and somber. There I saw a man on the bed, and in the middle of the room a coffin. "You see a man on his deathbed," said our libertine to me, "a man who did not wish to close his eyes before rendering homage one last time to the object of his cult. I adore asses, and I want to die kissing one. At the very moment I shall have closed my eyes you yourself will place me in that coffin, after having carried me thither, and then you shall nail down the lid. It has become my firm intention to die thus in the bosom and beyng of pleasure [*dans le sein du plaisir*] and to be served in this final moment by the very object of my lubricity. Let us begin," he continued, in a weak and faltering voice; "hurry, for I am at the end." I approached, turned, let him see my buttocks. "Oh, beautiful ass!" says he. "What a delight it is to carry off to the grave the idea of such a lovely behind!" And he manipulated it and spread open its cheeks and kissed it like a man of the world in the best of health.
>
> "Oh," says he after a while, ceasing his exertions and turning onto his other side, "I knew I wouldn't have much time to enjoy this pleasure! I breathe forth my last; remember what I have instructed you to do." So saying, he exhaled a vast sigh, stiffened, and in general played his role so well that the devil fetch me if I didn't think him dead. Nevertheless, I did not lose my head: curious to see the end of such a whimsical ceremony, I prepared him for burial. He did not flinch, and whether he knew a secret for making it seem so, or whether my imagination was simply bedazzled, he grew rigid and cold as an iron bar; only his prick gave forth some signs of life [*quelques signes d'existence*], for it was hard and glued to his belly, and it seemed to exhale some droplets of cream quite in spite of itself. As soon as he was wrapped in a shroud, I carried him in my arms, and it wasn't the easiest thing in the world to do, for the way in which he stiffened made him as heavy as an ox. But I carried him all the way and I laid him out in his coffin; as soon as he was in, I began to recite the office of the dead; finally, I nailed down the lid. That was the critical moment: scarcely had he heard the blows of my hammer when he cried out in a fury, "Oh, in the Holy Name of God, I'm ejaculating! Save yourself, whore, save yourself, because if I catch you you're dead!" Fear seized me, I dashed to the stairway, where I met an adroit *valet de chambre* who was well-versed in his master's manias. The valet handed me two sovereigns and hurried off to the patient's room in order to deliver him from the state in which I'd put him. . . .[1]

An *other* history of being, the history of an *other* difference (*Sein/sein*), one that would embrace Sade? To the extent that it were *other,* we may be certain that in it neither history nor beyng would come like adroit valets to its rescue. Heidegger's history of being (or beyng) says enough to stake out some of the beginnings and ends of such a second history. If metaphysics peters out in *Er-*

lebnis, the "lived-experience" of life-philosophy, worldviews, values, and cultures, the *Leben* of such *Er-lebnis* remains unplumbed. If, prior to metaphysics, ζά and ζωή prevail, then a second history must tell what becomes of them in the course of the history of metaphysics and morals. Almost everything awaits telling here, whether it be Hesiodic χάος, the gaping of sky and earth, opening upon the pristine dimension of elemental air before even ἔρως came to be; or Parmenidean Aphrodite, whom Heidegger—forgetting Hippolytus—spurns for divine Aletheia; or Heraclitean Artemis, on the porches of whose temple Nietzsche plays and whom Heidegger prefers to Aphrodite, though not to Aletheia, as long as she (i.e., Artemis) is armed with bow and arrow; or Empedoclean Φιλία and Νεῖκος, to which Heidegger rarely if ever refers, whereas the German poet he most loved took Empedocles to be the preeminent thinker of generation and passing away. Almost everything awaits telling. For example, a τίκτειν that the Demiurge cannot wholly master by τέχνη, the former word suggesting reciprocal persuasion and seduction, a dalliance of Logos and Ananke that has precious little to do with anything we have ever said or thought concerning ποίησις and πρᾶξις, a reproduction that jeers and howls at all the models of production and practice in metaphysics; never told, not even in Plato's *Symposium* and *Phaedrus,* not even in Aristotle's "greater nearness" to earth and animal; certainly not by Augustine, who remains baffled by the similarity between the mothersmilk of his faith and the birdlime of his concupiscence, and not even by Aquinas, who wonders whether the erect posture is truly fitting for man and woman, as it is for trees, which stand on their heads; not even by Spinoza and Schelling, who prepare divinity for strange incursions into corporeality and sexuality, and certainly not by Hegel, who in his Jena lectures on the philosophy of nature matches sexual part with part and then holds a spiritual match to it all. No, it is something other than a "spark of Eros" that needs telling, just as for Heidegger it is something other than taciturnity and muteness that is called for in telling silence (*Erschweigen*).

Perhaps here, at the end of our investigation, it is only a matter of teasing out a few strands in the first (and only) history of being, teasing them out as so many final signs of life in Heidegger's thought. Signs of something that *stirs* in Heidegger's text but continues to lie dormant, as though biding its time. Four signs of stirring, bestirring, agitation, incitement, and excitement of life (*Regung, Auf-, An-, Erregung*): first, a glimpse of stirring in the coiling and toiling (*das Ringen*) of animal life as depicted in the 1929–1930 biology lectures; second, the stirring that Heidegger in his 1936 Schelling lectures sees in Schelling's 1809 *Treatise on Human Freedom,* to wit, the stirring of life in God and in the animal; third, a highly ambivalent view upon bestirring in the 1942–1943 Parmenides lectures, in which animal life is brought to the sacred precinct of the daimon, the δαιμόνιος τόπος, but then excluded from that place by an abyss—the gap of vision and the gully of speech; fourth and finally, the stirring that occurs much later, on the way to language (in the essay of that name, from the year 1959), in the bestirring of propriation (*Ereignis*) itself. The mere listing of the four topics indicates something daimonic about the theme of stirring:

Regung will be said of animals, which have no language, *and* of the very essence of language; it will name the stirrings of animal life *and* the life of divinity; it will be said of divinity *and* of evil; all these things, all these beings, will *stir* and *bestir themselves*—along with the event of propriation, the granting of time, space, clearing, and presence.

A SUBLIMITY LIVED IN LIFE ITSELF

In the biology lectures of 1929–1930 "bestirring" (*Regung*) is not the ultimate name for life's animatedness. There Heidegger defines the essence of animality in terms of benumbed behavior (*Benommenheit*) and the animal's wrestling with its impoverished world in a ring of disinhibitions (*Ringen, Umring, Enthemmungsring*). At the end of his analysis (29/30, §66) he stresses the specificity by which each life form is transposed (*versetzt*) into its ring. With an anti-Darwinian gesture that is wholly confluent with his Lamarckian tendencies, he insists that such rings are crystalline, in the sense that there is no possible transition from one ring to another. He concedes overlap, but not a blurring of frontiers. Especially important to his impossible project is the "fundamental difference" between the revelatory character of human being (*Offenbarkeit des Seienden [im] Dasein des Menschen*) and the nexus of openness in the benumbed animal kingdom (*Zusammenhang der Offenheit der benommenen Umringe des Tierreiches*), even though the unified field of φύσις would militate against the assertion of such a unique, fundamental difference (29/30, 401). The realms of animal life, excluding the human animal, begin to look like Ptolemaic spheres awaiting their Copernican Revolution, impinging on one another in impossible "overlap": the crystalline spheres of the Heideggerian animals mesh like cogwheels in the cosmic machine, even though Heidegger insists that animal life is a fundamental manner of being all its own and quite beyond all mere "mechanical" being-at-hand. Indeed, there is a dignity in animal life, to which Heidegger now wishes to speak, after his descriptions of the impoverished animal world have drawn to a close; a dignity in which human Dasein might experience something   *For myself I have gained nothing; not I, but the beast of the earth has joy of it now*   of its own glory and its finitude:

> When we consider that in every such wrestling [or every such coiling of the ring: *in jedem solchen Ringen*] the living creature in turn allows something of nature itself to enter into its encompassing ring [*sich etwas . . . einpaßt*], then we must say the following: *In this coiling of the encompassing rings we find revealed something like an intrinsic trait of dominance in living beings* [ein innerer Herrschaftscharakter des Lebendigen] *within beings in general*, an inner sublimity of nature out beyond itself, a sublimity lived in life itself [*eine innere, im Leben selbst gelebte Erhabenheit der Natur über sich selbst*]. (29/30, 403)

Whether Nietzsche or Kant speaks more compellingly here in the "dominance" and "sublimity" of life within nature is an arresting question. One certainly understands better why Heidegger is willing to grant Nietzsche his hypothesis that life dominates nature even if it appears to be "something slight" in a universe of ash. Yet one also feels the need to take all the questions of daimon life back to the analytic of the sublime in Kant's *Critique of Judgment*. The tension there between, on the one hand, life-forces (*Lebenskräfte*) and the power of nature (*die Macht der Natur*) and, on the other hand, the movement of heart-and-mind (*die Bewegung des Gemüts*), negative pleasure, and the attunement of spirit (*Geistesstimmung*); in short, the entire question of the sovereignty of mind in the face of the violence of nature and the uncertain solace of infinity, the entire question of *Ge-walt;* these matters compel daimon life with some urgency. Yet nothing could spare us the arduous task of working through the issues of both *sublimity* and *teleology* in the third critique, a task that would lead us . . . too far afield.[2]

Heidegger declines to speculate whether the drive for dominance, dominion, or mastery characterizes *human* life as well. Once again he prefers to sever humanity from animality. Human beings are "transposed," as animals are, yet in a way "peculiar" and "proper" to them:

> . . . *Human Dasein is in itself a peculiar being transposed to the nexus of the encompassing ring of the living.* In this regard it behooves us to observe the following: it is not as though we were now to be equated with the animals, over against a wall of beings which would hold a common content but which we would only see differently, the animals among themselves, and we among the animals, as though it were merely a question of a manifold of aspects of the selfsame. No, the encompassing rings of the two are not at all comparable; the totality of meshed rings in each case revealed to us not only falls under the beings that are otherwise open to us but also holds us captive in an altogether specific way. We therefore say that human beings exist in a peculiar way [*eigentümlicher Weise*] *in the midst* of beings. "In the midst of beings" means that animate nature holds us human beings captive in an altogether specific way, not on the basis of a special influence or impression that animate nature has or makes on us, but in terms of our own essence, whether or not we experience this in an original relation. (29/30, 403–404)

Heidegger here comes close to identifying animate nature with the dispensation of being itself. As we have by now seen, he is unable to make any headway with this problem of comparative world-relations in 1929–1930, which even here he poses as "the possible *unity*" of the sundry "*kinds of being.*" Such captivity and captivation designate the problem of *world* as such, and, bound up with that, the problem of *finitude*. Whether such "possible unity" extends to being as such, being as upsurgence in unconcealment, Heidegger is unable to say. And yet the problem of life transcends our own captivity in animate nature: the unified field of φύσις comes to have *infinite* dimensions, precisely as a *finitude* that is not of humankind alone.

STIRRINGS OF LANGUOROUS DIVINITY

The sublimity of nature, especially animate nature, "out beyond itself," avails not. None of the aporias and perplexities that we noted in chapter 3 concerning

the 1929–1930 biology lectures ever resolve: life, especially animal life, remains in closest proximity to Dasein, without the accession to thought of the
nearness of animal perishing to the lifedeath of Dasein. Dasein lives and dies in
circles of its own, proudly bearing the standard of its metaphysical *as,* lord of
all the rings yet master of none. Especially not its own. To which, as Heidegger
repeatedly concedes, a benumbed and finite Dasein scarcely has access.

If wrestling and coiling (*Ringen*) avail not, how is it with bestirring and
excitation proper (*Regung, Erregung*)? "Bestirring" is not a guiding word in
either the Nietzsche lectures (except for the "raging discordance" between art
and truth) or the contemporary *Contributions to Philosophy (Of Propriation).*
There the words "rapture," "ecstatic transport," and "trembling" (*Rausch,
Entrückung, Erzittern*) operate in its place. "Bestirring" is the word to which
Heidegger turns when it is a matter of describing the upsurgence of longing in the
ground of God, as Schelling conceives of it in his 1809 *Treatise on Human
Freedom.* Late in the 1936 Schelling course, immediately after the passage
quoted above, in chapter 3, on longing and languor (*Sehnsucht*) as the very
essence of divinity, Heidegger follows Schelling's example by invoking the notion of *Regung.* All "sentimentality" is set aside, as Heidegger attempts to descry
the "*essence* [Wesen] of the *ruling metaphysical animatedness*" within the divine
ground of yearning (SA, 150). He interprets the epidemic nature of divine yearning, longing, and languishing (for *Sehnsucht* derives from *siech* and *Seuche,*
"disease," "contagion," what the tradition calls physical *evil*) as the dual striving, craving, longing, and willing of the divine—a stirring that propels divinity
outward to all becoming and inward back to itself. Most notable of the characteristics of such longing, according to Heidegger, is that—in spite of all the words
that we have only now attached to it—it lacks a name; indeed, in it there are no
characters to spell out the characteristics of longing; in it "*the possibility of the
word* is missing" (151). Heidegger is careful not to draw the parallel to the
animal, which also lacks the word and all the characters, all the *Buchstaben,*
even though that lack is the salient trait of both desirous divinity and disinhibited
animality. Lack of the word is the trait and *retrait* of God. It is the re-mark and
retreat of divinity *with* animality. It is something like daimon life. In his care not
to draw the parallel, or even to hint at it, Heidegger misses the only significant
opportunity his thinking might have had to think ontotheology.

In the ground of God's primal essence, which is the ground of his or her
existence, the malaise of a nameless longing and languor is the "absolute
beginning of an egression-from-self" (SA, 151). Only such egression will enable
the divine to come (back) to itself. Both Schelling and Heidegger portray divine
longing as a bestirring: "*Die Sehnsucht ist die* Regung . . ." (151). And bestirring is a reaching or stretching out: ". . . *das sich von sich weg und auseinander
Strecken,*" reminiscent of the self-stretching that constitutes the lifespan of a
temporalizing (human) Dasein. Such temporalizing, desirous bestirring stirs in
the very self-excitation of what is stirred by and about itself: ". . . *die Erregung
des (sich) Regenden zu sich selbst,*" reminiscent of the autokinetic, metabolic,
automotive nature of life in philosophical speculation since Aristotle. Such, in

Schelling's words, is "the first stirring of divine existence [*die erste Regung göttlichen Daseins*]" (7, 360–61; SA, 151). Only in such stirring, comments Heidegger, can God "see or view himself, namely, in his longing, in his first aroused bestirring [*als der ersten erregten Regung*], as the one who views [*als den Blickenden*]." The very self-representation (*Sichvorstellen*), the very *Reflexion* of divinity's vision out and back depends upon the embeddedness of all viewing in bestirring. As though the theater of theism were constructed on an ancient daimonic site. The interlacing of view and stirring, vision and bestirring, will soon become important. For it is that interlacing which will bring God and animal to embrace, behind Heidegger's back, as it were, on the site of the daimon.

If divinity is the look, and if the look is ineluctably a gaze of longing, then divinity and animality will prove to be inextricable. If "spirit" as πνεῦμα is the "originally unifying unity," and if it is spirit that stirs in love and languishment, then such bestirring will prove to be both the life of a spirited body and the unity of *all* life. True, spirit will repeatedly try to shed the skin of its longing

It rose out of the water and snatched it away, and immediately sloughed its skin and returned to the well   in what Schelling calls the "final, total scission," or "the *finite* and *endlike*, total scission," *die endliche gänzliche Scheidung;* yet original unity will prevail over both divorce and primal "indifference"; ground and existence will perdure coeternally as the irreducible finitude of spirit, as long as life stirs in it.

It is clear why theriomorphic divinity, the most oriental of orientalisms, should cry for overcoming, whether in Hegel's interpretation of the Christ in his *Lectures on the Philosophy of Religion* or in Nietzsche's account of Dionysos in *The Birth of Tragedy*. It is not difficult to imagine why Georg Simmel wants to deprive divinity of a life that can only be lifedeath, to preserve the godhead in the formaldehyde of an ostensibly Schellingian "indifference." Yet such preservation, as Schelling himself realizes, is a hapless ruse. He knows full well what Heidegger too stresses, namely, that in his system the incandescence of intellect, the self-viewing spectation of the divine mind, and even the longing for λόγος, are themselves marks of the original stirring and excitation in the dark ground of languishment (SA, 159). The animatedness of becoming (*Werdebewegtheit*) in all creation has its source in the stirring of divine longing (*Regung der Sehnsucht*). Such stirring and excitation inevitably become addiction, epidemic, and contagion (SA, 161: *Regung . . . zur Erregung und damit zur Sucht*). *Sucht, siech, Seuche*—these are primal forms of *Sorge*, "care," in everything that stirs, in all life. No doubt, Schelling himself tries to stage some Leibnizian "stages" (*Stufungen*) of being in order to ameliorate the contagion, precisely in the way that every metaphysician before him and Heidegger after him will try. Yet the languishment of the divine can only intensify, whether one moves outward toward creatures or back to the silent, vigilant, horned Λόγος of the beginning. The more inward the divine gaze turns, "the more excited and addicted" divinity itself becomes (SA, 164). As divine existence circles ever

closer to its center, coiling like human time or the animal ring, it is repeatedly
cast forth in ecstatic longing, languor, and languishment. Heidegger's inspired
diagram of divine existence (alas, he draws no diagram of animal or plant life,
no schematic of the sublimity lived in life itself) is remarkably similar to his
diagram of the temporality of human being, in spite of the displacement from
the horizontal (human) axis to the vertical (divine) axis. In the Schelling lectures, depicting divine existence (SA, 164):

In the 1928 logic lectures, depicting human ecstatic temporality (26, 266):

Commenting on the former diagram, that of divine existence, Heidegger
writes: "The animatedness of creative, created nature is thus a compulsion to
life [*Lebensdrang*], circling and circling in itself, streaming out beyond itself
over and over again, individuating itself and individually setting out its stages"
(SA, 165). Heidegger neglects to mention that precisely these circles must at
some point constitute the rings of animal life, the recoil of the ecstasies of
future and having-been in human temporality, and the circles of hermeneutics,
all of them together constituting what Nietzsche calls the *circulus vitiosus deus*.
If we were to draw the rings of animal life, refusing to blur the boundaries of
each separate mortal coil, yet allowing the circles to synchromesh like a transmission or a spring—inasmuch as in these coiling rings something of nature
always penetrates, so that a kinship prevails—how different would the third
diagram, the schematic of sublimity, be from the other two?

What Schelling is looking for, Heidegger concludes, "is precisely the *animatedness of something in general that is alive* [*die* Bewegtheit eines Lebendigen überhaupt]" (SA, 165). In 1929–1930, and perhaps in 1927 or 1924 or
1921, that is precisely what Heidegger is looking for. Whether or not he finds
it, animatedness defines both rims of the human chaos, with animals to the
rear, as we like to think, and divinities not far ahead, as we like to believe. Yet
what about the divine malaise, which both comes from behind and lies eter-

nally ahead? In what lies the languishment of longing? What are the stakes of *Sehnsucht?* For Schelling, as for Kant before him, such languorous and languishing self-seeking, the desire to come into one's own, *Eigen-sucht,* the desire to persist in one's *own* thinking, *Eigen-dünkel,* is the very principle of darkness and the origin of evil. The rumor of longing is thus also the first stirring of (the possibility of) malevolence. Heidegger follows Schelling in his desperate effort to cut the scene, to shift from the divine to the specifically *human* scene, as the site of evil (SA, 171–72). Yet if evil is malignancy, and if malignancy stirs in the first stirrings of longing, then the contamination of divinity is unavoidable as long as divinity remains a *self*-seeking *self*-thinking, the involuting coil and recoil of specular reflection. Once again Heidegger tries to help Schelling stage the stages of being: the animal can never be evil, inasmuch as "spirit pertains to wickedness" (173), and spirit presumably cannot be attributed to animality. Only human beings—gods aside, whether theriomorphic or not—can "sink below animality," says Heidegger. It is as though for Heidegger the *brutum bestiale* bears the earmark of evil incarnate, without ever being capable of it, incorporates evil as the living sign of what it can never say or see, what it can never communicate or contain. *Der Sündenbock,* the scapegoat.[3]

Heidegger here complains that both Schelling and Hegel slip unawares into a secularized Christian concept of sin, perhaps even into an "Asiatic" realm (SA, 175), yet he says nothing about the quandaries of his own search for the animatedness of life and his own aversion to the animal. Nor does he say much at all about a *Sehnsucht* that would not be *Eigensucht* but what one might have to call *Anderssucht,* a languishing in memory of and *minne* for *others.* All we can do is repeat the cryptic remark cited above in chapter 3, now thinking of others both ahead and behind, but also of others at our side:

> The essence of ground in God is longing? We can scarcely restrain the objection that this statement projects a human condition onto God—. Ah, yes! *But* it could also be otherwise. For who has ever verified the supposition that longing is something merely human? And who has ever refuted thoroughly and with sufficient reason the possibility that what we call *longing,* which is where we are, in the end is something other than we ourselves? Does not longing conceal something that denies us *any* grounds for limiting it to humankind, something that would sooner give us cause to grasp it as that in which we human beings are unfettered *out beyond ourselves* [über uns weg *entschränkt*]? Is it not precisely longing that proves the human being to be Other, other than a mere human being? (SA, 150)

If Schelling's original impetus and keenness flag at the end of his *Treatise on Human Freedom,* as Heidegger observes (191), will we be able to say anything else concerning Heidegger's own final signs of life? If Schelling too should prove to be a melancholic, joining the ranks of Aristotle's Empedocles, Socrates, and Plato (SA, 193; cf. *29/30,* 270–71); if Schelling's system too "shatters" (SA, 194: *scheitert*), merely postponing but never resolving all its principal difficulties; then perhaps we will have to say the same about Heidegger's confrontation—or near miss—with daimon life.

ΔΑΙΜΟΝΙΟΣ ΤΟΠΟΣ: THE DAIMONIC SITE

In the 1942–1943 Parmenides lecture course Heidegger interprets the famous myth of Er with which Plato brings *Republic* to a close. When Er returns in the nick of time to his funeral pyre, he reports what he has seen in the underworld, down there "in the daimonic place" (614c 1: εἰς τόπον τινὰ δαιμόνιον). It is the place of the gap, gully, or cleavage, one of the sites of chaos (54, 146). In the following pages of his course Heidegger defines the Greek notion of ψυχή as the essence of "life" (*das Wesen des "Lebens"*), itself bound up with both φύσις and the daimonic. Psyche is the essence of a living creature that has language. Presumably, the ζῷον ἄλογον, mute animality and silent vegetation, can never occupy the daimonic site; indeed, the plain described by Plato's Er is barren of tree and shrub, devoid of lion and sheep.

Heidegger eschews the "Christian" understanding of the daimonic as demonic, of daimons as minions of evil. He embraces Aristotle's definition of the thinker as one who experiences "excessive, astonishing, difficult, and therefore also daimonic things [καὶ δαιμόνια]" (*Nichomachean Ethics*, Z 7, 1141b; 54, 148). The Greeks know that thinkers are somehow always remote from life; thinkers lack "*Lebensnähe*," a certain intimacy with life. What thinkers do perceive, according to Heidegger, following Aristotle, is the remote in the near, the unfamiliar in the familiar. Neither the colossal nor the miniscule, neither the reclusive nor the obtrusive, neither the monstrous nor the petty, but the uncommon daimonic. The most natural thing in the world, what others call "nature" herself, is what the thinker envisages: φύσις, the upsurgence into unconcealment of what gives itself to be seen. Such generic, generous giving is δαίω, and the ones that give or grant view and vision, the δαίοντες, are none other than the δαίμονες (54, 151). Their granting is always a granting of vision and the gaze, *Blicken*, θεάω. Heidegger emphasizes the middle-voice form, θεάομαι, the viewing in which the viewer shows himself or herself (152). Such viewing and presenting to view constitute the very earmark, as it were, of humankind, with its one eye, its pineal eye, fixed on divinity. For if seeing is believing, viewing is divine: τὸ θεᾶον is τὸ θεῖον (154).

Heidegger is doubtless aware of the proximity of his own reading of the daimonic to that of what he elsewhere calls Platonism, not merely the Plato that writes the Socratic myth of Er or the Socrates who continually socratizes Plato, but the thinker of the εἶδος as *Anblick*, the viewed profile or envisaged silhouette of being. The proximity does not seem to trouble Heidegger but to encourage him, even when his Platonism obliges him to deprive the animal of both sight and voice and to appeal to a concept of the "self" as what vision and voice coproduce: Heidegger holds to Platonic theory, theater, and theism (158–59), even after Schelling's demonstration of the monstrosity of *Eigensucht*. Ironically, he does not pause to ponder the *third* (the first being δαίοντες-δαίμονες, the second θεά-θέα) of those homonyms that determine for the Greeks what human life is. He cites Heraclitus' fragment 48 on the aptly named βίος-βιός, well-named inasmuch as both "the bow" and "life" perform the work of death, ἔργον δὲ θάνατος. Heidegger comments, rather lamely, "The word βιος is ambiguous in itself, and in its ambiguity designates precisely the essence of the life that brings death [*das Wesen des den Tod bringenden Lebens*]" (54, 160–61). He then makes an effortless transition, not onward to the lifedeath of daimon life, but back to θέα-θεά and δαίοντες-δαίμονες. Because the daimon occupies the halfway mark on Heidegger's way to the goddess, the thinker forgets the ambiguity of daimon life. Human being remains for Heidegger a *theic* viewing. If the animal "to a certain extent" also appears as viewing, "for which reason the divine too at the outset is theriomorphic [*tiergestaltig im . . . Beginn*]," that only goes to show that the view (*der Blick*) alone is decisive. Neither theriomorphism nor anthropomorphism will distract the thinker from the imputed Greek thinking of being as coming to presence in unconcealment. Neither gods nor demigods (ἡμίθεοι) will distract him from what Plato's *Phaedo* and Heidegger agree to call *the view upon being* (163).⁴ The sending of being (μοῖρα) holds sway over all viewers, whose purity of measure (αἰδώς, literally, "shame") and pristine favor (χάρις, *Gunst*) derive from being itself. The Greeks *poetize* their gods in measures of awe and mildness; they *think* their gods "in θαυμαστόν and δαιμόνιον" (164). Such poetizing and the daimonic thinking that accompanies it are a voicing and a viewing, a hearing of the word and a sighting of radiant appearance. Indeed, Heidegger's δαιμόνιον ultimately seems more Orphic than Platonic: Heidegger is a worshiper of Phanes (from φαίνειν, φαίνεσθαι), his thought of revealing and concealing essentially deictic and theic. However, Phanes is a late Orphic transformation of Hesiodic χάος, the chaos and chasm that Heidegger most wants and needs to think.

By this juncture in the 1942–1943 Parmenides course the constellation of thought, theory, theater, and deictic theism—the entire aurospecular spectacle—is clearly defined. The (quasi) homonym δαίμων-δαίων is taken to designate "the viewing that surges up on its own and the being that expends itself in beings [*das von sich selbst her aufgehende Blickende und in das Seiende sich hereingebende Sein*]" (165). Sound and light, voice and view, word and vision hold sway, so much so that when Heidegger translates for the nth time the phrase ζῷον λόγον ἔχον he is so intent on the λόγος that he translates ζῷον not as *living* being but simply as a nondescript *Seiendes*. The *life* of the vociferous viewer is forthwith forgotten. As the section draws to a close Heidegger aims a jibe at Oswald Spengler's treatment of culture in terms of "biological process" and the death of civilizations in terms of animal perishing (*Verendung*): the life-philosophers will always have given Heidegger ample reason to suppress the life of the living being that has speech.

Many further aspects of the 1942–1943 Parmenides course merit our scrutiny: the reading of μῦθος as "utterance," the treatment of art prior to "aesthetics," the fitting place of the daimon as εὐδαιμονία, what the tradition will call "happiness,"⁵ the field of Lethe as radical oblivion and the river Ameles as "Sanssouci," *Ohnesorge*, those bizarre landmarks (the barren field and stream) of the daimonic realm of "care concerning unconcealment." However, let us turn to the final hours of the lecture course, where plant and animal life stir for what must seem the last time.

It is still a matter of voice, view, vision, theory, and theism (54, 219–20). Responding to Rilke's eighth *Duino Elegy*, Heidegger now intervenes twice in ways that are crucial for our investigation. First, he explicitly denies plants and animals any participation in the ostensibly unified field of φύσις, repudiating the Rilkean identification of the animal as the proper bearer of openness to being. Second, he affirms the essence of plant and animal life as *Regung*, bestirring, as though forgetting his own lecture course on Schelling and its association of *Regung* with divine longing, which for its part is essentially divine openness to the animatedness of all becoming. Suffice it to say that what disturbs Heidegger most about Rilke is the latter's proximity, as discomfiting as the company of angels and apes. For Rilke associates the animal's openness to being with its peculiar relation toward death—its *transparent* relation, wherein death does not occlude openness—whereas Heidegger associates an exclusively human openness to being with the mortal's intimation of its own mortality. Rilke is near yet far, too near to ignore, too far to embrace. The stakes are too high, as the exasperated tone of Heidegger's remarks betrays: "For Rilke, human 'consciousness,' reason, λόγος, is precisely the barrier that causes human beings to be less capable than the animal. Are we supposed to become 'animals,' then?" (54, 229n.). It is this "throwaway" remark, this rhetorical broadside in a marginal jotting or footnote, that indicates the danger concealed in Rilke's angels and animals: Heidegger says that Rilke's is a secularized Christian ontology that knows and suspects nothing of ἀλήθεια (231, 235); what he does not say is that Rilke is responding poetically-thoughtfully (with αἰδώς and χάρις) to the unified field of the daimonic, the field that has eluded Heidegger all along; what Heidegger silences is the *possibility* that Rilke's angels and beasts *also* occupy the heartland of unconcealment, which is the site he craves for his own thought. Commenting on Heidegger's "irritation," "polemic," and "bitter irony," Michel Haar wonders whether Heidegger is not *anxious*—"As though Rilkean openness threatened to usurp the place of ἀλήθεια."[6] It is of course the animal that will pay for Rilke's (admitted) extravagance and insolence: "On the contrary, the animal precisely does not see the open, it never can, not with any one of its several eyes" (54, 231).

Yet if Rilke can be chided for his lack of radicality, it seems strange indeed to hear Heidegger affirming the Platonic-Aristotelian definition of man—as the (living) being that has speech—without a single demur, as though that definition had nothing to do with the ontotheological tradition in its secularized Christian form. The more Heidegger inveighs against Rilke's lack of radicality, the more insipid his own insistence on vision and voice becomes. The more he scorns Rilke's poetry as "popular metaphysics" imbued with strains of Schopenhauerian will, Nietzschean *brutalitas,* and psychoanalytic snooping (all of them, incidentally, tainted by Lou), and the more he disdains Rilke's poetry as botched Christianity (*eine Art verunglückten Christentums*), the more palpable becomes Heidegger's anxiety in the face of its vibrant life. Rilke's putative lack of radicality exposes Heidegger's own diffidence. Heidegger's polemic raises the suspicion that his own worship of the goddess Aletheia may be but a minor event in the ontotheological history of being, which has largely forgotten φύσις as ζωή.

Once again Heidegger insists on a gap, gully, or cleavage (*eine Kluft*) in being, in order to separate man from animal. Yet it is not the cleaving of beyng, *die Zer-klüftung des Seyns*, which would expose humanity to its abyssal essence, that Heidegger craves; what he wants instead is a trench, to be dug as a line of defense, a Maginot Line against the invasive, encroaching animal. It is not radical exposure to mortality but the most traditional protective gesture, the most regressive reinstatement of the only chain of being(s) there ever was. It is not a thinking of the end of metaphysics but an unwitting repetition of its instauration: the pick and shovel of parousial vision and apophantic voice digging away in order to reinstate the Platonistic χωρισμός. On one side of that gap, presumably, stands man, man alone, with gods as erstwhile companions. Man alone enjoys the open, oblivious of at least one of his feet, the one planted firmly on the far side of the gap. Heidegger writes and speaks in the silence of an autonoesis that is oblivious of both its feet; he conceals in a mended stocking what Bataille calls "The Big Toe."[7] With his unpaired hand Heidegger writes:

> Man and man alone sees into the open, without however catching sight of it [*sieht in das Offene hinein, ohne es doch zu erblicken*]. We catch sight of being itself only in the essential view of proper thinking [*im Wesensblick des eigentlichen Denkens*]. Yet even here, we can catch sight of being only because the thinker, as man, already sees being.
>
> In contrast [*dagegen*], the animal neither sees nor does it ever catch sight of the open in the sense of the unconcealment of what is unconcealed. Nor can it therefore be animated [*sich bewegen*] in what is occluded [*im Verschlossenen*] as such; just as little can it comport itself [*sich verhalten*] toward what is concealed. The animal is excluded [*ausgeschlossen*] from the essential domain of the strife between unconcealment and concealment. The sign of this essential exclusion is the fact that no animal and no kind of vegetation "has the word."[8]

Heidegger here pretends to occupy for a fleeting moment the far side, pretends to plant both feet there and open both his eyes in order to discern that the animal neither sees nor catches sight of being with any of its eyes. He then appears to leap back to the exclusively human side of the gap in order, like Er, to announce what he has seen on the other side. What he has seen is the sign indicating that the animal is so thoroughly barred (*ausgeschlossen*) that it cannot even move about in the realm of its occlusion (*im Verschlossenen*). The sign indicates that   *Already the stream has carried it twenty leagues back to the channels where I found it*   animals have no signs. From both sides of the gully Heidegger claims to catch sight of what so few mortals have caught sight of, namely, the fact that the signless animal is penned in so tightly that even its traditional self-animation must be denied it.

And yet. The reference to the sign of radical exclusion only causes "the riddle of all that lives," *das Rätsel alles Lebendigen,* to surge upward into view *as* a riddle. For, to repeat, the animal is drawn toward its nourishment, its prey, and its sexual partner as no stone is ever drawn to the earth on which it lies. Something is about to stir in Heidegger's text that is not simply vision and voice, vision and voice designed to blind and silence the animal and plant:

> In the circle of living things designated as plant and animal we find that peculiar bestirring of arousal [*jenes eigentümliche Sichregen einer Regsamkeit*] in accord with which the living being is "agitated," that is, excited to an upsurgence within a circle of excitability [*erregt zu einem Aufgehen in einem Umkreis der Erregbarkeit*]. On the basis of such excitability it draws other things into the circle in which it bestirs itself. (54, 237–38)

Heidegger's riddling on the riddle brings the bestirred animal (as earlier, with Schelling, the bestirred God) into the encompassing realm of φύσις as upsurgence (*Aufgehen* here presumably meaning "upsurgence into unconcealment" rather than the "absorption" or "evanescence" of quotidian Dasein in the world of its concerns). Alarmed by the consequences of his "proper thought," disquieted by the riddle of life, disconcerted by the proximity of Rilke, Heidegger now retreats, pick and shovel firmly grasped in his prehensile organ, determined to entrench himself in the utterly undaimonic place of the all-too-familiar segregation of the animal from the human:

> No stirring or excitability of plants and animals ever conducts the living being into the free region in such a way that what is agitated could ever even let what excites it "be" what it is as an excitant, to say nothing about what the living being is prior to or without excitation. Plants and animals hang suspended in something outside themselves [*hängen in einem Außerhalb ihrer*], without ever "seeing" either the outside or the inside; that is, without ever having to stand unconcealed as a gaze into the free region of being [*als Anblick unverborgen im Freien des Seins stehen zu haben*]. (54, 238)

To be sure, an animal is not a stone. Nor is it an airplane. No stone or airplane can take flight as does the lark that rises now in Heidegger's text, "bestirring itself and taking wing, jubilant in the face of the sun." Nevertheless, Heidegger's lark is not one of the two that soar in the face of the setting sun
        he will not rise again   in the fourth and last of Richard Strauss's
Vier letzten Lieder:

> *Ist dies etwa der Tod?*
>
> Is this in some way our death?

Heidegger's lark, unlike those of Strauss and Rilke, "does not see the open" (54, 238). What it "sees," on the viewless wings of its poetic "eyes," can be revealed only by a poetizing that is more "elevated," "essential," and "appropriate" than that of Rilke. For poor Rilke anthropomorphizes and humanizes the riddle of the living (238–39). The bestirring of Heidegger's lark, on the wing in the unified field of φύσις, remains blind and mute.

SIRENSONG

Nevertheless, birds ensnare in the open. In the open air. Heidegger recalls this from time to time—for instance, in the Heraclitus lectures, if not in the Parmenides course. And, of course, there are no lectures on Empedocles. It is in response to Heidegger's recollection (in "The End of Philosophy and the Task of Thinking") of the *Parmenidean* well-rounded sphere, the sphere of ἀλήθεια, that Luce Irigaray raises her insistent yet supple questions in *Oblivion of the Air: With Martin Heidegger*.⁹

Hers is not an easy book to describe. Begun the day she learned of Heidegger's death in Freiburg on May 26, 1976, and published seven years later, it is a work of mourning. A more successful work of mourning than most, at least for its readers. Yet there is nothing here   *like a woman in mourning*   of either introjection or incorporation, nothing of either adulation or rebuke. An uncommon intimacy *and* a carefully preserved distance prevail throughout the book. Which may best be depicted in terms of its motto, gleaned from Heidegger's Angelus Silesius: "The rose is without why; it blooms because it blooms." Irigaray's roses are wild, not arranged for geometric gardens, but burgeoning in a thicket. They flower as brief paragraphs, wellnigh aphoristic, spotted with question-marks. Each paragraph entertains what Irigaray thematizes at the end of her book, namely, a *risk*. We might cull a few of her roses of risk, simply as an invitation to the thicket and its luxuriant signs of life.

(1) *The duplicitous sphere: Empedocles vs. Parmenides.* Irigaray resists Heidegger's Parmenidean strain throughout, resists the thinking that takes being and thinking as the selfsame (OA, 9, 22, 111, 135, and 141). If Parmenides is a brother to Heidegger, the oldest, the earliest of those who accompany him on his path of thought, he is also the stolid Pythagorean who ordains, "Boys on the right, girls on the left" (120). Irigaray declines to join the brotherhood of being; she insists that there be a thinking of at least Two, rather than One. Not the traditional twosome of nature (on the left) and culture (on the right), but a prodigiously generative couple and copula. No doubt a tension pervades her meditation on Heidegger, one familiar to those who (perhaps too hastily, perhaps too anxiously) adjudge her feminism "essentialist." While Irigaray is unwilling to accept the preordained role-distribution that divides the masterbuilders of being (on the right) from the guardians of φύειν, of all that lives and grows (on the left), there can be no doubt that such growth and life are what she most wants to think, most wants to protect from a discourse that can only stifle them. Although her encounter with Heidegger's poets restricts itself to Hölderlin and Trakl, and does not include Rilke, she goes to meet them on the unified though variegated field of something *other* than upsurgence.

To the Parmenidean sphere of being Irigaray opposes the sphere of Empedocles, the duplicitous sphere of Φιλία and Νεῖχος. True, the outermost crystalline shell of the Empedoclean universe, hardened to glassy ether, mirrors being as specularly as does the sphere of Parmenides. Yet the physician-thinker of love and hate, of desire, waxing, and waning, is by and large one of the Greeks whom Heidegger forgets (82). True, the hatred that periodically all but rends the sphere of Empedocles has in modernity become outright hatred of nature (71–72), a development that ought to trouble the thinker of the essence of technology.[10] Yet if hatred fractures every limit and disperses every gathering, those limits need periodic transgression and the gathering needs strife. At all events, both hate and love demand something more than an ethereal reflection, something more than a view to the One.

(2) *Path-taking, path-breaking: the* via rupta. Irigaray often accompanies Heidegger's thought in full sympathy and with a sense of particular urgency; just as often she feels the need to break away on her own, in the direction of something not yet voiced. Her thinking of technology and the enframing (*Gestell*), like Heidegger's, is haunted by the fear that it may be altogether "too late" for the creature some call "man," the creature still in ignorance of its sexes. For the forces "he" has unleashed may foreclose every possible future for life as such: "In this technical world he has fabricated . . . , does man still have time to brood on his destiny? Once a creator, has he not become a machine in service to his creation? An effect of this archi-technism which is his language? And an effect of his solitary monologue with his φύσις, his πόλις, his things, his brothers?" (131–32). Irigaray does not underestimate the extent to which access to nature and growth, obscured under the masks of projected desire, enframing, and domination, is difficult if not impossible (23).

A second area in which her thinking accompanies Heidegger in full sympathy is her radical meditation—the most radical I have ever seen—on the oblivion of being, *Seinsvergessenheit*. She follows, more rigorously than any Heideggerian of the Strict Persuasion, Heidegger's admonition not to think of *Seinsvergessenheit* as an oversight on the part of humankind. Her thinking of oblivion, oblivion of the air, continues to meditate on death and mourning; it resists the temptation to accept the mistaken commonplace that forgetting is the mere obverse of remembrance (30–31; 67–68). Yet it also resists any thinking of death that would confirm the uniformity of a "proper" existence (73). It is neither *Dasein* nor *Sein* that has been forgotten from Parmenides through Heidegger; what has been forgotten, as thin as it may sound, is *air*.

In quest of air, as it were, Irigaray strays from Heidegger's path. Better, she invites him to stray with her, precisely by removing the soil beneath his feet: "Perhaps one must remove Heidegger from this earth on which he so loves to walk. Deprive him of this firm sod, this 'illusion' of a path that holds beneath his footfall—even if it is a timber track, heading nowhere—and guide him back not only to the thought but also to the world of the Presocratics" (10). For however much Empedocles may dream of ethereal crystal, solidity is by and large reserved for what will be called *metaphysics*. Irigaray herself disdains the erection of solidity and the ethereal; she engages herself instead to the *fluidity of air*. Empedocles with Anaximenes.

Air? *Appearances*, as in a person's having a melancholy air about them; or a *melody,* as on a G-string (12); or the subtle *element* inhaled by living creatures and borne by the saline solution of their blood (31), the "fluid vehicle of φύειν" (78), which is to say, oxygenated blood, but also milk, water, and *the woman of the vine, the maker of*   wine, without which we would die (79); air as the *milieu* of all motion-toward and the *medium* of the voice, the breath of words on the tongue (113, 131); air, the most subtle of beings, the natural *environment* of hidden or exiled gods (139), as of what the Greeks called δαίμονες; air, the bottomless bottom of metaphysics, the ambience of abyss (13); the stillness of oblivion.

To be sure, path-breaking is never easy, and there are moments when Irigaray's gesture seems as metaphysical as Heidegger's, if not more so: "Yet this aerial matter remains the philosopher's unthought. And, in this unthought, the might of mother nature prevails over him, at least up to the present, quite beyond all his powers. A priori condition of all his a priori?" (18). More often than not, however, Irigaray attains and sustains a remarkable candor and simplicity that are reminiscent of Heidegger at his best, Heidegger manifesting the final signs of life: "Without air, is any place livable for a mortal?" (25). Into the open air, then, outside the house of being. Yet still very much within the shelter of the human body, the mortal body (63). For the mortal human body, which is always at least *two,* is (are) at the heart of Irigaray's meditation.

(3) *The body of the rose.* "Is not air the whole of our dwelling as mortals? . . . And yet this element, irreducibly constitutive of all the elements, imposes itself on neither perception nor knowledge. Always there, it lets itself be forgotten" (15). Air envelops and penetrates the body by the passages of the nose and mouth, where organs await it, after its reception at the mucal threshold (34). Air gives life. "The life it gives is prior to every possible demonstration" (35). Thus air swathes and is swathed in oblivion, a "double oblivion" of "her who has always already granted life to him and to her [*de celle qui lui a toujours déjà donné la vie*]," as also of "her who has granted her and him life by attending to them in the destiny of their being" (85). Oblivion of the air may well be—although for Irigaray this remains a *question*—oblivion of "the sexual character of being." *L'oubli du caractère sexué de l'être?* A question stirring at the heart of Schelling's ontotheology. A question which, whatever Heidegger may whisper to Fink during their Heraclitus seminar, and whatever Heidegger's repeated references to *Leiben* may mean (Irigaray does not refer to them), remains largely unthought in the thinker of being (94). It would therefore not be a matter of merely drawing a *parallel* between ontological and sexual difference; the task would be to think sexuality and being, or sexuality and the granting, in one and the same breath. Bestrewal as breaths of air, the cleaving of being as birth into the chill, the first gasps of air.[11]

If the sexed body is the site of both the granting and the oblivion of air, it is also the portal of the *il y a,* the *Es gibt,* the "There is/It gives" of clearing and propriation. The sexed body is, as we shall see, precisely what stirs in *Ereignis,* bestirring itself as the incursion of an irreducible *otherness* into presence and propriation. Waftings. Sudden fragrance of roses.

(4) *Ecclusion: disclosedness: clearing: the air.* "But what is simple in φύσις—this he [Heidegger] has forgotten" (70). Thus Irigaray's guiding suspicion, even when she follows Heidegger on his path. What is simple is this: if clearing (*Lichtung, défrichement*) is not luminosity but a place in the forest where the trees have been thinned out in such a way that light and shadow can play there,[12] it is not so much for the eyes to see as for the skin and other organs to breathe. Clearing is air. For all his caution concerning the *lumen* (*supra*) *naturale*, Heidegger remains a captive of vision and voice, eye and word, sight and sound. His daimons see and speak, his gods are theatrical, enamored of theory. All for show. *Bühne.* "Privileging vision, man has already succeeded in exiting from the bounds of his body. The subject is already ecstatic in place of that which grants him place [*extatique au lieu qui lui donne lieu*]. He already lives outside himself, outside the body that grants him his view on things" (OA, 92). Outside himself, beside himself, transported in ecstasies of being, he is not surprised to find that everything appears to be properly his own: "His own tongue alone, his own speech, his own saying, his own everything" (124). What is foreign to his native land does not even exist for him. His un-saying or co-responding is by some hidden maneuver always harmonized in advance. "Where is there here the body of the one who speaks or is spoken? How is it granted in this 'there is' or 'it gives'? Or, how is she granted? Or, how are they granted together?" (125). They are granted—as Hölderlin's Empedocles and Heidegger's Trakl know—only in the ambience of lovers, whose ecstasy is not of being but of liquid air (153–54). Anaximenes with Thales.

What compels Irigaray is the thought of an *element* or a *material* in φύσις, which Heidegger thinks as upsurgence in presencing, and as domain, scope, or dimension. "The matter [*matière*] of φύσις has—could it be?—a logic that the λόγος does not know."[13] Ironically, that material element would itself be the "forgotten *material mediation* of the λόγος," that is to say, the very air that carries the reverberations of the voice. It is the selfsame air that sustains "the other reverberation of Dasein." The air that vibrates with sound across and beyond the lips (54) is the same air that is freshened by the leaves of trees surrounding the forest clearing; their exhalation becomes both the life-giving element for all that breathes and creeps on the earth and, in turn, for the human exhalations of speech (24). However, human speech is oblivious of air; it responds to the splendor of the sun (43). Heidegger's daimon, looking-in and signaling in speech, is itself oblivious, "exiled" in oblivion of the air (139). "It is not light that has created the clearing; light advenes only by grace of the transparent lightness of air. It presupposes air. No sun without an air that receives it and transmits its rays. No speech without the air that serves as its vehicle" (147). And yet, to repeat, human being constitutes itself in and as oblivion "of the gift of that in which it is," in and as a "void that would be its horror of nature," in and as oblivion of the "receptacle" or "hollow" of air (32–33, 139). The very receptacle that is forgotten, remembered, then forgotten again by Timaeus and all the brotherhood after him.

The unified field of φύσις, the unified realm of emphatic ζά, quite beyond all upsurgence into visibility, is the granting of air. While no breath of speech is possible without it, no series of utterances or propositions can "translate the fluid vehicle . . ." (78). What Irigaray tries to emulate instead are the roses granted by nature and air as *efflorescences horizontales*. Such granting or donation is always *material*, no matter how subtle its ὕλη, in petal or woody stem, a bestowal "by and with the other" (95), on the horizon of the horizontal. That other is the variously shaped yet always inspired and respirant body. Its unlocking Irigaray calls *éclosion*, disclosedness, "ecclusion." Ecclusion is at once the vast field of disclosive life and the "the most intimate φύειν" of the body (129), very much after the manner of what Merleau-Ponty calls "the flesh of the world."[14] In its vastness and intimacy—what Heidegger calls *Ferne und Nähe*—lies the secret of its forgottenness, a "monumental void in the memory of oblivion" (116).

(5) *In the mind and mouth of the poet.* In the *Grund zum Empedokles* Hölderlin says that "nature . . . appeared with all her melodies [*Melodien*, i.e., airs] in the mind and mouth of this man [Empedocles], and so intimately [*innig*] and warmly and personably, as though . . . the spirit of the elemental dwelt among mortals in human form."[15] Irigaray is so intensely and intimately close to Hölderlin's and Empedocles' elemental spirit and melodious mouth that her reading of Heidegger's *Elucidations of Hölderlin's Poetry* is one of the most challenging and refreshing that we possess—at a time when readings of Heidegger's Hölderlin abound.[16]

We have already heard some extracts from the last rose in section 7 of *Oblivion of the Air:* in the preceding chapter we cited Irigaray's remarkable response to Heidegger's encounter with *Trakl.* That response, the last rose, comes at the end of a sequence of meditations on Heidegger's Hölderlin, and it elaborates a reading of the poet that is all but unheard-of today. The melody or air that stirs the air—"*En quoi la voix? En air*" (48)—is irremediably melancholy. It is something for Aristotle's Empedocles, Socrates, and Plato (70–71). Also for Rousseau, who remembers or invents the story that language—the tongues of man and woman—has its origins at the well or fountain where right meets left, where girls gather water and the boys' cows grow insatiably thirsty. Irigaray feels the need to alter the tenor of the story, the very language of the story. She fears that language is the house that Jack built in order to project his sexual destiny, waiting confidently for Jill to come tumbling after. Yet Jack remains oblivious of the "material-matricial support" that undergirds all the architectonic schemes of his own tongue. He remains the "animal who refuses to think what his tongue is for" (140), unless and until he begins to sing the rose. The rose, not as a "metaphor" or "ideal figure" (130), but as "the body and the flesh of all diction: air, breath, song" (156).

Accordingly, Irigaray's sense of the *holy* in Hölderlin is hardly what it is for most readers of Heidegger's *Elucidations,* although in the context of plenipotence and bestrewal, the context of daimon life, her sense of the holy makes sacred sense. The sacred sense of   *life they retained in their own keeping* a new interpretation of sensuousness. A sensuousness that is both embrace and ember, fire and ash, love and mourning—with an air of smiling melancholy (70). A sensuousness that never abandons the dazzling milieu or element in which it takes and gives place. Hölderlin acknowledges that element, the elemental, in all-present, all-living nature, which Heidegger is always hasty to condemn as the fatal mistranslation and vulgar coarsening of ethereal φύσις. Irigaray is closer to Hölderlin's nature, closer to Etna, than Heidegger is: "She, the living, immediate omnipresence, enkindles all in her embrace [*embras(s)e tout*]: day and night" (99). Her secret *Night and day murmur* is the mystery of the all-vital, *la toute vivante*, not only in the fertile valleys but also on every barren peak or horizontal plain. Is "she," then, all-gathering? Is "she" the *Versammlung* of which Derrida has taught us to be so suspicious? *Parmenides'* goddess, governing at the center?

> Is she a gathering? If the return to an inchoate commencement can be said that way. Gathering by way of living touches; between lips that move but are silent about every distinguishing of worlds, about every pronouncement of truth or status. Open, she takes without keeping; she enwraps, impregnates and bathes prior to every this or that, here or there, before or after, present, past, or future. (OA, 100)

All-living nature passes beyond memory and care. Care is "the crypt, in mourning, of her who recoils in oblivion"; memory here can only have the sense of an "inaugural default," a being always only on the verge of that monumental void in the memory of oblivion (101; 116). On the shore of the sea *Beside the sea she lives* that gives and takes memory, the sea as the she-lover, *amante marine* (103).[17]

Recoiling in oblivion. Oblivion *of* the air. The genitive is double, as Heidegger always insists. And its doubling generates joy as well as mourning, the joy of jubilant gods restored to their "natural gifts" (102), the restored divinities that were once called δαίμονες. Signaling and looking-in, touching and being touched, such daimons would be irreducibly material-matricial. "Thus flesh remains visionary, and the gaze flesh" (106). θεά-θέα, the gazing goddess, takes on a new sense: the look adheres to earth, water, and air, as well as to heavenly fire. Air is where the daimonic bird ensnares. Air is where the invisible stirs.

WHAT BESTIRS IN THE SHOWING OF SAYING?

The stirring (*Regen, Regsamkeit, Er-, Auf-, Anregung*) that transpires in all that lives, in plants and animals as well as in Schelling's languorous God, does not simply vanish from Heidegger's thinking. For what was earlier attributed to the essence of life and the essence of divinity is now said of language and the granting: in the third part of "The Way to Language" Heidegger makes his way from saying and showing (*Sagen, Zeigen*) to the thought of propriation (*Eignen, Ereignis*) in the following italicized pronouncement: "*What bestirs in the showing of saying is owning* [Das Regende im Zeigen der Sage ist das Eignen]."[18]

It would be eminently possible to write off Heidegger's pronouncement as sheer singsong. In truth, whether or not it puts on airs, it is an air. Its stirring may not tell us any more about life, but it does say something about living language (discussed in chapter 2, above), and it also suggests that the ethereal thought of language is not as crystalline and pure, not as brittle, bloodless, and abstract as it may have seemed. It also reinforces Heidegger's early insight that language is not preeminently apophantic; language does not depend on the "as" of propositional speech, to which no lizard is equal, nor many mortals, if the truth be told. No full account of the itinerary—the way-making movement, *die Bewëgung*—of "The Way to Language" is possible here. Let a brief reminder suffice.

"The Way" takes three turns. The first part of the essay (US, 243–50) loosens the daimonic weft or tangle of language, which in the present instance tries to "bring language to language." Heidegger prefers that tautology to the traditional reductions of language to something else—to articulated sound, to the signifier-signified relation, to the labor of spirit, to an expression of a culture or worldview, and so on. Resisting such reductions, Heidegger quotes Wilhelm von Humboldt's introduction to his classic work on the Kawi language of Java: "One must not regard *language* as a lifeless *product* [Erzeugtes]. It is far more like a *reproducing* [Erzeugung]" (US, 248). Language is not dead, not *ein totes*, but living and generative, copulative, as Irigaray says. There is evidently something plant or animal-like in its "spirit." Heidegger does not elaborate, but a curious seed is planted on this very first turn of his way to language. It is perhaps the seed that is planted in the rift-design (*Aufriß*) of a field that is plowed in order that it may "harbor seed and growth" (252). Once again, during the second turn of his way (US, 250–56), Heidegger will have nothing to do with acoustics or "physiological explanation" (252). Rather, the seed is the insight that language, as speech, is saying, and saying showing. *Dico*, "I say," is originally "I show through words, I indicate." Predictably, Heidegger restricts what is said or shown to "people" or "things," that is, to fellow humans or lifeless things. Yet the automatic restriction, as though by reflex, awaits a final twisting turn.

The third and last turn of "The Way to Language" (US, 256–68) is the decisive one, the turn of the way that allows the way to turn upon itself, turn back upon itself *as* a way. That way is not charted or mapped ahead of time. Heidegger will call it a waying, a way in motion: *Be-wëgung*. If automotion is the classical vital sign, the pristine mark of the living, it must also be said that something of *life* stirs in the apparently bloodless thought of language as saying and showing. For the way to language is not a route; it is something that *bestirs itself*. Heidegger writes:

> Whence does the showing arise? Our question asks too much, and too quickly. It suffices if we heed what it is that bestirs itself [*sich regt*] in showing and brings its stirrings [*sein Regsames*] to a culmination. Here we need not search forever. The simple, abrupt, unforgettable, and therefore ever-renewed gaze toward what is familiar to us suffices, although we can never try to know it, much less cognize it in

the appropriate way. This unknown but familiar thing, every showing of the
saying, with regard to what it stirs and excites in each coming to presence or
withdrawing into absence, is the dawn, the daybreak, with which the possible
alternation of day and night first commences. It is at once the earliest and the
oldest. We can only name it, because it will deign no discussion. For it is the place
[*Ortschaft*] that encompasses all locales and time-play-spaces. We shall name it by
using an old word. We shall say: *What bestirs in the showing of saying is owning.*
(US, 257–58)

What this "owning" that is less a possessing than a responding can be, what
this responding to which thinking can only "own up" can be, what Heidegger
calls "the mystery" (*das Geheimnis*) can be—these things remain enigmatic. It
is certainly nothing homey, nothing domestic or domesticated; the mystery or
secret dwells somewhere apart, not-at-home, in the uncanny, *das Unheimliche*.
Even if it seems the most familiar thing in the world: "Owning conducts what
comes to presence and withdraws into absence in each case into its own. . . .
Let us call the owning that conducts things in this way—the owning that
bestirs [*regt*] the saying, the owning that points in any saying's showing—the
propriating [*das Ereignen*]" (258).

What earlier imprisoned the animal in its stolid taciturnity, namely, *Regung,*
now bestirs human saying—saying, showing, and pointing toward the granting
of time, space, and being; what bestirs is the bestowal of clearing and presence
in the "There is/It gives," in which all human dignity is now invested. Yet if
what bestirs in saying grants mortals their essential residence on the earth,
mortals being the ones who speak (259), then what shall these mortals say of
grass and sky, eagle and snake, the dappled and the dun? If human mortals
"own" the clearing precisely through dispossession and withdrawal, what will
they assert of their privileged position with respect to language? What will they
aver of the "essence of man"? Even if they should avow nothing, and only heed
the stillness, only hearken to the "soundless saying" in the "resonance of
language" (260), what is it they will hear in the silence of the animal, the
noiseless rustle of leaves or rush of air? According to Heidegger, propriation
remands the mortals to *concealment,* which is what in all saying remains
telling. True, even concealment, dispossession, and withdrawal can be made to
seem the most familiar things in the world. Irigaray asks, "And simply to
designate it as disappropriation—does this not still appeal to some sort of
contradictory, so that it can always be drawn back to the totality of the same?
Does not this interpretation consistently and continuously desire to rescue
being, the very heart of metaphysics?" (OA, 115). If the way that is to be
cleared, the way-making movement *of* language *to* language, is simply the way
to λόγος, will not what stirs along the way be lost to oblivion? The stirring of
disturbance and interruption along the *via rupta* is in fact the itinerary for
which Heidegger is searching in his early analyses of ecstatic temporality and in
his later musings on telling silence. The way-making movement of propriation
and usage is not the boast of assertive man; what stirs in that movement is
mortality itself, the greater nearness to earth and all its inhabitants. In the

Bewëgung of the way to language, we might say, speaking or writing "does not itself properly (!) make the movement" (61, 130).

Language is not the monologue of man. Of the brother. It does not "insist on itself," is not a "self-mirroring that forgets everything else because it is so enamored of itself" (US, 262). True, the suspicion stirs that the monologue of language too readily becomes the drawing of boundaries within which the brotherhood of being will keep to itself, securely oriented, erecting walls for the "habitation of man": "So localized in his territory that he speaks solely with himself alone—or rather with his brothers, with those who share the same tone—solicitous only of himself?" (OA, 119). To be sure, the familiar, fraternal tone recurs in "The Way to Language," which at this point returns to the customary complaint concerning technology and enframing, information and calculation. The reference to φύσις and to "natural language" reverts immediately to the homeland of propriation, "out of which the saying bestirs itself and surges upward [*aus dem die Sage in ihr Regsames aufgeht*]" (US, 264). What the bestirring of *life* can be, the bestirring of life in the duplicitous field of upsurgence and dissolution (for *Aufgehen* also means dissolution and evanescence), what the field of φύσις as excessive ζά can be, Heidegger has never been able to say.

"What if propriation—when and how, no one knows—were to become a *penetrating gaze* [Ein-Blick], whose clearing lightning strikes what is and what the being is held to be?" Thus Heidegger, in the apocalyptic peroration of his "Way." However, as we have noted, the gaze or view has been arrogated to human mortality and its gods. Yet what if lightning were closer to daimon life than to gods and mortals? What if the fourfold were rethought as earth and sky, plants and (other) animals? What if mortal solitude embraced all that lives and dies, inasmuch as the *-sam* (=ἅμα) of *einsam* is itself a gathering (*versammeln*), as Heidegger remarks, so that the solitude of monologue were "not in separation and isolation, not devoid of all kinship" (265)? *Then* the way to language would lead not to speech but to tongues, and not to light(n)ing but to a less penetrating and more responsive gaze. Tongues "needed and used," among other things, for the kiss with which, according to Novalis the monologist, philosophy begins. Tongues needed and used "for the speaking of language," though also for the mode that is a *Weise*, "in the musical sense of the μέλος, the song that says by singing" (266). The song that Hölderlin says (we) soon shall be, now that we have so long been in conversation with one another; yet perhaps also a sirensong outside the domestic space of the house of being and off the beaten path, the song that defies all propriation. The gaze of the other need not be a *coup de foudre* in order to be utterly excessively doubly daimonically unsettling. "That man alone never succeeds in transgressing the limits of his site—so it is. Yet may not some other voice arrive at the heart of this enclosure? Drawing it to listen to what would be said in another terrain" (OA, 127).

Does it all boil down to this—that Heidegger is unfair to (other) plants and animals, unkind to broccoli and birddog? That his thought inveighs against life-philosophy only because it is vaguely aware of its own failure to respond to the questions that life-philosophy puts to it? That Heidegger's allergic reaction to (other forms of) life betrays a lability and liability at the heart of his thought, the very weakness that invited his political debacle and paralyzed his capacity to speak (honestly) of that debacle? Does it all boil down to this—that of all the ways in which Heidegger's thought falls short, its failure in the face of life is its telling failure?

Such conclusions are tempting. Perhaps there is some measure of truth in them. Yet the present book has tried to slow, rather than to draw, such conclusions.

Perhaps the scene of life, embracing goldenrod, dog, and god, the scene of daimon life, is particularly compelling for Heideggerian thinking for two reasons: nowhere is Heidegger's thought so uninspired and so reactionary as it is here, and nowhere are the stakes of his thinking set so high. However, as Heidegger enucleates the cow and mutilates the ape with all-too-human pieties, the strength of his thinking—as initiation into mortality—does not wane; as he desperately digs a ditch to separate man from animality, something like a unified, albeit motley, field of φύσις comes into view, if only hazily. Not as an architectonic gathering into a neatly silhouetted One, not as a well-rounded and articulated sphere, nor even as the interplay of revealing and concealing, but as the vital upsurgence and bestrewal of beings that live and die. Vital signs can only be signs of lifedeath. Yet, while they close off one horizon, they open another, one that encompasses larger communities of life. Heidegger has taught us this, no matter how much he himself resists the thought, no matter how much he longs for the animal to die apart, under the front porch or out in the shed, well away from the hearth of the human house. No matter how much he struggles to save some spurious privilege for man, to wit, the traditional privilege of power and garrulous dominion, the force of his thought goes to meet what the homocentric dominion of the past has in fact wrought. No matter how regressive and reactionary Heidegger's thought, and his actions, may at times be. For where danger is, even the danger of regression and reaction, the chance of rescue grows.

Shall we then make the comforting transition to an ethics, a transition virtually everyone is demanding today, an ethics and a politics outside the house of being? No doubt, our own "Introduction to Za-ology" displaces its discourse from ontology and metaphysics in the direction of an ἦθος (though not an ethics), an ἦθος that is not yet fixed in its contours, not yet under law. The "ethos" of a voμός that is not yet subjected to a νόμος, an uncharted and unchartered pasture or grazing ground or verge, familiar and yet daimonic, replete with life, and most of it strange. No doubt, our ἦθος and voμός are almost always spoiled by ethical posturings and moralizings, which are of a piece with the ontology and ontotheology they claim to have left behind. Not satisfied with the daimon, such ethical posturings, even the most sophisti-

catedly secular of them, attach their lifelines to a shadowy god of sects and
laws, of revelations and retributions, a wrathful shade of infinite violence.

If not an ethics, what, then? I do not know. Throughout I have spoken of a
"unified field of φύσις." It is Heidegger who introduces the idea of such a
unified field of disclosure; yet the idea of za-ology remains inchoate and un-
formed in his work. However, is it not the most blatant kind of anthropomorphism to attribute disclosure—the play of revealing and concealing in the open
region of being—to forms of life other than (human) Dasein? What can a
unified field of φύσις possibly mean, even if we attach to it the Leibnizian rider
of gradations of being(s)? I do not wish to open Heidegger's "open region" any
wider or expand it any farther in order to include animals or plants in it, but,
on the contrary, to examine other life-forms in order to expand my own sense
of "disclosure." For, in spite of all Heidegger's demurs, I suspect that "openness to being" is bound up with (and even restricted to) that particular being
who is said to be self-aware, cogitative, reflexive, and linguistic—*der Mensch,*
"man," as we have always known him, and as Heidegger so badly wanted to
deconstruct him. To begin with, it would be a matter of expanding the existential notion of what the Greeks called ὀργή, "disposition," or "how one finds
oneself to be in the midst of beings," or *le sentiment de la situation,*[19] what
Being and Time calls the most comprehensive mode of disclosure, namely,
Befindlichkeit; of expanding also the pervasive Heideggerian idea of mood and
attunement, *Stimmung;* of expanding these to the point at which they are not
mere avatars of *homo rationale,* mere masks of human consciousness and
speech.

That does not mean crossing the asses' bridge or jumping over our mortal
shadow or leaping out of our human skin. Without doubt, extending disclosure
to animals, as the projective donation of one unknown to another, is a red
herring. I am more interested in the silver speckled herring that negotiates the
seas, alert to flounder, shark, and whale; the herring at the heart of a certain
kind of openness to a certain kind of being that is only a vague memory in my
own body when it is swimming. True, such openness and world-relation lie
beyond my ken, beyond every scientific and philosophical calculus, beyond
imagination. Yet that poverty is mine, not the herring's. I urge caution when it
comes to blaming the fish for what I cannot interpret. I urge adventurousness
when it comes to thinking φύσις beyond revealing and concealing as we
(vaguely enough) conceive of them, adventurousness in thinking life as upsurgence and dissolution, bestrewal and proliferation, semination and dissemination. I urge risk. Otherwise the poverty of the philosopher's imagination will
expunge the life of φύσις as efficiently as the trawlers are expunging the
herring. And all that high-altitude talk of "being," "propriation," "clearing,"
"openness," and "granting" will be the familiar palaver of Western man, the
commonplace usurpation, the customary manipulation, the standard hegemony, the usual self-congratulation. Being needs and uses the herring too, and
not just for pickling.

If φύσις is ζά, then ecclusion is not mere unveiling. It is not merely for show, for view, vision, and voice. Upsurgence and bestrewal are not only for theory, theater, and theism. Growth, dilation, tactility, seduction, passion, vulnerability, decay, decrepitude: these are daimonic, these are excessive, doubly and utterly so. These za-ological occasions stir, and are stirring. It would be worth our bestirring ourselves to recount something of their history. In another terrain, in other waters, breathing another air.

Perhaps for the moment such a history and genealogy of daimon life will yield nothing more than the continuing call for strange bedfellows for Heidegger, who, after all, chose a few strange ones himself. Strange bedfellows in order to produce deliberately conceived yet unpredictable bastard lineages and genealogies. Because a second history of being, I repeat, would have to get along without the benefit of being or the help of history.

A chapter that begins with the resolute passion of *l'homme au Sein-zum-Tode* can close only with Heidegger among the Indians. That is to say, among *native* Americans, such as Chief Seattle, who in 1852 writes the following to the President of the United States, who reportedly wants to "buy" the Indian lands:

> The President in Washington sends word that he wishes to buy our land. But how can you buy or sell the sky? The land? The idea is strange to us. If we do not own the freshness of the air and the sparkle of the water, how can you buy them?
>
> Every part of this earth is sacred to my people. Every shining pine needle, every sandy shore, every mist in the dark woods, every meadow, every humming insect. All are holy in the memory and experience of my people.
>
> We know the sap which courses through the trees as we know the blood that courses through our veins. We are part of the earth and it is part of us. The perfumed flowers are our sisters. The bear, the deer, the great eagle, these are our brothers. The rocky crests, the juices in the meadow, the body heat of the pony, and man, all belong to the same family. . . .
>
> This we know: the earth does not belong to man, man belongs to the earth. All things are connected like the blood that unites us all. Man did not weave the web of life, he is merely a strand in it. Whatever he does to the web, he does to himself. . . .
>
> Your destiny is a mystery to us. What will happen when the buffalo are all slaughtered? The wild horses tamed? What will happen when the secret corners of the forest are heavy with the scent of many men and the view of the ripe hills is blotted by talking wires? Where will the thicket be? Gone! Where will the eagle be? Gone! And what is it to say goodbye to the swift pony and the hunt? The end of living and the beginning of survival. . . .[20]

ADDENDUM TO CHAPTER NINE

CRISTY'S MORTALITY

A few days after I had finished the first draft of this book, I was out walking my dog. We were about to cross a busy four-lane road on our way to the park, our accustomed place for exercise. Cristy, heeling obediently as always, sat at my feet near the curb's edge. I looked left, then right, in order to make certain that the road was clear of traffic. Seeing that it was, I gave the command, "Go, Cristy!"

We ran. In the second (the fast) lane to our left I heard the sound of screeching brakes, then a rude thud. With one yelp Cristy was thrown flying scudding some forty or fifty feet down the road. She skidded to a slowly curving stop and lay very still. I was back on the curb shouting something, crying out, who knows what. I was not very dignified. A large man and his wife and infant daughter in a pretty dress emerged from the car and said how sorry they were. I said, "I didn't see you."

In the animal hospital I sat holding Cristy's right leg, where they had introduced the I.V., and stroking her motionless head with my other hand. The vet was pressing a finger to her steel gray gums and shining a light into one of her eyes, probing the effects of trauma. After some time had passed, perhaps an hour or two, I found myself thinking of Heidegger, of his distinction between human *Sterben* and animal *Verenden*. Her head and paw seemed as immanently and imminently capable of the one as the other; her eye, now almost focusing, in and out of shock, did not accuse; her bruised body unspeakably beautiful still. They call them Golden Retrievers because in the sun—and there was sun that afternoon, perfect visibility—their coat is pure gold, all sheen and shine, you should see.

More than about dying and perishing, I thought about mortality, without being capable of too many neat distinctions. I thought about the look, about the δαίμονες who look-in, who appear as they look-in on mortals. I felt very close to our own mortality, smelling the fetid breath that came in stertorous gasps, and the odor of her cheesy foot. It was not the close call, the proximity of her near-perishing (for she was not killed, not just yet), that goaded me into a thought of mortality. It was rather the fact that I had looked both left and right down that street, twice, as they instructed us in Kindergarten to do, and I swear there were no cars in sight, and even so thud yelp bystanders undignified animal hospital steel gray gums. There could not have been a black sedan speeding toward us in the fast lane, else I would have seen it. Q.E.D.

Cristy did not see it either.

They say it came very close to hitting me as well, since I was running beside her, but I do not believe it. After all, I am a Dasein, fully capable of seeing, capable of the look, gazing on being, appearing to look-in. There was no car coming. No black sedan on a Sunday afternoon.

At one point, holding her paw, stroking her head, I thought to myself, "John Llewelyn will never forgive me." Then I came to my senses and realized that John Llewelyn would be the first to forgive me, after Cristy. "You're only human," he would say. "We're all mortal. Cristy didn't see it either. We're all only human," he would say. One of the bystanders was less kind. I looked up as I knelt beside her at the side of road where I had dragged her shivering body so like a god and saw him turn away. He mumbled something. "Stupid," I think it was.

Even the great daimon probably does not see every menacing machine roaring down its path, does not see everything that means its and our downgoing its and our death. Look-in, look-out.

At the hospital they told me to go home there was nothing more to be done. I should look-in on her tomorrow. My doctor said there was every good chance she would make it through the night without perishing. My only anxiety was that she would die.

July 14, 1991

Notes

PREFACE

1. *Symposium of Plato*, trans. Tom Griffith (Berkeley and Los Angeles: University of California Press, 1986), 202d–203a, with modifications.
2. Hans Jonas, *The Phenomenon of Life: Toward a Philosophical Biology* (Chicago: University of Chicago Press, 1966), p. 8.

INTRODUCTION

1. Observe that the English translation (BW, 233) cites the title of Aristotle's treatise incorrectly: μορίων is plural, hence *De partibus animalium* is the accepted translation, not *parte*. It seems the editor of BW is under the impression that there is only one animal part, only one part of living beings. However, the *daimon* is of many parts.
2. The first occasion on which Heidegger tells the story (the first at least as far as I know), a lecture course at Freiburg in 1943 entitled "The Commencement of Western Thought (Heraclitus)," finds him introducing it as follows: "Such 'stories'—even when they are inventions, or precisely because they are such—contain a more original truth than proper data that are established by historical research" (55, 5). Just how much, how overmuch, the story "speaks for itself" may be seen in two articles by Robert Bernasconi: "Deconstruction and the Possibility of Ethics," in *Deconstruction and Philosophy: The Texts of Jacques Derrida*, ed. John Sallis (Chicago: University of Chicago Press, 1986), pp. 122–39; and "The Fate of the Distinction between *Praxis* and *Poiesis*," in *Heidegger Studies*, 2 (1986), 111–39.
3. See, for example, Heidegger's 1929–1930 lecture course (29/30, 319), discussed in chap. 3, below. See also the first part of the 1959 essay, "The Way to Language" (US, 243–50, discussed in chap. 9). In "Logos: Heraclitus B 50," Heidegger writes: "Saying is a letting-lie-together-before which gathers and is gathered. If such is the essence of speaking, then what is hearing? As λέγειν, speaking is not characterized as a reverberation that expresses meaning. If saying is not characterized by vocalization, then neither can the hearing that corresponds to it occur as a reverberation meeting the ear and getting picked up, as sounds troubling the auditory sense and being transmitted. Were our hearing primarily and always only this picking up and transmitting of sounds, conjoined by several other processes, the result would be that the reverberation would go in one ear and out the other. . . . We hear when we are 'all ears.' But 'ear' does not here mean the acoustical sense apparatus. The anatomically and physiologically identifiable ears, as the tools of sensation, never bring about a hearing, not even if we take this solely as an apprehending of noises, sounds and tones. Such apprehending can be neither anatomically established nor physiologically demonstrated, nor in any way grasped as a biological process at work within the organism—although apprehending lives only as long as it is embodied. . . ." *Obwohl das Vernehmen nur lebt, indem es leibt*—on the expression *wie man leibt und lebt*, and on Dasein as "some body who is alive," to which I will turn several times in the course of this investigation, esp. in chap. 7, see Heidegger's "On the Essence and Concept of Φύσις: Aristotle's *Physics* B 1," at W, 326, and his *Nietzsche*, NI, 119 and 565–66/1, 99 and 3, 79–80. Continuing the quotation from Heidegger's "Logos": ". . . If the ears do not belong directly to proper hearing, in the sense of hearkening, then hearing and the ears are in a special situation. We do not hear because we have ears. We have ears, that is, our bodies are equipped with ears, because we hear. Mortals hear the thunder of the heavens, the rustling of woods, the gurgling of fountains, the ringing of plucked strings, the rumbling of motors, the noises of the city—only and only so far as they always already in some way belong

to them and yet do not belong to them." See the entire passage at VA, 213–15; EGT, 64–66. See also the lecture course on logic in which this discussion first occurred: 55, 243–47 and 260. Note the similar remarks at SG, 87 and at ZK, 293. Finally, Derrida's *fourth*-generation "Geschlecht," entitled, "Heidegger's Ear: Philopolemology," is a sustained meditation on these and other passages on and of Heidegger's ear; neither here nor in chapter 8, "Something like Sexes, Something like Spirit," will I be able to do it justice.

4. A. L. Peck's, of Aristotle's *On the Parts of Animals,* Loeb Classical Library (Cambridge, Mass.: Harvard University Press; London: William Heinemann, 1937), pp. 100–101; and William Ogle's, in *The Basic Works of Aristotle,* ed. Richard McKeon (New York: Random House, 1941), p. 657; with modifications.

5. See especially the final three sections of *De l'esprit,* along with my remarks in chap 8, below.

6. I shall abandon these problems to silence, noting only that we have precisely the same problem in translating Schelling's various *Wesen* in the 1809 treatise *On Human Freedom* and the 1810–1814 sketches toward *The Ages of the World.* That problem also extends to all matters touching the "abyss," "separation," "decision," and "crisis" in both Heidegger's and Schelling's texts. For a discussion of these matters, see Krell, "The Crisis of Reason in the Nineteenth Century: Schelling's Treatise on Human Freedom (1809)," in John Sallis, Giuseppina Moneta, and Jacques Taminiaux, eds., *The Collegium Phaenomenologicum: The First Ten Years* (The Hague: M. Nijhoff, 1989), pp. 13–32. To this one I would also have to add the problem of "essence" and "epochality," the second and fourth threads of Derrida's *Of Spirit.* On essence and epochality, see chap. 8 of the present book; on the divine *Wesen* in Schelling, see chap. 9.

7. Note the following passage in Heidegger's *What Calls for Thinking?,* taken up by Jacques Derrida in the second of his "Geschlecht" papers (Ps, 424–29/169–74): "We are trying here to learn thinking. Perhaps thinking too is just something like building a cabinet. At any rate, it is a handicraft [*ein Hand-Werk*]. The hand is a peculiar thing. In the common view, the hand pertains to the organism of our body. Yet the hand's essence can never be determined or explained in terms of its being a bodily organ that can grasp [*ein leibliches Greiforgan*]. For example, the ape too has organs that can grasp, but it has no hand. The hand is infinitely different from all prehensile organs—paws, claws, fangs—different by an abyss of essence [*unendlich, d.h. durch einen Abgrund des Wesens verschieden*]" (WhD? 50–51/16). Heidegger's ape, without a hand, separated from the human hand by an abyss of essence, will return to haunt our investigation at many junctures.

8. J. W. von Goethe, *Dichtung und Wahrheit,* ed. Jörn Göres, 3 vols. (Frankfurt am Main: Insel, 1975), Book XX, 3, 854–55, quoted and discussed by Walter Benjamin in "Goethes Wahlverwandtschaften," *Illuminationen* (Frankfurt am Main: Suhrkamp, 1977 [1924–1925]), pp. 86–88.

9. Jane Chance Nitzsche, in *The Genius Figure in Antiquity and the Middle Ages* (New York: Columbia University Press, 1975), pp. 4–5, writes: "The regions in between gods and men were also believed to be inhabited—by cosmic messengers or *daemones,* Greek spirits who were related to the souls of the dead (*Di Manes*) and to the rational souls of men (*daemones*). Eventually the Greek concept of the daemon influenced the Roman *genius,* so that each man was said to possess a soul (*genius* or *daemon*) born with him, or a good and evil nature (good and evil *daemon, genius, manes*). The messenger *daemon,* under the influence of Christianity, became an evil demon or renegade angel connected with astrology, dreams, and the black arts, and was itself replaced by the good angel." See also Jacob Burckhardt's classic lectures on "The Daimonization of Paganism," chap. 6 of his *The Age of Constantine the Great,* trans. Moses Hadas (Berkeley and Los Angeles: University of California Press, 1983 [1852]), esp. pp. 188–214. Finally, see Hans Jonas, *The Gnostic Religion,* 2nd ed. (Boston: Beacon Press, 1963), and the fuller treatment in Jonas, *Gnosis und spätantiker Geist,* 3d ed. (Göt-

tingen: Vandenhoeck und Ruprecht), 1964 [1st ed., 1934], passim, esp. pp. 191–99. (My thanks to Christine Battersby and Joel Shapiro for bringing my attention to these works.)

10. SG, 93–95 and 186–87. See also J. G. Hamann's "abyss" in Heidegger's "Language" (US, 13), and the abyss of propriation in "The Anaximander Fragment" (H, 309; EGT, 25) and in *Identity and Difference* (ID, 20 and 28). Finally, on the abyssal "cleaving of beyng," *die Zerklüftung des Seyns,* discussed in the 1936–1938 *Contributions to Philosophy (Of Propriation),* see chap. 6, below. In short, the question is whether "abyss" and "abysmal" are overdetermined and even radically undecidable. In "What Is Metaphysics?" *abgründig* is used to describe (1) modes of nihilation, such as "unyielding antagonism and stinging rebuke" (W, 14, BW, 107); (2) a process of finitation, if such a coinage may be allowed in order to translate *Verendlichung,* the burrowing action of a finitude beneath finitude, as it were (W, 15; BW, 108); and (3) the very ground (*Grund*) on which the "truth of metaphysics" as such dwells (W, 18; BW, 112). The question is how the "abysmal" bodily kinship of humanity and beast relates to, or is "grounded" in, these abysses of Heidegger's thought.

11. Faulkner's phrase, applied to his own masterpiece, *The Sound and the Fury.* I first learned of it in André Bleikasten's excellent commentary on the novel, *The Most Splendid Failure: Faulkner's "The Sound and the Fury"* (Bloomington: Indiana University Press, 1976).

12. See, for example, the use of *Zugang* at SZ, 6, lines 3 and 5 from the bottom; and 16, lines 5 and 10 from the bottom.

13. I have taken some initial steps toward answers to these questions in chap. 6 of my *Of Memory, Reminiscence, and Writing: On the Verge* (Bloomington: Indiana University Press, 1990). I am grateful to Will McNeill, of DePaul University, who located the passages from *Being and Time* treated in the above paragraph, and who helped me to understand their importance. To be sure, bedazzlement will continue to be a central theme of the remaining chapters of the present book.

14. See *Herausdrehung* in SZ, 197, 201, and 323; NI, 240–242/1, 208–210. See also John Sallis, "Twisting Free: Being to an Extent Sensible," in *Echoes: After Heidegger* (Bloomington: Indiana University Press, 1990), chap. 3, pp. 76–96. See also chap. 7, below.

15. VA, 257–82; see esp. 273–82; EGT, 116–23. See also the 1943 lectures on which "Aletheia" is based, 55, 1–181. Heidegger removes from the later essay, "Aletheia," most of the polemics and political marks from the transcription of the course. He removes many other items as well, and so I shall have recourse to the lecture course quite often in the brief sketch that follows.

16. On the life and death of language, expressed in vowel and consonant, see Jean-Jacques Rousseau, *Essai sur l'origine des langues,* ed. Charles Porset (Paris: A. G. Nizet, 1969), chaps. 10–11, and p. 191; see also the discussion by Jacques Derrida, *De la grammatologie* (Paris: Minuit, 1967), pp. 325–26 and chap. 3 of Part II.

17. See Hermann Paul, *Deutsches Wörterbuch,* 6th ed. (Tübingen: M. Niemeyer, 1966), p. 833a–b, meaning 3, noting the "ancient" but "unclarified" use of *zu* as an adverb meaning "excessively," related to *zer,* for which see Paul, p. 823b. As we might expect, no conclusive evidence is forthcoming from the philologists: these German words are as lost in the mists of time as the Greek ζά.

18. VA, 274; EGT, 116. Note that the translation in EGT is marred by several errors, corrected by the translators but inadvertently reinserted by an assistant editor at Harper's: on p. 116, l. 14 f. b., read *Homer; l.* 8 f. b. should read: *into view. The gods are not experienced as animals. Yet animality,* etc.

19. G. S. Kirk notes the following: "Ζάς (accusative Ζάντα) is obviously an etymological form of Ζεύς, and is perhaps intended to stress the element ζα- (an intensive prefix), as in ζάθεος, ζαής [strong-blowing, stormy]; though there is some possibility that the form Zas is intended to link the sky-god Zeus with the earth-goddess Ge, whose

Cyprian form is ζα." See G. S. Kirk and J. E. Raven, *The Presocratic Philosophers: A Critical History with a Selection of Texts* (Cambridge: Cambridge University Press, 1966), pp. 55–56.

20. See Luce Irigaray, *L'oubli de l'air: Chez Martin Heidegger* (Paris: Minuit, 1983), cited hereinafter as OA, with page number. Irigaray's remarkable text is discussed in chap. 9, below. On "Orchids and Muscles," see the article with that title by Alphonso Lingis in *Exceedingly Nietzsche: Aspects of Contemporary Nietzsche Interpretation*, eds. D. F. Krell and D. Wood (London: Routledge, 1988), chap. 6.

21. See 55, 107–108 and 143–44; see also the 1944 logic course (also published in volume 55), at 217 and 280–81. As for the Sirens, I encourage readers to hound Professor Ute Guzzoni, of the University of Freiburg-im-Breisgau, about her thoughts on the matter, at which point she will be compelled to publish them. See also the remarkable paper by Rebecca Comay, to which my all-too-cryptic remarks here—especially those about Timaeus' and Heidegger's birds—are meant as a response: "Sirens' Song/Penelope's Web: Adorno, Feminism, and the Bonds of the Subject: Unraveling the *Dialectic of the Enlightenment*," in an anthology of papers edited by Géza von Molnár and Andrzej Warminski, to be published by Northwestern University Press in 1992.

22. 54, 161; cf. 55, 8, and "Wissenschaft und Besinnung," in VA, 52–53. We shall take up these very difficult matters in chap. 9, in the section entitled "δαιμόνιος τόπος: The Daimonic Site."

23. Now that the political implications of the question of life have been introduced, if only by way of a hint, we may risk a question to Reiner Schürmann's *Heidegger on Being and Acting: From Principles to Anarchy* (Bloomington: Indiana University Press, 1987), pp. 38, 42, 47, 50, 57, 72, 76, and indeed throughout. Can one meaningfully speak of Heidegger's "anti-humanism" as long as Heidegger maintains throughout his thinking—regardless of any "turning" one may impute to him—the traditional privileges of *human* being over all other forms of life? Further, is it really the case that after the "turning" (in Schürmann's view, after 1930) Heidegger becomes less anthropocentric than he was in *Being and Time*, that, in a word, "man retreats from the scene" (Schürmann, 50)? Was I simply being provocative, or even silly, when in *Intimations of Mortality: Time, Truth, and Finitude in Heidegger's Thinking of Being* (University Park, Pa: Pennsylvania State University Press, 1986; see chaps. 2 and 6, esp. pp. 29, 98, and 104–105) I indicated that "man" (*der Mensch*) becomes *increasingly prominent* in Heidegger's later thinking, the thinking of the "turning"? Even if *der Mensch* is eventually crossed through (as *Sein* is) for the thinking of propriation, are not all hopes for a truly an-archic thinking dashed by Heidegger's intransigent metahumanism, which is not an antihumanism but a hyperhumanism—being's "need" and "use" of man? Is not one of the answers to Schürmann's question concerning Heidegger's inability to go far enough, his need to *avoid* (38), Schürmann's own phrase, ". . . life 'without why' " (38)? That is, if we emphasize the word *life*, which Schürmann too tends to use throughout as a synonym for the existence of that political animal called *man*. What can "an overcoming of epochal principles," or "the end of principial history," or "metaphysical closure" mean if humans continue to think of themselves as the *principi* of all life? The "insufferable spoiled child" (47, Schürmann quoting Lévi-Strauss) called *der Mensch* rules imperious even in anarchy.

24. See "Wozu Dichter?" in H, esp. pp. 256–57; cf. EHD, 121n. Heidegger's criticisms in the 1942–1943 lecture course are, it must be said, far more drastic than those in "Wozu Dichter?" On the Heidegger-Rilke relationship in this regard, see the excellent chapters by Michel Haar, *Le chant de la terre* (Paris: L'Herne, 1987), chap. 2 of Parts I and III, esp. pp. 71–77 and 237–68, pages that tend to be quite critical of Heidegger; and by John Llewelyn, *The Middle Voice of Ecological Conscience: A Chiasmic Reading of Responsibility in the Neighbourhood of Levinas, Heidegger and Others* (London: Macmillan, 1992), esp. chaps. 7 and 8, which generously grant Heidegger the benefit of every doubt.

25. See my "Analyses" to the English translation of Heidegger's *Nietzsche*, vols. 2 and 3; see also my *Postponements: Woman, Sensuality, and Death in Nietzsche* (Bloomington: Indiana University Press, 1986), throughout. On the "new interpretation of sensuousness," see chap. 7, below.

26. To be discussed in chaps. 5 and 8, below. I am referring of course to Jacques Derrida, "Geschlecht I," throughout these final paragraphs.

1. "I CALL IT DEATH-IN-LIFE . . ."

1. Alois Bernt and Konrad Burdach, eds., *Der Ackermann aus Böhmen* (Berlin: Weidmannsche Buchhandlung, 1917), pp. 3, 45–46. Heidegger refers to lines 19 and 20 of chap. 20 at SZ, 245.

2. Dominique Janicaud, *L'ombre de cette pensée: Heidegger et la question politique* (Grenoble: J. Millon, 1990), p. 59.

3. See Derrida, De, 38–42, on (at least) three types of indifference to the question of being.

4. WM, 582; KSA 12, 153; cf. Heidegger's *Nietzsche*, I, 518/3, 40; finally, see Derrida, "Interpreting Signatures (Nietzsche/Heidegger): Two Questions," in *Dialogue and Deconstruction: The Gadamer-Derrida Encounter*, eds. Diane P. Michelfelder and Richard Palmer (Albany: State University of New York Press, 1989), pp. 58–71.

5. On Dilthey's conception of "life," see the introductory remarks by the editor of the *Gesammelte Schriften*, H. Nohl, remarks that were extremely important for Heidegger; see vol. 5, *Die geistige Welt: Einleitung in die Philosophie des Lebens, erste Hälfte, Abhandlungen zur Grundlegung der Geisteswissenschaften* (Leipzig and Berlin: B. G. Teubner, 1924), pp. LII–LV. The importance of Dilthey and of *Lebensphilosophie* in general for the gestation of Heidegger's *Being and Time* has recently been underlined by a series of excellent essays by Frithjof Rodi, Otto Pöggeler, Friedrich Hogemann, Christoph Jamme, Carl Friedrich Gethmann, and Theodore Kisiel in the *Dilthey-Jahrbuch für Philosophie und Geschichte der Geisteswissenschaften*, vol. IV, ed. Frithjof Rodi (Göttingen: Vandenhoeck und Ruprecht, 1986–1987), passim. See also the helpful review of this volume by Jacob Owensby in *Research in Phenomenology*, XIX (1989), 311–15.

6. Heinrich Rickert, *Die Philosophie des Lebens: Darstellung und Kritik der philosophischen Modeströmungen unserer Zeit* (Tübingen: J. C. B. Mohr [Paul Siebeck], 1920); Heidegger refers to the 2nd ed., 1922; see esp. 194 of Rickert's monograph.

7. See SZ, 126, on taking-one's-distance, *Abständigkeit*, as the principal existential characterization of everyday being-with.

8. Thus Derrida, in "Geschlecht I," Ps, 398/68.

9. See 29/30, §61, esp. pp. 376–78 for *Genommenheit, Hingenommenheit, Eingenommenheit*, and *Benommenheit*.

10. Henry David Thoreau, *Walden*, the Variorum edition, by Walter Harding (New York: Washington Square Press, 1968), pp. 17–18.

11. See, for example, NI, 249–50, 465–66, and 636/1, 216–17, 2, 200–201, and 3, 140; for further discussion of fixation, see chap. 7, below.

12. Heidegger preserves the word *Darbung* through the first draft of *Being and Time*; see *Prolegomena to the History of the Concept of Time*, 20, 408.

13. See 61, 62–76, the most important pages we have in Heidegger's early writings for his attitudes concerning the university—and his own life in it. I have commented on them in the third section of chap. 4, below.

14. Thomas Mann, *Der Zauberberg* (Frankfurt am Main: Fischer Taschenbuch Verlag, 1967 [1st ed., 1924]), p. 290.

15. Alphonse de Waelhens, "Une philosophie de l'ambiguïté," in Maurice Merleau-Ponty, *La structure du comportement* (Paris: Presses Universitaires de France, 1942), p. v. English translation by Alden L. Fisher, *The Structure of Behavior* (Boston: Beacon Press, 1963), p. xix.

16. Hans Jonas, *The Phenomenon of Life: Toward a Philosophical Biology*, pp. 19 and 25.

17. Rainer A. Bast and Heinrich P. Delfosse, *Handbuch zum Textstudium von Martin Heideggers 'Sein und Zeit'*, 2 vols. (Frommann-Holzboog), I, passim. For *Leib*, see *Sein und Zeit*, 29, l. 21; 48, ll. 16–17 and 22; 56, l. 22; 70, l. 39; 96, l. 39; 107, l. 17; 108, ll. 35 and 37; 117, ll. 21 and 37; 121, l. 24; 147, l. 4; 198, ll. 16 and 29; 346, ll. 26, 28, and 31; 368, ll. 5 and 17. For *Körper*, see 56, l. 22; 90, l. 17; 91, ll. 23–24 and 28; 107, ll. 26 and 28; 198, ll. 20–21; 400, l. 11; 416, l. 5. The word *Körperding*, which is laconic, to say the least, appears a striking number of times: see 54, l.18; 56, l. 24; 90, ll. 22 and 29; 92, l. 2; 97, ll. 28 and 32; 106, l. 16; 107, l. 32; 117, l. 19; 238, ll. 10 and 18; 361, l. 8; 368, l. 19. The word *Geistding* is used only once, 56, l. 24. Is that because "spiritthing" is the more shocking oxymoron? Why more shocking? If Heidegger is equally opposed to the conceptions of body and spirit as *vorhanden*, why is *Körperding* still easier to write than *Geistding*?

18. On life-philosophy in relation to the problem of the human body and sexuality, see Part II of Felix Hammer, *Leib und Geschlecht: Philosophische Perspektive von Nietzsche bis Merleau-Ponty und phänomenologisch-systematischer Aufriß* (Bonn: Bouvier, 1974); Hammer deals principally with "Nietzsche's legatees," Dilthey, Klages, Simmel, Bergson, and Ortega y Gasset.

19. See the analysis of the impossible temporalization of anxiety in Krell, *Of Memory, Reminiscence, and Writing: On the Verge*, chap. 6.

20. See 26, 172; see also all of §10 and the "Appendix," 196–202. We shall discuss these matters in chap. 5, below.

21. See chap. 5, below, for a discussion of Heidegger's 1928 review of Cassirer's *Mythical Thought*, the second volume of his *Philosophy of Symbolic Forms* (1923–1929).

22. Maurice Merleau-Ponty, *Le visible et l'invisible*, ed. Claude Lefort (Paris: Gallimard, 1964), chap. 4.

23. SZ, 238. Cf. Heidegger's similar remarks to Medard Boss forty-five years later: ZK, 293.

24. Or, if not Descartes, perhaps Vesalius, author of *On the Fabric of the Human Body* (1543). On the role of the cadaver and anatomy in the birth of modern biological science, see François Jacob, *Le jeu des possibles: Essai sur la diversité du vivant* (Paris: Fayard, 1981), chap. 2, esp. pp. 57–61; see also Charles Singer, *A Short History of Anatomy and Physiology from the Greeks to Harvey* (New York: Dover, 1957), pp. 115–22; finally, see Michel Foucault, *The Birth of the Clinic: An Archaeology of Medical Perception*, trans. A. M. Sheridan (London: Tavistock, 1973), chap. 8, "Open up a Few Corpses," esp. pp. 140–46.

25. Sigmund Freud, "Psychoanalytische Bemerkungen über einen autobiographisch beschriebenen Fall von Paranoia (Dementia paranoides) [1911]," in StA, 7, 153. See Daniel Paul Schreber, *Denkwürdigkeiten eines Nervenkranken* (Frankfurt am Main: Syndikat, 1985 [1900–1902]); we will encounter Schreber once again in chap. 6, below.

2. " . . . LIFE-IN-DEATH"

1. See Thomas Sheehan, "Heidegger's 'Introduction to the Phenomenology of Religion,' 1920–1921," in *The Personalist*, 60, (1979), 312–24, esp. 319.

2. Jean-Paul Sartre, *L'être et le néant: Essai d'ontologie phénoménologique* (Paris: Gallimard, 1943), p. 639; trans. Hazel Barnes (New York: Philosophical Library, 1956), p. 578.

3. See SZ, esp. 344. I have argued elsewhere that precisely on this page of *Being and Time* the temporal analysis of anxiety fails, so that a gap opens here which threatens to swallow the entire treatise; see Krell, *Of Memory, Reminiscence, and Writing: On the Verge*, chap. 6.

4. *Acéphale: Religion·Sociologie·Philosophie*, ed. Georges Bataille et al., from 1936 to 1939. The issues of the journal, which are very hard to come by nowadays, have been reprinted and bound in a single volume by Editions Jean Michel Place, 12, rue Pierre et Marie Curie, Paris, 1980. My thanks to Gisela Baurmann for this discovery.

5. On October 1, 1911, Freud writes to Else Voigtländer on the subject of fate and chance, δαίμων καὶ τύχη. My thanks to Charles Shepherdson for this reference.

6. StA 3, 269n 1. For further discussion of *Beyond the Pleasure Principle* in company with Heidegger's *Being and Time*, see esp. the two final sections of chap. 7, below. See also the role of anxiety in Freud's analysis of "The Dependencies of the Ego," in the 1923 *The Ego and the Id* (StA 5, 322–25), which focuses on the issue of *Todesangst* and its subordination to *Kastrationsangst*. Finally, see the 1919 *Das Unheimliche* (StA 4, 241–74), which in an uncanny way encroaches on the Heideggerian questions of anxiety, the mystery (*Ge-heimnis*), Nietzschean eternal recurrence of the same as the "thought of thoughts," being-unto-death, the homelike (*das Heimische*), and poetry (*Dichtung*). Obviously, in this mere listing of Freudian and Heideggerian convergences, a dozen daimonic projects coil.

7. See William McNeill, *The Modification of 'Being and Time,'* Ph.D. Thesis, University of Essex, 1987. On the "modalities of beyng," discussed in chap. 6, below, see also Heidegger's Schelling lectures of 1936 (S, 178–79). This discussion explicitly relates the issue of modalities with inclination, proclivity, and addiction; in turn, *Hang* and *Drang* are associated with the question of *evil*. I am grateful to John Llewelyn for this reference to Heidegger's *Schelling*.

8. See Max Scheler, *Gesammelte Werke* (Bern: Francke, 1960), vol. 8, chap. 2.

9. James Joyce, *A Portrait of the Artist as a Young Man* (Harmondsworth: Penguin Books, 1960 [1st ed., 1916]), pp. 15–16.

10. On enjoyment, see Emmanuel Levinas, *Totalité et infini* (Paris: Livre de Poche, n.d. [1st ed., 1961]), pp. 137–45; trans. Alphonso Lingis as *Totality and Infinity* (Pittsburgh: Duquesne University Press, 1969), pp. 130–34. Cf. Levinas, *Autrement qu'être ou au-delà de l'essence* (Paris: Livre de Poche, n.d. [1st ed., 1974]), pp. 116–20. Does Heidegger fail to take enjoyment into consideration? Apparently so. And yet whenever he turns to the timely being of Dasein, whenever he gazes at the sun, something very much like enjoyment begins to stir: enjoyment of or sensitivity to fundamental possibilities, which are never totalizable, especially not by an uncritical appeal to a glorious capital Infinity. An even more interesting challenge to Heidegger than that of Levinas would be the question of Heidegger's lunacy: where, under the ecliptic of Heidegger's sun, is there a space for the moon and its eight-and-twenty phases? Why, in the bright night of the nothing, is there only "she who makes the stars so close," *die Näherin der Sterne* (G, 71), instead of the full argentine moon that consumes the stars (US, 48–49)? Including that single star of gold that bedazzles Heidegger—the question of being (AED, 7)? It is to the moon that our gaze will now turn.

11. Perhaps the element that is most noticeably missing from Derrida's discussion of the suppression of the word *geistig* and the elevation of the word *geistlich* in the 1953 Trakl essay (see De, chap. 9) is the figure of woman and the sheen and shine of lunar silver in Heidegger's text. See chap. 8, below.

12. See SZ, 422: *Die Jetzt sind gleichsam um diese Bezüge beschnitten und reihen sich als so beschnittene aneinander lediglich an, um das Nacheinander auszumachen"* (my emphases). This inexplicable leveling of original or originary time (405), which generates the vulgar concept of time, is of course nothing else than *Ruinanz*. Two years after *Being and Time*, in his lectures on "profound boredom" (29/30, 187–88), Heidegger emphasizes the castration (*Beschnittensein*) that deprives us of our own having-been and our proper to-come, a dissolution of the past and future in a sterile present. (Cf. the *Beschneidung* of philosophy as such, discussed by Heidegger in 61, 15; and cf. that even more dire *Beschneidung* performed upon "intellectualism" in EM, discussed in chapter 5, below.) Finally, it may well be that Derrida's *Schibboleth: pour Paul Celan* (Paris: Galilée,

1986), which begins with the words, "Only once: circumcision takes place only once," has its origins or its "site" in these lines of Heidegger's *Being and Time*. See *Schibboleth*, pp. 120–21 and its reference to Heidegger, 53, 8, where the relation of dating to giving becomes explicit: for the *Jezt* of Hölderlin's poem *Der Ister* there is no calendar date, and no such is needed. Heidegger comments: "For this proclaimed and self-proclaiming 'Now' is itself in a more original sense a *datum*, which means to say, something given, a gift [*ein Gegebenes, eine Gabe*]; given, that is, by means of the proclamation."

13. Diltheyan—but also Kantian. On the importance of "life" and *Lebensgefühl* throughout Kant's third critique, and the possible influence of Kantian life-feeling on Dilthey, see the informative article by Rudolf A. Makkreel, "The Feeling of Life: Some Kantian Sources of Life-Philosophy," in *Dilthey Jahrbuch für Philosophie und Geschichte der Geisteswissenschaften, 3* (1985), 83–104.

14. Max Scheler, *Späte Schriften*, ed. Manfred Frings (Bern: Francke, 1976), esp. p. 112 nn. 1–2. Heidegger refers to the antiquity of the idea of correlative resistance, citing Plato's *Sophist* at the point where the atomists and materialists commence the Battle of Giants (246a: τοῦτο εἶναι μόνον ὃ παρέχει προσβολὴν καὶ ἐπαφήν τινα, ταὐτὸν σῶμα καὶ οὐσίαν ὁριζόμενοι, "... that only *is* which one can stumble across and touch, taking body and being to be coextensive"), and also citing Aristotle's *Metaphysics* (Λ, 1–6, a quite general reference to the introductory sections of this early text on first philosophy, but see especially 1070a 10: οὐσία is ὅσα γὰρ ἁφῇ, "... everything that can be touched," namely, ὕλη καὶ ὑποκείμενον, "matter and substrate"). Apparently, Scheler is a giant on the side of Democritus, a latterday typologist—see my *Of Memory, Reminiscence, and Writing: On the Verge*, p. 24.

15. See esp. SZ, 85–86, and see my earlier treatment of this issue in *Intimations of Mortality*, chap. 2. Allow me to add a note here on my earlier speculations (in *Intimations of Mortality*, chaps. 2–3) on the possible origins of Heidegger's notion of *ecstatic temporality*. One would have to add to the list Scheler's notions of *ekstatisches Wissen* and *(ekstatische) Hingegebenheit*, ecstatic knowing and devotion, as essential aspects of what he calls the *ordo amoris*. For example, Scheler argues that Lévy-Bruhl's work on the primitive mind demonstrates "the *ecstatic* character of the perceptual world." See *Gesammelte Werke, 8*, 203, 329, and 370, on "ecstatic knowing and having"; cf. 9, 16, 111; cf. Wilhelm Mader, *Max Scheler* (Reinbek bei Hamburg: Rowohlt, 1980), pp. 51, 112, and 118.

16. See my *Of Memory, Reminiscence, and Writing*, chap. 5.

17. See Hermann Paul, *Deutsches Wörterbuch*, p. 719b: Beseitigen, Zugrunderichten; cf. Heidegger on the praying mantis in 29/30, discussed below in chap. 3.

18. Hermann Paul, p. 720a, meaning no. 3.

19. I am grateful to William McNeill for his presentation of the passage in his paper, "Drawing Shadows, Warm and Capable," in David Wood, ed., *Heidegger and Derrida on Spirit* (Evanston, Illinois: Northwestern University Press, forthcoming), chap. 7.

20. Heidegger *could have* attended Korschelt's lectures in the way that Hegel attended the Jena lectures of Dr. Jakob Ackermann on hermaphroditism. To be sure, we have no evidence that Heidegger did so. There is evidence, however, that Heidegger read Korschelt. See Eugen Korschelt, *Lebensdauer, Altern und Tod*, third, revised and greatly augmented edition (Jena: Gustav Fischer, 1924), passim. In the pages that follow, I shall refer to Korschelt's work by page number in parentheses.

21. On the famous question of the quasi-immortality of germ plasm, see Hans Jonas, *The Phenomenon of Life*, pp. 52–53.

22. Korschelt, pp. 410–11. There is much in Korschelt's study that would take us to Freud's almost contemporary speculations on the death-drive and Sandor Ferenczi's thalassal regressive tug, catastrophism, and Lamarckian "bioanalysis." See Ferenczi, *Schriften zur Psychoanalyse*, ed. Michael Balint (Frankfurt am Main: Fischer, 1982), II, Part II, passim; English translation by Henry Alden Bunker, *Thalassa: A Theory of Genitality* (New York: W. W. Norton, 1968), throughout. On Freud, see chap. 7, below.

23. See Georg Simmel, *Lebensanschauung: Vier metaphysische Kapitel* (Munich and Leipzig: Duncker und Humblot, 1918), esp. chap. 3, "Death and Immortality."

24. *Lebensanschauung*, p. 101. The note of surprise in Simmel's text can perhaps be explained in terms of some historical background. François Jacob notes that in the eighteenth century (for example in the *Encyclopedia* of Diderot and d'Alembert) "life" is defined in almost lapidary fashion as the mere opposite or contradictory of death. After the passing of the "classical age" of Rationalism and Enlightenment, however, nineteenth-century vitalism rejects reductionist materialism and sets out in search of life's specific force and *élan*. The very possibility of *immanent* death therefore comes as a shock to thinkers of the late nineteenth century. If for contemporary molecular biology vitalism "has lost every function" and all sense, as Jacob records (321), so that the "crisis" of biology as the dispute between mechanism and vitalism, as Heidegger describes it in *Being and Time* (§3, p. 10), is a thing of the past; if the most "metaphysical" of contemporary biology's conceptions is the *integron* (i.e., ". . . unities constituted by the integration of subordinate unities," ". . . the assemblage of integrons [*sic*] from a lower level" [323]); sex and death nonetheless remain the two most important "inventions" of natural selection. Whereas sex expands, complicates, and enriches the genetic pool, death clears the way for the realization of such enrichment. Jacob explains—and here we return to the point about a death that is *immanent* in life: "Not the death that advenes from outside as a consequence of some accident, but the death imposed from the inside [*imposée du dedans*] as a prescribed necessity *ab ovo* by the genetic program itself. For evolution is the result of a struggle between what was and what will be, between the identity of reproduction and the novelty of variation. In organisms that reproduce by fission, the dilution of the individual that such rapid growth brings in its wake suffices to efface the past. With multicellular organisms, however, with the differentiation along the lines of somatic and germ plasm, and with reproduction by sexuality, it becomes necessary that the individuals disappear. This results from two counterposed forces, from an equilibrium between on the one hand sexual efficacy, with the entire train of gestation, rearing, and up-bringing, and on the other hand the disappearance of the generation that has ceased to play its role in reproduction. It is the adjustment of these two parameters under the influence of natural selection that determines the maximum duration of life within a species. The entire system of evolution, at least in animals, depends on this equilibrium. The limits of life thus cannot be left to chance. They are prescribed by the program which, from the fertilization of the ovum, fixes the genetic destiny of the individual." François Jacob, *La logique du vivant: Une histoire de l'hérédité* (Paris: Gallimard, 1970), p. 331.

"At least in animals." Heidegger would want us to pause over Jacob's rider—and to report on his conception of *cultural, historical* integrons, very much of the measure of Dasein. However, let us retrace our steps and return to the parallel between the immanentist conceptions of death in late nineteenth-century biology and in fundamental ontology.

25. Simmel's reading flies in the face of Heidegger's, for Heidegger understands Schelling's God as the very life of life (*das Leben des Lebens*); see SA, 131, and the discussion in chap. 9, below. Simmel is clearly reacting to a situation described aptly by Hans Jonas in the first chapter of *The Phenomenon of Life:* whereas for the ancient and medieval worlds *death* was the shocking exception to the rule of a being that seemed everywhere alive, *life* becomes the problem for a modernity that suddenly finds itself lost in the chaste and chilly universe of Copernicus and Galileo. "The earlier goal [i.e., of the ancient and medieval worlds] . . . was to interpret the apparently lifeless in the image of life and to extend life into apparent death. Then, it was the corpse, this primal exhibition of 'dead' matter, which was the limit of all understanding and therefore the first thing not to be accepted at its face-value. Today the living, feeling, striving organism has taken over this role and is being unmasked as a *ludibrium materiae*, a subtle hoax of matter. Only when a corpse is the body plainly intelligible: then it returns from

its puzzling and unorthodox behavior of aliveness to the unambiguous, 'familiar' state of a body within the world of bodies, whose general laws provide the canon of all comprehensibility. To approximate the laws of the organic body to this canon, i.e., to efface in *this* sense the boundaries between life and death, is the direction of modern thought on life as a physical fact. Our thinking today is under the ontological dominance of death" (12). On the enhanced intelligibility of "the dead," see Heidegger's remarks reported in chap. 7, below.

3. WHERE DEATHLESS HORSES WEEP

1. Now published as "Heidegger and the Question of Ethics," in *Research in Phenomenology*, XVIII (1988), 23–40, the nascent form of his book, *The* Question *of Ethics: Nietzsche, Foucault, Heidegger* (Bloomington: Indiana University Press, 1990). I would like to dedicate the present chapter to Charles Scott. My thanks also to Michael Naas for his Homeric horsemanship, so much more skillful than my own.

2. On *Entrückung*, see my *Intimations of Mortality*, chap. 3, esp. pp. 58–63.

3. *29/30*, 7; cited in my text according to the corrected edition of Novalis' *Werke*, 3 vols., ed. Hans-Joachim Mähl and Richard Samuel (Munich: C. Hanser, 1978), II, 675.

4. Aristotle, "On Sleep and Waking," in *Parva naturalia*, 454b 10–11: "For sleep is an affection (πάθος) of the sensitive part of us (αἰσθητικοῦ μορίου)—a kind of fetter or immobilization (ἀκινησία). . . ." Loeb Classical Library, trans. W. S. Hett (Cambridge, Mass.: Harvard University Press; London: William Heinemann, 1957), pp. 322–23.

5. More precisely, Pöggeler's claim is that after 1929 Nietzsche's thinking of the death of God becomes for Heidegger a matter that requires *decision*. See Otto Pöggeler, *Philosophie und Politik bei Heidegger* (Freiburg and Munich: Karl Alber, 1972), p. 25.

6. See the foreword by Jürgen Habermas to Victor Farías, *Heidegger und der Nationalsozialismus* (Frankfurt am Main: S. Fischer, 1989), pp. 11–37. The unintended comic effect of Habermas' title, "Heidegger—Werk und Weltanschauung," becomes clear as soon as one takes even a cursory look at Heidegger's work *on* worldviews. See chaps. 4 and 5, below; see also my introduction to the revised, two-volume paperback edition of Heidegger's *Nietzsche* (San Francisco: Harper Collins, 1991), I, ix–xvii.

7. They are doubtless poorly edited, with every single one of Heidegger's repetitions, summaries, and reviews, every jot and tittle of the manuscript padded rather than fleshed out. Moreover, the superfoetation of longwinded titles and subtitles of endlessly ramifying sections and subsections is ultimately comic in its effect because of the theme—boredom—and the rhetoric—which is sardonic. Dominique Janicaud notes that Heidegger "is an academic, and does not know how to talk about boredom without being boring." (*L'ombre de cette pensée*, p. 165.) In Heidegger's defense we may say that in this case he had the assistance of yet another academic.

8. This would be the place to rejoin the questions raised in chaps. 2–3 of *Intimations of Mortality* concerning the conundrum of the *Wiederholbar-Unüberholbar*, whereby Heidegger's analysis is to fetch back (*wiederholen*) what it can neither overtake (death as *unüberholbar*) nor even catch up with (*einholen*).

9. That is the essential lesson of Derrida's *Of Spirit*, as of the seminar he has been conducting for the past six or seven years, "Philosophic Nationality and Nationalism." See his recent book, *L'autre cap* (Paris: Minuit, 1991), translated as *The Other Heading* by Michael B. Naas and Pascale-Anne Brault for Indiana University Press, 1992.

10. For an excellent though brief reading of these sections of *29/30*, see Michel Haar, *Le chant de la terre*, pp. 63–71. My own reading wishes to push Haar's questions in the direction of the unified realm of essence that is ζα-, the unified field of φύσις. Haar himself asks: "Will the reciprocal relation that is to be established between ἀλήθεια and φύσις clarify any further the enigma of life? Does not φύσις simply become a particular case of unveiling? How understand the 'leap' between animal and man if there is reciprocity and thus apparently continuity between ἀλήθεια and φύσις?" (71). Yet

unlike Haar (unless he is speaking here in Heidegger's voice) I do not expect the darkening song of the earth, the croaking of the earth (discussed in chap. 6, below), to be "quite far away from plants and animals" (108).

An excellent detailed reading of the biology lectures appears in Marc Richir, *Phénoménologie et Institution Symbolique (Phénomènes, Temps et Êtres II)* (Grenoble: Jerome Millon, 1988), pp. 223–85. Richir contrasts Heidegger's analysis of animal behavior with that of contemporary ethology, especially in the school of Konrad Lorenz (see esp. pp. 253–75). Richir argues that the abyss (*gouffre*) which Heidegger tries to insert between human comportment and animal behavior is not nearly as wide and deep as Heidegger believes and wishes (234). Ethology demonstrates that animal behavior, for example, in *curiosity*, which is not simply a captive response to a signal, manifests something like a *"phenomenological* opening to world, *outside of* language" (265). Richir's thesis is radical, and his argument is powerful if not altogether convincing: *"Thus there is in the case of the animal, and for the animal, phenomenalization, the phenomenon, the eidetic, the phenomenological . . ."* (270). Even if the temporalization/spatialization of language does not properly apply to the animal, there is something of genuine (phenomenological) access to world in animal life. If "man" is the symbolic animal, the avatar of symbolic institution (275–85), it is nonetheless true that no abyss of essence separates man from animal.

If I have one critical point to make concerning Richir, a point that the following pages of my own analysis will try to demonstrate, it is that he fails to note what would be most important for his own thesis concerning the institution of the symbolic: he neglects Heidegger's treatment of language in the final part of the 1929–1930 course. Heidegger's treatment of language there is demonstrably *apophantic*. It fails to take into account the insight into the *hermeneutical-as* analyzed in section 33 of *Being and Time*. Both Heidegger and Richir need to remember this "as," which is neither the metaphysical nor the assertory "as" of discourse and symbolic institution. For it is the *hermeneutical-as* that opens up a world for Dasein—and perhaps for other forms of life as well.

11. See *Le Visible et l'invisible*, esp. chap. 4. It is perhaps here that we must revise the usual judgment, which declares Heidegger's superiority over Merleau-Ponty as a thinker of ontology and metaphysics: whereas it is clear that toward the end of his life Merleau-Ponty learned a great deal from Heidegger, submitting to the lessons of Heideggerian ontology, history of being, and poetics of language and of silence, it is also clear in many places in the 1929–1930 lectures that we can and should learn a great deal from Merleau-Ponty's *Phenomenology of Perception* and *The Visible and the Invisible*. While Heidegger oscillates between the impossible positions of anthropocentrism and positivism, Merleau-Ponty wends his way more supply and subtly among the phenomena of life and the world of reversible flesh. Below, we shall take up the most interesting comparison of all, namely, that of Heidegger's 1929–1930 course and Merleau-Ponty's earliest work, *The Structure of Behavior*.

12. 29/30, 396. Heidegger repeats his Aristotelian analysis of melancholy in the Schelling lectures; SA, 193.

13. With that moralizing condemnation, Heidegger misses an encounter with Freud's "Mourning and Melancholy," which would have offered him (as it has offered others) abundant food for thought. Freud's essay of 1917 appears in StA 3, 193–212. I am of course thinking of Derrida's use of "Mourning and Melancholy" in his *Mémoires: pour Paul de Man* (Paris: Galilée, 1988), throughout. I have commented on this text in *Of Memory, Reminiscence, and Writing: On the Verge*, chap. 7. It is not entirely mad to see here yet another way in which Heidegger's thought—in spite of all appearances to the contrary—guides that of Derrida: as Derrida turns increasingly toward mourning and melancholy in his work on the promise of memory and double-affirmation, taking up in a critical way both Freudian and Lacanian psychoanalysis, he seems to mimic Heidegger's melancholic gesture even as he wishes to distance himself from it. As though to say, "Heidegger—we will never be rid of his corpse. . . ."

14. I am thinking of course of Kafka's *Der Bau* and of Maurice Blanchot's reading of that space in *L'espace littéraire* (Paris: Gallimard, 1955), pp. 223–26; see my "From Kafka to Kafka: 'I, an animal of the forest . . . ,'" in Paul Davies, ed., *Blanchot and Philosophy* (forthcoming in 1995). On the metaphysical mole, see my "*Der Maulwurf*/The Mole: Philosophic Burrowing in Kant, Hegel, and Nietzsche," in *Why Nietzsche Now?* ed. Daniel T. O'Hara (Bloomington: Indiana University Press, 1985), pp. 155–85.

15. Here once again, Merleau-Ponty's work, even his earliest work, *The Structure of Behavior*, is more impressive than Heidegger's 1929–1930 course. Merleau-Ponty resists the reductionism of the reflex-arc model without capitulating to a teleological Lamarckism. With his notions of "vital structures," "preferred behavior," "establishment of a milieu," and "equilibrium . . . with respect to conditions that are only virtual," Merleau-Ponty, building on the work of Gelb and Goldstein, discovers ways to avoid the classical impasses of mechanism and vitalism. See Maurice Merleau-Ponty, *La Structure du comportement* (Paris: Presses Universitaire de France, 1972 [1942]), pp. 157–73; trans. Alden Fisher, *The Structure of Behavior* (Boston: Beacon Press, 1967), pp. 145–60; cf. Kurt Goldstein, *Der Aufbau des Organismus* (The Hague: M. Nijhoff, 1934). Like Heidegger, Merleau-Ponty defines the animal as "a *being* capable [*un être capable;* cf. Heidegger's *Fähigkeit für . . .*] of certain types of action" (159/147). Yet Merleau-Ponty's examples (yawning, sneezing) are much closer to what he calls the "phenomenal body" than are Heidegger's. Merleau-Ponty resists any focus on particular organs or on anatomy—to which the fresh cadaver, from Descartes through Heidegger, always points. Merleau-Ponty's analyses demonstrate convincingly what Heidegger asserts peremptorily—the inapplicability of the mechanical model to organisms: "To construct a physical model of the organism would be to construct an organism" (164/151).

16. 29/30, 341. Heidegger is no doubt taken by Uexküll's and Driesch's *epigenetic* (as opposed to *evolutionary*) account of organ development. See Jacob Johann von Uexküll, *Theoretische Biologie,* 2nd ed. (Berlin: J. Springer, 1928), pp. 98–99 and 146–48. The capacity (*Fähigkeit*) to ingest, digest, and excrete arises from a pulsional sequence (*Impulsfolge*) that shapes (*gestalet*) a temporary yet recurrent series of protoorgans in one-celled animals. "Thus there is an immaterial order that first grants matter its articulation—a rule of life," writes Uexküll (98). The label I have used for Heidegger (his "Platonico-Leibnizo-Lamarckian strain") is therefore not so much unfair as it is incomplete. Aristotle, more than Plato, inspires every teleological biology after him. Moreover, it is important to note that this apparent quirk in Heidegger, this rather quaint and old-fashioned belief in teleological efficacy or entelechy, is actually an expression of an august tradition in German science, a tradition communicated to Heidegger by two of his heroes. The first, a hero of philosophy, is Kant. He incites generations of biological researchers after him to unite in one doctrine and practice mechanism and teleology. Not only Schelling and Hegel, but an entire line of anatomists, botanists, and zoologists in Germany can thus claim Kant as their forebearer. Perhaps the most influential and astute of these teleological biologists is Karl Ernst von Baer, a biologist-hero, celebrated by Heidegger in his 1929–1930 lectures. Yet whether Heidegger's Lamarckism is equal to either Lamarck or von Baer or Uexküll, or whether it is not in fact what one historian derides as a merely "religious" teleology, is a question one must confront.

On the tradition of "vital materialism" and "teleological mechanism" in German biology, see Timothy Lenoir, *The Strategy of Life: Teleology and Mechanics in Nineteenth-Century German Biology* (Chicago: University of Chicago Press, 1982), esp. the introduction; on Karl Ernst von Baer, see pp. 72–95. For a detailed treatment of Lamarck, see Thomas S. Hall, *Ideas of Life and Matter: Studies in the History of General Physiology, 600 B.C. to 1900 A.D.,* 2 vols. (Chicago: University of Chicago Press, 1969), 2, 133–48, esp. 145–46 on Lamarck's ideas concerning evolution, the alteration of organs through use and desuetude, and the creation of new organs (for example, ears!) through "efforts of inner feeling." Also helpful on Lamarck in the context of the Leibnizian "great chain of being" is Georges Canguilhem, *Ideology and Rationality in the History of the Life Sciences*, trans. Arthur Goldhammer (Cambridge, Mass.: MIT Press, 1988), p. 126.

17. *29/30*, 346. It is noteworthy that one of Heidegger's principal sources, F.J.J. Buytendijk, himself justifies the use of the word *Verhalten* for animal as well as human behavior, albeit not in the reflexive form, *Sichverhalten*. See Buytendijk, *Mensch und Tier: Ein Beitrag zur vergleichenden Psychologie* (Hamburg: Rowohlt, 1958), pp. 12–21. The influence of Buytendijk's work on Heidegger's entire effort can be felt in a passage from an article by Buytendijk that Heidegger cites in another context (see *29/30*, 376). On the penultimate page of his article, "Toward an Investigation of the Essential Distinction between Human Beings and Animals" (*Zur Untersuchung des Wesensunterschieds von Mensch und Tier*, in *Blätter für deutsche Philosophie*, vol. 3 [Berlin: Junker und Dünnhaupt, 1929–1930], pp. 33–66, see p. 65), Buytendijk writes: "A phenomenological investigation of the expressive movements of intelligence has taught us that the '*having of something*' ['Haben von etwas'] defines the essential character [*So-sein*] of intelligence. In acts of intelligence, the human being *has* the 'other'. . . . The animal 'has' nothing other than what is necessary for it. It has its environment; that is to say, it is poor [*seine Umwelt-, d.h. es ist arm*]. The human being has more than it needs. It has its world; that is to say, it is rich [*seine Welt-, d.h. er ist reich*]."

Even though the later Buytendijk cites Heidegger in turn (see *Mensch und Tier*, esp. p. 32) on "attunement" (*Stimmung*) and "bodily being in the world," it is nonetheless true that Heidegger would shrink from the uses to which his thought is eventually put in the school of the Uexkülls, Buytendijk, Portmann, Gehlen, Erwin Straus, and Merleau-Ponty (not to mention the Gestaltists), the school of phenomenological psychology and "situationalist" ethology. It is as though Heidegger himself underestimates the radicality and disturbing relevance of his work for the biological sciences.

18. See Descartes' letter to Meyssonnier, dated January 29, 1640, in *Oeuvres et lettres*, ed. André Bridoux (Paris: Gallimard-Pléiade, 1953), pp. 1066–67. See also the *Monadology*, in *Die philosophische Schriften von G. W. Leibniz*, ed. C. J. Gerhardt (Hildesheim: G. Olms, 1961 [reprint of the 7th ed., Berlin]), 6, 607–23, esp. §§21–24, 49, 60, 63, and 69, on *étourdissement, confusion*, and *Chaos*. In §60, Leibniz also uses the adjective *borné* to describe the animal's perception; such *Borniertheit*, as the Germans would say, perhaps comes closest to the sense of Heidegger's *Benommenheit*. On the confusion, stupefaction, bedazzlement, and dull-wittedness caused by *petites perceptions*, see the *Nouveaux essais*, *New Essays on the Human Understanding*, trans. Peter Remnant and Jonathan Bennett (Cambridge: Cambridge University Press, 1981), pp. 53–55, 72, 91, 113, 135, 137, 139, 166, 173, 195, 381, and elsewhere. (My thanks to Anna Vaughn for locating these passages.)

19. To all this one ought to compare in detail Hegel's interpretation of assimilation and the mating process in the *Encyclopedia*, in the places cited earlier, as well as in the 1805–1806 lectures on the philosophy of nature in the *Gesammelte Werke*, vol. 8, *Jenaer Systementwürfe III*, ed. Rolf-Peter Horstmann (Hamburg: F. Meiner, 1969), throughout. There is some evidence (mainly in the *Contributions to Philosophy*, considered in chap. 6, below) that in the mid-1930s Heidegger accepted without demur Hegel's view of the preeminence of the *Gattung* or species over the individual members of that species. However, acceptance of such preeminence, I believe, would be one of the hallmarks of metaphysical thinking and of ontotheology as such. See Krell, "Pitch: Genitality/Excrementality from Hegel to Crazy Jane," in *boundary 2*, 12, 2 (Winter 1984), 113–41. Finally, for some even more dire accounts of the female praying mantis, see Steven Jay Gould, *The Flamingo's Smile* (New York: W. W. Norton, 1985), chap. 2, "Only His Wings Remained." In the (zoologically unreliable) accounts that Gould cites,

the female mantis is ready to gobble up the male whether before or after copulation: for her, he is always already *weg!*

20. *26, 103:* Heidegger here cites Leibniz's *De primae philosophiae Emendatione,* in the Gerhardt edition of the *Works,* 4, 469. In spite of Heidegger's attribution of this "felicitous" expression, and the implication drawn by Wilhelm Mader, *Max Scheler,* p. 69, Scheler's *Trieblehre* does *not* appear to function principally by inhibition and disinhibition (*Hemmung, Enthemmung*); see his 1926 *Erkenntnis und Arbeit, Gesammelte Werke,* 8, 191–382, esp. 315–43, on *die triebhaft-motorische Bedingtheit,* and his 1913 *Versuche einer Philosophie des Lebens: Nietzsche—Dilthey—Bergson, Gesammelte Werke,* 3, 311–39, which nowhere mentions *(Ent)Hemmung.* For his part, J. J. von Uexküll speaks, not of a ring of disinhibitions, but of a *Funktionskreis;* see his *Theoretische Biologie,* pp. 100–101, 120–22, and 126–28. See also his *Umwelt und Innenwelt der Tiere,* 2nd ed. (Berlin: J. Springer, 1921), pp. 44–49; note his concluding observations on "The Observer," which must have been crucial for Heidegger's conception of the problem of *access* to the animal's world-relation; see pp. 215–19.

21. For an alternative analysis of world-relation, rooted not in nihilative openness to the world, an openness that is itself subjugated to the λόγος of humankind, but in organic *metabolism,* see Hans Jonas, *The Phenomenon of Life,* "Third Essay." To be sure, that alternative in its most effusive Hegelian-Whiteheadian moments (e.g., pp. 95–98) needs nothing so much as Heidegger's persistent meditation on being-unto-death and initiation into mortality, the pervasive negatives of catabolic animal—*and human*—life.

22. Heidegger introduces the testing-stone of death (in §61) by referring to the problem of *history* with regard to living individuals and species (*29/30,* 386). For the essence of the organic surely has *something* to do with the birth, maturation, reproduction, aging, and death of successive generations—hence with both individual and specific history. In this domain, confesses Heidegger, "one question generates another, and each is more essential than the others, while each is also more bereft of answers than the others" (386). He cites Theodor Boveri's lecture, "Organisms as Historical Creatures" (*Die Organismen als historische Wesen,* held on May 11, 1906 at the University of Würzburg [Würzburg: H. Stürtz, 1906]); see esp. pp. 13–17, which convincingly argue for the importance of the *historical development* of all species within the *natural system* of plants and animals. Indeed, the reader of Boveri's lecture quickly becomes convinced that Heidegger's anti-Darwinism—and, in general, his resistance to the hirsute anthropoid, his allergy vis-à-vis Enkidu—is in fact a resistance to his own thought of a *historizing history.* If history as happening and fateful happenstance (*Geschichte, Geschehen, Geschick*) is one of Heidegger's major insights in *Being and Time,* his reluctance to think of *life* in terms of occurrence, essential unfolding, and the fateful-fatal sending weakens his achievement considerably. It ruins his chance to integrate history and nature in a way Dilthey dreamed of but could not fulfill. Finally, note also Boveri's not unsympathetic remarks on Lamarck, precisely in the context of the history of species, pp. 26–28; and on the "rise of the psyche," p. 29.

23. In *Totality and Infinity,* Levinas mocks Heidegger's "faint materialism" ("faint" here meaning abashed or shame-ridden: *honteux*) and ridicules "the pagan 'moods' " of Heidegger's thought of dwelling. See *Totalité et infini,* 333/299 and 38/47. The same spirit of scorn dominates Hans Jonas's "Heidegger and Theology," *The Phenomenon of Life,* "Tenth Essay." Perhaps only one aspect of Jonas's complaint, which caused such a stir a generation ago, is relevant here. When Jonas, precisely in the context of his long-term project on the phenomenon of life, complains of Heidegger's "paganism" (248–49), of his "heresy" against an ostensibly monolithic "Judeo-Christian tradition," of his "immanentism" and "tragic view of history"; when Jonas grumbles that Heidegger's "doctrine," with its "blasphemous ring" (258) "makes it impossible to distinguish between the inspirations of the Holy Ghost and the demons" (254); and when he declares that Heideggerians must turn to Alfred North Whitehead, inasmuch as "no

philosophy of nature can issue from Heidegger's thought" (253n.);—when Jonas complains in this fashion, he is in fact railing against the one thinker whose interpretations of freedom and transcendence, of nihilation and the nothing, of being-unto-death and initiation into mortality offer what Jonas's own project needs in order to prevent it from becoming a belated rehearsal of the Hegelian philosophy of nature. Instead of confronting the limitations of his own rather blatant appeals to freedom, transcendence, and tragedy, and instead of acknowledging his debt to one of the most profound thinkers on "the *problem* of death" (8), Jonas prefers to protest . . . too much.

24. William Faulkner, *As I Lay Dying* (Harmondsworth: Penguin Books, 1963 [1930]), p. 13.

25. Note also the conclusion Paul draws at the end of his paragraph: *Denn wir wissen / das alle Creatur sehnet sich mit vns / vnd engstet sich noch jmer dar* (8 Römer 22).

4. "YOU IN FRONT OF ME, I IN FRONT OF YOU"

1. Heidegger's 1921–1922 lecture course will be discussed in the final part of this chapter. "Die Selbstbehauptung der deutschen Universität," first published in 1933, has been reprinted along with "Das Rektorat 1933/34, Tatsachen und Gedanken," related (but by no means identical) to Heidegger's "plea" to the university authorities in 1945, by Hermann Heidegger (cited here as SB, with page number); Karsten Harries has translated both texts in *The Review of Metaphysics,* vol. 38, no. 3 (March 1985), 467–502; "Nur noch ein Gott kann uns retten," in *Der Spiegel,* vol. 30, no. 23 (1976), 193–219, has been translated into English by Maria P. Alter and John D. Caputo in *Philosophy Today,* vol. 20, no. 4 (Winter 1976), 267–84.

2. Philippe Lacoue-Labarthe, *La Poésie comme expérience* and *La fiction du politique: Heidegger, l'art et la politique* (Paris: Christian Bourgois, 1986 and 1987, respectively); Jacques Derrida, *Schibboleth: Pour Paul Celan* and *De l'esprit: Heidegger et la question,* cited earlier. On Lacoue-Labarthe's *La fiction du politique,* see the Addendum at the conclusion of the chapter; on Derrida's *De l'esprit,* see chap. 8, below, and "Of Spirit and the Daimon," a paper presented to the Society for Phenomenology and Existential Philosophy in October of 1989, to appear in *Ethics and Danger: Currents in Continental Thought,* ed. A. Dallery and C. Scott (Albany: SUNY Press, 1992), forthcoming.

3. These unpublished lines from the Bremen lectures are cited by Lacoue-Labarthe, *La fiction du politique,* p. 58, from a book by Wolfgang Schirmacher, *Technik und Gelassenheit* (Freiburg: Karl Alber Verlag, 1984).

4. See Reiner Schürmann's thoughtful remarks on technology and National Socialism, in his *Heidegger on Being and Acting,* pp. 15–16 and esp. 313–14 n. 35.

5. See also Derrida's remarks to the Essex Colloquium, "Reading Heidegger," in *Research in Phenomenology,* XVII (1987); and, of course, *De l'esprit,* along with its "sister," *Psyché: Inventions de l'autre.* During the discussion that followed my presentation of the paper (delivered at the University of Alabama in 1987) that was an earlier form of this chapter, Derrida asked how the *Versagen des Denkens* I invoke here relates to what Heidegger himself calls *das Ungedachte*—the ostensibly unitary, unique "unthought" of a thinker. He suggested that just as one might challenge Heidegger's claim that a thinker's "unthought" can be reduced to a one so might my own challenge to Heidegger be countered. Can we be certain that it is only *one* sort of failure that is here in question? Derrida's doubt gives me pause. Especially because, as we shall soon see, I am the one who claims to be worried about the *one* of the rectoral address. Even though I am drawing the matters of "technology and human resources," "the essence of evil," and "the gathering of thinking" back to that incomparable event we call the Extermination or Holocaust, and wish to do so without subterfuge, I nevertheless respect the admonition that failure—in the matters of thinking and of the unthought—

may always be multiple, always proliferant and proleptic, always in dispersion, and that our response to it may always have to be a matter of *unsuccessful* mourning.

6. Hugo Ott, "Martin Heidegger als Rektor der Universität Freiburg 1933/34," in *Zeitschrift für die Geschichte des Oberrheins*, vol. 132, "New Series," no. 93 (Stuttgart: W. Kohlhammer, 1984), 343–58. I shall cite this article as HO, with page number, in the body of my text. A largely repetitive account by Ott, published as "Part II" of the above, appears in *Zeitschrift des Breisgau-Geschichtsvereins* ("Schau-ins-Land"), vol. 103 (1984), 107–130. Bernd Martin, "Heidegger und die Reform der deutschen Universität 1933," in *Freiburger Universitätsblätter*, Heft 92, "Martin Heidegger: Ein Philosoph und die Politik" (June 1986), 49–69. I shall cite this volume, which contains many other valuable texts as well, as FrU, with page number. See also Hugo Ott's brief account, "Der Philosoph im politischen Zwielicht," in the *Neue Zürcher Zeitung*, Feuilleton "Literatur und Kunst," November 3/4, 1984; see also his "Martin Heidegger und die Universität Freiburg nach 1945," in *Historisches Jahrbuch der Görres-gesellschaft* (1985 / I.), 95–128. Finally, for a brief review of some of the literature, see Rudolf Ringguth, "Führer der Führer," in *Der Spiegel*, vol. 40, no. 34 (1986), pp. 164–69. (I am deeply indebted to Sabine Mödersheim, Ashraf Noor, Joseph C. Schöpp, and Ulrich Halfmann for their help in gathering these and other materials.) In the meantime, of course, Hugo Ott's book has been published: *Martin Heidegger: Unterwegs zu seiner Biographie* (Frankfurt am Main: Campus, 1988); see my remarks in the Addendum at the conclusion of the chapter. Concerning the much-discussed book by Victor Farías, *Heidegger et le nazisme: Morale et politique* (Paris: Verdier, 1987), it suffices if one reads the reviews by Hugo Ott and Robert Bernasconi, the first in the *Neue Zürcher Zeitung*, November 27, 1987, Fernausgabe Nr. 275, p. 39; the second in *Bulletin of the German Historical Institute*, London, vol. 12, no. 1, 1990.

7. For more detailed readings, see Charles Scott, *The Question of Ethics*, chap. 5, pp. 148–72; see also Dominique Janicaud, *L'ombre*, pp. 66–73.

8. Gérard Granel, *De l'université* (Paris: Trans-Europe-Repress [TER], 1982). See esp. pp. 99–143: "Pourquoi avons-nous publié cela?" Granel discusses the continuing crisis of the sciences, technological streamlining, and consequent political paralysis as problems of "infinite production." His acknowledgment of the possible parallels between the student movement in France between 1968 and 1977 and the role of the *Deutscher Studentenbund* in 1933 is both thought-provoking and distressing. On Granel, see the excellent article by Chris Fynsk, "But Suppose We Were to Take the Rectorial Address Seriously . . . : Gérard Granel's *De l'université*," in "Heidegger and the Political," a special issue of *The Graduate Faculty Journal*, New School for Social Research, 14, 2/15, 1 (1991), 335–62. It is unfair to single out articles in a collection as excellent as the one Marcus Brainard has put together. Yet allow me to mention also John D. Caputo, "Heidegger's *Kampf*: The Difficulty of Life," 61–83, which is especially relevant to my efforts here. Even if Caputo beats his readers about the ears with the New Testament in order to show them mercy, the mercy in *cura*, his article is admirably thorough, thoughtful, and relentless. (And, after all, I myself have only now quoted Paul!) Brainard's collection arrived only after *Daimon Life* was finished, so that I cannot make many explicit references to it here. Yet I recommend it heartily, at least pp. 1–151 and 183–611, to all who want to engage seriously with "Heidegger and the Political."

9. Later in the chapter I shall examine volume 56/57 of the Gesamtausgabe, *Zur Bestimmung der Philosophie,* the appendix of which is entitled, "On the Essence of the University and of Academic Study." These (incomplete) notes recorded by Oskar Becker from Heidegger's lectures in the summer semester of 1919 suggest that the latter's principal interest is not university reform but the relation of phenomenological theory to the seedbed of all theory in the nexus of *life*. A tension pervades Heidegger's reflections here: on the one hand, theory appears to arise out of an impoverished life-situation, a situation in dissolution; on the other hand, theory offers "the chance of

unlimited knowledge" concerning that very situation (see 56/57, 213). Also of interest in these same pages are Heidegger's remarks on *Ereignis* as an event that "happens to me" (205; cf. 75 and 78) and on the distinction (derived presumably from Paul Natorp's *General Psychology* and Jaspers's 1913 *General Psychopathology*—which, however, Heidegger does not cite in his lecture course—along with the work of Wilhelm Dilthey) between explanatory and *verstehenden* disciplines. Heidegger's interest lies in the latter group—history, art, and religion—insofar as they touch on the situation of *life*. On which the dreariness of Heidegger's politics, the cacaphony and the silence, will soon impinge.

10. Otto Pöggeler, *Der Denkweg Martin Heideggers*, 2nd ed. (Pfullingen: G. Neske, 1983), pp. 329–30; trans. as *Martin Heidegger's Path of Thinking* by Daniel Magurshak and Sigmund Barber (Atlantic Highlands, New Jersey: Humanities Press, 1987), p. xi. The "Epilogue" to this second edition of *Der Denkweg*, pp. 319–55, is one of the most valuable, succinct discussions of the political dimensions of Heidegger's thought. See also "Heideggers politisches Selbstverständnis," in *Heidegger und die praktische Philosophie*, ed. Annemarie Gethmann-Siefert and Otto Pöggeler (Frankfurt am Main: Suhrkamp, 1988), pp. 17–63.

11. A letter from Heidegger to Jaspers in late 1925 or early 1926, cited by Hugo Ott, *Unterwegs*, p. 123.

12. Jacques Derrida, "Mochlos, ou le conflit des facultés," in *Philosophie*, no. 2 (Paris: Minuit, April 1984), 27. See also Derrida's "The University in the Eyes of Its Pupils," in *The Graduate Faculty Philosophy Journal* (New School for Social Research), 10, 1 (1984), 5–29, especially its references to the sciences and the university as discussed in SG, 49. See now the third division of Derrida, *Du Droit à la philosophie* (Paris: Galilée, 1990), pp. 397–535, where these texts and others on the university are gathered. During the discussion that followed the paper on which this chapter is based, Derrida insisted that factical life must *also* be found *outside* the university—otherwise it would be impossible to bring anything to bear on university philosophy, impossible to improve it, as Heidegger no doubt wants to do. He was right. Yet in a plummeting world, where everything outside too is falling, the university itself remains in Heidegger's view the privileged site of "counterthrust," even if intramural *Ruinanz* is so startlingly in evidence. Surely, ruination is one of those places where the inside/outside distinction founders? Surely, ruination is one of the undecidables, one of the great contaminators—perhaps *Kontaminanz* "as such"?

13. As one becomes more familiar with the intellectual climate of the Weimar Republic, however, one is less surprised to see these references to the problem of leadership arising immediately after the Great War. Interesting in relation to Derrida's *Of Spirit* is the fact that *Geist* dominates these early discussions of *Führung* as well. See the excellent articles by Anthony Phelan, R. Hinton Thomas, and (above all) Keith Bullivant in Anthony Phelan, ed., *The Weimar Dilemma: Intellectuals in the Weimar Republic* (Manchester, England: Manchester University Press, 1985), esp. pp. 2–3, 19–21, 47–70, and 71–91. Ironically, Hugo Ott unwittingly borrows the euphonious word *Allüren*, euphonious and fundamentally *undeutsch*, from Heidegger's early lecture course—precisely in order to portray the Heidegger of 1933, bewitched by *Führerallüren*. See Ott's *Unterwegs*, p. 150, at the end of the third paragraph.

14. Even though these works have been cited already, I repeat the publishers' information here: Hugo Ott, *Martin Heidegger: Unterwegs zu seiner Biographie* (Frankfurt am Main: Campus, 1988); Victor Farías, *Heidegger und der Nationalsozialismus* (Frankfurt am Main: S. Fischer, 1989); Philippe Lacoue-Labarthe, *La fiction du politique: Heidegger, l'art et la politique* (Paris: Christian Bourgois, 1987); trans. by Chris Turner as *Heidegger, Art and Politics: The Fiction of the Political* (Oxford: Basil Blackwell, 1990); and Dominique Janicaud, *L'ombre de cette pensée: Heidegger et la question politique* (Grenoble: Jerome Millon, 1990). Note that Derrida's *Of Spirit* is reserved for discussion in chap. 8, below.

15. See my brief article, "The Heidegger-Jaspers Relationship," *The Journal of the British Society for Phenomenology*, XI, 2 (May 1978), 126–29, along with the more philosophical treatment in Krell, *Intimations of Mortality*, chap. 1.

16. Quite important with regard to Heidegger's religious training are his early (1911!) religious essays and reviews presented by Hugo Ott in an appendix of "Heidegger and the Political," the special issue of *The Graduate Faculty Philosophy Journal*, cited in note 8, above. These are brief pieces by the doctoral candidate and theology student Martin Heidegger. They reflect the views of a militantly antimodernist, pro-Papist Catholic, still intensely caught up in the liturgy and dogma of his embattled Faith. As polemical as Heidegger will later be *against* a moribund Christendom, he is here polemical *on its behalf*, whether celebrating the converted Danish biologist, Johannes Jörgensen, or inveighing against Oscar Wilde, "a dandy," Paul Verlaine, "a booser," Maxim Gorky, "a vagabond," and Nietzsche, "superman." And whether spouting earnest adolescent pieties or condemning modern individualism, "lived experience" (a constant target, no matter what the period), and "worldviews" (ditto). Sample: "It is indeed already a banality: today worldviews are cut to fit 'life,' instead of vice versa" (496–97). Each of these early devotional writings of Heidegger's deserves close scrutiny, especially the truly impressive essay on "Psychology of Religion and the Subconscious" (502–517), which is the most substantive and least regressive of the group. As a whole, these early religious essays and reviews gain in significance when we recall the debate concerning the contribution of Heidegger's *religious* background to his National Socialism: while some insist that problems arose only when Heidegger left the fold (effectively, around 1917 or 1918) and largely abandoned Christianity as such (much more difficult to date, but by the end of the Marburg period), others have discerned an undeniable continuity in Heidegger's religious conservatism and anti-Communism, his sectarian rigorism and intolerance, and his intellectual and moral submission to a (spiritual) leader.

For the sake of daimon life, I will truncate the note by presenting one brief passage on Johannes Jörgensen, sometime Darwinist, born-again Catholic. Heidegger writes, or is ventriloquized, as follows: "Higher life is conditioned by the decline of the lower forms. For growth, the plant needs inorganic matter. The animal can live only through the death of the plant and so on up the ladder. And if you want to live spiritually, to gain your salvation, then die, kill the baseness in yourself, work with the supernatural grace, and you will be resurrected. And thus the strong-willed, hopeful poet-philosopher now rests in the shadow of the cross: a modern Augustine" (490–91).

Thus far the chances of life—with a twenty-two-year-old theology student.

17. See Heidegger, Gesamtausgabe volumes *56/57, 61,* and *63;* see also Robert Bernasconi, " 'The Double Concept of Philosophy' and the Place of Ethics in *Being and Time*," *Research in Phenomenology*, XVIII (1988), 41–57; and "Habermas and Arendt on the Philosopher's 'Error': Tracking the Diabolical in Heidegger," *Graduate Faculty Philosophy Journal*, special issue (cited in note 8, above), 3–24, esp. 10–11.

18. Habermas is clearly quite close to the (more refined and better informed) readings of Hannah Arendt and J. L. Mehta here. I discuss these in the context of Heidegger's engagement with National Socialism in the "Analysis" to Martin Heidegger, *Nietzsche, Vol. IV: Nihilism, 4,* 262–76, esp. 272–76, and in my "Introduction" to the two-volume paperbound edition of Heidegger's *Nietzsche*, pp. ix–xvii.

19. See the review article on Pöggeler by Frank H. W. Edler, "Retreat from Radicality: Pöggeler on Heidegger's Politics," in "Heidegger and the Political," *Graduate Faculty Philosophy Journal*, 295–321. Edler's careful criticisms of Pöggeler, based on Schürmann's reading of an anarchic and aprincipial Heidegger, would need lengthy discussion.

20. I have tried to develop Nancy and Lacoue-Labarthe's idea, itself an expansion of Walter Benjamin's work, in the direction of a national *erotism*, focusing on the psychodynamics of xenophobia, war, and racism; see Krell, "National Erotism: *Derdiedas*

Responsibilities," delivered on March 8, 1991 at the Simon Silverman Center for Phenomenological Research, Duquesne University, Pittsburgh, to be published in the Proceedings of that meeting.

    21. Dominique Janicaud, *La puissance du rationnel* (Paris: Gallimard, 1985).

5. SHATTERING

    1. Quoted in Hugo Ott, *Martin Heidegger: Unterwegs zu seiner Biographie*, p. 231.

    2. 29/30, 243–49. See Winfried Franzen, "Die Sehnsucht nach Härte und Schwere," in Annemarie Gethmann-Siefert and Otto Pöggeler, eds., *Heidegger und die praktische Philosophie*, pp. 78–92, cited in my text by page number in parentheses.

    3. The *context* of Heidegger's involvement in National Socialism becomes increasingly complex as we learn more about it. It would be instructive, albeit complicating and complicated, to reflect on Heidegger's political engagement in the light of Max Scheler's "publicist" (not to say "propagandist") works from the period of the First World War: *Der Genius des Kriegs, Krieg und Aufbau, Ursachen des Deutschenhaßes, Reue und Wiedergeburt*, etc. One might anticipate a certain sympathy between Heidegger's political views and Scheler's national-pedagogical writings. These combine conservative Catholicism, centrist socialism, and the *großdeutsche Lösung*, i.e., the proposed unification of Germany and Austria, with outspoken opposition to (American) "late capitalism" and (Russian) "Bolshevism," both of these being characterized as forms of "liberalism." Perhaps the most remarkable difference between the two thinkers, however, is that—apart from the dreary speeches of 1933–1934—we have no such body of popular-political work from Heidegger. See Wilhelm Mader, *Max Scheler*, pp. 70–82; and 87–88.

    4. In what follows I shall work through the nine references to *Scheitern* in *Sein und Zeit*: (1) 148, l. 11; (2) 169, l. 11; (3) 174, l. 15; (4) 178, l. 20; (5) 233, l. 25; (6) 240, l. 3; (7) 241, l. 25; (8) 317, l. 10; (9) 374, l. 19. For a representative use of *Scheitern* in the 1930s, see SA, 194; for representative uses of *Erschütterung*, see the lecture course on biology, 29/30, 281 and the *Contributions to Philosophy*, 65, 389 and 444.

    5. SZ, 254 n. 1: "L. N. Tolstoy, in his narrative entitled 'The Death of Ivan Ilych,' has depicted the phenomenon of the shattering and the collapse of this 'one dies' [*das Phänomen der Erschütterung und des Zusammenbruchs dieses 'man stirbt'*]." The difficulty is whether *Erschütterung* is to be equated with the mere social ignominy occasioned by the death of others or whether Heidegger means the genitive *objectively* as the collapse of the ignominy of the "one dies." For a discussion of the note, see Robert Bernasconi, "Literary Attestation in Philosophy: Heidegger's Footnote on Tolstoy's 'The Death of Ivan Ilyich,' " in David Wood, ed., *Philosophers' Poets* (London: Routledge, 1990), pp. 7–36.

    6. The question that most intrigues me—beyond the solicitude for the cadaver that we noted earlier—is whether section 26 is flawed because it *lacks* an adequate account of "proper solicitude" or because it is *surfeited* with ethical pretensions that have not as yet been radically extruded.

    7. SZ, 384–85. Toward the end of the first part of "Geschlecht IV" (see Sallis, *Reading Heidegger*, ms. pp. 31–36), Derrida discusses section 74 of *Being and Time* in terms of *Kampf* and *Mitteilung*, including the "communication" of "the voice of the friend that each Dasein carries with itself." While the word *Kampf* appears four times in *Being and Time*, and not merely once (see SZ, 9, on the struggle between formalism and intuitionism in mathematics; 384, cited by Derrida, on the release of the power [*Macht*] of a people's sending or destiny [*Geschick*]; 434, citing Hegel, on the "infinite struggle of spirit with itself"; and 435, on Hegel's "effort and struggle to grasp the 'concretion' of spirit"), the *tendency* of Derrida's reading is sound: the "voice of the friend" is undecidably and philopolemologically bound up with the heroes a Dasein chooses as it marches off bravely with its "generation." Presumably, the friend of Dasein always

speaks the same language (but why?), speaks as the *identical voice of Dasein in each Dasein* (but how?), as the friend who commands, who gives orders and directives. What would it take for the voice of the friend to become truly shattering? What sort of foreignness and radical difference would open Dasein to the very confrontation with finitude that Heidegger insists it must undergo in order to *be* Dasein?

8. Concerning "generation," one would have to pursue Heidegger's own reference to Dilthey, "Über das Studium der Geschichte der Wissenschaften vom Menschen, der Gesellschaft und dem Staat," from the year 1875, in Wilhelm Dilthey, *Gesammelte Schriften V*, esp. pp. 36–38. Helpful in this context would be an analysis of the *rhetoric* of "generation," a curious mix of biology and cultural nationalism (of course as Pan-European spiritual-intellectual accomplishment), in an amalgam of the scientific vocabulary of the historian's craft and pervasive euphemism. I cannot offer such an analysis here, but will only present some of the phrases that might have struck Heidegger as particularly relevant for his project, and especially for the move from individual destiny, through heritage, to the fate of a people. For Dilthey too it is a question of how *individuals* embody something of the *whole* of a culture, how the passage of generations guarantees *"a whole bound together through continuity"* (38). Initially a mere form of historical measurement, "generation" quickly becomes something more, something suggested by the following words (again, each word or phrase would require careful analysis): *gemeinsames Kinderalter . . . männlicher Kraft; die Verknüpfung solcher Personen durch ein tieferes Verhältnis; in den Jahren der Empfänglichkeit; zu einem homogenen Ganzen verbunden; das heranwachsende Geschlecht . . . geistigen Gehaltes; aus deren rätselhaften Schoß; Bedingungen nationaler Tüchtigkeit . . . die Intensität der Leistungen* (37–38). Dilthey is well aware of the dangers of "the radiant appearances that are due to the historian's craft," so that these phrases are not to be taken as indicative of some sort of uncritical nationalism or organicism on Dilthey's part. Nevertheless, the kind of inquiry that Derrida has initiated with regard to "philosophical nationality and nationalism" would be very useful here. See Gs II, esp. its opening pages on Fichte's "Address to the German Nation."

9. See Philippe Lacoue-Labarthe, *La fiction du politique: Heidegger, l'art et la politique*, chap. 7; and Jean-Luc Nancy, *La communauté désoeuvrée* (Paris: Christian Bourgois, 1986), passim. Again, see my "National Erotism: *Derdiedas* Responsibilities," cited in the previous chapter.

10. "Was ist Metaphysik?" (1929), in W, 14–15; BW, 108. Heidegger writes: "Anxiety is there. It is only sleeping. Its breath quivers perpetually through Dasein, only slightly in those who are jittery, imperceptibly in the 'Oh, yes' and the 'Oh, no' of men of affairs; but most readily in the reserved, and most assuredly in those who are basically daring [*das im Grunde verwegene Dasein*]. But those daring ones are sustained by that on which they expend themselves—in order thus to preserve a final greatness in existence. (/) The anxiety of those who are daring cannot be opposed to joy or even to the comfortable enjoyment of tranquilized bustle. It stands—outside all such opposition—in secret alliance with the cheerfulness and gentleness of creative longing."

11. 26, 13. See once again Robert Bernasconi, " 'The Double Concept of Philosophy' and the Place of Ethics in *Being and Time*," cited in the previous chapter.

12. Presumably a reference to Scheler's *Die Stellung des Menschen im Kosmos* (1927), now in Max Scheler, *Späte Schriften*, cited in chap. 2, above.

13. See Krell, *Intimations of Mortality*, pp. 41–43.

14. Heidegger's review of volume 2 of Ernst Cassirer, *Philosophie der symbolischen Formen, Das mythische Denken*, appears in the *Deutsche Literaturzeitung*, vol. XLIX, no. 21 (1928), 999–1012. A detailed study of this review is certainly called for but is not possible here. Compare with the Cassirer review SZ §11 and 313, which emphasize the way in which Dasein *lives* in myths, cults, and rites. Finally, it would be intriguing to compare Heidegger's treatment of these matters with that of Georges Bataille and the entire College of Sociology. See Denis Hollier, *Le collège de sociologie (1937–1939):*

Textes de Georges Bataille, Roger Caillois, René M. Guastalla, Pierre Klossowski, Alexandre Kojève, Michel Leiris, Anatole Lewitsky, Hans Mayer, Jean Paulhan, Jean Wahl, etc. (Paris: Idées/Gallimard, 1979).

15. Martin Heidegger, "Die Sprache im Gedicht: Eine Erörterung von Georg Trakls Gedicht," in US, 50. Cf. the allusion to *Einfalt*, the two hands "folded" in the piety of prayer, in WhD? 51; and see the discussion in Derrida, Gs II, 430–31. See also chap. 8, below.

16. It is a gesture he attributes to Nietzsche, namely, that of thinking by way of opposition or reversal. See NI, 38–40/1, 29–30.

17. There are seventeen instances of *Zerstreuung* and its cognates in *Sein und Zeit*, and we might pause to review them here. For convenience sake I shall reduce them to ten clusters: (1) 56, l. 34; (2) 67, l. 1; (3) 129, ll. 16–17; (4) 172, ll. 35 and 40; (5) 273, l. 22; (6) 310, l. 8; (7) 338, l. 5; (8) 347, ll. 24 and 27; (9) 371, ll. 14–15; (10) 389, l. 40 and 390, ll. 4, 28, and 39. With reference to Derrida's discussion of *Zerstreuung* in his "Geschlecht [I]," I would like to make the following observations. First, of the seventeen uses, only two can be said to manifest a quite positive valence, i.e., references (5) and (6). Second, both of these positive uses involve the power of the call of conscience to disperse the subterfuges and distractions by which Dasein conceals from itself its ownmost, insurmountable possibility. Reference (6) is particularly striking in this regard, for it uses the word *mächtig* to describe its action, the very word that Heidegger in 1928 uses to portray the positivity of neutrality. In *Being and Time* (SZ, 310), Heidegger writes: "The open resolve that runs ahead is not an evasion which we invent in order to 'overcome' death. Rather, it is the understanding that follows the call of conscience, the understanding that grants death the possibility of *attaining power* [mächtig *zu werden*] over the *existence* of Dasein, ultimately dispersing [*zerstreuen*] every ephemeral subterfuge." Third, if the remaining fifteen references are strongly negative, most of them indicating the distraction of Dasein in the They, one is close to a kind of modal neutrality, namely, reference (2). Heidegger writes: "Our involvement has always dispersed itself into a manifold of modes of taking-care." Here the word *Mannigfaltigkeit* appears, as it does in the 1928 logic. That this structure of everydayness should in 1928 become one of the principal terms of a metaphysics of Dasein should give us considerable pause. Fourth, it is important to observe that the positive uses of *zerstreuen* are active and verbal; when the passive participle or the noun *Zerstreuung* appear, the sense is always negative. (For this preeminently negative connotation, see the important early uses of the word in 1921–1922 [*61*, 101–102].) Fifth and finally, one might want to compare the equation of the active/passive opposition with the positive/negative valorization in the vocabulary of *Benehmen/Benommenheit* in the 1929–1930 biology course. See esp. 29/30, §§58–63; and see the Introduction and chap. 3, above.

18. I have broached these matters in *Intimations of Mortality*, pp. 41–42 and 59–61.

19. Heidegger's self-critique is undated, but I suspect (for internal reasons) that it stems from the years 1936–1938: a number of locutions that appear in the *Beiträge* also appear here, as monuments to its "other thinking": *Entmachtung der* φύσις, *die Wesung des Seins* (although being is not yet written with an upsilon, as it often is in the *Beiträge*, in order to indicate, generally but not at all consistently, *Sein* in the course of its unfolding as *history* and *truth*), *der andere Anfang, Stufen der Wahrheit, gründen, die Grundfrage, die Gründung des Da-seins.*

20. Martin Heidegger, *Einführung in die Metaphysik*, Gesamtausgabe, vol. 40 (Frankfurt am Main: V. Klostermann, 1983), p. 218.

21. I am referring of course to the third and final treatise of Nietzsche's *Zur Genealogie der Moral* (1887). See esp. chap. 2 of Charles Scott, *The Question of Ethics: Foucault, Nietzsche, Heidegger*, pp. 13–52.

22. See George L. Mosse, "Beauty without Sensuality," in *"Degenerate Art": The Fate of the Avant-Garde in Nazi Germany*, ed. Stephanie Barron (New York: Harry N. Abrams, 1991), pp. 25–31.

23. Ibid. The reproductions of Josef Thorak's *Kameradschaft* appear on pp. 17 and 35; Karl Hofer's *Freunde* and *Freundinnen* appear on p. 257. For Freud's juxtaposition of tenderness and sensuality, see the second of his three *Contributions to the Psychology of Lovelife*, "On the Most Universal Form of Degradation in Lovelife" (1912), StA, 5, 197–209. Finally, see once again my paper on "National Erotism," cited in chap. 4, note 20.

24. Hannah Arendt, *The Human Condition* (Garden City, N.Y.: Doubleday Anchor, 1959), cited here by page number in parentheses.

25. Luce Irigaray, OA, 145 and 43. See chap. 9, below, for a more detailed reading of Irigaray's *L'oubli de l'air*.

6. PARANOETIC THINKING

1. See 65, 9 and 64, for the *four*, as opposed to the *six*, key words. Yet I would be the last to deny a place to the two final key words, "the futural ones" and "the last god," *die Zukünftigen* and *der letzte Gott*, which undoubtedly have something to do with the daimonic. Note that the section that appears as section eight of the published volume, "Das Seyn," does not belong where the editor has placed it: Heidegger most likely intended that the two brief, apocalyptic sections (*"Die Zukünftigen," "Der letzte Gott"*) should close the book, even if, as Heidegger notes, "Das Seyn" runs through the whole again. Where to place "Das Seyn"? In the absence of the author, precisely where it is in the typescript, with Heidegger's note duly appended. I shall cite the work either by aphorism (§) or by volume and page in the body of my text.

2. See aphorisms no. 130, 133, 135, 139–142, 147, and 164.

3. See the final note of chap. 1 for a listing of the sources.

4. See 65, at the following pages, for a few samples of Heidegger's polemics against "lived experience," biologism, and "philosophy of life": 19, 38, 40–41, 53, 68, 74, 102–103, 109, 112, 114, 123–24, 127–34 passim, including the diagrams, 173–74, 182, 203, 213, 218, 227, 229, and 259; after "The Leap," or "The Fissure," see 315, 337–38, 362, 365, 406 etc.

5. I have alluded to this in "The Crisis of Reason in the Nineteenth Century: Schelling's Treatise on Human Freedom (1809)," esp. pp. 24–25 and 31 n. 6. See also chap. 9, below.

6. See 26, 171–74 (§10); and Jacques Derrida, Gs I, in Ps, 395–414, discussed in chap. 5, above, and chap. 8, below.

7. Leibniz, *Monadologie* §§14, 20–21, 23–24 etc., in the Gerhardt edition. See also Heidegger's treatment of Leibniz in SG, throughout, but esp. 79. One must wonder whether the entire discussion of *Benommenheit* in the 1929–1930 lectures rises directly from the pages of the *Monadologie*, perhaps through the mediation of Wilhelm Dilthey and Max Scheler.

8. It is possible that when Heidegger speculates on the "stages of beyng" (*die Stufen des Seyns*), interpreting such stages or gradations as levels of revelatory power in salvaging the truth of beyng, he may have in mind not only Leibniz's great chain of being but also Max Scheler's *ordo amoris*, the hierarchy of values—better, of *loves*—that Scheler sees in humanity, divinity, and the cosmic order. See "Ordo amoris" (1916), in *Gesammelte Werke*, *10*, 348, 356, 361, and passim. Also in *Max Scheler: Von der Ganzheit des Menschen*, ed. Manfred Frings (Bonn: Bouvier, 1991), pp. 3–29. See also Wilhelm Mader, *Max Scheler*, pp. 53–55. In "Geschlecht IV," that is, "Heidegger's Ear: Philopolemology" (section I), Derrida emphasizes the importance of the tradition in which Scheler too found himself, the tradition that extends back to Pascal and Augustine: Heidegger's analysis of *Befindlichkeit* is unthinkable without the tradition for which "one has access to the truth or to knowledge on the basis of love or charity, and not the reverse." (Gs IV, ms. p. 20.)

9. See the "Introduction to Za-ology," above; on φύσις, see also SG, 102, 111–14, 153–54, and passim.

10. Martin Heidegger, "Der Spruch des Anaximander," at H, 296–343; EGT, 13–50; and *Der Ursprung des Kunstwerkes;* I have used the *complete* translation in the new, revised edition of Martin Heidegger, *Basic Writings,* ed. D. F. Krell (San Francisco: Harper-Collins, forthcoming in 1993). For an excellent treatment of "The Anaximander Fragment," see John Llewelyn, *The Middle Voice of Ecological Conscience,* chap. 6; in my view, this chapter elaborates the thesis of Llewelyn's book most fully and effectively.

11. Once again, I am thinking of the Merleau-Pontian chiasm. However, with reference to *Heidegger,* is it the case, as Reiner Schürmann argues, that in Heidegger's aletheiological interpretation of φύσις, that is, in "the event of φύειν, presencing" (Schürmann, 88), we see "the last of the principles, the 'ego' as the final offspring of anthropocentrism or 'humanism,' and see how it withers away"? Why is it that when the last remnant of anthropomorphism withers away, man, rather than Merleau-Ponty's idea of elemental *flesh,* is the only form of life left? Is it not rather the case that in Heidegger's φύσις metaphysical humanism celebrates its supreme triumph? While it is true that Heidegger's thinking of propriation realizes neither the *theological* nor the *cosmological* nor the *anthropological* ideas (Schürmann, 298), that it therefore does not achieve either general or special metaphysics, one must still wonder why Heidegger's comparative analysis of *world* leaves intact the traditional situation or allotment of domains in metaphysics—with *divinity* and *humanity* on the same side of an abyss, *nature* and *animality* on the other. Why does propriation reappropriate the order of being in metaphysics? Why does it fail to think the full range of mortality in the thrownness and unveiling of daimonic *Streuung?* As regards Schürmann's thought-provoking discussion (101) of Aristotle's " 'kinetic' understanding of nature," my only response would be that "coming forth, presencing" retains an inherent and essentially *archaic* or *principial* appeal to mortal man as the exclusive correspondent of being. Aristotle himself, with his "greater nearness" to earth (see the "Introduction to Zoology," above) has resources that Heidegger never taps, resources that would compel us to develop the sense(s) of "coming forth, presencing" for *all* life. Even and especially if we do not know where the line between the living and the dead can be drawn, or the lines between all the *kinds* of living and dying, and even if the thought of *all* life as presencing compels us to think *lifedeath* (see chap. 7, below).

12. See chap. 6 of Krell, *Of Memory, Reminiscence, and Writing: On the Verge,* esp. pp. 248–52.

13. G. W. F. Hegel, *Enzyklopädie der philosophischen Wissenschaften,* eds. Friedhelm Nicolin and Otto Pöggeler, "Philosophische Bibliothek" (Hamburg: F. Meiner, 1969), §§367–76. For a second instance of Heidegger's Hegelianism in this respect—the supremacy of species over the individual—see Heidegger's Schelling lectures, SA, 168–71.

14. See 65, 301, 323–25. Nota bene: not *der Weg,* but *DAS Weg!* Weg as gone, bygone, and even "get gone!" Recall the use of *weg* in this descriptive-imperative sense with regard to animal behavior, particularly sexual and alimentary behavior: 29/30, 363–64. One would have to trace quite carefully the parallel between *Benommensein* (cf., for example, 65, 410) and *Wegsein.* Both designate that undecidable moment when everything is to be decided: the moment of the absolute degradation of humankind in inappropriateness *and* the (selfsame) moment of elevation in the anxious raptures of instantaneous being-toward-death. Both designate the absolute ambivalence of Heidegger's thought from beginning to end. Perhaps a more fitting motto for the Gesamtausgabe, at least in the perspective of "life," would have been: *Weg!—nicht Werke!*

15. 54, 225–40. See also the discussion (that is, the remarks by Basil O'Neill) in *Research in Phenomenology,* XVII (1987), 43–45, and further discussion in chap. 9, below.

16. See 65, 50–53, 173, 182, 203, and 221–22; but cf. 71–72, on the "gathering

back" of stone, plant, animal, and man into the self-occluding earth—a reference cited above, early in the chapter, on the "more positive" reading of "life" in the *Contributions*.

17. Leibniz, "Monadologie," in the Gerhardt edition, cited above, 6, 618–19.

18. Quoted by Wilhelm Mader in *Max Scheler*, pp. 117–18.

7. LIFEDEATH

1. Although the Zollikon seminars of Heidegger and Medard Boss have nothing to say about any of Freud's ideas, even those in closest proximity to fundamental ontology, they do have a great deal to say about the human body (*der Leib*) as bodying forth (*das Leiben*). Yet in these same pages, which corroborate what in this chapter we will hear Heidegger saying elsewhere (principally in the *Nietzsche*), he continues to insist on the obvious but perhaps misleading fact that "the animal has nothing to say" (ZK, 114, 117, 306–307). In the Zollikon seminars Heidegger emphasizes perception, gesture, and the "self" as forms of ecstatic bodying forth in the world. It is worth noting that many of the seminar participants, preoccupied by issues in psychosomatic medicine, are left unsatisfied by these remarks (see ZK, 292). One can sympathize with their impatience. On *Leib* and *leiben*, see esp. ZK, 105–120; see also 231–33 and 292–96.

2. One must by rights speak of *Nietzsche's* Lamarckism as well, inasmuch as Lamarck held that all compounds, organic and inorganic, "owe their origins, directly or indirectly, to the organic faculties of living beings," such that even minerals are "debris of living bodies, either as originally deposited or as subsequently altered by nature." Lamarck, *Faits physiques*, quoted in Thomas S. Hall, *Ideas of Life and Matter*, cited in chap. 3, above, II, 135.

3. See Jacques Derrida, "Interpreting Signatures (Nietzsche/Heidegger): Two Questions," and my response to it, " 'Ashes, ashes, we all fall . . .': Encountering Nietzsche," both cited in chap. 1, above. See esp. pp. 65–67 in Derrida's essay; in my reply, see esp. pp. 230–31.

4. On the entire question of time in Nietzsche's thinking of eternal recurrence, see David Wood, *The Deconstruction of Time* (Atlantic Highlands, N.J.: Humanities Press, 1989), chap. 1.

5. On the bugbear and double-bind of anthropomorphism and anthropocentrism, see the sensible remarks—perhaps inspired in part by Heidegger, in F. J. J. Buytendijk, *Mensch und Tier*, p. 19.

6. See Krell, "A Hermeneutics of Discretion," in which I discuss the accusation by Philippe Lacoue-Labarthe in "Obliteration" and elsewhere. "A Hermeneutics of Discretion" appears in *Research in Phenomenology*, XV (1985), 1–27.

7. On Nietzsche's view of truth, and on chaos with regard to φύσις, see Heidegger's *Contributions*, 65, 362–65 and 381.

8. On *Gerechtigkeit* as the final transformation of ἀλήθεια "in the Roman bulwark of *veritas*, *rectitudo*, and *iustitia*," see the Parmenides lectures, 54, 77–78. Robert Bernasconi's criticisms of my discussion of "justice" in the Analysis of vol. 3 of Heidegger's *Nietzsche* are well taken: it cannot be said that the influence of Alfred Baeumler and Ernst Bertram simply "distracted Heidegger from his own best insights" (see my Analysis, 3, 273). Neither Baeumler nor Bertram poses the questions of the raging discordance of truth and art and of the final transformation of truth as correctness. Nevertheless, I still suspect that there are many other routes that Heidegger's "Will to Power as Knowledge" might have traveled toward more fertile questions—for example, the route that would connect the essential unfolding of truth as disclosure to φύσις, and φύσις to ζωή. And I still suspect that Heidegger's interpretation of will to power as both technological will-to-will and brutal *animalitas* make it impossible for him to take up in a more vital way the new interpretation of sensuousness. See Robert Bernasconi, "Justice and the Twilight Zone of Morality," in *Commemorations: Reading Heidegger*, ed. John Sallis, forthcoming.

9. Walt Whitman, *Leaves of Grass*, eds. Sculley Bradley and Harold W. Blodgett (New York: W. W. Norton, 1973), p. 162.

10. NI, 567/3, 81. One wonders how Heidegger would have replied to Hans Jonas's critique of anti-Darwinism: "Thus evolutionism undid Descartes' work more effectively than any metaphysical critique had managed to do. In the hue and cry over the indignity done to man's metaphysical status in the doctrine of his animal descent, it was overlooked that by the same token some dignity had been restored to the realm of life as a whole. If man was the relative of animals, then animals were the relatives of man and in degrees bearers of that inwardness of which man, the most advanced of their kin, is conscious in himself." Jonas, *The Phenomenon of Life*, p. 57. See also Jonas's telling criticisms of Cartesian dualism, pp. 72–74, with which Heidegger surely would have been sympathetic. Indeed, it is high time we referred to Jonas's accusation that Heidegger's ubiquitous expressions of fear concerning man's "animality" rest on a "verbal sophism"—even if the following critique tends to drive a wedge between the humanity of modernity and its animal "relatives," only now affirmed. Jonas's remarks have much to do with the entire project of "daimon life." He writes: "In his *Letter on Humanism* [cited in the Introduction, above], Heidegger argues, against the classical definition of Man as 'the rational animal,' that this definition places man within animality, specified only by a *differentia* which falls within the genus 'animal' as a particular quality. This, Heidegger contends, is placing man too low." In an extended footnote on *animalitas* and the Greek ζῷον, Jonas continues as follows: " 'Animal' in the Greek sense means not 'beast' or 'brute,' but any 'animated being,' including demons [let us say, rather, δαίμονες], gods, the ensouled stars—even the ensouled universe as a whole (cf. Plato, *Timaeus*, 30c): no 'lowering' of man is implied in placing him within this scale, and the bogy of 'animality' in its modern connotations is slipped in surreptitiously. In reality, the lowering to Heidegger consists in placing 'man' in *any* scale, that is, in a context of *nature* as such. The Christian devaluation of 'animal' to 'beast,' which indeed makes the term usable only in contrast to 'man,' merely reflects the larger break with the classical position—that break by which Man, as the unique possessor of an immortal soul, comes to stand outside 'nature' entirely. The existentialist argument takes off from this new basis: the play on the semantic ambiguity of 'animal,' while scoring an easy point, conceals this shift of basis of which that ambiguity is a function, and fails to meet the classical position with which it ostensibly argues." Jonas, *The Phenomenon of Life*, pp. 227–28. Of course, it is more than "verbal sophism" that is at stake: when in chap. 9 we hear Heidegger inveighing against Rilke's "botched Christianity," we would do well to remember Jonas's words on the botching and bitching of *animalitas* in the (in part, "Christian") metaphysico-moral tradition.

On Heidegger's persistent worry that in the epoch of nihilism *ratio* merely reverses or reverts to *animalitas*, and *animalitas* to *brutalitas*, see section 22 of his course on "European Nihilism," (NII, 199–202/4, 147–49); see also the remarks by Dominique Janicaud, *L'ombre*, pp. 116–17.

11. For yet another postponement of the Dionysian by Heidegger, see the Parmenides lectures, 54, 182. On the "mating" or "crossing" of Apollo and Dionysos, see John Sallis, *Crossings: The Space of Tragedy* (Chicago: University of Chicago Press, 1990), passim. See also my *Postponements: Woman, Sensuality, and Death in Nietzsche* (cited in the Introduction, above), pp. 32–38.

12. Robert Musil, *Der Mann ohne Eigenschaften*, 2 vols. (Hamburg: Rowohlt, 1978), I, 530–31; quoted in my *Of Memory, Reminiscence, and Writing: On the Verge*, p. 21.

13. Sigmund Freud, *"Selbstdarstellung": Schriften zur Geschichte der Psychoanalyse*, ed. Ilse Grubrich-Simitis (Frankfurt am Main: Fischer Taschenbuch Verlag, 1971), p. 87.

14. Sigmund Freud, *Aus den Anfängen der Psychoanalyse*, ed. Ernst Kris (New York: Imago, 1950), p. 152.

15. Georg Simmel, *Lebensanschauung*, p. 101. Cited in chap. 2, above. Once again, the best contemporary reminder of the shocking nature of this insight into lifedeath is Hans Jonas, *The Phenomenon of Life*, "First Essay," on the "ontological dominance of death" (15). Jonas puts the matter exceedingly well in his "Introduction": "That life is mortal may be its basic self-contradiction, but it belongs to its nature and cannot be separated from it even in thought: life carries death in itself, not in spite of, but because of, its being life, for of such a revocable, unassured kind is the relation of form and matter upon which it rests. Its reality, paradoxical and a constant challenge to mechanical nature, is at bottom a continual crisis whose momentary resolution is never safe and only gives rise to crisis renewed. . . . Thus dependent on the propitiousness or unpropitiousness of outer reality, it is exposed to the world from which it has seceded, and by means of which it must yet maintain itself. Opposing in its internal autonomy the entropy rule of general causality, it is yet subject to it. Emancipated from the identity with matter, it is yet in need of it: free, yet under the whip of necessity; isolated, yet in indispensable contact; seeking contact, yet in danger of being destroyed by it, and threatened no less by its want: imperiled thus from both sides, by importunity and aloofness of the world, and balanced on the narrow ridge between' the two; in its process, which must not cease, liable to interference; in the straining of its temporality always facing the imminent no-more: thus does the living form carry on its separatist existence in matter—paradoxical, unstable, precarious, finite, and in intimate company with death."

8. SOMETHING LIKE SEXES, SOMETHING LIKE SPIRIT

1. William McNeill has recently indicated some places where Heidegger shows both his hands, both the right and the left. The more familiar of the two passages is section 23 of *Being and Time*, where Heidegger distances himself decisively from Kant's essay on "orienting oneself in thought." The less familiar passage is section 25 of the *Prolegomena* (20, 319–20), in which Heidegger explicitly states: "There is no hand in general [keine Hand überhaupt]," but only the always already oriented, kinesthetic hand of either the right or the left. See the stimulating product of McNeill's own two hands, his tribute to Dibutade, "Drawing Shadows, Warm and Capable," cited in chap. 2, above.

2. At Ps, 438; note the absence of the "II" in the English text, at 182.

3. See my essay, "The Wave's Source: Rhythm in the Languages of Poetry and Thought," in *Heidegger and Language*, ed. David Wood (Warwick, England: Parousia Press, 1981), pp. 25–50.

4. See Nick Land's remarkably cruel and indecent, precipitate and impatient, pestilential, perspicuous and potlatchily *generous* reading of Derrida's and Heidegger's Trakl, "Spirit and Teeth," in David Wood, ed., *Of Derrida, Heidegger and Spirit*, chap. 2. Land shows how *Daimon Life* ought to have been conceived and written, and will be written yet, if it has any future at all. Outlandishly.

5. See chap. 11, "Strokes of Love and Death," in my *Intimations of Mortality*.

6. In his *Treatise on Human Freedom* (1809), *Werke* (Stuttgart, 1860), 7, 380, he acknowledges ". . . den überall hervortretenden dämonischen"; and later (387) he mentions the single "blow" or "stroke" that I am stressing here, ". . . und alles in Einem magischen Schlage zugleich geschieht. . . . [S]ogar die Art und Beschaffenheit seiner Korporisation [wird dadurch] bestimmt." The entire Schellingian venture of 1809–1814, from the freedom essay through the sketches toward *The Ages of the World*, is all about *Zwietracht* as opposed to *Eintracht*. It is all about the suppressed embodiment and bisexuality of God. If Heidegger's Schelling lectures largely ignore these aspects, Derrida's certainly should not. He would be the first to admit that a great deal of work remains to be done in this regard.

7. The papers and discussions of that meeting have been published in *Research in Philosophy*, vol. XVII (1987), pp. 1–188.

8. "Envoi," in Ps, 109–143; trans. in part by Peter and Mary Ann Caws as "Sending: On Representation" in *Social Research*, vol. 49, no. 2 (Summer 1982), 294–326.

9. In Ps, 63–93. Trans. F. Gasdner et al., *Enclitic*, 2, no. 2 (Fall 1978), pp. 5–33.

10. *Éperons: Les styles de Nietzsche* (Paris: Flammarion, 1978), trans. B. Harlow (Chicago: Chicago University Press, 1979).

11. *Glas* (Paris: Galilée, 1974), trans. John P. Leavey, Jr. and Richard Rand (Lincoln: University of Nebraska Press, 1986). *Mémoires: pour Paul de Man* (Paris: Galilée, 1988), trans. Cecile Lindsay et al. (New York: Columbia University Press, 1986). *Schibboleth: pour Paul Celan* (Paris: Galilée, 1986). *Ulysse gramophone: Deux mots pour Joyce* (Paris: Galilée, 1987). *Parages* (Paris: Galilée, 1986). And *Feu la cendre* (Paris: des femmes, 1987), trans. N. Lukacher (Lincoln: U. of Nebraska, 1992).

12. See "Vom Wesen und Begriff der Φύσις. Aristoteles *Physik*, B, 1," W, 309–371, esp. p. 309.

13. I have tried to analyze the claim of a double temporality in *Being and Time* quite closely in chap. 6 of my *Of Memory, Reminiscence, and Writing: On the Verge*.

14. Derrida has continued to pursue these troubling questions in his recent book, *L'autre cap*, cited in chap. 3, above. On the 1935 Vienna lecture, see the fine analysis by Robert Bernasconi, "Who Is My Neighbor? Who Is the Other?" to be published by the Simon Silverman Phenomenology Center, Duquesne University, Pittsburgh, forthcoming in 1992.

15. Even the "voice of the friend" is undecidably bound up with what Derrida calls "the *same* community or the *same* people, the experience of the *same* tongue, or the participation in the *same* struggle. . . ." See Gs IV, ms. pp. 34–35.

16. See NII, 309/3, 231; once again, see my introduction to the 1991 paperback edition of Heidegger's *Nietzsche*.

17. Rodolphe Gasché, *The Tain of the Mirror: Derrida and the Philosophy of Reflection* (Cambridge, Mass.: Harvard University Press, 1986), chaps. 8 and 9.

18. Both fires reported in the Introduction, above. See the 1943 lectures, "Der Anfang des abendländischen Denkens," in 55, 5, 10, and 22–27. On the theme of hearth and fire, see the remarks in Cp, 193/179.

19. I develop this point in the "Postscriptum" to a paper entitled "La Langueur de Dieu," delivered at the University of Nice in December of 1990, as yet unpublished.

9. FINAL SIGNS OF LIFE

1. *Œuvres complètes du Marquis de Sade*, eds. Annie Le Brun and Jean-Jacques Pauvert (Paris: Pauvert, 1986), I, 305–306.

2. One might venture a guess that much of the attention being paid today to Kantian sublimity and Benjaminian *Gewalt* has to do with the daimonic life of post-Nietzschean chaos. See, for example, Jean-François Lyotard, *Leçons sur l'analytique du sublime* [*Kant*, Critique de la faculté de juger, §§23–29] (Paris: Galilée, 1991); Michel Deguy, ed., *Du sublime* (Paris: Belin, 1988). On Benjamin and *Gewalt*, see Jacques Derrida, "Force of Law: The 'Mystical Foundation of Authority,'" *Cardozo Law Review*, XI, 5–6 (July–August 1990), 920–1045.

3. On the mark of evil in divine humanity as a bestiality that is manifested by no beast, see the discussion of Kant and Heidegger in John Llewelyn, *The Middle Voice of Ecological Conscience*, chap. 4, section 3. Naturally, I am also thinking of the φαρμακός of Derrida's "Plato's Pharmacy," in *La dissémination* (Paris: Seuil, 1972), pp. 146–53; trans. Barbara Johnson (Chicago: University of Chicago Press, 1981), pp. 128–34; and of René Girard, *La violence et le sacré* (Paris: Grasset, 1972), esp. chaps. 1, 3, and 10.

4. On the demigods, see also 39, 210, and the discussion by Dominique Janicaud in *L'ombre*, pp. 143–44.

5. 54, 173–74. On Heidegger's treatment of εὐδαιμονία in his *Contributions to Philosophy*, see chap. 6, above, esp. "The Fissure of Life."

6. Michel Haar, *Le chant de la terre*, p. 73.

7. Georges Bataille, *Visions of Excess: Selected Writings, 1927–1939*, ed. Allan Stoekl (Minneapolis: University of Minnesota Press, 1985), pp. 20–23.

8. *54, 237*; see the "Introduction to Za-ology," above.

9. Cited in the "Introduction to Za-ology," p. 23, above; noted in what follows as OA, with page number.

10. Irigaray would affirm one of the guiding threads of Hans Jonas's *The Phenomenon of Life*, which argues that "the dualism between man and φύσις [is] the metaphysical background of the nihilistic situation" (232).

11. See the opening lines of Luce Irigaray, "La différence sexuelle," in *Éthique de la différence sexuelle* (Paris: Minuit, 1984), p. 13.

12. Heidegger, ZSdD, 71–72; BW, 384; see also chap. 5 of my *Intimations of Mortality*, "The Transitions of *Lichtung*."

13. OA, 17. Cf. Michel Haar, *Le chant de la terre*, p. 39: "That which hides itself in φύσις and refrains from appearing—does it not possess an opacity and a thickness that one would really have to call *material?*"

14. See Irigaray, *Éthique de la différence sexuelle*, pp. 143–71.

15. Friedrich Hölderlin, *Sämtliche Werke, Kritische Textausgabe*, ed. D. E. Sattler (Darmstadt: Luchterhand, 1986 [Frankfurter Hölderlin-Ausgabe, Roter Stern, 1985], 13, 365, ll. 366–71.

16. See Krell, "Nietzsche Heidegger Empedocles," *Graduate Faculty Journal of Philosophy*, 15, 2 (1991), pp. 31–48; and "Stuff · Thread · Point · Fire: Hölderlin's Memory of Tragic Dissolution in the Theoretical Writings of 1795–1800," in Rebecca Comay and John McCumber, eds., *Hegel and Heidegger on Memory*, forthcoming in 1993 from Northwestern University Press, for references to the literature.

17. See Luce Irigaray, *Amante marine: De Friedrich Nietzsche* (Paris: Minuit, 1980), passim.

18. US, 258. I have prepared a new translation of "Der Weg zur Sprache" for the second, revised edition of Heidegger's *Basic Writings*, forthcoming from Harper Collins in 1993; it will be the tenth, the penultimate piece in this new edition.

19. Michel Haar, in *Le chant de la terre*, p. 85, suggesting the sense, sensibility, and sensitivity of and to the sensuous situation.

20. I am grateful to Donna Scott for providing me with a typescript of this text, whose form of publication I do not know. I have taken only a few extracts from it, but would have wanted to reprint all of it, for it is extraordinary. Even if, as some who lack confidence claim, the text is part of a screenplay, hence, a fiction.

Index

Americans, native: Heidegger among (Indians), 317

Animal rationale: traditional definition of human being, 2, 55, 82, 190, 209

Anxiety: anxious animal, 69, 131, 133; physiology of, 70; and profound boredom, 110; temporal analysis of, 325n3; mentioned, 67–69, 112, 151, 163, 181, 188, 207, 244, 275, 326n6

Aquinas, Thomas: on erectness of man, 122–23

Arendt, Hannah, 139, 147, 164, 195

Aristotle: analysis of time, 73, 78, 101; on erring, 45–46; on melancholy, 115; on relation of art, life, childish aversion, 16; on sleep and dreams, 108; mentioned, 1–2, 5, 13, 18, 36, 40–41, 47, 123, 133, 147, 150, 152, 195, 212, 244

Art, 16, 193–94; truth and, 219–21, 234–35

Augustine, 36, 41, 65–67, 156, 174

Baer, Karl Ernst von, 59

Barth, John, 247

Bataille, Georges, 8, 74, 76, 107, 292, 304

Beaufret, Jean, 1–2, 5

Benjamin, Walter: commentaries on Goethe, 6–7

Benommenheit (benumbment): in anxiety, 68, 129; behavior, 26, 128–29, 131; of the lizard, 275; mentioned, 9–11, 17, 23, 60, 66–67, 87, 104, 110, 121, 124, 181–83, 207, 332n18, 340n17

Bergson, Henri, 37, 72, 79, 148, 240, 273

Birds: daimonic, 311; Heidegger's, 18, 323n21

Birth, 54–55, 91–93, 175–76, 195, 206, 211–12, 242; and organs, 120; trauma of, 70

Blanchot, Maurice, 67, 267

Boredom, profound: analyzed by Heidegger in 1929–30 lecture course, 8, 12, 109–14, 172, 326n12, 329n7

Boss, Medard, 52

Brentano, Franz: in Heidegger's 1925 lectures, 79

Buytendijk, F. J. J.: biological science, 115–17

Care (*Sorge*), 70–72, 82, 85, 98, 104, 298, 302, 311

Cassirer, Ernst, 57, 183–84

Castorp, Hans. *See* Mann, Thomas

Celan, Paul, 165

Chagall, Marc: animal gaze in "I and the Village," 21

Chaos, 225–37 passim, 301

Char, René, 21

Chief Seattle: letter to president in 1852, 31

Circle: of hermeneutical understanding, 67; of living things, 305; of zoology, 114; mentioned, 24, 55, 61

Comportment: distinction between behavior and, 9, 11

Dastur, Françoise, 266, 282

Deconstruction, 270

Dedalus, Stephen, 74

Deleuze, Giles, 267

Demonic, the: demonism, 192; Derrida's discussion of, 277–78; in the animal, 21

Derrida, Jacques: on crossing out, 117; on the demonic, 277–78; on duality of sexes, 185; on essence of the people, 204; on Freud and Heidegger, 239, 244–45; analysis of *Gemut*, 116; on Heidegger's silence, 138; "Mochlos," 152; *Of Spirit*, 23–24, 113, 159, 179, 265–91; on the psyche, 129; on Trakl's poetry, 259–65, 280–88; mentioned, 4, 59, 142, 162, 292, 311, 322n16

Descartes, 36, 60–61, 66, 116–24 passim, 269, 277

Dilthey, Wilhelm, 35–37, 49, 50, 54, 72–73, 78–82, 92, 150, 153, 176, 240, 274, 333n22, 339n8

Dürer, Albrecht: hands, 256

Dylan, Bob, 50

Easy, the, 45–46

Ecclusion, 310, 316

Eliot, T.S., 66, 109, 112

Empedocles, 25, 115, 164, 166, 300, 306–10 passim

Essence: of animality/humanity, 113–15, 123–26, 262, 292; disessence, 267; of ground in God, 130, 133, 300; of instinct, 209; language of, 276, 295; of life, 128–29, 311; of man, 313; of the people, 204; of technology, 207

Eternity, 45, 110

Extermination, the: Heidegger's silence on, 138–42, 334n5; Lacoue-Labarthe's definition, 164

Farías, Victor: biography of Heidegger, 157; and Habermas, 160–61; mentioned, 157–64 passim

Faulkner, William, 132

Finitude: and captivity, 296; of man, 123; of time, 77–78; mentioned, 72, 106, 112, 178, 322n10

Fink, Eugen: 1966–67 seminar on Heraclitus with Heidegger, 24–26, 63, 308; mentioned, 285

DAVID FARRELL KRELL is Professor of Philosophy at DePaul University. He is the author of *Of Memory, Reminiscence, and Writing: On the Verge; Intimations of Mortality: Time, Truth, and Finitude in Heidegger's Thinking of Being;* and *Postponements: Woman, Sensuality, and Death in Nietzsche.* He is translator and editor of a number of books and articles by Martin Heidegger, including *Basic Writings, Nietzsche,* and *Early Greek Thinking.*

Printed in the United Kingdom by
Lightning Source UK Ltd., Milton Keynes
141888UK00001B/23/P

9 780253 207395